Tamta's World

The Life and Encounters of a Medieval Noblewoman from the Middle East to Mongolia

This book tells the compelling story of a Christian noblewoman named Tamta in the thirteenth century. Born to an Armenian family at the court of Queen Tamar of Georgia, she was ransomed in marriage to nephews of Saladin, after her father was captured during a siege. She was later raped and then married by the Khwarazmshah and held hostage by the Mongols, before being made an independent ruler in eastern Anatolia under them. Her tale stretches from the Mediterranean to Mongolia and reveals the extraordinary connections across continents and cultures that one woman could experience. Without a voice of her own, surviving monuments – monasteries and mosques, caravanserais and palaces – build up a picture of Tamta's world and the roles women played in it. It explores how women's identities changed between different courts, with shifting languages, religions and cultures, and between their roles as daughters, wives, mothers and widows.

ANTONY EASTMOND is A. G. Leventis Professor of Art History at the Courtauld Institute of Art, University of London. He has published extensively on the world of eastern Christianity and its connections with the Islamic world around it, especially in Georgia and the Caucasus, and Trebizond. He has also published on Late Antique and Byzantine art, with a particular interest in ivories and the visual power of inscriptions. Notable among his works are *Royal Imagery in Medieval Georgia* (1998), *Art and Identity in Thirteenth-Century Byzantium: Hagia Sophia and the Empire of Trebizond* (2004), *The Glory of Byzantium and Early Christendom* (2013) and *Viewing Inscriptions in the Late Antique and Medieval World* (ed., 2015).

Tamta's World

The Life and Encounters of a Medieval Noblewoman from the Middle East to Mongolia

ANTONY EASTMOND
Courtauld Institute of Art, London

CAMBRIDGE
UNIVERSITY PRESS

University Printing House, Cambridge CB2 8BS, United Kingdom

One Liberty Plaza, 20th Floor, New York, NY 10006, USA

477 Williamstown Road, Port Melbourne, VIC 3207, Australia

4843/24, 2nd Floor, Ansari Road, Daryaganj, Delhi - 110002, India

79 Anson Road, #06–04/06, Singapore 079906

Cambridge University Press is part of the University of Cambridge.

It furthers the University's mission by disseminating knowledge in the pursuit of education, learning and research at the highest international levels of excellence.

www.cambridge.org
Information on this title: www.cambridge.org/9781107167568
DOI: 10.1017/9781316711774

© Antony Eastmond 2017

This publication is in copyright. Subject to statutory exception
and to the provisions of relevant collective licensing agreements,
no reproduction of any part may take place without the written
permission of Cambridge University Press.

First published 2017

Printed in the United Kingdom by TJ International Ltd. Padstow Cornwall

A catalogue record for this publication is available from the British Library

Library of Congress Cataloging-in-Publication data
Names: Eastmond, Antony, 1966– author.
Title: Tamta's world : the life and encounters of a medieval noblewoman from the Middle East to Mongolia / Antony Eastmond.
Description: Cambridge, United Kingdom : Cambridge University Press, 2018. | Includes bibliographical references and index.
Identifiers: LCCN 2016052045 | ISBN 9781107167568
Subjects: LCSH: Christianity and other religions – Islam. | Islam – Relations – Christianity. | Christian women – History – To 1500. | Middle East – History – To 1500.
Classification: LCC BP172 .E37 2018 | DDC 956/.014 – dc23
LC record available at https://lccn.loc.gov/2016052045

ISBN 978-1-107-16756-8 Hardback

Cambridge University Press has no responsibility for the persistence or accuracy of URLs for external or third-party internet websites referred to in this publication, and does not guarantee that any content on such websites is, or will remain, accurate or appropriate.

To Helen and Stephen

Contents

Illustrations   [*page* viii]
Acknowledgements   [xx]
Transliteration   [xxii]
Abbreviations   [xxiii]

1 A New World of Encounters: The Life of Tamta Mqargrdzeli   [1]

2 Tamta's Origins: The World of the Mqargrdzelis   [21]

3 Tamta, Ivane and Akhlat in 1210   [66]

4 Al-Awhad and Tamta's First Marriage   [79]

5 Women and Power   [103]

6 Akhlat: Identity and Life in the Medieval City   [124]

7 Tamta: Ayyubid Wife of al-Ashraf Musa   [172]

8 Tamta: A Christian at the Ayyubid Court   [206]

9 Tamta at Court   [242]

10 Akhlat, Builders and Buildings   [282]

11 Tamta and the Khwarazmians   [322]

12 Tamta and the Mongols   [342]

13 Tamta as Ruler of Akhlat   [368]

14 Afterlife   [391]

Bibliography   [395]
Primary Sources   [395]
Secondary Sources   [400]
Index   [425]

Color plates of the following after page 132 and again after page 292

Illustrations

Maps

Map 1: The Near East at the start of the thirteenth century   [*page* xxv]
Map 2: The Caucasus at the start of the thirteenth century   [xxvi]
Map 3: Anatolia at the start of the thirteenth century   [xxvii]
Map 4: The Mongolian world *c*. 1250   [xxviii]

Figures

1. View of the main church of the monastery of Akhtala, Armenia, in its fortified complex, built by Ivane Mqargrdzeli; *c*. 1205. © Antony Eastmond   [29]
2. Goshavank, Armenia; 1191–1291. General view from the south west of the cluster of buildings in the monastic complex around the catholicon (main church). © Antony Eastmond   [31]
3. Ground plan of the monastic complex at Goshavank, Armenia. A: catholicon of the Mother of God (1191); B: zhamatun (1197); C: church of St Gregory (1208); D: chapel of St Gregory (1237); E: library (1241, with church of the Holy Archangels built over it in 1291); F: scriptorium (thirteenth century); G: small chapels (thirteenth century)   [32]
4. Decoration on the east façade of the main church at Akhtala, Armenia; *c*. 1205. © Antony Eastmond   [33]
5. View of the apse, showing post holes for templon screen at Akhtala, Armenia; *c*. 1205. © Antony Eastmond   [34]
6. View of the apse of the catholicon, at Harichavank, Armenia, showing altar platform; *c*. 1200. © Antony Eastmond   [36]
7. Communion of the Apostles with Greek inscription, in the apse at Akhtala, Armenia; *c*. 1205. © Antony Eastmond   [37]
8. Bilingual Greek and Georgian inscription accompanying St John in the north-east pendentive in the church of St Gregory the Illuminator of Tigran Honents, Ani, Turkey; 1215. © Antony Eastmond   [38]

9. St Luke and trilingual inscription of the painter Abas in the Red Gospels of Gandzasar; early thirteenth century (University of Chicago Library, Goodspeed MS 949, fol. 139v; 26.5 × 20 cm). Special Collections Research Center, University of Chicago Library   [40]
10. Detail of the Last Judgement on the west wall at Akhtala, Armenia; *c.* 1205. © Antony Eastmond   [41]
11. The Glorification of the Cross in the dome of the church at Timotesubani, Georgia; *c.* 1220. G. Chubinashvili National Research Centre for Georgian Art History and Heritage Preservation (S. Kobuladze photo-laboratory)   [42]
12. Georgian monastic saints (Sts Ekvtime Mtatsmindeli, Hilarion Kartveli and Giorgi Mtatsmindeli) on the north side of the door on the west wall at Akhtala, Armenia; *c.* 1205. © Antony Eastmond   [44]
13. General view of the monastic complex at Harichavank, Armenia, from the south; 1201. Photo: Hiosn   [47]
14. Ground plan of the monastic complex at Harichavank, Armenia; 1201. A: church of St Gregory (seventh to tenth century); B: catholicon of the Mother of God (1201); C: zhamatun (*c.* 1224)   [49]
15. View of the the church of St Sargis at Khtskonk, Turkey, from the north; early eleventh century. © Antony Eastmond   [50]
16. Zakare and Ivane Mqargrdzeli on the east façade at Harichavank, Armenia; 1201. © Antony Eastmond   [51]
17. Canon tables from the Haghbat Gospels; 1211 (Yerevan, Matenadaran, MS 6288, fols. 8v–9r; 30 × 22 cm). The inscription by the figure holding the fish in the lower left corner reads, somewhat mysteriously: 'Sahak, next time bring fish!' © Matenadaran, Yerevan   [52]
18. The Anchiskhati icon; painted panel: seventh century; silver gilt frame by Beka Opizari, *c.* 1190 (gilt cover of the body of Christ: eighteenth century) (Tbilisi, Art Museum of Georgia; 105 × 71 cm). G. Chubinashvili National Research Centre for Georgian Art History and Heritage Preservation (S. Kobuladze photo-laboratory)   [56]
19. The vision of St Gregory the Illuminator in the west arm of the church of St Gregory the Illuminator of Tigran Honents, Ani, Turkey; 1215. © Antony Eastmond   [61]
20. The vision of St Nino and the life-giving pillar in the west arm of the church of St Gregory the Illuminator of Tigran Honents, Ani, Turkey; 1215. © Antony Eastmond   [61]

21. Khatchkar at Kosh, Armenia, set up to celebrate the liberation of Armenia from the Seljuk Turks; 1195. Photograph: Marina Kamenskaya   [68]
22. The massacre of monks by Seljuk Turks, depicted in the chapel of the martyrs (Motsameta) at Udabno monastery, Gareja desert, Georgia; *c.* 1200. Photo: © Antony Eastmond; drawing: © Zaza Skhirtladze   [70]
23. Lustreware dish showing a wedding procession. Kashan, Iran; first quarter of the thirteenth century (Metropolitan Museum of Art, New York, 1983.247; diameter 41.7 cm). © Metropolitan Museum of Art, New York, www.metmuseum.org   [95]
24. The arrival of the bride, from a Byzantine *epithalamion* (bridal poem) manuscript; late twelfth century (Biblioteca Apostolica Vaticana, gr. 1851, fol. 3v; 22.5 × 17 cm). © 2017 Biblioteca Apostolica Vaticana   [97]
25. Inscription commemorating al-Awhad's rebuilding of the walls of Mayyafariqin (Silvan), Turkey; 1203. © Antony Eastmond   [100]
26. King Giorgi III (r. 1156–84) and Queen Tamar (r. 1184–1210), north wall of the church of the Koimesis at Vardzia, Georgia; 1184–6. G. Chubinashvili National Research Centre for Georgian Art History and Heritage Preservation (S. Kobuladze photo-laboratory)   [114]
27. Queen Tamar (r. 1184–1210) and Giorgi IV Lasha (r. 1210–23), north wall of Bertubani monastery, Gareja desert, Georgia (now in Azerbaijan); *c.* 1210. After Chubinashvili   [115]
28. Gold dinar of Shajar al-Durr, minted in Cairo; 1250 (British Museum, inv. 1849,1121.294). © Trustees of the British Museum   [118]
29. Tree of Pearls mosaic in the conch of the *mihrab* in the mausoleum of Shajar al-Durr, Southern Cemetery, Cairo, Egypt; 1250–80. © Antony Eastmond   [122]
30. View of the Muslim cemetery at Akhlat, Turkey. © Antony Eastmond   [125]
31. View of Van, Turkey, from the south, showing the jumble of minarets and church domes rising above the city walls, with the Rock of Van behind (from C. Texier, *Description de l'Arménie, la Perse et la Mésopotamie* (Paris, 1842), 1: pl. 36) (the medieval city was razed to the ground after 1915). © British Library Board   [128]
32. Mosque of Minuchihr, Ani, Turkey, from the south-west; twelfth–thirteenth century. © Antony Eastmond   [131]

33. Cathedral (1000–1001) and Mosque of Minuchihr (twelfth–thirteenth century) seen from the east, at the edge of the ravine of the river Akurean, Ani, Turkey. © Antony Eastmond   [132]
34. The minaret outside the walls at Mayyafariqin (Silvan), Turkey, begun by al-Awhad in 1203, completed by his brother al-Ashraf in 1212. © Antony Eastmond   [135]
35. The minaret of the Great Mosque at Aleppo, Syria; 1090–2 (destroyed April 2013). Photograph: Michal Salaban. wikimedia (CC BY-SA 3.0)   [135]
36. Kars Gate at Ani, Turkey; thirteenth century. © Antony Eastmond   [137]
37. Mangonel from Murda b. ʿAli b. Murda al-Tarsusi, *al-Tabsira fi 'l-Hurub* (The explanation of the masters of the quintessence [of military knowledge]), made for Saladin; late twelfth century (Oxford, Bodleian Library, MS Huntington 264, fols 135a–134b; 25.5 × 39 cm). Oxford, Bodleian Library   [138]
38. Polychrome stonework cross and khatchkar on tower 5 at Ani, Turkey; thirteenth century. © Antony Eastmond   [139]
39. The Ulu Baden tower, Amid (Diyarbakir), Turkey, constructed by Nasir al-Din Artuq Arslan; 1207–8. © Antony Eastmond   [141]
40. The tower of Mamkhatun (tower 62) at Ani, Turkey; 1219. © Antony Eastmond   [143]
41. Bilingual inscription of Badr al-Din Abu Bakr, Emir of Simre, on the walls of Sinop, Turkey; 1214. © Catherine Draycott   [145]
42. Ceramic bowls (*bacini*) inserted into the walls of Ani, Turkey; thirteenth century. © Antony Eastmond   [146]
43. Re-used spolia on the walls of Konya (engraving from L. de Laborde, *Voyage en Orient* (Paris, 1838), fig. 117). Bibliothèque numérique de l'INHA – Bibliothèque de l'Institut National d'Histoire de l'Art, collections Jacques Doucet   [148]
44. Copper dirham of Najm al-Din Alpi, Artuqid ruler of Mardin, 1152–76. © The Barber Institute of Fine Arts, The University of Birmingham   [149]
45. Silver tetradrachm of Antiochos VIII, issued 121–113 BC. © The Barber Institute of Fine Arts, The University of Birmingham   [150]
46. Gateway at Konya (engraving in C. Texier, *Description de l'Asie Mineure faite par Ordre du gouvernement Français de 1833 à 1837* (Paris, 1839–49), 2: pl. 97). © British Library Board   [151]

47. Lion and bull relief at the citadel arch in Amid (Diyarbakir), Turkey; 1206/7. © Antony Eastmond   [152]
48. Processional gate to the north of Ani, close to Horomos monastery, Turkey; tenth–eleventh century (engraving by Julius Kästner in M. F. Brosset, *Les ruines d'Ani, capitale de l'Arménie sous les rois Bagratides, aux Xe et XIe siècles: histoire et description. Atlas* (St Petersburg, 1860), pl. 29). © Bibliothèque nationale de France   [153]
49. The so-called palace of the baron, Ani, Turkey; early thirteenth century. Image courtesy History Museum of Armenia. No. 611   [157]
50. Christian cemetery, Akhlat, Turkey (photo by Walter Bachmann, *c.* 1913). Image courtesy Deutsches Archäologisches Institut Berlin, Werner Bachmann Nachlass   [158]
51. Muslim cemetery, Akhlat, Turkey (photo by Walter Bachmann, *c.* 1913). Image courtesy Deutsches Archäologisches Institut Berlin, Werner Bachmann Nachlass   [159]
52. Tax inscription of 1269 on the exterior of the zhamatun of the church of Holy Apostles, Ani, Turkey   [164]
53. Albert Gabriel's 1931 reconstruction drawing of the Sultan Han, near Kayseri, Turkey; 1230s (from *Monuments turcs d'Anatolie I: Kayseri–Niğde* (Paris, 1931)). Reproduction with permission of the Orient-Bibliothek, Deutsches Archäologisches Institut, Berlin   [168]
54. Courtyard mosque with hall portal beyond, Sultan Han, near Kayseri, Turkey; 1230s. © Antony Eastmond   [169]
55. Portal of the Zor Han, near Iğdir, Turkey; early thirteenth century (from A. Loris'-Kalantar, 'Razvaliny drevniaiu karavansaraia', *Khristianskii Vostok* 3 (1914))   [170]
56. Portal to the Madrasa al-Atabakiyya, al-Salihiyya district, Damascus, Syria; 1229–42. © Dick Osseman, http://www.pbase.com/dosseman/profile   [182]
57. Dome of the Dar al-Hadith al-Ashrafiyya, al-Salihiyya district, Damascus, Syria; 1229–37. © Tom Nickson   [183]
58. Monastery of Dadivank, Nagorno-Karabagh, Azerbaijan (disputed); 1214. Photo: Dadivank   [187]
59. Plan of the vaulting of baths at the Sitti 'Adhra complex, Damascus, Syria; 1185   [190]

60. Entrance to the covered hall at the Hatun Han in the village of Pazar, north-west of Tokat, Turkey; 1238. © Antony Eastmond   [192]
61. Bridge over the river Debed at Sanahin, Armenia; 1192, built by Vaneni © Antony Eastmond   [193]
62. Albert Gabriel's 1931 reconstruction drawing of the Mahperi complex, Kayseri, Turkey; 1237–8 (from *Monuments turcs d'Anatolie I: Kayseri–Niğde* (Paris, 1931)). Reproduction with permission of the Orient-Bibliothek, Deutsches Archäologisches Institut, Berlin   [199]
63. Screen in front of the tomb of Mahperi Khatun, facing the gate into Kayseri, Turkey; 1238. © Antony Eastmond   [200]
64. Tomb of Malika 'Adiliyya, Kayseri, Turkey; 1247/8. © Antony Eastmond   [203]
65. Niche from the west façade of Deir Mar Benham, south-east of Mosul, Iraq; first half of the thirteenth century. © Amir Harrak   [208]
66. *Mihrab* niche from Great Mosque, Mosul, Iraq; first half of the thirteenth century. © Museum für Islamische Kunst, Staatliche Museen zu Berlin   [208]
67. View of the monastery of Gandzasar from the south, Nagorno-Karabagh, Azerbaijan (disputed): catholicon (1216–38); zhamatun (*c.* 1261). © Harout Tanielian   [216]
68. Wooden door with Arabic text from the church of the Nativity, Bethlehem, Palestine; 1227. © University of Haifa – the Library   [218]
69. Wooden door with Armenian text from the church of the Nativity, Bethlehem, Palestine; 1227. © University of Haifa – the Library   [219]
70. The Annunciation and a polo match; details from the 'Freer' basin made for Najm al-Din Ayyub, Sultan in Cairo. Brass with silver and gold inlay; 1247–9 (Freer Gallery of Art, Smithsonian Institution, Washington, DC: purchase, F1955.10; height: 22.5 cm; diameter: 50 cm). © Smithsonian Institution   [222]
71. Fragment of a marble vessel made for al-Muzaffar Mahmud, the Ayyubid ruler of Hama, d. 1244 (Kolaşin Collection, inv. Y730; 35 × 35 cm). © Ali Konyali   [223]
72. Syrian ceramic figurine showing a woman breast-feeding her child; thirteenth century. Height: 27.5 cm. © Philippe Maillard/akg-images   [230]

73. Detail of the Talisman Gate, Baghdad, Iraq, built by the Caliph Nasir li-Din-Illah; 1221 (destroyed 1917). © Museum für Islamische Kunst, Staatliche Museen zu Berlin   [232]
74. The angel of the course of the sun from the *Daqa'iq al-Haqa'iq*, copied in Aksaray and Kayseri, Turkey; 1272–3 (Paris, BNF, MS Pers. 174, fol. 115; 25.5 × 17 cm). © Bibliothèque nationale de France   [235]
75. *Minai* bowl with a noblewoman listening to a musician, Iran, early thirteenth century (Freer Gallery of Art, Smithsonian Institution, Washington, DC: purchase, F1938.12; diameter 23 cm). © Smithsonian Institution   [236]
76. Twenty of the XL Martyrs of Sebaste, from a Syriac lectionary, copied at the monastery of Mar Mattai, near Mosul, Iraq; 1219–20 (Biblioteca Apostolica Vaticana, Syr. 559, fol. 93v; 43.5 × 33.5 cm). © 2017 Biblioteca Apostolica Vaticana   [237]
77. The Resafa Hoard, a mixed set of Christian liturgical and other silver, buried at Resafa in Syria 1243–59. Photo © Thilo Ulbert. Image courtesy Resafa-Archiv DAI Berlin   [238]
78. Silver dirham of Kaykhusraw II, minted in Sivas; 1242. © Trustees of the British Museum, http://creativecommons.org/licenses/by-nc-sa/4.0/   [240]
79. Levon, prince of Cilicia, wearing a robe embroidered with roundels containing a lion beneath the sun, in a Gospel book presented to the prince by his godfather, Catholicos Constantine I; *c.* 1255 (Yerevan, Matenadaran, MS 8321, fol. 15r; 15.8 × 11.3 cm). © Matenadaran, Yerevan   [240]
80. The tents of a caravan, from the fourth *Maqama* of al-Hariri, *c.* 1230 (St Petersburg, Institute of Oriental Studies, Ms c-23, fol. 12a; 25 × 19 cm). Institute of Oriental Manuscripts, Russian Academy of Sciences, St Petersburg   [246]
81. Gateway to the palace in the citadel at Aleppo, Syria, built by al-Zahir Ghazi; 1186–1216. Photo © Dick Osseman, http://www.pbase.com/dosseman/profile   [248]
82. Ruler portraits from the opening of a copy of al-Hariri's *Maqamat* (the Schefer Hariri), probably made in Baghdad, Iraq, 1237 (Paris, BNF, arabe 5847, fols. 1v–2r; 37 × 28 cm). © Bibliothèque nationale de France   [250]
83. Niche with reliefs of warrior guards from the Gu'Kummet at Sinjar in Iraq, possibly made for al-Ashraf in the 1220s (National Museum of Iraq, Baghdad). © Yasser Tabbaa   [251]

84. Gate of the Two Baptisms, Deir Mar Benham, south-east of Mosul, Iraq; first half of the thirteenth century. © Amir Harrak [251]
85. View of the main iwan beyond the entrance to Geguti palace, near Kutaisi, Georgia; twelfth–thirteenth century. © Antony Eastmond [252]
86. Real and fantastic fights on the basin of al-'Adil II. Brass with silver and gold inlay; 1238–40 (Paris, Musée du Louvre, 5991; height: 19.2 cm; diameter: 47.2 cm). Photo © Musée du Louvre, Dist. RMN-Grand Palais/Hughes Dubois [254]
87. Ceramic fountain spout of a sphinx-like chimera, excavated from Rafiqa, early thirteenth century (Copenhagen, David Collection, inv. Isl. 56; height: 37 cm). The David Collection, Copenhagen. Photo: Pernille Klemp [256]
88. Tiles from the Seljuk palace at Kubadabad on the edge of Lake Beyşehir, Turkey, built by the Sultan Kaykubad; 1220s. Courtesy Rüçhan Arık (from R. Arık and O. Arık, *Tiles: Treasures of Anatolian Soil: Tiles of the Seljuk and Beylik Periods* (Istanbul: Kale Group Cultural Publications, 2008)) [257]
89. The killing of the dragon by the hero Amiran, from the Georgian poem *Amiran-Darejaniani*, painted on the south wall of the church of the Archangels, Lashtkhveri, Svaneti, Georgia; fourteenth century. © Antony Eastmond [259]
90. Stucco fragments excavated at Ani, Turkey, and Dvin, Armenia; twelfth–thirteenth century (Yerevan, History Museum of Armenia). Photo: Vram Hakobyan [260]
91. Stucco fragments from the Seljuk palace at Beyşehir and the kiosk at Konya, Turkey; early thirteenth century (Los Angeles County Museum of Art, The Madina Collection of Islamic Art, Gift of Camilla Chandler Frost, M.2002.1.675, 11.4 × 9.4 cm; M.2002.1.683a-h, height approx. 5.7 cm). Photo © Museum Associates/LACMA [262]
92. Badr al-Din Lu'lu' and his court entertained by female musicians, from volume 4 of the *Kitab al-Aghani*, Mosul, Iraq; 1219 (Cairo, Egyptian National Library, Ms Farsi 579, frontispiece). © Alfredo Dagli Orti/The Art Archive/Corbis [265]
93. Twelfth-century Iranian brass ewer, excavated at Ani by Nikolai Marr in 1906 (Yerevan, History Museum of Armenia, inv. 123-1322). Photo: Vram Hakobyan [267]
94. Crusader doorway from Acre, re-used as the entrance to the madrasa–mausoleum complex of the Mamluk Sultan

al-Nasir Muhammad in Cairo, Egypt; 1296–1303. © Antony Eastmond   [269]

95. Back of the astrolabe of al-Ashraf, made by ʿAbd al-Karim, Mesopotamia. Brass with gold and silver inlay; 1227 (Oxford, Museum for the History of Science, inv. 37148; diameter: 27.7 cm; weight: 3.75 kg). © Museum of the History of Science   [274]

96. Aries from a Georgian astrological treatise, 1188 (National Manuscripts Centre, Tbilisi, MS A-65, fol. 352; 23 × 30.5cm). © National Manuscripts Centre, Tbilisi. Courtesy Zurab Samarghanishvili   [276]

97. The preparation of the theriac of Aflaguras from the *Kitab al-Diryaq* [Book of antidotes], written and illustrated in Mesopotamia; 1199 (Paris, BNF, arabe 2964, fol. 15; 36.5 × 27.5 cm). © Bibliothèque nationale de France   [278]

98. Detail of the celestial globe of Frederick II, Holy Roman Emperor, a gift from al-Kamil Ayyub, showing Gemini and Cancer, with Orion and Hydra below. Brass with gold and silver inlay; 1225/6 (Naples, Museo di Capodimonte; diameter 22.1 cm). Museo di Capodimonte, Napoli. Photo © Luciano Pedicini/Archivio dell'Arte   [280]

99. North portal of the Alaeddin Camii, Konya, Turkey; 1219–20. © Antony Eastmond   [284]

100. Portal of the Sultan Han near Aksaray, Turkey; 1229 (photo by Gertrude Bell, 1907). Gertrude Bell Archive, Newcastle University. I_196   [285]

101. Sitte Melik, Divriği, Turkey, tomb of Shahanshah, Mengujekid ruler of the city; 1196. © Antony Eastmond   [289]

102. Tomb of Mumine Khatun, Nakhchivan, Azerbaijan, built for the first wife of Jahan Pahlavan, *atabeg* of Azerbaijan; 1186. © Steve Rapp   [290]

103. Portal of the mausoleum of Mama Khatun, Tercan, Turkey; early thirteenth century. © Antony Eastmond   [291]

104. Ground plan of the mausoleum of Mama Khatun, Tercan, Turkey, early thirteenth century   [292]

105. Tomb of Mama Khatun, Tercan, Turkey; early thirteenth century. © Antony Eastmond   [294]

106. Convent of the Virgin, Ani, Turkey, from the north; early thirteenth century. © Antony Eastmond   [295]

107. Ground plan of the convent of the Virgin, Ani, Turkey; early thirteenth century   [296]

108. Muqarnas stonework in the central vault of
 the zhamatun of the monastery of Harichavank, Armenia;
 c. 1224. © Antony Eastmond   [297]
109. Muqarnas stonework in the central vault of the Yakutiye Madrasa,
 Erzurum, Turkey; 1310. © Antony Eastmond   [298]
110. West façade of the chapel of St Gregory, Goshavank, Armenia; 1237.
 © Antony Eastmond   [299]
111. Tympanum over the west door of the zhamatun, Harichavank,
 Armenia; 1234. © Antony Eastmond   [300]
112. Cantilevered staircase in the main church at Harichavank, Armenia;
 1201. © Antony Eastmond   [301]
113. Armenian inscription on east façade of main church at Harichavank,
 Armenia; 1201. © Antony Eastmond   [302]
114. East façade of the zhamatun of the church of the Holy Apostles, Ani,
 Turkey; before 1217. © Antony Eastmond   [302]
115. Polychrome vaulting in the zhamatun of the church of the Holy
 Apostles, Ani, Turkey; before 1217. © Antony Eastmond   [303]
116. Polychrome vaulting in the mosque of Minuchihr, Ani, Turkey;
 twelfth–thirteenth century. © Antony Eastmond   [304]
117. Ground plan of the mosque–hospital complex at Divriği,
 Turkey; 1229   [305]
118. North portal of the mosque at Divriği, Turkey; 1229. © Antony
 Eastmond   [307]
119. Detail of rhombuses and foliate decoration on north portal of the
 mosque, Divriği, Turkey; 1229. © Antony Eastmond   [308]
120. Detail of interlace medallions and palmettes on north portal of the
 mosque, Divriği, Turkey; 1229. © Antony Eastmond   [309]
121. Detail of the depth of carving of the decoration on the north portal
 of the mosque, Divriği, Turkey; 1229. © Antony Eastmond   [310]
122. West portal of the mosque, Divriği, Turkey; 1229. © Antony
 Eastmond   [311]
123. West portal of the hospital, Divriği, Turkey; 1229. © Antony
 Eastmond   [312]
124. Detail of a vault in the south-east corner of the mosque, Divriği,
 Turkey; 1229. © Antony Eastmond   [313]
125. Iwan of the hospital, Divriği, Turkey; 1229. © Antony
 Eastmond   [314]
126. Detail of a tombstone at Akhlat; late thirteenth century. © Antony
 Eastmond   [315]

127. Side wall of the portal of the madrasa of the Mahperi Huand Hatun complex, Kayseri, Turkey; 1237. © Antony Eastmond [316]
128. View from the south-west of Hovhannavank monastery, Armenia: church (1215–21); zhamatun (1250–5). © Antony Eastmond [318]
129. Tympanum over the west entrance to the zhamatun at Saghmosavank monastery, Armenia; 1250–5. © Antony Eastmond [318]
130. Altar platform in main the church at Makaravank monastery, Armenia; 1205. © Antony Eastmond [319]
131. *Mihrab* commissioned by al-Muzaffar Ghazi in the Ulu Camii at Mayyafariqin (Silvan), Turkey; 1227. © Antony Eastmond [320]
132. Roman temple at Garni, Armenia; first century AD (rebuilt 1960s). © Antony Eastmond [323]
133. Detail of the ornate brick and tile work on the south iwan of the madrasa at Zuzan, Iran; 1218. © Sheila Blair and Jonathan Bloom [332]
134. Copper ingot of Jalal al-Din Khwarazmshah counterstamped by Queen Rusudan of Georgia; 1228 (Copenhagen, David Collection, inv. C330; 49.2 g). The David Collection, Copenhagen. Photo: Pernille Klemp [334]
135. *Minai*-ware dish showing a siege; c. 1210–20 (Freer Gallery of Art, Smithsonian Institution, Washington, DC: purchase, F1943.3; diameter: 47.8 cm). © Smithsonian Institution [334]
136. Black stone of Jalal al-Din Khwarazmshah; November 1230 (British Museum, inv. ME OA 1990.6–12.1; 47 × 29 cm) [337]
137. The great Buddha at Bamiyan, Afghanistan; sixth century AD (photo by Robert Byron, 1933/4). Image courtesy Conway Library, Courtauld Institute of Art, London [354]
138. Guillaume Boucher's drinks fountain at the Mongol court, as imagined by Pierre Bergeron to accompany *Illustrations de Voyages faits principalement en Asie* (Paris 1735). Muséum national d'histoire naturelle (Paris) – Direction des bibliothèques et de la documentation [359]
139. Design for a peacock fountain for cleaning hands, from al-Jazari's *Book of Knowledge of Ingenious Mechanical Devices*; 1206 (TSMK. Ahmet III, 3472, fol. 136a) [361]
140. Tiles from the summer palace at Takht-i Sulayman, Iran; 1270s (Los Angeles County Museum of Art, Shinji Shumeikai Acquisition Fund, AC1996.115.1–4; each tile 24.8 cm high). Image: Los Angeles County Museum of Art, www.lacma.org [365]

141. John, bishop of Grner and brother of King Hetum II, consecrating a priest, from a Gospel book made in 1289 (Yerevan, Matenadaran 197, fol. 341v; 26.3 × 18 cm). © Matenadaran, Yerevan [366]
142. Coin of Tamta from Akhlat; *c.* 1250 (Tübingen no. 99–14–54). Tübingen University coin collection, FINT inv. no. 99–14–54. [375]
143. Sts Constantine and Helena with Mongolian features, from a Syriac lectionary, copied at the monastery of Mar Mattai, near Mosul, Iraq; 1219–20 (Biblioteca Apostolica Vaticana, Syr. 559, fol. 223v; 43.5 × 33.5 cm). © 2017 Biblioteca Apostolica Vaticana [385]
144. Family mausoleum bell-tower for Zakare III and his wife Vaneni Mqargrdzeli at Kobayr, Armenia; 1279. © Antony Eastmond [387]
145. Usta Sakirt Türbe, Akhlat, Turkey; 1273. © Antony Eastmond [388]

Acknowledgements

Tracing Tamta's life has forced me to move far beyond the corners of the medieval world which I studied as a student. I am acutely conscious of how much I owe to the scholars who have mastered the languages, histories and cultures of each of the groups that Tamta encountered and who have written about them with such erudition and knowledge. This is truly a book that was written standing on the shoulders of giants. Wherever possible in this book I have used materials that are available in English or other European languages in the hope that it points readers usefully to the extraordinary work that historians have carried out over the past 150 years to bring the world in which Tamta lived to a wider audience, beginning with the travel accounts and translations of Marie-Félicité Brosset. Indeed, I could not have carried out my research without much of this material. However much I might wish I had the polyglot skills of Vladimir Minorsky, the first scholar to write seriously on the Mqargrdzelis in Ani and who had mastered all the languages of the region – as well as a plethora of European ones – I do not. I am only too aware of the limitations this imposes upon my research. However, I wrote this book hoping that the benefits of presenting a cross-cultural study might outweigh the weaknesses imposed by my access to the material in all its diversity.

This book was written whilst I held a Major Research Fellowship from the Leverhulme Trust, which gave me invaluable space and time to travel around (some of) Tamta's world, and then to think and write. I received generous financial support towards the cost of images from the A.G. Leventis Foundation and the Research Committee of the Courtauld Institute of Art. I am grateful to all of these foundations for their backing and their encouragement.

I am particularly grateful to Liz James, Ioanna Rapti, Scott Redford and Zaza Skhirtladze, who have either read parts of the manuscript or travelled through Tamta's world with me, and have shown unflagging interest in my work, whatever they were actually thinking or feeling. Others who have answered more specific questions and queries include Sussan Babaie, Doris Behrens-Abouseif, Massimo Bernabò, Anna Contadini, Eleni Dimitriadou, Theresa Fitzherbert, Eurydice Georganteli, Tim Greenwood, Judith

Herrin, Konrad Hirschler, Renata Holod, Lynn Jones, Hugh Kennedy, Irina Koshoridze, Bernard O'Kane, Bob Ousterhout, Andrew Peacock, Venetia Porter, Mariam Rosser-Owen and Christine Stevenson. My medieval colleagues at the Courtauld, Alixe Bovey, Joanna Cannon, John Lowden and Tom Nickson, have provided the supportive but critical research community that every scholar needs. Finally, I have recently been able to rehearse many of my ideas on site with my colleagues on two Getty Foundation Crossing Frontiers research expeditions to Tamta's world, where I was challenged and stimulated by, from A–Z: by Arpine, Christina, Diana, Elif, Gohar, Hadi, Hale, Ioanna, Maxime, Natia, Nato, Nazenie, Oya, Polina, Sima, Sussan, Zarifa and Zaza.

For photographs, I am enormously indebted to Karin Kyburz at the Courtauld, who has pursued images with a tenacity and vigour that is extraordinary. The obscurity of some of the images, and the range of sources from which they came, compelled her to be at her most enterprising, and she more than rose to the challenge. Additional help with images came from Ruçhan Arık, Sheila Blair, Jonathan Bloom, Mariam Didebulidze, Catherine Draycott, Nazenie Garibian de Vartanan, Amir Harrak, Oğuz Kolaşin, Richard McClary, Tom Nickson, Dick Osseman, Banu Pekol, Steve Rapp, Yasser Tabbaa, Harout Tanielian and Thilo Ulbert. Lara Frentrop very efficiently helped to prepare the index.

My wife, Marion, has had a greater impact on this work than perhaps she realises; but the book is dedicated to my children, Helen and Stephen, who continue to put my research into its proper perspective.

Transliteration

As anyone who has worked on materials that cross linguistic and alphabetic frontiers knows, trying to impose consistency of spelling is well nigh impossible, not helped by the absence of consistency in the primary sources. No single system can cope with the diversity of names and sounds employed by the peoples that Tamta met, spoke and wrote with, so I have preferred to present names in ways that do not deter the casual reader. Whilst Hałarc'in or *mcignobart'uxuc'esi* may please purists, they are not easy on the eye.

Abbreviations

BEO　　*Bulletin d'études orientales*
BSOAS　*Bulletin of the School of Oriental and African Studies*
DOP　　*Dumbarton Oaks Papers*
RCEA　*Répertoire chronologique d'épigraphie arabe*, 18 vols. (Cairo, 1936)
REArm　*Revue des études arméniennes*
REB　　*Revue des études byzantines*
RHCHO　*Recueil des historiens des croisades: historiens orientaux*
TEI　　*Thesaurus d'Epigraphie Islamique* (http://www.epigraphie-islamique.org/)

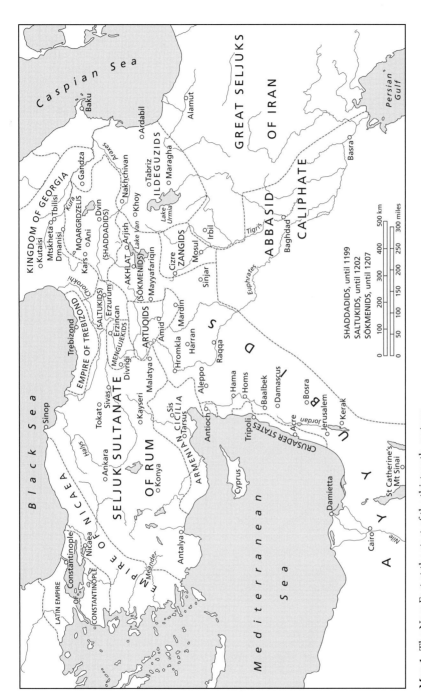

Map 1 The Near East at the start of the thirteenth century

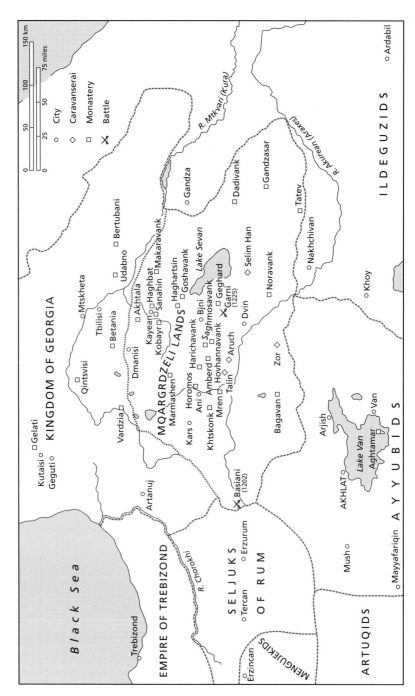

Map 2 The Caucasus at the start of the thirteenth century

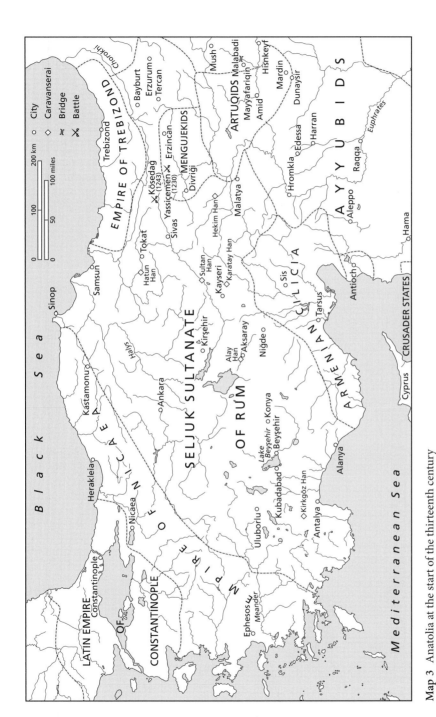

Map 3 Anatolia at the start of the thirteenth century

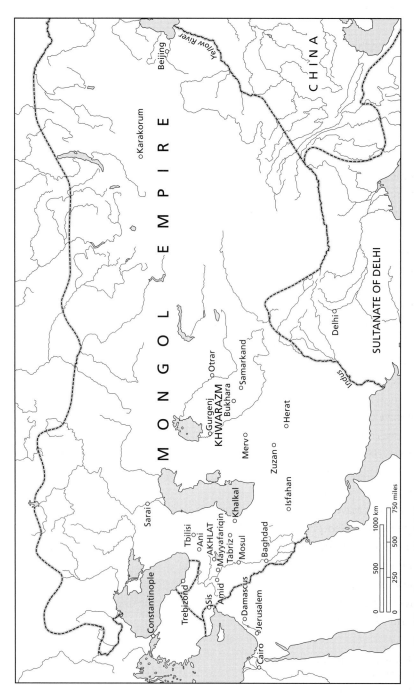

Map 4　The Mongolian world c. 1250

1 | A New World of Encounters

The Life of Tamta Mqargrdzeli

> The coming of this woman into the house of the sultans brought about much good.[1]

Some said it was the fault of the horse, which went lame just as he tried to escape. Others blamed the rider himself: he was drunk and, 'riding aimlessly', came too close to the walls of the besieged city. Yet others praised the city's defenders: they had dug a trap and carefully covered it in straw, and it was this that the horse blundered into.[2] All, however, agreed on what happened next. Ivane Mqargrdzeli, the commander of a combined Christian army of Georgians and Armenians, was captured outside the besieged walls of the Muslim-held city of Akhlat, on the north-west shore of Lake Van in what is now eastern Turkey. The year was 1210.

The consequences of Ivane's capture would resonate for the next forty years, particularly for one person, his daughter Tamta. Tamta became one of the rewards in the ransom negotiations that followed Ivane's capture and led to her diplomatic – forced – marriage to al-Awhad, the ruler of Akhlat, and a nephew of the Ayyubid Sultan, Saladin, the scourge of Christians. However, this was only the first in a series of defeats, marriages and rape that saw her passed between all the conquerors who eyed Anatolia in the first half of the thirteenth century. These encounters traversed a new world that stretched from the Mediterranean to Mongolia.

Tamta's travels show the mobility of the medieval world. Her life links together the Georgians and the Armenians – the Christian peoples of the Caucasus – with the Ayyubids, Seljuk Turks and other Turkish emirates – the Muslim groups that dominated Anatolia and Syria. She was involved with the Crusader states in the Holy Land and Byzantium. She also connects all these eastern Mediterranean and Caucasian cultures with the Central Asian world of the Khwarazmians and the East Asian Mongols – both of whom

---

[1] Kirakos, 83 (trans. Bedrosian, 46).
[2] These varied explanations are recounted by Abu'l-Fida, 85; V. Minorsky, *Studies in Caucasian History* (London, 1953), 150 n.1 (citing al-Qazvini). Kirakos, 82; al-Dahabi, 193; M. F. Brosset, *Additions et éclaircissements à l'Histoire de la Géorgie* (St Petersburg, 1851), 272–3, notes the silence of the Georgian sources concerning this defeat.

invaded Tamta's world in the 1220s and 1230s; shocking new arrivals with radically different cultures and terrifyingly ferocious armies. She travelled between Christianity, Islam and the shamanistic and Buddhist religions of the Mongol world, and between the cultures of the Mediterranean, the Caucasus, Eurasia and Asia. We do not normally think that all these culturally diverse and apparently separate worlds could be experienced by one person, let alone by a woman, in the thirteenth century. Tamta lived amongst all these different groups and, between about 1236 and 1245, she even travelled to Mongolia. Although she has left no account of her travels, she was one of the first Christians to undertake such an arduous journey, and she returned before the first of the better-known western missionaries, the Friar John of Plano Carpini, had even set out on his travels. In the mid-1240s the Mongols returned Tamta to Akhlat and, if she had first entered the city as a prize of war, a victim, she now returned to it as the city's independent ruler and was to govern there for the last decade of her life. Tamta's shift from forced bride to female ruler represents one of the great transformations of a woman in the thirteenth century.

Tamta's life can only be pieced together from a few off-hand mentions spread across histories written by contemporaries in Georgian, Armenian, Arabic and Persian. For them, women were hardly the stuff of history. But those occasional, sparse appearances in the historical sources give enough information to sketch out her history, and that is the aim of this chapter. The following chapters examine the nature of the religious and cultural encounters that she enjoyed or endured, and the ways in which her identity changed in consequence. The different names, peoples and cultures that appear in this chapter, in many cases fleetingly and with only the briefest of descriptions, will be explored and explained at much greater length in the next. This book re-traces Tamta's life, the cultures she encountered and the role played by women in them.

Tamta's Life

Tamta's presence as a bargaining chip in the ransom negotiations for her father is the first that we know of her in any historical source. Her life before then is purely surmise. It is an inauspicious beginning for a biography: we do not know when she was born, and this is compounded by the fact that we do not know when her father, Ivane, was born either; nor do we have any information about her mother, beyond her name, Khoshak.[3] The

---

[3] She is named in Kirakos, 159, and in Vardan, 212, where Vardan claims that she was responsible for the conversion of Zakare's son, Shahanshah, to Chalcedonianism: C. Toumanoff, *Les*

Mqargrdzeli family owned great estates in the province of Lore, on the marchlands between Armenia and Georgia in the Caucasus, and it was in this area of high plateaux and deep river gorges that she must have spent her first years. We know that Ivane took on an active role at the court of Georgia from the 1190s, and that Tamta was clearly of marriageable age by 1210. If we assume that she was over thirteen at her marriage, and given that her death is placed in the year 1254, we might assume that she was born around 1195.[4] Tamta had one brother, Avag, who was to succeed their father in his posts at the Georgian court in the 1230s, and who played an important role in Tamta's life in the decade before she died.

Tamta had been raised at a time when women seemed to be in the ascendant in the Caucasus. Her family held senior posts at the court of Tamar, the Queen of Georgia and the first woman to rule in her own name and in her own right in the region (r. 1184–1210). Taking advantage of internal power struggles all around Georgia among the Seljuk Turks, the Turkoman tribes in Anatolia and Azerbaijan, the Byzantines and the Armenians, Tamar's armies extended Georgian rule and influence through eastern Anatolia. By 1199 Georgia controlled most of Greater Armenia (the traditional name for the area comprising most of modern Armenia and parts of eastern Turkey), and by the end of the next decade it dominated many of the small Muslim emirates that lay beyond them. Tughrilshah, the Emir of Erzurum, acknowledged Tamar as his overlord and even placed a cross above his Islamic banners;[5] and the Mengujekid ruler of Erzincan similarly acknowledged his vassalship to her. Muslim historians worried about Georgian expansionism in this decade: Tamar's troops raided far into Khorasan in eastern Iran, and one writer feared the Georgians' ambition to replace the Caliph in Baghdad with their Christian Catholicos, and to turn the city's mosques into churches.[6] In 1210, then, Tamar's independent position as a woman ruler was secure, and, as her reign coincided with a period of Georgian territorial expansionism, it was already being hailed as a golden age, commanded by a living saint who was also the 'fourth member of the Trinity'.[7]

dynasties de la Caucasie chrétienne de l'Antiquité jusqu'au XIXe siècle. Tables généalogiques et chronologiques (Rome, 1990), 295, tab. 63:7.

[4] From the eighth century the legal age for a girl to marry was thirteen: *Ecloga*, 72; for the reality see C. Hennessy, *Images of Children in Byzantium* (Aldershot, 2008), 16–17.

[5] Ibn al-Athir, 3: 270.

[6] Juvayni, 2: 426. However, this is something of a cliché in Islamic sources: the same appears in Husayni, 36.

[7] Tamar was named as saint during her lifetime in the Vani Gospels (Tbilisi, National Center of Manuscripts, A-1335, fol. 272v): K. Sharashidze, *Sakartvelos sakhelmtsipo muzeumis kartul khelnatserta aghtseriloba: qopili saeklesio muzeumis khelnatserebi (A kolektsia)* vol. 4 (Tbilisi, 1954), 409; E. Taqaishvili, 'L'évangile de Vani', *Byzantion* 10 (1935), 655-63; Tamar as fourth member of the Trinity: *Kartlis Tskhovreba*, 239.

The Mqargrdzeli family played a formidable role in this expansion of Georgian power, although it was not itself a Georgian family.[8] It had risen to prominence in the 1170s under Tamar's father, Giorgi III, as he looked for fresh courtiers to counterbalance the established but fractious nobility that constantly sought to subvert or limit his royal power. For new, loyal allies he had looked beyond Georgia's traditional borders to an Armenian family of Kurdish descent whose head, Sargis Mqargrdzeli, had proved himself in battle and at court. Sargis was followed by his sons Zakare and Ivane, and it was their loyalty to Tamar that enabled her to exercise independent power as ruling Queen in a world in which women were more normally expected to move from father to husband as meek and obedient chattels.

Tamta's background, then, must be found within the mixed Georgian and Armenian milieu of the start of the thirteenth century. Tamta's early life was spent in this double world – divided geographically between Armenia and Georgia, divided linguistically between the different languages each country spoke, and divided religiously between the two different Christian confessions that each nation professed. Her uncle Zakare adhered to the Armenian Apostolic Orthodoxy into which members of the family had been baptised, but in around 1200 her father converted to the Chalcedonian Christianity of the Georgians.[9]

Ivane's capture at Akhlat in 1210 took place during the annual Georgian summer raids that sought to extend Tamar's territory south and west into Greater Armenia and Anatolia, or south and east into Iran. Akhlat was an important military goal because of its strategic location between the Caucasus, Anatolia and the Jazira. One of the explanations for Ivane's seizure offered by Armenian chroniclers claimed that it was divine vengeance for his apostasy from the Armenian faith.[10] The failed assault on Akhlat marked the high water mark of the Georgian adventurism that opened the thirteenth century. Two years later, soon after Zakare's death, Ivane set up a great public inscription around the entrance to the church at Haghartsin in northern Armenia in memory of his brother and to celebrate their joint successes:

> By the will of God, this inscription is a monument in perpetuity, in memory of the sons of the Great Sargis, Zakare and Ivane, of the Bagratid family. When the bounty of God was upon his creatures and allowed us to enter into possession of the heritage of our fathers, he placed first in our hands the impregnable castle of Amberd and the royal city of Ani, then the

---

[8] The family's origins are described in Kirakos, 81.   [9] *Kartlis Tskhovbreba*, 263–7.
[10] Kirakos, 82–3. His defeat at Garni in 1225 was similarly ascribed to his apostasy in the Sebastatsi chronicle: *Armianskie istochniki*, 23.

fortress of Bjni and Marand as far as Gushank; Tevriz [Tabriz]; Karnukalak [Erzurum] as far as Akhlat; Shaki, the Shirvan; Barda as far as Beluqan, and many other countries with their frontiers which we regard as futile to mention. This God, who never angers, loved Zakare, the crown of our head, and called this powerful hero to him. So I, I constructed this oratory, in our hereditary monastery of Haghartsin, carved in stone, red in colour, at the gate of the church of St Gregory, and I gave it a vineyard, located at Yerevan, in memory of my brother. The servants of this place must celebrate, without interruption, a liturgy in the principal chapel; those who will do this, may they be blessed by God.[11]

Given the fate of Tamta, the 'as far as Akhlat' appears particularly poignant. There is certainly no mention of his capture, or of Tamta's, in this bombastic text.

The price of Ivane's ransom in 1210 was high: a thirty-year peace in which the Georgians vowed not to launch new attacks to the south, the return of captured castles, the release of 5,000 Muslim captives and the payment of 100,000 dinars.[12] The final demand, the handing over of Tamta in marriage to the commander of the city, al-Awhad, was perhaps the most costly of all. Tamta's treatment shows the limits and exceptionalism of Tamar's hard-won position: the Queen may have eventually been able to determine her own fate, but her female subjects were not afforded a similar luxury.

Al-Awhad was one of the many nephews of al-Nasir Salah al-Din Yusuf, better known in the west as Saladin, the leader of the Ayyubid family that dominated the Muslim world in Syria and Egypt at the end of the twelfth century. Al-Awhad had only recently come into power in Akhlat. In the twelfth century the city had been an independent Turkish emirate, ruled by Muslim emirs who gave themselves the title of Shah-i Armen (King of the Armenians), but the years before Ivane's capture were marked by internal strife within the city. The last of the Shah-i Armen dynasty, an unnamed son of Beg-Temür, had been forced out of the city by its inhabitants. His malicious and incompetent rule fed a revolt, and he was replaced by one of his *mamluk*s (slave soldiers) named Balban. Al-Awhad was based in the nearby city of Mayyafariqin (modern Silvan) and his advance to the north was part of a concerted campaign organised by his father al-'Adil (the brother and successor of Saladin) to expand Ayyubid power out of Syria and the Jazira and into south-eastern Anatolia and Greater Armenia. In the face

---

[11] Brosset, *Additions et éclaircissements*, 271; S. La Porta, '"The Kingdom and the Sultanate were Conjoined": Legitimizing Land and Power in Armenia during the 12th and early 13th Centuries', REArm 34 (2012), 73–118, at 91.

[12] Abu'l-Fida, 85.

of these Ayyubid advances on the city Balban allied himself with Tughril-shah, the Seljuk ruler of Erzurum (and occasional vassal of Georgia), the most powerful of the emirates in eastern Anatolia. This kept the Ayyubids at bay, but awakened Tughrilshah's own ambitions. He betrayed and murdered Balban, hoping to take control of Akhlat himself. Once more the people of the city rose against a potential ruler, refusing Tughrilshah entrance into Akhlat. But to keep him out they needed support from elsewhere, and were now forced to open their gates to al-Awhad, who was clearly seen as the lesser of two evils.[13] Nevertheless, the Ayyubid ruler was not a popular choice and his garrison was virtually imprisoned in the citadel by the city's population.[14] Underlying this fierce distrust was ethnic tension between the Turkoman elites of Anatolia and the Arabicised rulers of Syria. Al-Awhad had been warned to be careful in Akhlat, as its people 'are averse to the Arabs' (although as we will see, such ethnic distinctions are by no means clear cut, and the identity of the Ayyubids was complex).[15]

It was at this moment that the Georgian raid on the city ended in failure with such disastrous consequences, and led to Tamta's marriage to its Ayyubid ruler. The marriage was a minor affair – al-Awhad was one of the less important of the sons of al-'Adil, only trusted with a relatively insignificant territory to rule, a long way from the heartland of Ayyubid power in Syria and Egypt. Al-Dahabi dismisses him as 'unjust and deceitful'.[16] Although the marriage had international ramifications in bringing Georgians and Ayyubids into contact with each other, it was essentially a border affair. However, this was to change very quickly, when Tamta found herself a widow after only a few months.[17] Al-Awhad died, probably of disease, and his lands were rapidly taken over by his brother al-Ashraf Musa, who assumed control of his government, and also took over his treaty with the Georgians. He clearly inherited al-Awhad's Caucasian wife as well, and he immediately married Tamta to preserve the blood-link that underlay the peace.

The replacement of al-Awhad by al-Ashraf appeared seamless. Al-Ashraf stressed his continuity with his brother, maintaining his policies and even completing his buildings.[18] But this appearance of continuity in fact disguised a radical change, as al-Ashraf was much more ambitious than his

---

[13] Bar Hebraeus, 363–5. [14] Minorsky, *Studies in Caucasian History*, 149.
[15] Ibn al-Athir, 3: 122. [16] Al-Dahabi, 198.
[17] C. D'Ohsson, *Histoire des Mongols, depuis Tchinguiz-Khan jusqu'à Timour Bey ou Tamerlan* (Amsterdam, 1852), 3: 42.
[18] As at the minaret extra muros at Mayyafariqin al-Ashraf completed in 1212 and that at al-Ruha: E. J. Whelan, *The Public Figure: Political Iconography in Medieval Mesopotamia* (London, 2006), 437–40.

brother, and sought to carve out a larger and more significant realm to rule. The second marriage moved Tamta into a very different league within the Ayyubid world: al-Ashraf, along with his older brothers al-Kamil and al-Muʿazzam, were the three major figures in their generation of the family and dominated its tensions, manoeuvrings and disputes over the next quarter of a century across the Jazira, Syria and Egypt. Initially, al-ʿAdil disapproved of his son's actions at Akhlat, fearing, with good reason, that it was evidence of his dangerous ambition, but al-Ashraf managed to persuade him of his loyalty to the family.[19] This second marriage lasted for more than a quarter of a century, until al-Ashraf's death in 1237.

As a wife of al-Ashraf, Tamta was closer to the heart of the Ayyubid world, but she had to move carefully. On the one hand she now potentially had access to much greater wealth and influence than she had ever enjoyed before, but on the other her status as a Christian wife in a Muslim court made her vulnerable. Indeed, her future must have looked bleak. She was just one of many wives in al-Ashraf's harem, and by no means the most favoured. She had little family around her and no leverage among the court elite. We know more about the activities of her co-wives, who came from the most powerful Islamic dynasties to the west and east, including an unnamed sister of the Seljuk Sultan of Anatolia, Kaykubad I (1219–37), and Terkan Khatun, the sister of the Zangid ruler of Mosul, Arslan Shah I (1193–1211).[20] We also know more about her sisters-in-law, such as Dayfa Khatun, who was to go on in Aleppo to become the first Muslim woman to exercise independent rule.[21] These other women were Muslims and allied to powerful families within the Ayyubid confederacy and its allies. Tamta had neither religious nor family ties to protect her. Akhlat was very much an outpost of al-Ashraf's pocket empire; it was separated from his heartlands around Harran and Raqqa in the Jazira by the Artuqids in Amid (modern Diyarbakir) and Mardin. And when, in 1229, he took control of the wealthy capital, Damascus, al-Ashraf relinquished control of most of his other lands in the Jazira, leaving the windswept lakeside town of Akhlat even more isolated.[22]

It is not clear how al-Ashraf used his new wife, and she does not seem to have borne him any children.[23] However, she was not required to convert to

---

[19] Ibn al-ʿAmid, 19.
[20] R. S. Humphreys, 'Women as Patrons of Religious Architecture in Ayyubid Damascus', *Muqarnas* 11 (1994), 35–54, no. 15.
[21] Y. Tabbaa, 'Dayfa Khatun, Regent Queen and Architectural Patron', in *Women, Patronage, and Self-Representation in Islamic Societies*, ed. D. F. Ruggles (Albany, 2000), 17–34.
[22] Al-Dahabi, 224.
[23] J. Sublet, 'La folie de la princesse Bint al-Ašraf (un scandale financier sous les Mamelouks Bahris)', *BEO* 27 (1974), 45–50 suggests that Tamta may have borne him a daughter; but the identity of the mother is unknown.

Islam, as the Christian brides of other Muslim rulers around her were often forced to. It seems unlikely that she accompanied her new husband on his journeys between the cities he controlled. Instead, the one source that takes an interest in the marriage suggests that she mostly resided in Akhlat. This is the Armenian historian Kirakos Gandzaketsi's comment on the aftermath:

> The coming of this woman into the house of the sultans brought about much good, for the lot of the Christians under their domination improved, especially in Taron since the monasteries which were there and had been under taxation, had the rate of their taxes lowered, and half of them had the whole tax discontinued. [The Muslims] ordered those under their domination not to despoil or trouble travellers going to Jerusalem for pilgrimage. The Georgians especially expanded [their influence], for Ivane was misled to the doctrine of Chalcedon (through which the Georgians were lost); for he loved the glory of man more than the glory of God. He became charmed by the queen named Tamar, daughter of Giorgi, while Zakare remained true to the orthodox confession of the Armenians. Therefore they honoured the Georgians even more, for they were not taxed in all their cities, and in Jerusalem as well. [Ivane's daughter] was named Tamta.
>
> Thus was friendship and unity achieved between the Georgian kingdom and the sultans' lordship.[24]

Kirakos, who was probably writing on behalf of a Mqargrdzeli patron, is our main source for Tamta's life.[25] He was a contemporary of Tamta and began writing his history in 1241. His assessment of Tamta's influence is clearly a retrospective view, so we must assume that it was these concerns with monastic and city taxation and freedom of travel that occupied her over the next decades; for she is mentioned in no source for the next fifteen years. Akhlat itself was administered by a governor installed by al-Ashraf, his *hajib* (chamberlain), Husam al-Din 'Ali, so any influence that Tamta might exert had to be exercised through him. As we will see, where women did rule in the Muslim world, they had to do so through a façade of male governors. Taron, the fertile agricultural plain to the west of Lake Van, clearly came under her purview. This province was still largely populated by Christians, mostly Armenian, but also Greeks and Syriacs, despite having been under Muslim rule for more than a century; and it was among the Christians living here that Tamta was able to have most impact. The two achievements that

---

[24] Kirakos, 83 (trans. Bedrosian, 46). When fighting broke out between the Georgians and Akhlat, the Georgians were able to appeal to al-Ashraf to restore the peace, which he did: Ibn al-Athir, 3: 242–3.

[25] B. Dashdondog, *The Mongols and the Armenians (1220–1335)* (Leiden; Boston, 2010), 13.

Kirakos lists for Tamta, the reduction in taxation and support for pilgrimage, were key state activities in the thirteenth century, and both indicate her active role in the government of the region. Tax exemptions and records of pilgrimages were frequently noted in inscriptions on Armenian churches and city monuments to provide a permanent record of their existence, but the Christian monuments of Taron are almost all now destroyed.

In 1220 al-Ashraf gave Akhlat to his brother al-Malik al-Muzaffar Ghazi to rule as part of a redistribution of fiefs among the Ayyubid clan, and so this is the one period when Tamta may have travelled south with her husband into the Jazira and Syria. Ghazi himself tried to replicate the Georgian alliance by demanding to marry Rusudan, the daughter of Queen Tamar (and now sister of the ruling King, Giorgi IV Lasha), but the negotiations came to nothing.[26] By 1224 al-Ashraf was fed up with his brother, who had started to conspire against him with al-Mu'azzam, their more powerful sibling in Damascus, and he returned to capture and rule the city once again.[27] Tamta was certainly back in the region, without her husband, when Akhlat changed hands once again in 1230, suggesting that once more al-Ashraf left her in the city as his regent.

Tamta's reappearance coincided with the appearance of a new threat to the society of eastern Anatolia and the Caucasus. It came from the east: the Khwarazmians, a Turkic–Persian people from Central Asia, based to the south of the Aral Sea (modern Turkmenistan and Uzbekistan). The first phase in the expansion of the Mongols in the 1210s and 1220s had forced them to retreat to the west, where the Khwarazmian ruler, Jalal al-Din Minguburnu, carved out for himself a new kingdom in Iran, Azerbaijan and the Caucasus. The Khwarazmian invasion of eastern Anatolia began in 1225, when Jalal al-Din set out from Tabriz. It was in the course of this invasion that Tamta re-emerges from obscurity; and once again her fate can, in part, be laid at her father's door. Jalal al-Din's freedom to establish a new realm in the region came from his crushing defeat of a Georgian–Armenian army under Ivane's control at the battle of Garni in 1225. Ivane had underestimated the power of the Khwarazmians, thinking them a spent force after their defeats by the Mongols; his army was massacred and he fled the battlefield, leaving Tamta's brother Avag to sue for peace on humiliating terms.

In 1225 Tamta is recorded as being in command of the castle of 'Aliabad; a site which Jalal al-Din passed by but spared on his way to capture the

---

[26] *Kartlis Tskhovreba*, 205.
[27] Ibn al-Athir, 3: 247–8; Minorsky, *Studies in Caucasian History*, 150.

Georgian capital, Tbilisi.[28] This castle was probably located somewhere on the modern frontier between Armenia and Azerbaijan, suggesting that Tamta was still associated with the politics of her family in Armenia at this time, as well as exercising power in Akhlat on behalf of her husband.[29] However, on 14 April 1230 she was in Akhlat again when the city was finally captured by Jalal al-Din – three-and-a-half years after his first attempt in November 1226 had been rebuffed by the *hajib* Husam al-Din 'Ali.[30] The siege was a long and brutal one: 'The people of Akhlat ate the sheep, then the cattle, then the buffaloes, then the horses, then the donkeys, then the mules, then the dogs and cats. We heard that they were catching rats and eating them. They showed endurance that nobody could match.'[31] Jalal al-Din attacked with giant mangonels that hurled burning naphtha into the city. It was still remembered as the most traumatic episode in the city's history as late as the 1890s when the Anglo-Irish traveller H. F. B. Lynch visited Lake Van.[32] With the city captured, Tamta was taken prisoner by Jalal al-Din himself, who then 'enjoyed his rights with her that very night'.[33] In other words, he raped her.

Here we begin to gain a more sober assessment of the position of elite women and the fragility of their position. The successful, independent reigns of Tamar in Georgia or Dayfa Khatun in Aleppo were exceptions that few other women could equal. Contemporary chroniclers presented Jalal al-Din's assault on Tamta as an act of retribution against Malika, one of his wives. Malika was the daughter of Toghril Shah III, the last Great Seljuk ruler of Iran, and had been married to Muzaffar al-Din Özbek, who, with the title of *atabeg* of Azerbaijan, dominated the government of Iran.[34] Malika seems to have been the effective ruler of Tabriz when Jalal al-Din first moved west, and she negotiated the surrender of the city to him in 1225. She then engineered an excuse to force a divorce from her husband (condemned as cowardly and incompetent) in order to marry the Khwarazmshah. This looks very much like an attempt to jump horses to the new power in the region. She moved with Jalal al-Din to the city of Khoy, but fell out with her new husband and escaped to Akhlat, where she incited the *hajib* Husam

---

[28] Juvayni, 2: 430–31; al-Nasawi, 295.
[29] On the location of 'Aliabad see Minorsky's note in Juvayni, 2: 431 n. 20.
[30] J. A. Boyle, 'Dynastic and Political History of the Īl-Khāns', in *The Cambridge History of Iran*, vol. 5: *The Saljuq and Mongol Periods*, ed. J. A. Boyle (Cambridge, 1968), 303–421, esp. 327–33.
[31] Ibn al-Athir, 3: 298.
[32] H. F. B. Lynch, *Armenia: Travels and Studies* (London; New York, 1901), 2: 295–6: 'the event still forms the centre of the slight historical knowledge which is possessed by [even] the least educated of the present inhabitants'.
[33] D'Ohsson, *Histoire des Mongols*, 3: 42.   [34] Juvayni, 2: 424.

al-Din ʿAli to attack the Khwarazmians in Azerbaijan.[35] Her fate when Jalal al-Din took Akhlat is unknown, but she seems to have escaped, and Jalal al-Din took out his anger on Tamta instead: 'He entered the palace where he passed the night in the company of the daughter of Ivane, who was the wife of Malik Ashraf, and so assuaged his anger at the elopement of Malika [his former wife].'[36] As one woman evaded retribution, another suffered in her place.

Jalal al-Din then formalised his treatment of Tamta by forcing her to marry him.[37] In the light of her rape, this next act served to prolong Jalal al-Din's humiliation of Tamta. Perhaps more surprisingly, the marriage hints at a more positive assessment of Tamta's position. Jalal al-Din had no need to marry Tamta, and so the fact that he did indicates that she had attained some form of local authority that the Khwarazmian deemed wise to harness to his own benefit. The legality of the marriage was dubious at best given its coercive nature and the fact that al-Ashraf was still alive and had never divorced Tamta.

The Khwarazmian invasion of Iran, the Caucasus and eastern Anatolia proved to be only short-lived, although it managed to deliver extraordinary devastation during that time. The destruction was caused as much by the Khwarazmians' reputation as by their army: in 1226 the invaders burned down all the churches in the city of Tbilisi, the capital of Georgia ('to the joy of all Muslims', says the chronicler Ibn al-Athir).[38] However, the complete destruction of the city, which is lamented in Georgian histories, was actually carried out by the Georgians themselves the following year. They pre-emptively razed the city to the ground as they feared they could never hold it against the Khwarazmians, who could then use it as a base against them.[39] With the capture of Akhlat, Jalal al-Din announced his further intentions in a *Fatihname* (victory proclamation):

> By this auspicious action a clime of this splendour has been added to the realms acquired and inherited by us (may God increase their extent!), as sooner or later the realms of Syria and Rum [i.e. Seljuk Anatolia] will likewise fall into the hands of the servants of our house (may God perpetuate it and grant it victory!).[40]

Such a proclamation forced the different powers of the region to ally against the Khwarazmians. In August 1230 the Seljuk ruler of Anatolia, Kaykubad,

---

[35] R. S. Humphreys, *From Saladin to the Mongols: the Ayyubids of Damascus, 1193–1260* (Albany, 1977), 216.
[36] Juvayni, 2: 445.   [37] Kirakos, 113.   [38] Ibn al-Athir, 3: 269.
[39] Ibn al-Athir, 3: 283; al-Nasawi, 209.   [40] Juvayni, 2: 448.

joined with al-Ashraf to fight against the Khwarazmians.[41] They were joined by Georgian and Armenian troops. All were united – for once – by the fear of continued Khwarazmian expansion. The Ayyubids may possibly also have been driven by the desire to redeem the mistreatment of al-Ashraf's wife; but no sources mention such a motive.[42] The armies met at the battle of Yassıçemen, near Erzincan on the north of the Anatolian plateau. Jalal al-Din's initial successes were gradually whittled away, and after three days of fierce fighting he was forced to retreat back to Khoy in Iran. Al-Ashraf was able to occupy Akhlat again, although Tamta was no longer there as she had been taken off to Azerbaijan by Jalal al-Din on his retreat.[43] She was released as part of the peace negotiations that followed; her third marriage had lasted just four months.

The battle weakened Jalal al-Din, but it did not destroy him. This was only achieved by his old foe from the east, the Mongols. It was the Mongol invasion of Khwarazm in the 1210s that had forced Jalal al-Din to seek new lands to rule to the west, and it was the second phase of Mongol expansionism under Ögödei Khan, son of Genghis (Chinggis) Khan, in the 1230s that now sealed his fate. The arrival in Azerbaijan of the Mongol general Chormaqan made escaping the Mongols Jalal al-Din's main preoccupation. He and his army were pursued around the south of the Caspian Sea throughout the winter of 1230–1. Finally in August 1231 he was cornered by the Mongols near Amid. Abandoning his army and fleeing his enemies he escaped in disguise into the mountains where he was captured by two Kurds. His brief, violent reign came to an equally brutal end when they murdered him, either simply for his clothes and his horse or, according to a second source, in revenge for his killing of one of their relatives.[44] His fearsome reputation was such that even two decades later rumours circulated that he had somehow survived and was planning a new campaign, leading to the torture and execution of at least one possible pretender to his name.[45]

The Khwarazmian invasion ended with Tamta restored to her previous husband, and returned to her invisibility in the historical record. The Mongol attack of 1230–1 was not followed up for six years, after which they returned with a permanent force. In the brief, uneasy interlude that this created the local rivalries around Akhlat resumed once more. This time the city was captured by the Seljuk Sultan Kaykubad I, whose *pervane* (chief minister), Kamyar, took possession soon after Jalal al-Din's death.[46]

---

[41] Al-Dahabi, 227.   [42] The closest hint comes in Ibn al-'Amid, 40.
[43] D'Ohsson, *Histoire des Mongols*, 3: 45.   [44] Juvayni, 2: 459.
[45] Bar Hebraeus, 421–2.   [46] C. Cahen, *Pre-Ottoman Turkey* (London, 1968), 130–2.

Nothing is recorded of Tamta's whereabouts or her position during these years. However, we can deduce that she was not with her husband, al-Ashraf. In 1229, on the death of his brother al-Muʿazzam, al-Ashraf had succeeded in taking control of Damascus, the spiritual capital of the Ayyubid dynasty. He took the city from under the nose of al-Muʿazzam's heir, al-Nasir Dawud, but had to give up all his lands in the Jazira to maintain the fragile overall family peace.[47] He retained control only of Akhlat, but this was now isolated from his main landholding and al-Ashraf made no effort to recapture the city after it fell to Seljuk control. He seems to have lost interest in the city and the Armenian–Georgian wife who had come with it. From then until his death in 1237 all his energies were directed to his life in the capital of Syria. We know that Tamta was not with him at the outset of this period as she was besieged in Akhlat; and we know again that she was not with him in 1236 when she faced the next calamitous disruption to her life: her capture by the Mongols. The circumstances around her capture are now obscure, but she was probably staying with her brother Avag in his castle at Kayean, in northern Armenia. It is doubtful that she was still in Akhlat, as this was only captured by the Mongols in 1245.[48] In 1236 the castle at Kayean was besieged by the Mongol general, Chormaqan, who had returned to the Caucasus, but now with a much larger and more determined army, which set out permanently to conquer the region.[49] Avag was unable to withstand the siege, and quickly had to surrender his castle (and his daughter) to the Mongols. It is likely that Tamta became their prisoner at the same time. Soon after this happened Tamta became a widow for the third time when, in 1237, al-Ashraf died.

It was at this point that Tamta entered the most extraordinary period in her long and difficult life. She was sent by Chormaqan to his Mongol overlords in Karakorum, an overland journey across the steppes of Asia of some 5,000 kilometres.[50] It was while she was at the Great Khan's court in Mongolia that Akhlat changed hands for the final time in the thirteenth century. The battle of Kösedağ in 1243 saw the comprehensive defeat of the

---

[47] Humphreys, *From Saladin to the Mongols*, 193–206.
[48] Sebastatsi in *Armianskie istochniki*, 26.
[49] Here I follow M. F. Brosset, *Histoire de la Géorgie depuis l'antiquité jusqu'en 1469 de J.-C* (St Petersburg, 1849), 515 (n.4, carried over from p.514), borrowed by Minorsky, *Studies in Caucasian History*, 156. Brosset seems to base his scenario on Kirakos' account of Avag's siege at Kayean, but this makes no explicit mention of his sister: Kirakos, 126–7 for his capture, 129–31 for him being sent to the Great Khan.
[50] Minorsky, *Studies in Caucasian History*, 156, giving no source. Brosset, *Histoire de la Géorgie*, 505–6, n.1, argues that Tamta only went as far as Batu's camp on the Volga, but this contradicts what we know of the travels of all the other rulers from this region under Mongol rule.

Seljuks, Georgians and Armenians by the Mongol army. In its aftermath the Mongols took over the structures of the Seljuk state and placed puppet governors under a puppet sultan in all the cities they now controlled.

It was into this new political system that Tamta entered when she returned to Akhlat nine years after her capture.[51] Her journey to Mongolia is not recorded, but we know she was there because the new Queen of Georgia, Rusudan (r. 1223–45), daughter of Queen Tamar, requested her return:

> Rusudan, queen of the Georgians, sent prince Hamadola as an envoy to the Khan, and when he was to return Hamadola requested Tamta from the Khan. He brought her with him with orders from the Khan that whatever had been hers while wife of Malik al-Ashraf be given back to her.
> They obeyed the commands of their king and gave to her Akhlat and the districts surrounding it.[52]

Rusudan's request for Tamta's release was probably arranged by Avag, who now dominated the Georgian court as *atabeg*, and played a leading role in its politics in the first decades of the Mongol invasion. Tamta's life had come full circle as she returned to rule Akhlat thirty-five years after she had first entered the city as the queen of its ruler. Now, however, she was the city's ruler in her own right, administering the region on behalf of her Mongol overlords.[53] This was exactly the same position as that in which the kings of Georgia, the Byzantine Emperor of Trebizond, the Seljuk rulers of Anatolia and the Lu'lu'id rulers of Mosul all found themselves. After spending so much of her life in the Ayyubid world, this last decade returned her to the politics of Anatolia and the Caucasus. The Mongols' failure to invade Syria created a border that ran roughly along the line of the modern Turkish–Syrian frontier, and which cut the links that had previously tied Akhlat and its region with the Jazira.

Tamta seems to have had a decade in power in Akhlat before her death, probably in 1254.[54] The Mongols' acknowledgement of Tamta confirmed her status and position in Akhlat, but those final years were by no means easy. Ruling as a vassal of the Mongols placed enormous burdens on all those that had submitted to them, and this made Tamta's role a difficult and

---

[51] Her return in 1245 is recorded in Sebastatsi: *Armianskie istochniki*, 26, yr 694/1245.
[52] Kirakos, 145.
[53] A slightly different account is reported in Sibt ibn al-Jawzi's *Mir'at al-zaman*: Sublet, 'La folie de la princesse'. This will be investigated in a later chapter.
[54] This is the year of her death reported by Toumanoff, *Les dynasties de la Caucasie chrétienne*, 296, tab. 63:8, but with no primary source cited. I have been unable to track down a date.

unpopular one: whilst before she had been known as a reducer of taxation, now she had to fulfil the Mongols' oppressive demands for money, tribute and goods.

Despite its complexity, Tamta's life can be summarised in one sentence. Of Armenian birth, she was raised at the Georgian court before being married to two Ayyubid rulers, raped and then married by the Shah of the Khwarazmians, captured by the Seljuks, transported by the Mongols, before finally returning to the city of Akhlat as its ruler for the last decade of her life.[55]

Medieval Biographies and their Limitations

Having outlined her life, we must now begin to understand who Tamta was, and how she was changed by the many events that she underwent in her tumultuous life. Given how little we know about Tamta, we cannot answer this question through the traditional concerns of biography. We have no internal evidence of thoughts or beliefs, no inner life. We can only guess at her emotions, actions or psychology at any point in her life; they are not recorded. Everything we know about her comes from the outside – the brief observations of the events that affected her. Instead, we must build up a picture of her life in different ways: by situating her in the cultures in which she lived and understanding their concerns and expectations, and the positions and choices available to women in them. We must also see the ways in which the movements and changes she witnessed could affect what she was able to do: her access to power, influence and patronage, and the ability to exercise these. Rather than a study of Tamta's internal character and personality, which can only ever remain surmise, this is a study of the public, outward display of her personality. Through acts of patronage women were able to present aspects of themselves in public, particularly concerning their grasp of power and wealth, the details of their beliefs and piety, and the nature of their education and cultural aspirations. These could all be conveyed through the buildings and other works of art that they commissioned, and the styles, languages and materials that they adopted. These features that we can study are not intrinsic qualities; like clothes, they can

---

[55] An excellent parallel account of Tamta's life and her family background has been published by S. La Porta, 'Re-Constructing Armenia: Strategies of Co-Existence amongst Christians and Muslims in the Thirteenth Century', in *Negotiating Co-Existence: Communities, Cultures and Convivencia in Byzantine Society*, eds. B. Crostini and S. La Porta (Trier, 2013), 251–72, esp. 264–5.

all be manufactured, contrived and altered. Their appearance can develop and change depending on when and where they are expressed, and different facets can be displayed simultaneously to different audiences. They reveal not so much personality as identity.[56] What identities did Tamta have, and how were they transformed and manipulated as she moved between cultures? What was Tamta, what did she become, and how did she change over the course of her life?

Tamta provides the narrative focus of this book; she is a figure who witnessed and so unites all the different cultures that this book explores. However, she is often invisible at its centre – Hamlet without the prince. In order to understand the world in which she lived, we have to exploit three parallel sets of evidence which can be overlaid to build up a picture of Tamta and her world. The first is the limited, but important, evidence that concerns Tamta herself. This amounts to no more than half a dozen references to her in chronicles written in Armenian, Georgian, Arabic and Persian (and even here, the mentions can be allusive and indirect). It is on these that the chronology of her life is based.

The second is the more frequent (but still by no means abundant) evidence about other court women in the thirteenth century. Here we can turn to the evidence about queens, princesses and noblewomen across the region. Like Tamta, these women were involved in diplomatic marriages that forced them to move between cultures and religions, often against their will. Like Tamta they had to find ways to establish themselves within the power structures of the new court and find ways to exercise authority to defend their own interests and those of their children; occasionally some, like Tamta, even came to rule in their own right. We are able to see the options and possibilities that were open to them and the limitations that restricted what they were able to achieve. They allow us to see how such women adapted their identities in the new settings in which they found themselves through marriage, and how they presented these new faces to the people around them.

In a world in which women's lives were closely circumscribed and their public appearances limited and constrained, the means open to them to give themselves a public presence were restricted. Personal appearances were curbed by social expectations that women should remain in the house (or palace) and only appear in public with due modesty and deference to the men around them. Women's own bodies, then, were largely hidden from sight. In their place, women found a substitute to give them an enduring presence by commissioning substantial public monuments, which had a

---

[56] L. Safran, *The Medieval Salento: Art and Identity in Southern Italy* (Philadelphia, 2014), 3–5.

permanent place in the city or countryside, an ever-visible reminder of their founders. These buildings – monasteries, mosques and madrasas; baths and bridges, caravanserais and city walls – became ciphers through which women could express their piety, their virtues, their wealth and their power. The buildings and objects introduced in this book provide the closest we have to first-hand evidence from these women – none has left any writings to reveal their character, temperament or desires.

Religious foundations allowed women to show their piety and their adherence to the faith of their fathers or husbands; the secular foundations also demonstrated their concern for the welfare and defence of their subjects and their desire to increase the wealth and prosperity of their lands. At the same time all these buildings provided other forms of self-advertisement: who was able to build reveals shifts in the balance of power within the regime, as some women prospered at the expense of others. They were the arena in which rivalries were fought out. Buildings celebrated dynastic victories and mourned the murdered victims of the succession disputes that erupted within the royal harem on the death of a ruler. The choice of materials and craftsmen could demonstrate the wealth and geographic reach of their builders as rare marbles and stones were imported from distant lands and prestigious craftsmen were sought from neighbouring states. Although the majority of foundations of all these building types were made by men, a significant minority were erected by the women who feature in this book. How the foundations of women related to those of their male relatives reveals much about the independence they could claim within the social structure of the family. The appearance of the buildings could act as a marker of identity: the revival of building types from older regimes allowed their builders to situate themselves within networks of power as the inheritors of older kingdoms with the implications that followed of innate legitimacy as well as the claim to a particular historic set of territories, usually rather larger than the land currently under their control. The importation of styles used by more powerful neighbours provided a means to display forms of allegiance to some of the major political, cultural and military players in the region, and this could easily slip over into forms of appropriation as the styles were adopted as a means to claim dominion beyond normal boundaries. These visual languages were reinforced by the textual languages of the inscriptions carved on to the buildings. The dedicatory and other texts that appear on almost all the monuments provided the most direct means by which a founder could put her own words in the public domain, setting out her status, piety, wealth and ambition. However, they could only be read by an educated minority in each country (and in the case of some particularly complex inscriptions not even by them), but most people would be able to recognise the alphabet used and the implications of culture and religious affiliation that went with that.

In addition to magnificent buildings we can also look at the smaller-scale objects that surrounded women at court: metalwork mirrors, basins and ewers, manuscripts and scientific instruments, tiles and ceramics. Whilst these were mostly commissioned by men, they show the ethos and beliefs of the court and the place it allotted to women. The range of building types and objects that this book explores – from Christian churches to Islamic Sufi hospices, from rural monastic complexes to great city mosques, from urban palaces to tented Asian encampments, from books of poetry to astrolabes – reflects the diversity of situations and cultures in which Tamta lived during her life as she moved between Christian, Muslim and shamanistic societies.

If women are the main protagonists of this book, there is one other actor of almost equal importance: this is the third strand. It is the city of Akhlat. Tamta's fate throughout her life was inextricably linked to this city. It is now a remote and sleepy small town which sits largely unnoticed on the northern shore of Lake Van. Its modern appearance (or lack of it) belies its strategic importance in the Middle Ages. Tamta's three marriages were all as much about control of Akhlat as they were about Tamta herself, as was the decision of the Mongols to return Tamta to the city as its governor in the last decade of her life. Like Tamta, Akhlat was a site of interaction between cultures and religions as different regimes and populations took control, and the fate of the city ran parallel with that of Tamta. Although little survives in the city itself beyond tombstones and tomb towers (the few other buildings that survived the succession of Khwarazmian and Mongol attacks in the 1230s were destroyed in two terrible earthquakes in 1246 and 1276), we can piece together much about the city by looking at the development of other towns in the region. These shared similar fates to that of Akhlat, and the move between different rulers, religions and cultures is reflected in the changing monuments that were commissioned and built. Thus, like Tamta, the identity of the city could change as it moved between different rulers; and it could present different identities to different viewers – defenders and invaders took different messages from city walls; Christians and Muslims structured their encounter with the city around different sets of monuments – mosques and madrasas or monasteries and churches – and viewed those of rival religions in different ways. From these we can build up a picture of the ways in which identities were mapped onto the urban fabric of the city. In other cases, we have more direct evidence of what the buildings in Akhlat may have been like: a number of sites in Turkey preserve monuments built during Tamta's lifetime by architects and masons who named themselves as coming from the city of Akhlat. These show us the skill and versatility of the men who trained in Akhlat, their technical accomplishments as well as the diversity of the stylistic motifs that they incorporated in their work showing evidence of knowledge of contemporary buildings in Turkey, Armenia, Iran and Syria. Studying the motifs allows us to recreate the network of cultures with which Akhlat engaged during Tamta's lifetime. Cities had identities too, and the parallel development of the identity of the city and that of Tamta each enrich our understanding of the other.

One obvious sign of Akhlat's multiple populations and its multiple identities is the number of names that the city has. Each community adapted the town's name to their own language. The modern Turkish name, Ahlat, is just one of many. To the Georgians it was Akhlat, and in Persian, Armenian and Arabic sources, it was Khlat or Khilat; to the Byzantines it was Khliat or Khaliat. The same is true of Tamta and her family. Georgian sources always give them the surname of Mqargrdzeli (Georgian for 'Longarm'), but this is not a name that is employed anywhere in the Armenian sources. These use no surname; but conventionally they are given the family name of 'the sons of Zakare' – the Zakarians. There is no consistency even within one language: Zakare is so named in Armenian chronicles, but in the Armenian-language inscriptions he ordered carved into the monasteries he supported he is called Zakaria or Zakharia (the same as the Georgian spelling of his name). To succeed in this world required formidable linguistic skills. Ibn Bibi reports that in around 1200 the *hajib* of the Seljuk sultan Kaykhusraw I, Zakariya (probably a Christian given his name – Zacharias), was 'fluent in the five languages of Anatolia' – Greek, Persian, Turkish, Armenian and Arabic; and that ignored Georgian, Syriac and Hebrew.[57] As new conquerors appeared, the requirements changed, and in the 1260s the Armenian nobleman Smbat Orbelian was reported to be 'unbeatable in discussions at court since he spoke five languages: Armenian, Georgian, Uighur, Persian and Mongolian'.[58]

Equally, every community gave its own date to events: for the Georgians in Ivane's army, the handing over of Tamta took place in *koronikon* 430,[59] whereas for the Armenian soldiers in the same army it was 658 of the

---

[57] R. Shukurov, 'Harem Christianity: The Byzantine Identity of Seljuk Princes', in *The Seljuks of Anatolia: Court and Society in the Medieval Middle East*, eds. A. C. S. Peacock and S. N. Yıldız (London; New York, 2013), 115–50, at 131–2.
[58] Stepanos Orbelian, 228.
[59] A paschal cycle of 532 years, beginning in AD 780: V. Grumel, *Traité d'études byzantines*, vol. 1:*La chronologie* (Paris, 1958), 151–3.

Armenian era;[60] the Ayyubid and Turkish troops opposing them regarded the year as *hejira* 608. Any Syriac Christians in Akhlat recognised it as the year 1522, taking a longer world view that originated in Alexander the Great's conquest of Babylon in 312 BC, and the Greek population of Anatolia used a chronology looking back even further to the creation of the world: this was *etos kosmou* 6719. The Syriac chronicler Bar Hebraeus, one of the main sources for the history of this region, was conscious of the diverse readership of his writings, and often cross-references between the different calendars, at one point using three of these systems on one page.[61] The arrival of the Mongols brought a new way of counting the years: the Georgian chronicle explained the cycle of twelve years and twelve animals beginning with the mouse and the cow that the new invaders used.[62] Only a Latin Crusader looking north from Acre might have dated Ivane's capture according to the incarnation of Christ, *anno domini* 1210, the basis of the Common Era dating I have used throughout for consistency.

Given the multiplicity of names, dates and languages, it is clear that identities were slippery things, hard to define, and easy to shift. This book explores the shifting nature of identity in this region in the thirteenth century. Tamta provides the spine around which it is focused, but as her life was subject to such change and fluctuation, the transformations of her identity are central. How then can we define who Tamta was? How was she perceived by those around her, and how did she see herself? What were the worlds of encounters between which she moved and how did these change her? Akhlat lies at the intersection of three of the medieval world's major economic and cultural blocs – between the Mediterranean, the Middle Eastern and the Asian circuits – and Tamta embodies the extraordinary results of the meeting of these many worlds.[63]

---

[60] A solar calendar beginning in AD 552: Grumel, *Chronologie*, 140–5.
[61] Bar Hebraeus, 375: the Hejira, the Syriac (which he calls the 'of the Greeks'), and the Armenian.
[62] *Kartlis Tskhovreba*, 318–19.
[63] J. Abu-Lughod, *Before European Hegemony: The World System AD 1250–1350* (Oxford, 1991), fig. 1.

2 | Tamta's Origins

The World of the Mqargrdzelis

> By the will of God, this inscription is a monument in perpetuity, in memory of the sons of the Great Sargis, Zakare and Ivane, of the Bagratid family. When the bounty of God was upon his creatures and allowed us to enter into possession of the heritage of our fathers, he placed first in our hands the impregnable castle of Amberd and the royal city of Ani… and many other countries with their frontiers which we regard as futile to mention.[1]

If Tamta's life is one of changing cultures and identities, as she moved from marriage to marriage and from culture to culture, then her childhood could be seen as a good preparation for such a life. Tamta was born into a family, the Mqargrdzelis, that itself hovered between two different cultures and religious confessions. For this initial stage in Tamta's life, we must first look at the way her family situated itself between Georgia and Armenia. The picture that emerges is of divergent family identities that were deliberately manipulated by its members in order to further their political, social and military aims in these two neighbouring cultures. Zakare and Ivane, Tamta's uncle and father, in particular, played with many different facets of their identity, often adopting apparently contradictory elements drawn from both Georgia and Armenia. The study of the two brothers establishes many of the themes of this book: the fluidity of identity and the ease with which it could be changed in the Caucasus at this time. It also shows the importance of buildings and art as ways of displaying these identities to the wider world.

Georgia and Armenia have shared a closely related, but often antagonistic, history. Situated side by side in the southern Caucasus, their history down to the Middle Ages followed a similar path. Their geographic location means that they were pulled between the Graeco-Roman world of Anatolia to the west and the Persian world of Iran to the east. Both countries adopted Christianity in the early fourth century, and developed alphabets alongside this. Both suffered terribly during the Arab invasions and the abolition of their monarchies between the fifth and seventh centuries, and kings were only recognised again in the ninth (in 884/5 in Armenia, four years later in

---

[1] Brosset, *Additions et éclaircissements*, 271.

Georgia). Both began a closer engagement with the Byzantine Empire from this period, but to different ends: the eleventh century saw the annexation of Armenian lands by Byzantium and the abolition of its monarchies; whereas the Georgian monarchy survived, to grow in power over the course of the twelfth century.

Any synopsis of either country's history, however, immediately falls prey to nineteenth-century notions of what a nation-state is – a group of people united by a common ethnicity, language and religion, living in a defined space, and ascribing to a shared history (to call them 'countries' before the twentieth century is anachronistic, but provides an easy short-hand here).[2] These terms simply cannot apply in the Middle Ages: the divisions between the two are complex and blurred, with populations that intermingled and intermarried. Rising to power in the border province of Lore, the Mqargrdzelis lived on both sides of the traditional frontiers between the two states, and they epitomised the fluid interrelationships between them at the start of the thirteenth century.

Even to define ethnicity is problematic. Although he was ambivalent about some branches of the Mqargrdzeli family (particularly those that converted to Georgian Chalcedonianism), the Armenian-speaking historian Kirakos Gandzaketsi essentially regarded them as Armenian, and celebrated their successes as successes for Armenia. However, his idea of what constitutes 'Armenian' fluctuates, as elsewhere in his history he notes that the family was of Kurdish descent.[3] Kirakos implies that Kurdishness was manifested by a distinct linguistic and cultural tradition, but it is clear that this was not immutable or precisely delineated. On the one hand, from it emerged the Christian Mqargrdzelis, and on the other – a bizarre coincidence – it produced their Muslim opponents at Akhlat in 1210. The Ayyubid family of Saladin into which Tamta was to marry are similarly recorded by Arab historians as being of Kurdish descent, originating from a village near the Armenian city of Dvin, later one of the richest cities under Mqargrdzeli rule.[4] They reinvented themselves as Arabic-speaking rulers, just as the Mqargrdzelis redefined themselves first as Armenians and then as Georgians.

---

[2] A. D. Smith, 'National Identities: Modern and Medieval?', in *Concepts of National Identity in the Middle Ages*, eds. L. Johnson, A. V. Murray, and S. Forde (Leeds, 1995), 21–46; B. Anderson, *Imagined Communities. Reflections on the Origin and Spread of Nationalism* (London; New York, 1991), 1–7; for a defence of the idea of the nation in the Middle Ages see J. A. Armstrong, *Nations before Nationalism* (Chapel Hill, NC, 1982), 1–34.

[3] For literary constructions of their identity see La Porta, '"The Kingdom and the Sultanate were Conjoined"', esp. 78–81.

[4] Minorsky, *Studies in Caucasian History*, 124–5, 138.

If it is impossible to define who an Armenian was in terms of their kin, it is equally hard to define them by place. The modern republic of Armenia – which largely overlaps with the area that the Mqargrdzelis controlled at the start of the thirteenth century – does little justice to the areas in which Armenian speakers lived in the thirteenth century. Their settlements were more broadly spread across Anatolia, occasionally ruled by Armenian princes, but more often located in areas controlled by Seljuk sultans or Turkoman emirs. Most of the Muslim-ruled cities of eastern Anatolia had large Armenian populations, not least Akhlat itself. Tamta would have shared the language of many of the people in the city into which she moved after 1210.

A further problem about associating identity with place came from a geopolitical shift in where Armenia actually was. The Mqargrdzelis ruled in the parts of the land traditionally labelled as 'Armenia', around Mount Ararat and Lake Van (often called 'Greater Armenia'), but there had been an exodus of Armenians after the annexation of the Armenian kingdoms by the emperors of Byzantium in the eleventh century. Many of these Armenians had settled much further south, between the Taurus mountains and the Mediterranean coast, and here in the thirteenth century a new Armenian kingdom was created around Tarsus and Sis: the Armenian kingdom of Cilicia.[5] The Armenian Patriarch had also moved, and was now based just to the east of Cilicia in the castle of Hromkla on the Euphrates (a small Armenian enclave surrounded by Muslim lands). There was an uneasy relationship between the two Armenias. Although spiritual authority resided with the Patriarch in Hromkla, many of the most important monasteries were in the north, and it was in these that many renowned Armenian intellectuals worked, such as the scholar and jurist Mkhitar Gosh, whose wisdom was celebrated in both Greater Armenia and Cilicia. Temporal authority was equally problematic: the Mqargrdzelis paid nominal deference to the kings in Sis, but they owed their control of Armenia to the queen of Georgia, under whose auspices they had taken back their lands from Seljuk control. This political and ecclesiastical split between the two Armenias lasted throughout the century and ensured that there was not a straightforward association between place and identity for the Armenians.

Finally, we must remember that the lands that the Mqargrdzelis controlled were not the sole geographical marker of their identities. They were defined as much by the lands in which they travelled on duty for the

---

[5] T. S. R. Boase, *The Cilician Kingdom of Armenia* (Edinburgh, 1978); C. Mutafian, *Le Royaume arménien de Cilicie, XIIe–XIVe siècle* (Paris, 2002).

Georgian crown. The family's allegiance first to the Georgian King, Giorgi III, then to his daughter Queen Tamar and then her heirs required the Mqargrdzelis to spend much of their time travelling with the Georgian court around Georgia. They spent much of their lives in this milieu and ruled over their lands as vassals of the Georgian crown. Queen Tamar regularly spent her winters in their city of Dvin, as did her son Giorgi IV Lasha (1210–23).[6] The unambiguous borders marked on maps (including those in this book) do not reflect the uncertainty of tracing them on the ground.

Being based in the Georgian court made language a more obvious marker of identity for the Mqargrdzelis. Language provided people with one clear way to mark their allegiance to one community or the other. The Armenians spoke an Indo-European tongue, the Georgians a completely unrelated language from the South Caucasian language group. Each was written in a different alphabet, and so the two shared nothing in common either orally or in written form. Language had implications beyond those of parentage and a notional 'national' community. This is the one area from which it is possible to identify the kernel of a distinct identity for each group, for language was intimately associated with religion. The language that you spoke was historically associated with the religious confession that you adhered to. Of all the many differences between the two Christian nations of the Caucasus, religion was the most significant. Georgians and Armenians held fundamentally opposed beliefs about the nature of Christianity, and on these theological distinctions entirely separate social and state differences had been built. Much of medieval identity was tied up in religion, and the fact that the two Churches had ethnic labels (contemporary chroniclers always refer to them as the 'Georgian' or 'Armenian' Church), rather than theological ones ('Dyophysite' or 'Miaphysite' – referring to the different ways in which each Church believed that the human and divine natures of Christ were related), shows that the confession that you espoused had greater implications beyond a personal relationship with God, or a particular view of the relationship between the two natures of Christ. It mattered not just for which Church you worshipped in, but also for issues about language (what language did your Church speak?), ecclesiastical affiliation (where did your Patriarch reside: Hromkla or Mtskheta?) and political allegiance (to which earthly authority did your Church administer: the queen in Georgia or the king in Armenian Cilicia?). Religion provided a core set of beliefs around which a community could coalesce, and a means to distinguish its members

[6] *Kartlis Tskhovreba*, 261, 270, 276.

from those with different beliefs. These separate beliefs then became associated with social and economic differences as each Church built up its own institutional and administrative structures which dealt as much with community issues to do with taxation and social conventions as with ecclesiastical affairs. The differences were embedded in the major physical structures in the landscape, the different churches and monasteries required for the different communities, and the languages they used, as each Church translated the bible into its own tongue.

By the thirteenth century these differences had been entrenched across the Caucasus for more than seven hundred years. In 451 the bishops of Armenia had refused to ratify the acts of the Fourth Ecumenical Council at Chalcedon and so had fallen out of communion with the Byzantine and Roman Churches. The Council had declared in favour of the Dyophysite doctrine of the equality of Christ's human and divine natures joined in one person, whereas the Armenian bishops (in conjunction with those from Syria and Egypt) argued that Christ had a single human and divine nature.[7] The Georgians had briefly taken the same step, but in the early seventh century had reversed their decision and were now aligned with the Byzantine Church in Constantinople once again.[8] Despite frequent attempts by the two Churches to reconcile their theological doctrines, they could never agree, and allegiance to one Church or the other was probably the most visible marker of identity to contemporaries. In this book for clarity I will use each Church's modern name – the Georgian Orthodox Church, the Armenian Apostolic Church – even though, of course, each Church regarded itself as Orthodox and the other as heterodox, rendering the modern usage of 'Orthodox' to refer only to the Greek and Georgian Churches deeply unhelpful.

All these facets of identity – family/kinship, language, place, religion and shared history – are equally problematic to define, particularly in a region like the Caucasus in the thirteenth century which was undergoing so much change. We must therefore build up a picture of identity in a different way, not in abstract terms of what people were, but more concretely in terms of what they did, how they presented themselves and how they wanted to be seen.

---

[7] For introductions to each see V. Nersessian, 'Armenian Christianity' and S. H. Rapp, 'Georgian Christianity', both in *The Blackwell Companion to Eastern Christianity*, ed. K. Parry (Oxford, 2007), 23–46 and 137–55 respectively.

[8] B. Martin-Hisard, 'Christianisme et église dans le monde géorgien', in *Histoire de Christianisme des origines à nos jours*, vol. 4, eds. J.-M. Mayeur, C. Pietri, L. Pietri, A. Vauchez and M. Venard (Paris, 1993), 549–603.

Whatever the origins of Tamta and her family, the Mqargrdzelis rose to prominence not in Armenia but in Georgia. Following their father Sargis, Ivane and his elder brother Zakare found promotion at the Georgian court of Queen Tamar (r. 1184–1210). Tamar, the only daughter of King Giorgi III, had faced considerable opposition to her elevation to the throne on her father's death. However, after a decade of rebellion and plot she managed to establish herself as the legitimate, sole ruler. This later enabled her daughter, Rusudan, to succeed to the throne after her son, Giorgi IV Lasha, died without legitimate heirs. This paints a picture of female emancipation and power that Tamta's life cruelly undermines. What Queens could get away with few others could manage.

Towards the end of the twelfth century Zakare, the elder brother, was appointed by Queen Tamar to the post of *amirspasalar*, commander of her army, and Ivane was made *msakhurtukhutsesi*, chamberlain (later, after Zakare's death, Ivane also claimed a new title, *atabeg*, tutor to the heir to the throne; a title borrowed from the neighbouring Muslim world). They were thus at the very centre of the Georgian court hierarchy, even though both at this point still belonged to the Armenian Church. They presided over a combined army of Georgians and Armenians, with which they were able to reconquer Greater Armenia from the Turks. They were then granted this region to rule as a semi-autonomous fiefdom. Thus they established themselves within a Georgian context at the Georgian court before returning to Armenia to take power there. The nature of their rule is unclear. At the Georgian court, and in many of their inscriptions in Armenia, they proclaimed their power through their Georgian court titles, and simply transliterated these into Armenian.[9] Whilst this must have rendered the titles effectively meaningless to an Armenian audience, it made those deliberately foreign words signifiers of the non-Armenian source of their power. This would have been bolstered by the regular appearances of the Georgian Queen in their territory.

However, their identities were dual. In one inscription on the palace church on the citadel of Ani, the brothers' principal city and the former capital of Armenia, they refer to themselves as 'the kings of Ani', suggesting loftier ambitions, independent of Georgia,[10] and in the inscription at

---

[9] For example, both *amirspasalar* and *mandaturtukhutsesi* (lit. 'master of ceremonies', in effect interior minister) were transliterated in inscriptions at Ani: K. J. Basmadjian, *Les inscriptions arméniennes d'Ani, de Bagnaïr et de Marmachèn* (Paris, 1931), nos. 35, 36, 38; I. A. Orbeli, *Corpus Inscriptionum Armenicarum*, vol. 1 (Yerevan, 1966), nos. 15, 11, 23.

[10] A. M. Lidov, *The Wall Paintings of Akhtala Monastery: History, Iconography, Masters* (Moscow, 2014), 342. The authenticity of this inscription is in doubt, however.

Haghartsin quoted in the first chapter, they claimed descent from the Bagratunis, the Armenian kings of the region until the eleventh century. The extent of their ambitions was broader still: an inscription set up at the castle of Amberd in 1195 also claimed descent for them from the rival Armenian royal family, the Artsrunis, who had ruled in Vaspurakan (the region including Lake Van and the lands to its east) in the tenth century.[11] This inscription was set up in Arabic on the castle wall to broadcast these claims even to their Muslim subjects. The conflicting claims of the brothers, as vassals in Georgia but as independent kings in their own lands, are reflected in the modern disagreement about the family's name: Mqargrdzeli in medieval Georgian sources, Zakarian in modern Armenian histories. No compromise seems possible in the modern histories of Georgia and Armenia. Although most of the evidence I draw on about the brothers comes from the modern-day territory of Armenia, I have used their Georgian surname in this account in order to hint at their ambivalent position within Armenia and to stress the way they lie outside any simple 'national' categorisation.

Tamta's identity before her first marriage was intimately bound up with that of her father. In a patriarchal society, it was his career and decisions that moulded the fate and status of the rest of his family, and determined how they were perceived until they were in a position to break away from him, or were taken from him as in Tamta's case. We can be sure that Tamta was forced to follow the path Ivane carved out for himself. In Ivane's case, we can trace his changing religious identity with particular clarity. As noted in the first chapter, Armenian chroniclers blamed his capture at Akhlat on one root cause: his conversion from Armenian to Georgian Orthodoxy. Religion was a central concern of the thirteenth century: it provided the means to salvation, and this could be influenced by men's actions on earth, in particular by their support for the Church and its institutions. In addition, it gave people a community and an identity; it provided a means of defining oneself in contrast to others (both other 'heretical' Christians and adherents of other religions, notably Islam). Thus, when Ivane converted to Georgian Orthodoxy he publicly signalled a major shift in his identity and that of his family. The Georgian Chronicle records that when Ivane converted many chose to follow him.[12] Conversion was about community and family, not just individuals. The ritual surrounding the conversion itself was a great public event. It took place in front of the whole court after a week of

---

[11] A. A. Khachatrian, *Korpus arabskikh nadpisei Armenii* (Yerevan, 1987), 47: the inscription reads 'Amir spasalar Zakaria Ivana al-sarruni [i.e. Artsruni]'; see also La Porta, '"The Kingdom and the Sultanate were Conjoined"', 90 n.87.

[12] *Kartlis Tskhovreba*, 267.

debates between the Georgian and Armenian clergy. The Georgians claimed victory (not surprising since the debates are only recorded in a Georgian source), and this was confirmed, in their eyes, when two dogs, starved for three days, were each offered a piece of communion bread consecrated by the Catholicoses of the two different Churches. The Georgian dog refused to eat the (transubstantiated) Georgian host, but the Armenian dog wolfed down what was still just Armenian bread.[13] Even dogs, it seems, belonged to 'national' religions.

The fact that his elder brother, Zakare, did not convert made Ivane's decision stand out even more. Zakare's decision also suggests that the conversion involved more mundane pragmatic decisions alongside spiritual imperatives. The split within the family with one brother adhering to each of the two local branches of Christianity allowed them to provide a leadership to the army that appealed to both sides of the religious rift, and that minimised the divisions between them. For a sense of what it meant to Ivane to convert we can look at the foundation he established soon after his conversion to pray for his soul: his mausoleum church at Akhtala. Located on the west bank of the river Debed in Lore province in northern Armenia, Akhtala is on the marches between Georgia and Armenia, the heartland of the Mqargrdzeli family.

Akhtala and Religious Identity

The importance of Akhtala and the amount Ivane invested in it are now most visible in the scale of the church surviving at the heart of the monastery, and the quality of its carved and painted decoration, but originally it extended far beyond this to the gift of villages, land and shops that would support the work of its monks. The monks' prime duty was to pray for Ivane's soul for all eternity, in order to expedite his passage into paradise. Contemporary documents from Byzantium provide fuller details of the way such personal foundations were expected to work. The foundation documents, called *typika*, spell out the number of clergy to be employed, the nature of all services, the number of candles and lamps to be lit at each service (and the additional numbers required on the Great Feast days of the year); they record the acts of charity to be financed by the foundation and the number and frequency of the prayers to be said for the donor after his death.[14] Ivane was buried

---

[13] *Kartlis Tskhovreba*, 263–7. The event is dated to *c.* 1200 in S. Meskhia, *Sashinao politikuri vitareba da samokheleo tsqoba XII saukunis sakartveloshi* (Tbilisi, 1979), 257–8.

[14] All the Byzantine *typika* are now translated: *Byzantine Monastic Foundation Documents: a comparative translation of the surviving founders' typika and testaments*, eds. J. Thomas and A. C. Hero, Dumbarton Oaks Studies 35 (Washington, DC, 2000).

Figure 1 View of the main church of the monastery of Akhtala, Armenia, in its fortified complex, built by Ivane Mqargrdzeli; *c.* 1205

in the monastery after his death (probably in 1227) and later was followed by his son, Avag, and other members of their family. Akhtala allows us to see the way in which Ivane framed and presented his religious identity, and through this we can also begin to understand Tamta's.

The church at Akhtala, dedicated to the Mother of God, is located in a fortified compound above a valley filled with copper mines [Fig. 1].[15] The waters that run down the hill from the monastic site still stain the ground a bright, cuprous blue. This is reflected in the medieval Armenian name for the site, Pghndzavank, the copper church. A church had been founded at the site in the twelfth century by the previous rulers in the region, the Armenian Apostolic Kwirikid family. However, the site was taken over by Ivane in around 1205. He forcibly converted the monastery and its monks to Georgian Chalcedonian Orthodoxy and replaced the original church with a new construction. Ivane's church stands today, although its original conical dome collapsed some time before the nineteenth century and has never been replaced, giving the church the truncated, squat appearance it has today. Alongside it is the small chapel in which Ivane is thought to have been buried.

---

[15] Lidov, *The Wall Paintings of Akhtala*, 332–3; B. Kirion, *Akhtal'skii monastyr'* (Tbilisi, 2005); N. Thierry, 'Le Jugement dernier d'Axtala: rapport préliminaire', *Bedi Kartlisa* 40 (1982), 147–85; E. Taqaishvili, 'Gruzinskiia nadpisi Akhtaly', *Sbornik materialov dlia opisanie mestnostei i plemen Kavkaza* 29 (1901), 138–45.

Akhtala is surrounded by Armenian monasteries that populate this section of the Debed gorge. The concentration was possible because of the wealth that came from the mining and agriculture in the gorge and on the plateaux on either side. On the east bank of the river, just 5 kilometres from Akhtala, are the major complexes of Haghbat and Sanahin, both founded in the tenth century, and a little further south on the plateau above the west bank is the eighth-century church of Odzun. Akhtala lies in what, theologically, was contested territory, with other Georgian monasteries further south down the valley, including Kobayr, where later generations of the Mqargrdzeli family were to be buried.[16] The church at Akhtala employs the same carefully squared tufa masonry as its Armenian neighbours, and it shares the same architectural tradition of constraining the ground plan of the church to fit within a strict rectangular frame. Yet, despite these common origins, it is visibly distinct. Ivane intended his religious affiliation to be made manifest on a monumental scale.

The differences would have been apparent to visitors to the church from afar. Long before they arrived at the site they would have known whether they were entering a Georgian, rather than an Armenian, site. Two differences alerted them to the distinction: the way the buildings in the monastic complex were grouped together; and the monumental architectural decoration of their façades.[17] Although it is surrounded by a fortified wall, the main church at Akhtala stands alone in the centre of the complex; subsidiary buildings were placed against the curtain wall, leaving the church as the central focus of the complex. Both from afar and close to, the main church dominates the site. With the loss of almost all the ancillary buildings this isolation is now starker than it would have been in the thirteenth century; but the monasteries of Mount Athos allow us to envisage how such complexes could develop, with a curtain of low buildings surrounding the main church, which remained the dominant central focus.[18] In contrast, Armenian monasteries of the early thirteenth century tended to cluster their buildings all around the main church, until it was almost completely surrounded. Large low zhamatuns (entrance halls), often larger than the

---

[16] Kobayr: I. Drampian, *Freski Kobaira* (Yerevan, 1979), 6–8; N. Thierry, 'A propos des peintures de la grande église de Kobayr', *Revue des études géorgiennes et caucasiennes* 2 (1986), 223–6; G. Kalandia and K. Asatiani, 'Koberis I da II sametsniero eskpeditsiis pirveladi shedegebi (sainpormatsio mimokhilva)', *Saistorio krebuli* 2 (2012), 170–91.

[17] V. Beridze, 'Quelques aspects de l'architecture géorgienne à coupole de la seconde moitié du Xe siècle à la fin du XIIIe', in *Communication faite à Bergamo (Italie) le 29 juin 1974 au 'Primo simposio internazionale sull'arte Georgiana'* (Tbilisi, 1976), 74–96, esp. 90–2.

[18] S. Ćurčić, *Architecture in the Balkans, from Diocletian to Süleyman the Magnificent* (New Haven; London, 2010), 300–7.

Figure 2 Goshavank, Armenia, 1191–1291. General view from the south west of the cluster of buildings in the monastic complex around the catholicon (main church)

church itself, hide the main façade of the church completely. Zhamatuns are completely unknown in Georgian or Byzantine architecture, but at Haghbat, the monastery on the opposite bank of the river Debed, which had been the mother house of Akhtala before it was taken over by Ivane, the tenth-century church was almost entirely enclosed in surrounding chapels, zhamatuns and covered passageways by the middle of the thirteenth century. The hillside setting of Haghbat means that no photographs can show the overall impression of the cluster of buildings; but this is apparent at Goshavank, to the south-east of Haghbat. The monastery at Goshavank was founded in 1191 for Mkhitar Gosh, and even though it was an Armenian Apostolic foundation, it was supported by Ivane Mqargrdzeli. The central church was quickly enclosed, and by 1241 it had been surrounded on three sides by a zhamatun, library and numerous chapels [Figs. 2 and 3].

As visitors climbed up the side of the valley to the Akhtala complex from the river below other differences became clear. The road took them opposite the east façade of the church, the most symbolically important because of its proximity to the high altar of the church just inside. At Akhtala this façade is ornamented in a distinct way, unlike any other church in

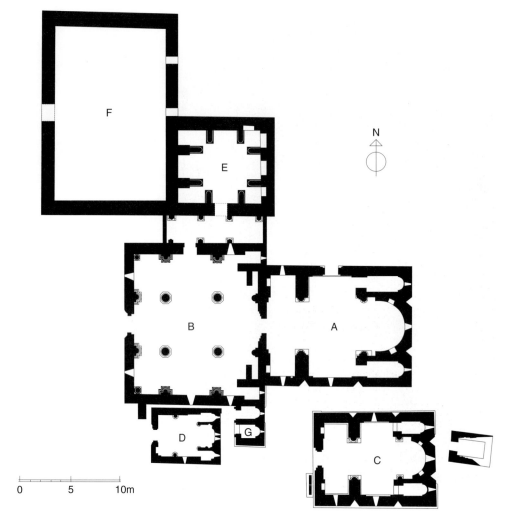

Figure 3 Ground plan of the monastic complex at Goshavank, Armenia. A: catholicon of the Mother of God (1191); B: zhamatun (1197); C: church of St Gregory (1208); D: chapel of St Gregory (1237); E: library (1241, with church of the Holy Archangels built over it in 1291); F: scriptorium (thirteenth century); G: small chapels (thirteenth century)

Armenia [Fig. 4]. A cross in relief crowns the apex of the façade and establishes a strong vertical axis that dominates the end of the church. The cross is bordered by a pair of pipe-like mouldings which descend down the centre of the façade, dividing in succession to act as the frame for a small boss, and for the window in the centre of the main apse. Below this the pipes divide again, this time to create a pair of squares, each balancing on one corner to form an angular figure eight set on its side. Each square encloses a circular

Figure 4 Decoration on the east façade of the main church at Akhtala, Armenia; c. 1205

disc with a distinct interlace foliate relief and an elaborately carved boss at its centre. The overall arrangement of the façade produces a bold composition that stands out from afar. More importantly, it stands out from the much more austere and plainer façades of the Armenian monasteries that surrounded it. To onlookers in the thirteenth century the façade was an eloquent proclaimer of identity. Although it contained no theological message, this design would quickly and easily have been recognised as belonging to a Georgian tradition. Similar east ends can be traced back in Georgia to the early eleventh century, most famously, and most perfectly in the church at

Figure 5 View of the apse, showing post holes for templon screen at Akhtala, Armenia; c. 1205 (For the colour version, please refer to the plate section. In some formats this figure will only appear in black and white)

Samtavisi, to the west of Tbilisi.[19] In as much as stones could speak, those at Akhtala shouted out for the triumph of Georgian Chalcedonian orthodoxy.

These external architectural distinctions continued as visitors entered the churches. Churches are designed as theatres for the liturgy, and the

---

[19] G. Sokhashvili, *Samtavisi: masalebi tadzris istoriisatvis* (Tbilisi, 1973). The continuing tradition can be traced into later centuries at Ikorta (1172), and Metekhi in Tbilisi (1278–89): V. Beridze, G. V. Alibegashvili, A. Vol'skaia and L. Xuskivadze, *The Treasures of Georgia* (London, 1984), 38–9, 46. Hovhannavank monastery, built by Vache Vachutian, a vassal of the Mqargrdzelis in 1215, employs a similar façade design.

Georgian and Armenian liturgies had developed in different ways, requiring different stages. In the Georgian church the liturgy was a theatre of entrances, orchestrated by the appearances and retreats of the officiating priests through the doors of the templon screen that hid the altar from the congregation in the nave (the precursor of the modern iconostasis in Orthodox churches). The screen at Akhtala is now destroyed, but post holes for a horizontal wooden beam to run across the face of the apse still remain on the two pillars to either side [Fig. 5]. This beam, the epistyle, rested on columns, and the space between the columns was blocked by a low stone screen. The mysteries of the Eucharist took place at the altar in secret, and only later was the sanctified bread and wine revealed triumphantly to the worshippers in the nave of the church. The Armenian liturgy, on the other hand, was celebrated more openly and more theatrically, and the majority of churches built to accommodate it placed the clergy on a raised stage, at least a metre above the congregation. This is visible, for example, at Harichavank, which was built by Tamta's uncle, Zakare (and to which we will return shortly) [Fig. 6]. It is possible that the altar was concealed by a curtain, and Kirakos records that the weaving and embroidery of such curtains was deemed a suitable job for a noblewoman:

> Arzu Khatun [the builder of the monastery at Dadivank in Artsakh in 1214] and her daughters made a beautiful curtain of the softest goats' hair as a covering for the holy altar, a marvel to behold. It was dyed with variegated colours like a piece of carving with pictures accurately drawn on it showing the Incarnation of the Saviour and other saints. It astonished those who saw it. Beholders would bless God for giving women the knowledge of tapestry-making and the genius of embroidery, as it is said in Job, for it was no less than the altar ornaments fashioned by Bezalel and Oholiab [the consummate artists of Exodus 31]. Nor is it bold to make this statement, for the same spirit moved them both. Not only did the woman make a curtain for this church at Getik, but for other churches as well – Haghbat, Makaravank and Dadivank; for she was a great lover of the church, and very pious.[20]

More noticeable today as a difference is the presence of wall paintings in Akhtala. Although the Armenian Church did not ban wall paintings, they are much less common than in Georgia or Byzantium. Armenian sources reveal a suspicion of monumental art: to use paintings was to 'become'

---

[20] Kirakos, 107–8 (trans. Bedrosian, 62); interestingly, Nerses of Lambron makes no mention of curtains in his commentary on the liturgy written at the end of the twelfth century: *Explication de la Divine Liturgie*, ed. and trans. I. Kéchichian (Beirut, 2000).

Figure 6 View of the apse of the catholicon at Harichavank, Armenia, showing altar platform; c. 1200 (For the colour version, please refer to the plate section. In some formats this figure will only appear in black and white)

Georgian. Stepanos Orbelian's late thirteenth-century history of Siunik, the south-eastern province of Armenia, shows the ambivalence to paintings that existed. In chapter forty-nine he writes with admiration of the paintings that were commissioned from a Frankish artist at the monastery of Tatev in 930 (extraordinarily, some of these still survive).[21] But three chapters later he records the expulsion in 969 of Vahan, the Catholicos of Armenia, for introducing images 'like the Georgians' and thereby threatening to

[21] J.-M. Thierry and N. Thierry, 'Peintures de caractère occidental en Arménie: l'église Saint-Pierre et Saint-Paul de Tat'ev', *Byzantion* 38 (1968), 180–242.

Figure 7 Communion of the Apostles with Greek inscription, in the apse at Akhtala, Armenia; *c.* 1205 (For the colour version, please refer to the plate section. In some formats this figure will only appear in black and white)

'insinuate the heresy of the Greeks' into the Church.[22] The majority of paintings that survive in Armenia come from these two periods: either the sporadic flirtation with monumental art in the early period,[23] or the more frequent occurrences in the Mqargrdzeli period in the thirteenth century.

In Akhtala wall paintings once covered every surface. In the church they are characterised by a vibrant, rich blue background. There are two layers of paintings visible today, the older of which was completed before 1216, but the second is not much later.[24] The layout and details of the paintings add precision to Ivane's Georgian allegiance. The first point that jumps out is the use of language: the inscriptions in the church are in a combination of two languages: Greek and Georgian. The scene of the communion of the Apostles that runs across the entire apse beneath the gigantic (but sadly partly destroyed) image of the Mother of God is all inscribed in Greek [Fig. 7]; the Church Fathers beneath have their names written first in Greek (beside their heads) and secondly in Georgian (between their waists). Interestingly, fragments of red underpainting that have emerged from beneath these

---

[22] Stepanos Orbelian, 1: 166–7.
[23] N. Kotandjian, 'Les décors peints des églises d'Arménie', in J. Durand, I. Rapti and D. Giovannoni, eds., *Armenia Sacra: mémoire chrétienne des Arméniens (IVe–XVIIIe siècle)* (Paris 2007), 137–44.
[24] Lidov, *The Wall Paintings of Akhtala*, 325, 465–6.

Figure 8 Bilingual Greek and Georgian inscription accompanying St John in the north-east pendentive in the church of St Gregory the Illuminator of Tigran Honents, Ani, Turkey; 1215 (For the colour version, please refer to the plate section. In some formats this figure will only appear in black and white)

figures give the artists' identifying labels in Armenian and Greek, a different linguistic competence.[25] Elsewhere many of the narrative scenes on the side walls, and the figures of saints on the west wall, are written only in Georgian. The use of Greek inscriptions was symbolic rather than functional. It is doubtful whether more than a few of the most educated monastic visitors to the church could ever have read the Greek inscriptions – it was here as a marker of theological allegiance and the alliance between the Georgian and Byzantine Churches. Greek is similarly used alongside Georgian in the other Chalcedonian churches that were built in Armenia in the first half of the thirteenth century, including the church of St Gregory the Illuminator built in Ani by the merchant Tigran Honents (1215) [Fig. 8] and those at Kirants (c. 1220) and Kobayr (mid-thirteenth century).[26] Although Greek was theologically important, it was not necessarily well understood. The uncertain status of Greek is visible in the Red Gospels of Gandzasar (now University of Chicago Library, Goodspeed MS 949), an Armenian manuscript probably made for a Chalcedonian (i.e. Georgian Christian) patron some time

---

[25] Lidov, *The Wall Paintings of Akhtala*, 180–1.
[26] J.-M. Thierry and N. Thierry, *L'église Saint-Grégoire de Tigran Honencʻ à Ani (1215)* (Louvain; Paris, 1993); Drampian, *Freski Kobaira*.

before 1237.²⁷ When the artist Abas signed his name in a trilingual inscription in Greek, Armenian and Georgian beneath the portrait of St Luke on folio 139v, it is evident that his knowledge of Greek was very basic: compared to the Armenian and Georgian texts either side, the Greek letters ΑΠΑΣ ζοΓραφ (Abas the painter), are uneven and awkwardly formed [Fig. 9]; he mixed upper and lower case and added a large hanging serif to his gamma (which makes it look more like a reversed 'e' in the old Georgian alphabet (*asomtavruli*).²⁸

The use of Georgian in the inscriptions in Akhtala might suggest that this was the key language of faith for its monks, but other evidence suggests that while some monks and worshippers were bilingual in Armenian and Georgian, most needed to say the liturgy in Armenian. Georgian may have been the official language of the court, and was presumably spoken and understood by Ivane and his family, but most of the followers who converted with him spoke only Armenian. To aid them, the monks at Akhtala were commissioned to translate theological texts from Georgian into Armenian. Their task was to make available important texts that explained the meaning and working of the Georgian Chalcedonian liturgy to the brethren in the new faith in a language they could understand. This tradition continued after Ivane's death. The colophon of a translation of a major Neoplatonic text, Prochlus Diadochus' *Elements of Theology* made at Akhtala in 1248, proclaims the importance of the text, and the need for the monks to have access to it: 'All the new theologians founded their works on this book. This is the foundation and the root and the mother of everything, from this book they did all take everything. But insofar as they showed only small parts, I have translated so that our people should not be lacking in it.'²⁹

The early thirteenth century also saw the translation of the compilation of Georgian chronicles known as *Kartlis Tskhovreba*, into Armenian.³⁰ The sole extensive narrative record of Georgian history, its Armenian translation joined a rich and varied tradition of Armenian history writing. It seems likely that this project was sponsored by the Mqargrdzelis, and was designed

---

²⁷ T. F. Mathews and R. S. Wieck, eds., *Treasures in Heaven: Armenian Illuminated Manuscripts* (Princeton, 1994), 86–7, and cat. 24; A. Taylor, 'Armenian Art and Armenian Identity', in Mathews and Wieck, eds., *Treasures in Heaven*, 133–46, at 135.

²⁸ http://goodspeed.lib.uchicago.edu/view/index.php?doc=0949&obj=282. On fol. 4r the word is spelled ζωΓραφ, but with the same hanging serif on the gamma. I. Rapti, 'La peinture dans les livres (IXe–XIIIe siècle)', in Durand et al., eds., *Armenia Sacra*, 176–83, at 182, describes the writing as 'a curious melange of Greek and Coptic'.

²⁹ Lidov, *The Wall Paintings of Akhtala*, 336–7.

³⁰ R. W. Thomson, *Rewriting Caucasian History: The Medieval Armenian Adaptation of the Georgian Chronicles. The Original Georgian Texts and the Armenian Adaptation* (Oxford, 1996).

Figure 9 St Luke and trilingual inscription of the painter Abas in the Red Gospels of Gandzasar; early thirteenth century (University of Chicago Library, Goodspeed MS 949, fol. 139v; 26.5 × 20 cm)

Figure 10 Detail of the Last Judgement on the west wall at Akhtala, Armenia; c. 1205 (For the colour version, please refer to the plate section. In some formats this figure will only appear in black and white)

to inculcate a sense of shared history with the Georgians.[31] It is noticeable that the translators made very few alterations to the text even when it gave the Georgian view of disputes between the two countries, which one might expect if the history were being prepared for an Armenian audience that was more antagonistic to Georgia.[32]

The programme of the paintings at Akhtala also formed part of this attempt to forge a clearer Georgian identity among worshippers. The general absence of monumental painting in Armenia meant that the painters had to turn to the Chalcedonian world for models of how to decorate a church. The overall layout – the Mother of God presiding in the conch of the apse, the life of Christ and the saints on the side walls, and the Last Judgement on the west wall [Fig. 10] – all looked to Georgia or Byzantium for precedents. Similar church designs can be found in Georgia at Vardzia

[31] S. H. Rapp, ed., *K'art'lis c'xovreba: The Georgian Royal Annals and their Medieval Armenian Adaptation* (Delmar, NY, 1998), 7–8.
[32] Compare Thomson, *Rewriting Caucasian History*, xlvii–xlix.

Figure 11 The Glorification of the Cross in the dome of the church at Timotesubani, Georgia; *c.* 1220 (For the colour version, please refer to the plate section. In some formats this figure will only appear in black and white)

(1184–6), Betania, Qintsvisi, Timotesubani and Bertubani.[33] The collapse of the dome means that we cannot know what was depicted at the highest point of the interior: Greek tradition placed the bust of Christ Pantokrator there; the Georgians preferred the image of the cross being lifted to heaven by angels, the Glorification of the Cross. The only hint comes from the one surviving fragment of the great liturgical inscriptions that ran around the crossing arches beneath the dome. Just four words (in Georgian) survive from the west side of crossing, '[the sun] knoweth his going-down'. These words come from Psalm 104.19, and the same verse is found in the exactly same location in the contemporary Georgian church of St George at Timotesubani, in which the dome is dominated by the vision of the cross [Fig. 11].[34] This suggests that the dome programme was planned in line with Georgian churches of the period.

The church programme is not a simple clone of Georgian interiors. Some elements are not found in Georgian churches of this period, such as the Communion of the Apostles that runs across the width of the apse. Of the churches built in Georgia in this period, only one, Qintsvisi, contains

---

[33] A. Eastmond, *Royal Imagery in Medieval Georgia* (University Park, PA, 1998); S. Amiranashvili, *Istoriia gruzinskoi monumental'noi zhivopisi*, vol. 1 (Tbilisi, 1957).

[34] Lidov, *The Wall Paintings of Akhtala*, 355–6; E. Privalova, *Rospis' Timotesubani* (Tbilisi, 1980), 37–8.

the scene.³⁵ For this iconography the painters had to look further west to Byzantium. The inclusion of the scene subtly emphasises a difference between the two churches, notably the converts' desire to adhere to trends from the centre of the Orthodox world, rather than more local Georgian fashions. The same scene was painted at Haghbat later in the century when its interior was decorated on the order of the local lord, Qutlu Bugha.³⁶ At Akhtala the inscription in Greek unusually repeats the phrase 'this is my blood', stressing this element of the liturgy.³⁷ The blood is similarly stressed in the image of the Crucifixion in the Red Gospels (fol. 6v), highlighting the different interpretations the Churches had of the mixing of wine and water in the Eucharist.³⁸ This was one area in which the Georgian and Armenian Churches visibly differed during the performance of the liturgy.

These fine theological differences may have been lost on many of the congregation, but other elements in the painting provided a clearer, less ambiguous demonstration of Ivane's new Byzantine/Georgian/Chalcedonian allegiance. The paintings particularly celebrated Georgian saints. To either side of the west door, a location where everyone leaving the church must see them, parade six monastic saints. They are labelled in Georgian as Sts Shio Mghvimeli, Ioane Shuvamdinareli and Evagre on the south [left] side of the door; Sts Ekvtime Mtatsmindeli, Hilarion Kartveli and Giorgi Mtatsmindeli on the north [Fig. 12]. These saints were only revered in Georgia, and are clearly present here as paragons of a local form of Chalcedonian virtue to which the newly converted monks could aspire. Two of the saints, Ekvtime and Giorgi Mtatsmindeli, were celebrated for their work at the start of the eleventh century translating texts from Greek into Georgian.³⁹ Their goal had been to make the latest Greek theological texts accessible to Georgian monks at a time when the Georgian Church was seeking to bring its liturgy closer to that in Constantinople, providing a saintly model for the work of the Akhtalan monks now to translate those same works into Armenian. Nearby these monastic saints on the attached south column against the west wall stands a seventh specifically Georgian saint, Nino. St Nino was the female Evangelist of Georgia, and her cult became particularly prominent at

---

³⁵ G. Babić, 'Les programmes absidaux en Géorgie et dans les Balkans entre XIe et le XIIIe siècle', in *L'Arte Georgiana dal IX al XIV secolo: Atti del Terzo Simpozio Internazionale sull'arte Georgiana*, ed. M. Calo'Mariani (Bari, 1981), 117–36.

³⁶ N. I. Marr, 'Freskovoe izobrazhenie parona Khutlu-bugi v' Akhpat' (hAibatp)', *Khristianskii Vostok* 1/3 (1912), 350–3.

³⁷ T. S. Qaukhchishvili, *Berdznuli tsartserebi sakartvelo*, vol. 1 (Tbilisi, 1951), 356–7.

³⁸ Taylor, 'Armenian Art and Armenian Identity', 135. Lidov, *The Wall Paintings of Akhtala*, 375–6, sees the phrase in relation to Armenian differences with the Church of Rome.

³⁹ B. Martin-Hisard, 'La vie de Jean et Euthyme et le statut du monastère des Ibères sur l'Athos', *REB* 49 (1991), 67–142.

Figure 12 Georgian monastic saints (Sts Ekvtime Mtatsmindeli, Hilarion Kartveli and Giorgi Mtatsmindeli) on the north side of the door on the west wall at Akhtala, Armenia; c. 1205

the end of the twelfth century, when she was promoted as a model of female leadership in a country now ruled by a woman, Queen Tamar.[40] The status of images is further accentuated by the inclusion among the saints on the south wall of St Stephen the Younger, a martyr of Byzantine iconoclasm, who is rarely seen in Georgian art. He holds icons of Christ and the Mother of God. Two saints particularly venerated in Armenia, Sts Gregory the

---

[40] A. Eastmond, 'Royal Renewal in Georgia: The Case of Queen Tamar', in *New Constantines: The Rhythm of Imperial Renewal in Byzantium, 4th–13th Centuries*, ed. P. Magdalino (Aldershot, 1994), 283–93.

Illuminator and Jacob of Nisibis, do also appear, but they are included among the sixteen Church Fathers in the lowest register of the apse of the church. Uniform in dress and appearance with the other Church Fathers, and hidden from view behind the templon screen, their appearance is much less prominent.[41]

The design, decoration and painting of Akhtala all suggest that Ivane wanted his body and soul to be preserved within a Georgian community in order to promote his salvation. As has been seen, there are nuances within this programme which do not fit entirely within usual Georgian practice, but which would still have been alien to Armenian practice. In modern histories the ownership of the Church has been contested by Georgian and Armenian scholars: copies of the frescoes appear in both the Art Museum of Georgia in Tbilisi and in the History Museum of Armenia in Yerevan, and the church is incorporated into the narrative of the history of art of both countries.[42] My reading of the evidence, set out here, suggests that the church fits more closely within the Georgian tradition, but the fact that it has been claimed for both shows not so much the ambiguity of the monument as the problems inherent in trying to define either 'Georgian' or 'Armenian' in this period. A possible solution to this has been proposed more recently by some scholars who have argued that Ivane and his fellow converts were seeking to create a distinct confessional group, which they have termed 'ethno-confessional self-aware Chalcedonian Armenians'.[43] Their thesis is that although these were men who converted from the Armenian to the Georgian Church they deliberately sought to promote themselves as a distinct, separate social and ethnic group.[44] They highlight all the unusual elements in Akhtala (and elsewhere) that makes the group stand out from the Georgian Church to support this. To an extent they must be right: the use of a distinct liturgical language, the extensive employment of Greek in

---

[41] Lidov, *The Wall Paintings of Akhtala*, 373.
[42] S. Amiranashvili, *Istoriia gruzinskogo iskusstva* (Moscow, 1963), 218–19; B. Brentjes, S. Mnazakanjan and N. Stepanjan, *Kunst des Mittelalters in Armenien* (Vienna; Munich, 1982), 240.
[43] V. A. Arutiunova-Fidanian, 'The Ethno-Confessional Self-Awareness of Armenian Chalcedonians', *REArm* 21 (1988), 345–63; V. A. Arutiunova-Fidanian, 'Les Arméniens Chalcédoniens en tant que phénomène culturel de l'Orient Chrétien', in *Atti del quinto simposio internazionale di Arte Armena* (Venice, 1992), 463–77; A. M. Lidov, 'L'art des Arméniens Chalcédoniens', in *Atti del quinto simposio internazionale di Arte Armena* (Venice, 1992), 479–95; all building on the fundamental work of N. I. Marr, 'Arkaun, mongol'skoe nazvanie khristian, v sviazi s voprosom ob armianakh-khalkedonitakh', *Vizantiiskii Vremennik* 12 (1906), 1–68.
[44] But contrast the actions of Kiwrion, who converted in the sixth century and kept his conversion secret: Kirakos, 24.

inscriptions and the incorporation of specific iconographies rarely seen in Georgia do accord with the idea of there being distinct local practices.

However, the idea misses the mark as it loses sight of the ultimate goal of these conversions in the early thirteenth century. However sincere their change of beliefs, it is difficult to avoid thinking that they were also driven by a more cynical motive: to seek promotion at the Georgian court, the most prosperous and active Christian centre of patronage and employment in the region. This required them to assimilate, not to stand apart. The idea of an ethno-confessional, self-aware identity also implies a single, set identity. But as everything above shows, no facet of identity was immutable: parentage, language, religion and place could all change over a person's lifetime, and each change led to a shift in the ways in which identity was expressed by that person and perceived by those around them. This is not to say that it was always successful. To move between confessions, in particular, was a precarious business, as Ivane found out from the hostile reaction of the Armenians around him when he converted. He might have learned from an earlier example: the twelfth-century *Chronicle* of the Armenian Apostolic Matthew of Edessa, condemned the general Philaretos, an Armenian convert to Chalcedonianism: '[He] was a superficial Christian and was disavowed by both the Armenians and the Romans [Greeks]; he professed the Roman faith and followed their customs but he was Armenian through his father and mother, having grown up with his uncle in the monastery of Zorvi-Kozern.'[45] Such people were in danger of excluding themselves from both the community they were abandoning and that which they were seeking to join. One key difference for Ivane was that Queen Tamar's support meant that he was at least assured a welcome in the Georgian, Chalcedonian camp. But his Armenian ancestry was not so easily left behind. The role of the Georgian queen in his conversion also suggests that it was not allied with the idea of a distinct confessional identity, but rather one that moved him, his family and his followers within the mainstream of the Georgian court.

Nevertheless, it does point to a fascinating aspect of the patronage of Ivane and his family. To take Akhtala on its own paints a one-sided aspect of his character. Ultimately it must be seen as the most important aspect of his identity as it was the Church through which he envisaged his salvation would be achieved. But church patronage had many other functions as well. Whilst Ivane's spiritual concerns drove him to patronise his

---

[45] Matthew of Edessa, 137; C. J. Yarnley, 'Philaretos: Armenian Bandit or Byzantine General?', *REArm* 9 (1972), 331–53.

Figure 13 General view of the monastic complex at Harichavank, Armenia, from the south; 1201 (For the colour version, please refer to the plate section. In some formats this figure will only appear in black and white)

mausoleum church in a very particular way, his piety could also be demonstrated in other ways. These begin to undermine the clear Georgian identity that Akhtala presents, and replace it with a more nuanced identity that seems more concerned with maintaining a body of support among the Armenians and with blurring distinctions between the two different communities. Beyond Akhtala, Ivane's religious identity appears more fluid and contingent. Inscriptions claim Ivane's support and offer of gifts to many other monasteries in Armenia. These include such bulwarks of Armenian Apostolicity as Haghbat and Sanahin, Haghartsin and Geghard. He is recorded as paying for the building of new churches and zhamatuns, as well as giving tracts of land, vineyards and the income from shops to support each site. This continued long after his conversion. Haghartsin, whose inscription was mentioned in Chapter 1, was built nearly a decade later.

In the light of these donations to Armenian sites, Ivane's Georgian identity looks much more fragile. And this may have been a deliberate act. This can be suggested by looking at another site with which Ivane is linked, the monastery of Harichavank [Fig. 13]. This was founded in 1201 by Ivane's brother, Zakare. The donor inscription on the north wall of the church proclaims Zakare as founder, but includes Ivane, even though he had probably already converted to Chalcedonianism by this time:

> By the grace [and the mercy] of God, the lover of mankind, I, Zakare [*mandaturtukhutsesi* and] *amirspasalar* of Armenia and Georgia, son of the great Sargis, I have bought the famous and holy monastery of Harich with its hereditary properties for the well-being of my sovereign, the pious queen Tamar and for my salvation, for that of my brother Ivane and of our children... and our parents. I have built there at great expense a citadel and a katholikon, I have ornamented it with all sorts of religious vessels and I have offered to the Mother of God [St Astuatsatsin] my village of Moghorio near the holy monastery with all its areas of land with the mountain and water which is part of its domain; I have given a mill situated at Getik which is called Diwaghats, a mill at Ani Klijor, a garden at Caghkajor, a vineyard in Yerevan and a vineyard at Talin; and on the first boundaries which were its original property I erected a boundary cross at the Harich river cemetery... and the ancient Harich. I have... made a covenant to have the sacrifice of Christ celebrated in my name in perpetuity. Now those who observe this my memorial are blessed by God and by all the saints; but the one who opposes it or tries to annul it, great or small, he will inherit the curse of Cain and of Judas and will be cursed by God doubly. If someone takes away my gifts by force, may he be accursed by 318 pontiffs and by all the Saints... and this authentic testament was written in 1201.[46]

The final reference to the 318 pontiffs is a pointed reference to the Armenians' own claims to Orthodoxy. It refers to the body of churchmen, including Armenian bishops such as Aristakes, the son of St Gregory the Illuminator, who agreed the canons of the Council of Nicaea in 325. The oath refers to the common beliefs of all Christians, before the later councils refined these canons in a way the Armenians could not agree to.

As at Akhtala, the architecture and decoration of the main church at Harichavank had political and religious resonances that spoke to onlookers, and which are particularly interesting when seen in conjunction with Akhtala, begun at about the same time. In the same way that the distant view of Akhtala revealed the confession of the complex, so too with Harichavank. The agglomeration of buildings shows the clustering that is a feature only seen in Armenian churches. The main church is preceded by a large zhamatun that was placed around the west façade of the church in

---

[46] L. Der Manuelian, 'The Monastery of Geghard: A Study of Armenian Architectural Sculpture in the Thirteenth Century' (Ph.D. thesis, Boston University, 1980), 99–100; M. F. Brosset, *Les ruines d'Ani, capitale de l'Arménie sous les rois Bagratides, aux Xe et XIe siècles: histoire et description* (St Petersburg, 1860), 82–3.

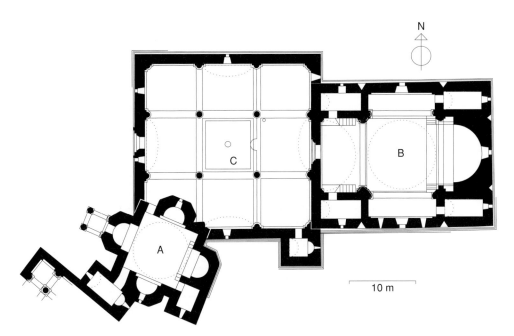

Figure 14 Ground plan of the monastic complex at Harichavank, Armenia; 1201. A: Church of St Gregory (seventh to tenth century); B: catholicon of the Mother of God (1201); C: zhamatun (*c.* 1224)

the decade after the church was finished [Fig. 14]. The zhamatun absorbs the earlier centralised church at the site into its south-west bay to produce a picturesquely asymmetric view from the south or west. And to the south of the earlier church were further subsidiary chapels and zhamatuns. Whilst the overlapping of the buildings at first sight looks like incompetence on the part of the builders (why did they simply not build the main church a few metres further east to allow more space for the zhamatun?), comparison with other contemporary sites soon reveals it to be a deliberate desire to create this form of distinctive asymmetric clustering.

If the overall appearance of the monastery suggests a general cultural allegiance to Armenia, some of its details point to a more precise political claim. This is most evident in the design of the dome.[47] The upper edge of the drum has a zig-zag profile which determined the umbrella-like form of the conical roof of the dome itself. This dome design had a long history in Armenian architecture, but this was the first time that it had been

---

[47] This dome was restored in the twentieth century. P. Donabédian and J.-M. Thierry, *Les arts Arméniens* (Paris, 1987), 536 shows a pre-restoration photograph of the church with a plain conical dome. However, the profile of the drum of the dome shows that the current restoration does reflect the original design.

Figure 15 View of the the church of St Sargis at Khtskonk, Turkey, from the north; early eleventh century

used in nearly two hundred years. The umbrella dome had been devised at the end of the tenth century, and survives in the main church at Marmashen (986–1029), Amberd (1026) and the church of St Sargis at Khtskonk (eleventh century) [Fig. 15]. What all these buildings share is their location: all were erected in the old kingdom of Ani. This had been established in 885 when the Bagratuni family were acknowledged as kings by the Caliph in Baghdad and the Emperor in Constantinople, and had made Ani their capital in 971. The kingdom had ended with its annexation by the Byzantine Emperor Constantine IX Monomachos in 1045. As Zakare's inscription from the palace church at Ani reveals, the Mqargrdzelis had pretensions to revive that kingdom, which had been lost for more than a century. In the

Figure 16 Zakare and Ivane Mqargrdzeli on the east façade at Harichavank, Armenia; 1201

inscription at Haghartsin they even claim descent from the Bagratuni kings of Ani. This church design seems to give those regal desires a concrete form, and associate them with a long-standing architectural tradition. The association is taken further at Marmashen, which was restored in 1225 by Ivane and his nephew Shahanshah, commemorated in an extensive inscription on the north wall of the church.[48] The design was taken up by relatives and supporters of the Mqargrdzelis at other churches built in the first half of the thirteenth century such as Gandzasar, Gtchavank and Hovhannavank.[49]

Ivane's close association with the church at Harichavank can be inferred from the fact that he is depicted prominently on its exterior. He appears in a relief sculpture alongside his brother on the east façade of the church [Fig. 16]. Like the profile of the dome, the donor portrait also looks back to Bagratuni precedents of the tenth century. Two double portraits were carved in relief on the east façades of the main churches in the monastic complexes at Haghbat and Sanahin.[50] These showed Smbat II, King of Ani (r. 977–89),

[48] Brosset, *Les ruines d'Ani*, 65–6, 148–51.
[49] Donabédian and Thierry, *Les arts Arméniens*, 532.
[50] And also revived at the same time on the east façade of Dadivank.

Figure 17 Canon tables from the Haghbat Gospels; 1211 (Yerevan, Matenadaran, MS 6288, fols. 8v–9r; 30 × 22 cm). The inscription by the figure holding the fish in the lower left corner reads, somewhat mysteriously: 'Sahak, next time bring fish!' (For the colour version, please refer to the plate section. In some formats this figure will only appear in black and white)

and his brother Gurgen, who went on to become King of Albania-Lori. The two panels were both set up by the brothers' mother, Khosrovanush. The parallels are clear: the images are set up in the same location on all three churches, and they each show a pair of brothers in an act of piety. At

Figure 17 (*continued*)

Harichavank the clothes have been updated to reflect contemporary fashion, with its sharbushes (the high, peaked hats) and bright kaftans, as can be seen when comparing the image with those in contemporary manuscripts, such as the Haghbat Gospels (Matenadaran 6288) of 1211 [Fig. 17].[51]

[51] Durand et al., eds., *Armenia Sacra*, cat. 69, executed at the monastery of Horomos in 1211, but given to the monastery at Haghbat soon after.

The similarities between the three sets of portraits have led to a major misapprehension about the Mqargrdzeli image. At Haghbat and Sanahin the two pairs of brothers offer God their churches, shown as miniature models that they hold between them. The images refer to the donation of the monastery as a whole. At Harichavank it has long been assumed that the brothers were doing the same, but that the model of the church has been lost.[52] However, detailed scrutiny of the carving suggests that it did not follow the same pattern. They can never have been directly holding a church; instead, their hands support the lower edge of what appears to be a window frame.[53] It has a delicate vegetal scroll decoration running round it. But this is no window – it has no corresponding opening inside the building. Instead, it is the frame for a shallow niche. The niche is now filled with a late alabaster relief image of the Mother of God and Christ; the question is, what did it hold in the thirteenth century?

It is possible to make a strong argument for the niche originally holding an icon, either painted or carved. The size and shape of the niche, as well as its height above the ground, leaves little scope for any alternatives. This is significant because it shows that Zakare was trying to change the religious practice of the Armenian Church in a radical way. Unlike in Georgia and Byzantium, icons were not part of Armenian religious tradition. Instead, like wall paintings, they were largely shunned by the Armenian Church. (It is important to note that this Armenian concern about images only referred to particular types of image: Armenian manuscripts are full of some of the most sumptuous paintings to have survived from anywhere in the medieval world. The concern seems to be about images made independent of biblical texts and the worry that they might elicit the wrong sort of veneration, i.e. the danger of idolatry.) The promotion of an icon on the exterior of Zakare's church made public his desire to introduce the Georgian veneration of images to Armenia.

The presence of an image at Harichavank reflects the impact of the Georgian court on Zakare and the time he spent there. Although Zakare remained faithful to Armenian Apostolicity throughout his life he was exposed to the Georgian promotion of icons throughout his time working

---

[52] Donabédian and Thierry, *Les arts Arméniens*, 536; see also Der Manuelian, 'The Monastery of Geghard', 105–6.

[53] This was noted in the mid-nineteenth century by Chahkhathounof: Brosset, *Les ruines d'Ani*, 81 n.2. However, in the same note Brosset records that Father Sargis claimed they held a church between them. I am unable to trace either of these texts from Brosset's citations, and so it is impossible to gauge their accuracy, although Brosset records that Chahkhathounof was working from second-hand notes. However, his record remains closest to what is visible today.

for Queen Tamar. Icons were at the heart of Georgian religious worship: numerous religious images, painted and hammered in metal, survive from the decades around Tamar's rule, and they attracted huge donations to fund their embellishment with gold, silver and jewels. Prayers to icons were believed to be highly efficacious in securing salvation. Icons were also credited with greater powers: they were central to the waging of war. The Georgian army had for centuries been preceded by miraculous icons as it marched to battle. Queen Tamar regularly prayed before such icons on the eve of her generals' battles, and she devoted much of the spoils of war to them and the monasteries that housed them. The material investment in icons is still visible from two surviving examples that were particularly venerated at the Georgian court. The great tenth-century enamel icon of the Mother of God from Khakhuli monastery attracted many donations, and was continually improved and expanded over the centuries.[54] The Anchiskhati, the seventh-century icon of Christ from Ancha, which was believed not to have been painted but to have been miraculously imprinted from the face of Christ himself, was similarly given a new golden frame at Tamar's command, made by the leading goldsmith of his day, Beka Opizari [Fig. 18].[55] An inscription of 1184 at the monastery of Haghartsin shows that the Georgian interest in icons was being transferred to Armenia in the late twelfth century. Anton Glonistavisdze made a donation to the monastery, leaving it under the protection of the icon of the Holy Mother of God of Vardzia.[56] The exposure of the Mqargrdzeli to icons was extensive, and there can be no doubt that the Georgians credited much of the Mqargrdzelis' military success to the divine support that they received through these images.

Zakare's desire to display an icon on the exterior of his church, a visual device without parallel in the Caucasus, must partly be credited to the belief that these images were instrumental in bringing victory to the army. But the desire was also driven by pragmatic issues. In the combined army of Georgians and Armenians that the brothers led, the promotion of icons by the Georgians and the hostility to them on the part of the Armenians caused frequent disputes. Ivane's conversion had, partially at least, been an attempt to bypass the differences between the two groups by providing each army faction with a Mqargrdzeli leader, but this had never been entirely successful. The tensions between the two sides came to a head in 1204, when the

---

[54] L. Z. Khuskivadze, *The Khakhuli Triptych* (Tbilisi, 2007).
[55] S. Amiranashvili, *Beka Opizari* (Tbilisi, 1964).
[56] S. T. Eremian, 'Agartsinskaia nadpis 1184g.', in *Issledovania po istorii kultury narodov vostoka: sbornik v chest' akademika I.A. Orbeli* (Moscow, 1960), 78–87.

Figure 18 The Anchiskhati icon; painted panel: seventh century; silver-gilt frame by Beka Opizari, c. 1190 (gilt cover of the body of Christ: eighteenth century) (Tbilisi, Art Museum of Georgia; 105 × 71 cm)

different religious practices of the troops whilst on campaign became too divergent: the Georgians took decorated tents with them to use as portable churches in which they could set up altars and icons and so celebrate the liturgy. The Armenians did not do this, and were accused by their Georgian colleagues of impiety for not celebrating the liturgy whilst on the march, and also of delaying celebrating particular feast days until they reached a church. Different rules about when fasts began and ended also caused problems as one part of the army went hungry whilst the other ate. Zakare demanded a change in Armenian practice to bring it into line with the Georgians' acts, but was told by the Armenian priests that it needed approval from the Armenian Catholicos in Hromkla, and from Levon, the Armenian King in Cilicia.

Whilst the authorities in Cilicia may not have wanted to change their traditions, they were fearful that Zakare would convert like his brother, leading to the wholesale persecution of the Armenian Church in its homeland. As a result they quickly acceded to his demands, and promulgated eight new canons after a Church council held in Lore, of which the fourth is the most significant:

> First: the mass should be performed with blessed clerks and deacons, as the law is.
> Second: the feast of the Annunciation to the Mother of God should be celebrated on April sixth, on whatever day it falls. The feast of the Assumption should be held on the fifteenth of August, on whatever day [of the week] it occurs, and the feast of the Holy Cross on the fourteenth of September, on whatever day it occurs. Similarly, other feasts of the martyrs should be celebrated on the actual days they occurred on according to the traditional commentary.
> Third: the fasts of the blessed Revelation of Christ and of Easter should be kept until evening, and not broken with anything except fish and olives.
> Fourth: icons of the Saviour and all the saints should be accepted, and not despised as though they were pagan images.
> Fifth: mass should also be performed for the living.
> Sixth: clerics must not eat meat.
> Seventh: one should first be ordained as a clerk and, only after many days as a deacon, and as a priest, in full maturity.
> Eighth: coenobites [communal monks] should reside in monasteries. No one [in the monasteries] should receive things separately [as private property].[57]

Whilst some of these canons concern other issues relating to the behaviour and training of priests and monks, most address the concerns of Zakare and the Armenians in his army. It is immediately apparent that none of the clauses concerned matters of doctrine or faith. Instead, they all addressed the external practice of religion: where services were held, on what days, and with what accompaniments – images. It was these differences that had previously visibly separated the two different factions of the

---

[57] Kirakos, 84–5 (trans. Bedrosian, 47).

army. Once adopted, it would be harder to tell the Georgian and Armenian troops apart on campaign: they would now all celebrate saints' days on the same day, they would fast at the same time, and they would all be permitted the use of icons. Even religion was being made less of a marker of identity under the Mqargrdzelis.

The alacrity with which Zakare's demands were met was a sign of the general fear that he would convert like Ivane if refused. He was further helped by a separate dispute between the Armenian King and his Catholicos, who each wanted Zakare's backing against the other. This produced further results, including the gift of a domed tent in the shape of a church with marble and decorations from the Catholicos. The fact that the Catholicos sent such a gift suggests that Zakare's acts were weakening the Armenian opposition to images even at the highest level of the Armenian Church.

Although it took place after Harichavank was built, the council marked an end-point in the debate about the propriety of monumental images in the Armenian world, not the beginning. The development of a joint Georgian and Armenian army in the second half of the twelfth century meant that the discrepancy in the treatment of images, and the consequent tensions between the factions, must have been apparent much earlier. It is therefore plausible to see the double donor portrait at Harichavank as a religious manifesto: the two brothers, each belonging to a different religious confession, shown together holding a sacred image. It is evident that the dominance of the Georgian faction required the Armenians to compromise; Harichavank presents that compromise as a positive feature, a clever play on longstanding traditions of donor imagery.

The interest in icons had one further effect on the design of Harichavank. The internal arrangements of the main church reflect the usual needs of the Armenian liturgy, notably with the apse raised on a high platform with an elaborately carved front. However, in the middle of the south wall inside the church is a second niche. This one is at eye level and stands above a shallow, projecting shelf. It is surrounded by a large rectangular frame which projects forward from the smooth, vertical surface of the wall. The combination of niche and frame resembles a stone triptych that has been opened to reveal its contents. Again the shallowness of the shelf and the size of the niche suggest that it could only have been suitable to house a thin painted panel – an icon. The fact that the current users of the church have painted an image in the niche shows how that idea has resonated down the centuries. This feature does not appear in earlier Armenian churches, although it does recur in a number of churches built in the years immediately after Harichavank was completed and the canons of the church council were approved. A niche appears, for example, in an identical location in the monastic complex at Makaravank, erected in 1204/5.

Thus, it seems that in the early thirteenth century there was a clear desire on the part of the ruling elite to diminish outward signs of distinction between Georgians and Armenians. The donor panel on the east façade was therefore not just an image of pious donation but of politically driven imagery. Identity was being deliberately blurred. Policy does not always indicate success, however. There was resistance to many of Zakare's changes, not least from the Armenian monastery of Haghbat. Its monks attacked Minas, the bishop, and his entourage who came to deliver the rules of the new observances, leaving his men half-dead and their mules driven over a cliff and killed.[58] In retaliation the abbot, Grigores, was imprisoned and threatened with death; it is likely that it was the monastery's opposition to the council that allowed Ivane to seize its daughter house at Akhtala and convert it to Georgian Orthodoxy. At the same time, however, both Mqargrdzeli brothers continued to offer their patronage to Haghbat.[59] This can only have been a deliberately disorientating use of carrot and stick simultaneously in order to destabilise the monastery and keep its monks more compliant.

When examined in detail like this, much of the patronage of the Mqargrdzelis appears contradictory and confusing, and it seems highly likely that this was intentional: to support, cajole and threaten the two communities of Armenia and Georgia to make them uncertain whether they would continue to receive support from their lords. Others sought to play the Mqargrdzelis at their own game. Mkhitar Gosh was the most esteemed Armenian monk of his age. He was a theologian, lawyer, writer of fables and patron of architecture; his advice was sought by the Mqargrdzelis and by the King in Cilicia; and Zakare took him as his spiritual father. Grigores of Haghbat fled to him for protection after the attack on Minas, hoping that Gosh's influence over Zakare would protect him. Yet when he came to compile his will in 1213, Mkhitar Gosh left his home monastery of Nor Getik (later renamed Goshavank after its founder) in the care not of an Armenian Miaphysite nobleman, but of the Chalcedonian Ivane.[60] Presumably he hoped that this

---

[58] Kirakos, 86.
[59] M. F. Brosset, *Description des monastères Arméniens d'Haghbat et de Sanahin par l'archimandrite Jean de Crimée* (St Petersburg, 1863), 6.
[60] Kirakos, 109–10; Lidov, *The Wall Paintings of Akhtala*, 344.

would place a burden of responsibility on Ivane to protect the monastery in the form in which it was left, as an Armenian foundation.

One final church shows the impact of the Mqargrdzeli brothers on the next level of society in the region, among the wealthy merchant class. In 1215 the foremost such merchant, Tigran Honents, built a church dedicated to St Gregory the Illuminator, in Ani.[61] Its exterior includes a very extensive inscription, effectively his testament. It names Tigran as the servant of Zakare and his son Shahanshah, and includes an oath at the end swearing in the name of the first three ecumenical councils, i.e. the three convened before the meeting at Chalcedon in 451 at which the Armenian Church left communion with the Byzantine Church.[62] Both elements suggest that the merchant was an adherent of Armenian beliefs. Yet the inscription also includes a list of objects given to the church:

> I have ornamented it with all kinds of adornments, of signs of the Lord, of holy crosses in gold and silver, of figurative icons (*khati*), enhanced with gold and silver with pearls and precious stones, of lights in gold and silver and of reliquaries of the holy apostles, with a fragment of the cross of the lord that received God, and all sorts of precious vases, in gold and in silver, with many other jewels.[63]

The 'signs of the Lord' seems to refer to Armenian crosses, whereas the 'figurative icons' is a borrowed word from Georgian, *khati*, meaning painted or metalwork panel images. It would seem that Tigran Honents, for one, followed the canons of the council of Zakare in 1204/5. The interior of his church is also covered in wall paintings. There remains some controversy about whether these were painted at the time the church was built (i.e. for Tigran himself) or slightly later (after the church was possibly taken over by a Chalcedonian group). The programme of images and the style in which they were painted was similar to those at Akhtala; the church likewise employs bilingual Greek and Georgian inscriptions. However, whoever had the images painted was still interested in the syncretistic vision of the two churches that Zakare and Ivane seem to have wished for. The western part of the church is filled with a cycle devoted to the conversion legends of Armenia and Georgia. A set of seventeen scenes devoted to the

---

[61] Thierry and Thierry, *L'église Saint-Grégoire*.
[62] Equally, at Horomos in 1201, Tigran described himself as 'loyal to my baron' Zakare: E. Vardanyan, ed., *Hoŕomos Monastery: Art and History* (Paris, 2015), no.40.
[63] J.-P. Mahé, 'Le testament de Tigran Honenc': la fortune d'un marchand arménien d'Ani aux XIIe–XIIIe siècles', *Comptes Rendus de l'Académie des Inscriptions et Belles-Lettres* 145/3 (2001), 1319–41, esp. 1323–6.

Figure 19 The vision of St Gregory the Illuminator in the west arm of the church of St Gregory the Illuminator of Tigran Honents, Ani, Turkey; 1215 (For the colour version, please refer to the plate section. In some formats this figure will only appear in black and white)

Figure 20 The vision of St Nino and the life-giving pillar in the west arm of the church of St Gregory the Illuminator of Tigran Honents, Ani, Turkey; 1215 (For the colour version, please refer to the plate section. In some formats this figure will only appear in black and white)

life of St Gregory tells of the establishment of the Church in Armenia, culminating in the saint's vision of heaven [Fig. 19]. But the cycle ends with an eighteenth scene on the neighbouring wall showing a miracle performed by St Nino, the Evangelist of Georgia [Fig. 20 The image shows St Nino, aided by angels, miraculously setting up a column that no one else could lift in the cathedral of Svetitskhoveli at Mtskheta, the old capital of Georgia. This was the symbol of the foundation of the Georgian Church, celebrated in a sermon by the Georgian Catholicos Nikoloz Gulabrisdze at about the same time.[64] Whilst there is an imbalance in favour of the Armenian saint in the

---

[64] Nikoloz Gulaberisdze, *Sakitkhavi suetis tskhovelisay kuartisa sauploysa da katolike eklesiisa* (Tbilisi, 1908).

cycle as a whole, the message of the parallel creation of the Churches is clear, and the inscriptions that accompany each scene were all written solely in Georgian.[65]

This spirit of compromise is evident in one more case, which was potentially explosive and divisive. In 1216 Tamta's father Ivane was issued with a summons to court in Dvin. He was accused of the illegal possession of a fragment of the True Cross. The relic had come to him as the spoils of war against the Muslims, but the Muslims had earlier seized it from the monastery at Noravank. Its previous owners now argued that it should be returned to them.[66] The political danger of the case lay in the cross having come from an Armenian site, but now being in the possession of the Georgian Ivane, who had deposited it at Akhtala. It inflamed the tensions between the two sides, which had already erupted into violence at Haghbat. The case was to be decided before a large bank of judges drawn from Georgia, including the archbishop of Chqondidi (who also doubled as the prime minister of Georgia), the abbot of Vardzia (the first and most favoured of Queen Tamar's foundations) and the newly Chalcedonian abbot of Akhtala (where the relic was being kept). Arrayed against them were a number of Armenian judges, including the bishops of Ani and Bjni and the abbot of Haghbat. This was a formidable array of some of the most powerful ecclesiastics in both countries. Alongside these judges sat a third group of men: the three Muslim *qadi*s (judges) of Tbilisi, Ani and Dvin and the 'celebrated' sheikh of Surmari. Given the tensions between the Georgians and the Armenians, the four Muslims on the bench were presumably recruited as more impartial judges. Being forced to side with either their pro-Georgian ruler or the majority Armenian population that they lived amongst put them in an invidious, impossible position. It must have severely tested their disinterestedness. The inclusion of Muslim judges also seems to run against all the work that Mkhitar Gosh had undertaken a few years earlier when he compiled his law code, since this was primarily established to help the Armenians avoid contact with the Islamic legal system![67] The final judgment was a brilliant compromise – a classic political fudge. Ivane was deemed the true, legal owner of the relic, since he had captured it in war. But it was agreed that it should be returned on loan to its

---

[65] Thierry and Thierry, *L'église Saint-Grégoire*; see also A. Eastmond, '"Local" Saints, Art and Regional Identity in the Orthodox World after the Fourth Crusade', *Speculum* 78/3 (2003), 707–49.
[66] Stepanos Orbelian, 1: 201–3.
[67] R. W. Thomson, *The Lawcode [Datastanagirk'] of Mxit'ar Goš* (Amsterdam; Atlanta, GA, 2000).

previous owners in perpetuity, on the grounds of the expense they had gone to through the legal system to reclaim it. Although the judgment effectively went against Ivane, he retained the legal moral high ground and no one lost face. It is easy to imagine the relief of the four Muslim judges at such an ingenious resolution to the affair.

The make-up of the judging panel reminds us of the importance of Muslims in the medieval Caucasus. Although Queen Tamar and her nobles ruled over territories with long Christian histories, they were lands that had large Muslim minorities, particularly in the urban centres. The buildings and icons that we have examined here show how the Mqargrdzelis manipulated their Christian identities. However, the Muslim presence throughout the region also had an impact on how the family presented itself in public. This was of course of particular importance for Tamta, whose life was more intimately connected to the Muslim world through her marriages to the Ayyubids in the Jazira, and so it will be examined later.

Tamta

The various forms of Mqargrdzeli Christian identity that this chapter has explored have presented predominantly male identities. Women have been less visible, and Tamta has remained invisible throughout. She is not named in any inscription set up by any member of her family. Nor is she ever referred to even indirectly. The colophon added to a translation of the homilies of Gregory of Nazianzus from Georgian to Armenian that was made at Akhtala in 1227 records: '[This book] was compiled in the reign of *atabeg* Ivane, the builder of this monastery, to whom God grant long life, together with his sons [Avag, and Ivane who died in childhood].'[68] Tamta, along with any other women in the family, are simply passed over in silence. Where daughters are mentioned, as in the exceptional Armenian inscription of 1241 at Kiz in Cilicia, which talks about the three daughters as well as the five sons of Constantine of Paperon (the father of King Hetum I of Cilicia), it is only to mention their marital status, as determined by their father:

> And his eldest daughter, a virgin, he prepared her for monastic orders. And the other, he married her to the king of the Cypriots. As for the third,

---

[68] Lidov, *The Wall Paintings of Akhtala*, 336.

he gave her in marriage to the baillis of Cyprus, who was lord of Beirut and Jaffa.[69]

Whilst the sons are also listed in the same way, their fate decided by their father, they are at least listed by name: 'by the grace of God, he made him king of Armenia, the superb and very beautiful and full of virtue, Hetum'. The omission of women such as Tamta from inscriptions was not solely determined by sex. Even sons could find themselves ostracised if they were not the designated heir. An eleventh-century inscription in the city of Ani weeps with the wounded love of one such son to his brother and father that survived their disregard of him:

> although I was neglected by my father because of the fact that I was the younger son, even so I was moved by love for my parents to restore this place of repose for my father Grigor and my brother Hamza and my sister Seda…[70]

The fact that Tamta is ignored in these donor inscriptions underlines the way in which her identity was determined by that of her father. She was simply expected to follow the plans, the mores and the beliefs that Ivane established. His conversion gave her two parallel identities, depending on whether she wished to trade on her father's ethnic, familial background with its roots in Armenian culture, or his present religion and court affiliations, which placed him at the heart of the Georgian court of Queen Tamar. The different religious paths taken by her father and her uncle, the different languages needed to communicate with the Georgian and the Armenian nobilities that she lived amongst, and the different cultural traditions of the two different communities ensured that Tamta grew up with a flexible, fluid mind-set, able to accommodate changing environments quickly. As we will see, she was able to exploit these different identities and skills in her later life, using both simultaneously to enhance her usefulness to her Ayyubid husbands and so establish for herself a more powerful position at their courts in Akhlat.

Whilst the absence of references to Tamta before 1210 can perhaps be ascribed to her being too young, her omission after that is more revealing. It shows the way in which the marriage process was conceived in her father's

---

[69] M. Geopp, C. Mutafian and A. Ouzounian, 'L'inscription du régent Constantin de Paperōn (1241): redécouverte, relecture, remise en contexte historique', *REArm* 34 (2012), 243–87, at 255.

[70] Orbeli, *Corpus Inscriptionum Armenicarum*, no. 97; Basmadjian, *Inscriptions arméniennes d'Ani*, no. 16.

mind. Once she was married, she was no longer a member of his family. Responsibility for her conduct and her salvation was transferred to her husband and his family. Effectively, ownership had been reassigned. Women, as we will see in later chapters, were able to exercise both power and patronage in this period, in Georgia, Armenia and the Islamic lands that surrounded them; but these forms of authority had to be gained and fought for; they were not simply inherited.

3 | Tamta, Ivane and Akhlat in 1210

> This city is the border town between the Muslims and the
> Armenians ... In the city of Akhlat they speak three languages, Arabic,
> Persian, and Armenian.[1]

Tamta's life in recorded history begins in 1210 with the failed siege of Akhlat by Ivane Mqargrdzeli and the Georgian–Armenian army of Queen Tamar. Before we move on to consider Tamta's marriage and her life among the Ayyubids, we must examine the conjunction of events that led to her arrival in the city: why was Ivane fighting? Why was he fighting at Akhlat? And why was he fighting in 1210?

Why War?

The attack on Akhlat formed part of the annual military campaigns conducted every summer by all the states in eastern Anatolia in the early thirteenth century. It therefore has the appearance of inevitability. But the motivations for war were varied and not all were obvious. The primary aim of war was to increase each state's territory and to secure its frontiers; and the main justification for war was the Will of God. It was incumbent on the army of Georgians and Armenians to support their fellow Christians, and to fight what they saw as the scourge of Islam. Homilies and sermons preached the righteousness of these religious wars, and chroniclers fuelled hatred with their vilification of those 'demon-infested', 'perfidious', 'lascivious-mouthed caterpillars'.[2] The substantial Armenian and Christian population of Akhlat (William of Rubruck, a Franciscan friar who travelled through Anatolia in the 1250s, reckoned the population was 90 per cent Greek and Armenian Christian, but under Muslim rule) was a reminder that this whole region

---

[1] Nasr-e Khosraw, 6.
[2] See the entertaining list of insults collected in S. La Porta, 'Conflicted Coexistence: Christian–Muslim Interaction and its Representation in Medieval Armenia', in *Contextualizing the Muslim Other in Medieval Christian Discourse*, ed. J. C. Frakes (London, 2011), 103–23, at 107–8, 109–11.

had been in Christian hands before it had been conquered by Arabs and then Turks, and it was easy to paint the population as being oppressed by its Muslim governors. War, to 'liberate this realm from the bitter servitude of the Tajiks [i.e. Turks]' (in the words of the Armenian bishop and historian, Stepanos Orbelian), and to prove that the Christian God was the true God, was an imperative.[3] A 6.8-metre-high khatchkar (Armenian cross-stone), decorated with elaborate geometric interlace designs around the central cross, was set up at Kosh in 1195 to celebrate that 'our land was purified and the churches of Armenia were made radiant' by Zakare and Ivane's conquests [Fig. 21].[4] It was just as much an imperative on the Muslim forces to defend their territories in return. One of the factors that gave Saladin's reconquest of Jerusalem and the Holy Places such importance was his propagandists' ability to cast it as *jihad*, Holy War fought in the name of Allah.[5]

The desire to demonstrate the power of the rival gods through war was supplemented by more human motives. Across eastern Anatolia, the Caucasus and Azerbaijan from the mid-twelfth century onwards the lust for war was fuelled by accounts of atrocities and outrages perpetrated by the enemy. Each side accused the other of committing them, and equally all sides celebrated their brutal, but in their eyes justified, treatment of defeated opponents. In the year of Tamta's marriage, the 'sultan' of Ardabil (presumably a mamluk soldier of Jahan Pahlavan, the *atabeg* of Azerbaijan) attacked the Mqargrdzeli capital, Ani, as its gates opened at dawn on Easter Sunday. The citizens had crowded into the churches for the services on this holiest of feast days, and were burned to death there; 12,000, it is claimed, were 'massacred like lambs'.[6] The Christian chroniclers particularly condemned this massacre as it was conducted outside the normal rules of such incursions. Instead of sacking and pillaging all the way to the city, which gave everyone fair warning to prepare themselves for what was to come and to hide their possessions and move out into the countryside, the sultan had kept his approach a secret by making no other attacks en route. In revenge, Tamta's uncle Zakare attacked the Azeri city of Ardabil in north-west Iran at the start of Ramadan:

> Many of the inhabitants together with their prayer-callers (who are called *mughri*) took refuge in their prayer houses. Zakare ordered that grass and stalks be brought. He had oil and naphtha poured on this kindling until [the mosques] were blazing with flames; and he burned [the Muslims]

---

[3] Stepanos Orbelian, 1: 222.
[4] La Porta, '"The Kingdom and the Sultanate were Conjoined"', at 95 n.109.
[5] Ibn Shaddad, 28. [6] *Kartlis Tskhovreba*, 271.

Figure 21 Khatchkar at Kosh, Armenia, set up to celebrate the liberation of Armenia from the Seljuk Turks; 1195

to death saying: 'Here are princes and laymen in return for the Armenian princes whom the Tajiks immolated in the churches of Nakhchivan, Qur'an-readers in return for the priests of Bagavan who were slaughtered and whose blood was splattered on the gates of the church – a place which is darkened to this day.'[7]

These two massacres were simply the most recent in a long and ignominious tradition of tit-for-tat slaughters. In 1161 Christian chroniclers claimed that the minaret of the main mosque in Dvin had been built from the freshly

[7] Kirakos, 91 (trans. Bedrosian, 52).

boiled skulls of recently slain Christians;[8] this led the Georgian King, Giorgi III (r. 1156–84), to attack the city in revenge: 'with sword and fire he cruelly afflicted them'. The Muslim response a year later saw 4,000 Christians at Mren 'killed as a burnt sacrifice for Christ'.[9] The Christian martyrs created in such attacks were commemorated in wall paintings to perpetuate the memory of the animosity, and the promise of an eternal reward for the victims. At the Georgian desert monastery of Udabno on the modern frontier between Georgia and Azerbaijan a small funerary chapel was decorated at the end of the twelfth century with a scene of Seljuk soldiers beheading monks [Fig. 22].[10] It was set above a charnel trough in which the monks' bones were housed for veneration.

These accounts all come from Christian sources. The numbers, no doubt, are exaggerated – as are many of the incidental details. The pathos of the 1210 massacre taking place over Easter, with church altars as the place of sacrifice, and with Queen Tamar still in mourning for the death of her beloved second husband Davit Soslan, all helped to inflame the passions of the chroniclers' Christian audience. However, the brutality was real, and Kirakos Gandzaketsi's account clearly approves of Zakare's Old Testament eye-for-an-eye revenge.[11] This voracious appetite for violence is conveyed in Vardan Areweltsi's almost identical account of the 1210 massacre, which opens with a parallel devastation in the natural world: 'In [this year], locusts ruined many provinces.'[12] It echoes a Georgian description of the Persian army being 'as innumerable as locusts or the sands of the sea'.[13] To farmers and city dwellers alike the wholesale destruction caused by the ravenous insects and the rapacious armies must have been difficult to tell apart.

The picture is identical when seen through the eyes of Muslim chroniclers; only the victims and oppressors are reversed. Ibn al-Athir, a chronicler based in Mosul, provided a sober summary of life around Akhlat in the early thirteenth century: 'This frontier region had always been one of the most dangerous for those living near it, the Persians before Islam, and after

---

[8] Al-Fariqi in Minorsky, *Studies in Caucasian History*, 92; Vardan, 206.
[9] Vardan, 206.
[10] A. Eastmond and Z. Skhirt'ladze, 'Udabno Monastery in Georgia: The Innovation, Conservation and Reinterpretation of Art in the Middle Ages', *Iconographica: Rivista di iconografia medievale e moderna* 7 (2008), 23–43, at 36–7; T. Khoshtaria, 'The Wall Paintings of the Chapel–Martyrium Motsameta in the Rock-Cut Monastery Complex of Udabno David-Gareji', *Inferno: University of St Andrews School of Art History Postgraduate Journal* 9 (2004), 15–22.
[11] Exodus 21:24. [12] Vardan, 212.
[13] *Kartlis Tskhovreba*, 330 (trans. Vivian, 129), referring to the Persian army at the battle of Shamkhori.

(a)

(b)

Figure 22 The massacre of monks by Seljuk Turks, depicted in the chapel of the martyrs (Motsameta) at Udabno monastery, Gareja desert, Georgia; *c.* 1200

them the Muslims from the beginning of Islam until now.'[14] As noted in Chapter 1, the ferocity of the Georgian army led Ibn al-Athir to fear for the very existence of the caliphate in Baghdad (and when the Mongols finally

[14] Ibn al-Athir, 3: 270.

destroyed the city and its institutions in 1258 – one of the most notorious calamities in all Muslim history – many chronicles record that at the forefront of the Mongol army was a Georgian contingent).[15] The chroniclers dress up the battles, sieges and massacres as crusade or *jihad*, with the violence endorsed by God and Allah respectively. Victories were celebrated with suitably partisan feasts: Davit Soslan, the husband of Queen Tamar, enjoyed a great feast of pork served at the Sultan's throne after he briefly occupied the city of Gandza in 1195.[16]

Religious fervour was undoubtedly a motivation for war. However, the importance of religion should not be overemphasised. Anti-Christian or anti-Muslim sentiment appears more often as a gloss to justify local wars that were primarily fought for territorial and financial gain with little concern about whether the opponent was of a different faith or a co-religionist. Seljuk expansionism at the start of the thirteenth century was at the expense of Muslim neighbours – the Mengujekids in Erzincan, the Saltukids in Erzurum – as much as of Christian opponents, whether the Byzantines to the west or the Georgians to the east. Equally, Ayyubid expansion into Anatolia could only be at the expense of Muslim principalities. The multi-faith alliances against the Khwarazmians and then the Mongols in the 1230s showed the ease with which former enemies, Christian and Muslim, could combine in the face of a greater threat.

Medieval warfare is perhaps more accurately characterised as a core economic function of the state. New lands provided new populations to tax, and captured booty paid for armies' upkeep. Both filled the state's coffers and individual soldiers' purses and thereby funded the next year's campaign. The chronicler al-Husayni describes the horror of Nasir al-Din Sökmen II, the Shah-i Armen of Akhlat, and his soldiers when told by his ally Shams al-Din Ildeguz, the *atabeg* of Azerbaijan, that he was considering cancelling their joint campaigns of 1161 (following the sack of Dvin) after receiving a peace embassy from the Georgian King, Giorgi III.[17] The Akhlati complaints centred on the amount they had already invested in preparation for the war (although they balanced this with appeals to religious motives). Their horror is understandable when you read the accounts of what could be gained in a campaign. Shortly after the massacre at Dvin, a royal Georgian castle had been captured on the river Gergeri:[18]

---

[15] Bar Hebraeus, 431.   [16] *Kartlis Tskhovreba*, 293.
[17] Husayni, 104–6; see also A. C. S. Peacock, 'Georgia and the Anatolian Turks in the 12th and 13th Centuries', *Anatolian Studies* 56 (2006), 127–46, at 132.
[18] All the following quotations are from al-Fariqi, trans. in Minorsky, *Studies in Caucasian History*, 93–4.

> Of their property so much booty was taken that it could not be described or counted. The king's stables were seized in which the mangers were of silver. The king's cellar was seized with all that was in it, including the silver vats. One of the latter was brought to the sultan; together with its fellow, it required for its transportation one [whole] wagon. The sultan sent it home along with booty to the amount of 2,000 current dinars. He had sent away drinking vessels of gold and silver and offered them to the cathedral mosque of Hamadan so that people should use them for drinking water.

And this was only part of the treasury, for as the Georgians fled they abandoned their field camp, which was captured three days later:

> The Shah-i Armen [ruler of Akhlat] seized three separate loads, one of which contained gold and silver vessels, in the second of which there was the king's chapel with gold and silver crosses set with gems, gospels illuminated with gold and set with jewels of inestimable price the like of which could not be found; the third contained the king's treasure of gold, silver and jewels, the price of some of which could not be estimated in view of the numbers.

On his return to Akhlat, the victory was celebrated with the slaughter of 300 oxen, and the display to the people of 'all kinds of peerless specimens of valuables and jewels'. Equally Georgian victories were celebrated by the import of booty.[19] The victorious campaign of the Georgians into northwest Iran in 1210 ended not with any strategic victory, but when the army had too much treasure to be able to carry back.[20] Later, when Jalal al-Din Khwarazmshah captured Tbilisi after a bitterly cold siege in the winter of 1226–7 his biographer claimed that his fingers were worn out from counting the spoils that were captured, and there was simply not enough paper to list them.[21] All this is hyperbole, no doubt, but indicative of the symbolic and financial benefits of victory.

Almost nothing of this plunder survives; most was destined to be melted down for coinage or returned to circulation when it was transformed into booty once more in the next defeat on either side. Monasteries, mosques and madrasas were mostly financed by the gems and precious metals seized, and so provide some concrete evidence for its lucrative extent. The tenth-century icon of the Mother of God of Khakhuli, the most revered of all Georgian icons, was enlarged into a triptych with gold captured at the start of the twelfth century from the Seljuks at the battle of Didgori (1121).[22] It was

---

[19] D. Rayfield, *Edge of Empires. A History of Georgia* (London, 2012), 112–13.
[20] *Kartlis Tskhovreba*, 274.   [21] Al-Nasawi, 204.
[22] On the booty from Didgori: *Kartlis Tskhovreba*, 180–1.

further adorned with gems by Queen Tamar after the battle of Shamkhori (1195), when she also donated the captured banners of the Abbasid Caliph of Baghdad to the icon.[23] War could lead to cultural as well as monetary gains. After the Georgian victory at Basiani in 1202 Anton Glonistavisdze, the Georgian archbishop of Chqondidi and prime minister, captured a copy of an Arabic treatise on medicine, which he had translated into Georgian – *The book for doctors* [*Tsigni saakimoy*]; one of the earliest works on Galenic medicine available in the country.[24]

The shifting alliances between all the powers in the region, the poor training of most troops, the depredations of disease and injury, and the problems of communication and food supplies made campaigning a risky and dangerous activity; but the potential rewards, spiritual, territorial and financial, ensured that there was no lack of men prepared to undertake it. When Ivane and Zakare set out on campaign in the spring of 1210, they did so in the belief that their actions were sanctioned by God, and that success would bring both material and heavenly returns. The recent decades of almost unbroken success in battle must have given them confidence that victory was as good as guaranteed.

Why Akhlat?

Looking at Akhlat today, it is hard to imagine why it was worth fighting over in 1210. It is now a small provincial town on the north-west shore of Lake Van in eastern Turkey, its population of just 20,000 dispersed over a wide area. The modern centre of the town has just one short row of shops and businesses, and the only surviving medieval monuments are the mausolea and tombstones in the cemeteries to the west of the town (discussed in Chapters 6 and 11). There is no sense of what the living city was like; its old buildings were burned down during the Khwarazmian and Mongol sieges of the 1220s and 1230s, and what was left was destroyed in two devastating earthquakes that followed in 1246 and 1276; and that only describes the depredations of the thirteenth century.

Of itself, Akhlat had few natural resources to offer invaders. Whilst the region had a rich soil, and a pleasant climate in the summer, it stands at an altitude of more than 1,600 metres and the town is buffeted by the winds that sweep across Lake Van in winter. 'Akhlat is one of the coldest places and one

---

[23] *Kartlis Tskhovreba*, 259–60; Khuskivadze, *The Khakhuli Triptych*, fig. 25.
[24] Rayfield, *Edge of Empires*, 114; D. Rayfield, *The Literature of Georgia: A History*, 2nd edn (Oxford, 2000), 97.

with the most snow' was all that Ibn al-Athir (d. 1233) could summon up to say about it.[25] Indeed, the cold and the snow are clichés in all the medieval descriptions of the town: the two words are indivisible in the Persian writer and traveller Nasr-e Khusraw's description of the eleventh century as well as in Yaqut's *Dictionary of Countries* of the 1220s; they appear together again in Marco Polo's travel account in 1299.[26] The weather often proved a more formidable defence for the town than its armies. The limited pasture barely supported the few thin cows and even thinner sheep and goats that roamed between the factories of the only thriving industries that are recorded: fruit, beehives to produce vast quantities of honey, and salting factories to preserve the abundant stocks of tirrikh, a herring-like fish, that was caught in the lake and exported as far as Balkh in modern-day Afghanistan.[27] There is an irony in that the Mongols' failure to settle in the region after 1245 was caused by a summer heatwave.[28]

But, at the start of the thirteenth century, Akhlat was a much more substantial prize. Its key value lay in its location: it was the meeting place of four different worlds. This was recognised in the earliest description of the town to survive, written in the eleventh century by Nasr-e Khusraw, who regarded the city as the epitome of converging cultures on the frontier: 'We arrived in the city of Akhlat on 18 Jumada I [20 November 1046]. This city is the border town between the Muslim and the Armenians... In the city of Akhlat they speak three languages, Arabic, Persian, and Armenian. It is my supposition that this is why they named the town Akhlat.'[29] This etymological explanation was based on Khusraw's (mistaken) belief that the name of the town was derived from an Arabic root, *kh-l-t*: *to mix*.

The four worlds that converged at Akhlat were all very different. To the north-east stood the Christian kingdoms of the Caucasus, Georgia and Armenia. It was from here that Ivane drew his army that was to face defeat in 1210 by the walls of Akhlat. The soldiers had much in common with the people of Akhlat, as the city's population was largely Christian and Armenian. Throughout the twelfth century the Muslim Sökmenid rulers of the city took the title of Shah-i Armen, which translates as King of the Armenians. It is likely that the majority of the population of Akhlat was still Armenian in the thirteenth century, and they only needed to sail across Lake Van

---

[25] Ibn al-Athir, 3: 297; see also 292.
[26] Nasr-e Khosraw, 6; Yaqut cited in G. Le Strange, *The Lands of the Eastern Caliphate: Mesopotamia, Persia, and Central Asia from the Moslem Conquest to the Time of Timur* (New York, 1905), 183; Marco Polo, 45–6.
[27] Nasr-e Khosraw, 6; Le Strange, *The Lands of the Eastern Caliphate*, 183.
[28] Kirakos, 145. [29] Nasr-e Khosraw, 6.

to the island of Aghtamar and its remarkable tenth-century palace complex with the church of the Holy Cross for a reminder of the heyday of Armenian rule, when the land around the lake was the centre of the Armenian kingdom of Vaspurakan.[30] To the north and west was the plateau of Asia Minor. Although historically a province of the Byzantine Empire, much of this territory had come under the control of Turkish tribes in the course of the twelfth century. Its population was mixed and undergoing rapid transition; nevertheless, it still contained a majority Christian population, mostly Greek speaking but also Armenian and Syriac.[31] To the south lay Syria and the Jazira, a confederation of Arabic city-states, divided among the Ayyubid family of Saladin. Finally, to the south-east lay the Persian world of Azerbaijan and Iran. And, as we have seen, from the 1220s Akhlat became a frontier for yet more groups to cross and conquer, the Khwarazmians from Central Asia and then the Mongols.

At the start of the thirteenth century none of the great powers, whether the Seljuks in central Anatolia to the west, the Georgians in the Caucasus to the north-east, or the Ayyubids in the Jazira and Syria to the south, was able to control south-eastern Anatolia. It had broken down into a political no man's land, a patchwork of small principalities that looked easy to capture, but each of which maintained a tenacious grip on its small territory. Before the capture of the city by al-Awhad in 1207, Akhlat was ruled by local princes, the Sökmenids. To the north were other minor Turkic families: the Mengujekids in Erzincan and the Saltukids in Erzurum. To the south, the Artuqids controlled the fortified cities of Mardin and Amid (modern-day Diyarbakir), both in south-eastern Turkey, and to their east, the Zangids, the former power across the region, were now restricted to the region around Mosul, in present-day north-western Iraq. In Azerbaijan the Pahlavuni family ruled. The Ayyubid base in Mayyafariqin (modern-day Silvan), from which al-Awhad captured Akhlat, was isolated from the heartlands of the Ayyubids in the Jazira and Syria, connected only by a strip of land squeezed between Artuqid-controlled cities. These principalities acted as buffers between the larger powers that surrounded them; they survived by playing the major powers off against each other.

Of all these minor principalities, Akhlat stood out because of the strategic importance of its location. With a defensible citadel, it could launch raids in every direction and so could act as a stranglehold on trade caravans

---

[30] L. Jones, *Between Islam and Byzantium: Aght'amar and the Visual Construction of Medieval Armenian Rulership* (Aldershot, 2007).
[31] S. Vryonis, *The Decline of Medieval Hellenism in Asia Minor and the Process of Islamization from the Eleventh through the Fifteenth Century* (Berkeley; Los Angeles; London, 1971), 42–55.

moving between Asia, the Caucasus and Europe. A tenth-century Armenian itinerary has Akhlat as a major stop on a north–south route that runs from Dvin in Armenia to Damascus and then Jerusalem.[32] The Arab geographer Ibn Hawqal places Akhlat on an east–west trade route from Ardabil and Tabriz in Persia on to Khoy then Akhlat and down to Amid. In Akhlat's hinterland (at Arjish) a branch of the road moved north to Erzurum and Sivas.[33] These trade routes, which took silks and spices from east to west, and slaves from north to south, were the same as those taken by invading armies: Akhlat stood on everyone's path to expansion. As Husam al-Din 'Ali, Al-Ashraf's chamberlain in Akhlat, warned his sultan in 1225: 'Jalal al-Din is close by, and if he takes Akhlat he will conquer the whole region.'[34] The town's strategic importance had long been recognised by the Ayyubids: Saladin himself had tried to take the city in the 1180s, as had his nephew, Taqi al-Din, in 1191.[35]

Why 1210?

The year 1210 was perhaps the first, and certainly the last, year that the Georgians were in a position to be able to attack Akhlat. That year marked the greatest extent of the Georgian kingdom, pushing towards the coastline of the Caspian Sea to the east, and stretching far into Anatolia to the west. Zakare and Ivane's army had already forced some of the minor principalities, notably the Saltukids of Erzurum and the Mengujekids in Erzincan to accept Georgian suzerainty. They had also begun to force other Muslim powers out completely, not least the Shaddidids, who were conclusively expelled from Ani in 1199. The list of cities recaptured listed in Vardan Areweltsi's history shows how fast Georgian expansion took place at the start of the thirteenth century: 'By their own valour, they [Zakare and Ivane] expelled the Turks from all the fortresses and provinces in a short time. For in 1191 they took the land of Shirak; in 1196 they took Anberd; in 1199 they took Ani; in 1201, they took Bjni; in 1203 they took Dvin; in 1206 they took the royal Kars, then Getabakk and Charek' (his list echoes that inscribed on the church at Haghartsin, quoted in Chapter 1).[36] These were more permanent conquests than the temporary seizures of these cities that

---

[32] H. Manandian, *The Trade and Cities of Armenia in Relation to Ancient World Trade* (Lisbon, 1965), 169.
[33] Manandian, *The Trade and Cities of Armenia*, 157.
[34] Humphreys, *From Saladin to the Mongols*, 216.
[35] Minorsky, *Studies in Caucasian History*, 148.   [36] Vardan, 211.

Giorgi III had enjoyed in the 1160s. The Mqargrdzelis' confidence was aided by spectacular victories over Abu Bakr, *atabeg* of Azerbaijan, at Shamkhori in 1195, and over Rukn al-Din Suleymanshah II, the Seljuk Sultan, at the battle of Basiani in 1202. In 1204 Queen Tamar had successfully intervened in Byzantine politics, establishing a breakaway state in Trebizond for exiled members of the imperial Komnenian dynasty, and this may have encouraged her to play an ever more active role in international affairs across the region.[37] Akhlat was the next target in the creation of a Georgian empire, to be built for Queen Tamar by the Mqargrdzelis.

These battles and expansions were testimony to the growing experience and training of the Georgian–Armenian army, but also to weaknesses among their neighbours in both Azerbaijan and Seljuk Rum caused by internal disputes. Although the Seljuks in Anatolia had begun to consolidate their control in central Anatolia, they were not yet in a position to expand to the east. Equally, Syria took a decade to resolve the inheritance of Saladin after his death in 1193. By 1210 all these neighbours were beginning to resolve their internal problems, and the Georgians were never able to repeat the gains they had made before. Akhlat marked the end of the expansionist phase of the Georgians and their allies.

Akhlat had one other attraction in 1210: the state of the city itself. Under its Sökmenid rulers the fabric of the city had been transformed over the previous fifty years using the income it earned from its position on the trade routes between Anatolia and Iran as well, perhaps, as the spoils it had taken from the Georgians in the 1160s. This had enabled Shahbanu, the wife of the Shah-i Armen Nasir al-Din Sökmen II, to begin an extensive building programme in the city. Like Tamta, she had come to Akhlat as a diplomatic bride to form an alliance with the neighbouring emirate of Erzurum; she was the daughter of 'Izz al-Din Saltuk II (ruler of Erzurum, 1132–68). The record of her work shows how active she was on behalf of her new home: a campaign had begun to renew and repair all the roads leading to Akhlat; the old wooden bridges were replaced with new stone ones and a series of caravanserais was established along the roads leading to the city.[38] Unfortunately nothing now survives of her work. However, it left Akhlat a more tempting prize for its neighbours than it had ever been before.

---

[37] A. Eastmond, *Art and Identity in Thirteenth-Century Byzantium: Hagia Sophia and the Empire of Trebizond* (Aldershot, 2004), 18–22; A. A. Vasiliev, 'The Foundation of the Empire of Trebizond', *Speculum* 11 (1936), 3–37.

[38] O. Pancaroğlu, 'The House of Mengüjek in Divriği: Constructions of Dynastic Identity in the Late Twelfth Century', in *The Seljuks of Anatolia: Court and Society in the Medieval Middle East*, eds. A. C. S. Peacock and S. N. Yıldız (London; New York, 2013), 25–67, at 54.

The background to 1210 shows how important control of Akhlat was, and how much rested on Tamta's marriage. The treaty that sent Tamta to wed al-Awhad was contracted under high pressure against a background of regional hostility that had rumbled on in the region for at least two generations. The marriage was expected to stop a similar legacy of enmity emerging between the Georgians and the Ayyubids, who had never before shared a common border. In 1210 it was these two groups who looked to be becoming the regional superpowers, but neither yet had a strong enough army and a settled enough internal state structure to be able to claim dominance in eastern Anatolia. The next chapter explores the nature of diplomatic marriages in the thirteenth century, and whether the union of two individuals, albeit both highly placed in their respective societies, could overcome the larger religious and economic imperatives of war, and the centuries of enmity that had built up between Christians and Muslims.

4 | Al-Awhad and Tamta's First Marriage

> When he [Abu Bakr] saw that he was incapable of protecting his lands with the sword, he turned to protecting them with his penis.[1]

The ransom negotiations conducted after the capture of Ivane at Akhlat introduce Tamta to history in an inauspicious light: she is presented as a bride and as a pawn in the desperate political manoeuvrings of her father. The combination might seem uncomfortable, but it is by no means unusual for the Middle Ages, when sisters, daughters and nieces were frequently regarded as commodities for their brothers, fathers and uncles to dispose of however they saw fit to further their own ends. This chapter charts the marriages of Tamta to al-Awhad and then, very soon afterwards, to his brother, al-Ashraf Musa, both nephews of the great Muslim hero Saladin. It examines the additions and changes to Tamta's identity brought on by marriage; her shift from being the daughter of a Christian nobleman to the wife of a Muslim Ayyubid ruler. In order to understand the politics behind the marriage, the expectations that both sides brought to the union, and the symbolism and practical results of the wedding, we need to look more broadly at the phenomenon of diplomatic marriage in the thirteenth century.

The Ayyubids: The Family of the Groom

Tamta's first husband, al-Awhad, was one of the less well-known members of the Ayyubid family. The Ayyubids had risen to prominence in the Islamic world from their obscure Kurdish origins in the Caucasus under the charismatic warrior al-Nasir Salah al-Din Yusuf, better known in the west as Saladin, the opponent of Richard the Lionheart and the Third Crusade. Saladin's recapture of Jerusalem in 1187, after almost a century of occupation by crusaders from western Europe, gave him and his family extraordinary prestige and a reputation as jihadists – holy warriors – which resounded

---

[1] Ibn al-Athir, 3: 113.

among contemporaries across the Islamic world.[2] Before taking Jerusalem he had ousted two Muslim powers, the Fatimids in Egypt in 1171, and three years later the Zangid *atabeg*s (governors) of Syria, in whose service he had first started his career as a military commander. He even extended his rule down through Arabia and into the Yemen. This record of military success, all achieved in a very short space of time in the 1170s and 1180s, gave the Ayyubids vast territories and wealth, and some of the richest, most cosmopolitan cities in the Mediterranean, including Aleppo, Damascus and Cairo.

Saladin's conquests also furnished the family with great spiritual authority. The victories in Arabia gave them control of Mecca and Medina, so that after the recapture of Jerusalem they possessed the three holiest Islamic cities. The last Islamic dynasty to have ruled all three had been the Fatimids, who were Shi'a Muslims; the Ayyubids were Sunnis, as were the majority of the populations in Egypt, Syria and Arabia. The Ayyubid revival of Sunni Islam added lustre to the family's reputation among their co-believers.[3] The Sunni cause was promoted by the Ayyubid sponsorship of mosques, and particularly of madrasas that would promote this branch of Islam against Shi'a Islam and other heterodox sects that might threaten to undermine their status. Even though they had only emerged from relative obscurity in the middle of the twelfth century, their military achievements enabled them within two generations to compete with the Abbasid Caliph in Baghdad as the spiritual leaders of the Islamic world.

However, whilst Saladin's legacy was one of military and religious strength, it lacked political unity. On Saladin's death in 1193 he was succeeded in most of the Ayyubid territories by his brother al-'Adil, who then followed family practice by dividing his inheritance between his thirteen sons. The lands that had been retained by Saladin were divided between his seven sons, and the remaining territories he had conquered were split among his other brothers and their sons (the dispersed nature of the family and the absence of a contemporary historian interested in the whole dynasty means that it is impossible to be precise about the exact numbers of sons, nephews and cousins involved, but Saladin's empire was split between at least twenty-five men in the next generation). Whilst this ensured that all the sons had land to rule, it undermined the cohesion of the state and weakened the overall power of the dynasty. This fragmented Ayyubid control across

---

[2] M. C. Lyons and D. E. P. Jackson, *Saladin: The Politics of Holy War* (Cambridge, 1982), 201–20, 267–78, 365–74, taking full note of Saladin's detractors as well.

[3] Y. Tabbaa, *The Transformation of Islamic Art during the Sunni Revival* (Washington, DC, 2001), 11–24, 68.

the Middle East, creating what has been called a confederacy of rulers, most based in cities and strongholds.[4] The divisions inevitably encouraged political dissension within the family, leading to civil war between brothers and cousins as they competed with each other to defend or increase their own lands, power and wealth.

The common Caucasian, Kurdish roots of the Ayyubids and the Mqargrdzelis underline the capacity for medieval people to reinvent themselves: two families from the same region rising to power in different states, using different languages and professing different religions.[5] The impression given by medieval chronicles is that the Ayyubids were fully Arabicised: they used Arabic as their official language (Kurdish was not a written language in the twelfth century),[6] and they resided in the predominantly Arabic-speaking cities of the Jazira, Syria, Egypt and Arabia. It seems likely that there was a division between the public, Arabicised face of the Ayyubid family and its private, Kurdish roots which seem to have remained hidden to all but the most assiduous of researchers, such as Ibn Khallikan, writing in the 1280s, who was the first to research Saladin's origins in his biographical encyclopaedia.[7]

Al-Awhad: The Groom

Al-Awhad does not appear with any prominence in any Ayyubid histories. He was established by his father, al-ʿAdil, as the ruler of Mayyafariqin (modern-day Silvan), at the northern tip of the Ayyubid world. Mayyafariqin stood on open plains, just to the south of the Anatolian plateau. Al-ʿAdil was determined to expand Ayyubid power on to the plateau using Mayyafariqin as the base for his operations. He repeatedly attempted to capture Akhlat without success. Al-Awhad's posting to the city was therefore an opportunity for an astute warrior to carve out a new realm for himself, but al-ʿAdil does not seem to have trusted his son's capacity to wage war on his own. Most of the Ayyubid expeditions in the region involved al-Awhad, but only as a minor member of an army led either by al-ʿAdil himself or by al-Awhad's younger brother, al-Ashraf Musa, who controlled the important cities of Harran and Raqqa in the Jazira to the south. For

---

[4] Humphreys, *From Saladin to the Mongols*, 41–2, 67–9.
[5] For the prehistory of the Ayyubids see Minorsky, *Studies in Caucasian History*, 107–37.
[6] B. James, 'Les Kurdes au Moyen Âge', in *L'Orient de Saladin: l'art sous les Ayyoubides*, ed. É. Delpont (Paris, 2002), 24.
[7] Ibn Khallikan, 4: 479–80; Minorsky, *Studies in Caucasian History*, 124–32.

al-Awhad it is perhaps more accurate to see the Mayyafariqin posting as a relatively obscure place to park a son in whom his father had little confidence.

The fact that it was al-Awhad who captured Akhlat in 1207 probably came as a surprise both to himself and to his father and brothers. It was a case of being in the right place at the right time. His army had only recently been repulsed from the city by the combined forces of Balban, the former mamluk (slave commander) then in control of Akhlat, and Tughrilshah of Erzurum. But when the two allies fell out, leading to Balban's assassination by his supposed partner, al-Awhad with the remnants of his army was able to enter Akhlat unopposed, as its citizens now saw the Ayyubids as the least-worst option to provide the security the city needed to prosper.

Whose Marriage was it Anyway?

Although al-Awhad was still in command of Akhlat three years later when Ivane was fortuitously captured, it seems that he was barely in control: his army was effectively besieged in the town's citadel by its population. Indeed, even al-Awhad's marriage to Tamta seems to have been organised without his knowledge: he was as much a victim of events as Tamta was. The inclusion of Tamta as part of the ransom package for the release of her father lay outside both the Georgians' and the Ayyubids' control. According to Kirakos Gandzaketsi's account of the debacle at Akhlat, the capture of Ivane was carried out by the 'men of the city';[8] and it was they, rather than the Ayyubid governing elite, who organised the marriage. Al-Awhad was away from the city, and the people were too worried about their security to send Ivane all the way to join him, as Zakare was threatening reprisals: 'release my brother from your city, or I shall destroy it, I will take your soil to Georgia, and destroy your population.'[9] To avoid this, they demanded that Tamta be given to the city as a substitute hostage for her father, effectively presenting the sultan with a new wife as a *fait accompli* in order to seal the peace.

As a result, the marriage was not simply an expression of Ayyubid victory. Instead, it balanced the needs and bargaining strengths of three different groups. The Mqargrdzelis, in the weakest position, gained the release of Ivane, but the marriage also gave them a link to the Ayyubid ruling clan. This had potential strategic advantages in terms of fostering alliances against

---

[8] La Porta, '"The Kingdom and the Sultanate were Conjoined"', 87, for discussion of the terminology used to describe the citizens.
[9] Kirakos, 82.

other common foes in the region, notably the Seljuk Turks to the west in Anatolia. The Ayyubids also gained from the marriage: they effectively neutralised a worrying military threat to the north-east of their lands, and similarly may have hoped for strategic alliances against common enemies. However, it was the predominantly Christian people of Akhlat who perhaps gained the most. They used the ransoming of Ivane to protect their rights and improve their own position under Ayyubid rule. Organising the marriage of Tamta to al-Awhad enabled them to introduce a Christian princess into the heart of the Islamic dynasty that now ruled over them. The previous regime in Akhlat had been careful to show tolerance to the Christian population: Sökmen II, the Shah-i Armen of Akhlat (1128–85), is reported by an Armenian source as being 'friendly to Christians and solicitous for the country'.[10] The largely Armenian population of Akhlat had no means of knowing whether the Ayyubids would continue such a policy, but the marriage of al-Awhad and Tamta presented them with one means of influencing their treatment by the Ayyubids; although they cannot have known at the outset whether it would be successful or not. The Arabic historians Ibn Wasil, al-Nuwayri and Ibn al-Furat record explicitly that Tamta was to be allowed to retain her Christian faith, suggesting that her religion was a key factor in the marriage.[11]

The selection of Tamta shows how different facets of her dual identities were picked up on by the different parties in the negotiations. To the Ayyubids she represented a link to the court of Georgia, but to the people of Akhlat it was her Armenian origins, and her membership of the wider Mqargrdzeli family, that was most important. These were all potent elements in her persona that each side hoped it could draw on to further its own interests in Akhlat, whether this was the short-term goal of the release of Ivane, or longer-term plans to neutralise the Georgian threat to the city, or to retain a voice for the Christians in the ruling of the city. Tamta emerges from this as an intermediary between all the competing interests that converged at Akhlat. Although she started off simply as a pawn in the power plays of others, and clearly had no say in her involvement at this moment, she stood to be transformed by the wedding. The act of marriage provided a new and potentially powerful dimension to her identity as the figure that each party in the negotiation needed in order to placate the others. She now overlaid the position of wife of an Ayyubid ruler onto her paternal

---

[10] Vardan, 204.
[11] Ibn Wasil, 3: 201; al-Nuwayri, 29: 48; Ibn al-Furat, 5: 105 (who says that Ivane requested that Tamta remain a Christian), with thanks to Scott Redford for these references; see also La Porta, '"The Kingdom and the Sultanate were Conjoined"', 88 n. 79.

family identity as an Armenian and a Georgian, but above all as a Christian. This put her in a position to act as a figurehead to represent the interests of all the Christian groups to the new Ayyubid regime. Kirakos Gandzaketsi's comments on Tamta's ability to reduce taxation of monasteries and improve access for pilgrims to Jerusalem (both of which will be explored in more detail in later chapters) show that she was able to capitalise on this, and convert her position into one with real power. Tamta's authority necessarily originated in her evolving and increasingly mixed identity, otherwise the marriage would have had no value for the people of Akhlat who had organised it. The aim of the marriage can never have been simply to assimilate her into an Ayyubid role, supplanting her paternal identity, as this would have given nothing to the parties involved.

Thus, despite having no say in her marriage and appearing to be a pawn in the whole business, it was Tamta who gained most from it. Indeed, the source of her power was the wedding and the way it gave an official and public sanction to the layering of her paternal and uxorial identities.

The Theory of Marriage

For Tamta, marriage was central to the establishment of her identity. As we saw in Chapter 2, she had no visible presence before her marriage. She is mentioned in no inscriptions, chronicles or other written sources. This fits a more general pattern in which female members of families are generally unrecorded until they are betrothed. This invisibility, this dependence on the father, ensures that we are right to think of Tamta as sharing her father's identity during this first stage of her life. Marriage changed the lives of women irrevocably. When Tamta was transferred from her father's family to that of her new husband, she was forced to become part of a new family with a new identity. As we will see, the effect this had on women varied from case to case, depending on the circumstances of the marriage and its consequences: first as wife; then as mother; and finally as widow. The dowries that they brought with them to their marriages gave them a degree of financial independence. If they had children, they had a means by which they could exert influence within their families into the next generation. As widows, women had access to resources and legal status that they had lacked before, and were often able to maintain their independence.

In the case of Tamta and other women like her, marriage had a further layer of significance. As a diplomatic alliance, it represented the coming together of two different states, and so the participants in the wedding came to take on the trappings of personifications of those states. Thus questions of identity became increasingly important. At this point it is worth stepping back to see how diplomatic weddings were regarded in the thirteenth century. Within the normal confines of international diplomacy alliances were forged and broken in order to further each state's political and territorial interests. Such diplomatic encounters were lubricated by gifts. The exchange of robes of honour, of gold and silver, of fine horses and foodstuffs allowed each party to indicate their approval of the other and to establish a means of communication. As has so often been observed, the key feature of such gifts was reciprocity: the need to return gifts of equal value to maintain the engagement.[12] They formed part of the extended world of gift exchange which bound rulers together across political and religious frontiers. The ransoming of captured noblemen formed part of this almost chivalric code. It was only in exceptional circumstances that it was abandoned, as in July 1202 when Queen Tamar captured Nasir al-Din Bahramshah, the Mengujekid Emir of Erzincan (r. 1165–1225) at the battle of Basiani. In anger at the attack of this former vassal, she ordered him to be sold into slavery for the price of one iron horseshoe.[13] The punishment gained its potency from the deliberate abandonment of diplomatic norms (and the waiving of Tamar's chance to charge a huge ransom for his release).

Marriages should be seen within the same context of gift and exchange, with the bride as a special category of offering, which created a tie of kinship between the parties. She represented the most prized commodity available to any ruler, his own flesh and blood. The daughter's value derived largely from this rarity: this is certainly the case for Tamta, whose exchange for her father gave her almost equal value to him. Unlike silks and silver, daughters were very limited in supply. Georgian chroniclers even went so far as to invent a Byzantine princess for a later King of Georgia, Davit VII Narin (r. 1254–93), the son of Queen Rusudan. They passed off an illegitimate daughter of John Palaiologos as the legitimate daughter of his elder brother, the Emperor Michael VIII Palaiologos (r. 1259–82), in order to increase the prestige of the union, and to afford Davit a higher status in the community of kings than he actually enjoyed.[14]

---

[12] C. Hilsdale, 'Gift', *Studies in Iconography* 33 (2012), 171–82.

[13] *Kartlis Tskhovreba*, 299; Bahramshah had been a patron of Nizami of Gandza, whose poems celebrated him as 'the captor of Georgia': O. Pancaroğlu, 'The Mosque–Hospital Complex in Divriği: A History of Relations and Transitions', *Anadolu ve Çevresinde Ortaçağ* 3 (2009), 169–98, at 175.

[14] *Kartlis Tskhovreba*, 355, 364, 371; E. Trapp, ed., *Prosopographisches Lexikon der Palaiologenzeit* (Vienna, 1976–96), 3: no. 5017; the 'real' identity is given by Georgios Pachymeres, III.21, 286.

Very occasionally, a bride could be provided in return, but more often the reciprocity came in a different coin (for Ivane it was his release and a non-aggression treaty). In the longer term a bride could provide the next generation. She could give birth to an heir to the throne and could nurture more daughters to supply the royal marriage market. Herein lay their greatest power, as we shall see in future chapters. However, in Anatolia and Greater Armenia, as Tamta demonstrates, they also had power as a mediating force in a world in which the majority population was often not of the same religion or ethnicity as its ruler.

Tamta's position can be contrasted with a diplomatic marriage that had taken place just five years earlier, when the boot was on the other foot. In the 1160s the lands of Shams al-Din Ildeguz, the *atabeg* of Azerbaijan, had stretched as far west as Akhlat, but by the start of the thirteenth century the family were restricted to a region corresponding to the modern-day borders of Azerbaijan and north-west Iran, and faced devastating annual incursions from the Georgians.[15] The army of Ildeguz's grandson, Abu Bakr (r. 1186–1210), was insufficient to defend his lands and he lacked the luck of the defenders of Akhlat. Rather (if we are to believe the Muslim chroniclers who despaired of his failures against the Georgians), Abu Bakr was a habitual incompetent and drunkard.[16] It reached the stage that he was so demoralised that he forbade his ministers even from mentioning any further Georgian raids.[17] But Abu Bakr's solution was simple: '[when] he saw that he was incapable of protecting his lands with the sword, he turned to protecting them with his penis.'[18] Abu Bakr arranged a marriage with a woman Ibn al-Athir names only as 'the daughter of the king of Georgia'. Who this woman is remains something of a mystery. The Georgian chronicles' account of the episode has the negotiations ending without a marriage taking place.[19] Georgia, of course, was ruled by a woman, Queen Tamar, and the marriages of her only daughter, Rusudan, are fully accounted for. The only possible candidate is Tamar's sister, also called Rusudan, but such are the vagaries of the medieval sources when it comes to women that it is not clear whether this Rusudan ever existed, or is simply a confusion or even invention on the part of the chronicler. However, the reality of this marriage is largely beside the point. What concerns us is the perception of marriage as a means to bind enemy forces together, and the symbolic role it gave the wife as the link between the two sides.

---

[15] C. E. Bosworth, *The New Islamic Dynasties. A Chronological and Genealogical Manual* (Edinburgh, 1996), no. 99.
[16] Ibn al-Athir, 3: 113.   [17] Husayni, 125; Rayfield, *Edge of Empires*, 113.
[18] Ibn al-Athir, 3: 113.   [19] *Kartlis Tskhovreba*, 255–6.

What makes the Abu Bakr story stand out is its gender politics. The interpretation of the marriage as a failure was determined by the fact that the groom was forced to give himself away – to become the junior partner in the union, the role usually reserved for the bride. The sarcastic tone in which Ibn al-Athir reports Abu Bakr's tactics shows that his marriage was clearly seen as the feeble ruse of a deficient ruler by his Muslim contemporaries. However, it did work. The Georgians reduced their attacks on Azerbaijan (until the attack on Marand and Ardabil of 1210), and Abu Bakr was able to pass his lands on to his half-brother, Özbeg (r. 1210–25), in reasonably peaceful conditions at his death the same year.[20]

Other cases show the extremes to which men would go to achieve the marriage alliance they wanted. In 1164 the Danishmendid ruler of Malatya, Yağibasan (r. 1142–64), sought to strengthen his power by marrying his nephew to the daughter of the 'Izz al-Din Saltuk II, the ruler of neighbouring Erzurum (r. 1132–68). Unfortunately, there was a problem: she had just married his greatest enemy, Kılıç Arslan, the Seljuk Sultan (r. 1156–92), who obviously did not want to dissolve the marriage, not least because she was promised with a trousseau of 'inestimable value'. Yağibasan's solution was ingenious and elegantly pragmatic, if theologically suspect. He seized her whilst she travelled to join her husband, and then 'ordered her to repudiate Islam – which she did – in order to invalidate her marriage to Kılıç Arslan. Then she converted back to Islam and he married her to his nephew.'[21]

Paternal Identity

The importance of the bride's paternal identity is shown by other examples, which also hint at the fragility of the alliance brought together at a wedding. Marriage was by no means the lifetime union that Christian and Muslim theologians alike desired. In 1232 Tamta's Ayyubid brother-in-law al-Kamil, the ruler of Egypt and most powerful of al-Awhad's brothers, arranged for his daughter 'Ashura Khatun to marry his nephew, al-Nasir Dawud, who ruled the region around Kerak, to the south-east of the Dead Sea. When he suspected al-Nasir Dawud of plotting against him the following year he simply forced the couple to divorce.[22] She remained her father's daughter even after the marriage. Al-Nasir had to flee to Baghdad to seek the

---

[20] Özbeg's wife was later to divorce him to marry Jalal al-Din Khwarazmshah. It was her decision to leave Jalal al-Din and flee to Akhlat that incited his attack on the city and his rape of Tamta.
[21] Ibn al-Athir, 2: 157; Peacock, 'Georgia and the Anatolian Turks', 129.
[22] Abu'l-Fida, 112.

protection of the Caliph, the nominal leader of all Muslims. Defended by the Caliph's considerable moral power, al-Nasir Dawud was able to make peace with al-Kamil and return to Kerak. Later, in 1236, during a second family conspiracy against al-Kamil, al-Nasir Dawud stayed loyal to the Egyptian ruler, rather than siding with his other Ayyubid uncles and cousins, and his reward was to have the wedding to 'Ashura Khatun renewed, this time with a grand procession through the streets of Cairo.[23]

Anecdotes reveal other, seemingly more innocent, ways in which marriage negotiations could be manipulated. Badr al-Din Lu'lu', the *atabeg* of Mosul (r. 1234–59), complained that his daughter had been taught obscene language by her husband, al-Mas'ud Shahanshah, the Zangid ruler of Jazirat ibn 'Umar (modern-day Cizre on the frontier between Turkey and Syria).[24] This was deemed a valid enough excuse to allow Badr al-Din to abandon his alliance with his Zangid neighbour, opening the way to the invasion of his small territory. In both these cases the father was able to intervene because the daughter clearly retained an element of her paternal identity throughout her life. Tamta's father was not able to exploit this link in the same way that al-Kamil and Badr al-Din Lu'lu' were, but nevertheless it was this paternal link that was crucial to her future value to al-Awhad.

Tamta's Armenian–Georgian origins gave her status, not through the military power of her father and the threat he offered, but through the agency of the people of Akhlat. The city was probably controlled by confraternities of young men, modelled on the idea of Muslim *futuwwa* brotherhoods, an idea revived at the start of the thirteenth century.[25] These brotherhoods could be charitable and philanthropic, but they could also act as assertive militias within towns. The position of al-Awhad's garrison, almost permanently besieged in the citadel and only allowed to operate around the city with the town's permission, gave its population the degree of power locally over al-Awhad that al-Kamil had been able to exercise over al-Nasir Dawud in Kerak. Cut off as he was from the rest of the Ayyubid world, al-Awhad could not operate without their consent. The town's power was partially at least transferred to Tamta by the marriage, giving her a say as their representative in al-Awhad's court. This is not to say either that Tamta simply did

---

[23] Humphreys, *From Saladin to the Mongols*, 222, 228–31.
[24] D. Patton, *Badr al-Dīn Lu'lu', Atabeg of Mosul, 1211–1259* (Seattle; London, 1991), 44.
[25] S. Dadoyan, 'A Case Study for Redefining Armenian–Christian Cultural Identity in the Framework of Near Eastern Urbanism – 13th Century: The Nāṣirī Futuwwa Literature and the Brotherhood Poetry of Yovhannēs and Konstandin Erznkac'i – Texts and Contexts', in *Redefining Christian Identity: Cultural Interaction in the Middle East since the Rise of Islam*, eds. J. J. van Ginkel, H. L. Murre-van den Berg and T. M. van Lint (Leuven; Paris; Dudley, MA, 2005), 237–64; Cahen, *Pre-Ottoman Turkey*, 195–200, 336–40.

their bidding or that the town now deferred to her policies, but that her position required her to become a mediator between the parties. Tamta's long career shows that she was clearly intelligent and sharp enough to be able to exploit this position, in which both sides needed her advocacy, to establish her own independent authority.

Marriage Symbolism and Hierarchies

We can place Tamta's situation in a broader context by examining other cases in which women took on a similar role. Indeed, diplomatic marriages could only have a place in international relations if some kind of symbolic or actual transferral of paternal power and identity moved with the bride. Tamta's marriage was an exceptional one because of the intermediary role required of her by the population of the town. In other cases the bride's paternal identity became a symbol through which the status of nations could be fought out: rapacious grooms and victimised brides.[26] The negotiations behind a diplomatic marriage were a delicate balancing act between the concrete gains to be won from the alliance and the potential losses in terms of the symbolism that accompanied the wedding.

The case of Abu Bakr, cited earlier, shows the way in which marriage could act as an indicator of (in his case declining) international prestige and status. However, the most shocking example of this came at the end of the thirteenth century; a case which underlines the potential symbolic dangers of such unions, even between countries sharing the same religion. Contemporaries saw the participants in the marriage effectively as personifications of their countries and could see in their relationship a metaphor for the affiliation of the two countries involved and the balance of power between them. This emerges from the accounts of the marriage of Simonis, the daughter of the Byzantine Emperor Andronikos II Palaiologos (r. 1282–1328), to Stefan III Milutin, the King of Serbia (r. 1282–1321).[27] In 1299 the Byzantine Emperor was forced to agree to the marriage: Byzantine power was on the wane, and he needed a way to prevent further incursions from Serbia into his territory. Simonis' dowry was Byzantine lands in the north-west of the empire, which were already in Milutin's hands; presenting them as a dowry

---

[26] As characterised by K. Hopwood, 'Byzantine Princesses and Lustful Turks', in *Rape in Antiquity: Sexual Violence in the Greek and Roman Worlds*, eds. S. Deacy and K. F. Pierce (London, 1997), 231–42.

[27] A. Eastmond, 'Diplomatic Gifts: Women and Art as Imperial Commodities in the Thirteenth Century', in *Liquid and Multiple: Individuals and Identities in the Thirteenth-Century Aegean*, eds. G. Saint-Guillain and D. Stathokopoulos (Paris, 2012), 105–33.

legalised the transfer of ownership and allowed the Emperor to save face. But this was the only way in which Andronikos saved face. In every other way the marriage was a humiliation.

Simonis was just five when the marriage was agreed. Milutin was in his forties. This would be his fourth marriage (possibly his fifth),[28] and his sexual appetite was legendary: his opponents gleefully scandalised contemporaries with their tales of his supposed affair with a nun. Simonis' age outraged Byzantine society. Andronikos had to plead forgiveness from the Patriarch of Constantinople, wringing his hands like Pilate and claiming that it was a matter beyond his control. The scandal grew. Simonis was forced to go to live at her new husband's court in Serbia, supposedly to be looked after until she reached puberty. But within three years – when Simonis was at most only eight – she was repeatedly raped by her husband, leaving her unable to have children. Over the years that followed she tried to escape and get back home on more than one occasion; but even when she succeeded (she had been allowed to return to Thessaloniki for the burial of her mother) she was forcibly returned by her own brother. Adopting a nun's habit had proved no defence: her brother simply ripped the clothing off her back and tied her to her horse for the return.

The horror of the case lay not in the fact that Andronikos was powerless to intervene in his daughter's fate, but in that he was a willing accomplice in her continued mistreatment; as were other members of the family, including her brother and mother. On the Serbian side, Milutin's ability to mistreat his bride with impunity clearly symbolised the impotence of the empire: the once-supreme Byzantine Empire was now personified as a small girl, to be used and abused at will.

Similar symbolic dangers arose with all attempts to form marriage alliances with Georgia during the reign of Queen Tamar (1184–1210) and then that of her daughter Rusudan (1223–45). Georgia was in the exceptional position of having women in the supreme position of power twice within half a century, and so the presumption of the male ruler taking a bride from abroad was turned on its head. This caused disruption to the usual mechanics of diplomatic marriage. Attempts had been made to impose patriarchy on Queen Tamar. Rukn al-Din Suleymanshah II, the Seljuk Sultan of Rum (r. 1197–1204), had written to force a marriage upon her. His letter to her opened, 'Every woman is feeble of mind', and his ambassador added that she might be allowed to become Rukn al-Din's wife if she

---

[28] L. Maksimović, 'War Simonis Palaiologina die fünfte Gemahlin von König Milutin?', in *Geschichte und Kultur der Palaiologenzeit*, ed. W. Seibt (Vienna, 1996), 115–20.

converted to Islam; she would be forced to be his concubine if she did not.[29] Rukn al-Din's bravado only lasted as long as it took Tamar to raise her army, which crushed the Seljuk forces at the battle of Basiani. Thereafter male suitors had to tread more carefully. When in the 1220s Tughrilshah of Erzurum sought an alliance with Rusudan's Georgia (to re-establish the link that had existed under Queen Tamar, and which gave the Mengujekids some defence against the encroachment of the Seljuks), he offered his son in marriage to the Queen. Rusudan agreed, but argued that as her husband would be the consort of a Christian Queen, he should convert to Christianity; he was duly baptised. As Ibn al-Athir put it, this was 'a strange turn of events without parallel'.[30] No other account of the willing conversion of a male member of a Muslim ruling family to Christianity is known, although the Georgian chronicles tell us that 'Izz al-Din Saltuk II had previously offered his grandson to Queen Tamar, with an offer that he would convert to Christianity. Tamar toyed with the idea, before rejecting him in favour of Davit Soslan. He was fobbed off with 'a concubine's daughter, reputedly of royal blood'.[31] The idea of Muslims converting to Christianity for a marriage was largely a fantasy confined to Byzantine novels.[32]

Whilst the apostasy from Islam of women given in diplomatic marriages might be overlooked in silence, that of a man could not easily be missed. Yet, apart from Ibn al-Athir's laconic comment, there is no record of the controversy caused by the conversion of Rusudan's husband. Ibn al-Athir could not avoid including the event in his history, but he minimised its impact by omitting the prince's name; he appears only as the son of Tughrilshah. The marriage failed to protect Tughrilshah, and it did little for Muslim–Christian relations. Rusudan was unfaithful to her husband and soon divorced him. She married again and was again unfaithful. However, the military and economic problems that Georgia faced in the 1220s meant that Rusudan did not have the complete control of her court that her mother Tamar had had. When she announced a third marriage, this time to a Muslim who refused to convert, the Georgian nobles led by Ivane as her chief minister opposed her and forced her to abandon the match.

There are few examples of women converting from Islam to Christianity in this period. This must reflect the general predominance of Muslim powers across the region. Where they exist, they seem to mirror the conversions that went the other way. At the Armenian monastery of Horomos to the north of Ani is a funerary chapel built by Khutlukhatun for her mother

---

[29] *Kartlis Tskhovreba*, 268.   [30] Ibn al-Athir, 3: 244.   [31] *Kartlis Tskhovreba*, 246–7.
[32] E. Jeffreys, *Digenis Akritis: The Grottaferrata and Escorial Versions* (Cambridge, 1998).

Rusukan, who had converted from Islam to Christianity in order to be married to Khawras, one of the nephews of Zakare and Ivane.[33] Nothing in the inscriptions she set up in the chapel to commemorate her mother reveals her pre-Christian past. Her identity was completely transformed by her marriage. The same is true of Jigda Khatun, the wife of the Georgian King Davit VII Ulu. When she was commemorated in an inscription with her husband at the church of Abelia in south Georgia, it was with the Christian, and royal, name of Tamar Khatun.[34] Her origins are unknown, and scholars have proposed either that she was a Seljuk Turk or that she was a Mongol.[35]

Tamta's marriage seems to fit these cases of women usually being the representative of the weaker partner in the negotiations. To everyone at the Georgian court, Ivane's need to give her up in order to secure his own release was an obvious sign of his failure during the siege of Akhlat. Equally, the marriage reinforced the Ayyubids' sense of growing power in south-eastern Anatolia, and its neutralisation of the threat from Georgia. However, in other ways Tamta's case is less typical. It seems that the need for her to act as an intermediary between the people of the city and its ruler meant that she was not forced to convert to Islam, allowing her to continue to support Christian monasteries in the region over the next decades.

Marriage Symbolism and the Rhetoric of the Bride

One final aspect of diplomatic marriages remains: the ceremonies themselves. Whilst the alliance brought about by marriage was personified in the figures of the groom and bride, the actual power of the union came from the rituals and ceremonies that surrounded the wedding. The marriage ceremony was itself probably the least important of these, and is rarely described in any account. It was simply the final performance in a series of formal encounters during which each party was able to assess and weigh up the other. The wedding between Abu Bakr and that unknown Georgian princess was preceded by meetings between the *atabeg* and Queen Tamar, which became a form of war by proxy. This war was fought through protocol and ostentation in which each party sought to out-dazzle the other.

---

[33] J.-P. Mahé, 'Les inscriptions de Hoŕomos', in *Le couvent de Hoŕomos d'après les archives de Toros Toramanian*, eds. A. Baladian and J.-M. Thierry (Paris, 2002), 147–213, R1; she is also mentioned in an inscription at Bagnayr: Basmadjian, *Inscriptions arméniennes d'Ani*, no. 165; and in a colophon of 1232. No Khawras appears in Toumanoff, *Les dynasties de la Caucasie chrétienne*, 295, tab. 63:7.

[34] I. Gomelauri, 'Khurotmodzghvruli dzegli sopel abeliashi', *Matsne* 1 (1968), 255–74, at 255–6.

[35] Toumanoff, *Les dynasties de la Caucasie chrétienne*, 137, tab. 22:9 (Seljuk); I. Javakhishvili, *Kartveli eris istoria* vol. 3 (Tbilisi, 1982), 55, 70 (Mongol).

Weeks were spent exchanging gifts of fine silk robes and foodstuffs, hunting and feasting, and tournaments in which Zakare, Ivane and the other leaders of Tamar's army ranged themselves against Abu Bakr's family and supporters. The Georgian chronicles asked 'Who can describe the tents and the tapestries, the menageries and the towers, the decorations and ornaments worthy of Bezalel and the temple of God consecrated by Solomon [taken from Exodus 36]?'[36] Ibn Bibi's description of Kayka'us I's marriage to Seljuk Khatun, the daughter of Fakhr al-Din Bahramshah of Erzincan, in around 1210 provided just one such attempt to capture the expense and lavishness of the food and decorations:

> On the next day the *qadis* of the town and the senior imams gathered at the Sultan's palace for the wedding ceremony. The Sultan ordered golden sugar moulds to be made of a thousand, of five hundred, of two hundred, of one hundred and of fifty *mitqal* in weight and placed on gold and silver plates, and he ordered that the water basins in the court of the palace be filled with ambergris and coral, and that the fountains should discharge sherbet rather than water. Each guest was given a dish according to his position and his rank. And the representatives and witnesses of both parties were present.[37]

The marriage itself was a time to display the bride and her dowry and so reveal the true wealth and value of the bride's family. In 1212 Tamta's sister-in-law, Dayfa Khatun, was married by her father al-'Adil to her first cousin, al-Zahir Ghazi, the ruler of Aleppo. Ibn Wasil (d. 1298) was the first to describe the arrival of the bride. His account, written a generation or so after the event, already has the ring of legend:

> The khatun arrived in Aleppo in great ceremony. She was received by al-Malik al-Zahir along with the emirs of Aleppo, its turbaned [scholars], and its notables. Her entry into the citadel was a famous day. She had with her textiles, furnishings, and diverse jewellery that required fifty mules, one hundred Bactrian camels, and three hundred dromedaries to carry... It is also mentioned that she had in her retinue one hundred slave girls who could make various wonderful crafts... When she entered the court of al-Malik al-Zahir he arose and took several steps towards her and showed her great respect.[38]

By the time the Egyptian scholar al-Maqrizi recalled the event two hundred years later, legend had triumphed: the numbers were shamelessly inflated

---

[36] *Kartlis Tskhovreba*, 255, 438.   [37] Ibn Bibi, 76–81.
[38] Quoted in Tabbaa, 'Dayfa Khatun', at 21.

to imagine a procession that now had two hundred Bactrian camels and an extra century of female singing-slaves. And to these Dayfa Khatun could add another twenty bags of textiles, an extra twenty handmaidens and another ten slaves, all gifts from her new husband.[39] The account closely echoes the dowry prepared by Kayka'us I for his bride, which had required craftsmen to work day and night for three months to prepare:

> bejewelled diadems, ambergris-perfumed bangles, precious rings and armbands, costly dresses embroidered with a variety of jewels, mules with golden hooves, horses as lightfooted as the morning breeze, and rows of mountainous dromedaries bearing immeasurable and uncountable loads of money and goods.[40]

Similar hyperbole is found in the description of the dowry offered to the legendary Byzantine frontiersman in the epic poem *Digenis Akritis*.[41]

It seems unlikely that Tamta's wedding was accompanied by similar magnificence. The need to exchange Tamta for her father quickly, before Zakare took revenge on the city, suggests that in this case the niceties were dispensed with. In contrast, the status of Dayfa Khatun, the honour paid to her and the sense of change through her movement to a new home is clear. However, in both cases the physical movement of the bride from her father to her husband symbolised her changing identity. There is also a sense in both examples that the bride was simply one item in the inventory of beauty and splendour (or ransom conditions, in Tamta's case) that actually reflected the father's wealth and status.

The Paradoxes of Marriage

The rhetoric that surrounded royal marriage in the Middle Ages was contradictory and paradoxical. It emphasised the centrality of the bride, whilst simultaneously marginalising her, and it depended on the paternal link of the bride whilst simultaneously imagining that it was erased by the marriage itself. This tension is evident in the different ways the bride was envisioned by artists.

A lustreware dish, now in the Metropolitan Museum of Art in New York, gives some impression of the spectacle involved. Probably made in Kashan in Iran at the start of the thirteenth century, it reflects the common practices of such events throughout the region [Fig. 23].[42] It shows a wedding procession, with the veiled bride at the centre of the composition, in a litter with its richly embroidered curtains drawn back. She is surrounded

---

[39] Maqrizi, 156–7. [40] Ibn Bibi, 77. [41] Jeffreys, *Digenis Akritis*, book 4.
[42] Metropolitan Museum of Art, New York, inv. 1983.247.

Figure 23 Lustreware dish showing a wedding procession. Kashan, Iran; first quarter of the thirteenth century (Metropolitan Museum of Art, New York, 1983.247; diameter 41.7 cm)

by a retinue of forty-four other figures, most on horse- or camel-back. Some ride forward with the bride, others play polo and still more watch the events. All wear elaborately decorated robes. A second procession of elephants bearing howdahs winds its way round the inner rim of the bowl. With a diameter of 41 centimetres and technically highly refined to produce its glittering metallic sheen, the dish is itself a luxury object, its size and materials chosen to match the subject that it portrays.

The inscription around the edge of the dish celebrates love and beauty: 'If the reflection of your cheek had fallen into the darkness, immediately [a hundred suns] would have been checkmated. If Alexander had put a kiss on our lip, he would have been free from the search for the Water of Life.'[43] This

---

[43] A. Schimmel, at http://www.metmuseum.org/Collections/search-the-collections/453209.

evocation of the transformative emotions of marriage highlights the rhetorical expectations of the union, and the pretence of the importance of love in the match. However, the image on the dish reveals the true significance of the event: the display of wealth and opulence. It is telling about the status of the bride. She is the central figure on the dish, but she is effectively invisible: just two eyes staring out from a white veil and headdress, set against a white background. She is a void in the densely illustrated space of the dish, visibly smaller than all the figures around her. The paradox of her centrality and her insignificance reduces her to simply the means by which the wealth surrounding her will be conveyed to her husband.

A second paradox in diplomatic marriages lay in the identity of the bride herself. Whilst the bride's importance to the marriage came from her paternal identity – it was the link to her father that gave the marriage its diplomatic purpose and established an alliance – at same time the bride, the potential mother of the next king, was required to assimilate into the new culture/family that she was joining, and so break the relationship to her own family. This is the conflict that faced Tamta after her marriage: the need on the one hand to secure her own position within al-Awhad's household, surrounded by a new language and religion and with many different customs and traditions, and on the other to retain her Christianity and her Caucasian background as the leader of the Christians of Akhlat.

The tension between assimilation and separation is played out in a slightly earlier Byzantine *epithalamion* (bridal poem) manuscript, which also hints at some of the other issues raised by the marriage in terms of the relative hierarchy of the states involved and perceptions of cultural superiority. The twelfth-century manuscript was commissioned for the marriage of a Frankish princess into the Byzantine royal family. It describes the reception of the foreign bride at Constantinople; but it is written from the point of view of the groom's family and shows the transformation of the bride that they envisioned. In a series of miniatures in the manuscript (now in the Vatican Library: Vat. gr. 1851), the young foreigner is shown blossoming into a Byzantine princess once she has been embraced by the women of the Byzantine court.[44] At the outset the manuscript speaks of the bride's

---

[44] I. Spatharakis, *The Portrait in Byzantine Illuminated Manuscripts* (Leiden, 1976), 210–30; M. Jeffreys, 'The Vernacular εἰσιτήριοι for Agnes of France', in *Byzantine Papers: Proceedings of the First Australian Byzantine Studies Conference* (Canberra, 1981), 101–15; C. J. Hilsdale, 'Constructing a Byzantine Augusta: A Greek Book for a French Bride', *Art Bulletin* 87/3 (2005), 458–83. A fourteenth-century date has been argued for the manuscript by C. Hennessy, 'A Child Bride and her Representation in the Vatican *Epithalamion*, cod. gr. 1851', *Byzantine and Modern Greek Studies* 30/2 (2006), 115–50.

Figure 24 The arrival of the bride, from a Byzantine *epithalamion* (bridal poem) manuscript; late twelfth century (Biblioteca Apostolica Vaticana, gr. 1851, fol. 3v; 22.5 × 17 cm)

distress at her separation from her loving father, but by the end, where the text breaks off, she is described as the twin-star of the Emperor's own daughter. As Cecily Hilsdale has noted, the idea is conveyed both in the images and the text. On folio 3v the bride is depicted three times to show her transformation [Fig. 24]. In the upper register she approaches the city, visibly smaller and less elaborately dressed than those around her; once she has crossed the bridge into the city she reappears both larger and now in Byzantine dress. The transformation is complete in the lower register of the image, where she is presented enthroned as a Byzantine empress. She is now much larger than the courtiers who surround her; her immobility and statuesque frontality give her the aura of an imperial icon. The foreigner has become Byzantine. It is thanks to this process that she is able to greet the Porphyrogenneta, her 'twin-star', as an equal in a later image (folio 6r).[45]

Thus, for an incoming bride, the transformation was to be one of assimilation and conversion. Any foreign element in her appearance (or depiction) has been removed, and she has been assimilated into the domestic world of the new court. At its core, this manuscript inculcates ideas about passivity and identity: none of the former identity or personality of the bride survives the process. It is clear that she no longer represents her home country or her father, but rather is now a member of an idealised court. This totally ignores the bride's role as emblematic representative of her paternal family, but plays instead to a sense of superiority in which it is assumed that all peoples want to emulate and become – in this instance – Byzantine. Such transformations were rarely fixed or immutable, however, and could prove to be a double-edged sword. The arrogance of the groom's family rarely worked in the shifting political and military positions of the Anatolian world, or even in Byzantium itself. The symbolic power of Milutin's rape of Simonis actually relied on her remaining a cipher of Byzantium; her violation explicitly pricked any idea of Byzantine superiority. Jalal al-din Khwarazmshah's rape of Tamta similarly exploited his bride-to-be's existing and earlier identities to demonstrate a shift in regional power; it was a double victory over both the Ayyubids and the Georgians. However, the manuscript hints at the embedded worldviews that ambassadors had to overcome. Whilst the brides' families had to endure these humiliations, there was one potential justification for them. The implicit acknowledgement that the bride still had a connection back to her paternal family maintained a link that they no doubt hoped could be exploited in future. The bride's intimate relationship to her husband, her future position as the mother of the next king, gave her access to the heart of the court, and a possible means by which the paternal family might influence the policies of their new ally in their own interests.

The evidence of wives who continued to aid their paternal families and those who sided with their husbands' families splits evenly. Some brides seem to have maintained close links to their paternal cultures. Mahperi

---

[45] Indeed, Hilsdale, 'Constructing a Byzantine Augusta', 474 and 476, notes that the poem even places the new bride above the Porphyrogenneta.

Khatun, a relatively minor Armenian noblewoman who was married to the Seljuk Sultan Kaykubad I (r. 1219–37), and became mother to his successor Kaykhusraw II (r. 1237–46), fled to her compatriots in Cilicia after her son's defeat by the Mongols in 1243 at the battle of Kösedağ rather than stay among the Seljuks (we will encounter her at greater length in Chapter 7). Her co-wife of Kaykubad (an Ayyubid sister of al-Ashraf), who was murdered with her sons in order to promote Mahperi's son Kaykhusraw II as the new sultan, similarly emphasised her paternal descent, not that of her husband's family, on her tomb.[46] Others, such as Mahperi's Georgian daughter-in-law, Gurji Khatun, the wife of Kaykhusraw II, moved more decisively into their new families. Although Gurji Khatun was the daughter of Queen Rusudan of Georgia (she was christened Tamar, after her grandmother), she became central to the administration of the Seljuk realm, ruling in her husband's absence, and later marrying his vizier and effective successor, the *pervane* Muin al-Din Sulayman.[47] It is clear that such women could gain substantially more power within their husbands' families than they could within their fathers'. Eudokia Palaiologina, a legitimate daughter of the Byzantine Emperor Michael VIII, was able to act independently of her family once she had been married. Her father had married her to John II Grand Komnenos, Emperor of Trebizond (r. 1280–97), the maritime empire on the northern fringes of Anatolia, in order to try to bring the outpost back under Byzantine rule, but Eudokia consistently refused to support this policy, siding with her husband instead.[48] Even after she had been widowed she remained independent: it was her refusal to follow her brother's wishes for her to marry Milutin in Serbia that forced Andronikos to offer his own child, Simonis, instead. She clearly had gained independent wealth from her position in Trebizond; she was buried in the city in 1302.

Tamta certainly gained power and influence through her marriage to al-Awhad, and then al-Ashraf. Some of this power, her support for monasteries in Taron (the Armenian name for the region to the west of Lake Van), seems to have been limited just to this region, but in other areas, notably her support for pilgrims, her influence seems to have worked throughout the Ayyubid confederacy. Tamta's advocacy for pilgrims indicates that she also still retained contacts with the Georgian and Armenian heartlands in which she had grown up. As we will see in a later chapter, she seems to have

---

[46] See Chapter 7.
[47] A. Eastmond, 'Art and Frontiers between Byzantium and the Caucasus', in *Byzantium. Faith and Power (1261–1557): Perspectives on Late Byzantine Art and Culture*, ed. S. T. Brooks (New Haven; London, 2007), 154–69.
[48] Eastmond, 'Diplomatic Gifts'.

Figure 25 Inscription commemorating al-Awhad's rebuilding of the walls of Mayyafariqin (Silvan), Turkey; 1203

become involved in the politics of her family as well towards the end of her life. The constantly changing circumstances of Tamta's life required her to deal with both her paternal and her marital families.

Al-Ashraf

If Tamta had remained married to al-Awhad it is unlikely that we would have heard more about her in medieval sources. The marriage sealed al-Awhad's control of Akhlat, but probably little more. He was essentially a local governor who did what he was told by his father, al-ʿAdil, the man who remained in ultimate control of Ayyubid policy on the northern frontier. Al-Awhad's only real material legacies are the walls of Mayyafariqin, which he rebuilt, and the copper coinage that he minted. The walls proclaim al-Awhad's name and titles and show him as a royal lion beneath the sun [Fig. 25]:

> This was made on the order of our master the sultan al-Malik al-Awhad, the wise, the just, Najm al-Din, the pillar of Islam and of Muslims, [Ayyub, son of] our [master] al-Malik [al-ʿAdil … the supporter of the emir of] the believers – may Allah perpetuate his kingdom! – in Ramadan of the year 599 [May/June 1203].[49]

[49] RCEA IX, 3555; *TEI*, 8288.

The real change in Tamta's life came in the immediate aftermath of al-Awhad's sudden death after only a few months of marriage. Al-Awhad's younger brother, al-Ashraf Musa, happened to be nearby with his army, and quickly rushed to Akhlat to assume power there. Al-Ashraf had been made governor of the cities of Harran and Raqqa in the Jazira to the south-west of al-Awhad's territories, and had often led joint campaigns with his brothers in Armenia. Al-Ashraf's takeover of his brother's power was complete, and was designed to convey a sense of continuity and stability. For example, he completed the minaret of the mosque outside the city walls of Mayyafariqin, which al-Awhad had started after 1203. Al-Ashraf also produced coins similar to those of his brother at the city mint.

It was as part of this policy of continuity that al-Ashraf took on his brother's Caucasian wife, Tamta. However, the fact that he retained her, rather than sending her back to her family as a penniless widow, shows that she must already have gained some symbolic or strategic leverage in Akhlat. There seems to have been little other reason for al-Ashraf to marry her. She had no direct link to the city, and so he was not marrying into its traditional power hierarchies by taking her; yet he clearly regarded it as an expeditious act in order to consolidate his authority there.

The importance of having a Christian bride with close links to Georgia in Akhlat was highlighted a decade later, when al-Ashraf appointed his younger brother al-Muzaffar Ghazi as his viceregent in Armenia, with control of Akhlat and Mayyafariqin. Al-Ashraf handed over the city in order to rationalise his disparate fiefdoms and concentrate all his personal land in the Jazira. His aim was to free himself up from the extensive travel required so that he could assist his brother al-Kamil in the defence of Egypt, then under attack from the Latin forces of the Fifth Crusade; but it was a policy he regretted, and reversed, four years later. Al-Muzaffar Ghazi's first act in Akhlat was to replicate al-Ashraf's wedding and seek his own marriage alliance with Georgia. He wrote to Tamar's son, Giorgi IV Lasha, who was now King of Georgia (r. 1210–23), seeking the hand of his sister, Rusudan (who, at that point, no one expected would go on to rule Georgia in her own right, even after the precedent of her mother's long reign). According to the Georgian Chronicle he wanted Giorgi Lasha's sister 'in order to have someone to rule at Akhlat'.[50] Giorgi took this seriously, and travelled to Bagavan to the north-east of Lake Van to organise it – although ultimately it came to nothing, suggesting that Georgian ambitions no longer looked so far south,

---

[50] *Kartlis Tskhovreba*, 205.

and that the alliance was not equal to the value that could be gained from offering the King's sister for marriage.

Al-Ashraf and al-Muzzafar Ghazi's attempted unions with the Georgian court suggest that the Ayyubids realised that trying to maintain power in Armenia simply through force of arms was unrealistic, especially here on the fringes of the Ayyubid confederacy. This was the fact that Tamta had to exploit in order to establish her own position in the Ayyubid world. The various cases outlined here for the ways in which women were treated by their husbands show that there was no consistent role for women in these diplomatic marriages. Although women were usually in the inferior position at the outset of the marriage, Tamta shows how it was possible to turn this on its head. However, to do so required careful manipulation of the different roles and identities that Tamta now had. Marriage gave her new possibilities, and the ways in which she interwove these with the already multifaceted identities inherited from her father shows how women could work within the symbolism and actual institutions of marriage in the thirteenth century.

5 | Women and Power

> You, as a woman, cannot control a city.[1]

> Though indeed she is a woman, still as sovereign she is begotten of God. She knows how to rule. We say this not to flatter you; we ourselves, in your absence, often say so. Her deeds, like her radiance, are revealed bright as sunshine. The lion's cubs are equal, be they male or female.[2]

Tamta's access to power came from her association with Akhlat. We know that she must have remained in the city for long periods whilst her second husband, al-Ashraf, was absent, embroiled in the politics and his wars in Syria and Egypt. He was alongside his brother al-Kamil in Egypt for much of 1221, fighting against the forces of the Fifth Crusade. He was effectively a captive of another of his brothers, al-Mu'azzam, in Damascus from September 1226 to June 1227.[3] This latter period coincides with a report in al-Nasawi's history of Jalal al-Din Khwarazmshah that the queen 'Tamestsaha Belmikour' was at her castle at 'Aliabad (probably to be located to the east of Akhlat, in the region to the south of Lake Sevan) when the invader arrived in the region.[4] This invented name can only refer to Tamta – a corruption formed from the collision between her name and that of Beg-Temür, the last ruler of Akhlat before it was taken over by the Ayyubids in 1207. The two can never have met (it was Beg-Temür's death that opened up Akhlat to all the wars from 1207 on), but both were linked with Akhlat, suggesting that it was this that caused al-Nasawi's faulty memory to link them in this garbled way. The confusion of names implies a degree of authority for Tamta in the Akhlat region and an association of her name with the city. Certainly Tamta was at Akhlat, away from her second husband, al-Ashraf, when Jalal al-Din captured the city in 1230; and she was away from him again in 1236 when she was seized by the Mongols. Finally, the fact that the Mongols later

---

[1] This is the Georgian reaction to the attempt of the widow of King Gurgen II (d. 941) to succeed her husband in the city of Ardanuj: *De Administrando Imperio*, 46.
[2] Shota Rustaveli, stanza 39.   [3] Humphreys, *From Saladin to the Mongols*, 166–9, 182–3.
[4] Al-Nasawi, 295. The castle at 'Aliabad is now impossible to identify. Numerous villages in modern-day Azerbaijan bear the name, but Juvayni 2: 430–1 reports that Jalal al-Din passed the castle after defeating the Georgians at Lore, suggesting the site near Lake Sevan.

returned Tamta to rule in Akhlat implies that she had by then long been identified with the town and its hinterland, and was firmly regarded as its de facto ruler.

We can, then, locate Tamta in Akhlat for much of her married life to al-Ashraf. The question that this chapter addresses is what power she had access to during this period. What authority could women wield in Christian and Muslim societies in the early thirteenth century? Among all the societies in which Tamta lived – Georgian, Armenian, Ayyubid, Khwarazmian and Seljuk – none had any formal expectation that women should be able to exercise power. Only in Mongolia was it different, as we will see in Chapters 12 and 13. Indeed, the conjunction of women and authority is almost always seen as a negative, detrimental to the state and contrary to the laws of nature. Yet Tamta managed to find means to wield power in Akhlat, as did women in other cities around in the region. In a few cases in the early thirteenth century, women managed to manipulate state structures to gain officially recognised power for themselves. This chapter explores the frameworks within which women in positions of power had to work.

Women and Theories of Power

Tamta's rule in Akhlat and the other cases that follow reveal a sharp disparity between theory and practice. The theory was simple: women should not (indeed, could not) exercise power. Manuals on how to rule a state, whether from Christian or Muslim sources, are equally misogynistic in their assessment of women. Nizam al-Mulk's *Book of Government*, an eleventh-century handbook of advice for Persian kings that was still essential reading in the thirteenth century, is damning in its estimation of women and power. He discussed them in chapter XLII: 'On the subject of those who wear the veil':

> The king's underlings must not be allowed to assume power, for this causes the utmost harm and destroys the king's splendour and majesty. This particularly applies to women, for they are wearers of the veil and have not complete intelligence. Their purpose is the continuation of the lineage of the race, so the more noble their blood the better, and the more chaste and abstemious their bearing the more admirable and acceptable they are. But when the king's wives begin to assume the part of rulers, they base their orders on what interested parties tell them, because they are not able to see things with their own eyes in the way that men constantly look at the affairs of the outside world. They give orders following what they are told by those who work amongst them such as chamberlains and servants. Naturally their commands are mostly the opposite of what is right, and

mischief ensues; the king's dignity suffers and people are afflicted with trouble; disorder affects the state and the religion; men's wealth is dissipated and the ruling class is put to vexation. In all ages nothing but disgrace, infamy, discord and corruption have resulted when kings have been dominated by their wives.[5]

Nizam's paradoxical expectation of chastity and child-bearing and his correlation of invisibility (the veil, abstemious bearing) with virtue firmly put women in their place. His observation that women when they did rule had to do so through men was, as we will see, largely correct, but he provided the most negative interpretation of this that he could imagine.

Sentiments were similar in the Christian world.[6] The thirteenth-century Byzantine encyclopaedist Theognostes answered his own question 'What is a woman?' with an inventively repellent litany of insults:

> What is a woman? A fish-hook of the devil, a trap and a net through which having been deceived we are put to death. What is a woman? A source of evil, a shipwreck on land, a treasury of filth, a fatal mischance, a slipperiness of the eyes, a spear for the heart, a perdition for young men. What is a woman? The soul's damnation, Hades' sceptre, precipitous desire, slander of the saints, a serpent's lair, the devil's consolation. What is a woman? Inconsolable anguish, incurable wickedness, the cause of sin for those who have been saved, a daily penalty, a guide into darkness, a master of blunders, a discloser of secrets. What is a woman? A shameless beast, an unbridled mouth, a wicked delight, a cause of eternal hell, an earthy arrogance, men's indolence, insatiable desire. What is a woman? Winter in the home, a battle self-incurred, a husband's shipwreck, incontinence as a bedfellow, an ever-nagging worry. What is a woman? A poisonous snake, an untameable lioness, a venom-spitting viper, a wild leopard, the devil's weapon, a passionate frenzy, a worldwide plague, an irrepressible evil, an untameable she-dragon. All other wickedness is small when compared to the wickedness of a woman.[7]

Whilst this language damned all women, it also provided a well of invective to draw on to libel women who had gained positions of power. Theognostes' contemporary, the equally unpleasant and argumentative monk Nikephoros Blemmydes, borrowed almost identical phrases in his attack on

---

[5] Nizam al-Mulk, 179–80.
[6] C. Galatariotou, 'Holy Women and Witches: Aspects of Byzantine Conceptions of Gender', *Byzantine and Modern Greek Studies* 9 (1984), 55–94, at 62–3; B. Hill, *Imperial Women in Byzantium 1025–1204: Patronage, Power and Ideology* (Harlow, 1999), 78–95.
[7] Theognostus, *Theognosti Thesaurus*, II, §11, pp. 11–12 (trans. Munitiz, 45). With thanks to Eleni Dimitriadou.

Marchesina, a mistress of the Byzantine Emperor John III Vatatzes (r. 1221–54). She had arrived at the Byzantine court as a lady-in-waiting to Costanza, an illegitimate daughter of the Holy Roman Emperor Frederick II, and diplomatic bride to John III. Blemmydes felt she was overreaching her position through her liaisons with the Emperor (he was particularly incensed when she arrived late for a service at which he was officiating: he barred her from entering; she had her bodyguards beat him almost to death): 'Hardly had I enjoyed a little respite from the onslaught of troubles when Satan brought against me the licentious female, the evil-doer, the world's stumbling block, the universal disgrace... attempting with her neck, her brow, her prancing, to overbear and overcome me.'[8]

Even women were complicit in these assessments: writing in the middle of the twelfth century Anna Komnena, the daughter and sister of Byzantine emperors and a challenger for the imperial throne herself at one point, consistently belittles women (other than her mother and her grandmother) in her history of her father, the *Alexiad*: women are easily given to shed tears, to fear and panic; they are of low intelligence and incapable of dealing with serious matters, frivolous, morally unstable and unreliable.[9] In 1222 Vaneni, an Armenian noblewoman, acquired a manuscript which she then gave to the monastery of Havptuk. In the colophon she added to commemorate her act, she wrote simply: 'As there was no king in Georgia, the throne was occupied by the daughter of Tamar [i.e. Rusudan].' Women were only acknowledged in power when there was no alternative. However, this rhetoric of misogyny, whether explicit or implicit, was wrapped around a world in which women actually had rather a closer grip on power – as wives and mothers, but also as representatives of husbands in their absence; and occasionally in their own right.

The Male Façade: Tamta as a Wife and Governor

As outlined at the opening of this chapter, we know that Tamta spent much of her married life in Akhlat, often apart from her husband. The implication is that she acted as her husband's representative there in his absence. Combined with Kirakos Gandzaketsi's account of her achievements there as a reducer of taxes and supporter of pilgrims, this suggests that Tamta had a substantive and powerful place in the city. The employment of Tamta as the Sultan's personal representative in Akhlat would have been a sensible

[8] *PG* 142, 605; trans. in Nikephoros Blemmydes, 139–43.
[9] Anna Komnena, III, 3, 7, 8; IV, 4; XV, 2.

policy for al-Ashraf for a number of reasons. She could act as an intermediary who could understand both sides in any negotiations. Tamta's paternal background allowed her to act as a mediator between the largely Armenian, Christian population of the town and its Arab rulers; she was well placed to appease the anxieties of the native population about the intentions of its Ayyubid rulers. At the same time, she was separated from the direct support of her father, and so her status and wealth were dependent on her husband, whose interests she needed to support in order to maintain her own position. As al-Ashraf's interests increasingly moved away from Anatolia towards Syria in the course of the 1220s, the need for a loyal regent in Akhlat became ever more important. This became most evident in 1229 when he took possession of Damascus on the death of his brother al-Mu'azzam. In return he had to give up his lands in the Jazira, including the cities of Harran and Raqqa. The only exception was his northern outpost at Akhlat, which al-Ashraf retained. Now cut off from all his other landholdings, it made little sense for al-Ashraf to keep Akhlat; the decision is only explicable through Tamta. The city was effectively her domain, and al-Ashraf kept it in order to maintain her position.

Tamta's dependence on her husband for her position meant that al-Ashraf could assume that her interests coincided with his. However, Tamta's gender meant that she could hold no official position in the government, and so al-Ashraf was also required to appoint a male governor to act as his public mouthpiece in the city. The motives and policies of these appointees could not be guaranteed to coincide with those of the Sultan in the same way those of a wife could be. For much of the 1220s the appointed governor of Akhlat was al-Ashraf's *hajib* (chamberlain), Husam al-Din 'Ali.[10] Even though the *hajib* had a proven record of loyalty and demonstrable success in protecting Akhlat from the Khwarazmian invasions between 1226 and 1229, he fell foul of the internal politics of the Ayyubids. In 1229, shortly before he took Damascus, al-Ashraf ordered his execution. Contemporary chroniclers claimed that this decision was incomprehensible and that Husam al-Din 'Ali's loyalty was unquestioned.[11] Whatever the reason for his fall, it is clear that the role of governor was seen as a threat since it could be used to build up a personal power base that threatened members of the ruling Ayyubid clan.

---

[10] R. Ward, 'The Inscription on the Astrolabe by 'Abd al-Karim in the British Museum', *Muqarnas* 21 (2004), 345–57.

[11] Humphreys, *From Saladin to the Mongols*, 216. The execution seems to have been at the instigation of al-Ashraf's senior brother, al-Kamil; the quandary surrounds al-Ashraf's agreement to it. Ibn al-'Amid, 40, claims that al-Ashraf had him executed for failing to save his Georgian wife.

Tamta was by no means the only wife left to protect her husband's interests whilst he travelled or fought. A number of cases are recorded in the states around Akhlat in which wives were left in charge of areas of a state whilst their husbands resided or fought elsewhere. These better-documented examples support the claims that we are able to make for Tamta's own exercise of authority in Akhlat. They also all show that while women could exercise power and make decisions, they had to do so from behind a façade of male government, as Nizam al-Mulk had observed in the eleventh century. Zahida Khatun, one of the wives of Jahan Pahlavan, the *atabeg* of Azerbaijan, is recorded as controlling the fortress at Alanjar and through it the nearby city of Nakhchivan. When her husband died in 1187 she took the decision that her garrison should support her nephew, Abu Bakr, in the succession crisis that followed. She summoned the fortress's male governor and made him swear an oath of allegiance, and instructed the town's governor to allow Abu Bakr to take control of the city. The other side in the dispute was organised by a second wife of Jahan, Inanch Khatun, who equally acted through other local male governors in support of her own chldren.[12] The dispute revolved around that cliché of harem politics, the rivalry between wives, but it was played out through the control of fortress garrisons. For Tamta to have had the success she had, she must have found a way to work with or through the *hajib* in Akhlat.

A further example of the command that women could take and the breadth of their international networks came a generation later in Azerbaijan when Malika acted as regent on behalf of her husband, Muzaffar al-Din Özbek. He was another son of Jahan Pahlavan, who came to power after Abu Bakr's death in 1210. Malika was left in charge of the important trading city of Tabriz in the early 1220s, and controlled it whilst her husband fought ineffectually against the Georgians on the one hand, and the new Khwarazmian threat on the other.[13] Acceptance of her rule was no doubt aided by the fact that she was the daughter of the Great Seljuk sultan of Iran, Toghril Shah III (r. 1177–94). When Jalal al-Din Minguburnu Khwarazmshah attacked the city, it was she who recognised that the city could not withstand a siege, and she who called together the emirs and notables of the town to negotiate the surrender. After handing Tabriz over to Jalal al-Din she was then able to force her husband to divorce her in order to free herself to marry the new conqueror. The details are murky, but Ibn al-Athir explains that Özbek had taken an oath that he would divorce her if he ever killed a particular slave; and so when he finally did execute him (for reasons that are never

[12] Husayni, 119–20. [13] Juvayni, 424.

explained), she was able to make him fulfil what he had sworn.¹⁴ Malika corresponded with imams in Damascus and Baghdad who issued the fatwas that legitimated the divorce. Malika's actions reveal that women were well versed in the mechanisms of power and influence, and that they were able to manipulate and control them both to defend their lands and to further their own causes. Malika was subsequently given Khoy to rule by her new husband, along with two towns that had not been under the city's purview before.¹⁵ Malika had been able to turn Jalal al-Din's attacks to her own advantage, and the results of his violence opened opportunities for other women as well. Ibn Wasil also reports that the strategic castle of Ruyindiz in Azerbaijan was taken over by an (unnamed) woman after her two brothers had been killed in battle against the Khwarazmian army.¹⁶

These were women with considerable power, acting in the absence of their husbands and brothers. The decisions they made had wide-reaching implications; they were not simply petty, local matters. Zahida Khatun shows that it is feasible to expect that a woman could dictate policy to be implemented through her governor. Malika even oversaw a complete change of regime in Tabriz as it was handed over to the Khwarazmians before going on to govern Khoy. However, all these women required a male mouthpiece through which to act. The implications of this are that Tamta was able to exercise a degree of power independent from her husband, but not openly. She was probably regarded by al-Ashraf as some kind of check or balance against the power of the appointed governor in the city.

Wives and Mothers

Tamta's access to power came from her separation from her husband. More normally, women were most effectively able to gain power through direct contact with their husbands. It was wives' intimate access to their husbands in bed that gave them their most potent and direct means of influence. The Artuqid ruler of Amid, for example, became infatuated by a singing-girl and ignored his more important diplomatic brides. It was this concubine 'whom Nur al-Din married and showed preference for. She exercised authority over his land and his treasury, meanwhile he neglected Kılıc Arslan's daughter [his first wife, Seljuka Khatun (d. 1188/9), through whom he had gained control of the city] and left her forgotten and abandoned.'¹⁷ Such influence

---

¹⁴ Ibn al-Athir, 3: 256–8.   ¹⁵ Al-Nasawi, 197.
¹⁶ Ibn Wasil, 4: 308; cited in Ibn al-Athir, 3: 302 n.14.
¹⁷ Ibn al-Athir 2: 271–2; Ibn Jubayr, 240.

could then be continued through the birth of heirs, and the mother's role in their upbringing. The degree of intimacy between Tamta and al-Ashraf is suspect: not only was he away from her for long periods, there is also evidence that he preferred men to women (the impact of this on Tamta in Akhlat will emerge in later chapters). Al-Ashraf is only recorded to have had one child, a daughter, and it is possible that Tamta was her mother (although there is no direct evidence for this and al-Ashraf had at least three wives).[18] If Tamta were this girl's mother, she could not have used her as a means to exert influence over her husband as she was brought up away from Tamta in Damascus and Cairo.

However, it is possible to see the potential advantage of becoming a mother by looking at one of Tamta's Ayyubid sisters-in-law, Dayfa Khatun, whose wedding procession we encountered in the previous chapter. She emerged as regent Queen in the city of Aleppo, one of the major cities in northern Syria. On Saladin's death in 1193, Aleppo was one of the few cities that his brother al-'Adil did not take possession of. Instead it was passed to one of Saladin's own sons, al-Zahir Ghazi. It was in response to this division that al-'Adil arranged the marriage of al-Zahir Ghazi to his own daughter, Dayfa Khatun, in order to bring the two branches of the family together.

After her magnificent wedding, Dayfa Khatun took on the traditional roles of a wife and performed her principal function, to give birth to a son, in 1213. Thereafter, like Tamta, she disappears from historical record for more than two decades, during which her husband (d. 1216) and then her son, al-'Aziz Muhammad, ruled. Only on al-'Aziz Muhammad's death in 1236 did she re-emerge, now as regent for her grandson, Salah al-Din II, who was only seven years old. She acted as his regent until her own death in 1243. This long period in power was possible because of the care with which she acted. Dayfa Khatun remained carefully veiled from public view: she acted through a regency council, led by Jamal al-Dawla Iqbal al-Zahiri al-Khatuni, her personal slave. It was through the careful placement of such loyal men that she could act; they were her mouthpieces in the city.

This was rule in a most discreet way; it went almost unrecorded by medieval historians, and it remained largely unnoticed by modern scholars until rescued from oblivion by Yasser Tabbaa.[19] Dayfa Khatun issued coins in her grandson's name and ordered that his name be recited at

---

[18] Tamta as mother is proposed by Sublet, 'La folie de la princesse'.
[19] Tabbaa, 'Dayfa Khatun'.

Friday prayers in the *khutba* – the public acknowledgement of his legitimacy to rule. However, it was clear that she was in charge. She formed an alliance with al-Ashraf to fight against al-Kamil, her father and his brother, when they began to fear his growing power in Syria.[20] Ibn Wasil summarised her achievements: 'She was just to her subjects, very charitable and loving towards them. She removed various taxes in all the regions of Aleppo. She favoured jurists, ascetics, scholars and people of religion, and extended to them many charities.'[21] This was effectively rule from behind the throne – or from within the harem. The one public expression of her power came in the buildings she founded in Aleppo. But even these shrouded her power. The foundation inscription of the Firdaws Madrasa, which she built in Aleppo in 1235–6, describes its patron as 'the elevated curtain and impregnable veil'.[22] Both analogies are traditionally used to describe fortifications, but here they are equally appropriate as metaphors of modesty and chastity, and even as allusions to her discreet exercise of power. Dayfa's access to power came through her marriage, and the opportunity it allowed her to establish herself within the city of Aleppo and slowly gather power through courtiers. Her example is an appropriate model for Tamta, coming as it does from within the Ayyubid world.

Women as Independent Rulers

When Tamta moved to Akhlat to be married, there existed one paradigm for the independent exercise of power by a woman in the region: Queen Tamar of Georgia. Given that Tamta grew up in a region ruled by a woman, that she was based in Akhlat when Tamar's daughter Rusudan inherited the throne, and that her father and brother served both rulers, these queens must have had an impact on how women like Tamta regarded their own positions, and the possibilities that they too might control power. A quick survey of Tamar's life allows us to see the issues faced by a woman who could claim legitimacy to rule in her own right. More importantly, it allows us to see how Tamar's power was reconciled and presented to the world around her.

By 1210 Tamar had been ruling for a quarter of a century, and her hold on the throne was secure.[23] A manuscript completed for her in Constantinople

---

[20] Abu'l-Fida, 112.   [21] Quoted in Tabbaa, 'Dayfa Khatun', 22.
[22] *RCEA* XVI, 4084; *TEI*, 2536.
[23] Eastmond, *Royal Imagery in Medieval Georgia*, 93–184; R. Metreveli, *Mepe tamari* (Tbilisi, 1991).

at about this time names her as a living saint.[24] The chronicles that look back on her reign similarly portray her as a sun around which all else revolved; extraordinarily, she was even a fourth member of the Trinity.[25] She had a personal grip on power: she appointed and dismissed her ministers; it was she who determined policy and taxation; and although she could not fight, she did lead her army to the battlefield before retreating to a monastery to pray before icons for her troops' victory.

Tamar's grasp of power had been hard won and her rise had been anything but straightforward. Her father, Giorgi III, who had no male heirs, had foreseen the problem of his succession, and so had had her crowned as his co-ruler in 1178 to try to secure loyalty for her. With no legitimate alternate candidate the nobles of Georgia had no choice but to accept Tamar, but it is clear that they planned to use her as a vehicle to manoeuvre a male ruler into power. They congregated and demanded that Tamar marry, 'pointing out that she was childless and the kingdom without an heir, demanding a leader for the army'.[26] Their complaints in a nutshell encapsulated their opposition: women should just bear children, and men were needed to fight wars. This demand effectively undid the divinely ordained coronation ceremony. During this service the Queen had been anointed with chrism by the Catholicos, the conferring of God's approval, and then she had been girded with a sword by the nobility, their acknowledgement of her earthly authority (and by implication of her leadership of the army).[27] The importance of the two elements of the coronation, divine and earthly, is shown by their appearance together in a unique image of the coronation of Tamar's grandfather, Demetre I, at Matkhsvarishi in the high mountains of Georgia, painted in 1140.[28] The presentation of the sword to Tamar was clearly seen as a hollow symbol by those who gave it, given that she could not wield it personally. The nobles were also concerned about the image of the country abroad. As the demands of Rukn al-Din for her to convert and marry him discussed in the previous chapter showed, even in 1202 – after she had been in power for nearly twenty years – her sex was seen as a weakness that could be exploited.

After her coronation factions among the nobles first sought to choose her ministers for her, and then to select her husband. They summoned a

---

[24] Vani Gospels (Tbilisi, National Center of Manuscripts, A-1335, fol. 272v): Sharashidze, *Sakartvelos sakhelmtsipo muzeumis kartul khelnatserta aghtseriloba*, 409; Taqaishvili, 'L'évangile de Vani'.

[25] *Kartlis Tskhovreba*, 239. [26] *Kartlis Tskhovreba*, 289. [27] *Kartlis Tskhovreba*, 287.

[28] M. Qenia, *Upper Svaneti: Medieval Mural Painting* (Tbilisi, 2010), fig. 116; T. Virsaladze, 'Freskovaia rospis' khudozhnika Mikaela Maghlakeli v Matskhvarishi', *Ars Georgica* 4 (1955), 169–231, repr. in T. Virsaladze, *Izbrannye trudy* (Tbilisi, 2007), 145–224; Eastmond, *Royal Imagery in Medieval Georgia*, 73–91.

Russian prince from Novgorod, Iurii Bogoliubskoi (a potentially useful Christian ally to the north of the Caucasus), and eventually she was compelled to marry him. This was hardly a promising start to her reign, recalling both Christian and Muslim invectives against women rulers. Over the next two years Iurii sought to take complete control of the state from his wife. This was what most Georgians no doubt expected to happen, but Tamar fought back to reclaim power for herself. She was able to call on the ancestral legitimacy of her bloodline, the religious legitimacy of her coronation with holy chrism and the oaths sworn to her by her nobles. However, the most potent reason for many of her court to side with her was their disillusionment with Iurii himself. This reduced Georgia to civil war, which ended when Iurii's faction was defeated by the Mqargrdzelis and others loyal to Tamar. Her husband was divorced and exiled to Constantinople (from where he continued to lay claim to the Georgian throne for the next four years, until his death in 1192). Tamar's rise to power was almost certainly initially due more to her husband's deficiencies than her own skills; but her real achievement lay in retaining the loyalty of her court after his dismissal. The problem of an heir still remained, but for her second husband Tamar had a greater say, choosing the Ossetian Davit Soslan, who was prepared to rule as her ally rather than her rival, and who fathered her two children.

The unease in Georgia about having a woman as ruler can be seen in the scale of the response to it: Tamar's reign presents endless apologies for her gender.[29] In royal documents Tamar's sex is excused by giving her joint titles; she is simultaneously both 'king of kings' and 'queen of queens'.[30] The literature associated with Tamar's reign is similarly careful to bolster her position. *The Knight in the Panther's Skin*, Georgia's great epic poem composed by Shota Rustaveli during Tamar's reign, opens with the coronation of the princess Tinatin by her father King Rostam as his legitimate heir. It describes Tinatin in terms unambiguously reminiscent of Tamar's position:

> Though indeed she is a woman, still as sovereign she is begotten of God. She knows how to rule. We say this not to flatter you; we ourselves, in your absence, often say so. Her deeds, like her radiance, are revealed bright as sunshine. The lion's cubs are equal, whether they are male or female.[31]

---

[29] Eastmond, *Royal Imagery in Medieval Georgia*, 108–10.
[30] T. P. Enukidze, V. I. Shoshiashvili and N. Sologava, *Kartuli historikuli sabutebi XI–XIII s* (Tbilisi, 1984), no. 14 (p. 77). S. H. Rapp, 'The Coinage of Tamar, Sovereign of Georgia in Caucasia: A Preliminary Study in the Numismatic Inscriptions of Twelfth- and Thirteenth-Century Georgian Royal Coinage', *Le Muséon* 106 (1993), 309–30.
[31] Shota Rustaveli, verse 39.

Figure 26 King Giorgi III (r. 1156–84) and Queen Tamar (r. 1184–1210), north wall of the church of the Koimesis at Vardzia, Georgia; 1184–6

Even ecclesiastical literature in Tamar's reign tried to find role models among the saints for the empowerment of women. Georgian clerics found a convenient example in the figure of St Nino, the female Evangelist of Georgia from the fourth century. New versions of her life were written and new homilies composed that sought to naturalise the association of women and authority in Georgia. Equally, St Nino began to flourish in church paintings, often alongside or opposite images of Queen Tamar herself. St Nino's appearance in the paintings at Akhtala and in Ani, discussed in Chapter 2, must also be part of this wider phenomenon of using monumental painting

Figure 27 Queen Tamar (r. 1184–1210) and Giorgi IV Lasha (r. 1210–23), north wall of Bertubani monastery, Gareja desert, Georgia (now in Azerbaijan); *c.* 1210

to promote a female ruler. In art, Tamar is always associated with men. In the earliest depiction of her, painted between 1184 and 1186 in the monastery of Vardzia, she is shown meekly following her father, even though he had already been dead for two years by the time the church was painted [Fig. 26].[32] She is also shown slightly smaller than her father, but as she proffers the model of the church to Christ and the Mother of God, her pre-eminence is still signalled. The abundant use of gold, silver leaf and lapis lazuli in the painting all underscored the ideas of wealth, power and confidence that the Queen needed to convey. Her title is listed simply as *mepeta mepe* – king of kings.

In later churches she appears with combinations of her father and other ancestors, her second husband, and her son, Giorgi IV. These all adhere to the demands made of Tamar when she came to power – to be a mother, and wife of a military ruler.[33] The paintings present fictions to show that the correct (male) order is maintained and respected, even when it had evidently been overturned. Only at the very end of her reign was Tamar given first place in the donor images [Fig. 27]. But even here, in the rock-cut church at

---

[32] Eastmond, *Royal Imagery in Medieval Georgia*, 103–8.
[33] Eastmond, *Royal Imagery in Medieval Georgia*, 124–30, 141–9, 154–64, 169–78.

Bertubani painted in about 1210, she is still associated with a man: her now adult son who follows her, just as she followed her father at Vardzia. In total, five portraits of the Queen survive, a staggering quantity given what must have been lost over the centuries.[34] The number is testament not just to her piety, but to the need to give the Queen a visual presence, constantly to articulate and reiterate her power. But whilst the paintings at Bertubani might demonstrate the triumph of her gender over entrenched views of women, the absence of her daughter, Rusudan, from all these churches shows how deeply ingrained the expectation of male power still was.

Monumental art was a particularly important means for a woman such as Tamar to demonstrate her power. The churches in which she was painted were public spaces. They were a legitimate arena for the disbursement of state funds, demonstrating wealth, piety and proximity to God. The use of haloes and appropriation of Byzantine imperial dress further emphasised the difference between the ruling family and the other donors depicted in the church. Tamar's nobles, like the Mqargrdzelis at Harichavank, are depicted wearing kaftans and sharbushes (peaked, fur-lined hats) which tied them in to more local modes of dress that can be found across eastern Anatolia. It is likely that Tamta would have been dressed in this fashion, more familiar in the Ayyubid world than the antiquated ceremonial robes of Byzantium, and without their explicitly Christian associations.

It was the precedent of Tamar that enabled her daughter Rusudan to succeed to the throne, when the only alternative was the illegitimate son of Rusudan's brother, Giorgi IV Lasha. Rusudan was again able to exercise power in her own name: the letters sent to Pope Honorius III seeking aid against the Mongols are signed by her alone, and the Pope's replies address her as 'Russutane illustri regine ... Georgianorum' [Rusudan, illustrious queen of the Georgians].[35] But equally she was required to marry, both to supply a (male) heir to the throne and to establish an alliance with the Muslim states in Anatolia. Although these were traditional tasks for a woman, the dominance of Georgia and the established precedent for a woman in Georgia to retain power in her own right meant that now Rusudan's husband was expected to convert to fit with her Christian demands.[36] Ultimately this second essay into the world of female leadership in Georgia failed. Chronicles blamed Rusudan's dissolute lifestyle for the fate of Georgia, but these read dangerously like a return to type on the chroniclers' part,

---

[34] Z. Skhirtladze, 'Another Portrait of Queen Tamar?', in *Anadolu Kültürlerinde Süreklilik ve Değişim, Dr. A. Mine Kadiroğlu'na Armağan*, eds. C. Erel, B. Işler, N. Peker, and G. Sağir (Ankara, 2011), 505–23.

[35] *Regesta Honorii*, 2: 246, no. 4979.   [36] Al-Dahabi, 216.

seeking to blame the weakness of a woman for the calamities caused by first the Khwarazmian and then the Mongol invasions, which no male rulers in the vicinity had been able to repulse either.

The Georgian examples provide an attractive model for Tamta's own role at Akhlat. Both Tamar and Rusudan ruled in Tamta's lifetime, but ultimately they can have had little impact on her status. Tamar's ability to rule was ensured by her exceptionalism. She effectively rose above her gender to become something more than a man or a woman. Declaring her a saint during her lifetime was the clearest way of announcing this; and the failure of the Georgian state under a woman, Rusudan, confirmed it. The principal difference between Georgia and everywhere else was that in Georgia female power was exercised openly and with official sanction. In theory Georgia and the Islamic states to the south shared their attitudes to women and power – as we have seen, Christian and Muslim writers were equally aghast at the prospect of this combination – but the different structures of their states meant that placing women in power had to be justified (or explained away) by different arguments. In the Christian Caucasus, the ruling dynasties claimed that their legitimacy came from God and that it was inherited through blood. Tamar could trace her bloodline back in a direct line to the first Bagrationi King of Georgia in 888 (and he in turn claimed descent from the Old Testament King David). The Muslim dynastic tradition was less well entrenched. Legitimacy to rule lay with the Abbasid caliphate in Baghdad, whose rulers could claim to trace their ancestry back to the Prophet Muhammad's uncle. However, the Abbasids had long since lost actual control of the Muslim world among the mosaic of rulers who now exercised real power. These men all derived their legitimacy by paying (nominal) deference to the Caliph, but the source of their power more frequently lay in their individual military might and personal authority. As such, there was much greater acceptance of changes of ruling family, so long as each new one continued to acknowledge the Caliph. So when a woman came to power, it was easier to supplant her with another man.

This is evident from the one case in Tamta's lifetime when a Muslim woman did seek to take power in her own name. In 1249 Shajar al-Durr, a former slave, emerged as ruler of the Ayyubid domains in Egypt, when her husband al-Salih Ayyub (the son of al-Kamil, and so nephew of al-Ashraf) died suddenly.[37] His death came just as Louis IX of France landed at

---

[37] For the early sources on her life: G. Schregle, *Die Sultanin von Ägypten: Šaǧarat ad-Durr in der arabischen Geschichtsschreibung und Literatur* (Wiesbaden, 1961), 9–29, 33–6; brief accounts of her life: P. Thorau, 'Shadschar ad-Durr, Sultanin von Ägypten', in A. Wieczorek, M. Fansa and

Figure 28 Gold dinar of Shajar al-Durr, minted in Cairo, 1250 (British Museum, inv. 1849, 1121.294)

Damietta with the soldiers of the Seventh Crusade, hoping to take back control of Jerusalem by first attacking the Ayyubids in their Egyptian heartlands.[38] Shajar al-Durr helped to keep her husband's death secret in order not to undermine the Egyptian defence against the crusaders. Al-Salih Ayyub had signed many blank papers before his death, allowing her to continue to issue decrees in his name. The invasion was thwarted when the Frankish forces were defeated and Louis IX was captured by the Egyptians. At this stage the plan was to pass the throne on to al-Salih Ayyub's son, Turanshah, then resident in Hisnkeyf in south-eastern Turkey. The transition was effected successfully, but Turanshah fell out with both his mother and her mamluks, who killed him in the middle of the river Nile in May 1250 (supposedly his heart was cut out by his killer and offered to Louis IX of France, then still a captive in Cairo, in hope of a reward). Thereafter Shajar al-Durr was installed by the mamluks to rule in her own right. She began to hand out robes of honour to her emirs and to issue coins in her own name [Fig. 28].[39] She also claimed the prerogative of being named in the *khutba*, the official Friday sermon in mosque.[40] These were the standard

---

H. Meller, eds., *Saladin und die Kreuzfahrer* (Mannheim, 2005), 167–69; A. Levanoni, 'Šağar al-Durr: A Case of Female Sultanate in Medieval Islam', in *Egypt and Syria in the Fatimid, Ayyubid and Mamluk Eras*, vol. 3, eds. U. Vermeulen and J. Van Steenbergen (Leuven, 2001), 209–18; F. Mernissi, *The Forgotten Queens of Islam* (Cambridge, 1993), 90–3, 97–9.

[38] J. R. Strayer, 'The Crusades of Louis IX', in *A History of the Crusades*, vol. 2, eds. R. L. Wolff and H. W. Hazard (Madison; Milwaukee; London, 1969), 487–518.

[39] Coins: S. Lane Poole, *Catalogue of Oriental Coins in the British Museum* (London, 1879), vol. 4: *The Coinage of Egypt (AH 358–922) under the Fátimee Khaleefehs, the Ayyoobees, and the Memlook Sultans*, no. 469 (and commentary on pp. xvii–xxi); robes of honour: al-Dahabi, 257.

[40] Schregle, *Die Sultanin von Ägypten*, 61–2.

means by which a ruler's sovereignty was announced; no woman had ever claimed them before. Other titles she adopted, such as 'al-Malikat Ismat al-Din Umm-Khalil Shajar al-Durr' (the Queen Ismat al-Din Shajar al-Durr, mother of Khalil) and 'al-Malikat al-Muslimin' (Queen of the Muslims) exacerbated the sense of hubris.[41]

Shajar al-Durr's rule immediately faced opposition, especially from al-Musta'sim, the Abbasid Caliph in Baghdad, the nominal leader of Islam: 'If there is not a man left among you whom you can appoint, tell us and we will send you one.'[42] It is easy to imagine Tamar's nobles uttering remarkably similar words when they demanded that she marry. Within just three months this forced Shajar al-Durr to find a new man to front her throne. She adopted the leading mamluk commander, Aybak, who quickly manoeuvred her into marrying him to consolidate his rule (although ostensibly power now lay with the infant al-Ashraf Musa, a nephew of al-Salih Ayyub). After seven years of marriage and co-rule this pair fell out as well, when Aybak announced an alliance with Badr al-Din Lu'lu' of Mosul, to be sealed by marrying his daughter. Shajar al-Durr arranged for the Sultan's murder (another watery death, this time in his bath). However, now Shajar al-Durr lacked sufficient support, and three days later she was arrested and killed by Aybak's supporters. They, symbolically, had her killed by Aybak's female slaves, who beat her to death with their wooden clogs; her body was dumped in a ditch. Even her death was gendered.

Whilst Rusudan had been able to rule in her own name in Georgia at almost exactly the same time, she could look to the precedent of her mother, and was anyway more careful in the external presentation of power (the use of husbands). Shajar al-Durr did not obey these rules: her self-promotion scandalised the remaining Ayyubid rulers in Syria, and her reliance on her mamluks alienated her from them. With her the Ayyubid dynasty ended, and the mamluks who were to rule in Syria and Egypt for the next three hundred years established their power.

Another crucial difference between Tamar and Rusudan's grasp of power and that of Shajar al-Durr was in their ability to present their power in visible terms. Islamic culture had no equivalent of the church paintings that presented Tamar's piety and authority in public. Whilst Muslim rulers commissioned portraits (in manuscripts and palaces, as we will see in the next chapters), they were visible to a much more limited audience. Shajar al-Durr was

---

[41] Schregle, *Die Sultanin von Ägypten*, 62–3, citing al-Maqrizi.
[42] This later story is recounted in Mernissi, *The Forgotten Queens of Islam*, 29; and B. Lewis, 'The Coming of the Steppe People: 2: Egypt and Syria', in *The Cambridge History of Islam*, vol. 1A, eds. P. M. Holt, A. K. S. Lambton and B. Lewis (Cambridge, 1970), 175–230, at 210.

able to conceive a more permanent commemoration for herself in Cairo: her mausoleum.⁴³ She commissioned it in a prestigious location, in the cemetery to the south of the citadel; it lay close to the burials of female relatives of the Prophet, including Sayyida Ruqayya and Sayyida Nafisa. All that now survives is the tomb itself, but Doris Behrens-Abouseif has found evidence for it being at the centre of a large madrasa complex with an impressive minaret. The tomb itself was not immediately visible to passers-by, standing away from the street. It was certainly more modest than the mausoleum she built for her first husband, al-Salih Ayyub. This was the first mausoleum to be built inside the walled city of Qahira on the Bayn al-Qasrayn, the road between the old Fatimid palaces.⁴⁴ His tomb projected out into the middle of this vital thoroughfare, where it stood as an unavoidable obstacle, ensuring he would never be forgotten. Shajar al-Durr used the building indirectly to legitimise her own position, by presenting herself as the widow of a martyr to the Christian warriors of the Seventh Crusade. This was spelled out in the largely fictitious inscription that adorned the tomb building:

> He died in the grace of God in combat in the place of Mansurah against the cursed Franks, presenting his throat to their swords, offering his face and chest in battle, hoping to be rewarded by Allah for his fine conduct before the enemy through his courage... He died in the night of 15 Shaban 647. (23 November 1249)⁴⁵

Shajar al-Durr similarly sought to determine her own commemoration in the inscription she had carved at her mausoleum:

> In the name of God, here lies the dust of the elevated curtain and impregnable veil, 'Ismat al-Dunya wa'l-Din, mother of the victorious king al-Mansur Khalil, son of our master the sultan al-Malik al-Salih Najm al-Din Abu'l-Fath Ayyub, son of our master sultan the good king Nasr al-Din Abu'l-Ma'ali Muhammad, son of Abu Bakr, son of Ayyub, devoted commander of the faithful, may God sanctify his soul and illuminate his grave! The pen has extolled her virtues across the pages of the Book, great deeds bear witness to her eternal glory from the highest of heavens, where the brilliant suns of the kingdom rise for her, and the opinions of the emirs are obedient and hear her orders. May God strengthen her supporters, multiply her strength and elevate her radiance... May God make heaven her

---

⁴³ For all that follows: K. A. C. Creswell, *The Muslim Architecture of Egypt*, vol. 2: *Ayyūbids and Early Bah.rite Mamlūks, AD.. 1171–1326* (Oxford, 1959), 136–41; D. Behrens-Abouseif, *Cairo of the Mamluks: A History of the Architecture and its Culture* (London, 2007), 113–16.
⁴⁴ Creswell, *The Muslim Architecture of Egypt*, 94–103.
⁴⁵ *RCEA* XI, 4298; M. van Berchem and H. Edhem, *Matériaux pour un Corpus Inscriptionum Arabicum*, part 1, *Egypte* I(i) (Paris, 1903), no. 66.

highest abode. She was victorious and supported by God, and by Muhammad, his family and companions, the good, pure and honourable.⁴⁶

Whilst the opening words echo the modesty of those of Dayfa Khatun at the Firdaws Madrasa in Aleppo, the rest presents a more regal and imposing persona for the Queen. This testimony proved too much in the aftermath of her death, and at some point the inscription was concealed by thick black paint, presumably added by her enemies to efface her memory.⁴⁷ This verbal portrait of the Queen found an echo inside the building. The conch of the *mihrab* niche is filled with a mosaic showing the curling leaves and tendrils of a plant, set against a rich gold background. The fruits of the plant are made from pearls [Fig. 29]. At first sight it echoes the mosaic decoration set up in the Dome of the Rock in Jerusalem, but the design also provides a direct representation of Shajar al-Durr herself: her name translates as 'tree of pearls'. This is the closest we will come to a portrait of any Muslim woman ruler in this period. However, it may not be a self-portrait, as it has been argued that the mosaic was inserted by a later Mamluk ruler.⁴⁸ The association of the medium of mosaic with the early Umayyad caliphs (the niche may even have been made of tesserae brought from the Great Mosque in Damascus) associated Shajar al-Durr with the prestige of the first Muslim ruling dynasty.⁴⁹ Muslim women simply did not have the visual means to underwrite their power in any more direct way than this.

No images of Tamta are known to us, but the fact that she was permitted to remain a Christian during her marriage to al-Ashraf means that if she commissioned any portraits, it is most probable that they would have appeared in churches, either carved in stone like those of her father and uncle, or painted like those of Queen Tamar. These would have given Tamta a visible presence among the majority Christian population of Akhlat, and this would have bolstered her image among them as a co-religionist and supporter.

---

⁴⁶ Van Berchem and Edhem, *Matériaux* 1: *Egypt I(i)*, no. 70; *RCEA* XI, 4321; *TEI*, 2780; trans. in C. O. M. Wolf, '"The Pen Has Extolled her Virtues": Gender and Power within the Visual Legacy of Shajar al-Durr in Cairo', in *Calligraphy and Architecture in the Muslim World*, eds. M. Gharipour and I. C. Schick (Edinburgh, 2013), 199–216, at 208–9.

⁴⁷ D. Behrens-Abouseif, *Islamic Architecture in Cairo: An Introduction* (Leiden; New York, 1989), 91–2.

⁴⁸ M. Meinecke, 'Das Mauseoleum des Qala'un in Kairo: Untersuchungen zur Genese der mamlukischen Architekturdekorationen', *Mitteilungen des Deutschen Archäologischen Instituts. Abteilung Kairo* 27 (1971), 47–80, at 55–8.

⁴⁹ F. B. Flood, 'Umayyad Survivals and Mamluk Revivals: Qalawunid Architecture and the Great Mosque of Damascus', *Muqarnas* 14 (1997), 57–79.

Figure 29 Tree of Pearls mosaic in the conch of the *mihrab* in the mausoleum of Shajar al-Durr, Southern Cemetery, Cairo, Egypt, 1250–80 (For the colour version, please refer to the plate section. In some formats this figure will only appear in black and white)

The inconsistency between the actual and theoretical position of women in the medieval world shows both the possibilities and the problems faced by any woman who sought to take power, whether openly or from behind the veil, in the thirteenth century. This discrepancy allowed women to take power, but the ever-present reminder of that patriarchal structure acted as a constant threat to them. It was easy to recall the distrust of women in the texts and so undermine their power. The women who succeeded, among whom we must now number Tamta, walked a tightrope between their abilities and the expectations placed on them by social restrictions that were common in both Christian and Islamic cultures. It was as wives and widows that women were most easily able to access power. The relative power and autonomy that the women in this chapter enjoyed shows that they were an important part of the structure of the state. They may not have had any official position, beyond that of wife and mother, but they were needed by their husbands given that the states that they ruled were often geographically disparate, spread over large areas with poor communication, and contained large populations from different ethnic and religious groups. In these circumstances husbands were required to trust their wives.

6 | Akhlat

Identity and Life in the Medieval City

Before we move on to consider Tamta's actions as wife of al-Ashraf, we must establish the nature of the other main actor in this book: the city of Akhlat, the centre around which Tamta's adult life revolved. Akhlat today is a city of the dead. It is famed for its tower mausolea and fields of tombstones which stand between the modern houses and frame views of the mountains of eastern Anatolia in the distance [Fig. 30]. The western approach to the town is through an extensive cemetery covering more than two square kilometres marked with thousands of tall, slender tombstones. The romance of the site was captured by Austen Henry Layard, who passed through the city on his way to excavate at Nineveh in 1853:

> At our feet, as we drew nigh to the lake, were the gardens of the ancient city of Akhlat, leaning minarets and pointed mausoleums peeping above the trees. We rode through vast burying-grounds, a perfect forest of upright stones seven or eight feet high of the richest red colour, most delicately and tastefully carved with arabesque ornaments and inscriptions in the massive character of the early Mussulman age. In the midst of them rose here and there a conical *turbeh* of beautiful shape, covered with exquisite tracery. The monuments of the dead still stand, and have become the monuments of a city, itself long since crumbled into dust. Amidst orchards and gardens are scattered here and there low houses rudely built out of the remains of earlier habitations and fragments of cornice and sculpture are piled up into walls around the cultivated plots.[1]

These great funerary monuments began to appear towards the end of Tamta's lifetime, whilst she was governing in the city. Of the city of the living, however, nothing now survives.

The destruction of Akhlat means that we cannot recreate the exact shape and appearance of that city; rather, we must create a composite picture of the ways in which the form and structure of cities helped to construct the

---

[1] A. H. Layard, *Discoveries in the ruins of Nineveh and Babylon: with travels in Armenia, Kurdistan and the desert: being the result of a second expedition undertaken for the trustees of the British Museum* (London, 1853), 24; and 31 on the similarity of the Christian and Muslim tombstones.

Figure 30 View of the Muslim cemetery at Akhlat, Turkey

identities and communities of those that lived in them.[2] To do this we can draw on evidence from other cities in the three worlds that met at Akhlat. Evidence comes from across the Caucasus – Ani, Dvin, Van, Tbilisi; from Anatolia and the Jazira – Amid (Diyarbakir), Kayseri, Konya; and Syria – Aleppo, Damascus.[3] Whilst these regions differed in many ways, all provide insights into the ways in which cities worked, and all were linked to Akhlat through its geographical location on the edge of those different worlds. They intersect in the figure of Tamta herself, who was related to rulers in all of them.

Urban centres dominated all these regions in the thirteenth century: they were the focus of trade and industry, and so also the goals of war. Cities should not just be seen as inanimate collections of buildings. Rather, it is possible to see them as characters in themselves, with their own identities. Astrologers famously created horoscopes for cities, just as they did for

---

[2] H. Kennedy, 'How to Found an Islamic City', in *Cities, Texts and Social Networks, 400–1500. Experiences and Perceptions of Medieval Urban Space*, eds. C. Goodson, A. E. Lester and C. Symes (Farnham; Burlington, VA, 2010), 45–63; A. H. Hourani, 'Introduction: The Islamic City in the Light of Recent Research', in *The Islamic City: A Colloquium*, eds. A. H. Hourani and S. M. Stern (Oxford, 1970), 9–24, esp. 20–3 on factors involved in recreating a 'typical' Islamic city.

[3] For a historiography of definitions of the Islamic city: A. Raymond, 'The Spatial Organization of the City', in *The City in the Islamic World*, vol. 1, eds. R. Holod, A. Petruccioli and A. Raymond (Leiden; Boston, 2008), 47–70.

individuals.⁴ And just as Tamta's identity was multi-layered and complex, and changed over time, so too were those of cities. Cities' identities were expressed through their urban fabric and by the people and trades that operated in them. To explore the city is to explore the physical world in which Tamta moved and lived.

First we must recognise the particular qualities of cities in eastern Anatolia and the Caucasus. The revival of cities was essentially a Muslim phenomenon, so the very fact that Tamta's life can be constructed around one city is already an implicit recognition of the importance of Muslim culture in her life, and its impact on the social structures of eastern Anatolia. Although Armenian and Georgian cities were important – such as the centres like Ani, Dvin, Van or Tbilisi – they were essentially an alien import in the Middle Ages.⁵ In every case these cities had developed during long periods of Muslim rule, and their established position encouraged their Christian conquerors to continue to invest in them. Christian aristocratic life still revolved around castles and fortresses at the heart of great estates. The majority of the population of Georgia and Armenia was based in small rural settlements, from which they worked the land, and much Christian intellectual life was concentrated in remote monasteries, such as Sanahin and Haghbat in Armenia, or Gelati and Iqalto in Georgia. However, cities were becoming increasingly important as centres of trade and manufacturing, and the concentration of money that resulted opened new opportunities for literary, scientific and legal developments. The city of Ani, for example, was the home of three major Armenian historians in the twelfth and thirteenth centuries,⁶ as well as their Muslim contemporary, Burhan al-Din ʿAli, who acted as *qadi* (judge) in the city under Mqargrdzeli domination, and composed poetry and chronicles.⁷ At the same time Mkhitar Gosh (d. 1213), the great Armenian jurist, poet and theologian, worked for the Mqargrdzelis from the monasteries of Getik and then Goshavank, both of which were sited well away from any large settlements.

---

⁴ Aleppo was believed to have had an ancient Greek horoscope inscribed on an arch by the Antioch Gate: Ibn al-Shihna, 11–16; see also G. Saliba, 'The Role of the Astrologer in Medieval Islamic Society', *BEO* 44 (1992), 45–67, at 57–8.

⁵ N. G. Garsoïan, 'The Early-Medieval Armenian City: An Alien Element?', *Journal of Near Eastern Studies* 16–17 (1984), 67–83.

⁶ R. W. Thomson, 'Medieval Chroniclers of Ani: Hovhannes, Samvel, and Mkhitar', in *Armenian Kars and Ani*, ed. R. G. Hovannisian (Costa Mesa, CA, 2011), 65–80.

⁷ Minorsky, *Studies in Caucasian History*; A. C. S. Peacock, 'An Interfaith Polemic of Medieval Anatolia: Qāḍī Burhān al-Dīn al-Anawī on the Armenians and their Heresies', in *Islam and Christianity in Anatolia and the Caucasus*, eds. A. C. S. Peacock, B. De Nicola and S. N. Yıldız (Farnham, 2015), 233–61.

Cities were the constructions of their citizens, governors and rulers over time. It was they who determined (whether through rigid design or a more haphazard form of evolution) the urban layout of the city, the clarity of its street plan, the prominence of its buildings, the extent and location of its industry and palaces. At the same time, the entity of the city began to determine the ways in which citizens interacted with each other and the authorities raised over them. This symbiotic relationship, constantly in flux as the governorship of cities changed hands and as the buildings and appearance of the city fabric changed, played an important role in the ways in which identities could be formulated and displayed – both for individuals and for a corporate sense of identity expressed by each city.

This chapter explores the appearance of the city – the character conveyed by its layout, its range of architecture, its walls and its gardens; the following chapters explore what Tamta did in the city: how she was able to use its people and resources to carry out her acts.

The Anatomy of the City

Silhouette

The identity of the city was first established from afar by its profile: its silhouette against the skyline. With most buildings relatively low, two or at most three storeys high, cities were dominated by their defensive and religious institutions: walls, churches, mosques. Towers, domes and minarets rose above the dwellings of the citizens and the palaces of rulers to impose the city upon its surrounding landscape and to mark it from afar. In eastern Anatolia this was most dramatically visible in the settlement closest to Akhlat on Lake Van, the city of Van itself. Completely destroyed between 1915 and 1920, only Charles Texier's 1838 engraving now records the church domes and minarets that rose above the city wall, all in the shadow of the citadel on the great Rock of Van above [Fig. 31].

The mixed populations of all the cities in these regions meant that both churches and mosques rose above the city walls, whether in conversation or competition on the skyline. As cities changed hands between Christian and Muslim rulers, so the skyline changed in response. The ways in which buildings could be used to manipulate the religious identity of a city can be seen in Ani, one of the two principal cities of the Mqargrdzelis, which provides a model that also applies to Akhlat. Ani had been founded as a new capital for the Bagratuni rulers of Armenia in 971, but after less than a century it had changed hands; first annexed by the Byzantines in 1045, and

Figure 31 View of Van, Turkey, from the south, showing the jumble of minarets and church domes rising above the city walls, with the Rock of Van behind (from C. Texier, *Description de l'Arménie, la Perse et la Mésopotamie* (Paris, 1842), vol. 1: plate 36) (the medieval city was razed to the ground after 1915)

then falling to the Seljuk Turks in 1064.[8] In 1072 the Sultan Kılıç Arslan sold Ani to the Shaddadid family, who ruled it during the twelfth century. Periodically, it was captured by the Georgians (in 1124, 1161–4, 1174), but they were never able to hold it for long, until the Mqargrdzeli victory of 1199. As a Mqargrdzeli-controlled city, it is likely that this is the city that Tamta knew best from her childhood. Abandoned gradually in the course of the fourteenth century, the city's skeleton still rises above the eastern Anatolian plateau, forming one of the most haunting sights in Turkey. Whilst the skin and organs of the city – its houses, mills, markets and gardens – have decayed over the centuries, the bones – its walls, churches and mosques and gates, and the shadows of its major roads – have survived. The skeleton of the city was created from the local stone of the Caucasian plateau, a volcanic tufa that varies from orangey-red to rusty brown. It was easy to square and carve, and the natural variation in colour allowed builders to incorporate patterns, motifs and even words into their stonework. A similar tufa was abundant in Akhlat, and was the ubiquitous building material for the surviving medieval tombstones and mausolea; the only difference being that it has a deeper, richer red-brown than the stone around Ani.

---

[8] For a historical overview see C. Mutafian, 'Ani after Ani, Eleventh to Seventeenth Century', in *Armenian Kars and Ani*, ed. R. G. Hovannisian (Costa Mesa, CA, 2011), 155–70.

Figure 31 (*continued*)

By the time of the Seljuk capture of Ani from the Byzantines in 1064, its Christian skyline was clear – dominated by the conical dome of the cathedral (now lost). Even among Muslims, Ani was known as the city of 1,001 churches;[9] the dome of the cathedral rose above many other conical roofs, and those of a dozen other churches are still visible or are known from nineteenth-century travellers' accounts. At Ani the original Christian profile of the city may have been largely uniform, as the majority of its citizens belonged to the Armenian Apostolic Church. It was only in the twelfth century, as Georgian influence in the city grew, that evidence emerges of churches of other confessions being built, such as the church of the Georgians just inside the Kars Gate.[10] In Akhlat the situation was different, as many more Christian confessions jostled for place inside the city walls. The majority may have been Armenian, but there was a large Greek population too.[11] Nearby Malatya also had a thriving Greek population that was in regular communication with the Greek Patriarch, Germanos II; he described the community there in 1226 as populous and prosperous.[12] In addition, there were at least two other confessional sects, each of which had ethnic

---

[9] Burhan al-Din cited in Peacock, 'An Interfaith Polemic', 238.
[10] P. Cuneo, A. Zarian, G. Uluhogian, J.-M. Thierry and N. Thierry, eds., *Ani* (Milan, 1984), 91.
[11] William of Rubruck, 276.
[12] D. Korobeinikov, 'A Greek Orthodox Armenian in the Seljukid Service: The Colophon of Basil of Melitina', in *Mare et litora: Essays Presented to Sergei Karpov for his 60th Birthday*, ed. R. Shukurov (Moscow, 2009), 709–24, at 719; V. Laurent, *Les regestes des actes du patriarcat de Constantinople*, vol. 1: *Les actes des patriarches*, fasc. 4: *Les regestes de 1208 à 1309* (Paris, 1971), no. 1240.

and regional affiliations with which they were aligned. These were the Syrian Orthodox and Nestorian Christians: Akhlat was the birthplace of Solomon of Akhlat, who was to become Nestorian bishop of Basra on the Tigris in southern Iraq in about 1222,[13] and the residence towards the end of the century of Abdishoʿ Bar Brikha, the Nestorian bishop of Nisibis.[14] Each confession required its own churches, designed to suit their own traditions and configured to match their liturgies, and with profiles to advertise their presence in the city.

The Turkish conquest of eastern Anatolia began to change this Christian silhouette. The most striking and politically important alteration at Ani came when the mosque of Minuchihr was built by the entrance to the citadel [Fig. 32]. The date of both mosque and minaret are disputed: the minaret takes up the north-west corner of the mosque, and stands at a slightly awkward angle to it, suggesting that it pre-dates the hall of the mosque, which appears to have been rebuilt towards the end of the twelfth century.[15] However, their impact on the cityscape is not. The octagonal minaret rose 23 metres above the city, and unambiguously spelled out Minuchihr's religious affiliation in the *bismallah* that was built into the fabric of the stonework. Even more significant was its location: it was erected on the edge of the ravine immediately above the main bridge that connected Ani with the lands to its east. This location put it in direct competition with the cathedral just 100 metres further east [Fig. 33]. The cathedral, finished at least one hundred and fifty years earlier in 1000, was taller (to the base of its dome, it was already 24 metres high), but it was set further back from the ravine. The other mosque that is known from the city, that of Abu Maʿmaran, was also built in a strategic location, halfway along the main road between the Lion Gate and the citadel.[16] This had a substantially taller minaret (the Anatolian equivalent of Venetian *campanilismo*?), and must have

---

[13] Best known for the *Book of the Bee*, a theological treatise on everything from the creation of the world to the last judgement: Solomon, Bishop of Basra, *The book of the bee: the Syriac text edited from the manuscripts in London, Oxford, and Munich with an English translation*, ed. E. A. W. Budge (Oxford, 1886).

[14] Abdishoʿ Bar Brikha, 422: 'This useful book was written in the month of September, in the year of Alexander 1609 [=1298], in the blessed city of Khlat, in the Church of the blessed Nestorians.'

[15] B. Karamağaralı, 'Ani Ulu Cami (Manucehr Camii)', in *9th International Congress of Turkish Art, Summary of Contributions* (Ankara, 1995), 323–38. This date is based on the similarity between its stone vaults and those of the zhamatun of the church of the Holy Apostles, which has a *terminus ante quem* of 1217, determined by the earliest surviving inscription there: Orbeli, *Corpus Inscriptionum Armenicarum*, no. 56; Basmadjian, *Inscriptions arméniennes d'Ani*, no. 49.

[16] William of Rubruck, 270, records the city had 1,000 churches and 'two Saracen synagogues' (i.e. mosques).

Figure 32 Mosque of Minuchihr, Ani, Turkey, from the south-west; twelfth–thirteenth century

dominated the heart of the city (it collapsed only in 1890). In the thirteenth century, minarets were emerging as visual shorthand for the Islamic city, as in the cityscapes depicted in early thirteenth-century copies of al-Hariri's *Maqamat*.[17]

These changes to the city's silhouette affected existing buildings as well. In Ani, the capture of the city from the Armenians by the Seljuks in 1064 had been celebrated by the removal of the silver cross from the dome of

---

[17] O. Grabar, *The Illustrations of the Maqamat* (Chicago, 1984), 92–96 [43rd *maqamah*]; O. Grabar, 'The Illustrated Maqamat of the Thirteenth Century: The Bourgeoisie and the Arts', in *The Islamic City: A Colloquium*, eds. A. H. Hourani and S. M. Stern (Oxford, 1970), 207–22, esp. 214.

Figure 33 Cathedral (1000–1) and mosque of Minuchihr (twelfth–thirteenth centuries) seen from the east, at the edge of the ravine of the river Akurean, Ani, Turkey (For the colour version, please refer to the plate section. In some formats this figure will only appear in black and white)

the cathedral and its transfer to the mosque in Nakhchivan, where it was placed under the threshold, destined to be trodden upon by all those coming to pray.[18] It was replaced by 'that hated symbol': a crescent.[19] Sixty years later Vardan Areweltsi's chronicle celebrated the reversal of this procedure and the installation of a new cross after one of the brief expulsions of the Shaddadids by the Georgians that punctuated the city's history in the twelfth century.

With the exception of the ornament on the top of the cathedral dome, the changes to Ani's identity appeared through a process of accumulation rather than replacement. The skyline was continually added to, creating a richer and denser silhouette in which minarets and domes competed for attention. This coexistence was certainly determined by pragmatic politics: the fact that the Christian population was always in the majority meant that Muslim rulers needed to retain Christian support, or at least acquiescence, in order for the commerce of the city to survive. Equally, the Muslim

---

[18] Matthew of Edessa, 104.   [19] Vardan, 202.

Plate 5 View of the apse, showing post holes for templon screen at Akhtala, Armenia; c. 1205

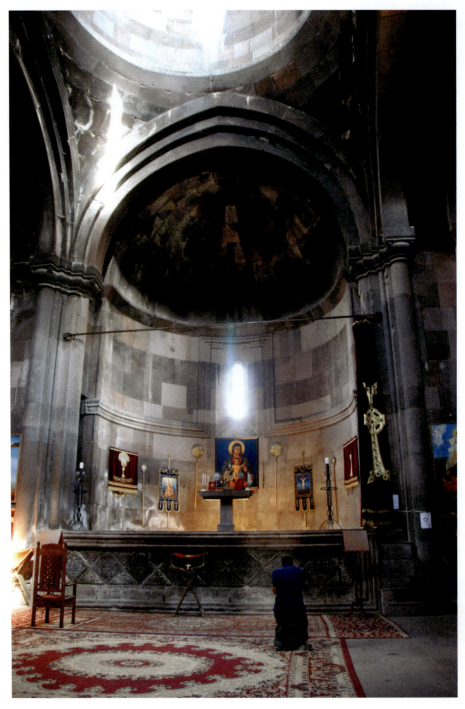

Plate 6 View of the apse of the catholicon at Harichavank, Armenia, showing altar platform; *c.* 1200

Plate 7 Communion of the Apostles with Greek inscription, in the apse at Akhtala, Armenia; *c.* 1205

Plate 8 Bilingual Greek and Georgian inscription accompanying St John in the north-east pendentive in the church of St Gregory the Illuminator of Tigran Honents, Ani, Turkey; 1215

Plate 10 Detail of the Last Judgement on the west wall at Akhtala, Armenia; *c.* 1205

Plate 11 The Glorification of the Cross in the dome of the church at Timotesubani, Georgia; *c.* 1220

Plate 13 General view of the monastic complex at Harichavank, Armenia, from the south; 1201

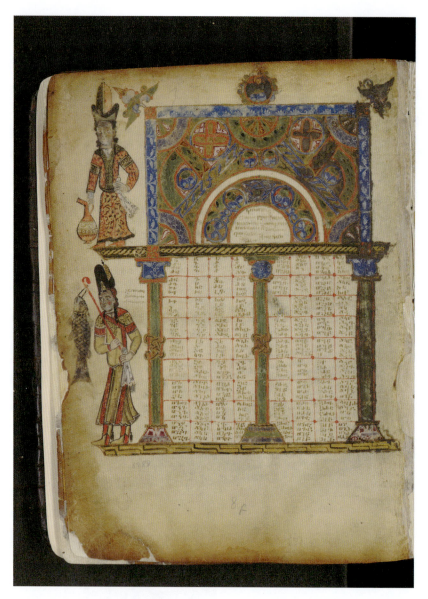

Plate 17 Canon tables from the Haghbat Gospels; 1211 (Yerevan, Matendaran, MS 6288, fols. 8v–9r; 30 × 22 cm). The inscription by the figure holding the fish in the lower left corner reads, somewhat mysteriously: 'Sahak, next time bring fish!'

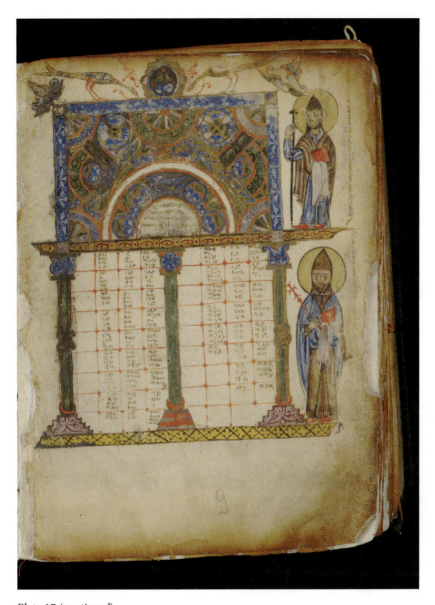

Plate 19 The vision of St Gregory the Illuminator in the west arm of the church of St Gregory the Illuminator of Tigran Honents, Ani, Turkey; 1215

Plate 20 The vision of St Nino and the life-giving pillar in the west arm of the church of St Gregory the Illuminator of Tigran Honents, Ani, Turkey; 1215

population by 1199 was large enough, and the commercial links with Islamic neighbours extensive enough, for its Christian conquerors to be unable or unwilling substantially to alter the Muslim structures. The two communities were interdependent, however reluctantly. Given this rough tolerance,[20] what became important was the placement and scale of buildings: the two known mosques certainly punched above their weight in terms of their location, dominating the main vistas and public spaces in the city.[21] After the Georgian conquest of 1199 there was presumably relatively little free space in the centre of the city for the Mqargrdzelis and their supporters to erect new buildings without causing extensive disruption and discord. The only churches built by Zakare and Ivane were in the palace on the citadel, away from the densely populated centre of the city. The one major new foundation that we know about in the city itself, the church dedicated to St Gregory the Illuminator in 1215 by the wealthy merchant Tigran Honents, was sited on the very edge of the walled city, clinging to the cliff face above the river Akurean. Given what we know of Akhlat, the situation there must have been very similar: it too had a Christian majority under a Muslim government throughout the twelfth century, requiring a similar, uneasy accommodation between the two religions, and a similarly shared skyline.

In Akhlat we know that a new church was built for Tamta by al-Awhad after her arrival in the city.[22] Rulers elsewhere in the region were less tolerant, and there is evidence that the Muslim rulers of Mardin allowed churches to be transformed into mosques in the second half of the twelfth century. In Aleppo and Hisnkeyf efforts were made to prevent the construction of new churches at this time. Equally, when Christian rulers triumphed, they turned mosques into churches, as happened in Sinop during its brief decades of rule by the emperors of Trebizond from 1245 to 1264.[23] However, these examples of persecution do not seem to have been long-lasting, and were anyway matched by examples elsewhere of more tolerant practices, as in Amid (Diyarbakir), where a number of churches were restored in the period after 1150.[24] Equally, in Cairo, the church of the Virgin at Haret al-Rum, located

---

[20] C. MacEvitt, *Rough Tolerance: The Crusades and the Christian World of the East* (Philadelphia, 2008).

[21] Compare also the minaret in Aleppo that was sited expressly to dominate the synagogue in the street of the Jews: Sibṭ ibn al-'Ajami, 155.

[22] Al-Nuwayri, 29: 47–8; La Porta, '"The Kingdom and the Sultanate were Conjoined"', 88 n. 79.

[23] A. A. M. Bryer, 'A Byzantine Family: The Gabrades, c.979–c.1653', *University of Birmingham Historical Journal* 12 (1970), 164–87, at 181.

[24] N. M. Lowick, S. Bendall and P. D. Whitting, *The 'Mardin' Hoard: Islamic Countermarks on Byzantine Folles* (London, 1977), 51.

within the walls of the Fatimid city, was reconstructed in 1186, after the city came under Ayyubid control. The restoration followed a short period of persecution in which the many churches had been attacked.[25]

The erection of new minarets or domes to reconfigure the city's skyline was not limited to cities that flipped between Christian and Muslim power; they could equally mark changes of regime within each religion. The revival of the umbrella zig-zag dome in the region around Ani was certainly intended to be a visual signifier of Mqargrdzeli dominance to other Christians, and an advertisement of the family's pretensions to revive the glories of the former Bagratuni kingdom. On the other side of the religious frontier, architecture had an equally important symbolic power. In 1212 al-Ashraf completed the minaret of a mosque at Mayyafariqin [Silvan] that his brother had begun a decade earlier, adding the top four storeys [Fig. 34].[26] The act of completion was a symbol of continuity, but the foundation of the minaret in the first place had been as much a political act on al-Awhad's part as a pious one. The minaret was located at a strategic point to the south of the city; it was actually well outside the city's walls and so difficult to defend, but its placement dominated all approaches from the south and the east. The inscription that al-Ashraf added turned the minaret as a whole into an advertisement of his universal lordship in the region, with its tripartite claim to rule over the Armenians, the Persians (i.e. the Turks) and the Arabs:

> This is what our master ordered to complete and to make, the Sultan al-Malik al-Ashraf, the wise, the just, the champion of the faith, the defender of the borders, Muzaffar al-Dunya wa'l-Din, the mainstay of Islam and Muslims, the lord of nations, king of the Arabs and the Persians, the Shah of the Armenians, Abul-Fath Musa, the defender of the emir of the believers, in the days of the caliphate of our master the imam Abul-Ma'ali Ahmad al-Nasir li-din Allah, the emir of the believers, may God glorify his victories and double his power! This [was completed] at the date of al-Muharram of the year 609 [June 1212].[27]

A second political claim was embedded in the form of the minaret itself, which addressed the Muslim population of the city more directly. The minaret's square plan, with five distinct storeys, is a close copy of the minaret of the Great Mosque in Aleppo [Fig. 35]. This had been built in 1090–2

---

[25] O. H. E. Khs-Burmester, *A Guide to the Ancient Coptic Churches of Cairo* (Giza, 1955), 68.

[26] A. Gabriel, *Voyages archéologiques dans la Turquie orientale* (Paris, 1940), 344–5, inscriptions nos. 125, 126; Whelan, *The Public Figure*, 437–40. See also J. M. Bloom, *The Minaret* (Edinburgh, 2013), 255, 269 n.47.

[27] *RCEA* X, 3709; *TEI*, 2974 (compare *RCEA* X, 3670; *TEI*, 2934, which inexplicably names al-Awhad as al-Afdal).

Figure 34 The minaret outside the walls at Mayyafariqin (Silvan), Turkey, begun by al-Awhad in 1203, completed by his brother al-Ashraf in 1212

Figure 35 The minaret of the Great Mosque at Aleppo, Syria; 1090–2 (destroyed April 2013)

by the Seljuk Sultan Tutush, and became a symbol of north Syrian Islamic architecture up until its destruction during the Syrian civil war in 2013. Copying the design tied the city of Mayyafariqin explicitly to Syria and so associated it with the Ayyubid realms there. Similar rectangular minarets dominated the skyline of Maʿarat al-Nuʿman (between Aleppo and Hama) and al-Ashraf's capital, Harran, either built or restored under Saladin at the end of the twelfth century.[28] Another minaret, built in 1211–12 at the Maqam al-Khalil in Edessa (modern-day Urfa), probably by al-Ashraf, also adopted the angular form.[29] These square masonry minarets, which were built as freestanding structures separate from the mosque itself, stood in clear visual contrast to the cylindrical minarets, often built in brick, that

---

[28] Bloom, *The Minaret*, 91–2 (Harran), 254 (Maʿarat al-Nuʿman).

[29] M. van Berchem, 'Arabische Inschriften', in *Inschriften aus Syrien, Mesopotamien und Kleinasien gesammelt im Jahre 1899*, ed. N. von Oppenheim (Leipzig; Baltimore, 1909), 1–156, no. 79.

had been imported into Anatolia with the Seljuks from Iran (such as that built for the Ulu Camii in Sivas in 1212–13).[30] Whilst the different forms of these minarets were partly determined by expediency – the availability of materials and craftsmen – they were still the result of particular decisions on behalf of their patrons, who wished to associate themselves with each tradition. This is apparent from the building works of the Artuqids in Amid (Diyarbakir) and Dunaysir (modern-day Kızıltepe). Squeezed between the Ayyubid territories in northern Syria and those around Mayyafariqin, they also began to build similar square minarets at the end of the twelfth century to signal their general cultural allegiance with Syria.[31] The minaret at Mayyafariqin thus brought the city within a distinct visual tradition; and in doing so it also served to distinguish the city from the rival Turkish-led Muslim communities in central Anatolia.

Walls

Whilst the skyline of the city gave the first clues as to its religious identity, the cumulative nature of the silhouette created, with its mixture of church domes and minarets, may have left those approaching it uncertain as to which religion or faction dominated, and who was in charge. Such issues began to be resolved as they drew nearer to the city, to encounter its walls. In the culture of campaigning that was endemic across the Caucasus, Anatolia and Syria, walls were an essential feature of all cities, whether controlled by Christians or Muslims.

City walls were primarily about defence, and so their form and development responded to changes in military technologies and tactics. This led to many common features that can be found in city walls across the region at the start of the thirteenth century. Massive towers began to be included in wall circuits: at Ani, the towers either side of the Kars Gate [Fig. 36]; at Amid the massive Ulu Baden tower and its partner the Yedi Kardeş of 1207–8, with diameters of 25 metres; at Damascus the new towers of the citadel of around 1200, nearly 30 metres in diameter; and at Alanya the Red Tower of 1226, with a diameter of 29 metres.[32] All were probably built on this scale in order to allow counterweight trebuchets to be mounted on top of them. These weapons had been developed at the end of the twelfth century to attack cities, but could also now be employed to defend them; mounted on the city walls, their long range prevented attacking forces from being able to

[30] O. Aslanapa, *Turkish Art and Architecture* (London, 1971), 100.
[31] J. M. Bloom, *Minaret: Symbol of Islam* (Oxford, 1989), 166.
[32] P. E. Chevedden, 'The Citadel of Damascus' (Ph.D. thesis, UCLA, 1986), 277–86.

Figure 36 Kars Gate at Ani, Turkey; thirteenth century

set up their own weapons within striking distance. The new invention was celebrated in a luxury manuscript produced for Saladin [Fig. 37].[33]

The walls demarcated the extent of the city – what was in and what was out – creating a defined space with which its inhabitants could identify. The increased scale of the walls presented new opportunities to exploit their surfaces as ways of displaying the city and its identity to those approaching it. The design of walls and the decoration incorporated into them became fields onto which the civic, corporate ideals of the city could be projected. They also provided the theatrical backdrop against which ceremonies could be performed, and made statements about the ambitions of their rulers.

[33] C. Cahen, 'Un traité d'armurerie composé pour Saladin', *BEO* 12 (1948), 103–63.

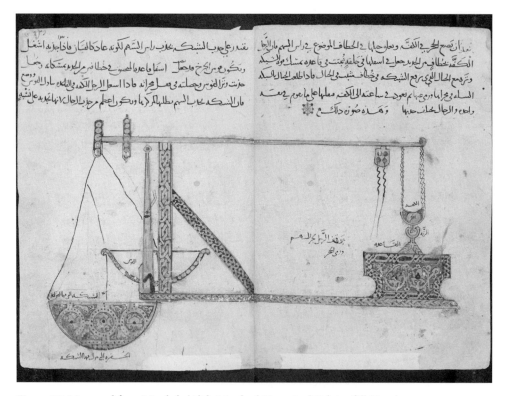

Figure 37 Mangonel from Murda b. ʿAli b. Murda al-Tarsusi, *al-Tabsira fi 'l-Hurub* (The explanation of the masters of the quintessence [of military knowledge]), made for Saladin; late twelfth century (Oxford, Bodleian Library, MS Huntington 264, fols. 135a–134b; 25.5 × 39 cm)

All these can be investigated through the walls of Ani. The double line of walls, a lower outer bastion and a higher inner wall, that still exists today, was constructed by the Mqargrdzelis between their capture of the city in 1199 and about 1220. They created a formidable barrier along the northern edge of the city, the one side of the triangular site that was not protected by natural ravines. However, the Mqargrdzeli walls were not built *ex-novo*; their impressive run of gates, towers and walls was made simply by adding cladding around earlier walls. The original tenth-century walls of the Bagratunis had already been extended in the twelfth century by the Shaddadids, but now the Mqargrdzelis encased all those earlier defences to create thicker and substantially taller fortifications. This allowed the Mqargrdzelis to change completely the character of what had gone before.[34]

[34] J.-P. Mahé, N. Faucherre and B. Karamağaralı, 'L'enceinte urbaine d'Ani (Turquie Orientale): problèmes chronologiques', *Comptes Rendus de l'Académie des Inscriptions et Belles-Lettres* 143/2 (1999), 731–56.

Figure 38 Polychrome stonework cross and khatchkar on tower 5 at Ani, Turkey; thirteenth century

The Arabic inscriptions which had been set up to mark each new addition to the walls during Ani's century of Shaddadid rule were simply bricked in behind the new walls. This memory of Islamic rule was effaced, to be replaced by the apparent permanence of the Christian fortifications. Only since the gradual collapse of the walls have some of the earlier Muslim texts been revealed. Thus the inscription of Minuchihr, first Emir of the city, which was originally set up beside the Lion Gate, the most important and prominent gate along the circuit of walls, was lost for centuries.[35] In place of these Muslim texts, new inscriptions were added to the walls. Monumental writing thereby became a marker of identity, and defence.

Sections of the wall used the different coloured tufas available in the quarries around the city to create crosses in the masonry and so fuse them into the very core of the defences [Fig. 38]. In addition, khatchkars, Armenian memorial cross-stones, were mortared in to the ashlar faces of the walls, or placed in niches by the city gates. These were symbols of both military and spiritual victory. But even these were not unambiguous markers of the religion of the city's rulers: visitors to Ayyubid-ruled Mayyafariqin would

[35] M. N. Khanykof, 'Excursion à Ani, en 1848', in M. F. Brosset, 'Ire livraison: 3e Rapport: Edchmiadzin, Ani', in *Rapports sur un voyage archéologique dans la Géorgie et dans l'Arménie exécuté en 1847–48* (St Petersburg, 1849), 121–52, at 142–3. Other inscriptions are noted in Mahé, Faucherre, and Karamağaralı, 'L'enceinte urbaine d'Ani' at 755; and Minorsky, *Studies in Caucasian History*, 106, addition to p. 88: a mutilated Kufic inscription in poor Arabic which names the builder of a gate as Fakhr al-Din Shaddad. Arabic inscriptions are now gathered in Khachatrian, *Korpus arabskikh nadpisei Armenii*, nos. 24–5.

also have faced a great cross that still stood on the city's south-west tower, believed by all to have been made by the same craftsman who made the cross that stood atop the church of the Holy Sepulchre in Jerusalem, and so an especially venerable and efficacious object.[36]

Walls tried to specify the nature of their defence. At Kars, just to the west of Ani, inscriptions proclaimed that the walls had been built 'by Christians' and were 'against foreigners',[37] whereas at Bayburt, further west again, the walls built by Mugith al-Din Tughrilshah in 1213 included honorifics proclaiming him as 'the glory of Islam and Muslims, the crusher of infidels and polytheists'.[38] Even to those who could not read, the ability to recognise an alphabet, and so to observe the switch at Ani from Armenian to Arabic lettering and back, announced the ascendant force inside the city. To those who could read (and were prepared to take the time to do so), inscriptions were able to proclaim even more.[39]

Inscriptions could be used to proclaim imperial ambitions. At Antalya the Seljuk sultan Kayka'us I set up a vast inscription to celebrate his reconquest of the city in 1216 (its citizens had rebelled in 1212, following the initial conquest in 1207 by his father, Kaykhusraw I). Set up on the ends of forty-two marble columns, the inscription was spaced out along the walls of the city, effectively encircling it; this was Kayka'us' victory text, a *Fatihname*, to recount the history of the rebellion and his subsequent recapture of the city after a month-long siege.[40] However, such an extensive and well coordinated programme of inscriptions was exceptional. More often city walls were marked by a whole series of separate inscriptions that commemorated the building of individual parts of the walls and which celebrated the power and titles of the city's ruler. At Ani, the Mqargrdzeli family are named in eleven inscriptions set up along the walls between 1207 and 1223; they rejoice in rehearsing their Georgian court titles of *atabeg* (borrowed from the Islamic world), *mandaturtukhutsesi* and *amirspasalar*, simply transliterated into Armenian, as well as some of the Armenian ones they adopted, including *sparapet* and *baron* (borrowed from the Frankish Crusaders). At Amid (Diyarbakir) we find the Artuqid equivalent. The great towers

---

[36] Le Strange, *The Lands of the Eastern Caliphate*, 112.
[37] I. A. Orbeli, 'Armianskie nadpisi na kamne', in *Izbrannye Trudy* (Yerevan, 1963), 469–76, at 470–1.
[38] S. Redford, *Legends of Authority: The 1215 Seljuk Inscriptions of Sinop Citadel, Turkey* (Istanbul, 2014), 271; Khachatrian, *Korpus arabskikh nadpisei Armenii*, no. 117.
[39] A. Eastmond, 'Inscriptions and Authority in Ani', in *Der Doppeladler: Byzanz und die Seldschuken in Anatolien vom späten 11. bis zum 13. Jahrhundert*, eds. N. Asutay-Effenberger and F. Daim (Mainz, 2014), 71–84.
[40] S. Redford and G. Leiser, *Victory Inscribed: The Seljuk Fetihnāme on the Citadel Walls of Antalya, Turkey* (Antalya, 2008).

Figure 39 The Ulu Baden tower, Amid (Diyarbakir), Turkey, constructed by Nasir al-Din Artuq Arslan; 1207–8

erected in 1207–8 at the south-west corner of the city, the Ulu Baden and the Yedi Kardeş, are both dominated by huge inscriptions displaying the titles and universal pretensions of its ruler, Nasir al-Din Artuq Arslan (r. 1201–22 in Diyarbakir, to 1232 in Mardin) [Fig. 39].[41]

The quantity of inscriptions set up on walls gives other information that can provide insights into the social structure of the city and the way in which it wished to display this to all viewers. It was common practice throughout Anatolia for the overall design of city walls to be overseen by the ruler, but for wealthy courtiers to 'sponsor' individual towers (often at swordpoint). This was the practice adopted at Sinop on the Black Sea coast, which was captured from its Byzantine rulers by Kayka'us I in 1215, just before he turned to besiege Antalya. After taking the city, the sultan immediately set about rebuilding its walls, and co-opted the finance of his emirs to complete the work. As a dubious reward for this, twelve emirs from nine different cities were permitted to include their names in the inscriptions.[42] The size

---

[41] M. van Berchem, *Amida: Matériaux pour l'épigraphie et l'histoire musulmanes du Diyar-Bakir* (Heidelberg, 1910), 91–3.

[42] S. Redford, 'Sinop in the Summer of 1215: The Beginning of Anatolian Seljuk Architecture', *Ancient Civilizations from Scythia to Siberia* 16 (2010), 125–49, 538; Redford, *Legends of Authority*, 153–233.

of the inscribed block, the length of the text and the prominence of its placement on the city walls were carefully controlled, and so reveal the relative seniority and importance of each emir, as well as the jealousy between them. As an ensemble the inscriptions bear witness to the emergence of a sense of a cohesive body to the Seljuk state, now conceived of as more than just a collection of separate cities, although marked by internal rivalries between its emirs. The rewards for the emirs did not always match the expenditure. When Kayka'us' brother Kaykubad tried the same trick in 1221 after his capture of Kalonoros (which he renamed Alaiya after himself; now Alanya), the cost of the new fortifications ruined his emirs: 'all of their wealth was spent and hatred of the sultan filled their hearts'.[43] Occasionally we find royal women involved in the construction of defences, as at Bayburt in 1213, where the Mengujekid princess Khalisat al-Dunya wa'l-Din commissioned the most impressive tower at the citadel (with equally impressive calligraphy to celebrate her contribution).[44]

At Ani, the variety of inscriptions reveals a very different social agenda. The foundation texts reveal that the citizens who were expected (or permitted) to pay for walls came from a much broader social base than the emirs who financed Seljuk walls. For example, in 1219 an otherwise unknown Christian Armenian woman, Mamkhatun, left money in her will for the construction of a tower on the north-eastern ramparts of the city [Fig. 40]; and her mother, Shanush, paid for a second tower nearby.[45] Mamkhatun's inscription reads:

> In 668 of the era, through the grace of Christ I Mamkhatun, daughter of Khacheres Loretsi went to Christ unexpectedly. From the legitimately earned silver of my father which he had given to me, so that I would not be forgotten, I built this tower in memory of me to Christ. Now I beg you who read, plead for our forgiveness from Christ.

The form of the women's inscriptions is very close to that of donations in churches, suggesting that they viewed their gifts to the walls as pious endowments, which both invoked Christ's aid in the defence of the city and served to preserve their memories among the living, who might then pray to expedite their entry into heaven. However, once more reflecting the mixed world in which these people lived, the phrasing borrowed words from Arabic: the silver funding the tower is described as 'halal'.

---

[43] H. Crane, 'Notes on Saldjuq Architectural Patronage in Thirteenth Century Anatolia', *Journal of the Economic and Social History of the Orient* 36 (1993), 1–57, at 9–10, citing the *Tarikh Al-i Saljuq*.
[44] Redford, *Legends of Authority*, 112–18, 270.
[45] Orbeli, *Corpus Inscriptionum Armenicarum*, nos. 5 and 8.

Figure 40 The tower of Mamkhatun (tower 62) at Ani, Turkey; 1219

Other towers at Ani were paid for by men who appear to have held no title or position at court, including Eghbayrik, who called himself 'servant of his lord Tigran' in his inscription. This Tigran was almost certainly Tigran Honents, the wealthy merchant who founded the church in the eastern corner of the city, and who also paid for the repair of the cathedral in 1213.[46] The relationship to Tigran suggests that Eghbayrik too was a merchant. This public acknowledgement of men outside the ranks of the nobility and of women in the defence of Ani suggests a degree of social mobility and inclusion not apparent in Muslim-controlled cities. This finds corroboration in inscriptions set up on the walls of the neighbouring city of Kars: 'Summer 683 of the Armenian era [= 1234]. By the grace of God and the favour of our king Rusudan, we, the Christians of Kars, great and small, built these towers in our memory and that of our [royal] mistress'; a neighbouring inscription says much the same, appending 'at our own expense'.[47] At Ani, many towers include plaques prepared for inscriptions that were never added, suggesting that in these instances the individual finance was not forthcoming.

---

[46] Orbeli, *Corpus Inscriptionum Armenicarum*, no. 20; Mahé, 'Le testament de Tigran Honenc'', 1323 n.18; for Honents' inscription at the cathedral: Orbeli, *Corpus Inscriptionum Armenicarum*, no. 100.

[47] Orbeli, 'Armianskie nadpisi na kamne', 471.

The inscriptions at Ani and Kars show that these Christian cities were governed in a different way from those under Muslim control. It appears that their citizens had greater control over their cities, and consequently were expected to be more closely involved in their maintenance and defence. The decision to celebrate the communal nature of the financing of their fortifications in such a public way is strikingly different from that of Muslim-run cities. Akhlat seems to fall between these two models. Given that it was under Muslim government, first under the Shah-i Armens and then the Ayyubids, Akhlat's fortifications would most likely have been financed by the city's emirs. However, the role played by the citizens of Akhlat during the negotiations for Tamta's marriage and their ability to keep the Ayyubid garrison confined to its barracks in the citadel suggest that despite its Muslim rulers, the city was still dominated by its Christian inhabitants. It is therefore possible that they may have equally been involved in the organisation of the city's defences, perhaps commemorated in a similar way to those at Ani and Kars.

The choice of language and alphabet for each inscription meant that they were directed at different audiences. A decision to use Armenian, Arabic or Georgian prioritised one group in the population of each city at the expense of others.[48] In only one case is a bilingual text known: an Arabic–Greek inscription at Sinop (1215), showing for once recognition of the multiple audiences that witnessed these texts [Fig. 41].[49] For other inhabitants in each city the language was an alienating factor, a reminder of the dominant power at the time. However, for every group of viewers the very presence of writing may have conferred some symbolic protection upon the city defences, as all the peoples in the region recognised the intimate link between writing and divine power. Both Islam and Christianity were religions of the Book, and both therefore placed great weight upon the power of the word, most explicitly recognised in the opening verse of St John's Gospel: 'In the beginning was the Word, and the Word was with God, and the Word was God.'

Elsewhere on the walls other visual protective symbols were incorporated.[50] A final layer of defence on Mamkhatun's tower at Ani (as well as a second tower just to its west) came in the form of two serpent-like dragons, who wrap themselves around the tower, binding its masonry together

---

[48] Eastmond, 'Inscriptions and Authority in Ani'.
[49] Redford, *Legends of Authority*, 235–43.
[50] A. Eastmond, 'Other Encounters: Popular Belief and Cultural Convergence in Anatolia and the Caucasus', in *Islam and Christianity in Anatolia and the Caucasus*, eds. A. C. S. Peacock, B. De Nicola and S. N. Yıldız (Farnham, 2015), 183–213.

Figure 41 Bilingual inscription of Badr al-Din Abu Bakr, Emir of Simre, on the walls of Sinop, Turkey; 1214

like the tie-hoops on a barrel. At one level this imagery was talismanic. Ferocious beasts, dragons were known to lurk around thresholds, destined forever to lie on the boundary between inside and out, between real and mythic, between order and disorder.⁵¹ At another level, animals could be seen as symbols of authority. The most common such motif was the lion, whose easy association with grace, power and intelligence meant that it was employed throughout the region by all different factions. A striding lion was placed over the main gate at Ani, where it was equally appropriate to the city's Armenian and then Seljuk rulers (the name of the Seljuk conqueror

---

⁵¹ S. Kuehn, *The Dragon in Medieval East Christian and Islamic Art* (Leiden; Boston, 2011), 5–13. Talismanic imagery is discussed further in Chapter 8.

Figure 42 Ceramic bowls (*bacini*) inserted into the walls of Ani, Turkey; thirteenth century

of the city, Kılıç Arslan, translates as 'Sword Lion'). And in 1203 al-Awhad included two lions either side of the sun above his foundation inscription on the walls at Mayyafariqin [Fig. 25].[52] Falcons and eagles were also popular in this role, most visibly on the Ulu Baden and Yedi Kardeş towers at Amid, where they appear alongside other beasts and extensive inscriptions. The inscriptions and animals worked in unison to tie the city's wall together: the Arabic texts seems to stretch round the walls much like the serpents at Ani, and the inscription on the Yedi Kardeş tower incorporates Turkic vocabulary in its Arabic text to describe the Sultan as a falcon.

The functions of other forms of decoration are less clear. The walls of Ani and Bayburt both have hollowed-out depressions into which blue-green ceramics were embedded, similar to the *bacini* added to churches in Italy from the twelfth century on [Fig. 42].[53] It is possible that these were also apotropaic, or were designed to convey a dynastic message about the walls' builders. They certainly demonstrate the expense that was invested in the walls.

These visual symbols may once have been much more common than the few surviving reliefs suggest. Recently the ramparts of the citadel at Antalya

---

[52] RCEA IX, 3555; *TEI*, 8288.
[53] Redford, *Legends of Authority*, 122–8; figs. 102–12; compare K. R. Mathews, 'Other Peoples' Dishes: Islamic Bacini on Eleventh-Century Churches in Pisa', *Gesta* 53/1 (2014), 5–23.

have been discovered to have been painted with pseudo-heraldic images of lions and griffins.⁵⁴ Indeed, extensive external painting, often employing a striking red-and-white zig-zag, has been noted on many Seljuk buildings and walls.⁵⁵ Anyone approaching these cities would have been able to recognise the many common elements that they shared in terms of their visual vocabulary of defence and power; however, they would equally have been able to recognise the religious and cultural differences between them. The shared visual language was being put to very different uses.

Walls and Spolia

Walls could be exploited in one further way to convey aspects of a city's identity, through the public display of spolia: reused stones, reliefs and sculptures.⁵⁶ These established a city's relationship to the past, demonstrating its history and building an image of continuity or rupture. Such a practice could only be undertaken in regions rich in earlier ruins (although, as we will see in Chapter 9, there was a market for the transport of such spolia, often of vast size and over considerable distances). Even when spolia were available, it was a conscious choice whether and how to exploit them. The Ayyubids in Syria, with the wealth of antiquities and ancient structures that were available from the long histories of occupation in cities such as Aleppo, Damascus or Harran, do not seem to have chosen to make visual statements with these antiquities, despite the extensive use of spolia by the Zangids who preceded them in these cities.⁵⁷ The minaret in the Great Mosque at Aleppo, for example, may well have been built with stones taken from the earlier Byzantine cathedral on the site, but this re-use was not made visible.⁵⁸ The Ayyubids' cousins in Egypt did use spolia, but in a very limited way. In a number of monuments, including the madrasa of al-Salih Ayyub (built 1242–4), the threshold is built around a pharaonic granite

---

⁵⁴ N. Krabbenhöft, 'A Veneer of Power: Thirteenth-Century Seljuk Frescoes on the Walls of Alanya and Some Recommendations for their Preservation' (MA thesis, Koç University, 2011), online at http://nkrabben.com/docs/PaintedCityWallsofAlanya_Krabbenhoeft_Thesis.pdf.

⁵⁵ S. Redford, *Landscape and the State in Medieval Anatolia: Seljuk Gardens and Pavilions of Alanya, Turkey* (Oxford, 2000).

⁵⁶ S. Redford, 'The Seljuqs of Rum and the Antique', *Muqarnas* 10 (1993), 148–56; S. Redford, 'Words, Books, and Buildings in Seljuk Anatolia', in *Identity and Identity Formation in the Ottoman World: Essays in Honor of Norman Itzkowitz*, eds. B. Tezcan and K. K. Barbir (Madison, WI, 2007), 7–16.

⁵⁷ T. Allen, *A Classical Revival in Islamic Architecture* (Wiesbaden, 1986), ix–x, 100–1; J. Raby, 'Nur al-Din, the Qastal al-Shu'aybiyya and the "Classical Revival"', *Muqarnas* 21 (2004), 289–310, esp. 300–1.

⁵⁸ Bloom, *The Minaret*, 254.

Figure 43 Re-used spolia on the walls of Konya (engraving from L. de Laborde, *Voyage en Orient* (Paris, 1838), fig. 117)

slab, its hieroglyphs still visible.[59] In the same way that worshippers at Nakhchivan stepped on the cross taken from Ani, the worshippers in Cairo were expected to trample down the ancient religions that had once dominated the Nile valley.

In Anatolia, the Seljuks took a very different approach to the material evidence of earlier cultures. The walls of Konya and Ankara were rebuilt in the early thirteenth century, and at both cities they made the most of the Roman antiquities that surrounded them. Classical statues and reliefs were embedded in the cities' walls. At Konya a male nude – possibly a statue of Herakles – was set up outside the city gate [Fig. 43]; at Ankara Roman altars, herms and classical inscriptions were built into the walls. The placement of these works advertised the cities' rulers as the legitimate successors of the Roman world. The Byzantines always referred to themselves as 'Romans' ('Byzantine' is an anachronistic label applied only since the sixteenth century), and the Seljuks similarly referred to the state they created on former Byzantine territory as the land of 'Rum' – i.e. Rome. The Byzantines had long used the

---

[59] Creswell, *The Muslim Architecture of Egypt*, 101.

Figure 44 Copper dirham of Najm al-Din Alpi, Artuqid ruler of Mardin, 1152–76

classical past to underpin their rule in the present, and they could look to Constantinople, whose walls and public spaces (up to 1204 at least) were adorned with classical statuary, to support this claim.[60] The Golden Gate, the main ceremonial entrance to Constantinople, was adorned with reliefs showing the twelve labours of Herakles.[61] There was certainly a local audience for antiquities in Anatolia in the thirteenth century. Najm al-Din Alpi, Artuqid ruler of Mardin 1152–76, produced coins imitating tetradrachms of Antiochos VIII (r. 121–96 BC) (although only the portrait of the ruler, not the statue of Zeus on the reverse) [Figs. 44 and 45]; his son, Qutb al-Din Ghazi II (r. 1176–84), produced portraits imitating those of Constantine the Great (r. AD 303–37).[62] In both cases the rulers sought to associate their own power with that of great rulers from the past, regardless of their religious beliefs.

However, the monumental spolia of the Seljuks were differently conceived. The visibility and prominence of the classical reliefs – usually located close to city gates – were clearly to announce the Seljuks' (largely fictional) links to the past, but the details of their placement suggest a desire to dissociate themselves from their specific meanings of each antiquity. The statue outside Konya was headless, and the herms, inscriptions and altars at Ankara were all inverted or placed sideways. The care with which this was done shows a recognition of the alien beliefs that each stone represented,

---

[60] S. G. Bassett, *The Urban Image of Late Antique Constantinople* (Cambridge, 2004).
[61] As recorded by Manuel Chrysoloras, *PG* 156, 45; cited in C. Mango, 'Antique Statuary and the Byzantine Beholder', *DOP* 17 (1963), 55–75, at 70.
[62] E. Georganteli, 'Transposed Images: Currencies and Legitimacy in the Late Medieval Eastern Mediterranean', in *Byzantines, Latins, and Turks in the Eastern Mediterranean World after 1150*, eds. J. Harris, C. Holmes and E. Russell (Oxford, 2012), 141–79, coins 3b and 4b.

Figure 45 Silver tetradrachm of Antiochos VIII, issued 121–113 BC

and a desire to constrain and harness any ancient powers they might contain; suitably tamed they could now be used to bolster rather than subvert the defences of each city. The relationship to the past was a complex one: at the same time as fearing the pagan power of classical imagery, Kaykhusraw II celebrated that of its rulers, and called himself a second Alexander in the inscription he set up at Kirkgöz Han to the north of Antalya in 1238-9.[63] The alien reliefs at Konya were further domesticated by being placed alongside modern relief carvings, such as the jinn over the bazaar gate, which also function as guardians of the city's safety and security [Fig. 46].[64] The placement of the statues gave them an apotropaic, talismanic quality; the serpents on the towers at Ani may well have been an attempt to replicate this in an area that did not have access to antiquities. This supranatural universe that ran in parallel to the physical world is one we shall return to in Chapter 9.

Citadels

Once within the city, the visitor would have faced one further line of fortification, which guarded the government and palace quarters from the rest of the city. Akhlat had such a citadel, of which only the ruins of a later Ottoman fort now remain, but it must have been a well-defended site within the city, given that its prime purpose at the start of Ayyubid rule was to protect the garrison from the population. At Ani the remains of the Bagratuni

---

[63] S. Redford, 'The Inscription of the Kirkgöz Han and the Problem of Textual Transmission in Seljuk Anatolia', *Adalya* 12 (2009), 347–60, at 350.

[64] C. Texier, *Description de l'Asie Mineure faite par Ordre du gouvernement Français de 1833 à 1837* (Paris, 1839–49), 2: pl. 97.

Figure 46 Gateway at Konya (engraving in C. Texier, *Description de l'Asie Mineure faite par Ordre du gouvernement Français de 1833 à 1837* (Paris, 1839–49), 2: pl. 97)

Figure 47 Lion and bull relief at the citadel arch in Amid (Diyarbakir), Turkey; 1206/7

walls that cut off the palace complex at the tip of the city are still discernible by the mosque of Minuchihr. More formidable defences survive elsewhere, most famously the citadel on the rock at Van that loomed over the medieval city, or that in the heart of Aleppo, which was largely rebuilt under Ayyubid rule. With its stone-clad slopes, and heavily fortified entrance reached only across a viaduct, the Aleppo citadel still dominates the city, and gives some idea of the aura of power that these strongholds could project. Like outer city walls, the citadel defences, a complex sequence of gates, passageways and sharp turns begun in 1182, were complemented by visual guards: more inscriptions and talismanic images of entwined serpents and lions. The entrance to the citadel at Amid, built in 1206/7, was similarly protected by inscriptions and reliefs: lions subjugate bulls in an elegant allegory of the triumph of graceful strength and cunning over brute force and unthinking rage [Fig. 47].

Roads

Between the outer walls and the citadel were the roads of the city, lined with houses, shops and workshops. They were punctuated by markets, caravanserais, baths, fountains, churches and mosques, and interspersed with gardens. These were the spaces for life, commerce and industry, but they also served ceremonial functions. Visitors' encounters with the city were structured by the road system, which progressively led up to the city walls,

Figure 48 Processional gate to the north of Ani, close to Horomos monastery, Turkey; tenth–eleventh century (engraving by Julius Kästner in M. F. Brosset, *Les ruines d'Ani, capitale de l'Arménie sous les rois Bagratides, aux Xe et XIe siècles: histoire et description. Atlas* (St Petersburg, 1860), pl. 29)

and then through them into the streets, which then framed the approach to the ruler in the citadel.

Before even entering it, the ceremonial nature of the city and its roads was declared. On the road to the north of Ani, near the monastery of Horomos, stood an isolated arch flanked by small towers containing chapels, a symbolic gateway to the city [Fig. 48].[65] It marked a notional outer limit of the city, and presumably acted as a staging point for processions. The interior of Ani does not seem to have had a planned road structure, but the major monuments and public spaces clustered along the principal road from the Lion Gate to the citadel, passing the mosque of Abu Maʿmaran, with its market, before moving on to the cathedral and mosque of Minuchihr, beyond

[65] R. H. Kévorkian, *Ani: capitale de l'Arménie en l'an mil* (Paris, 2001), pl. 53; from Brosset, *Les ruines d'Ani*, pl. XXIX; A. Kazaryan in Vardanyan, ed., *Hoṙomos Monastery*, 158–67.

which stood the walls to the citadel. In a city like Amid, which retained a memory of its Roman origins, the original grid plan survived in the two main roads, which bisected the city to meet at right angles at its centre. This gave the interior of the city the formal layout to match the grandeur of the walls. Streets were distinguished in a hierarchy of major and minor roads, following Islamic urban practice. Tigran Honents' inscription at Ani mentions the gift of houses in the alley of the grain merchants.[66] The term for alley, *zuqaq*, is an Arabic loan word, designating the smallest alleys, the third class of streets each set aside for particular trades, running off the secondary roads of the town.

Medieval texts are full of accounts of the citizens and nobility gathering outside the city to welcome returning heroes, diplomatic envoys or incoming brides to escort them back into the city. Nasir al-Din Sökmen II (r. 1128–85), the Shah-i Armen ruler of Akhlat, is recorded as coming out of his city to meet an ascetic Christian holy man 'to meet him with great pomp, and seeking his prayers, [he] escorted him with honour into the city'.[67] (Unfortunately this over-zealous holy man went on to criticise the 'fornicating' priests of the city, who then denounced him as a spy; he was stoned to death.) The same ruler celebrated his defeat of the Christian king Giorgi III of Georgia with a public feast and procession of the vast wealth he had captured from the Georgians before the city walls. We have already encountered the extensive procession in which Tamta's sister-in-law, Dayfa Khatun, arrived at Aleppo in 1212. Two decades later Dayfa Khatun's brother, al-Kamil, led his daughter 'Ashura Khatun on a grand procession through the streets of Cairo to celebrate her second marriage to her cousin al-Nasir Dawud (al-Kamil had previously forced them to divorce when he suspected the groom's loyalty).[68] Some idea of the magnificence of these processions comes from Ibn Jubayr's description of the arrival of two princesses at Mosul:

> They had adorned the necks of their camels with coloured silks and ornamental collars. The Mas'udi princess [Saljukshah] entered at the head of her troop of handmaidens, while before her was a body of the men who had conducted her. The dome of her litter was adorned with pieces of gold shaped like new moons, with dinars the size of the palm of the hand, and with chains and images of pleasing designs, so that hardly any part of the dome could be seen. The two beasts that bore her advanced with jaded steps, and the clatter of their trinkets filled the ears. The golden ornaments

---

[66] Mahé, 'Le testament de Tigran Honenc'', 1324, and discussion on 1332–3.
[67] Vardan, 205.

on the necks of her beasts and the mounts of her maidens formed together a sum of gold beyond estimation. It was indeed a sight that dazzled the eyes.[69]

The journey out of the city to meet the visitor was not only a sign of that visitor's status, but also an opportunity for the ruler then to use the city as an important part of his or her own display of pomp as they returned. The range of decoration and inscriptions, particularly around gates, shows the magnificent effect this might have. The walls could equally be used to humiliate visitors. After his defeat at the battle of Yassıçemen in 1230, where he foolishly allied himself with the Central Asian invader Jalal al-Din Khwarazmshah, Rukn al-Din Jahanshah, the ruler of Erzurum, was led back to his city and paraded before its walls in ridicule on the back of a mule, before being brutally killed.[70]

The Domestic World

The individual buildings that made up the city – its domestic and functional structures – are now harder to visualise: at ruined cities such as Akhlat, Ani or Harran, relatively few of these more mundane aspects of the city have attracted the attention of archaeologists. In surviving cities such as Aleppo, Amid or Raqqa the modern has buried the medieval beyond reach.[71] The private and public buildings of the city were sites for the display of individual identities. How people's lives were organised varied from city to city, and these offer different strategies for how they might have proclaimed themselves. It is likely that different groups clustered in different quarters, although there is little evidence for how carefully monitored these divisions were. In the thirteenth century the Crusader city of Acre was divided into self-governing fortified quarters, the largest controlled by the Venetians, the Genoese and the Hospitaller Knights, but this degree of separation was exceptional.[72] At Amid the separation occurred in a more subtle way, still evident in the city today. Identities there are now hidden behind

---

[68] Humphreys, *From Saladin to the Mongols*, 222, 228–31.   [69] Ibn Jubayr, 246.

[70] S. Redford, 'Paper, Stone, Scissors:'Alā' al-Dīn Kayqubād, 'Iṣmat al-Dunyā wa l-Dīn, and the Writing of Seljuk History', in *The Seljuks of Anatolia. Court and Society in the Medieval Middle East*, eds. A. C. S. Peacock and S. N. Yıldız (London; New York, 2013), 151–70, at 163, gives all the variant accounts of Rukn al-Din's fate.

[71] A. Yoltar-Yıldırım, 'Raqqa: The Forgotten Excavation of an Islamic Site in Syria by the Ottoman Imperial Museum in the Early Twentieth Century', *Muqarnas* 30 (2013), 73–93.

[72] D. Pringle, *The Churches of the Crusader Kingdom of Jerusalem: A Corpus*, 4: *The Cities of Acre and Tyre* (Cambridge, 2009), 5; D. Jacoby, 'Crusader Acre in the Thirteenth Century: Urban Layout and Topography', *Studi Medievali series 3* 20/1 (1979), 1–45.

compound walls. Even if you can see a church tower or a minaret ahead of you across the city, finding the building itself is difficult in the warren of streets, which provide only fleeting glimpses before a corner is reached and another high wall blocks any further view. All buildings are set back in their compounds behind unvariegated blank, black basalt walls with small, inconspicuous entrances. They suggest that discretion was an important element in everyone's identity, providing security through anonymity. This was presumably the result of the contested nature of public spaces. Tigran Honents' church in Ani was similarly secluded from the city behind a compound wall. Located on the side of the ravine down to the river Akurean, the church was a prominent monument facing visitors approaching from the east, but its dome would not have been visible from within the city itself. Given the tensions in all the cities in the region throughout this period, it is likely that such strategies were common, in order to maximise individual security without ever compromising on faith: buildings were secluded, not hidden. The monuments proclaimed their faith from afar, and only became invisible on closer inspection.

Even among those individuals with the wealth and confidence to show off their status, it is difficult to establish their identity through architecture. A description of Konya in the thirteenth century implies that the only distinctions came from wealth:

> The houses of the merchants and *ikdish* [implying converts to Islam, or people of mixed race] are more elevated than those of the artisans; the palaces of the emirs are more elevated than those of the merchants; the domes and palaces of the sultans are yet more elevated than all the others.[73]

This is confirmed by the one major private residence that survives in Ani, on the west side of the city [Fig. 49]. With extensive substructures to act as warehousing facilities, it was presumably a wealthy merchant's residence, and has an impressive street façade. It has been given many names by visitors since the nineteenth century – the house of the baron, the palace of the merchant, the sultan's serai – and it has been linked both with Christian owners, such as the merchant Tigran Honents or the semi-royal Pahlavuni family who controlled extensive territories around Ani, and with Muslims (on the basis of no concrete evidence in either case). This variety reflects the problems in associating the structure with any clear individual or group. The entrance façade is decorated with polychrome stone tiles, eight-pointed

---

[73] Aflaki, 164; C. Cahen, *The Formation of Turkey. The Seljukid Sultanate of Rum: Eleventh to Fourteenth Century* (London, 2001), 114.

Figure 49 The so-called palace of the baron, Ani, Turkey; early thirteenth century

stars in a reddish-brown stone, each decorated with a different interlace design, are interspersed with cross-shaped tiles in a black tufa. This tile design is identical to that employed in Seljuk palace and bath architecture in the early thirteenth century, appearing in the Seljuk palace at Kubadabad and the baths of Mahperi Khatun in Kayseri (1237–38) [Fig. 88]. The language of wealth and luxury was not tied to any cultural or religious divisions.

City of the Dead

The final city was the city of the dead, with which this chapter opened. This too contributed to the city's identity, and indeed may have helped form

Figure 50 Christian cemetery, Akhlat, Turkey (photo by Walter Bachmann, *c.* 1913)

the first impressions of it, along with its silhouette and its walls. Tombs and cemeteries were placed alongside the roads leading up to cities. At Ani tombs were cut into the cliffs on the further side of the ravines opposite the town; at Akhlat great cemeteries surrounded the town. The Muslim cemetery at Akhlat still survives; its tombstones include the earliest surviving monuments from the city, dating to the lifetime of Tamta. The cemeteries now cover a huge area and are the principal draw to the area for tourists. However, in the thirteenth century the cemeteries were even more extensive; for alongside the Muslim cemeteries were Christian ones, which are now completely destroyed. They are only known through one photograph taken by Walter Bachmann before 1913 [Figs. 50 and 51], showing a member of his expedition standing beside an Armenian khatchkar (cross-stone). From a distance the Christian khatchkars and Muslim stones would have been hard to tell apart. In Bachmann's photograph the Muslim stones appear taller and thinner than their Christian equivalents, but most khatchkars that we know of from the thirteenth century tend to be similarly proportioned to their Muslim cousins. Both types also usually have overhanging cornices at the top to protect the main face of the stone from the weather; and both were set up to face west. It is only on closer inspection that their symbolic repertoire – dominated by the cross on the khatchkars – and their choice of alphabet became apparent, allowing the different communities of the dead to be distinguished.

Figure 51 Muslim cemetery, Akhlat, Turkey (photo by Walter Bachmann, c. 1913). The photographs reinforce the religious identity of each cemetery by the careful choice of companion and dress

Life in Akhlat

The fabric of the city provided many ways of displaying an identity: it enabled shows of faith, of power, status and wealth; it allowed a city's cultural orientation to be manifested, in relation to the cultures around it, but also to those that had preceded it. Akhlat and the other cities of eastern Anatolia emerge from this account as places of mixed populations, whose identities fluctuated thanks to the wide movement of invaders coming in, of traders passing through, and of inhabitants moving out as employment took them elsewhere in the region. At no point are we dealing with hermetically sealed groups, but intermingling communities, with extensive and extended religious, political and cultural exchanges. These realities of life were determined by the nature of life in the city.

Economy

Akhlat's economy was primarily monetary. The city was able to generate taxation from three sources: land, manufacturing and trade. These sources underwrote most medieval economies, and the relative importance of each varied from city to city, depending on the quality of the agricultural land, the proximity of mines and natural resources and the local craft expertise built up over generations. Akhlat's location ensured that agriculture and trade were both important to its economy alongside manufacturing. To the west of Akhlat lay the plain of Taron, some 3,000 square kilometres of fertile soil, irrigated by the river Aratsani, a tributary of the Euphrates.[74] For trade, it lay on the north–south roads that linked the Black Sea and the Mediterranean, and the east–west routes that led from the Mediterranean to Iran and the Silk Road.

The main north–south trade that passed through Anatolia in the thirteenth century was the trafficking of slaves. The Ayyubid army was predominantly made up of Kipchaq Turkish slave-soldiers (mamluks). Taken as slaves from the Crimea and the steppes of the Volga basin, young boys were transported across Anatolia to Egypt and Syria where they were trained in *furusiyya* (the art of cavalry warfare), taught Arabic, and converted to Islam before being set free and enlisted in the army. In the early 1230s Baybars, the first great Mamluk sultan of Egypt, passed through Anatolia to be sold at auction in Sivas. Divriği, which had close links to Akhlat in the 1220s, similarly thrived on the slave trade. Other trade goods, notably furs, are also recorded as being imported from the north, but slaves dominated.

East–west trade was more diverse. Long-distance goods were dominated by the light and easily transportable silks and spices from which the Silk Road took its name, and by high-value materials such as lapis lazuli from Afghanistan. However, the bulk of goods came over shorter distances, including ceramics, metalwork and textiles. Excavations from the major Mqargrdzeli city of Dvin have found evidence for the extensive import of glazed ceramics from Iran[75] and glass from Aleppo and Damascus, and from Rustavi in Georgia. The city also had its own local manufacturing expertise. It was famed for its red cloth, and had a large quarter for its own ceramic production.[76] There is extensive evidence for ceramic production in Tbilisi, Dmanisi and Rustavi in this period in Georgia.[77] The diversity of goods manufactured and transported was staggering: a thirteenth-century Persian geographer listed as 'Tiflis-goods' (i.e. from Tbilisi in Georgia) saddles, bridles, quivers, ivory-encrusted bow-cases, sweetmeats, garnets, beaver and otter skins, glass, drinking bowls, excellent cut glass and slaves. It goes on to mention ceramics, glass, weapons, jewellery, furs and other high-value goods.[78] And from the 1272 *waqf* document for a madrasa founded

---

[74] R. H. Hewsen, 'The Historical Geography of Baghesh/Bitlis and Taron/Mush', in *Armenian Baghesh/Bitlis and Taron/Mush*, ed. R. G. Hovannisian (Costa Mesa, CA, 2001), 41–58, at 42.
[75] A. A. Kalantarian, *Dvin: histoire et archéologie de la ville médiévale* (Neuchâtel; Paris, 1996), 136.
[76] Kalantarian, *Dvin*, 92–3.
[77] M. Lordkipanidze, *Georgia in the XI–XII Centuries* (Tbilisi, 1987), 38.
[78] Lordkipanidze, *Georgia in the XI–XII Centuries*, 39.

in Kırşehir by its Emir, Nur al-Din ibn Jaja, we learn of a multiplicity of trades in that city, including saddlemakers, painters, kebab sellers, butchers, cobblers, carpenters, tailors, bakers, grocers, millers, ice sellers and tanners.[79]

Taxation

The corollary of economy is taxation. The cities of the region preserve extensive evidence about the nature of taxes collected in the city, and these records provide the background to Tamta's work to reduce taxes on monasteries in Taron and on Georgians in al-Ashraf's realm. A secondary function of city walls was to demarcate the area in which taxable activities could be undertaken, and the taxes levied on them. A fragmentary inscription from Mayyafariqin, set up on the city gate called the Gate of Deliverance (it had previously been known as the Gate of the Mirror) rebuilt by al-Ashraf between 1210 and 1215, hints at the range of goods and services that were being regulated inside his city walls: 'dyeing, salt, cheese, measuring [grain], the market for food products, ... cotton, sesame, the sheep market, the market for the beasts of burden, beverages, ... '.[80] And a Persian inscription set up on the mosque of Abu Maʿmaran in Ani in 1199 was aimed at the regulation of the sale of cotton goods in the city.[81]

Long before visitors to Ani saw that 1199 inscription, they would have been aware of the city's mercantile nature. It was presented to them before they even entered the city. The inscription set above the keystone over the main, inner arch of the Lion Gate, the most public and prominent of locations, did not concern the glories of its rulers, but rather the range of tolls and duties levied in the city:

> Through the mercy of the immortal Word of God, and for the long life of the king of kings, the God-crowned padishah, and of the country-builder prince of princes, possessed with God's wisdom, and under the reign of the country of Georgia, of which the capital of Ani has become part, and

---

[79] A. Temir, *Kırşehir emiri Caca oğlu Nur el-Din'in 1272 tarihli Arapça-Moğolca vakfiyesi = Die arabisch-mongolische Stiftungsurkunde von 1272 des Emirs von Kirşehi Caca Oğlu Nur el-Din* (Ankara, 1959), German summary, 281–301.

[80] Gabriel, *Voyages archéologiques*, 342, no. 119; no.118 gives the name of the gate and the name of al-Ashraf; *RCEA* X, 3827; *TEI*, 3904.

[81] L. T. Giuzal'ian, 'Persidskaia nadpis' Key-Sultana Sheddadi v Ani', in *XLV Akademiku N.Ia.Marru*, ed. I. I. Meshchaninov (Moscow; Leningrad, 1935), 629–41, at 633; translated, with amendments, in Minorsky, *Studies in Caucasian History*, 100. M. Khanykof, 'Quelques inscriptions musulmans, d'Ani et des environs de Bakou', *Bulletin de la classe des sciences historiques, philologiques et politiques de l'Académie Impériale des Sciences de Saint-Pétersbourg* 6/13–14 (1849), 193–200 also has a slightly erroneous transcription, unsurprising given the freezing temperature (-24°C) in which he worked.

during the rulership of the God-beloved patrons of the city, Grigor Agha and Hovhannes, and during the episcopacy of Lord Hovhannes, God the compassionate looked upon the hardship of this city and inspired an excellent plan in the hearts of *barons* Grigor and Hovhannes who restored this city of ours and reduced the collection of tax: the *mrur* and the *taghar*, the *hetsel*, the *ghapchun*, the *aiwsrtamar*, and the *drnagir* became the *daghma* and *muslajut*. And the tax of the episcopal see, which had been demanded was reduced as well, becoming again as it was in the beginning.[82]

The inscription runs over five lines, but fills less than a third of the block on which it was incised, suggesting that its creators were leaving ample space for extensive further tax information to be added in the future. The welcoming nature of the text – it concerns those taxes that have been remitted, after all – was presumably just a reminder of how many remained in place. The bewildering array of charges, most untranslatable and unknown, that are listed in this inscription (and who would have had the chance to read it, given that it was placed at the busiest, narrowest point in the city, with a constant flow of carts, horses, cattle, market goods and people in and out?) can easily be supplemented from the many other taxation inscriptions that appear throughout Armenia. They display the bureaucrats' eternal love of complication, interference and addition, commemorated through the Armenians' love of leaving a permanent record in stone of their words and edicts.

The inscriptions concerning city taxes cover all forms of import duties, as well as taxes on mills, sellers of dyes and other producers of foodstuffs. They give precise rates for the levies on pack animals entering the city, as well as the head taxes on cows, oxen and sheep going to market. Other inscriptions demarcated where products could be sold in the city, presumably in an effort to keep all the trade under the eyes of the tax assessors and collectors.[83] The economic imperative behind the announcements and their increasing number as the thirteenth century wore on reflected the declining fortunes of the city as trade dwindled; they represented the authorities' ultimately futile attempts to lure it back. However, the inscriptions dress the remissions up as pious rather than fiscal acts. Blessings are called upon those who observe the various tax remissions, and curses on those who disobey – 'may he share the fate of Judas and Cain', 'may he be charged with the sins of the city'. This final curse was added to one of the rare laws that increased restrictions, in this case a law banning Sunday trading introduced in 1269 in response to an

---

[82] Orbeli, *Corpus Inscriptionum Armenicarum*, no. 1; trans. in Basmadjian, *Inscriptions arméniennes d'Ani*, no. 24. Basmadjian argues it pre-dates 1072; but the reference to Ani becoming part of Georgia suggests that it dates to the twelfth century at the earliest.

[83] Eastmond, 'Inscriptions and Authority in Ani'.

earthquake. (Evidently the earthquake was seen as a judgement from God. In the 1280s Yovhannes of Erzincan proposed a similar ban as a means for Armenians in the city to re-establish their morals and distinguish themselves from their Muslim neighbours.)[84] The placement of these announcements on the walls of a church in the city underscored the religious nature of tax in Ani.

These were great public texts, requiring a high level of literacy among the population.[85] The densest concentration of such edicts in Ani comes from the church of the Holy Apostles. This seems to have become a public noticeboard for Armenian tax announcements over the course of the thirteenth century. The walls of the zhamatun (porch), both interior and exterior, are covered with multiple inscriptions about tax demands and remissions. Ten carved over the course of the century survive. They were set up at the instigation of both male and female members of the ruling Mqargrdzeli family, including Khuandza, the granddaughter of Tamta's brother Avag, as well as by city officials including the customs officers and their entourages.[86] The layout of these tax decrees even reflects the form of the original documents that they transcribe: they appear as unfurled scrolls with the year and issuing authority at the top in a seal-like medallion and the name of the responsible scribe reproduced at the bottom [Fig. 52].[87] The legal document was carved, often with great labour and exquisite calligraphy, as an eternal record. The tax documents reflect the multilingual nature of the populations in these cities and the changing languages and cultures of their rulers. Elsewhere in Ani tax documents were set up in their original languages – Georgian, Arabic, Persian – depending on the regime in power at the time; but these all appeared with Armenian postscripts, confirming their importance and legality to the local population.[88] This multi-ethnic relevance even extended

---

[84] P. S. Cowe, 'The Politics of Poetics: Islamic Influence on Armenian Verse', in *Redefining Christian Identity: Cultural Interaction in the Middle East since the Rise of Islam*, eds. J. J. van Ginkel, H. L. Murre-van den Berg and T. M. van Lint (Leuven; Paris; Dudley, MA, 2005), 379–403, at 388–9; see also Dadoyan, 'A Case Study for Redefining Armenian–Christian Cultural Identity'.

[85] Compare later tax inscriptions produced in Anatolia under the Mongols: P. Blessing, *Rebuilding Anatolia after the Mongol Conquest: Islamic Architecture in the Lands of Rūm, 1240–1330* (Farnham, 2014), 179–83.

[86] Orbeli, *Corpus Inscriptionum Armenicarum*, nos. 56 (inscribed in the year 1217), 88 (between 1253 and 1276), 75 (1269), 74 (1270), 72 (1276), 80 (1276), 85 (1276), 76 (1280), 84 (1303), 82 (1320); trans. Basmadjian in *Inscriptions arméniennes d'Ani*, nos. 49, 67, 68, 69, 72, 73, 74, 75, 81, 87.

[87] This example is Orbeli, *Corpus Inscriptionum Armenicarum*, no. 75 (1269); trans. Basmadjian in *Inscriptions arméniennes d'Ani*, no. 68.

[88] Eastmond, 'Inscriptions and Authority in Ani'.

Figure 52 Tax inscription of 1269 on the exterior of the zhamatun of the church of the Holy Apostles, Ani, Turkey

to finding relevant curses on those who disobeyed them, as on a slightly later inscription in the church of the Holy Apostles, produced in the decades of Mongol rule:

> Anyone who attempts to interfere with our arrangements, whether he be Armenian, Georgian, or Tajik, may he be judged and convicted by God, may he share the fate of Satan and become his co-inhabitant in hell; may the Georgian be excommunicated and cursed; may the Tajik be covered in shame and found guilty before the prophets glorified in God; but those who observe our provisions until the end of the world, may they be blessed by God Almighty. May whoever opposes this be anathema as Judas and as Cain.[89]

---

[89] Orbeli, *Corpus Inscriptionum Armenicarum*, no. 82; trans. in Basmadjian, *Inscriptions arméniennes d'Ani*, no. 87.

The earliest of the tax decrees set up on the church of the Holy Apostles was placed there in 1217, while Tamta's father and cousin still ruled the city. It concerned charges levied by priests. As well as having a pious purpose, this tax also indulged in the local politics and rivalries between the Georgians and the Armenians.[90] It was issued by the Armenian Archbishop of Ani and required Armenian priests to charge less for services, particularly at Easter – it ended a diocese-wide annual tax of two bushels of wheat per village/parish and a sheepskin per church. At first sight it looks like an innocuous and generous reduction in the payments required to the Archbishop. But it also sought to lure worshippers away from the Georgian churches in the city with the promise of cheaper tithes. We know of this potential effect because the following year the Georgians had to issue their own proclamation in the city. Incised in an enormous eighteen-line inscription on the exterior of a Georgian church near the main gate out of the city, the Georgian Catholicos, Epiphane, set out a series of reductions which resulted in the Georgian priests price-matching their Armenian rivals.[91]

Coinage

The extent of trade is witnessed by the diversity of coins recovered from these cities. Most have never been analysed, but the range of coins found at Ani (admittedly covering the tenth to fourteenth centuries) shows that the city was closely linked in to broader trading networks. Most coins found came from Byzantium, Georgia and Azerbaijan, suggesting that the east–west trade routes were most important.[92] All these coins were made of a similar quantity and purity of silver (approximately 3 grams) minted to a similar size. They were variations on the Seljuk dirham. The coins minted by the Grand Komnenos Emperors of Trebizond, the Greek outpost on the northern edge of Anatolia, employed a similar standard, and the quantities that were produced from their flourishing silver mines at Gümüşhane ensured that these coins gained wide currency in the region and were adopted in

---

[90] Orbeli, *Corpus Inscriptionum Armenicarum*, no. 56; trans. in Basmadjian, *Inscriptions arméniennes d'Ani*, no. 49; J.-P. Mahé, 'L'étude de P. M. Muradyan sur les inscriptions géorgiennes d'Arménie', *Bedi Kartlisa* 38 (1980), 295–309, at 296–8.

[91] The inscription was reconstructed by Marr, but is now lost: N. I. Marr, 'Nadpis Epifaniia, katalikosa Gruzii (iz raskopok v Ani 1910 g.)', *Izvestiia Imperatorskoi Akademii Nauk* 4 (1910), 1433–42; E. Taqaishvili, 'L'inscription d'Épiphane, Catholicos de Géorgie', *Revue de l'Orient Chrétien* 30 (1935–6), 216–24; Mahé, 'L'étude de P. M. Muradyan', 296–7.

[92] K. A. Mousheghian, A. Mousheghian and G. Depeyrot, *History and Coin Finds in Armenia: Inventory of Coins and Hoards (7th–19th c.)* (Wetteren, 2002, 2003), 1: 4–5; Kévorkian, *Ani*, 150–7.

Georgia, where close imitations were minted, known as *kyrmanueli* after the Emperor Manuel I in whose reign they were first were minted (1238–63).[93] By the early fourteenth century the Florentine merchant Francesco Pegolotti was reporting that the weights and measures of Trebizond were the same as those used in Tabriz, 650 kilometres to the south-east in Iran.[94] Much like the modern euro, these coins were valid in a number of different states. There were clearly extensive networks of commerce and trade that connected all the cities in the region, including Akhlat, with neighbouring towns. The coins facilitated communications networks and the movement of people, goods and services. Merchants were able to move between cities and regimes with apparent ease, something observed by Ibn Jubayr in the 1180s during Saladin's siege of Kerak, then still in Crusader hands:

> One of the astonishing things that is talked of is that though the fires of discord burn between the two parties, Muslim and Christian, two armies of them may meet and dispose themselves in battle array, and yet Muslim and Christian travellers will come and go between them without interference.[95]

The merchant Tigran Honents certainly built his fortune up under Muslim rule before the rise of the Mqargrdzelis in Armenia.[96]

Caravanserais and Trade

Trade was encouraged through roads and caravanserais, and the early thirteenth century was the heyday for their construction.[97] The Seljuks in particular invested huge sums to build a network of caravanserais across their territory, mostly along the lines of old Roman roads, to attract trade to cross Anatolia to the Mediterranean ports of Antalya and Alanya, rather than to go further south into Syria and the ports of the Levant. Lying in a string across Anatolia, about 200 are known, mostly built between 1220 and 1250, which stretch from west to east between Antalya, Konya and Kayseri, with northern branches heading up to Sinop, which had been captured in 1215

---

[93] E. Georganteli, 'Trapezuntine Money in the Balkans, Anatolia and the Black Sea, 13th–15th Centuries', in *Trebizond and the Black Sea*, ed. T. Kyriakides (Thessaloniki, 2010), 93–112; Eastmond, *Art and Identity in Thirteenth-Century Byzantium*, 22; W. Wroth, *Catalogue of the Coins of the Vandals, Ostrogoths and Lombards and of the Empires of Thessalonica, Nicaea and Trebizond in the British Museum* (London, 1911), lxxviii, 256, weight 44.

[94] Pegolotti, 29. [95] Ibn Jubayr, 300–1.

[96] Confirmed by the early date at which he was supporting building at Horomos monastery: Mahé, 'Les inscriptions de Horomos', 185–6, inscription Ži2.

[97] Blessing, *Rebuilding Anatolia*, 173–9.

to give the Seljuks a port on the Black Sea. They provided a series of nightly stopping points, usually about 25–30 kilometres apart. The caravanserais are great fortified buildings, with castle-like curtain walls, windowless and heavily buttressed. The most impressive included space for travellers to rest securely with stables for their animals and their goods, covered halls in which to conduct business, as well as other facilities including kitchens, baths and mosques [Fig. 53].[98] The *waqf* for the Karatay Han, built to the east of Kayseri in the early 1240s, stipulates the inclusivity and generosity of its welcome. Every traveller staying at the caravanserai, whether Muslim or Christian, man or woman, slave or free, was granted a daily ration of 'good' bread, a bowl of cooked food containing a specified quantity of meat, as well as the promise of honeyed sweets on Friday nights.[99]

The expense lavished on these buildings meant that they acted as much more than merely functional overnight hostels. They were also instruments of state policy, announcing the permanence of each ruler's power and the geographical extent of their realm. They were carefully built with ashlar masonry and high rectangular entrance porches that provided a locus for intricate decoration, including elaborate interlace designs and muqarnas vaults. These closely resemble the porches of contemporary mosques, indicating the degree of prestige intended for these commercial buildings.

The prospect of encountering such a building every day as traders travelled across Anatolia became a powerful reminder of the reach of the sultan and the resources available to him. The scale and quality of the greatest of the Seljuk caravanserais, such as the Sultan Han near Kayseri [Fig. 54], enabled them to be used as royal residences and guesthouses; equally, they acted as suitably grandiose and impressive backdrops for international diplomacy.[100] The largest *han*s seem to have been designed as much for royal use when travelling between principal cities as for commerce; an idea taken over by invaders, such as the Mamluk Baybars, who used the Karatay Han at Kayseri as his base during his invasion of Anatolia in 1277 (this was his first return to the region since he had passed through as a slave four decades earlier).[101]

---

[98] A. T. Yavuz, 'The Concepts that Shape Anatolian Seljuk Caravanserais', *Muqarnas* 14 (1997), 80–95.

[99] O. Turan, 'Selçuk devri vakfiyeleri III: Celaleddin Karatay, vakıfları ve vakfiyeleri', *Belleten* 12 (1948), 17–171.

[100] A. T. Yavuz, 'Anatolian Seljuk Caravanserais and their Use as State Houses', in *Turkish Art: Proceedings of the 10th International Congress of Turkish Art*, eds. F. Déroche, C. Geneguard, G. Renda and J. M. Rogers (Geneva, 1999), 757–65.

[101] Yavuz, 'Anatolian Seljuk Caravanserais'. See Umari's description of the glories of the Karatay Han, written in 1349 of the 1277 expedition: K. Erdmann, *Das Anatolische Karavansaray des 13. Jahrhunderts* vol. 1 (Berlin, 1961), 117–18, trans. in Blessing, *Rebuilding Anatolia*, 176–7.

Figure 53 Albert Gabriel's 1931 reconstruction drawing of the Sultan Han, near Kayseri, Turkey; 1230s (from *Monuments turcs d'Anatolie I: Kayseri–Niğde* (Paris, 1931))

The Seljuks' caravanserai routes inspired their neighbours to follow suit, all trying to erect similar buildings as a way to attract trade through their lands. The Mqargrdzelis tried to muscle in on the lucrative trade routes, building a series of caravanserais to lure merchants north to Ani from the traditional routes between Erzurum and Tabriz.[102] At least four sites have

---

[102] The link with the Mqargrdzelis has been persuasively argued by J. M. Rogers, 'The Mxargrdzelis between East and West', *Bedi Kartlisa* 34 (1976), 315–25.

Figure 54 Courtyard mosque with hall portal beyond, Sultan Han, near Kayseri, Turkey; 1230s

been identified: three at Aruch, Talin and Chrplu seem to lead south-east from Ani towards Iran, and a fourth, at Zor, west of Mount Ararat, on a route that would link Ani to the Erzurum–Akhlat road. The Zor caravanserai is the best preserved of this group [Fig. 55]. Its design is very close to the Seljuk examples, a rectangular hall with three vaulted aisles to house the caravans overnight. Its porch with interlocking blocks and geometric interlace also resembles the Seljuk examples, and so the overall appearance of these *han*s seems designed to insert them visually into the Seljuk system. However, many of the details of the masonry and carving can also be found in the decoration of Armenian churches: the moulding around the entrance that alternates Λ- and Π-shaped notches is comparable both to the design used on the porch of the mosque at Niğde of 1233, as well as on the narthex of the church of St Gregory the Illuminator of Tigran Honents in Ani (1215).[103] This Armenian element is even more evident in the varieties of different vaulting techniques used in the three rooms of the entrance bay, which closely resembles the work in the zhamatun of the church of the Holy Apostles at Ani, built by 1217.[104] Later caravanserais built in Armenia to extend this network to the south-east, such as the Selim Han of 1332

---

[103] This comparison has been noted at http://www.virtualani.org/zor/ (accessed 26 April 2013).
[104] A. Loris'-Kalantar', 'Razvaliny drevniaiu karavansaraia', *Khristianskii Vostok* 3 (1914), 101–2, plate X; J.-M. Thierry, 'À propos de quelques monuments chrétiens du vilayet de Kars (IV)', *REArm* 19 (1985), 285–323, esp. 293–307; R. H. Ünal, 'Iğdir yakmlannda bir selçuklu

Figure 55 Portal of the Zor Han, near Iğdir, Turkey; early thirteenth century (from A. Loris'-Kalantar', 'Razvaliny drevniaiu karavansaraia', *Khristianskii Vostok* 3 (1914))

and that at Kotrets, preserve bilingual inscriptions in Armenian and Persian, showing the international clientele for whom all these buildings were erected. Similarly, Badr al-Din Lu'lu''s al-Han near Sinjar of the 1230s seems to have been a bid on the part of the ruler of Mosul to tie in the east–west trade routes to the north–south trade to Baghdad.[105] The one benefit of the

kervansarayi ve Doğubayazit–Batum kervan yolu hakkmda notlar', *Sanat Tarihi Yilliği* 3 (1970), 7–15.

[105] G. Reitlinger, 'Medieval Antiquities West of Mosul', *Iraq* 5 (1938), 143–56, at 149–51; F. P. T. Sarre and E. Herzfeld, *Archäologische Reise im Euphrat- und Tigris-Gebiet* (Berlin, 1911), 1: 13–15.

Mongol invasions was the creation of a single power to administer trade all the way from China to the Mediterranean in the second half of the thirteenth century.

The role of the city was crucial in Tamta's world. It was the economic and social hub of all the cultures with which she was involved before her capture by the Mongols in 1236. Like Tamta, cities were versatile and adaptable. They were embedded in networks of trade which depended on communication and exchange throughout the region between Christians and Muslims, between Georgians and Armenians, between Turks, Arabs and Persians. The need to reconcile and accommodate all these different cultures and communities required cities to present different facets of their character and identity to each. Even the most bombastic features, such as the overt Christian nature of the walls at Ani, were counterbalanced by the visibility of the Muslim monuments within the city. The physical fabric of cities did not simply reflect their changing governments over time, but played an active role in determining how those governments could act, by defining the prominence and permanence of each community's presence. There are many parallels between the development of the city and the ever-changing nature of Tamta's public identity. Both comprised many layers built up over time and through each new contact with a different society and culture. Indeed, the examination of the city is perhaps the closest we can ever get to understanding, or at least visualising, Tamta's own character.

7 | Tamta

Ayyubid Wife of al-Ashraf Musa

Once Tamta was married into the Ayyubid royal family, her identity had to change to accommodate her new position. To the core of being an Armenian–Georgian noblewoman, she added the role of wife of an Ayyubid prince. Her Christian upbringing now had to be reconciled with entering a Muslim culture. Unlike in a Christian marriage, she was now in a polygamous society, in which she was just one wife among several. Tamta's marriage also placed her at the heart of the court, the richest and most cosmopolitan element of society. The Ayyubid court, through its expenditure on luxury goods and palaces, was able to translate its interests in poetry, music, hunting and science into material objects – inlaid metalwork, glazed tiles, illuminated manuscripts. These in turn helped to shape and reinforce the nature and interests of the courtiers. The following chapters examine Tamta's life among the Ayyubids. Each chapter takes a different aspect of her identity to explore the life she led, what she was able to achieve and what aspects of society were familiar or alien to her. This chapter examines Tamta's life as a wife; the following explores her role as a Christian in a broadly Islamic world; and the third, her life as a courtier among the elite of society. As ever, Tamta is an elusive presence, and much of what we can learn about her must be gleaned from the lives of women in comparable positions around her.

Other Wives

To build up a picture of Tamta's role as a wife in Ayyubid society it is necessary to look more broadly at the positions of wives at the Ayyubid court, the freedoms women had and the limits and expectations placed on them. This establishes the contexts against which we can judge Tamta's own achievements, which Kirakos Gandzaketsi described as supporting Christian monasteries and pilgrims in Ayyubid territories. The geopolitical position of Akhlat means that we must also consider what we mean by the Ayyubid world, as the city was located on the very fringe of their territories. Although she was married to an Ayyubid prince whose life and political interests lay predominantly in the Jazira, Syria and Egypt, Tamta resided at the one outpost of al-Ashraf's world that was situated in a region with a predominantly Christian population, but which had had rulers from Turkic–Persian cultures for the previous century. The physical geography of her life on these borderlands between Anatolia and Greater Armenia must be balanced against the political and cultural geography of her husband's life further south. This underlines the tension between the Arabic and Turkic worlds that Tamta had to negotiate throughout her life. We should also remember that the Ayyubids themselves had moved across this same frontier. The family was Kurdish in origin, before shifting its focus further south, and so their Arabicised rule was as much a reinvention as the Mqargrdzelis' adoption of Georgian court positions. So, as well as looking at the Ayyubid world into which Tamta was married, this chapter also looks at the actions of women in the Turkic world, among the Seljuks and Turkoman principalities of Anatolia. Finally, we must also consider the role of the Armenian, Christian population in Akhlat and the surrounding area, and the cultural freedoms and expectations that this group placed on women. Tamta, living in Akhlat on the edge of these three worlds, moved between them all.

The closest comparisons we have for Tamta are her fellow wives. Although the sources for women in the Ayyubid world are very sparse, we know that al-Ashraf had already married at least once before he encountered Tamta. In 1208/9 he had agreed a marriage to Terkan Khatun, the sister of Nur al-Din Arslanshah, the Zangid *atabeg* (governor) of Mosul in what is now north-western Iraq (r. 1193–1211).[1] As with so many of the marriages described in Chapter 4, this one had been forced on Nur al-Din in a time of weakness: al-Ashraf's army was threatening to overrun the city and its surrounding lands, and the marriage obviated the need for this. By offering his sister, Nur al-Din established an alliance with al-Ashraf, which allowed him to remain in power in the city, but ensured that Mosul would remain an ally of the Ayyubids. Indeed, the city's alliance with the Ayyubids would outlast the Zangid dynasty and continue under their *atabeg* successors, the Lu'lu'ids, until the Mongol invasions. As with Tamta, the marriage was not actually organised by al-Ashraf: in this instance the diplomacy that underlay the wedding had been undertaken by his father, al-ʿAdil, who then still controlled overall Ayyubid policy across the region.

---

[1] Patton, *Badr al-Dīn Luʾluʾ*, 9. According to H. Sauvaire, 'Description de Damas [II]', *Journal Asiatique*, IXe série 3 (May–June 1894), 385–501, at 445 n.1, the wedding took place in 600 AH [1203/4].

Later al-Ashraf possibly also married a Seljuk princess. In 1219 the Seljuk Sultan Kaykaʿus I died, and was succeeded by his older brother ʿAla al-Din Kaykubad I (r.1219–37). In the inevitable uncertainty following any succession Kaykubad sought alliances. Worrying in particular about the threat from the Byzantine west, he turned to al-Ashraf to make an alliance and so secure his south-eastern frontier: 'they undertook to be sincere partners and to cooperate, and they made marriage alliances'.[2] No sources give any precise details of what these alliances were: Kaykubad certainly married a sister of al-Ashraf,[3] and the reference to alliances (plural) suggests that al-Ashraf married a sister of Kaykubad in return. From al-Ashraf's point of view, he was now married in to the three major powers that surrounded him to the north: the Seljuks, the Georgians and the Zangids. The wives clearly had a major diplomatic function in al-Ashraf's life in linking him to powerful families in each state; however, their other roles are more complex. Despite this diplomatic importance, the women's public presence was rarely recognised. Few are given names; more often than not they are only recorded by titles or descriptive names. Hence, the sister of al-Ashraf married to Kaykubad is only known as Malika ʿAdiliyya – the Queen, Daughter of al-ʿAdil. Others are given honorific names such as Ismat al-Dunya wa'l-Din – Virtue of the World and Religion (for royal daughters within the dynasty), or Safwat al-Dunya wa'l-Din – Purity of the World and Religion (accorded to women marrying into a dynasty).[4] It is only in exceptional cases that a personal name is recorded for these women, usually for Christian brides, whose names are recorded in Christian chronicles. In Islamic texts these women who married into Muslim dynasties were given ethnic titles: Kurjiyya or Gurji Khatun – both meaning the Georgian Lady – are the titles used to describe both Tamta and Tamar (the daughter of Queen Rusudan of Georgia who was married to the Seljuk Sultan Kaykhusraw II).[5]

Harem Politics

The relationship between wives is difficult to assess. There is no legal definition of the relationship between wives of one husband. The easiest

---

[2] Ibn al-Athir, 3: 199.   [3] *RCEA* XI, 4273; *TEI*, 2731 names her as a daughter of al-ʿAdil.
[4] S. Yalman, 'Building the Sultanate of Rum: Memory, Urbanism and Mysticism in the Architectural Patronage of ʿAla al-Din Kayqubad (r. 1220–1237)' (Ph.D., Harvard University, 2010), 106–8.
[5] J. Sublet, 'La folie de la princesse Bint al-Ašraf (un scandale financier sous les Mamelouks Bahris)', *BEO* 27 (1974), 45–50.

English expression to describe it is as 'co-wives' or 'sister-wives', but such a description may be too fraternal in tone. In the same year that al-Ashraf died, 1237, his sister, who had married the Seljuk Sultan Kaykubad, was murdered, along with her two sons, to the benefit (and possibly at the instigation) of her 'co'-wife Mahperi Khatun, from a relatively minor Armenian family, in order to secure the throne for Mahperi's son, Kaykhusraw II.[6] And we have seen, in Chapter 5, other examples of wives manoeuvring against each other to promote their own children. The book of Leviticus suggests a more accurate term for the relationship: 'rival-wives'.[7]

In these battles the status of the mother could be very important. When Jahan Pahlavan, *atabeg* of Azerbaijan, died in 1187 he left four sons. Two had been born of Inanch Khatun, the daughter of a senior emir and an influential figure at court. However, his eldest son was Abu Bakr (whose later incompetence we have already encountered), born of a Turkish slave girl. Abu Bakr quickly seized power, aided by Zahida Khatun, another of Jahan Pahlavan's wives, but Inanch Khatun manoeuvred against him in favour of her own sons. She rallied support with a simple call: 'How can you be happy in mind that the son of a slave girl should be loftier in rank and greater in status than my own two sons?'[8] Inanch Khatun went on to support her claim by marrying Toghril Shah III, the last Great Sultan of Iran, but she was never able to supplant Abu Bakr during his lifetime, despite his terrible reputation as a ruler. Other tactics could also benefit the children of lesser wives, as we have seen with the more brutal tactics employed by Mahperi Khatun to ensure that her son came to power.

Other Loves

A further source of competition for the favour of the ruler came from the appearance of beautiful men at court. Al-Ashraf's sexual desire was not restricted to the women and concubines in his harem. He wrote love poems to a young Turk whom he put in charge of his treasury:

> May I be the ransom for a full moon whom description is at a loss to encompass,

---

[6] S. N. Yıldız, 'The Rise and Fall of a Tyrant in Seljuq Anatolia: Sa'd al-Din Köpek's Reign of Terror, 1237–8', in *Ferdowsi, the Mongols and the History of Iran: Studies in Honour of Charles Melville*, eds. R. Hillenbrand, A. C. S. Peacock and F. Abdullaeva (London, 2013), 92–103; Shukurov, 'Harem Christianity' has her as a Greek Christian. For a recent account, which ignores the role of women completely: S. Mecit, *The Rum Seljuqs: Evolution of a Dynasty* (Abingdon; New York, 2014), 116–21.

[7] Leviticus 18:18. [8] Husayni, 114–15.

> One who is liberal with my blood, despite being honest and trustworthy.
> Should I marvel? He keeps my wealth safe,
> But sees my soul destroyed by him and pays it no mind![9]

Ibn Khallikan (d.1282) records in his monumental collection of biographies that al-Ashraf at one point became so enamoured of a musician that, after hearing him play, he offered him whatever he wanted. The musician, thinking of his retirement, chose the 'government of the city of Akhlat' for the rest of his life, which gives some indication of the wealth of the city.[10] Al-Ashraf granted his wish, and it was left to the city's governor, the *hajib* (chamberlain) Husam al-Din 'Ali, to sort out the mess. Al-Ashraf's gift reflects his legendary generosity to his courtiers, but also the importance of relationships between men at court. A large portion of the love poetry written at the Ayyubid court in this period is homoerotic in content.[11] That it still has the capacity to shock modern readers is evident from the introductory chapter to the *Cambridge History of Arabic Literature*. Published as recently as 2006, it is clearly queasy about its subject matter. Writing of the Damascus poet Ibn 'Unayn, who died in 1233, it concludes that 'He was a self-declared lecher, notorious in his day for the wantonness of his invective and the obsessive and often repugnant relish with which he depicts utterly reckless sexual escapades.'[12] It cannot bring itself to cite any of this poetry.

Similar themes are much less visible in the Christian literature of the Caucasus, but they can still be traced. The great Georgian epic poem of the reign of Queen Tamar, the *Knight in the Panther's Skin*, is centred on a relationship between its male heroes Avtandil and Tariel, the eponymous wearer of the panther's skin. It reflects the bonds between men that were common in the poetry of the Persian world, and although it is never presented in a sexualised way it is modelled on the same ideals of male intimacy that could lead to such encounters.[13] As the apparent hypocrisy of al-Ashraf's support for the Hanbalis (the Sunni theological school that took the hardest

---

[9] E. K. Rowson, 'Homoerotic Liaisons among the Mamluk Elite in Late Medieval Egypt and Syria', in *Islamicate Sexualities: Translations across Temporal Geographies of Desire*, eds. K. Babayan and A. Najmabadi (Cambridge, MA, 2008), 204–38, at 212.

[10] Ibn Khallikan, 3: 490–1.

[11] J. Sharlet, 'Public Displays of Affection: Male Homoerotic Desire and Sociability in Medieval Arabic Literature', in *Islam and Homosexuality*, ed. S. Habib (Santa Barbara, CA, 2010), 37–56.

[12] S. K. Jayyusi, 'Arabic Poetry in the Post-Classical Age', in *The Cambridge History of Arabic Literature*, vol. 6: *Arab Literature in the Post-Classical Period*, eds. R. Allen and D. S. Richards (Cambridge, 2006), 25–59, at 44.

[13] Rayfield, *The Literature of Georgia*, 3rd edn, 69–82.

line on homosexuality, arguing that it was a crime deserving of the death penalty),[14] and his infatuation with his favourites shows, the social practice and acceptance of homosexual infatuation was often in conflict with the clear condemnation of it in both the Qur'an and the hadith, and the Bible.

As mothers, none of al-Ashraf's wives can be considered a success in terms of the traditional roles that were assigned to women. None produced a male heir for him, although this may well reflect al-Ashraf's own sexual proclivities rather than their fertility. The only record of a child concerns a daughter; she is scarcely mentioned in the sources, and the few existing references were not interested in naming her (or her mother).[15] If she were Tamta's daughter then it is clear that she was brought up away from her mother: she was certainly a Muslim, and she was brought within the world of Ayyubid family politics. She was married off to her cousin, al-Mansur Mahmud (son of al-Salih Isma'il, al-Ashraf's successor in Damascus). Their lives were played out primarily in Cairo, at the very opposite end of the Ayyubid empire from Tamta in Akhlat.

With no male heirs to fight over, the harem politics of al-Ashraf's court was less acute than at the Seljuk or Azeri court, but the rivalry between wives and other lovers and the financial implications that followed as gifts were handed out or redistributed shows that it could still be fraught. Al-Ashraf's surrender of the revenues of Akhlat shows how quickly and capriciously Tamta's political position and her economic independence could be undercut. Tamta's status in the hierarchy of al-Ashraf's wives was a complex one. Coming from outside the Muslim world, she was certainly al-Ashraf's least advantageous marriage in terms of the internal politics of the family in the Jazira, Syria and Egypt – the dominant concern of Ayyubid politics. This was further exacerbated by her role as a Christian. However, it was those same points that made Tamta so important for al-Ashraf in Akhlat. As his representative in the city, her Christianity, her parentage and her independence from internal Ayyubid pressures were essential to his continuing rule. Thus

---

[14] W. G. Clarence-Smith, 'Same-Sex Relations and Transgender Identities in Islamic Southeast Asia from the Fifteenth Century', in *Sexual Diversity in Asia, c. 600–1950*, eds. R. A. Reyes and W. G. Clarence-Smith (New York, 2012), 67–85, at 71, citing the views of the Hanbali jurist Ibn Taymiyya (1263–1328). Al-Ashraf also personally ordered the punishment of the Sufi sheikh Abu-l Hasan 'Ali al-Hariri, accused of corrupting young boys: Rowson, 'Homoerotic Liaisons', 212; L. Pouzet, *Damas au VIIe/XIIIe siecle: vie et structures religieuses d'une métropole Islamique* (Beirut, 1991), 367–8.

[15] H. Sauvaire, 'Description de Damas [VII]', *Journal Asiatique*, IXe série 6 (Sept.–Oct. 1895), 221–313, at 309–10, citing al-Saqqay's brief biography of her. Also Abu'l-Fida, 113; Sublet, 'La folie de la princesse'.

Tamta stands apart from her fellow wives. Nevertheless, it is important to see what these wives were capable of as this then provides a control against which to measure Tamta's own achievements.

Female Virtues

The standard tropes of good wifely behaviour and actions in medieval Islam centred on ideas of fecundity, modesty, obedience, piety and good works. The record that these virtues leaves behind is partial at best. One model was provided by Sitt al-Sham, the sister of Saladin and al-ʿAdil, who died in Damascus in 1220. Her good works are praised by Abu Shama in terms that reflect the traditional limits and expectations imposed upon women in medieval societies:

> She was first in rank among the princesses, intelligent, deeply pious, and greatly devoted to prayer, good works and alms. Every year thousands of dinars were expended in her residence on the manufacture of potions, narcotic electuaries, and medicinal plants, and she would distribute these to the people. Her gate was a refuge of seekers and a sanctuary for those who mourn. She provided a generous endowment for the two madrasas [she founded] and she received an impressive funeral.[16]

Much of this largesse was domestic, ephemeral and unseen; it was only her religious endowments that left a physical legacy, and it is on such acts of patronage that this chapter therefore focuses. The easiest feminine virtue to trace should be fecundity, but as we have seen, none of al-Ashraf's wives produced a male heir, in contrast to his father, who provided al-Ashraf with more than twelve male siblings and at least four sisters too.

Modesty

Modesty and obedience are the enemies of history. Women who accepted their role to be demure and hidden and to remain the willing instruments of their husbands were unlikely to attract the attention of their contemporaries, and so conspired to conceal their own lives from later generations. Yet women could, paradoxically, use their modesty to aggrandise themselves and make their invisibility in the urban fabric a means of attracting rather than deflecting attention. In the same way that the lustreware dish with

---

[16] Humphreys, 'Women as Patrons', 47.

a procession [Fig. 23] managed to extend the presence of the diminutive, invisible bride at its centre to encompass the whole surface through the retinue that surrounds her, so too could women swamp their surroundings, as Ibn Jubayr's account of his encounter with Saljukshah, the sister of the Seljuk Sultan Kılıc Arslan II on pilgrimage at Medina in 1184, makes clear:

> Among the strange affairs that are discussed and listened to by men we witnessed the following. One of the aforementioned khatuns, the daughter of prince Mas'ud ... came to the Mosque of the Apostle of God – may God bless and preserve him – on the evening of Thursday, 6 Muharram, the fourth day of our arrival at Medina, riding in her litter, surrounded by the litters of her ladies and handmaidens and led by Qur'an-readers, while pages and eunuch-slaves, bearing iron rods, moved around her driving the people from her path until she arrived at the venerated mosque. Wrapped in an ample cloak, she descended and advanced to salute the Prophet – may God bless and preserve him – her servants going before her and the officials of the mosque raising their voices in prayer for her and extolling her fame. She came to the small *rawdah* between the venerated tomb and the pulpit, and prayed there wrapped in her cloak while the people who thronged around her were kept back by the rods. She then prayed in the *hawd* beside the *minbar*, and moving thence to the west wall of the venerated *rawdah*, sat in the place where it is said that the angel Gabriel – peace be upon him – came down. The curtain was then lowered on her, and her pages, slaves and chamberlains remained behind the curtain receiving her commands. She had brought with her to the mosque two loads of provisions as alms for the poor, and stayed in her place until night had fallen.[17]

What is striking here is the way women could turn the expectations of seclusion, separation and concealment to their own advantage. They made themselves visible through the requirement for them to be invisible. The beating back of people to preserve Saljukshah's space in the streets, the setting up of curtains in the mosque – which presumably blocked the view and easy access of the men into its holiest parts – and the attraction of crowds of the poor to receive her alms all disturbed the normal, male-dominated life of the streets and mosque. The combination of violence, shouted proclamations of Saljukshah's fame and dispensations of charity must have caused considerable disruption in the city and so announced her presence forcefully, but at the same time her 'ample cloak' and veiling curtains ensured that her female modesty was protected.

---

[17] Ibn Jubayr, 207–8; this passage has previously been noted and discussed in Tabbaa, 'Dayfa Khatun'.

In all that follows we must bear this ephemeral presence and intrusion into the male world in mind. It both acts as a balance to the idea that women's influence came primarily through the marital bed – the secluded world of harem politics – and also substantiates the impact of the buildings that will be discussed below. The women who founded these buildings and ensured that their names were commemorated in inscriptions already had public presences. The foundations did not arrive without context.

Piety

It is only in the realm of piety that we can find more concrete information about the actions of al-Ashraf's wives, and those of other women at the Muslim courts in Anatolia and Syria: the buildings erected by these women to serve Allah, but also to commemorate themselves. This evidence of Muslim piety acts as an important balance to the evidence of Tamta's Christian piety, which will be examined in the next chapter. The evidence comes from two sources, the limited accounts in texts of the kinds of philanthropic acts that women carried out, and the physical remains of the religious and other buildings set up for the public good that they financed. The quantity and types of building that these women were responsible for, the designs they employed and the inscriptions that they commissioned to commemorate their acts all reveal much about the capacity of women to undertake such work, and the nature of their piety. They also reveal some of the other motives that lay behind patronage, as rival wives used architecture to jockey for position with their rivals, sought to protect their wealth against future depredation when they became widows, and sought to flatter their own egos.

The evidence that we have for al-Ashraf's other wives comes from late in his reign, the years after 1229 when, with the connivance of his brother al-Kamil in Egypt, he seized control of Damascus from his nephew al-Nasir Dawud. In the years before then al-Ashraf moved between the cities he controlled in the Jazira, Harran [now in Turkey on the Syrian border], Raqqa and Akhlat. Both Harran and Raqqa were important Muslim cities, major centres since the Abbasid period.[18] However, both cities were largely destroyed by the Mongols in the 1250s and 1260s. Almost nothing is left of them – the modern city of Raqqa was built over the old city at the start of the twentieth century with almost no archaeological excavation; Harran remains an isolated ruin on the Turkish–Syrian frontier. No buildings of al-Ashraf or his wives survive from either site.

[18] EI², *s.v.* Harran, al-Rakka.

The most concrete evidence concerns al-Ashraf's first wife, Terkan Khatun, the daughter of the Zangid *atabeg* of Mosul.[19] After twenty years of silence in the sources, she emerges after 1229 as the patron of two buildings in Damascus, a *ribat* (a hospice for Sufi mystics) and a funerary madrasa.[20] Her patronage in the city suggests that she, unlike Tamta, travelled with her husband. Both buildings imply an interest in the display of piety, as well as access to independent sources of funding to finance them. Statistical data collated by Stephen Humphreys suggests that Terkan's choice of institutions to support was typical among women: among all the known foundations by women in Syria in this period, madrasas and hostels feature disproportionately highly as commissions.[21]

Terkan's madrasa is known as the Atabakiyya Madrasa (the madrasa of the daughter of the *atabeg*), showing the importance of her paternal family to her identity in the Ayyubid world. It survives in the al-Salihiyya district at the foot of Mount Qasiyun to the north of Damascus.[22] It was built opposite the Dar al-Hadith al-Ashrafiyya, a foundation established by her husband, al-Ashraf.[23] The Atabakiyya Madrasa had a dual role as madrasa and mausoleum for its founder. Its only external decoration is on its porch, recessed back from the street down a narrow passageway. It is built from alternate courses of black and brown stone (known as *ablaq* (bicoloured) masonry), with a muqarnas vault over the door [Fig. 56]. The narrowness of the entrance accentuates its verticality, but this compressed location also undercuts the impact of the carefully dressed masonry. Its interior is unadorned. The Dar al-Hadith that al-Ashraf constructed opposite the madrasa is an even more austere building [Fig. 57]. It was built as a centre for the study of the hadith, the sayings of the Prophet Muhammad, but it also housed an important relic of the Prophet, one of his sandals. Al-Ashraf had learned about this relic whilst he was in residence in Akhlat, when it was first brought to show him.[24] He had been unable to acquire it then, and

---

[19] Humphreys, 'Women as Patrons', 43 for brief biography.
[20] All that follows is from Humphreys, 'Women as Patrons', no. 15.
[21] Humphreys, 'Women as Patrons', 35–6.
[22] Atabakiyya Madrasa: M. Meinecke, 'Der Survey des Damaszener Altstadtsviertels aṣ-Ṣāliḥīya', *Damaszener Mitteilungen* 1 (1983), 189–241, no. 69; Sauvaire, 'Description de Damas II', 385–7; *ribat*: H. Sauvaire, 'Description de Damas [VI]', *Journal Asiatique*, IXe série 5 (May–June 1895), 377–411, at 381. The name of the madrasa comes from the title held by Terkan Khatun's father: the *atabeg* 'Izz al-Din Mas'ud I b. Qutb al-Din Mawdud b. Imad al-Din Zangi b. Aqsunqur.
[23] Meinecke, 'Der Survey des Damaszener Altstadtsviertels aṣ-Ṣāliḥīya', no. 72. Women were able to attend classes at the Dar al-Hadith al-Ashrafiyya: M. A. Nadwi, *al-Muḥaddithāt: The Women Scholars in Islam* (Oxford, 2013), 83; al-Dahabi, 227, for his other Dar al-Hadith.
[24] The different accounts of how al-Ashraf acquired the relic are discussed in J. W. Meri, *The Cult of Saints among Muslims and Jews in Medieval Syria* (Oxford, 2002), 109–11.

Figure 56 Portal to the Madrasa al-Atabakiyya, Salihiyya district, Damascus, Syria; 1229–42

was reluctant to remove a small fragment for himself, fearing it would set a precedent that would quickly lead to the complete dismemberment of such a precious relic. He only took possession of the sandal when its owner left it to him in his will, in thanks for his earlier forbearance. The building thus had an unusual dual role as study centre and shrine.[25] Its entrance is constructed in just the local sandstone, and its only decoration is the foundation inscription over the door. This makes a clear allusion to Damascus' classical past as the text is presented in a rectangular frame with triangular 'handles',

[25] Humphreys, *From Saladin to the Mongols*, 212–13, citing the *Mirat* of Sibt ibn al-Jawzi.

Figure 57 Dome of the Dar al-Hadith al-Ashrafiyya, Salihiyya district, Damascus, Syria; 1229–37

a Roman convention for inscriptions known as a *tabula ansata*. The building has more prominence than Terkan's madrasa as it is surmounted by a dome, but it is still an undemonstrative edifice. Only the variation in shapes of the heads of the windows around the dome show any hint at decoration.

The visual distinction between the two edifices echoed a theological difference between them as well. Terkan Khatun's madrasa was given over to scholars of the dominant theological school in Syria in this period, the Shafi'ites; whereas al-Ashraf's was built for the smaller and more conservative school, the Hanbalis. Al-Ashraf's main city, Harran, was dominated by Hanbali madrasas, and his support for them stood apart from many of his brothers.[26] His brother, al-Kamil, had recently rebuilt the tomb of Imam al-Shafi'i, the founder of the Shafi'ite school, in Cairo in 1212. It was constructed on a grandiose scale, with a dome to match that of the Dome of the Rock in Jerusalem, and al-Kamil later chose to be buried there with his mother.[27] This promotion of the Shafi'ites has recently been interpreted as an attempt by the Ayyubids to promote a 'correct' school of Sunni belief, as proclaimed in the foundation inscription at the imam's shrine: 'for the jurists who are disciples of al-Shafi'i, may Allah favour them, are characterised by

---

[26] D. S. Rice, 'Medieval Ḥarrān: Studies on its Topography and Monuments, I', *Anatolian Studies* 2 (1952), 36–84, at 41.

[27] S. Mulder, 'The Mausoleum of Imam al-Shafi'i', *Muqarnas* 23 (2006), 15–46.

their firm, unified, Ash'ari doctrinal foundation against vain reasoners and other innovators'.[28] That jibe against 'vain reasoners and other innovators' seems to have been aimed specifically at Hanbalis, even though their interpretation of Islam was conservative and literal, emphasising strict adherence to the five daily prayers (the *salat*), and advocating that the hadith should be treated on a par with the Qur'an.[29] Al-Ashraf's patronage reflected his Hanbali beliefs, concentrating on congregational mosques (where the *salat* was performed) and madrasas, and building two schools of hadith, of which the building opposite Terkan Khatun's madrasa was one.

The different affiliations of these two neighbouring foundations shows the freedom available to al-Ashraf's wives in expressing their Islamic faith. A third building that was erected beside al-Ashraf's Dar al-Hadith supports this idea. It was a funerary madrasa built by Khadija Khatun, the sister of al-Nasir Dawud (the nephew al-Ashraf ousted from Damascus in 1229).[30] She remained in the city even after her brother had been expelled. Khadija Khatun's madrasa was given over to a third school of Islamic jurisprudence, the Hanafi.[31] Although these women were able to choose whom and what they supported, they were nevertheless tied to the senior male member of the Ayyubid family in the city in other ways – notably the location of their foundations. Al-Salihiyya was established as a predominantly Hanbali district, just beyond the city of Damascus, which explains al-Ashraf's interest in sponsoring an institution there. A second Hanbali madrasa was established there in 1231 by Rabi'a Khatun, the sister of Saladin, apparently at the instigation of her confidante, the daughter of the madrasa's first professor, Nasih al-Din 'Abd al-Rahman.[32] The choice of so many family members to follow al-Ashraf in building in al-Salihiyya rather than in the centre of Damascus itself seems to have been determined by their need to be close to the royal (male) foundation. Women were able to support any religious foundations that they chose, but their patronage was still structured around that of al-Ashraf. This provides a model against which to consider

---

[28] RCEA X, 3682; Mulder, 'The Mausoleum of Imam al-Shafi'i', 22–3. The inscription belongs to Saladin's work at the site in the 1170s. On the association of Ayyubid madrasas with the Sunni revival see Humphreys, *From Saladin to the Mongols*, 209–12; Y. Tabbaa, *Constructions of Power and Piety in Medieval Aleppo* (University Park, PA, 1997), 100–8.

[29] Humphreys, *From Saladin to the Mongols*, 210–12.

[30] Meinecke, 'Der Survey des Damaszener Altstadtsviertels aṣ-Ṣāliḥīya', no. 71. Khadija Khatun had been offered in marriage to Jalal al-Din Khwarazmshah by her father, al-Mu'azzam, but the plan came to nothing.

[31] Humphreys, 'Women as Patrons', 44. Her father, al-Mu'azzam, promoted Hanafi Sunnism.

[32] Meinecke, 'Der Survey des Damaszener Altstadtsviertels aṣ-Ṣāliḥīya', no. 73; Humphreys, 'Women as Patrons', 40–1, 46.

Tamta's actions. Whilst she may have decided which Christian confessions, and which Christian institutions, to support in Akhlat and Taron, the direction of that policy may well have had to accommodate al-Ashraf's overall policies. Thus the division of her support between Armenian monasteries in Taron and Georgian Christians on pilgrimage may have been as much a response to the Georgians' greater international standing in the Holy Land and al-Ashraf's desire not to incur their enmity as a sign of Tamta's own personal beliefs or allegiances. This issue is explored in the next chapter.

Terkan Khatun's other foundation, a *ribat* for Sufi mystics, is now lost, and all that is known about it is its name. It can also be fitted into a broader trend of female patronage in Ayyubid Syria. Terkan's sister-in-law, Dayfa Khatun (sister of al-Ashraf), who was married to her cousin, al-Zahir Ghazi, the ruler of Aleppo, similarly founded a hostel, the Khanqah al-Farafra (a Sufi hospice, which might have acted as a refuge for widows), and a madrasa, the Madrasa al-Firdaws, in Aleppo in the 1230s. The madrasa is the finest Ayyubid foundation in Syria, built on a scale and magnificence that is only paralleled in Egypt. It doubled as a home for Sufis, and includes extensive poetic inscriptions around its courtyard that evoke Sufi beliefs.[33] It has been suggested that women's support for Sufism reflected the fact that they could participate more actively in this mystical branch of Islam than they could in the more formal institutions around the mosque and madrasa. Women are also well documented as the builders of tombs, both for themselves and for members of their families. There was a long tradition of such buildings in the Ayyubid world, such as the tomb for Farrukhshah, a cousin of al-Ashraf, which was built in Damascus by his mother in 1183.[34] The tomb reveals both the financial independence of widows and the importance of maintaining familial links even after death.

With the exception of Dayfa Khatun's foundations in Aleppo, one striking aspect of all these Ayyubid female foundations is their scale. All are relatively small buildings, with little architectural aspiration. This stands in marked contrast to the buildings erected by their counterparts in Anatolia. The complexes that were erected by women in Seljuk and Turkoman territories in the first half of the thirteenth century are both larger in size and more ambitious in execution. The two great foundations by women in Kayseri, the mosque–hospital complex partly financed by Gevher Nesibe, sister of Kaykhusraw I in 1205, and the even more imposing complex built by Mahperi

---

[33] Tabbaa, 'Dayfa Khatun'; Tabbaa, *Constructions of Power*, 173–80.
[34] *RCEA* IX, 3381; *TEI*, 8111; J. Sauvaget and M. Écochard, *Les monuments ayyoubides de Damas, etc.* (Paris, 1938–48), 2: 25.

Khatun in 1238, both dwarf their equivalents in Syria.[35] In Divriği, the hospital founded by Turan Malik in 1229, as part of a larger complex built with Ahmadshah, her cousin and husband, is equally imposing, although in this case through the extraordinarily dense carving that surrounds each of the building's entrances. In addition to the hospitals and madrasas these women founded, we also have evidence of support for Sufi hospices and shrines. Mahperi Khatun built a mausoleum shrine to a local holy man, Sheikh Turesan. Her daughter-in-law, Gurji Khatun, the former Christian daughter of Queen Rusudan of Georgia turned Muslim wife of Kaykhusraw II, financed the tomb in Konya of Jalal al-Din Rumi Mevlana, the great Sufi poet and mystic.[36] All these buildings will be considered at greater length later on.

Although the types of Seljuk foundation are similar to those erected by women in the Ayyubid world, their form and appearance is very different. Some aspects were certainly determined by pragmatic regional issues, notably about the availability of types of building material and craftsmen, which in turn determined the forms of decoration that could be executed. However, it is less clear whether similar cultural explanations can account for the differences in scale between the foundations of the Ayyubid and Turkish worlds. Does this reflect differences in the freedoms and expectations of women in each society, or their access to independent finances that could match their ambitions? The fact that the largest female Ayyubid foundation, the Firdaws Madrasa, was erected by a woman in independent control of Aleppo suggests that access to money was key.

The evident extent of female patronage at elite level among the Seljuks and Ayyubids suggests that it was an important duty of wives and widows. It therefore seems probable that Tamta also commissioned buildings in Akhlat, although none survive. However, given the location of Akhlat, it is less clear which model of patronage she would have followed: the grander buildings erected by Seljuk women, or the smaller foundations of their Ayyubid counterparts. Moreover, Tamta had access to a third model of female patronage: that exercised by her fellow Christians in the lands controlled by her Mqargrdzeli relatives and their Georgian overlords. In scale the churches and monasteries commissioned in the Caucasus at this time matched that of their Turkish neighbours to the west. At Dadivank in the eastern region of Artsakh (now the disputed territory of Nagorno-Karabagh), a magnificent new church dedicated to the Mother of God was funded by a local noblewoman, Arzu Khatun, the senior female member of

[35] Gabriel, *Monuments turcs d'Anatolie I*.   [36] Eastmond, 'Art and Frontiers'.

Figure 58 Monastery of Dadivank, Nagorno-Karabagh, Azerbaijan (disputed); 1214

a family loyal to the Mqargrdzelis [Fig. 58].[37] Completed in 1214, its inscription sets out the role of the widow who founded it, and the pain it cost her:

> By the grace of... God and of his only son Jesus Christ and the gift of the Holy Spirit, I, Arzukhatun, the servant of Christ, daughter of the great prince of princes Kurd and wife of Vakhtang of the royal family of the house of Haterk and of all of Upper Khachen, I have built with great hope this holy catholicon as the resting place for my husband and my children Hasan, my eldest, and Grigor who have passed unto the Lord in the middle of their days; for the Lord admonishes in stripping from my head its double crown of joy. My elder son Hasan perished in fighting against the Turks for his Christian faith and three months after, my much younger son Grigor, was called by the Lord... departed from life and passed unto Christ, both of them leaving their unhappy mother with an inconsolable grief. But, because during their lives they had hoped to build a church in this place and could not because of their untimely death they passed on to me [the task] of carrying out the wish in their hearts, and I took it upon myself, with great hope, and with much labour, and I built [this church] in expiation for the salvation of their souls and mine and my daughters and all my family. Now I beseech you who worship at this altar to remember in

[37] Donabédian and Thierry, *Les arts Arméniens*, 511–12.

your prayers what I have written above. This was written in the Armenian year 662 [= 1214].[38]

As in the Muslim world, these larger foundations seem to have been funded by women after they were widowed, a time when they had greater freedom of action but still had access to funds. They also tend to be additions or rebuilds of earlier churches at existing sites rather than *ex-novo* foundations. This closely echoes the stress on familial association that we have seen in conjunction with Muslim foundations in this period. However, there are exceptions to this. Another vassal of the Mqargrdzelis, Mamakhatun Vachutian, built her own church at Tegher in 1213. This church was on the same scale as the two nearby Vachutian family churches at Hovhannavank and Saghmosavank that her husband, Vache, began in 1215.[39]

Tamta's life in Akhlat placed her within the orbit of all three of these contexts for female foundation: as a Christian, her commissions would have been seen alongside those created by her contemporaries in the lands ruled by her father and uncle. In Akhlat, a city that still remembered its century of Turkic rule, she would have been measured against the splendour of royal patronage that locals had come to expect. Tamta therefore needed to consider how her power could be displayed both in terms of what women were producing in Seljuk Anatolia and what they had produced in previous generations in Akhlat. The extensive works of Shahbanu in the 1160s to rebuild the city must have loomed large over all who wanted to portray their own prestige in the city in the generations that followed. Shahbanu's work included the maintenance of roads and the replacement of wooden bridges with stone ones. She was also responsible for the building of caravanserais around Akhlat. This suggests that Tamta was likely to have undertaken similar activities.

Finally, Tamta had to act within the constraints established by her husband. The expectations placed on women's patronage in Syria were, as we have seen, more restrictive. This suggests that limits were placed on the finances available to Tamta and her fellow wives. It is not clear which model of patronage Tamta would have been able to follow. Presumably there was a tension between all three, and a need to negotiate the different expectations and expenditures that each exemplar represented. However, Tamta's general independence in Akhlat, and the city's relative isolation from its Ayyubid-controlled counterparts, suggests that she may well have been free to produce grander buildings than her fellow wives in Syria.

---

[38] Der Manuelian, 'The Monastery of Geghard', 124.
[39] Donabédian and Thierry, *Les arts Arméniens*, 585 (Tegher), 567–8 (Saghmosavank), 591–2 (Hovhannavank).

Good Works

Members of the female elite were able to express their virtues in other forms of patronage as well: the commissioning of secular buildings for the public good – baths, fountains, roads, bridges and caravanserais. In so doing, they were fulfilling the strictures of Nizam al-Mulk in his *Book of Government* that the good ruler should improve the lives of his people; he recommended enhancements to infrastructure as one way of achieving this. The account of Shahbanu's activities in Akhlat exactly matches this. Of all the building types in Nizam's list the first two were those that would have gained their founders most visibility, as they were located in urban centres. Whilst Tamta would not have been involved in the foundation of madrasas and *ribat*s, it is much more likely that she would have joined her fellow wives in the sponsorship of these secular public buildings.

The most expensive of these public buildings were baths. In addition to the bathhouses themselves, expenditure was required on their heating systems, and on the canals and aqueducts that would bring in the water. Baths had important social functions as meeting places in the city, a local focus for the community to gather. They could be particularly important social spaces for women, as they provided a private space within the public realm in which women could meet; a legitimate destination away from the confines of the house. Bathing was central to Muslim culture, with its stress on the need for cleanliness before God and the ritual ablutions before prayers. These injunctions justified the building of bathhouses, legitimising their social role (even in the early twentieth century the baths in Damascus still had extremely low prices to enable the poor to use them).[40] Ibn Jubayr claims that Damascus had more than a hundred hammams and forty ablution houses, and Jean Sauvaget found reference to some 200 in Aleppo in the thirteenth century alone.[41] It was just as important in the cities that Tamta and the Mqargrdzeli family ruled. Bathhouses have been excavated at Ani and at Dvin, and the foundation of Tbilisi was determined by the discovery of hot sulphurous springs there. It is inconceivable that Akhlat did not also have its own bathhouses too.

In around 1185 ʿAdhara Khatun, a sister of Saladin, built the Sitti ʿAdhra baths in Damascus [Fig. 59]. In contrast to the austerity of the madrasas that survive from Ayyubid Syria, the bathhouse shows the versatility and playfulness that contemporary architects delighted in when given the opportunity. Unfortunately, ʿAdhara Khatun's baths were destroyed in 1924 by the new

---

[40] M. Écochard and C. Le Coeur, *Les bains de Damas* (Beirut, 1942–3), 1: 45–52.
[41] Ibn Jubayr, 302; J. Sauvaget, 'Un bain damasquin du XIIIe siècle', *Syria* 11/4 (1930), 370–80.

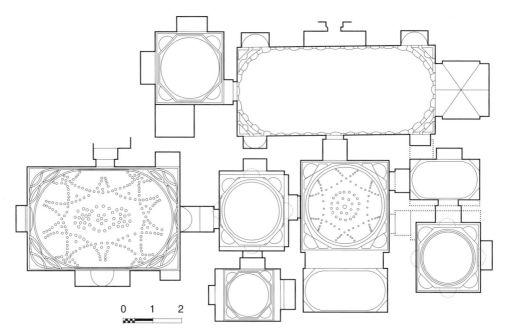

Figure 59 Plan of the vaulting of baths at the Sitti 'Adhra complex, Damascus, Syria; 1185

tyrant in Damascus, the motor car, but not before the building had been recorded.[42] As bathers moved from room to room they encountered spaces of different size and temperature, discovered endless variation in the design of the muqarnas niches in the pendentives and squinches below the dome, and witnessed different patterns of light cast from the many tiny piercings in the dome, with no pattern ever repeated. Through the steam thin, piercing shafts of light illuminated small areas of each room, providing a contrast of brilliant moments of illumination in the otherwise shaded spaces. 'Adhara Khatun's baths were part of a larger complex of *waqf* foundations, at the centre of which was her madrasa, to the north of the baths. A similar example can be found in Kayseri in Turkey, where Mahperi Khatun's huge complex opposite the city's castle had a bath complex beside its main entrance.[43] Fountains had a similar social role, as meeting place and public good; such as that established in Tokat in the 1270s from money left in the

---

[42] Écochard and Le Coeur, *Les bains de Damas*, 1: 56 (2: 23–6 notes recording part of the structure in 1929); Sauvaget, 'Un bain damasquin du XIIIe siècle', 378, n.1 on its destruction.

[43] A. Eastmond, 'Gender and Patronage between Christianity and Islam in the Thirteenth Century', in *Change in the Byzantine World in the Twelfth and Thirteenth Centuries*, eds. A. Ödekan, E. Akyürek and N. Necipoğlu (Istanbul, 2010), 78–88.

will of an unidentified woman.⁴⁴ Excavations in Ani have revealed extensive networks of waterpipes running under the city's streets, indicating a similar concern for the provision of water there as well.

One other area in which there is good evidence of female patrons promoting the public good (and themselves) is buildings to support trade. In Seljuk Anatolia, two wives of Kaykubad I, Ismat al-Dunya wa 'l-Din and Mahperi Khatun, both built a number of caravanserais in the 1230s.⁴⁵ The Kirkgöz Han, a large courtyard caravanserai with central raised mosque, was built to the north of Antalya by Ismat al-Dunya wa 'l-Din, and reflects her independent wealth (on which more below).⁴⁶ A series of seven caravanserais have been linked to Mahperi Khatun on the roads leading into Amasya, from Kayseri to the south, Sivas and Tokat to the south-east and Samsun to the north. The best preserved of these, the Hatun Han in the village of Pazar to the north-west of Tokat [Fig. 60], proclaimed its patron proudly on inscriptions set up over its porch and overlooking its courtyard:

> The construction of this han, may Allah bless it, was ordered in the reign of the great Sultan [and glorious Khan, the shadow of Allah in this world, Ghiyath al-Dunya] wa'l-Din Kaykhusraw, son of the fortunate sultan Kaykubad, associate of the prince of the believers, by the good queen Safwat al-Dunya wa'l-Din, mother of the Sultan of Sultans, Mahperi Khatun, in the year 636 [= 1238/9].⁴⁷

In each case the location of the new buildings was to encourage trade, but may also have reflected the locales in which each woman held her own independent lands under the Sultan.

The final infrastructure project required to promote trade was good roads and bridges, and both formed part of women's patronage. Whilst roads tend not to have survived, bridges have. A bridge over the river Yeşilırmak, very close to the Hatun Han, may have been linked to Mahperi's patronage, although no inscriptions survive on the structure. We can be more sure in Armenia, where the medieval bridge at Sanahin, a rare crossing-point over the river Debed, was built in 1192 by Vaneni, possibly a relative of Zakare and Ivane, in memory of her husband Abas II Kwirikid [Fig. 61]. As pinchpoints on roads, bridges provided excellent opportunities

---

⁴⁴ *RCEA* XII, 4789; *TEI*, 2436.
⁴⁵ P. Blessing, 'Women Patrons in Medieval Anatolia and a Discussion of Mahbari Khatun's Mosque Complex in Kayseri', *Belleten* 78 (2014), 475–526.
⁴⁶ Redford, 'The inscription of the Kırkgöz Han'.
⁴⁷ Erdmann, *Das Anatolische Karavansaray*, 138; *RCEA* XI, 4157, 4158; *TEI*, 2610, 2611; Eastmond, 'Gender and Patronage'; Crane, 'Saldjuq Architectural Patronage'.

Figure 60 Entrance to the covered hall at the Hatun Han in the village of Pazar, north-west of Tokat, Turkey; 1238

for rulers to promote themselves. Vaneni spelled out the details of her donation on a khatchkar beside the bridge.[48] Even more impressive is the huge dedicatory inscription set up by Gurji Khatun's second husband, the *pervane* Muin al-Din Sulayman, on his bridge at Tokat of 1250.[49] Both emphasise the pious intent of such constructions, and their role in promoting the social good. The devotion of female patrons to good deeds

---

[48] N. I. Marr, 'Nadpis' Sanahinskaiu mosta', *Khristianskii Vostok* 4 (1915), 191–2.
[49] *RCEA* XI, 4327; *TEI*, 2792; A. Gabriel, *Monuments turcs d'Anatolie II: Amasya–Tokat–Sivas* (Paris, 1934), 106–7.

Figure 61 Bridge over the river Debed at Sanahin, Armenia, built by Vaneni; 1192

was widespread, but in every case it was only possible because of the woman's marriage.

Patronage and Pensions

The great public foundations that women supported were all concerned with the piety of their founders and their concern for the public good. However, they had other ancillary roles as well. In addition to being a pious foundation and a demonstration of familial loyalty to Ayyubid beliefs, Terkan Khatun's madrasa in Damascus was set up to commemorate her name and body in perpetuity. In this it was successful: it is only thanks to the structure that we have any tangible record of her existence. It was also founded with a more immediate function: to preserve the founder's income and provide her with a pension. The chronicler al-Dahabi records that the madrasa and tomb were built some time during al-Ashraf's reign in Damascus (i.e. between 1229 and 1237), but were formally endowed with their *waqf* only in 1242, on the night of Terkan's death.[50] This suggests that in the interval Terkan used the income from the properties for her own upkeep,

---

[50] As reported in Sauvaire, 'Description de Damas II', 385–6.

and only transferred them to the madrasa when she was certain she was about to die. Given that she outlived her husband by five years, this was a sensible precaution. The last member of her family to reign in Mosul, her great-nephew Mahmud b. Masud II, had died in 1234, and the region had now passed into the hands of the *atabeg* Badr al-Din Lu'lu', so she had no prospect of support from her family or the city of her birth. The properties were presumably her main source of income, and by promising them to the madrasa she effectively protected them from seizure during her lifetime. Similarly Zahra Khatun, al-Ashraf's much younger sister, endowed a madrasa, the 'Adiliyya Sughra in eastern Damascus, in 1257, employing a particularly convoluted legal trick to ensure that its income would benefit her as well as her relatives, freedmen and eunuchs.[51]

The value of such properties is shown by the fate of al-Ashraf's daughter, his only known offspring, albeit without a recorded name. She was married to her cousin, al-Mansur Mahmud, and moved with him to Cairo. After the murder of Shajar al-Durr and the fall of the Ayyubid regime in Egypt in 1250, and its replacement by the new Mamluk rulers, her husband's lands were seized. She was allowed to retain the properties she had inherited from her father in Damascus and Harran. These included a grand mansion in Damascus, and a series of palaces, audience halls, villages, farms and grazing lands in the region around the city and in southern Syria. Gradually she was forced to sell these off one by one as she had no other income. Her husband died in 1269, and she outlived him by a quarter of a century and so eventually began to run out of money. Only some clever legal manoeuvring by her supporters saved her. First they had her declared as suffering from dementia, which allowed them to sequester her lands (now declared to have been illegally sold); then with her lands and her sanity legally restored she was able, once again, to sell them all off. 'Which gave rise to some remarks', her biographer al-Saqqay adds somewhat laconically.[52]

There are many overlaps between the pious foundations of the Ayyubids and those of Tamta's family in Armenia. Obviously, the forms of the buildings – mosques, madrasas, monasteries, churches – varied considerably, but all were underpinned by the same ideas. All were to make public statements of piety and particular branches of faith – whether Christian confessions or Islamic schools of law. In each case the architectural form was a key element in the ways in which that set of beliefs was expressed to the world around, supplemented by the use of inscriptions in prominent locations. Both also worked in the same way in terms of being individual

---

[51] Humphreys, 'Women as Patrons', 45. *RCEA* XII, 4427; *TEI*, 3951.
[52] Sauvaire, 'Description de Damas VII', 310; Sublet, 'La folie de la princesse'.

acts of patronage that were designed to ensure individual salvation. Whether a mosque, a madrasa or a monastery, each building type (and the clergy employed to maintain it) was funded with an eye on the world to come. The personal nature of the foundation inscriptions underscored this, even if Armenian inscriptions provide considerably more autobiographical information than Arabic ones. The extent of the common conception that underlies these foundations is evident in the similarity of their foundation texts. The idea of *waqf* (pious endowment) that underpins the Islamic foundations is paralleled by the list of donations that are inscribed on the walls of Armenian monuments (or listed in Byzantine foundation texts – *typika*). The extent of the slippage is such that terminology began to transcend culture. Starting with an inscription dated 1173 at Sanahin, the Arabic word *waqf* was simply transliterated into Armenian in donor inscriptions on churches to denote the legal status of the properties bequeathed to the monastery.[53]

A key point here is the ability of women to undertake these foundations. As noted above, in many cases they were set up in order to preserve the women's incomes during their lifetimes, and protect them against downturns in their fortunes, particularly after their husbands died. R. Stephen Humphreys' research into Ayyubid patronage in Damascus has shown that almost a quarter of the madrasas built were founded by women, and just over a fifth of the Sufi hospices.[54] Given the absence of women from the historical record, these numbers are surprisingly high. The evidence of female patronage in the Ayyubid world can be matched by that in the Armenian and Georgian worlds, as we have seen. In all communities, religious foundations were a means to present each donor's piety and provide a means of support in old age. Ultimately, they also acted as mausolea to provide a memorial to the body and its memory for all eternity. Thus the foundation of the Atabakiyya Madrasa in Damascus with its tomb for its founder is directly analogous to the buildings at Dadivank or Harichavank that were to contain their female founders' bodies until the end of time.

Other Motives/Patronage and Politics

The discussion so far has presented an idealised view of female patronage, inspired by welfare, piety and higher spiritual goals. However, architecture

---

[53] S. La Porta, 'Lineage, Legitimacy and Loyalty in Post-Seljuk Armenia: a reassessment of the sources of the failed Ōrbēlean revolt against king Giorgi III of Georgia', *REArm* 31 (2008–2009), 127–65, at 135, with discussion.

[54] Humphreys, 'Women as Patrons', 35.

allowed wives to give public expression to other concerns as well, particularly related to their power struggles against their rivals within the harem. This is not about petty squabbles between indolent wives, the stuff of Orientalist fables, but rather the impact of internal disputes about the succession on external affairs. This is most evident at the court of Tamta's Seljuk contemporary, Kaykubad I (1219–37). He married at least three women: a sister of al-Ashraf (known only from one inscription as Malika ʿAdiliyya – the princess, daughter of al-ʿAdil); Ismat al-Dunya wa 'l-Din, his cousin, a daughter of Mugith al-Din Tughrilshah, the governor of Erzurum; and Mahperi Khatun, the daughter of the Armenian governor of the city of Alanya, captured by Kaykubad in 1221. The foundations of some of these wives have already been mentioned, but they can now be revisited in a different light, to see how all three used commissions as a means to fight out their campaigns for legitimacy and succession. The range of buildings they erected, and the ways in which they described themselves in the texts they had inscribed on them, allow us to see how they used these foundations to manipulate their public status.

Ostensibly the best-placed wife was the daughter of al-ʿAdil, as she had the most powerful family connections, and she appears to have been most favoured by Kaykubad.[55] But there is no record of her financing any buildings. The wealth of her family and its power in Syria and Egypt do not seem to have been translated into anything that could benefit her practically in Anatolia, and there is no sign that she was able to take sufficient funds from her husband. Instead, it was the daughter of Mugith al-Din Tughrilshah of Erzurum who was the first to make a mark as the dominant wife of Kaykubad. She was also Kaykubad's cousin, and so came to court well connected and well financed. Her main commission was the erection of the Ulu Camii in Uluborlu, a town to the west of Konya, in 1232. This was the principal Friday mosque in the town, in which the Sultan and Caliph's names would be pronounced in the *khutba*, the weekly ceremonial acknowledgement of their authority in the town. The mosque's foundation inscription declares its patronage:

> This blessed mosque was built during the days of the empire of the august Sultan, the magnificent king of kings, the shadow of Allah on earth, ʿAla al-Dunya wa'l-Din, Abul-Fath Kaykubad, son of Kaykhusraw, by the fortune of the queen, the wise, the just Ismat al-Dunya wa'l-Din, the purity of Islam and of the Muslims, daughter of the martyred king Tughrilshah,

---

[55] Ibn Bibi, 151.

son of Kılıç Arslan – may her prosperity endure – in Rajab of the year 629 [May 1232].[56]

The queen's declaration of her paternal descent and his martyrdom made the nobility of her blood and the piety of her father abundantly clear. To this noble bloodline, she could add independent wealth: the explicit proclamation that the mosque was paid for out of the personal fortune of the queen, which distinguished the mosque from other buildings erected out of the royal finances.[57] As such the building became an assertion of her family's importance, and her own independence. Both enhanced her claim to pre-eminence among the rival wives of Kaykubad. We have already encountered the caravanserai she was responsible for, the Kirkgöz Han to the north of Antalya. Here again the foundation inscription gives much more space to her praise than that of her husband, the Sultan.[58]

However, whilst this rival wife may have had a superior bloodline, and a higher private income, both she and Malika ʿAdiliyya were ultimately out-manoeuvred by Mahperi Khatun in the one contest that really mattered: the succession. The historian of the Seljuks, Ibn Bibi, records that Kaykubad wanted to be succeeded by Rukn al-Din, his elder son by Malika, his diplomatic Ayyubid wife whom he had married in Malatya in 1227. Whilst this may have been motivated by Rukn al-Din's personal qualities, it undoubtedly also fitted the need for increased rapprochement between the Seljuks and the Ayyubids in the face of the arrival of the Khwarazmians and Mongols in the Caucasus in the 1220s, who were greedily looking both west into Anatolia and south into Syria. But Kaykubad's wishes were not to be obeyed. He died in 1237, poisoned by his emirs; subsequent events show that the assassination was exploited by Mahperi.[59] Both Rukn al-Din and his brother Kılıç Arslan were strangled, along with their mother, Malika. These murders are mentioned in Ibn Bibi's Persian-language chronicle, but are passed over in silence by the Ayyubid and other Arabic chroniclers of the period.[60] Malika seems to have gone to her grave unmourned, even unnoticed. Nothing shows Mahperi's seizure of power in her son's name more

---

[56] RCEA XI, 4044; TEI, 2493.
[57] J. M. Rogers, 'Waqf and Patronage in Seljuk Anatolia: The Epigraphic Evidence', *Anatolian Studies* 26 (1976), 69–104, at 74; and now a fuller discussion in Redford, 'Paper, Stone, Scissors', 152–8.
[58] Redford, 'The Inscription of the Kırkgöz Han'.
[59] Yıldız, 'The Rise and Fall of a Tyrant'; in contrast, Redford, 'Paper, Stone, Scissors', 157–8, suggests that the murders may have been instigated by Ismat al-Dunya wa'l-Din to promote Kaykhusraw II, as both had long connections with Erzurum.
[60] Ibn Bibi, 203–4.

clearly than this ability to kill a rival wife with apparent impunity. With no rivals to dispute the accession, Mahperi's own son, Kaykhusraw, came to the throne. In 1237 he was still only around fifteen years old, and so still open to his mother's influence (only in the 1240s was Mahperi's influence to be supplanted by that of Kaykhusraw's Georgian wife, Gurji Khatun). Over the next six years Mahperi was able to work through her son, effectively to rewrite her own history and to present herself as a suitable *walida*, mother of the Sultan.

In the same way that the daughter of Tughrilshah had used patronage to display her lineage and wealth, so too Mahperi erected major public buildings to transform her own identity. The first major commission with which she is associated is the complex named after her, the Mahperi Huand Hatun complex in Kayseri, one of the major cities of Seljuk Rum [Fig. 62].[61] This was an intensely public building, with a very prominent location at the heart of the city, and significant inscriptions naming the founder. Built immediately to the east of the citadel, it faced all those approaching and leaving the city.[62] The complex comprised a mosque, madrasa, bath complex and Mahperi's tomb. Built in the local black basalt, the complex has a looming presence, despite its relatively low proportions.

Mahperi's complex was centred on her mausoleum. The tomb structure itself appears deliberately modest; close-up views are blocked by walls, so screening Mahperi from close investigation [Fig. 63]. It is a physical manifestation of the idea of 'the elevated curtain and impregnable veil' used by Ayyubid wives in their foundation inscriptions. However, although the tomb is difficult to see, it is harder to avoid. The conical dome was the most prominent element of the complex's silhouette (the present dome over the mosque and the minaret are both later additions). The tomb also lies at the very centre of the complex, a permanent reminder to all worshippers of the building's patron; this required the internal vaulting structure of the mosque to be altered to accommodate it, and forced all those entering the mosque to pass by the tomb. The location of the tomb in turn seems to have determined the overall placement of the complex, lining the tomb up directly opposite the Yeni Kapı (the New Gate) into the city.[63]

---

[61] Blessing, 'Women Patrons in Medieval Anatolia'; Eastmond, 'Gender and Patronage'.
[62] Gabriel, *Monuments turcs d'Anatolie I*, 39–51.
[63] On the tomb itself see Ü. Ü. Bates, 'The Anatolian Mausoleum of the Twelfth, Thirteenth and Fourteenth Centuries' (Ph.D. thesis, University of Michigan, 1970), 141–5; and H. Karamağaralı, 'Kayseri'deki Hunad Camiinin Restitüsyonu ve Hunad Manzumesinin Kronolojisi Hakkında Bazı Mülahzalar', *A.Ü. Ilahiyat Fakültesi Dergisi* 21 (1976), 199–243, at 213–14.

Figure 62 Albert Gabriel's 1931 reconstruction drawing of the Mahperi complex, Kayseri, Turkey; 1237–8 (from *Monuments turcs d'Anatolie I: Kayseri–Niğde* (Paris, 1931))

Figure 63 Screen in front of the tomb of Mahperi Khatun, facing the gate into Kayseri, Turkey; 1238

Given the scale of the buildings and the alterations to its fabric to accommodate the tomb, the fact that the date of completion given in the inscriptions is just a year after the accession of Kaykhusraw suggests that it was probably begun before Kaykubad's death, possibly by the Sultan himself, and only completed by his widow. What is noteworthy, however, is that whatever the building history of the complex, the inscriptions claimed it all for Mahperi and her son:

> The construction of this blessed mosque was ordered in the days of the august Ghiyath al-Dunya wa'l-Din Abu'l-fath Kaykhusraw, son of Kaykubad, by his mother, the great queen, the wise, the ascetic, Safwat

al-Dunya wa'l-Din – may God prolong the days of her son and double his power – in Shawwal of the year 635 [May–June 1238].[64]

Indeed, Kaykubad receives no significant mention in the texts, despite the fact that it was only through him that Mahperi had gained the position she now held. She made it a monument to herself, distinct from that of the dynasty into which she married (Kaykubad was buried in the Alaeddin Camii in Konya along with all his predecessors, bar his brother, Kayka'us I, buried in the Şifaiye Medrese in Sivas, 1217–18).[65] It is perhaps to be seen as the central focus of a new element of the dynasty, legitimating Kaykhusraw's reign and providing a status for his mother and regent that she cannot have held during her husband's lifetime, when she was certainly the least significant of his wives.

The decision to complete such a large complex is also significant: it moved Mahperi beyond the realms both of her rival-wives, but also of the vast majority of female patrons in thirteenth-century Anatolia, who are most visible through the patronage of individual tomb towers. It established her within that funerary tradition, but allowed her to express ambitions far in excess of those small structures. Within Kayseri, Mahperi's complex was the largest structure. The mosque alone was larger than the main city mosque, the Ulu Camii.[66] The complex also outdid the building that acted as its principal model, the Çifte Medrese, the hospital–madrasa complex built a generation earlier by Kaykhusraw I in execution of the will of his sister Gevher Nesibe on the north side of the city (completed in 1205/6).[67] This too was a double foundation, with madrasa and hospital side-by-side as well as the patron's tomb. It was built for a woman and, judging by the wording of the foundation inscription, was funded out of her own independent wealth, albeit only posthumously.[68] However, it was further away from the citadel, considerably smaller in size and the decoration of its portals far less elaborate. The *coup de grâce* was the way in which Mahperi shifted the site of her tomb to the centre of the complex; at the Çifte Medrese the tomb for its founder was more anonymously sited at one end of the complex, within its walls.

---

[64] Gabriel, *Monuments turcs d'Anatolie I*, 46; *RCEA* XI, 4146, 4147; *TEI*, 2599, 2600. On the relationship between inscriptions and reality in patronage see E. S. Wolper, 'Princess Safwat al-Dunya wa al-Din and the Production of Sufi Buildings and Hagiographies in Pre-Ottoman Anatolia', in *Women, Patronage, and Self-Representation in Islamic Societies*, ed. D. F. Ruggles (Albany, NY, 2000), 35–52.

[65] Two other tombs were later added to the mausoleum: one for Mahperi's granddaughter, Seljuk Khatun, and one which is now unidentified.

[66] Gabriel, *Monuments turcs d'Anatolie I*, 32–5. [67] Gabriel, *Monuments turcs d'Anatolie I*, 60–2.

[68] *RCEA* X, 3616; *TEI*, 2877.

The Huand Hatun complex allowed Mahperi to overcome the earlier disparities between the wives, their access to money, and their influence at court. It enabled her to portray herself as a truly pious woman, and so suitable to be the mother of the Sultan. The impression of piety was furthered by other foundations that she funded in the region around Kayseri. To the west of the city, on a mountain on the way to Nevşehir, she erected a shrine to a local holy man, Sheikh Turesan. Given Mahperi's origins as a Christian concubine, and the murky background to her son's accession to the throne, the months immediately after Kaykubad's death must have been a crucial time for the establishment of the new ruler and his regent mother. The immediate takeover of the Huand Hatun complex and the sponsorship of an important local shrine enabled Mahperi to display herself anew as a pious Muslim queen, with access to wealth and power clearly in a most forceful and permanent way.

The importance of buildings as the means to construct and present a particular identity, and to entrench that as a communal memory, can be seen in the long-delayed reaction to the murder of Malika 'Adiliyya. Whilst her death went unmourned in Arabic chronicles, it remained an open wound to her surviving children. Malika's daughters had not been killed along with her sons – a clear indication of their insignificance in the world of dynastic politics. In 1247/8 the daughters were finally able to erect a funerary monument to their murdered mother [Fig. 64]. By that time Mahperi had lost power. After the disastrous battle of Kösedağ in 1243, at which the Seljuks were routed by the Mongols, the ruling Sultan, Kaykhusraw, fled to Ankara with his wife and sons, but his mother, Mahperi, sought protection in Cilicia from her Armenian kinsman Baron Constantine, the effective ruler of the Armenians in Cilicia in the name of his son Levon II. Constantine took little account of her Armenian origins and immediately betrayed her to the Mongol general Baiju (confirming the Seljuks' already low opinion of his reliability and fidelity), in order to prevent the Mongols from invading his lands. As Bar Hebraeus concludes: 'and this most hateful and blameworthy act appeared in the sight of all kings as a thing which should never have been done. And the queen was carried away into captivity, and behold, she is there to this day, and is not released.'[69] Whilst she was imprisoned by the Mongols, and once her son Kaykhusraw was dead, the daughters were finally able to commemorate their mother.

The tomb they erected for Malika was set up on the road from Kayseri to Sivas, some 6 kilometres east of Kayseri itself. This was a relatively remote

---

[69] Bar Hebraeus, 406–8. She had actually returned to Anatolia by 1254, when she is mentioned in an embassy of Kaykubad II: Ibn Bibi, 264.

Figure 64 Tomb of Malika ʿAdiliyya, Kayseri, Turkey; 1247/8

location, suggesting that the daughters did not have the political connections to find a site closer to the city walls, but its situation beside the main road to Sivas shows that its visibility was still an important factor in its planning. The octagonal tomb tower is relatively simple in design and makes no overt political statement, but the foundation inscription commissioned by the daughters reveals that the building was intensely partisan:

> This is the martyrium of the queen, the virtuous martyr, the wise, the ascetic, Ismat al-Dunya wa'l-Din, the innocent woman of Islam and the Muslims, the lady among women of this world, the Zubaida of her time, who possessed the most glorious qualities, the princess of this world and the next, queen of queens, source of goodness and blessings, daughter of al-Malik al-ʿAdil Abu Bakr, son of Ayyub. May God enlighten her tomb,

perfume her soul and her breath. Its construction was ordered by her daughters, of noble conduct, may God grant them a good fate. In the year 645 [1247–8].[70]

If Mahperi's inscriptions played down her husband to promote her son, this text ignores the Seljuks completely, excluding any reference to Malika's husband or to the ruling Seljuk Sultan, and even ignores her murdered sons. Malika 'Adaliyya is memorialised solely in terms of her Ayyubid family, tracing her descent back three generations to the founder of the dynasty. The comparison to Zubaida placed her on a par with the wife of the eighth-century Abbasid Caliph Harun al-Rashid. Zubaida had been a famous patron, recorded as the builder of a string of wells, reservoirs and artificial pools that provided water for Muslim pilgrims along the hajj route from Baghdad to Mecca.[71] Her fame lasted into the thirteenth century, and she was the subject of one of Ibn Khallikan's biographies. The trope of being a patron of pilgrims was, of course, what Kirakos Gandzaketsi highlighted in his account of Tamta's life.

However, whilst the inscription presented Malika as an Ayyubid princess, the form of the tomb was resolutely Seljuk. It was clearly built by local masons, used to working in the readily available stone of the region, and well versed in the decorative vocabulary of the area. Presumably Malika's daughters had either been cut off from their Syrian roots for too long and so were unaware of how to present their mother in a suitably Ayyubid fashion, or they lacked the resources to carry it out.

It is possible that Malika's tomb inspired a final response from Mahperi, from beyond the grave. Mahperi's executors placed an inscription on the sarcophagus inside her tomb. Its phrasing is very similar to that on Malika's tomb, but with different comparisons.[72] Mahperi is compared to Maryam, the mother of Christ, venerated by Muslims and Christians alike (a possible reflection of Mahperi's own mixed background?), and Khadija. This seems a deliberate riposte to Malika's comparison to Zubayda. Khadija was the first wife of the Prophet Muhammad. She was a wealthy businesswoman and trader with a noble ancestry, and she supported him morally and financially during his prophecy. She therefore represented a link to the family of the Prophet himself, rather than merely to the wife of a caliph, however

---

[70] *RCEA* XI, 4273; *TEI*, 2731. See also Y. Özbek, 'Women's Tombs in Kayseri', *Kadın/Woman 2000* 3/1 (2002), 65–85, Turkish text 86–114, at 78–9 n.17.

[71] Ibn Khallikan, 1: 533; V. Porter and M. A. S. Abdel Haleem, eds., *Hajj: Journey to the Heart of Islam* (London, 2012), 95–6.

[72] *RCEA* XI, 4259; *TEI*, 2718; see also Özbek, 'Women's Tombs in Kayseri', 78 n.8.

esteemed. This example of the politics of patronage among one cohort of wives shows the potential of buildings to define relationships. The types of building chosen, their locations and the ways in which the wives were presented in inscriptions all worked to give each wife a public memorial. The concentrated nature of the Seljuk state was different from the more diffuse world of the Ayyubids but nevertheless shows the options open to Tamta to present herself to the people she ruled over.

The role of wife in the Seljuk and Ayyubid worlds was a problematic one. It required women to balance the virtues of seclusion and modesty with the realpolitik of succession crises and the need for personal security. The life of a Muslim wife had a very different structure from that of a Christian wife, who – in theory at least – faced no threat to her position or to the inheritance of her sons. Adapting to the new role was perhaps the most challenging change that Tamta had to face. Her unique position as a Christian and as a semi-permanent resident in Akhlat, far away from the centre of Ayyubid politics, perhaps protected her from many of the dangers other wives faced. The failure of al-Ashraf to produce any male heirs must have reduced tensions between the wives, although at the same time it made it even more important for each of them to prepare carefully for the trials of widowhood: none had a son to support them, and none could be guaranteed to remain welcome in the court of their husband's successor.

Patronage was a crucial tool that these women could turn to to try to find a solution to these problems. The evidence from Anatolia, from Syria and from the Caucasus suggests that the functions of patronage were shared by women in all three areas, but at the same time, the mechanics varied greatly. Regional variations in style remained despite the movement of these women (and the architects who may have accompanied them) between courts and cultures. So too did the types and scale of the buildings they could afford. Ayyubid female patronage appears on a much smaller scale than either Seljuk or Caucasian patronage, but Tamta stood on the cusp of all these worlds, and had to negotiate between the expectations and resources each offered.

8 | Tamta

A Christian at the Ayyubid Court

The previous chapter provided an overview of female patronage in Tamta's world; this chapter focuses more closely on the works of Tamta herself, and the position of Christians in the Islamic world. To what extent were Christians tolerated at court and in wider Muslim society, and what impact did the Christians have on the Islamic culture around them? Although Tamta's position was unique in the Ayyubid family – no other Ayyubid ruler married a Christian of such importance – interreligious marriages were an important part of international diplomacy, as we have already seen. Indeed, it was a widespread practice elsewhere in the region in this period. The best-documented examples come from the Ayyubids' most formidable Muslim rivals, the Seljuks in Anatolia. Christian wives are recorded for five successive generations of sultans across the twelfth and thirteenth centuries, usually as part of diplomatic engagements with the Byzantines to the west, or the Armenians and Georgians to the south and east. In 1243 Baldwin II, the Latin Emperor in Constantinople, sought one of his French nieces as a possible diplomatic bride to marry to the Sultan Kaykhusraw II. He wrote to the French queen, Blanche of Castile, to reassure her about the number of Christians at the court: 'For the Sultan himself is the son of a Christian woman, whom his father kept in the Greek Christian faith for the whole of her life. Many of the pagan nobles in those parts have Christian wives, who persevere in their own faith.'[1] He went on to explain that Kaykhusraw guaranteed his bride that she would be allowed to remain Christian after the marriage, with her own chaplain and a fully Christian household. He would even offer to pay for the building and upkeep of churches in all his cities. He even hinted that the Sultan might convert to Christianity if she proved an affectionate (presumably a euphemism for fertile) bride, although here the letter is surely moving into the realms of fantasy.[2] Having said that, many of

---

[1] Du Chesne and Du Chesne, 5: 425; Hendrickx, nos. 219–21; the correspondence is summarised in R. L. Wolff, 'The Latin Empire of Constantinople, 1204–1261', in *A History of the Crusades*: 2, eds. R. L. Wolff and H. W. Hazard (Madison; Milwaukee; London, 1969), 187–233, at 223.

[2] Du Chesne and Du Chesne, *Historiæ Francorum*, 5: 424–6; Hendrickx, 'Régestes', nos. 219–21. Nikephoros Gregoras, 1: 110, implies that in 1266 Kaykaʿus II was involved in negotiations to be baptised. Vryonis, *The Decline of Medieval Hellenism*, 487–8.

these brides retained their Christian faith throughout their lives, even when their sons went on to rule as sultans.³ The Christian queens sometimes converted to Islam (accounts, unsurprisingly, tend to be mixed: Seljuk sources imply the conversions are sincere, whereas Christian ones claim the affected queens were beaten and their conversions were forced upon them).⁴

Archaeological evidence bears out the claim of tolerance of religious practice. A small Byzantine church in the Seljuk citadel at Alanya was carefully maintained as a chapel even as Kaykubad built a new palace around it after his capture of the city in 1221.⁵ And in Konya a church dedicated either to St Plato or to St Amphilochios was recorded in 1215 by al-Harawi on the fortified acropolis near the Alaeddin Camii and royal palace.⁶ Thus places were maintained for Christian worship throughout the Seljuk period at the heart of royal palaces. The model presented by the Seljuks seems to have been adopted by Tamta's Ayyubid husbands, who similarly allowed her 'to stay in her religion' and built a chapel for her in the citadel at Akhlat.⁷ The large Christian populations in Akhlat, Alanya and Konya meant that they already had churches for each confession, but the palace chapels gave the Christians and their faith added legitimacy within the state.

The appearance of these churches is unknown: whether they were made inconspicuous within the palace, or were more overt symbols of the continued presence of Christians at the heart of power. As the discussion of the appearance of cities in Chapter 6 has shown, there was a great deal of architectural intermingling in all these centres. So whilst the evidence of Alanya implies a distinct, Byzantine appearance to the church there, that from elsewhere suggests that churches might take on many of the visual trappings of the dominant Muslim culture around them. The Syriac monastery of Mar Benham, just to the south-east of Mosul, which thrived in the early thirteenth century, used many decorative features that appear to have been taken over from contemporary Muslim buildings.⁸ The unusual niche in the west façade of the church has the same form and arabesque designs as the

---

³ Shukurov, 'Harem Christianity'.
⁴ As is the case with the conversion of Gurji Khatun: Eastmond, 'Art and Frontiers'.
⁵ Redford, *Landscape and the State in Medieval Anatolia*, 15.
⁶ V. Macip Tekinalp, 'Palace Churches of the Anatolian Seljuks: Tolerance or Necessity?', *Byzantine and Modern Greek Studies* 33/2 (2009), 148–67; it survived into the twentieth century as the Eflatun masjid – mosque of Plato – probably finally converted in the fifteenth century. For two further, but more problematic, examples, see R. Shukurov, 'Churches in the Citadels of Ispir and Bayburt: An Evidence of "Harem Christianity"?', in *Polidoro: Studi offerti ad Antonio Carile*, ed. G. Vespignani (Spoleto, 2013), 713–24.
⁷ Al-Nuwayri, 29: 48; La Porta, '"The Kingdom and the Sultanate were Conjoined"', 88 n.79.
⁸ B. Snelders, *Identity and Christian–Muslim Interaction: Medieval Art of the Syrian Orthodox from the Mosul Area* (Leuven, 2010), 257–335.

Figure 65 Niche from the west façade of Deir Mar Benham, south-east of Mosul, Iraq; first half of the thirteenth century

Figure 66 *Mihrab* niche from Great Mosque, Mosul, Iraq; first half of the thirteenth century

contemporaneous *mihrab* niche in Mosul's Great Mosque [Figs. 65 and 66], distinguished only by the cross at the heart of the ornament. The shared aesthetic may have been employed in a desire to blend in, but more probably it was to demonstrate status by employing what was universally recognised by the elite as sophisticated, cultured, but above all expensive.[9]

The palatine churches may not have been generally open to the Christian population given their locations in royal citadels, but they would have found their congregations in the large numbers of Christians who worked or resided at court. In the 1220s John Komnenos Mavrozomes, a Greek Christian, served as an emir at the court of Kaykubad II, and helped to rebuild the walls of the city of Konya.[10] At the same time, Basil of Malatya, a Chalcedonian Armenian, held the position of *protonotarios* (notary). He

---

[9] Deir Mar Benham: C. Preusser, *Nordmesopotamische Baudenkmäler altchristlicher und islamischer Zeit* (Leipzig, 1911), 3–13, pl. 13 and 14; Great Mosque, Mosul: Sarre and Herzfeld, *Archäologische Reise*, 2: 227, 237–49; 3: pl. 90.

[10] S. N. Yıldız, 'Manuel Komnenos Mavrozomes and his Descendants at the Seljuk Court: The Formation of a Christian Seljuk–Komnenian Elite', in *Crossroads between Latin Europe and the*

commissioned a gospel book in Kayseri that year in which he called the Sultan 'my holy sovereign the most high Great Sultan of Romania, Armenia, Syria, and the places and countries of all Turks on land and on sea, Kaykubad, son of Giyath al-Din Kaykhusraw'.[11] Like the author of the Red Gospels, introduced in Chapter 2, Basil must have been a recent convert to Chalcedonianism (Greek and Georgian Orthodoxy): the colophons naming the scribe and artist are in perfect Armenian, but the Greek text describing Basil himself is full of spelling mistakes and other grammatical errors. Many men split their allegiance in similar ways. Basil Giagoupes, a Christian emir of the Seljuk ruler Mas'ud II in the 1280s, paid his Sultan homage in the inscription in the funerary church commissioned by his wife, Tamar (who might feasibly be identifiable as Gurji Khatun, the daughter of Queen Rusudan of Georgia, now married for the third time), in the Ihlara gorge in Cappadocia to the west of Kayseri.[12] Basil's political identity as a general in the Seljuk army required him to show his allegiance to his Sultan, but his religious identity as a Christian ensured that he simultaneously acknowledged the Byzantine Emperor in Constantinople, Andronikos II.[13]

The skills that Christians and Jews developed gave some of them high-ranking posts at the courts of both the Ayyubids and the Seljuks. We have already encountered notaries such as Basil of Malatya or Zacharias, fluent in the five languages of Anatolia.[14] Saladin employed a Copt as his personal secretary in Egypt.[15] Jews and Syriacs found fame as doctors, including Moses Maimonides, who was Saladin's physician, and Amin al-Dawla Abu al-Karim Sa'id, who 'was wholly loved and honoured' for ministering to the Caliph al-Nasir in Baghdad.[16] Through their work at the Seljuk and Ayyubid

---

Near East: Corollaries of the Frankish Presence in the Eastern Mediterranean (12th–14th Centuries), ed. S. Leder (Würzburg, 2011), 55–77, esp. 69–70.

[11] Athens, Gennadios Library, MS Gr. 1.5: Korobeinikov, 'A Greek Orthodox Armenian'; A. Mitsani, 'The Illustrated Gospel Book of Basil Meliteniotes (Caesaria, 1226)', *Deltion tes Christianikes Archaiologikes Hetaireias* 26 (2005), 149–64; the colophon on fols 166r–v is transcribed by Mitsani, 158. See also R. L. Wolff, 'The Lascarids' Asiatic Frontiers Once More', *Orientalia Christiania Periodica* 15 (1949), 194–7.

[12] Eastmond, 'Art and Frontiers'; R. Shukurov, 'Iagupy: tiurkskaia familiia na vizantiiskoi sluzhbe', in *Vizantiiskie Ocherki: trudy rossiiskikh uchenykh k XXI Mezhdunarodnomu kongressu vizantinistov* (St Petersburg, 2006), 205–29, at 210–17.

[13] V. Laurent, 'L'inscription de l'église Saint-Georges de Bélisérama', *REB* 26 (1968), 367–71; S. Vryonis, 'Another Note on the Inscription of the Church of St George of Beliserama', *Byzantina* 9 (1977), 11–22.

[14] Korobeinikov, 'A Greek Orthodox Armenian'; Shukurov, 'Harem Christianity', 131–2.

[15] K. J. Werthmuller, *Coptic Identity and Ayyubid Politics in Egypt, 1218–1250* (Cairo; New York, 2010), 46–7.

[16] Amin al-Dawla: Bar Hebraeus, 385–6. For the unfortunate Jewish doctor brought in to cure the Mongol lord Khul, see Grigor Aknertsi, 331: he was killed after encouraging Khul to bathe his feet in the stomachs of thirty red-headed local (i.e. Armenian) youths.

courts, such men grew wealthy enough to be able to endow institutions, such as the caravanserai between Sivas and Malatya that was founded in 1218 by an Armenian–Syriac doctor from Malatya, Abu Salim bin Abil-Hasan al-Sammas, who celebrated his new institution with a trilingual inscription in Armenian, Syriac and Arabic.[17] Tamta, allowed to retain her faith, was not alone as a Christian at the heart of a Muslim court. Equally, Muslims were appointed at Christian courts. The Georgian kings had a tradition of employing Muslim secretaries that looked back to the twelfth century, when Ibn al-Azraq from Mayyafariqin worked for Davit IV the Builder, and this must have continued into the thirteenth century, given the need for Tamar to communicate with all her Muslim neighbours.[18] The Mqargrdzelis certainly employed Muslim *qadi*s (judges) to help administer justice in their lands, even in cases solely between Christian litigants.[19]

The picture presented by this evidence is one of religious tolerance at court, particularly in Seljuk Rum, which has been celebrated by modern historians.[20] The case of Tamta might suggest that such tolerant interreligious marriages were more common in the Islamic world, but as no other marriages are recorded between Ayyubid rulers and Christian women of high status it is impossible to substantiate this further (and remember that al-Awhad had at least twenty-five brothers and male first cousins who were in need of brides, preferably ones who could bring them political or territorial advantage). It is highly likely that these other Ayyubid males had Christian or ex-Christian slave girls in their harems, but none of these was considered important enough to warrant even a fleeting mention in any text or inscription. Tamta emerges as a unique woman in a unique position. However, the work that she did, as we have already seen, fits a known model for elite women in the Ayyubid world – the only difference is that she supported Christian, not Muslim, institutions.

Tamta in Akhlat

The information we have about Tamta's actions comes from Kirakos Gandzaketsi's account of her life in Akhlat, cited in the opening chapter.

---

[17] Erdmann, *Das Anatolische Karavansaray*, no. 18.
[18] V. Minorsky, 'Caucasica [I] in the history of Mayyafariqin', *BSOAS* 13 (1949), 27–35; see also F. Micheau, 'Les médecins orientaux au service des princes latins', in *Occident et Proche-Orient: Contacts scientifiques au temps des Croisades*, eds. I. Draelants, A. Tihon and B. van den Abeele (Leuven, 1997), 95–115.
[19] See Chapter 2.
[20] Cahen, *The Formation of Turkey*, 123–4: 'a degree of religious toleration superior to that in the rest of the Islamic world'.

Kirakos was a contemporary of Tamta, writing between the 1240s and 1260s, and his main interest in Tamta concerned her work on behalf of Christians under Ayyubid rule.[21] It is worth quoting Kirakos Gandzaketsi's account once more:

> The coming of this woman into the house of the sultans brought about much good, for the lot of the Christians under their domination improved, especially in Taron since the monasteries which were there and had been under taxation, had the rate of their taxes lowered, and half of them had the whole tax discontinued. [The Muslims] ordered those under their domination not to despoil or trouble travellers going to Jerusalem for pilgrimage. The Georgians especially expanded [their influence]... Therefore they [the Muslims] honoured the Georgians even more, for they [the Georgians] were not taxed in all their cities, and in Jerusalem as well. She was named Tamta.
>
> Thus was friendship and unity achieved between the Georgian kingdom and the sultans' lordship.[22]

She may have been involved in military affairs as well. When fighting broke out between the Georgians and Akhlat in 1222 (when the city was controlled by al-Muzaffar Ghazi), the Georgians appealed not to the governor but to al-Ashraf to restore the peace, presumably because Tamta was seen as an intermediary.[23]

Taxation

For Tamta to have been able to reduce taxes on monasteries in Taron required her to have a deal of influence over the government of the region. As we have seen, she probably exercised this power in the name of al-Ashraf, but through his *hajib* Husam al-Din 'Ali, in al-Ashraf's all-too-frequent absences. However, neither Tamta nor Husam al-Din 'Ali was left solely in charge, and both had to deal with al-Ashraf's interference, such as the occasion when al-Ashraf, apparently on an infatuated whim, gave the entirety of the city's revenues to a musician who had caught his eye.[24] Taxation was an area of government in which women could actively participate. Indeed, it was a particularly valuable form of social intervention for women. It required no outlay of capital, and so was a very useful tactic for people without the land holdings or other wealth that was needed to endow a

---

[21] R. Bedrosian, 'The Turco-Mongol Invasions and the Lords of Armenia in the 13th–14th Centuries' (Ph.D. thesis, Columbia University, 1979), 22–7.
[22] Kirakos 83 (trans. Bedrosian, 46).
[23] Ibn al-Athir 3: 242–3; P. Balog, *The Coinage of the Ayyubids* (London, 1980), 7–9.
[24] Ibn Khallikan, 3: 490–1.

monastery or madrasa. Tax remission merely limited future income, and exchanged that reduced income for credit in heaven.

As a result, the remission of taxes was not simply about economics: it was primarily an act of piety. The large number of inscriptions relating to taxation that have survived from Ani and from various Armenian monasteries in the region, such as Horomos, show the religious weight that was attached to them in this period.[25] Reducing particular duties was a good act to be remembered by others before God. Taxation was particularly onerous for Christians under Ayyubid or Seljuk rule, because of the *jizya*, the additional poll tax levied on the *dhimmi*, the non-Muslim peoples of the Book – primarily Christians and Jews. The burden this imposed and the consequent need for remission of other taxes can be seen from the legacy of coins used to pay the *jizya* in Taron in the decades before Tamta came to reside there. In 1972 a large hoard of Byzantine copper coins was found, including many with prominent Islamic counterstamps. Some of these name Akhlat's Sökmenid rulers, Sayf al-Din Begtimur (r. 1183–93) and his successor Badr al-Din Aqsunqur (r. 1193–7), indicating that the coins had been taken over into the economy of eastern Anatolia. Other counterstamps bear the word *dhimam*, indicating the coins' particular association with non-Muslims in Akhlat. It is likely that these counterstamped coins were the required currency for the payment of the *jizya*.[26] This system required the non-Muslims to exchange their normal coins for these special issues, presumably at a very unfavourable exchange rate. They were thus charged twice for the same tax.

For Tamta to have become involved in the taxation of Christians within the Muslim court fits what we know of the activities of her female in-laws in the Ayyubid world who were similarly involved in taxation policy in the areas of Syria where they lived and ruled. When Ibn Wasil summed up the achievement of Dayfa Khatun, the youngest sister of al-Ashraf, the regent in Aleppo for her infant grandson, taxation lay at the heart of her virtues, most of which form the staple tropes of good rule: 'She was just to her subjects, very charitable and loving towards them. She removed various taxes in all the regions of Aleppo. She favoured jurists, ascetics, scholars and people of religion, and extended to them many charities.'[27] Remission of taxes was given as much prominence in Muslim hands as in Christian: an inscription set up on the Great Mosque in Amid in 1230s set in stone the reduction of

---

[25] Mahé, 'Les inscriptions de Horomos'.
[26] Lowick, Bendall, and Whitting, *The 'Mardin' Hoard*, 53–4, where the idea is proposed; coins nos. 7–8, 23–5. One coin (no. 5) is explicitly counterstamped *dhimam*.
[27] Tabbaa, 'Dayfa Khatun', 22.

an import duty levied at three of the city gates – the Hill Gate, the Gate of the Greeks, and the River Gate: 'as a pious donation of alms, in perpetuity and in favour of the citizens of the well-protected Amid'.[28] In contrast, it was Queen Tamar's introduction of new taxes on her Muslim subjects in Georgia that provided Abu Bakr with the justification he needed to invade Georgia in 1202 (leading to his defeat at the battle of Basiani): 'every woman is simple-minded... you... are a simpleton of a queen... a killer and taxer of Muslims'.[29]

Pilgrimage

The second achievement with which Tamta is credited is expediting pilgrimage to Jerusalem. Her main role in this must have been to persuade al-Ashraf and his brothers, particularly al-Mu'azzam (who controlled Jerusalem and the region around it), to allow Christian pilgrims to travel through Ayyubid lands without undue hindrance. It is possible that she also offered more practical support through the endowment of hostels in which pilgrims could stay during their journeys, and the provision of letters of passage to facilitate their dealings with Ayyubid officials. Tamta's role needs to be seen against the broader background of women's involvement in commercial activities outlined in the last chapter: trade routes and mercantile connections between towns facilitated the movement of pilgrims. Support for pilgrimage was also an activity deemed appropriate for pious women of all faiths: Saljukshah, whom we encountered in Medina in Chapter 7, was praised for helping public water supplies and other expenses on the pilgrim road to Mecca, driven by 'a strange admixture of pious work and regal pride' (although Ibn Jubayr who informs us of this was not above gossiping about the secret assignations of this 'much indulged princess' when she occasionally disappeared en route).[30]

Pilgrimage was a social activity of great importance and its effects were widespread throughout the region. In the 1250s William of Rubruck noted a number of Christian pilgrimage sites in Seljuk-controlled Kayseri and Sivas when he travelled through the region,[31] but Jerusalem remained the principal goal for pilgrims throughout this period. It was control of the Holy Places that had sparked the First Crusade in 1095, and the defence of the Holy Land remained a central concern of the Ayyubids after Saladin's

---

[28] Van Berchem, *Amida*, no. 35; *RCEA* XI, 4200; *TEI*, 2657.
[29] Rayfield, *Edge of Empires*, 113.   [30] Ibn Jubayr, 190, 246.
[31] William of Rubruck, *The Mission of Friar William of Rubruck: His Journey to the Court of the Great Khan Möngke, 1253–55* (London, 1990).

recapture of Jerusalem in 1187. The Ayyubid capture of Jerusalem was a decisive defeat for the Latin Crusaders, but it proved to be good for the Georgians, who had not participated in the battle and who went on to become the leading Christian faction in the city in the first decades of the thirteenth century. Queen Tamar negotiated with Saladin for the relic of the True Cross held in the church of the Holy Sepulchre after his recapture of the city; and although she was not successful, she had reclaimed all Georgian possessions in the city by 1192.[32] Thereafter Georgians also wrested control of the keys to the aedicule containing the tomb of Christ in the Holy Sepulchre, as well as chapels elsewhere in the complex, cementing their dominance over the other Christian confessions.[33] In 1219 the Georgians still felt powerful enough to threaten al-Mu'azzam after he razed the walls of Jerusalem without consulting them.[34] Georgians also controlled a number of other monasteries around the city, as well as the principal Georgian monastery of the Holy Cross to the west of the city walls.[35]

James of Vitry, who became Latin Bishop of Acre in 1216, reports that alone among all Christian groups, Georgians were able to raise their flags whilst on pilgrimage to the Holy Sepulchre and were exempted from the usual payments (unlike Wilbrand of Oldenburg and other Latin pilgrims who, in 1211/12, were charged an entrance fee of eight and a half drachmas (dirhams) for access to the Holy Sepulchre, payable to the city's Ayyubid rulers).[36] When relations between Latins and Ayyubids deteriorated even more in 1217 with the landing of the troops of the Fifth Crusade in Damietta, it became even more dangerous for Latin pilgrims, but still not for Georgians. As a result, another pilgrim, Magister Thietmar, tried to disguise himself as a Georgian monk to approach Jerusalem; his disguise failed and he was imprisoned outside the city walls until he could pay for his release.[37] Thietmar recorded quite how distinctive the Georgians were: 'The Georgians, who venerate St George, are vigorous in arms and trouble the Saracens

---

[32] Ibn Shaddad, 202, 230.
[33] D. Pringle, *The Churches of the Crusader Kingdom of Jerusalem. A Corpus* vol. 3: *The City of Jerusalem* (Cambridge, 2007), 33.
[34] J. Pahlitzsch, 'The People of the Book', in *Ayyubid Jerusalem: the Holy City in context, 1187–1250*, eds. R. Hillenbrand and S. Auld (London, 2009), 435–40, at 438, citing James of Vitry.
[35] Pringle, *The Churches of the Crusader Kingdom of Jerusalem*, 3: 157 (no. 308: St Basil), 158 (no. 309: St Catherine); 160 (no. 312: St Demetrios the Great); 338 (no. 347: St Nicholas). Georgian domination continued under the Mamluks, when they gained the churches of St George (165, no. 315), St Thekla (382, no. 362) and Sts Theodores (384, no. 364).
[36] D. Pringle, *Pilgrimage to Jerusalem and the Holy Land, 1187–1291* (Farnham, 2012), 88; Pahlitzsch, 'The People of the Book'.
[37] Pringle, *Pilgrimage to Jerusalem*, 107.

greatly. They cultivate their beards and hair. All have tonsures, both laymen and clerics, the laymen's being quadrate, the clerics' round. They have their own writing and wear felt hats on their heads one ell high.'[38]

In contrast to the Georgians, the Armenians in Jerusalem had gained most under Latin rule, and so had most to lose when it was reconquered by the Ayyubids. The loss of the city fell heavily on them, and it was often mourned in the colophons of Armenian manuscripts and in monumental inscriptions in churches.[39] However, the Armenians managed to regain their possessions in the city as well, and over the following decades there is increasing evidence of Armenian patronage of the Holy Sites. Kirakos' account of Tamta's support for pilgrims claims that it was entirely for the benefit of the Georgians (the paragraph includes one of his recurring jibes at Ivane's conversion to Georgian Christianity), but the material evidence suggests that there was more general toleration of Christians in the Holy Land in the early thirteenth century when Crusades were not threatened. Whilst this may partly have been the influence of Tamta, we should be careful not to overestimate her role; Christian access was aided by other diplomatic engagements. The most important of these occurred in 1229, just as Tamta was under siege in Akhlat from Jalal al-Din Khwarazmshah. It was a treaty between al-Kamil and Frederick II, the Holy Roman Emperor, in which the Sultan agreed to hand the Holy City over to the Christian Emperor without a fight, thereby preventing a more damaging war that would divert his resources from Egypt, where he already faced a revolt.[40] Frederick was granted control of all Jerusalem, bar the Temple Mount, although he was not allowed to rebuild the city walls that al-Mu'azzam had demolished a decade earlier. The treaty was due to last ten years, but in fact lasted until 1244, during which period Christians once again had easier access to the sites associated with Christ's life and passion. Whilst it was a success on the ground, it was politically very damaging for the two rulers, both of whom were berated by their allies for treating with the enemy and betraying their religion. The treaty effectively formalised the support for pilgrims that Tamta had managed to arrange informally before.

---

[38] Pringle, *Pilgrimage to Jerusalem*, 132.

[39] G. Dédéyan, 'Les colophons de manuscrits arméniens comme sources pour l'histoire des Croisades', in *The Crusades and their Sources: Essays presented to Bernard Hamilton*, eds. J. France and W. G. Zajac (Aldershot, 1998), 89–110, at 105–10; I. Augé, 'Gošavank', un complexe monastique au regard des sources littéraires et épigraphiques', *Le Muséon* 125/3–4 (2012), 335–65, at 349–50.

[40] T. C. Van Cleeve, 'The Crusade of Frederick II', in *A History of the Crusades*, vol. 2, eds. R. L. Wolff and H. W. Hazard (Madison; Milwaukee; London, 1969), 429–62.

Figure 67 View of the monastery of Gandzasar from the south, Nagorno-Karabagh, Azerbaijan (disputed); catholicon (1216–38); zhamatun (*c.* 1261)

It is now impossible to evaluate any further the means by which Tamta was able to expedite pilgrimage to the Holy Land, but there is ample evidence of the results of her work. This comes from the records of pilgrims who made the journey as well as those who also commissioned offerings for the churches they visited or left their mark by other means. The most impressive account of a pilgrimage made during Tamta's time as wife of al-Ashraf comes away from Jerusalem, at the monastery of Gandzasar [Fig. 67], located in the eastern Armenian province of Artsakh (the now disputed territory of Nagorno-Karabagh in Azerbaijan). It concerns a woman named Khorishah, a senior member of the ruling family of the region and a close ally of the Mqargrdzelis.[41] The record forms part of an inscription set up on the north side of the nave in 1240 by Khorishah's son:

> In the name of the Holy Trinity, Father, Son and the Holy Spirit, I, Jalal-Dola Hasan, son of Vakhtang and grandson of Hasan the Great, legitimate sovereign of the great and large land of Artsakh, a province with vast

[41] B. Ulubabian and M. Hasratian, *Gandzasar* (Milan, 1987); M. Hasrat'yan and J.-M. Thierry, 'Le couvent de Ganjasar', *REArm* 15 (1981), 289–316.

territories... my father had prescribed through his will, before leaving this world, to me and to my mother Khorishah, daughter of the great prince of princes Sargis, that I build this church and sepulchre of my fathers at Gandzasar, which was begun in the year... 1216 with the help of the good Lord, but when the east window was completed, my mother became a nun and went three times to Jerusalem. There, from the gate of the Holy Resurrection, she took herself to the dwelling of the nuns wearing a hair shirt and, after many years spent in... penitence, she passed into Christ, adorned with the seal of light, and her remains are preserved there.

Given that she travelled from Armenia to Jerusalem three times between 1216 and her death in 1238, Khorishah was surely one of the beneficiaries of Tamta's work, showing that the protection afforded Caucasian pilgrims extended as much to women as men. Khorishah clearly enjoyed independence in her widowhood in order to be able to leave her family to undertake these journeys and to settle in Jerusalem at the end of her life. Once in the Holy City she earned her own living by making and selling embroideries.[42] Indeed, this was the one form of employment that was deemed honourable for (noble) women to undertake. Queen Tamar is recorded as weaving robes for priests, and Kirakos Gandzaketsi records that Arzu Khatun (whom we have encountered as the builder of the monastery at Dadivank) and her daughters made tapestries embroidered with the images of saints for the monasteries at Getik, Haghbat, Makaravank and Dadivank.[43]

Khorishah was just one of many people from the Caucasus who visited the Holy Land on pilgrimage or settled there in one of the many monasteries and churches built by and for the Georgians and Armenians that have been recorded by historians and archaeologists.

Further evidence for the presence of pilgrims in the Holy Land comes from the quantity of graffiti that they left in the churches they visited. The church of the Holy Sepulchre, for example, has many examples of graffiti from throughout the Middle Ages incised in its columns and walls, testimony to the time pilgrims spent in these religious buildings and their desire to leave a permanent testimony to their faith.[44] Varying from texts in Armenian, Georgian, Syriac, Greek and Latin to simple crosses, the graffiti reveal the breadth of education and social standing of the pilgrims. Wealthier patrons had the option to create more formal memorials. The best

---

[42] Kirakos, 132.   [43] *Kartlis Tskhovreba*, 262; Kirakos, 107–8 (trans. Bedrosian, 62).
[44] Pringle, *The Churches of the Crusader Kingdom of Jerusalem*, 3: 69. For the graffiti at the entrance to the Holy Sepulchre see http://rockinscriptions.huji.ac.il/site/index inscriptions nos. 6517–6633.

Figure 68 Wooden door with Arabic text from the church of the Nativity, Bethlehem, Palestine; 1227

example from the thirteenth century is the pair of doors commissioned for the church of the Nativity at Bethlehem by two Armenian priests. Placed at the entrance from the narthex into the main body of the church, the doors had great prominence (they were later removed and only rediscovered and photographed in the 1930s, nailed to the roof beams of the church; they are now lost) [Figs. 68 and 69].[45] The form of the doors is predominantly Christian. The large crosses take their designs from Armenian khatchkars, the great stone crosses that were set up across Armenia throughout the Middle Ages. However, many of the details in the backgrounds around the crosses and on the wood that connects the cross panels are Ayyubid-style arabesques (*waqwaq*). These designs should not be seen as evidence of Islamic 'influence' on Christian art, but as an indicator of the existence of a common visual decorative language that could only be aligned with

---

[45] Z. Jacoby, 'The Medieval Doors of the Church of the Nativity at Bethlehem', in *Le Porte di Bronzo dall'Antichità al Secolo XIII*, ed. S. Salomi (Rome, 1990), 121–34; L.-A. Hunt, 'Eastern Christian Art and Culture in the Ayyubid and Early Mamluk Perids: Cultural Convergence between Jerusalem, Greater Syria and Egypt', in *Ayyubid Jerusalem: The Holy City in Context, 1187–1250*, eds. R. Hillenbrand and S. Auld (London, 2009), 327–47.

Figure 69 Wooden door with Armenian text from the church of the Nativity, Bethlehem, Palestine; 1227

any particular religious community by the insertion of explicit religious symbols.

The mixed artistic heritage of the doors is confirmed by the bilingual inscription that adorns them. The left door has a text in Arabic: 'This door was finished with the help of God, be he exalted, in the days of our Lord the Sultan al-Malik al-Muʿazzam in the month of Muharram in the year 624 [= 1226/7].' That on the right is in Armenian: 'The door of the Blessed Mother of God was made in the year 676 [= 1227] by the hands of Father Abraham and Father Arakel in the time of Hetum, son of Constantine, king of Armenia. God have mercy on their souls.'[46] The two priests who commissioned the doors thus pay homage both to the local ruler, the Ayyubid Sultan of Jerusalem, al-Muʿazzam (al-Ashraf's brother, who died the year the doors were made, opening the way for al-Ashraf to take Damascus), but also to the Armenian King in Cilicia, Hetum I (r. 1226–69). The inscriptions are further testimony to the multiple political allegiances that all were required to acknowledge in a world in which perhaps the majority of people were ruled by an elite belonging to a different religious tradition to their own.

---

[46] Jacoby, 'The Medieval Doors'; Hunt, 'Eastern Christian Art', 333–5.

Tamta and Indigenous Christians

Tamta's support for her Christian subjects can also be set against a broader background of the many indigenous Christians who lived under Muslim rule. The Jazira, Syria and Anatolia all had cities with large Christian populations, which necessarily had to engage with their Muslim rulers and deal on a day-to-day basis with their Muslim neighbours. The relationship between Christians and Muslims living together was frequently tense, and their protection and welfare largely depended on the will of the ruler. In 1212 the Coptic Patriarch processed through the streets and markets of Cairo with candles and crosses held high to celebrate the return of treasures which had been stolen from the monastery of St Makarios in the Wadi al-Natrun. Normally such an open celebration of Christianity could lead to riots, of which many are recorded, but on this occasion the Patriarch had the support of the city's Ayyubid ruler so it 'was hard to bear for those who were evil-disposed, but no one dared to utter a word or stretch out his hand, on account of fear of al-Malik al-Kamil'.[47] Similar resentments became visible in Seljuk lands during the celebration of the defeat of Jalal al-Din Khwarazmshah at the battle of Yassıçemen in 1230:

> Now when 'Ala al-Din [Kaykhusraw II] reached Caesarea of Cappadocia [Kayseri], the entire multitude of the city, including the Christians with their priests with crosses and bell-ringers, came a good day's journey out on the road before him. When the Sultan approached, the Tajik multitude did not allow the Christians to go near to mingle in their adoration of him. Instead, they shoved them to the rear. But the Christians went up onto a hill opposite the army. When the Sultan asked who those people were, and learned that they were Christians, he himself left his troops and went up among them alone, ordering them to worship aloud sounding their bells. And thus he entered the city with them, gave them gifts, and dispatched each to his place.[48]

These occasions on which violence was close to breaking out seem to have been provoked primarily by public professions of faith in communal spaces. However, they must be set against a parallel set of evidence which shows that at other times and in other circumstances, relations between the different communities were more relaxed and open.[49] Some cases reveal ideological overlaps between the rival religions at shared shrines, but others show simply that the communities shared a common visual vocabulary, albeit

---

[47] *History of the Patriarchs of the Egyptian Church*, cited in Werthmuller, *Coptic Identity*, 87–8.
[48] Kirakos, 114 (trans. Bedrosian, 67).   [49] Ibn Jubayr, 300–1.

with no sense of a shared meaning being associated with it. There was no consistency of view or action.

Visual Infiltration

The presence of so many Christians at the heart of Muslim courts had an undoubted impact on the visual environment of those courts. Christian brides brought icons and other religious objects with them when they were married to Muslim husbands as part of diplomatic alliances, and the Christians at court commissioned religious manuscripts for their use in the palace chapels. We can see the impact of this on art more traditionally associated with Islamic patrons, particularly brass and ceramic vessels commissioned from within the Ayyubid court in the 1230s and 1240s. The usual repertoire of images on these vessels concerned secular themes (which are explored in the next chapter), but some have more unusual iconographies that show an awareness of Christian art. Eighteen brass vessels made in the first half of the thirteenth century include scenes from the life of Christ or images of Christian priests.[50] Among the finest of these is a basin decorated with five episodes from Christ's early life, interspersed among the more usual array of polo-playing and hunting imagery [Fig. 70]. Its destination for the very heart of the Ayyubid court is clear from the dedication inscribed around its rim: it was made for al-Ashraf's nephew, al-Salih Najm al-Din Ayyub, the husband of Shajar al-Durr and last Ayyubid Sultan, whose death in 1249 during the invasion of the Seventh Crusade was presented as a martyrdom.[51] Similarly, a fragment of a marble jar made for al-Muzaffar Mahmud, the Ayyubid ruler of Hama (d. 1244), is decorated with an image of an Evangelist [Fig. 71].[52]

Many attempts have been made to analyse these curious objects: it has been noted that the narrative imagery only ever shows Christ's infancy and ministry, never his passion, and so were images that did not immediately offend Muslim beliefs; it has been suggested that they were made as diplomatic gifts to Crusader neighbours of the Ayyubids (or conversely

---

[50] E. Baer, *Ayyubid Metalwork with Christian Images* (Leiden, 1989); R. A. Katzenstein and G. D. Lowry, 'Christian Themes in Thirteenth-Century Islamic Metalwork', *Muqarnas* 1 (1983), 53–68; E. R. Hoffman, 'Christian–Islamic Encounters on Thirteenth-Century Ayyubid Metalwork: Local Culture, Authenticity, and Memory', *Gesta* 43/2 (2004), 129–42.

[51] E. Atil, W. T. Chase and P. Jett, *Islamic Metalwork in the Freer Gallery of Art* (Washington, DC, 1985), cat. 18.

[52] Kolaşin Collection, inv. Y730 (currently in Istanbul, Türk ve Islam Eserleri Müzesi).

Figure 70 The Annunciation and a polo match; details from the 'Freer' basin made for Najm al-Din Ayyub, Sultan in Cairo. Brass with silver and gold inlay; 1247–9 (Freer Gallery of Art, Smithsonian Institution, Washington, DC: purchase, F1955.10; height: 22.5 cm; diameter: 50 cm) (For the colour version, please refer to the plate section. In some formats this figure will only appear in black and white)

as gifts from Crusaders to the Ayyubids).[53] Equally, they have been seen as triumphalist tokens of Muslim sovereignty of the Christian Holy Places, and as iconographies re-employed to present biographical accounts of their owners' lives.[54] Iconographic parallels with Christian imagery in Syriac manuscripts have suggested that they may have been made for indigenous Christian patrons, and this must remain the most probable patronage of most of the lower-quality pieces. However, the great pieces, such as al-Salih Ayyub's basin with its unambiguous evidence of patronage, remain outside such an analysis.[55] The existence of Christian women such as Tamta at the heart of the Ayyubid court, however, presents an alternative context

---

[53] Baer, *Ayyubid Metalwork with Christian Images*; Hoffman, 'Christian–Islamic Encounters on Thirteenth-Century Ayyubid Metalwork'.

[54] R. Ward, 'Style versus Substance: The Christian Iconography on Two Vessels Made for the Ayyubid Sultan al-Salih Ayyub', in *The Iconography of Islamic Art*, ed. B. O'Kane (Edinburgh, 2005), 309–24.

[55] For the recent association of the Freer canteen with pilgrimage to the shrine of Mar Benham, near Mosul, see H. Ecker and T. Fitzherbert, 'The Freer Canteen Reconsidered', *Ars Orientalis* 42 (2012), 176–93.

Figure 71 Fragment of a marble vessel made for al-Muzaffar Mahmud, the Ayyubid ruler of Hama, d. 1244 (Kolaşin Collection, inv. Y730; 35 × 35 cm)

in which to view them. These objects could have been made by the sultans, but presented to their Christian wives or concubines. Such women were potential viewers or users of the dishes who were able to interpret the Christian scenes alongside the astrological and courtly imagery with which they appear. Alternatively, these Christian women may have had a more indirect influence on the vessels' designs. What matters is the reminder that Christian women were present at Muslim courts. We know that such women brought Christian art with them and this could have provided the source of a new visual language to the metalworkers. Thus it was the presence of Christians that might have been most significant, not their active participation in the design of the imagery or its consumption. It gave the metalworkers access to a new range of imagery, and encouraged them to broaden the already cosmic sweep of the imagery that they worked with. The inclusion of Christian scenes placed an even richer world of reality and myth in the hands and before the eyes of their patrons. The often incoherent iconography of the 'Christian' scenes and their lack of consistent narrative programmes fit the episodic nature of the metalwork in general and its desire to juxtapose the real and the imaginary, history and myth. In this interpretation, rather than seeing the scenes as being 'Christian', we should recognise them simply as representations of Christian myths, no different from the wealth of other imagery on the vessels: they represent stories, not beliefs. We should distinguish between the scenes' theological meaning to Christians and their artistic significance as the visual equivalents of the unicorns, hunters, feasters, wrestlers, rams and so on that they appear amongst; after all, on al-Salih Ayyub's basin the images of Christ are given considerably less prominence than the polo matches that appear below them.

The paucity of information about Tamta in the Ayyubid sources (as about women in general) means that we tend to neglect the significant female element of the Ayyubid court; but their involvement should not be discounted. A dish now in Munich, made at the same time as al-Salih Ayyub's basin for Badr al-Din Lu'lu', the ally of the Ayyubids in Mosul, has an inscription on its base stating that it was 'One of the things which the lowly Lu'lu' (may God reward him well) ordered to be made for the virtuous Khawanrah Khatun'.[56] This woman is not known from any other source, but was presumably a wife of Badr al-Din Lu'lu'. This secondary text about the ownership of the dish by a woman belies the complete absence of women's names from the main inscription on the dish, which concentrates only on the usual sonorous and lengthy litany of titles and virtues possessed by Badr al-Din Lu'lu' himself.[57] This discrepancy between the two inscriptions means that we cannot exclude any of these metalwork objects from being female possessions. Moreover, other metalwork pieces, either with only generic honorific inscriptions or uninscribed, were clearly made for sale on the open market, suggesting a wider social clientele for this kind of material. We can be confident that Tamta was familiar with these vessels as al-Ashraf's first wife Terkan originated in Mosul, the main source of this metalworking tradition.

Muslim Interest in Christianity

There is more evidence of Muslim interest in Christian art at court level, and of the impact of Christians at court on the making and perception of art.

---

[56] D. Jones and G. Michell, eds., *The Arts of Islam* (London, 1976), catalogue of an exhibition at the Hayward Gallery, 8 April–4 July 1976 180, cat. 197; F. Sarre and M. van Berchem, 'Das Metallbecken des Atabeks Lulu von Mosul in der Königlichen Bibliothek zu München', *Münchner Jahrbuch der bildenden Kunst* 1 (1907), 18–37, at 33.

[57] Jones and Michell, eds., *The Arts of Islam*, 180, cat. 197.

Many of these concern icons, the most potent visual tool in the Orthodox world. We have already seen how, under the Mqargrdzelis, icons began to make inroads into Armenian visual culture in ways it had hitherto resisted. Icons also had an impact at the Seljuk and Ayyubid courts, especially those images that had an association with the miraculous. A Christian source, the *Life of Sts Barnabas and Sophronios* by Akakios Sabaites, tells of the visit of a sultan in Anatolia, probably Kaykhusraw I, to a church in Antalya in the hope of seeing an icon of the Mother of God perform a miracle.[58] He expected to see the icon spontaneously raise up a purple cloth, itself a touch-relic of the Virgin, that was draped over it during the liturgy. The miracle is reminiscent of one performed every Friday by another icon of the Virgin at the Blachernae monastery in Constantinople (so regular that it became known, somewhat wearily, as the 'usual' miracle).[59] Predictably, as the tale is told in a Christian source, the miracle refused to happen whilst the Sultan and his entourage were in the church; only when he left was the miracle revealed, and its power was such that all the Turks outside were struck to the ground, and only able to get up again when rescued by the Archbishop.[60] Whilst the tale may be apocryphal, it was clearly written with an eye to plausibility: there was an expectation that a sultan might be intrigued by miraculous images and might attend church to witness it. Given the number of Christians at court, it becomes easier to see how such an interest could be generated. Later, when Kayka'us II sought refuge in Constantinople, he openly venerated the icons that he saw (according to Christian chroniclers, at least).[61]

Whilst this might be explained away as simple curiosity, other episodes show how elements of Christian practice with regard to images might infuse the entire court, and subvert the relationship between the Sultan, his wife and their emirs. Most are related to Tamar, the daughter of Queen Rusudan of Georgia, who was married to Kaykhusraw II.[62] Although Tamar began her life at the Seljuk court as a Christian, bringing icons and priests with her, she later converted to Islam. According to Georgian sources this conversion was forced onto her by Kaykhusraw, who reneged on his agreement with the Georgians to allow her to remain a Christian. The conversion was

---

[58] Translated by Veronica Kalas in Redford and Leiser, *Victory Inscribed*, 143–4.
[59] B. V. Pentcheva, *Icons and Power: The Mother of God in Byzantium* (University Park, PA, 2006), 145–61.
[60] Redford and Leiser, *Victory Inscribed*, 143–4.   [61] Nikephoros Gregoras, 1: 110–11.
[62] See Eastmond, 'Art and Frontiers'; A. Eastmond, 'Un'eco della leggenda del Mandylion nell'Islam', in *Intorno al Sacro Volto: Genova, Bisanzio e il Mediterraneo (secoli XI–XIV)*, eds. A. R. C. Masetti, C. D. Bozzo, and G. Wolf (Florence, 2007), 175–80.

marked by the expulsion of her priests and the smashing of her icons. This suggests a revival of the more orthodox Muslim hostility to religious images. Thereafter we hear of Tamar in the more traditional roles of wife and mother, a woman subsumed into the Seljuk world. Indeed, in medieval literature she is universally called by her Turkish appellation, Gurji Khatun, the Georgian Lady. The conversion may actually have been (or certainly later became) sincere, as Gurji Khatun is recorded as a major supporter of the Sufi mystic Jalal al-Din Rumi Mevlana, who settled in Konya in around 1228. On his death in 1273 she paid for the erection of his mausoleum. A number of stories about her relationship with Mevlana are recorded in the *Menaqib al-Arefin* (the Feats of the Knowers of God), a series of hagio-biographies of Mevlana and his followers written by Shams al-Din Ahmet-e Aflaki in about 1320.

In one tale, Gurji Khatun, forced to stay in Kayseri to advise her husband the Sultan, commissioned an artist to paint a portrait of Mevlana in Konya. For this she employed a Greek, Christian artist, named 'Eyn al-Dowla, with instructions to draw Mevlana in the 'extreme of beauty', so that the image could be her 'consoler' during her absences from him. Given her support for Mevlana, she must have been a Muslim by this stage, but the act of commissioning such a portrait had no Islamic sanction. The artist quickly encountered problems with his portrait:

> ['Eyn al-Dowla] took a look [at Mevlana] and began to depict his appearance. He drew a very lovely picture on a sheet of paper. The second time he looked, he saw that what he had seen at first was not the same. On another sheet of paper he drew another drawing. When he was finished with the picture, Mevlana displayed a different form again. In the end he sketched different pictures on twenty sheets of paper, and as often as he looked he beheld a different portrait of the figure.[63]

Given the Muslim context of this story, 'Eyn al-Dowla's inability to capture Mevlana's likeness is not unexpected. But while the moral of the story reflects Islamic theology, its core echoed Christian beliefs. The story has two elements, the desire for the portrait, and the inability of the artist to complete it. Both had long traditions in the Christian world: Byzantine hagiographies included many instances of artists seeking to capture the likeness of a saint for his followers to venerate.[64] These Christian accounts also included

---

[63] Aflaki, 293.
[64] For example, St Nikon Metaneiotes: C. Mango, *The Art of the Byzantine Empire 312–1453* (Englewood Cliffs, NJ, 1972), 212–13.

the inability of the artist to capture a true likeness, although the difficulties were usually resolved when divine intervention interceded to produce one. This trope looked back to one of the most important images of Christ, the Mandylion. According to the legend, an artist sent by King Abgar of Edessa to paint Christ from life was unable to capture his essence because of his divinity. However, Christ himself made the portrait by miraculously imprinting his likeness on a cloth he held to his face. The Mandylion became one of the major relics of the east Christian world. The image could even miraculously replicate itself on anything that was rested against it, allowing both Byzantium and Georgia to claim to house it. The Georgian version, known as the Anchiskhati (the icon of Ancha), was particularly celebrated at the start of the thirteenth century, having received a new gold frame from Gurji Khatun's grandmother, Queen Tamar, in the 1190s [Fig. 18]. The miracle guaranteed the veracity of the portrait, and underpinned the theological need for precision in portraiture. Thus ideas about the multiple facets of human essence and the difficulty of artists to capture one true essence would have been well known to Gurji Khatun. The only difference in the story in the *Menaqib* is that the final, definitive image is never produced. Instead, the twenty portraits simply capture twenty different aspects of the holy man. Despite this, however, Gurji Khatun was satisfied: she collected the twenty sheets, which then accompanied her wherever she travelled: 'And in whatever situation [when] she felt overwhelmed by passionate longing for Mevlana, he immediately took on form and shape so that she would grow calm.' The portraits have a dual function: they are a moral exemplar of the impossibility of images for the Islamic audience of the tale, but yet remain a potent force, dependent on a Christian understanding of the nature of the image for their principal viewer, the formerly Christian queen of the Seljuk Turks.

The presence of icons in Seljuk society, as well as an awareness of their potential power, is demonstrated by another tale in Aflaki's history, once again featuring the artist 'Eyn al-Dowla. In this story, a second Greek painter in Konya, called Kaluyan-e Naqqash (i.e. Kaloioannes the Painter), tells 'Eyn al-Dowla of a picture of Mary and Jesus in Constantinople which has no equal: 'Painters have come from all over the world but are not able to fashion anything like this picture.'[65] This description immediately conjures up the great miraculous icons of the Mother of God that resided in Constantinople – the Blachernitissa or the Hodegetria.[66] Infatuated by the idea of such an image, 'Eyn al-Dowla travels to Constantinople, works in the

---

[65] Aflaki, 382.   [66] Pentcheva, *Icons and Power*, 109–64.

monastery where it is kept and, after a year, when he has gained the trust of the monks, he steals the icon and takes it to Konya, where he shows it to Mevlana:

> After looking at it a long time, Mevlana said: 'These two beautiful images are complaining greatly about you, saying: "He is not honest in his love for us and he is a false lover."'
>
> 'Eyn al-Dowla said: 'How is this?'
> Mevlana replied: 'They say: "We never sleep and eat, and we continually stay awake at night and fast during the day. 'Eyn al-Dowla leaves us at night and goes to sleep, and during the day he eats. He does not do as we do."'
>
> 'Eyn al-Dowla said: 'Sleeping and eating are absolutely impossible for them, nor can they speak and say things. They are figures without a soul.'

Mevlana then asks 'Eyn al-Dowla why he should abandon God, whom he calls the painter of everything on the earth and in the sky, in favour of unaware images without soul or higher meaning. Seeing the error of his ways, 'Eyn al-Dowla repents and converts to Islam. This is the only known instance of a Christian icon working to convert a man to Islam. This complex interweaving of Christian ideas about images with Muslim theology and morals highlights how close the different cultures could be.

A similar shared interest in images is evident in Syria, at the major local pilgrimage site of Saidnaya. The monastery, to the north of Damascus, survived in the Middle Ages as a fortified complex looming over the valley below. There is evidence of joint veneration by Christians and Muslims here as early as the mid-twelfth century.[67] What is striking is that this was not veneration of a tomb or other holy place (as occurred at other sites, such as the church of the Nativity at Bethlehem, discussed earlier), but of an image. This was the icon of Saidnaya, an image of the Mother of God with the Christ child in her arms. The icon had particular importance as it performed miracles: the painting of the Virgin exuded a holy substance, variously described as sweat, oil or milk running from her breasts (some pilgrims even claimed the paint had transubstantiated into her flesh). The liquid was gathered in ampoules that could be purchased by pilgrims and taken home; it had healing properties, particularly sought after by

---

[67] M. Bacci, 'A Sacred Shrine for a Holy Icon: The Shrine of Our Lady of Saydnaya', in *Hierotopy: The Creation of Sacred Spaces in Byzantium and Medieval Russia*, ed. A. M. Lidov (Moscow, 2006), 373–87.

pregnant women.⁶⁸ Pilgrims reported that the icon was almost invisible, hidden behind a veil, lamps, candles and a plethora of votive objects that crowded the niche in which the icon sat.

Stepping outside the normal parameters of Islamic religion, pilgrimage to Saidnaya necessitated that Muslim pilgrims behave in unusual ways. For a Muslim to visit the site broke many fundamental taboos: it required them to enter a Christian church in a predominantly Christian village; it required them to venerate a religious image (of a man they did not recognise as a god); and it required them to accept the miraculous nature of the oil that was gathered from a basin below the icon. Magister Thietmar, a German pilgrim who visited in 1217–18, noted that the pilgrimage also released them from some lesser prohibitions: visiting the shrine allowed Muslims the opportunity to drink wine, and smuggling wine back into Damascus must have become a serious problem, as the guards on the gates of Damascus were ordered to keep a particularly careful eye out for it.⁶⁹

The Christian cult may have one reflection in Ayyubid art. A curious series of Syrian ceramics take the form of a woman breast-feeding her child [Fig. 72].⁷⁰ Their function is unknown, and whilst they cannot be seen as a direct copy of the appearance of the icon (the exact appearance of which is unclear, to say the least, as chroniclers give different accounts of what they were able, or unable, to see), they represent a similar desire to invest the same concerns and hopes about childbirth in a physical object. These figurines may just have been decorative, they may have simply acted to comfort their owners, but given the widespread belief in talismanic symbols, they may have been endowed with more powerful significance.

These stories show that although Christian and Muslim beliefs remained as sharply divided as ever, they increasingly drew on a shared Graeco-Roman and Christian heritage. Other records support this view of a society in which people and ideas might mix more freely. At Mevlana's death his funeral cortège was accompanied not just by Muslims, but also by Christians and Jews, who would not leave even when beaten with sticks and swords, proclaiming, 'this king of religion is our chief, imam, and guide ... we recognize him to be the Moses of the era, and the Jesus of the age'.⁷¹ He even spent time at a Christian monastery near Konya, dedicated to St Plato

---

⁶⁸ L.-A. Hunt, 'A Woman's Prayer to St Sergius in Latin Syria: Interpreting a Thirteenth-Century Icon at Mt Sinai', *Byzantine and Modern Greek Studies* 15 (1991), 96–145, at 119–20.

⁶⁹ Pringle, *Pilgrimage to Jerusalem*, 106; Bacci, 'Our Lady of Saydnaya', 376.

⁷⁰ É. Delpont, ed., *L'Orient de Saladin: l'art sous les Ayyoubides* (Paris, 2002), cat. 138.

⁷¹ Aflaki, 405.

Figure 72 Syrian ceramic figurine showing a woman breast-feeding her child; thirteenth century. Height: 27.5 cm

(similar to the dedication of the church on the acropolis, indicating the scale of veneration of the saint in this region).

Other Interminglings

The complex mix of the population of Syria was largely determined by the long history of the region. Each new religion did not immediately replace those that preceded it. Rather, it overlay them, building up an ever more complex mesh of beliefs and practices.[72] The conversion of the population to Islam was a gradual affair, and it incorporated existing Christian ideas, just as Christianity before it had absorbed earlier Graeco-Roman ideas and rituals. Elements of all these layers are visible in Muslim practice under the

---

[72] Eastmond, 'Other Encounters'.

Ayyubids. In some instances the place of veneration remained the same, but the older religion was ousted. At the town of Ruhin to the west of Aleppo the Muslims (and then the Mongols) annexed the veneration of an existing Christian holy site. To justify this behaviour the scholar Ibn Shaddad simply notes that Muslims venerated it with twice the fervour of their Christian predecessors.[73] In other cases, veneration at holy sites was shared between all the religions: the geographer al-Harawi (d. 1215) noted a shrine dedicated to an unknown prophet in northern Syria, and Sibt ibn al-Jawzi recorded a spring in Crusader-controlled Acre, both of which were venerated by Jews, Christians and Muslims alike.[74] In Anatolia, the Emir of Sivas sent his wife to be cured at the shrine of St Athanasios in Trebizond.[75]

These examples of common shrines, venerated by all the religions in Syria and Anatolia, indicate the entrenched nature of local worship that seems to have survived the many changes in regime and religion among the ruling class. In some cases, the practices that survived looked back to Graeco-Roman beliefs, which led adherents into even more unorthodox areas of belief and practice. Yaqut, the compiler of a geographical encyclopaedia in the early thirteenth century, reported that Jews, Muslims and Christians all made pilgrimage to pour perfumes and rose water on a stone by one of the gates of Aleppo (supposedly marking the burial place of a prophet), which would guarantee that wishes made there would come true.[76] In a village nearby statues were believed to hold special powers: the nose of the statue of a black man was rubbed by women to ensure they would become pregnant; elsewhere a statue of a scorpion kept snakes and scorpions away; and Ibn Shaddad notes that a tower on the city walls at al-Ashraf's early capital of Harran had two bronze statues of jinn regarded as talismans against snakes.[77] The surprise here is not so much the nature of the superstitions

---

[73] D. Sourdel, 'Rūḥīn, lieu de pèlerinage musulman de la Syrie du Nord au XIIIe siècle', *Syria* 30 (1953), 89–107, at 93; discussion in M. Frenkel, 'Constructing the Sacred: Holy Shrines in Aleppo and its Environs', in *Egypt and Syria in the Fatimid, Ayyubid and Mamluk Eras: Proceedings of the International Colloquium Organized at the Katholieke Universiteit Leuven*, vol. 6, eds. U. Vermeulen and K. D'Hulster (Leuven, 2010), 63–78.

[74] Harawi, 9; Sibṭ ibn al-'Ajami, 9. For other examples see M. Bacci, '"Mixed" Shrines in the Late Byzantine Period', in *Archeologia Abrahamica: issledovaniia v oblasti arkheologii i khudozhestvennoi traditsii iudaizma, khristianstva i islama*, ed. L. A. Beliaev (Moscow, 2009), 433–44.

[75] A. Papadopoulos-Kerameus, 'Symbolai eis tin istorian Trazepzountos', *Vizantiiskii Vremennik* 12 (1906), 132–47, at 141; A. A. M. Bryer, 'Last Judgements in the Empire of Trebizond: Painted Churches in Inner Chaldia', in *Mare et Litora: Essays presented to Sergei Karpov for his 60th Birthday*, ed. R. Shukurov (Moscow, 2009), 519–52.

[76] Ibn al-Shihna, 84–5 n.3.

[77] Ibn al-Shihna, 135–6; Rice, 'Medieval Ḥarrān', 37; C. Cahen, 'La Djazira au milieu du treizième siècle d'après 'Izz ad-din ibn Chaddad', *Revue des études islamiques* 8 (1934), 109–28, at 111.

Figure 73 Detail of the Talisman Gate, Baghdad, Iraq, built by the Caliph Nasir li-Din-Illah; 1221 (destroyed 1917)

as the existence of statues on which to focus them. Their survival seems to run counter to the aniconic orthodoxy of the Ayyubids, particularly under al-Ashraf. The account is similar to al-Harawi's pilgrimage guide, written shortly before 1215, which notes a statue of a double-headed snake in Mayyafariqin, a talisman against serpents.[78] The same town had a black marble basin near the synagogue containing a relic of Joshua that cured all diseases regardless of faith.[79]

These apotropaic images had counterparts elsewhere in the region, both among Christians and Muslims. In Armenia, Kirakos Gandzaketsi reports statues of two dragons (or rather, two dragons turned to stone by Lord Yovhannes in the eighth century, but 'they exist today') that produced water from their bellies that cured snake-bites.[80] Similar imagery can be found also among the Seljuk Turks to the west and in Baghdad, the capital of the Islamic world, to the east. The example from the east wall of Baghdad is perhaps the least ambiguous, since it was known as the Talisman Gate [Fig. 73]. It was built in 1221 by the Caliph Nasir li-Din-Illah, and fortunately it was photographed by the German archaeologist Friedrich Sarre before its own

---

[78] Interestingly, al-Harawi records that the talisman was kept in the church of Dart Maris: Harawi, 145.
[79] Le Strange, *The Lands of the Eastern Caliphate*, 112.   [80] Kirakos, 36.

luck ran out, blown up by the Ottomans as they retreated from Baghdad in 1917.[81] The name came both from the inscription that ran round the circumference of the gate tower and from the spandrels over the gate itself. These were decorated with the writhing figures of dragons, whose anatomy incorporates the body of a snake, the torso of a lion, the wings of an eagle, with other more fantastical inventions. Their scaly bodies loop and curl into knots, while their jaws open to reveal forked tongues and wicked fangs. They appear to be about to eat the ruler, who sits cross-legged between them, but he contains their fearsome power by calmly grasping their tongues in his hands. The dragons are reduced to little more than guard dogs. A similar device was used a decade or so later when Badr al-Din Lu'lu' built a caravanserai to the west of Sinjar, with similarly sinuous dragons over its entrance, this time being speared in the mouth by a bearded man.[82] Dragons also appear around the gates of the Syriac monasteries that thrived during his rule.[83] All clearly fit the same tradition and beliefs that underlay Mamkhatun's decision to decorate her tower at Ani with dragons [Fig. 40].

This religious world was a blurred and ambiguous one, in which different ideas about the way in which supernatural powers could manifest themselves all overlapped. Built up over a thousand years of changing religions, pagan statues, Christian icons and Islamic reliefs could all serve to help and protect those who chose to honour them. The evidence of al-Ashraf's religious patronage and his concern for Sunni orthodoxy suggests that he may not have followed these beliefs. But whilst his patronage promoted a conservative form of Islam, he seems to have left these informal practices alone: Saidnaya continued to thrive during his rule in Damascus, and the jinn at Harran remained standing, as did the miraculous cross on the city wall of Mayyafariqin (see Chapter 6). Al-Ashraf's tolerance of Tamta's Christianity is easier to understand when set against this regional background of shared practices and shrines. No rulers had sufficient power to be able to enforce their beliefs absolutely; compromise was an unavoidable policy.

Common Visual Worlds

The overlaps of belief between the Christian and Muslim communities can be seen alongside the existence of common visual traditions. We have

---

[81] Sarre and Herzfeld, *Archäologische Reise*, 1: 34–42; 2: 151–5; inscription: *RCEA* X, 3873; *TEI*, 4041.
[82] Sarre and Herzfeld, *Archäologische Reise*, 1: 13–15; dated by them to AH 631 or 637–57 (1233/9–58); better photograph in Preusser, *Nordmesopotamische Baudenkmäler*, pl. 17.
[83] Snelders, *Identity and Christian–Muslim Interaction*, 289–94.

already encountered the Ayyubid vessels with Christian scenes and the doors at Bethlehem which intertwined the designs of Armenian khatchkars with Ayyubid arabesques. A second door, made for a Frankish church in Syria in about 1215, now in the Musée des arts décoratifs in Paris, combines complex geometric star interlace and floral details in the interstices with a Latin inscription.[84] The workmanship on the wood carving is comparable to that produced at Ayyubid religious sites, such as the sarcophagus of Imam al-Shafi'i in Cairo.[85] Muslim artists similarly borrowed Christian iconography. The depictions of angels and dragon-slayers in a Persian-language magical treatise, the *Daqa'iq al-Haqa'iq*, compiled in Aksaray and Kayseri in 1273–4, show an awareness of contemporary Christian sources [Fig. 74].[86]

These overlaps need to be set in a broader context of the shared visual vocabulary of the medieval world. A very different form of relationship can be found in a comparison of a Syriac manuscript with an Iranian bowl. A dish in the Freer Gallery, probably made in Iran around 1200, shows a seated couple, the man playing the lyre, the woman holding a glass on a long stem [Fig. 75]. Both wear elaborately woven silks, but the woman, wearing a jewelled headdress, clearly outranks the man who performs for her.[87] The woman's robes feature seated figures wearing red in octagonal frames, with stars in between. In 1219/20, at about the same time as the bowl was painted, a Syriac miniaturist decorated a lectionary copy of the four gospels, now in the Vatican (Vat. Syr.559) [Fig. 76].[88] He chose to depict the XL Martyrs of Sebaste, setting out all forty of the martyrs as individual saints (fols. 93v–94r). Each saint was placed in an octagonal frame. Both manuscript and bowl are dominated by red and blue, by octagons whose frames interlace to created four-pointed stars with central quadripartite motifs. The visual similarity between the two must be unintentional. There can be no deliberate meaning attached to the appearance of this design in such different

---

[84] J.-P. Roux, ed., *L'Islam dans les collections nationales* (Paris, 1977), no.486; inv. 7674; J. Folda, *Crusader Art in the Holy Land, from the Third Crusade to the Fall of Acre, 1187–1291* (Cambridge, 2005), 137.

[85] Mulder, 'The Mausoleum of Imam al-Shafi'i'; R. Hillenbrand, 'The Art of the Ayyubids – an Overview', in *Ayyubid Jerusalem: The Holy City in Context, 1187–1250*, eds. R. Hillenbrand and S. Auld (London, 2009), 22–44; B. O'Kane, ed., *The Treasures of Islamic Art in the Museums of Cairo* (Cairo, 2006), no. 85.

[86] F. Richard, *Catalogue des manuscrits persans I: Anciens fonds. Bibliothèque Nationale, Département des manuscrits* (Paris, 1989), 191–5; M. Barrucand, 'The Miniatures of the Daqa'iq al-Haqa'iq (Bibliothèque Nationale Pers. 174): A Testimony to the Cultural Diversity of Medieval Anatolia', *Islamic Art* 4 (1990–1), 113–42.

[87] Freer 38.12: E. Atil, *Ceramics from the World of Islam* (Washington, DC, 1973), no. 41.

[88] J. Leroy, *Les manuscrits syriaques à peintures conservées dans les bibliothèques d'Europe et d'Orient* (Paris, 1964), 280–302, esp. 288–91 on the XL Martyrs.

Figure 74 The angel of the course of the sun from the *Daqa'iq al-Haqa'iq*, copied in Aksaray and Kayseri, Turkey; 1272–3 (Paris, BNF, MS Pers. 174, fol. 115; 25.5 × 17 cm)

Figure 75 *Minai* bowl with a noblewoman listening to a musician, Iran, early thirteenth century (Freer Gallery of Art, Smithsonian Institution, Washington, DC: purchase, F1938.12; diameter 23 cm) (For the colour version, please refer to the plate section. In some formats this figure will only appear in black and white)

media and such different contexts. But it is that coincidence that gives the repetition its importance. It speaks of a widely disseminated range of patterns, colours and motifs that was not out of place in any setting, religious or secular, Christian or Muslim.

These intertwinings show motifs and styles mixing together on one object, but other examples demonstrate how the distinct styles could coexist. In 1982 a silver hoard was discovered at the pilgrimage site of St Sergios at Resafa in eastern Syria. It had been buried between 1243 and 1259, presumably in fear of the Mongol invasions [Fig. 77].[89] It contained a mixture of objects made by artists from the Latin west, by members of the

---

[89] Folda, *Crusader Art in the Holy Land*, 87–92; T. Ulbert and R. Degen, *Der kreuzfahrerzeitliche Silberschatz aus Resafa-Sergiupolis* (Mainz am Rhein, 1990).

Figure 76 Twenty of the XL Martyrs of Sebaste, from a Syriac lectionary, copied at the monastery of Mar Mattai, near Mosul, Iraq; 1219–20 (Biblioteca Apostolica Vaticana, Syr. 559, fol. 93v; 43.5 × 33.5 cm) (For the colour version, please refer to the plate section. In some formats this figure will only appear in black and white)

indigenous Syriac community of the region, and by the Arabs of the Jazira. The paten was brought from France, probably by a knight of the Third Crusade; the chalice with a Syriac inscription was made locally; and the censer, decorated in niello with sphinxes, was probably made in the Jazira. A cup

Figure 77 The Resafa Hoard, a mixed set of Christian liturgical and other silver, buried at Resafa in Syria, 1243–59

with a French coat of arms on the front had an Arabic inscription on the reverse: 'This has been given by Zayn al-Dar, daughter of the master Abu Durra, to the church of the blessed Qalat Jabar.'[90]

It would be wrong to describe this as a syncretistic culture, since the ultimate aims and beliefs of the different communities could never be reconciled, and their adoption of a common heritage was put to such different ends.[91] The stories of potential conflicts during processions remind us of the importance not to over-romanticise the idea of *convivencia* – living together – between different religious communities.[92] Any common elements lay alongside a deep and well-founded distrust between the Christians and the Muslims. The Muslim soldiers' wariness of the Christians was not just a fear of an internal fifth column biding its time to overthrow the

---

[90] Delpont, ed., *L'Orient de Saladin*, cat. 85.
[91] T. Krstic, 'The Ambiguous Politics of "Ambiguous Sanctuaries": F. Hasluck and Historiography on Syncretism and Conversion to Islam in 15th and 16th Century Ottoman Rumeli', in *Archaeology, Anthropology and Heritage in the Balkans and Anatolia: The Life and Times of F. W. Hasluck, 1878–1920*, ed. D. Shankland (Istanbul, 2013), 247–62.
[92] For recent critiques of this notion: M. Soifer, 'Beyond *convivencia*: Critical Reflections on the Historiography of Interfaith Relations in Christian Spain', *Journal of Medieval Iberian Studies* 1/1 (2009), 19–35; A. Novikoff, 'Between Tolerance and Intolerance in Medieval Spain: An Historiographic Enigma', *Medieval Encounters* 11/1–2 (2005), 7–36.

regime. It was also a fear of the ways in which the Christians might corrupt the regime from within with their beliefs. Al-Ashraf's expulsion of teachers of the 'rational sciences' – the study of logic and the philosophy of the ancients – derived from a similar suspicion of ideas alien to Islam.[93]

The consequences of this distrust between the communities, and a belief that Christians at a Muslim court were in some way corrupting the Sultan and his entourage, are clear from one final piece of evidence. From 1240 on the Seljuk Sultan Kaykhusraw II started to mint coins in Sivas with a new design. The reverse was purely epigraphic, naming the Sultan as the great sultan Kaykhusraw, son of Kaykubad. The obverse included imagery, showing the sun blazing over a striding lion [Fig. 78].[94] This was a common enough zodiac image, and can be found across eastern Anatolia in this period. It appears on both the Malabadi (1146) and Cizre (1163) bridges,[95] and a close variation had been used by al-Awhad on the walls of Mayyafariqin in 1203 [Fig. 25]. Its appearance on coins gave it an emblematic quality, suggesting that it was becoming a more consciously political symbol – the sultan as lion bestriding all the world beneath the sun. It is therefore plausible that when Levon, prince of Armenian Cilicia, was depicted wearing silk robes woven with an identical device in a Gospel book in around 1255, it was an acknowledgement of his vassalship to the Seljuk ruler (Yerevan, Matenadaran, MS 8321, fol. 1r) [Fig. 79].[96] However, the very nature of an emblem means that it was open to alternative interpretations. Rather than seeing the coin as a symbol of Kaykhusraw's power, some viewers regarded it as a portrait of his weakness. Whilst the lion represented the Sultan, they said, the sun represented his Georgian queen and her ever-present, blinding domination over him. She had become a powerful figure at court, and acted as regent for her husband when he was away (hence her need for paintings of Mevlana when she travelled). She was acknowledged as 'the queen of the age, the lady of the hereafter'.[97] Disaffected members of the court, resenting her power, complained that

---

[93] Sauvaire, 'Description de Damas VII', 263.

[94] G. Leiser, 'Observations on the "Lion and Sun" Coinage of Ghiyath al-Din Kai-Khusraw II', *Mésogeios* 2 (1998), 96–114.

[95] Cizre bridge: Preusser, *Nordmesopotamische Baudenkmäler*, 26–8; Malabadi: Gabriel, *Voyages archéologiques*, 232–6, 345.

[96] S. Der Nersessian, *Miniature Painting in the Armenian Kingdom of Cilicia from the Twelfth to the Fourteenth Century* (Washington DC, 1993), 54, 154, and fig. 639; H. C. Evans, 'Kings and Power Bases: Sources for Royal Portraits in Armenian Cilicia', in *From Byzantium to Iran: Armenian Studies in Honor of Nina G. Garsoïan*, eds. R. W. Thomson and J.-P. Mahé (Atlanta, GA, 1997), 485–507.

[97] Aflaki, 292.

Figure 78 Silver dirham of Kaykhusraw II, minted in Sivas; 1242

Figure 79 Levon, prince of Cilicia, wearing a robe embroidered with roundels containing a lion beneath the sun, in a Gospel book presented to the prince by his godfather, Catholicos Constantine I; c. 1255 (Yerevan, Matenadaran, MS 8321, fol. 15r; 15.8 × 11.3 cm)

the coin was simply a crypto-portrait of Gurji Khatun, a substitution for the real portrait of his queen that Kaykhusraw had originally wanted to use before being advised against such an unambiguous and self-defeating gesture.

The commonness of the image in the Islamic world shows just how distrustful people could become of art given the Christian presence at the Seljuk court. An innocent and apparently positive image of power was reinterpreted instead as an insidious and dangerous revelation of the influences that the ruler was subject to – forces that were not just foreign, but female and Christian in origin. Such distrust might have been well grounded. Less than a decade later coins in the Crusader states started including overtly evangelising texts and imagery. When the papal legate Eudes de Châteauroux arrived in the Holy Land in 1250 he was shocked to discover the degree of complicity between the different communities in a supposedly Christian state, notably the inclusion of Islamic inscriptions and the name of Muhammad on the coins minted there. At his instigation Pope Innocent IV ordered the practice to cease, and in response a new series of coins was minted that continued to have Arabic inscriptions, but now proclaiming Christian articles of faith, such as 'The Father, the Son and the Holy Spirit, One Divinity', often accompanied by a cross. These were unambiguously aimed at the Arabic-speaking communities as deliberate attempts to place Christian doctrine into the everyday life of commerce.[98]

Tamta's presence as a Christian at al-Ashraf's court in Akhlat placed her in an ambiguous and difficult position. However, the evidence of mutual veneration at shrines and other common beliefs and interests suggests that there was much to ameliorate Tamta's position. She was neither as unique nor as isolated as at first sight appears. The number of Christians living under Muslim rule throughout the region, and their presence at court as secretaries, physicians, soldiers and officials, meant that there could never be a complete division between religions and cultures. This, combined with al-Ashraf's need for a Christian figurehead to help him keep the largely Christian population of Akhlat cooperative, gave Tamta the leverage to work in the way she did for the Christians of the Caucasus.

[98] Georganteli, 'Transposed Images', esp. 152, coin 7.

9 | Tamta at Court

It is a paradox that wars were fought over perceived differences between communities but that those who prosecuted the wars, the elites of each state, belonged to a shared culture of power and privilege with many of the same interests, values and beliefs. We have already seen some of the cultural overlaps through religion and the expectations it brought. In the mixed communities of the region – al-Ashraf ruling a majority Christian Armenian population in Akhlat, the Seljuks a largely Greek Christian one in Anatolia; the Georgians and Armenians with substantial Muslim populations in the Caucasus – this form of common identity was probably true. It was easier for the ruling class to present themselves in terms that their social equals would comprehend than to explain themselves to their subjects. This chapter explores the overlaps between the elites of states: the international fellowship of kings and queens.[1]

All ruling dynasties in the region were united by a series of ties, shared interests and beliefs that circumvented the divisions caused by religion, language, ethnicity and culture. These common values were essential to brides such as Tamta who were forced into diplomatic marriages: they provided a core of ideas and practices that were familiar and could perhaps act as the foundation on which to build a relationship to the new court that they were entering. These ties can be explored through the material world of the court: its palaces and gardens and their decorative schemes, the images of its pastimes, and the books and instruments connected to its intellectual and cultural interests. Ultimately, all these buildings and objects reflected the power of the ruler. They demonstrated his wealth, his erudition and his status among the international fellowship of kings. The ruler's majesty was partly evoked through solemn pomp and ceremonial, but partly also through leisure. To indulge in hunting, feasting, music and dancing proved that the ruler had the excess money, time and resources available to celebrate pleasure. Participation in these elite pastimes was a core characteristic of all courts in the medieval world. It is possible to find other common

---

[1] R. Cormack, 'But Is it Art?', in *Byzantine Diplomacy*, ed. J. Shephard, S. Franklin (Aldershot, 1992), 218–36.

strands as well, notably patronage of poets, musicians, scientists and writers. Finally, a number of other common beliefs and intellectual interests can be found across the region, notably a commitment to astrological observation and occasionally even to occult practices. Each court found different visual means to celebrate all these different pursuits depending on local artistic traditions, but whilst the ideas might be expressed through different conventions, the underlying structures of power and belief that determined them were largely the same. These common interests surrounded Tamta during her upbringing in the Georgian–Armenian courts of the Mqargrdzelis and their overlords, as well as in the court of al-Ashraf and the Ayyubids. They also provided a foundation of shared interests among the neighbouring principalities around Akhlat, and among the Seljuks and Byzantines to the west, and the Persian states to the east. As we will see later, adherence to astrology was even to provide a point of reference among the incomparably more alien cultures that Tamta encountered after the arrival of the Khwarazmians and the Mongols.

The world of the court was predicated on wealth, and the importance of displaying rather than hoarding it. As we have seen in the previous two chapters, much of that wealth was expended on works for the public good, whether religious or secular, but a large proportion was retained for the ruler to expend on himself and his court. Al-Ashraf was spectacularly rich. In 1240, 'Izz al-Din Ibn Shaddad, a bureaucrat and historian who died in Aleppo in 1285, was sent to audit the revenues of the city of Harran, and he calculated the income of the city as 2 million dirhams a year. But he added with a note of regret that this was a steep decline from the 3 million dirhams per year that al-Ashraf had enjoyed when he had controlled the city just a decade earlier (before he gave it up when he moved to Damascus in 1229).[2] By any standards this was an exceptional sum, and to it we must add his income from Raqqa, from Akhlat and from all the lands around these cities.

Al-Ashraf made good use of this money. The biographer Ibn Khallikan recounts that 'he was so profuse of his gifts that nothing was ever to be found in his treasury, though the kingdom he ruled over was very extensive'.[3] His reputation was equally widespread among his Christian subjects, as reported by the Syriac chronicler Bar Hebraeus: 'There was no limit to the generosity of this man, and he was a great lover of dainty meats and luxurious repasts.'[4] Whilst such excess was no doubt resented by those whose taxes funded it, it was also a necessary element in the exercise of

---

[2] Cahen, 'La Djazira au milieu du treizième siècle', 111.
[3] Ibn Khallikan, 3: 490.   [4] Bar Hebraeus, 404.

power: the display of conspicuous wealth reinforced the ruler's authority and confirmed his legitimacy. The world of the courtier was one in which status was lived out through ostentatious architecture, through excessive generosity and the flaunting of leisure, none of which were available to the vast majority of the population, who had no surplus time or money. Whilst not all members of the Ayyubid family were as rich as al-Ashraf (and he was probably poorer than his senior brothers, al-Kamil and al-Muʿazzam, who controlled the wealthier regions of Egypt and Syria in the 1220s), they and their neighbouring courts in Anatolia and the Caucasus would still have had incomes far in excess of those they ruled. Even under Mongol rule the Mqargrdzelis were still reported by William of Rubruck as having 'an abundance of everything', despite the poverty their subjects endured.[5]

At first sight the courtly world of the Ayyubids is a very different one from the public face the regime presented through its religious patronage. The austere design of the mosques, madrasas and hospices erected by al-Ashraf and his family suggest a puritanical view of the world and man's place in it. However, as we turn to the world of their palaces and bathhouses, we enter a more opulent and visually vibrant world that was designed to display the ruler's power, wealth and erudition. The world of the court was dominated by men. It was the ruler's interests that were served by the palace and its design, and the ruler's pastimes that determined the range of imagery shown. The royal images of Queen Tamar of Georgia are the only exception to this across the region, but even they were given a façade of male legitimacy. Very few personal buildings or objects survive that can explicitly be linked to wives, sisters and daughters themselves. Those objects that were made for women, such as jewellery, probably tell us more about their husbands: the wife becoming a further trophy through whom to demonstrate his access to gold and exquisite craftsmanship.[6] It is therefore difficult to discern the ways in which women were able to relate to or to exploit the art of the court. Tamta's relative independence in Akhlat suggests that she may have enjoyed more control over court expenditure there, but it is doubtful whether anything she commissioned would have reflected a specifically female view of the court.

Palaces

Royal display centred on the person and the housing of the ruler. For much of their lives the rulers of Anatolia, Syria and the Caucasus were on the

---

[5] William of Rubruck, 269. [6] S. de Beauvoir, *The Second Sex* (New York, 1989), 158.

move, living in tents on campaign and whilst travelling between their different territories. Nothing of these tents survives, but their luxury and scale is well attested. Al-Ashraf's brother, al-Kamil, had a travelling encampment of sixteen great pavilions to house himself and all the princes who travelled on campaign with him,[7] and when the Seljuk Sultan Kaykhusraw II fled the Mongol assault on Anatolia in 1239, he left behind him his large and beautifully coloured tent, to the door of which were tethered his leopard, his lion and his panther.[8] The chronicler ʿAta al-Malik Juvayni described the opulent tent of his father, the finance minister of Khorasan in eastern Iran, in the same year: 'My father provided another great tent of marvellous artifice and wondrous colouring with everything in keeping in the way of gold and silver vessels. He pitched this tent and feasted in it for days on end.'[9] Depictions in other media conjure up the magnificent textiles used to decorate tents, as in the early thirteenth-century copy of al-Hariri's *Maqamat*, now in St Petersburg (Russian Academy of Science, S-23, fol. 12a) [Fig. 80].[10]

Tents were the portable equivalent of the permanent palaces built in every city. These palaces were manifestations of power in stone, brick, stucco and wood. Although they had many functions as residences, military garrisons and governmental offices, palaces primarily worked as spaces in which to display the ruler. This was most evident in the locations chosen for palaces, usually in elevated, well-defended locations, literally looking down on the local population. Al-Ashraf is said to have built palaces (plural) in a huge citadel enclosure, measuring 140 × 140 metres outside the walls of Raqqa. He then demolished five of the city's defensive towers to provide him with better views and easier access to the city.[11] At Akhlat, the palace must have been in the citadel, although the present ruins there are all of Ottoman date. Location affected local populations in other ways as well: al-Salih Ayyub's new palace on the Roda island in the Nile in Cairo was built in around 1240 at the expense of an entire neighbourhood. All the pre-existing houses were seized and destroyed and their inhabitants forcibly evicted.[12]

Palaces were not single buildings, but rather were large complexes, with multiple buildings and pavilions, set in lush gardens. The gardens were as important as the buildings they contained, and were a key feature in Islamic culture, as the German pilgrim Magister Thietmar discovered when he

---

[7] Abu'l-Fida, 110.   [8] Grigor Aknertsi, 311.   [9] Juvayni, 2: 501.
[10] O. G. Bolshakov, 'The St Petersburg Manuscript of the Maqāmāt by al-Ḥarīrī and its Place in the History of Arab Painting', *Manuscripta Orientalia* 3/4 (1997), 59–66.
[11] S. Heidemann, 'The Citadel of al-Raqqa and Fortifications in the Middle Euphrates Area', in *Muslim Military Architecture in Greater Syria: From the Coming of Islam to the Ottoman Period*, ed. H. Kennedy (Leiden, 2006), 122–50, at 134–5.
[12] R. Arık and O. Arık, *Tiles: Treasures of Anatolian Soil: Tiles of the Seljuk and Beylik Periods* (Istanbul, 2008), 244; Creswell, *The Muslim Architecture of Egypt*, 84.

Figure 80 The tents of a caravan, from the fourth *Maqama* of al-Hariri, *c*. 1230 (St Petersburg, Institute of Oriental Studies, Ms c-23, fol. 12a; 25 × 19 cm) (For the colour version, please refer to the plate section. In some formats this figure will only appear in black and white)

passed through Damascus in 1217–18. He only encountered suburban gardens, but his account perhaps allows us to consider the scale and resources of the royal gardens in the palace:

> For in every house and along every street pools or washing places, rounded or quadrate in form, have been wonderfully provided through the folly

and extravagance of the rich. Around the city are most pleasant gardens, watered by natural watercourses and artificial aqueducts, abounding in every kind and species of tree and fruit, made lovely by the temperance of the weather, the playfulness of the birds, and the brightness of all the colours of the flowers. For the beauty of the whole of nature wanted to be visible in this place to such a degree that the place could truly be said to be another paradise.[13]

Ibn Wasil suggests that it was al-Ashraf's first encounter with the lush greenery and flowing waters and the fragrance of the fruit trees of Damascus in 1228 that made him determined to live there, a more luxurious retirement home than the cities he had lived in up until then.[14] Having said that, gardens had been a central feature of al-Ashraf's Jaziran palaces. At Raqqa the palace gardens became a device to display the reach of his power and the extent of his resources: 'he imported seedlings from every country, even palm trees and bananas'.[15] Stefan Heidemann has suggested that the magnificent 15-metre-high Baghdad Gate at Raqqa, which stood just outside the city walls and on an axis with his citadel, may have been employed by al-Ashraf primarily as a monumental entrance to these gardens.[16]

If the scale of the gardens and the variety of plants they contained did not make the point about the ruler's wealth and political reach sufficiently clear, then more direct means could be adopted. The extraordinary display of wealth of the Seljuks of Anatolia reached the ears of Jean de Joinville, the French chronicler of Louis IX's Crusade in 1248. Scattered through the Sultan's gardens, he says, were giant ingots of solid gold. 'These enormous lumps' – made by pouring molten gold into giant earthenware jars, which were then smashed to reveal the gold – were left strewn around the palace gardens for everyone who entered the gardens to see and to touch.[17] The impression of the Sultan's wealth was literally tangible, and its apparent casualness overwhelming. Gold was everywhere. If it was not on the jewellery that adorned their wives, it was on the palaces in which they lived. 'Imad al-Din al-Isfahani says of Saladin's residence in Damascus that: 'it was gilded with pure gold... [it] overlooked the fields... and was solidly constructed with a spacious court and a beautiful covered gallery'.[18]

[13] Pringle, *Pilgrimage to Jerusalem*, 101.
[14] Ibn Wasil quoted in Humphreys, *From Saladin to the Mongols*, 200.
[15] Cahen, 'La Djazira au milieu du treizième siècle', 112; Heidemann, 'The Citadel of al-Raqqa', 144.
[16] Heidemann, 'The Citadel of al-Raqqa', 144.
[17] Joinville, 199; Redford, *Landscape and the State in Medieval Anatolia*, 1.
[18] 'Imad al-Din al-Isfahani, 113; Chevedden, 'The Citadel of Damascus', 50.

Figure 81 Gateway to the palace in the citadel at Aleppo, Syria, built by al-Zahir Ghazi; 1186–1216

Design

The design of palaces reflected their functions. As well as residences and government offices they were sites for the reception of embassies and for public meetings with the ruler. Buildings therefore framed the ruler in these encounters, and their design and decoration became a means to display both the ruler's wealth (the visible expense of the materials used) and his learning and his taste (the design and decoration). These then informed and influenced the perception of him among those who were admitted to these spaces, his wives and close courtiers.

No medieval palaces survive intact, but remaining fragments and materials found in excavations allow us to see how palaces worked. The design of the palaces reveals the theatricality of the court. This is evident from the reasonably well-preserved remains of the palace in the citadel in Aleppo, erected by al-Ashraf's cousin al-Zahir Ghazi in 1209–12.[19] To the outside world (which, in the context of the heavily fortified citadel at Aleppo, must already have been a limited group), the palace presented a grand façade, elaborately worked with *ablaq* masonry, inlaid designs, joggled voussoirs and muqarnas vaulting [Fig. 81]. However, this façade concealed more than it revealed. There are few other openings between this world and that of

---

[19] Tabbaa, *Constructions of Power*, 71–96.

the palace within. It is an inward-looking building – largely, no doubt, for security, but partly also to inculcate a sense of seclusion and to highlight the exceptionality of the court, at a remove from the mundane world beyond. The ruler's twice-weekly public audiences usually took place in a separate building, the *dar al-'adl* (palace of justice), away from the citadel.[20] Those who did have permission to enter the palace itself to see the ruler faced further obstacles before their final entrance into his presence. The route from the portal to the courtyard where the ruler sat was narrow and circuitous (and, at Aleppo, this followed the tortuous route through the entrance gate of the citadel itself). This dark and winding passageway disorientated visitors, and left them unprepared for the contrastingly light and spacious central courtyard. Here, they finally encountered the ruler himself – dazzled, literally by the sun, and metaphorically by the persona and magnificence of the Sultan in his ceremonial robes.

Nine palaces of the early thirteenth century in the Jazira and southeastern Anatolia have been studied, and all share the same core design. They were designed around a central courtyard, each side of which had an iwan, a deep, vaulted recess.[21] It was in the iwan, which framed and shaded the ruler and raised him above his supplicants and courtiers, that the encounter took place. Draped with embroidered textiles, set with vessels in precious metals, surrounded by guards and officials, and accompanied by running water – that most extravagant of features in the Mediterranean heat – the iwan was the stage for the execution of power. The impact of the encounter was visualised in the frontispiece miniatures of manuscripts produced in the early thirteenth century. The opening bi-folio of a copy of al-Hariri's *Maqamat* (BNF, arabe 5847 (the Schefer Hariri), fols. 1v–2r, probably from Baghdad, 1237), shows two (unnamed) rulers, each seated beneath a canopy, richly dressed, and surrounded by their courtiers, who cluster in front of him, pushing to gain his attention [Fig. 82].[22] The miniatures replicate the architecture and decoration of the iwan as well as its effect to amplify the status of the ruler. This is achieved through his enormous scale, raised above his courtiers on his throne, and his richly embroidered robes. It is further enhanced by the jinn who draw back the textile canopy above his head and his dazzling golden halo. The dense floral interlace of the image's frame,

---

[20] Y. Tabbaa, 'Circles of Power: Palace, Citadel, and City in Ayyubid Aleppo', *Ars Orientalis* 23 (1993), 181–200.
[21] Tabbaa, *Constructions of Power*, 84–8.
[22] R. Hillenbrand, 'The Schefer Ḥarīrī: A Study in Islamic Frontispiece Design', in *Arab Painting: Text and Image in Illustrated Arabic Manuscripts*, ed. A. Contadini (Leiden; Boston, 2010), 117–34; his identification of one of the figures as al-Hariri is unconvincing.

Figure 82 Ruler portraits from the opening of a copy of al-Hariri's *Maqamat* (the Schefer Hariri), probably made in Baghdad, Iraq, 1237 (Paris, BNF, arabe 5847, fols. 1v–2r; 37 × 28 cm)

filled with falcons, hunting dogs, rabbits, foxes, hares and deer, evokes the decoration that filled the rest of the space (as we will see below), and the fact that the viewer is forced to view the ruler over the back of the heads of the central two courtiers in the densely packed row across the bottom gives the ruler the necessary sense of aloofness and distance.

One piece of evidence survives that allows us to focus on how al-Ashraf himself sought to project his power within his palace. A carved stone niche, excavated from a palace complex known as Gu'Kummet at Sinjar in Iraq, probably dates to the period when he regularly visited the city before relinquishing control of it in 1229 [Fig. 83].[23] Seated before the niche, the Sultan appeared surrounded by his mamluk guards, each presented with their emblem of office in miniature in tri-lobed frames around the edge of the niche. Interestingly, an almost identical solution to frame an important

---

[23] E. J. Whelan, 'Representations of the Khāṣṣakīyah and the Origins of Mamluk Emblems', in *Content and Context of the Visual Arts in the Islamic World*, ed. P. Soucek (University Park, PA; London, 1988), 219–53.

Figure 83 Niche with reliefs of warrior guards from the Gu'Kummet at Sinjar in Iraq, possibly made for al-Ashraf in the 1220s (National Museum of Iraq, Baghdad)

Figure 84 Gate of the Two Baptisms, Deir Mar Benham, south-east of Mosul, Iraq; first half of the thirteenth century

space was adopted by Christians in the region at Deir Mar Benham.[24] The Gate of the Two Baptisms, commissioned by an unnamed local woman, has similar tri-lobed niches, although now populated by monks and saints rather than warriors [Fig. 84].[25] It is further evidence of the congruence of all communities in this region when it came to finding ways to present authority, whether political or religious.

The gender separation of the Ayyubid court may have prevented Tamta from accessing these public spaces whilst the men of the court were present, but their organisation would certainly have informed her life at court. They demarcated spaces to which she had access, and the surroundings in which she would have been seen by others. Tamta would already have been familiar with the layout and operation of palace buildings from her childhood. One Georgian palace, probably of the thirteenth century, survives in a ruined state at Geguti to the south of Kutaisi [Fig. 85]. The site was a favourite of

---

[24] Snelders, *Identity and Christian–Muslim Interaction*, 257–335.
[25] A. Harrak, *Syriac and Garshuni Inscriptions of Iraq* (Paris, 2010), 1: inscription AE.01.20, 2: fig. on p. 138.

Figure 85 View of the main iwan beyond the entrance to Geguti palace, near Kutaisi, Georgia; twelfth–thirteenth century

the Georgian monarchy; in 1191 it was briefly used by Iurii Bogoliubskoi as his headquarters during his rebellion against Queen Tamar. Set on a plain away from any city, the context of the palace is very different from the urban Islamic palaces so far discussed; but its design suggests that it was expected to function in much the same way. It was a fortified complex that looked inwards rather than outwards, and its surviving walls show that its internal layout owed much to Islamic palace designs. As at Aleppo and Harran, it centred on a large courtyard on each side of which was a deep, vaulted recess. This can only be a variation of the four-iwan plan that dominated Muslim palatial architecture at this time, suggesting that the Georgian rulers had adopted the same habit of public display as their Muslim neighbours.[26] The only significant difference is that squinches suggest that the central courtyard may have been covered by a dome, a concession to the local climate.

Islamic designs filtered down to inform the architectural design of buildings made for other rich members of Caucasian society. The so-called palace of the baron at Ani, built during the Mqargrdzeli period (whose façade we encountered in Chapter 6), is again focused on its central courtyard and iwan opposite the main entrance, and there may have been a similar

[26] V. Cincadze, 'Der Königspalast in Geguti', in *L'Arte Georgiana dal IX al XIV secolo: Atti del Terzo Simposio Internazionale sull'arte Georgiana*, ed. M. Calo'Mariani (Bari, 1981), 105–10.

arrangement in the southern part of the main palace on the citadel at Ani, although the excavations of Nikolai Marr of 1907–8 are inconclusive.[27] Gardens were also a significant element in these Christian palaces. An inscription added to the seventh-century cathedral at Mren, just to the south of Ani, describes the building of a new palace there by Shams al-Din (the brother of the Persian historian Juvayni), who had bought the land from Artashir Mqargrdzeli, a distant cousin of Tamta, in 1261: 'I planned it myself, without the help of any craftsmen, along with the designs, and I set out the foundations of this palace and garden, which I completed after ten years. May God grant grace to the baron Shahmadin [i.e. Shams al-Din] to use it, and for his children and their children. The total cost of this palace was 40,000 gold dinars.'[28] The role of gardens in Caucasian buildings was certainly informed by their use in the Islamic world. The *Knight in the Panther's Skin*, the Georgian epic poem, delights in the mixture of nature and man-made beauty in its description of fantastic royal palaces and their gardens, a romantic vision drawn from Persian poetry:

> I saw the garden fairer indeed than all places of delight: the voice of birds was heard, sweeter than a siren's, there were many fountains of rose-water for baths, over the door were hung curtains of cloth of gold.[29]

Decoration

The world of the ruler was further elaborated in the decoration of his palaces. Ibn Shaddad calls al-Zahir Ghazi's palace in Aleppo the Palace of Pictures (Dar al-Shukhus), and celebrated it for the abundance of its images of people. He goes on to say that this palace replaced an earlier one, the Palace of Glory (Dar al-'Izz), which had burned down on his wedding night, destroying all its 'furniture, jewellery, vessels, and other things'.[30] The visual world of the ruler was painted and carved on that furniture as well as on the

---

[27] N. I. Marr, *Ani: knizhnaia istoriia goroda i raskopki na meste gorodishcha* (Leningrad; Moscow, 1934), 66–72. The northern part of the palace seems to have had rooms each with a different vista over the city.

[28] Manandian, *The Trade and Cities of Armenia*, 188; original in N. I. Marr, 'Novye materialy po armianskoi epigrafike', *Zapiski vostochnogo otdeleniia imperatorskogo russkogo arkheologicheskogo obshchestva* 8 (1894), 69–103; H. Margarian, 'Ṣāḥib-Dīvān Šams al-Dīn Muḥammad Juvainī and Armenia', *Iran and the Caucasus* 10/2 (2006), 167–80, at 168–9.

[29] Shota Rustaveli, stanza 392.

[30] Cited in Ibn al-Shihna, 44–5. The text cites a poem by Rashid 'Abd al-Rahman ibn al-Nablusi, which describes the many perfumes to be smelled around the palace, the abundance of aromatic flowers set in terraces among sculptures, and an image of a fierce lion facing a herd of oxen, now living in harmony.

Figure 86 Real and fantastic fights on the basin of al-ʿAdil II. Brass with silver and gold inlay; 1238–40 (Paris, Musée du Louvre, 5991; height: 19.2 cm; diameter: 47.2 cm)

vessels that he owned. However, much of it was also replicated on a larger scale on the textiles – those curtains of cloth of gold – that hung from the palace walls, on the tiles that were fixed to the walls, and on the carved stucco that acted as cornices and other mouldings at a higher level.

In the absence of any complete surviving wall decorative scheme from the Ayyubid world, we must turn to a different medium – the metalwork vessels of the type destroyed in the Aleppo fire of 1212 – to see an overview of the range of imagery employed. Large numbers of engraved metalwork vessels survive from the second quarter of the thirteenth century, the majority originating from Mosul, the home of al-Ashraf's first wife, Terkan Khatun. We have already encountered one of the less typical examples, the basin with Christian scenes made for al-Salih Ayyub. Another basin, now in the Louvre, made for al-Ashraf's nephew, al-ʿAdil II, between 1238 and 1240 is perhaps more representative of the variety of decoration on such objects [Fig. 86]. The diversity of images reflects the interests, beliefs and fashions of the early thirteenth century. The base of the basin displays the zodiac and planets, presenting them as the central features of the cosmos around which all else revolves. They are surrounded on the walls of the basin by a rich vision of the real and imagined wonders of the courtly world. On the exterior, thirty medallions have acrobats and dancers mix with hunters and wrestlers, and these human figures are interspersed with real and mythical animals, including rams and monkeys, griffins attacking deer, and sphinxes. The interior walls were given over to a series of multi-register images of hunting that evoke the chaos and thrill of the chase in their complex compositions of horsemen and animals. Below, a further sequence of medallions has separate images of individuals hunting, music-making, and feasting.[31] The absence of any visual division between the earthly and the planetary or between the real and the wondrous reveals a worldview of astonishing breadth, and gives some small clue as to their ability to combine these different perceptions of the cosmos, the tangible and the intangible.

The range of subjects is matched by the virtuosity of their execution, the one aspect of the bowl's decoration that is exceptional, and which marked it out as a work of truly royal status. The application of the silver inlay to both the interior (a very constricted space) and exterior walls of the basin was a display of unrivalled technical mastery by its maker, who signed his name as Ahmad ibn ʿUmar al-Dhaki. Other works by al-Dhaki include his *nisba*, al-Mawsili (of Mosul). The fact that his work was being exported to Cairo, and also to other parts of the Ayyubid and Turkish world, shows how widespread interest in these objects and their decoration was.[32]

Two surviving tiles found at Raqqa showing a lion and a peacock,[33] and fountain spouts excavated from Rafiqa that show a cock and a concoction of a sphinx and a chimera [Fig. 87],[34] show that the monumental decoration of the Ayyubid world mixed the real and the fantastical, and they provide some small indication of the colourfulness and figural inventiveness that was possible. The tiles suggest that the larger decorative programme was built up, like the basin, of many smaller individual figures. This is certainly the case with contemporary palaces decorated for the Seljuk sultans of Anatolia. The most extensive collection of tiles is that excavated from the Seljuk palace at Kubadabad, built by the Sultan Kaykubad I in the 1220s on the edge of Lake Beyşehir, 100 kilometres west of Konya. Hundreds of eight-pointed-star tiles with figural decoration have been found at the site, designed to be set up on walls interspersed by cross-shaped tiles with vegetal and geometric ornaments [Fig. 88]. These created walls covered in a dense array of individual images. The tiles present the cosmos in all its variety and complexity – birds,

---

[31] The most recent publication of the basin is S. Makariou, ed., *Islamic Art at the Musée du Louvre* (Paris, 2012), 175–7.

[32] In 1293 the Mamluk Sultan Qalaʾun ordered 200 candlesticks from Damascus, 50 each in silver and gold, and 100 in brass emblazoned with his titles: al-Maqrizi, cited in L. E. M. Mols, *Mamluk Metalwork Fittings in their Artistic and Architectural Context* (Delft, 2006), 155.

[33] K. Brisch, ed., *Museum für Islamische Kunst Berlin: Katalog* (Berlin-Dahlem, 1979), cat. 379; Wieczorek et al., eds., *Saladin und die Kreuzfahrer*, cat. B.11–12; Delpont, ed., *L'Orient de Saladin*, cats. 33, 34.

[34] K. von Folsach, *Art from the World of Islam in the David Collection* (Copenhagen, 2001), 158, inv. Isl. 57, Isl. 56.

Figure 87 Ceramic fountain spout of a sphinx-like chimera, excavated from Rafiqa, early thirteenth century (Copenhagen, David Collection, inv. Isl. 56; height: 37 cm)

animals, humans, mythical creatures, calligraphy and floral designs. The range of courtly interests is very close to that on the basin of al-ʿAdil II, but executed in a style more heavily influenced by Persian art. Like the basin, they cannot be combined to create a simple iconographic programme, or reduced to tell one clear message about the ruler and his court. The juxtaposition of such diverse images has a precedent in the hundreds of individual figures and animals that adorn the ceiling of the audience chamber in the palace of Roger II in Palermo, Sicily, built about a century earlier, which seems to have reflected contemporary practice in Fatimid Cairo.[35] Although

[35] J. M. Bloom, *Arts of the City Victorious: Islamic Art and Architecture in Fatimid North Africa and Egypt* (New Haven; London, 2008), 189–93; E. J. Grube and J. Johns, *The Painted Ceilings of the Cappella Palatina* (Genoa; New York, 2005).

Figure 88 Tiles from the Seljuk palace at Kubadabad on the edge of Lake Beyşehir, Turkey, built by the Sultan Kaykubad; 1220s (For the colour version, please refer to the plate section. In some formats this figure will only appear in black and white)

made for a Christian ruler, the ceiling images drew much of their inspiration from the Islamic world. In both instances attempts to find a cohesive, single programmatic meaning have been unconvincing. Instead, we should see them as deliberately varied. They celebrated the diversity of the cosmos, in just the same way as the brass vessels.[36] A further warning against looking for simple iconographic programmes in these image ensembles comes from the chronicler Ibn Bibi: his description of Kubadabad chose not to focus on the contents of the tiles at all; instead, he celebrated only the visual effect: 'turquoise and dark blue wall coverings on its walls, so beautiful that the colours of the rainbow fade with jealousy'.[37]

Other tiles reflected another major interest of the ruling elites of the region: poetry. Verses from the *Shahname*, the great Persian epic, composed by Firdowsi in about 1000, were inscribed in texts on the walls of

---

[36] For image Arık and Arık, *Tiles*, 253–9, fig. 195, 196 for Huand Hatun.
[37] Arık and Arık, *Tiles*, 300. Compare Ibn Bibi, 148.

Konya and Sivas by the Seljuk Sultan Kaykubad I,[38] and long tile inscriptions (unfortunately mostly illegible) have been excavated both at Kubadabad and at the Artuqid palace at Amid.[39] The epic was also represented visually, most notably Bahram Gur's display of archery for his slave-girl Azade, which is known in almost every medium in the early thirteenth century. Books of poems were deemed a suitable setting for displays of royal magnificence. A twenty-volume copy of the *Kitab al-Aghani*, a tenth-century compendium of poetry, made 1216–19 for the ruler of Mosul, Badr al-Din Lu'lu', included a series of portraits of the *atabeg* engaged in a range of royal pursuits including hunting and feasting (six portraits survive in the seven remaining volumes).[40] However, with poetry and art we run once more into the problem of the frontier between the Arabic and the Persian worlds, with Tamta's place in Akhlat right on this borderline. It is unclear whether the visual world of the palaces she inhabited shared more with the Turkic/Persian world that surrounded Akhlat or with the Ayyubid world from which her husband came. This is highlighted by the *Shahname*. The poem was hugely popular in the Persian and Turkic worlds, and although we know that its stories were familiar in the Ayyubid world as well, we do not know what impact they had. No *Shahname* images survive from an Arabic-speaking region,[41] although its tales of royal prowess were of obvious interest to all rulers, and Al-Ashraf's brother (and predecessor in Damascus) al-Mu'azzam commissioned a translation of the poem into Arabic from Fath al-Din al-Bundari, which was eventually completed in 1257.[42] This distinction between text and image is important because it suggests a very different attitude to the use of extended narrative images in court culture. The apparent preference for isolated, individual vignettes on tiles and metalwork seen in the Ayyubid world indicates that visual story-telling was constructed in a more complex and less literal way.

The evidence from the Caucasus suggests that when Tamta first encountered the range of images in Ayyubid palaces she may not have been familiar with the style and medium in which they were made, but she was certainly

---

[38] A. Bombaci, 'Die Mauerinschriften von Konya', in *Forschungen zur Kunst Asiens. In Memoriam Kurt Erdmann*, eds. O. Aslanapa and R. Naumann (Istanbul, 1969), 67–73; L. T. Giuzalian, 'Otryvok iz Shahname na glinianykh izdeliiakh XIII–XIV vv', *Epigrafika Vostoka* 4 (1951), 40–55 and 5 (1951), 33–50 on *Shahname* texts on ceramics.

[39] S. S. Blair, *The Monumental Inscriptions from Early Islamic Iran and Transoxiana* (Leiden, 1992), 11, citing Ibn Bibi.

[40] D. S. Rice, 'The Aghānī Miniatures and Religious Painting in Islam', *Burlington Magazine* 95/601 (1953), 128–35.

[41] E. Atil, 'The Freer Bowl and the Legacy of the Shahname', *Damaszener Mitteilungen* 11 (1999), 7–12.

[42] C. Brockelmann, *Geschichte der arabischen Literatur*, vol. 1 (Leiden, 1943), 392.

Figure 89 The killing of the dragon by the hero Amiran, from the Georgian poem *Amiran-Darejaniani*, painted on the south wall of the church of the Archangels, Lashtkhveri, Svaneti, Georgia; fourteenth century

familiar with the range of subject matter. The Arabic tales of *Kalila wa Dimna* and the Persian *Shahname* were well known in Georgia in the thirteenth century, and both are cited in the Georgian chronicles.[43] Firdowsi's poem was also translated into Armenian at this time.[44] We know that scenes from epic poetry were depicted in monumental art. The killing of the dragon by the hero Amiran, from the Georgian poem *Amiran-Darejaniani*, was depicted twice in Georgia (in both cases it survives on the exteriors of churches in Svaneti in the high Caucasus [Fig. 89]).[45] The *Amiran-Darejaniani* and Shota Rustaveli's *Knight in the Panther's Skin*, a tale of love lost and won which ranges across Persia and India and nowhere explicitly mentions Christianity, were both free reworkings of Persian poetic forms into Georgian.[46] These epic scenes appeared alongside historical and biblical imagery. The Byzantine epic *Digenis Akritis*, set on the eastern

---

[43] *Kartlis Tskhovreba*, 233.
[44] P. S. Cowe, 'Models for the Interpretation of Medieval Armenian Poetry', in *New Approaches to Medieval Armenian Language and Literature*, ed. J. J. S. Weitenberg (Amsterdam; Atlanta, GA, 1995), 29–46, at 35.
[45] N. A. Aladashvili and A. Vol'skaia, 'Fasadnye rospisi Verkhnei Svaneti', *Ars Georgica* 9 (1987), 94–120, façade paintings in Upper Savaneti; Qenia, *Upper Svaneti*, 241 (Lashtkhveri, church of the Archangels) and 287 (Chazhashi, church of the Saviour).
[46] Amiran-Darejaniani; Rayfield, *The Literature of Georgia*, 3rd edn, 75–83.

(a)

Figure 90 Stucco fragments excavated at Ani, Turkey, and Dvin, Armenia; twelfth–thirteenth century (Yerevan, History Museum of Armenia)

frontier of the Byzantine world, describes its hero's palace as being decorated with pictures of battles from the Old Testament, intermingled with duels from ancient mythology: David's defeat of Goliath was painted beside Bellerophon's victory over the Chimera.[47] A description of Queen Tamar's palace at Isani, near Tbilisi, similarly mixes myth and biblical imagery in a manner analogous to such paintings.[48] The closest comparison in the Islamic world to these battle scenes is a fragment of wall painting from Seljuk Iran, now in the Metropolitan Museum in New York, which shows a ruler killing a serpent or dragon.[49]

Alongside these narratives, however, were more emblematic images that also seem to have come from the Persian visual world. Stucco fragments excavated at Ani and Dvin reveal a familiar repertoire of birds, sphinxes and harpies, mixing the real and the fantastic in a similar way to that encountered in Islamic decoration [Fig. 90a, b, c].[50] They are remarkably close in imagery, style and technique to fragments from the Seljuk palace at Beyşehir and the kiosk at Konya [Fig. 91a, b].[51] Other borrowings from the

---

[47] Jeffreys, *Digenis Akritis*, book 7 (Grottaferrata version).
[48] *Kartlis Tskhovreba*, 238. NB the English mistranslates Achilles as Archil.
[49] E. Sims, *Peerless Images: Persian Painting and its Sources* (New Haven; London, 2002), cat. 38; http://www.metmuseum.org.
[50] N. I. Marr, *Ani: Rêve d'Arménie* (Paris, 2001), figs. 108, 128, 138.
[51] D. J. Roxburgh, ed., *Turks: A Journey of a Thousand Years, 600–1600* (London, 2005), cat. 58.

(b)

(c)

Figure 90 (*continued*)

Islamic world uncovered in secular buildings in Ani include six-pointed-star tiles (non-figural),[52] and window grilles.[53] Additionally we know that the Artuqid designer al-Jazari designed brass door-knockers for the palace of Nasir al-Din Mahmud in Amid in the form of two opposed dragons;

[52] Marr, *Ani: Rêve d'Arménie*, figs. 97–8, 102.   [53] Marr, *Ani: Rêve d'Arménie*, fig. 129.

(a)

Figure 91 Stucco fragments from the Seljuk palace at Beyşehir and the kiosk at Konya, Turkey; early thirteenth century (Los Angeles County Museum of Art, The Madina Collection of Islamic Art, Gift of Camilla Chandler Frost, M.2002.1.675, 11.4 × 9.4 cm; M.2002.1.683a-h, height approx. 5.7 cm)

an almost identical pair was found in Tbilisi early in the twentieth century (although their earlier provenance is less clear).[54] Finally, a large stucco figure discovered in the medieval palace at Rustavi to the south-east of Tbilisi suggests that the Georgians may even have borrowed the idea of monumental sculptural figures of rulers from the Seljuks in Iran.[55] However, whilst the medium and the use of extended narratives were not familiar in the Ayyubid

---

[54] E. Diez, 'Ein Seldschukischer Türklopfer', *Zeitschrift für bildende Kunst* 56 (1921), 18–20; Roxburgh, ed., *Turks*, fig. 33 and cat. 87.

[55] The relief is unpublished. S. Heidemann, J.-F. de Lapérouse and V. Parry, 'The Large Audience: Life-Sized Stucco Figures of Royal Princes from the Seljuq Period', *Muqarnas* 31 (2014), 35–72; M. Ekhtiar, P. Soucek, S. Canby and N. N. Haidar, *Masterpieces from the Department of Islamic Art in the Metropolitan Museum of Art* (New York, 2011), cats. 62 and 63.

(b)

Figure 91 (*continued*)

world, the underlying messages conveyed by these royal images were much the same. So although Tamta may have found the decoration of Ayyubid palaces unfamiliar at first sight, its portrayal of royal virtues and heroism in war, hunting and feasting was essentially the same.

Women

Women do not have a presence in this world. When higher-ranking women are depicted, they are secluded from the main spaces of the palace.

In the early thirteenth-century *Kitab al-Diryaq* manuscript in Vienna (Nationalbibliothek, MS A.F. 10, fol. 3a), women are shown veiled, and away from the palace in which the ruler prepares a feast of shashlik. However, while elite women may not be visually significant within these images of power, we know that they were certainly among the audience for them. We have already seen that the inlaid dish in Munich with courtly scenes was a gift from Badr al-Din Lu'lu', the ruler of Mosul, to a woman, Khawanrah Khatun,[56] despite the bombastic and militaristic tone of its main inscription. In Seljuk Anatolia, Mahperi Khatun, the Armenian wife of Sultan Kaykubad I, employed tiles identical to those her husband had commissioned for his palace at Kubadabad in the bathhouse attached to her mosque-madrasa-mausoleum complex in Kayseri.[57] The courtly imagery formed the major part of the visual environment in which the women had to live, and so it helped to determine the ideals and behaviours that they had to adopt. Inevitably these behaviours demoted the appearance and status of women, although the image did not of course reflect reality. The imagery provided an obstacle to women by always presenting them as secondary creatures, but may also have facilitated their manipulation of power by creating a façade of male dominance behind which they could act. From the point of view of Tamta, the design and decoration of palaces suggest that her identity continued to be framed through the men who controlled her, just as it had been by her father before her marriage. The details of the identity of male power that these palaces evoked was probably also consistent with that in which she had been brought up.

The one role in which women were recognised within the palace was as servants, musicians or dancers, the objects of men's attention and desire. It is in this guise that they appear in front of the ruler in vol 4 of Badr al-Din Lu'lu''s *Kitab al-Aghani* (Cairo, Egyptian National Library, Ms Farsi 579, frontispiece) [Fig. 92]. This was a role that could be exploited by the determined or the lucky: those that caught the eye of the ruler and were able to use their access to him to further themselves. The consequences of Nur al-Din of Amid's infatuation with a singing-girl (see Chapter 5), or of al-Ashraf's desire for his (admittedly male) musician (see Chapter 7), in which the objects of their affection were able to accrue power or money for themselves, have already been noted.

---

[56] Jones and Michell, eds., *The Arts of Islam*, 180, cat. 197; Sarre and van Berchem, 'Das Metallbecken des Atabeks Lulu', 33.
[57] Arık and Arık, *Tiles*, 253–9.

Figure 92 Badr al-Din Lu'lu' and his court entertained by female musicians, from volume 4 of the *Kitab al-Aghani*, Mosul, Iraq, 1219 (Cairo, Egyptian National Library, Ms Farsi 579, frontispiece)

Exchange

The common palace imagery that we have seen across the Caucasus, Anatolia and Syria reflects the shared interests of the elites of each region. It also provides evidence of how such visual imagery was exchanged. The work was carried out by craftsmen who travelled between courts producing similar work in each location. Objects travelled too. The metalwork from Mosul that was being made for clients across the region allowed a standard repertoire of images to be disseminated. The diplomatic value of these brass objects was observed by Ibn Saʿid, an Andalusian visitor to Mosul in 1250: 'There are many crafts in the city, especially inlaid brass vessels which are exported (and presented) to rulers, as are the silken garments woven there.'[58] Tamta would have been familiar with such objects from her childhood, as Islamic metalwork circulated throughout the Caucasus. A twelfth-century Iranian ewer was excavated at Ani by Nikolai Marr in 1906 [Fig. 93],[59] and such vessels must have been familiar sights: an object of almost identical design was depicted in the Haghbat Gospels, illuminated in Ani in 1211 (Matenadaran 6288, fol. 8v) [Fig. 17]. Many decorated ceramics imported from the Ayyubid world have also been excavated at Ani and Dvin as well. These exchanges encompassed all the states in the region, and moved in every direction. Evidence from the Kiosk of Kılıç Arslan in Konya and the palace at Kubadabad shows that their patrons imported ceramics from Iran, made in the technically complex minai technique as well as expensive lustreware tiles.[60]

The shared court culture was also interpreted in a much more literal sense. In addition to decorative motifs travelling between courts, we have evidence from the thirteenth century of whole palaces moving too. When Constantinople fell to the Latins of the Fourth Crusade in April 1204, the city, which had stood un-taken for nine hundred years, was looted with abandon. Its collections of sculptures – at least three hundred classical bronze and marble statues adorned the Hippodrome in the centre of the city alone – were either melted down for their bullion value or divided and exported among the victors. Great monolithic columns made their way from Constantinople through the Black Sea to Trebizond and up the

---

[58] D. S. Rice, 'Inlaid Brasses from the Workshop of Ahmad al-Dhaki al-Mawsili', *Ars Orientalis* 2 (1957), 283–326, at 284 n.9, explains his interpolation of 'and presented' to indicate that the Arabic here indicates that the vessels 'were of high quality and fit for kings'.
[59] Durand, Rapti, and Giovannoni, eds., *Armenia Sacra*, cat. 94.
[60] Arık and Arık, *Tiles*, 225–38.

Figure 93 Twelfth-century Iranian brass ewer, excavated at Ani by Nikolai Marr in 1906 (Yerevan, History Museum of Armenia, inv. 123–1322)

Adriatic to Venice.[61] The sculptures that ended up in Venice, the four bronze horses on the west façade of San Marco or the porphyry tetrarchs on the exterior of the church's treasury, are the most famous to survive. They were symbols of Venice's new claim to rule one quarter and one half of one

---

[61] Eastmond, *Art and Identity in Thirteenth-Century Byzantium*, 43–4; F. W. Deichmann, 'I pilastri acritani', *Rendiconti Atti della Pontificia Accademia Romana di Archeologia* 50 (1980), 75–89; R. S. Nelson, 'The History of Legends and the Legends of History: The Pilastri Acritani in Venice', in *San Marco, Byzantium, and the Myths of Venice*, eds. H. Maguire and R. S. Nelson (Washington, DC, 2010), 63–90.

quarter of the Byzantine Empire. However, this constituted only a small fraction of the trade in antiquities, and only one motive for their movement. Most were carried around the Mediterranean for sale on the open market, in the straightforward pursuit of profit.

The Ayyubid historian Abu Samah records that when the Venetians captured Constantinople, 'they plundered it, seized the marble sculptures from the churches, and transported them to Egypt and Syria where they sold them. A great number of these marble sculptures arrived in Damascus.'[62] Usama al-Halabi, one of the mamluks of al-'Adil, used such marbles and sculptures from Constantinople to embellish his hammam in the city.[63] The glut of marble and columns emanating from Constantinople must have led to a buyer's market, perhaps enabling Usama to buy his sculptures relatively cheaply. When he fell from grace in 1211, his lands were seized, his castles demolished and he was fined one million pieces of gold, before being imprisoned at Kerak until his death. Such was the luxury of his palace, however, that it was taken over by al-Nasir Dawud, the son of al-Mu'azzam.

Usama's sculptures from Constantinople were only the tip of the iceberg of international palace transfers. The extent of the removals could be enormous. A generation later, when Theodore Metochites, the prime minister of Byzantium, fell from grace in 1328, the *opus sectile* marble floor of his palace was carefully lifted and sent to the King of the western Scyths (i.e. the local Mongol ruler) so that it could be reinstalled in his palace.[64] The surviving marble floor and cladding of his monastery in Constantinople, the Chora, give some impression of the variety and richness of the marbles he was able to collect. The infrastructure required to manoeuvre these stones, especially to non-coastal cities such as Damascus, was enormous. It was testimony above all to the industrial prowess and expertise of the Venetians that they could undertake such work; skills developed through their proto-factory, the Arsenale, which enabled the mass building of boats from the late twelfth century on.

The one major surviving example of such a large-scale transfer is found on the façade of the madrasa–mausoleum complex of the Mamluk Sultan

---

[62] 'Abd al-Rahman ibn Isma'il, 154.
[63] 'Abd al-Rahman ibn Isma'il, 154; Sauvaget, 'Un bain damasquin du XIIIe siècle', 379; F. Barry, '*Disiecta membra*: Ranieri Zeno, the Imitation of Constantinople, the *Spolia* Style, and Justice at San Marco', in *San Marco, Byzantium, and the Myths of Venice*, eds. H. Maguire and R. S. Nelson (Washington, DC, 2010), 7–62, at 24.
[64] 1328: Nikephoros Gregoras, II/2: 239–40 (trans. Schopen and Bekker, 459). See P. Magdalino, 'Theodore Metochites, the Chora, and Constantinople', in *The Kariye Camii Reconsidered*, eds. H. A. Klein, R. Ousterhout and B. Pitarakis (Istanbul, 2011), 169–87, at 179.

Figure 94 Crusader doorway from Acre, re-used as the entrance to the madrasa–mausoleum complex of the Mamluk Sultan al-Nasir Muhammad in Cairo, Egypt; 1296–1303

al-Nasir Muhammad in Cairo.[65] To celebrate the capture of Acre in 1291, the final Crusader stronghold on the east coast of the Mediterranean, al-Ashraf Khalil had dismantled the porch of a church in Acre, and carried it stone by stone to Cairo, where al-Nasir Muhammad later reassembled it to form the main entrance into his complex [Fig. 94].[66] Located

---

[65] Behrens-Abouseif, *Cairo of the Mamluks*, 152–4; Pringle, *The Churches of the Crusader Kingdom of Jerusalem*, 3: 24–5, and 67–8 where he notes that the assumption that the portal is from the church of St Andrew has no archaeological or medieval support.

[66] A second Crusader spoil has been identified on the Sultan Hasan complex: C. A. Fleck, 'Crusader Spolia in Medieval Cairo: The Portal of the Complex of Sultan Ḥasan', *Journal of Transcultural Medieval Studies* 1/2 (2014), 249–99.

opposite the mausoleum of al-Salih Ayyub, built fifty years earlier by Shajar al-Durr, it marked the transformation of the city's rulers' relationship to the Crusades: al-Salih Ayyub had been buried as a martyr to the Franks; al-Nasir Muhammad's tomb was a symbol of triumph over the European invaders. The contrast between the porch, with its Crusader trefoil arch, thin piers and foliate capitals, and the austere blocked masses of the rest of the building and its ziggurat crenellations made the message of victory unavoidable.

These large-scale architectural removals could be dangerous, however. In 1200 Nur al-Din Muhammad, the Artuqid ruler of Hisnkeyf, was crushed to death by a marble column he was trying to remove from a church in Amid (Diyarbakir) to decorate his palace.[67] The story has survived only in a Christian source, which saw Nur al-Din's fate as divine punishment for his treatment of a Christian place of worship. The business of removals mixed pragmatism and politics. It allowed expensive materials to be endlessly recycled, each time at a profit for the seller. At the same time it allowed the buyers to parade their new possessions as a proclamation of triumph, whether over a defeated enemy city or a subjugated rival religion.

Tamta's position was clearly awkward. In many ways she shared the same symbolic status as these transported spoils; moved and installed in a new location as a reminder of (Ayyubid) victory. However, all such symbols remained open to reinterpretation, and it is likely that they could have been turned to Tamta's advantage. Tamta could claim both the forms of decoration that she encountered with the Ayyubids and those imported from the Caucasus with equal force.

Astrology

The most striking feature of the range of imagery in palace decorations – on tiles, on metalwork, whether in Christian or in Muslim settings – is the way that they blur different realms – the earthly and the heavenly, the real and the fantastic – moving the court beyond the normal mortal world and setting it apart. The lack of distinction between these worlds perhaps explains another major interest of courts: astrology.

Astrology lay on the edge of respectability, both socially and theologically. Its acceptability was ambiguous to say the least, and was simultaneously celebrated and denigrated by official religions. Al-Ashraf, for example, was a fervent adherent of astrology, and his concern for it shows

---

[67] Michael the Syrian, 3: 396.

the unique place it held in Muslim belief. Simultaneously, the Hanbali theologians he supported in Damascus were amongst the most prominent to write against astrology in this period.[68] Al-Ashraf himself is recorded as having clamped down on other forms of learning which he deemed to be potentially insidious.[69] However, such was the blurred line between theology, science and astrology that in al-Ashraf's view this did not extend to astrology. He employed a number of full-time astrologers on his staff whom he consulted about all important decisions. In this he followed most of his family, including his uncle Saladin, who had also employed an astrologer receiving the same salary as the court physician, 30 dinars per month.[70] The Christian Church also officially condemned astrology as it interfered with the belief in free will, leading to some vehement polemics against the practice. But this never undermined actual beliefs: in the 1160s the Byzantine Emperor Manuel I Komnenos had imprisoned his court poet Michael Glykas when he criticised the Emperor's belief in astrology.[71] Sceptics such as Glykas were more than outweighed by believers, even among the Church hierarchy. Bar Hebraeus (the Syriac primate of the East, d. 1286) blamed natural disasters in 1284 on the conjunction of the stars in the house of Aquarius with the planets in Capricorn.[72] Astrology determined the safety of bridges, such as that built in 1163/4 over the river Tigris at Jazirat ibn 'Umar (modern-day Cizre). Its piers are adorned with zodiac imagery, to add supernatural strength to their stonework.[73] The zodiac was also used to establish the iconography of coinage. Artuqid coins show Mars in Aries and Jupiter in Sagittarius, seeking to transfer the particularly auspicious conjunctions of the stars to the economy.[74] The international importance of astrology was most apparent during the rare alignment of the sun, moon and all five planets on 16 September 1186. This had been calculated by astronomers from Spain to the Near East, and was widely predicted by

---

[68] J. W. Livingston, 'Science and the Occult in the Thinking of Ibn Qayyim al-Jawziyya', *Journal of the American Oriental Society* 112/4 (1992), 598–610.

[69] Sauvaire, 'Description de Damas VII', 263.

[70] Saliba, 'The Role of the Astrologer', at 64; E. Ashtor, *Histoire des prix et des salaires dans l'Orient médiéval* (Paris, 1969), 264.

[71] D. George, 'Manuel I Komnenos and Michael Glykas: A Twelfth-Century Defence and Refutation of Astrology', *Culture and Cosmos* 5/1 (2001), 3–48, 5/2 (2001), 23–51, 6/1 (2002), 23–43; discussion in P. Magdalino, *The Empire of Manuel I Komnenos, 1143–1180* (Cambridge, 1993), 377–82.

[72] Bar Hebraeus, 473.

[73] Whelan, *The Public Figure*, 110–13, figs. 61–3; Lane Poole, *Catalogue of Oriental Coins*, vol. 3: *The Coins of the Turkumán Houses of Seljook, Urtuk, Zengee, etc.*, nos. 429–37.

[74] R. Hillenbrand, *Islamic Art and Architecture* (London, 1999), 133.

astrologers to lead to a terrible catastrophe.[75] According to one contemporary French historian:

> In this year, the astrologers of the East and the West, the Jews, the Saracens and even the Christians had sent letters across the diverse regions of the world, in which they predicted, without any doubt, that in September there would take place a most powerful tempest of winds, followed by earthquakes, a great mortality among men, sedition and trouble, as well as upheavals among kingdoms and a series of other menaces of this kind.[76]

Nothing occurred on the fateful day.

The ubiquity of astrology stretched from the street to the court, and attracted both men and women. Despite official condemnations of astrology, it could never be erased, and laws tended to be more pragmatic in attempts to regulate its practice and prevent fraud. Surviving Mamluk laws from the start of the fourteenth century required astrologers to work out of doors, and only on main streets in order to ensure that they could be regulated, as well as to protect the moral standing of the many women who wanted to consult them.[77] Women could train as astrologers too: Ibn Bibi, the historian of the Seljuks, says that his mother was an astrologer.[78] It is unlikely that the women of the court would have waited on street corners to consult astrologers, but they certainly had access to its beliefs and practices. A Seljuk bronze mirror with images of the seven planets, made in 1153, was designed to protect and aid women in childbirth, and it derived its power from the auspicious alignment of the sun and planets when it was made. This is revealed by its inscription:

> Bismallah. This blessed mirror was made in the ascendant of blessed augury and it will serve for curing the paralysis of the mouth, alleviate the pains of childbirth and also other pains and sufferings, if Allah permit. This was achieved in the months of the year 548 [1153] ... It was made of seven metals as the Sun passed through the sign of Aries.[79]

The seven metals were clearly thought to embody the seven planets depicted on the back.

---

[75] G. de Callataÿ, 'La grande conjunction de 1186', in *Occident et Proche-Orient: contacts scientifiques au temps des Croisades*, eds. I. Draelants, A. Tihon and B. van den Abeele (Leuven, 1997), 369–84.

[76] Rigord, 73–4 (with two examples of their doom-laden letters, 73–7).

[77] Saliba, 'The Role of the Astrologer', 61–2.   [78] Kuehn, *The Dragon*, 135.

[79] S. Carboni, *Following the Stars: Images of the Zodiac in Islamic Art* (New York, 2005), 6; D. S. Rice, 'A Seljuq Mirror', in *Proceedings of the First International Congress of Turkish Art* (Ankara, 1961), 288–90.

At court, astrology could be studied with greater rigour, accompanied by all the methodical trappings of scientific accuracy: instruments, calculations, observations. It decided everything in al-Ashraf's life, from war to medicine. In 1232 he called for the advice of Shams al-Din Yusuf, the one astrologer in his entourage whose name is recorded, to determine the time of the attack with his brother al-Kamil against al-Malik al-Mas'ud, the last Artuqid ruler of the city of Amid (Diyarbakir). In turn, Amid's walls were themselves protected by astrological symbols: on one tower a seated figure holding a scorpion represents Mars in the constellation of Scorpio, commonly regarded as an auspicious time for military victory.[80] Al-Ashraf's reliance on astrology suggests that he would also have consulted his astrologers in the months before his death: he needed to find an auspicious time for the surgery in which his skull was trepanned to deal with 'boils within the head'; he survived the immediate surgery, but not its after-effects.[81] His fellow rulers turned to oracles to confirm the propitiousness of their choice of bride.[82]

Given the weight al-Ashraf placed on his astrologers in the timing of his decisions, it is easy to see how the business as a whole began to take on its own place in the ceremonial life of the court. The importance of astrology was reflected in material form by the commissioning of astrolabes, the key instrument required to determine the placement of the planets at any time. Al-Ashraf is connected with a number of astrolabes, including two commissioned from 'Abd al-Karim, the most celebrated scientific metalworker of the day from the Jazira.[83] One of these astrolabes, made in 1227 and now in the Museum for the History of Science in Oxford, is among the most intricate astrolabes to have survived [Fig. 95].[84] The expense of the object is evident from its size and weight. It has a diameter of 27.7 centimetres, and weighs 3.75 kilograms. It is also visible in the care and detail with which it was engraved. The upper half of the front of the astrolabe is taken up by the

---

[80] Cahen, 'La Djazira au milieu du treizième siècle', 116; Saliba, 'The Role of the Astrologer', 58 n.81; Eastmond, 'Other Encounters'.

[81] Sauvaire, 'Description de Damas VII', at 266–7. Alternatively, Abu'l-Fida, 113, has al-Ashraf dying of dysentery.

[82] Ibn Bibi, 77.   [83] Ward, 'The Inscription on the Astrolabe'.

[84] The twelve rings are described by W. Hartner, 'The Principle and Use of the Astrolabe', in A. U. Pope, ed., *A Survey of Persian Art from Prehistoric Times to the Present*, vol. 3 (London; New York, 1939), 2530–54, at 2547–50; see also R. T. Gunther, *The Astrolabes of the World: Based upon the Series of Instruments in the Lewis Evans Collection in the old Ashmolean Museum at Oxford, with Notes on Astrolabes in the Collections of the British Museum, Sir J. Findlay, Mr S. V. Hoffman, the Mensin Collection, and in Other Public and Private Collections*, vol. 1: *The Eastern Astrolabes* (Oxford, 1932), 233–6, no. 103, but 'with grave errors'.

Figure 95 Back of the astrolabe of al-Ashraf, made by ʿAbd al-Karim, Mesopotamia. Brass with gold and silver inlay; 1227 (Oxford, Museum for the History of Science, inv. 37148; diameter: 27.7 cm; weight: 3.75 kg)

almacantar lines, representing each degree of space above the horizon. The skills required to incise all ninety lines, each less than one millimetre apart as they converge towards the centre of the instrument, are remarkable.

The size and quality of al-Ashraf's astrolabe bear testimony to its status as a royal statement of learning, wealth and taste. This was reinforced by the inscription inlaid in gold around the rim, which aimed to manifest al-Ashraf's erudition, his orthodoxy and power in the most sumptuous manner possible. The grandiose text, which matches anything inscribed in monumental art, shows how astrology and power were inextricably intertwined:

> This is made by order of our master King and Sovereign: the most noble, and the Great Prince, the glorious and magnanimous; the learned and the just; the warrior and the constant, the strong and the victorious, the conqueror of the world of nations; the extoller of the true faith; the king of Muslims, the helper of Princes, the auxiliary of mankind, the treasure of the Empire; the accomplishment of the people; the glory of the religion; master of kings and monarchs; the shelter of the troops of the state, the destroyer of the infidels and idolaters; the subduer of the schismatics and the rebels; the extirpator of the atheists; the consumer of pertinacy; the dissipator of the injurious and the insolent people, the expeller of seditions from towns; the hero of the world; the Chosroes of Iraq; the protector of the universe; the guardian of the defiles; the adjutor of the people; the King of Arabia, Persia and Armenia; and the victorious commander of the true believers; Abul-Fath Musa, son of the victorious king Abul-Bakr, son of Ayyub. May God Almighty render him victorious.[85]

The appeal of astrology and power was revived in the early twentieth century when Kaiser Wilhelm II sought to buy this astrolabe. He planned to replace al-Ashraf's name with his own as part of his attempt to seduce the Orient.[86]

Astrology was an important means of conveying erudition and power in the Caucasus as well. It would have been familiar to Tamta long before she moved south for her marriage. In 1188 an important astrological treatise was prepared in Georgia, which survives in the National Centre for Manuscripts in Tbilisi (MS A-65).[87] Surviving only in fragmentary form, it presents an astrological account of the key characteristics of each zodiac sign, starting with Aries [Fig. 96]. The astrological text forms part of a compilation of five works, including homilies of Anastasios of Sinai, once again showing the inextricability of religion and astrology, despite Orthodox teaching. The quality of the drawings in the treatise and its large scale suggests an elite, possibly royal, patron. The form of the text and the miniatures shows the debt that Christianity owed to Islamic societies in astrology. It was the Arabic and Persian worlds that were at the forefront of astrological science in this period. The Georgian text is essentially a paraphrase of an

---

[85] This is the translation in Gunther, *The Astrolabes of the World*, no. 103.
[86] This story from Gunther, *The Astrolabes of the World*, no. 103; for Wilhelm's other efforts – repairing the tomb of Saladin, building a new fountain in the Hippodrome in Istanbul: Wieczorek et al., eds., *Saladin und die Kreuzfahrer*, 459–70.
[87] S. Amiranashvili, *Gruzinskaia miniatura* (Moscow, 1966), 28–30; MS A-65.

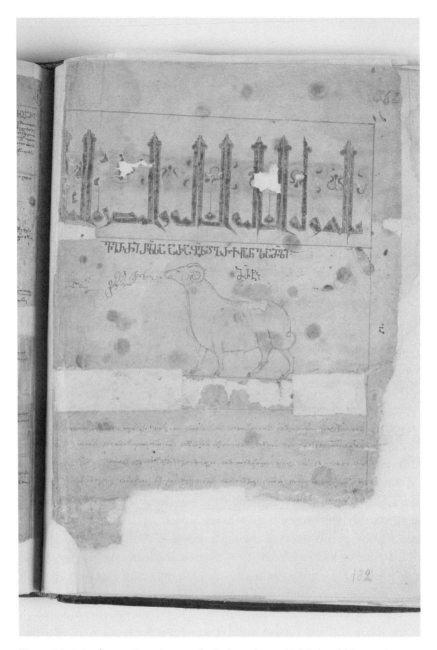

Figure 96 Aries from a Georgian astrological treatise, 1188 (National Manuscripts Centre, Tbilisi, MS A-65, fol. 352; 23 × 30.5 cm)

Arabic precursor, and throughout the author is careful to explain the Arabic words that lie behind the terms he employs. The opening title reads: '*Verdzi* [i.e. Aries], which is called in Arabic *Hamali* [i.e. al-haml]'.[88] The incomplete Kufic inscription at the head of the page, with its angular forms and tall risers and its foliate background, suggests that the text's Arabic origins lay in the Jazira. This region produced manuscripts with very similar calligraphy, such as a copy of pseudo-Galen's *Kitab al-Diryaq* (Book of antidotes), written and illustrated in 1199 (BNF arabe 2964) [Fig. 97].[89] The images are equally indebted to Islamic art, both in their style and iconography. Each of the surviving zodiac signs is rendered in a delicate pen outline, with just a hint of blusher on the cheeks of humans. This echoes images of the constellations in Arabic and Persian texts of al-Sufi's *Kitab Suwar al-Kawakib* (Book of the fixed stars). The figure of Sagittarius shooting an arrow at its own dragon-headed tail echoes the copper coins of Nasir al-Din Artuq Arslan, the Artuqid ruler of Mardin (r. 1184–1200). Similar translations were made from Arabic to Armenian at the same time for members of the Mqargrdzeli court in Armenia. Mkhitar of Ani, the keeper of the keys of the city's cathedral, translated a Persian text on astronomy in the early thirteenth century.[90] At the same time, in 1222, a manuscript on oneiromancy entitled 'An explanation of dreams' was translated into Armenian in the city.[91]

Because it was believed to have a relevance to every aspect of life, astrology crossed all frontiers in this period. This then gave it additional importance, as a common interest in the international fellowship of kings. Interest stretched from the Caucasus in the east to Spain in the west, where Alfonso X of Castile (r. 1252–84) employed men to translate from Arabic the *Liber del Saber de astrología*, which contained detailed instructions and diagrams on how to build an astrolabe.[92] Astrology became a tool in international diplomacy. In 1232 al-Ashraf sent the Holy Roman Emperor Frederick II a 'planetarium in which astral bodies worked in gold and jewels moved in

---

[88] A. Shanidze, *Etlta da shwidta mnatobtatwis: astrologiuri tkhzuleba XII saukunisa* (Tbilisi, 1948), 16.

[89] Most recently J. J. Kerner, 'Art in the Name of Science: The *Kitāb al-Diryāq* in Text and Image', in *Arab Painting: Text and Image in Illustrated Arabic Manuscripts*, ed. A. Contadini (Leiden; Boston, 2010), 25–40.

[90] K. A. Matʻevosyan, 'Scriptoria et bibliothèques d'Ani', *REArm* 20 (1986–7), 209–21, at 212.

[91] R. W. Thomson, 'The Eastern Mediterranean in the Thirteenth Century: Identities and Allegiances. The Peripheries: Armenia', in *Identities and Allegiances in the Eastern Mediterranean after 1204*, eds. J. Herrin and G. Saint-Guillain (Farnham, 2011), 197–214, at 207.

[92] Manuscript online at http://biblioteca.ucm.es/ (accessed 13/11/2015).

Figure 97 The preparation of the theriac of Aflaguras from the *Kitab al-Diryaq* (Book of antidotes), written and illustrated in Mesopotamia, 1199 (Paris, BNF, arabe 2964, fol. 15; 36.5 × 27.5 cm)

their orbits by a hidden mechanism'.[93] Conradus de Fabaria, abbot of St Gall, was told by Frederick that only his son, Conrad, was more precious than this

---

[93] J. D. North, 'Opus quarundam rotarum mirabilium', *Physis* 8 (1966), 337–72; reprinted in J. D. North, *Stars, Minds and Faith: Essays in Ancient and Medieval Cosmology* (London, 1989), 162–3; *Chronica regia Coloniese, continuato IV* (Hanover, 1880), p. 263; Ward, 'The Inscription on the Astrolabe', 356 n.29.

'astronomical heaven, of gold stellated with gems', which had 'within itself the course of the planets'.[94] In return al-Ashraf was offered a menagerie of rare and unusual beasts, including a white bear and a white peacock. These exchanges formed part of the embassies between the Ayyubids and Frederick II for control of Jerusalem and the Holy Places.

Al-Ashraf's planetarium was lost during Frederick's failed assault on Parma in 1248, but a celestial globe commissioned in 1225 by his brother, al-Kamil, can still be found in Italy, in Naples [Fig. 98].[95] This globe, which may well represent a rival diplomatic engagement with Frederick II, is engraved with the forty-eight Ptolemaic constellations, each star being marked by a circle of inlaid silver whose size corresponds to its magnitude in the night sky.[96] The alliance of technical brilliance, artistic refinement and scientific knowledge embedded in this globe gives some idea of the resources of expertise, time and materials that diplomacy required. Correspondingly, the fact that unusual animals were deemed to be an acceptable gift in exchange shows again the value placed on rarity and bloodstock in diplomacy.

The universality of astrology meant that there was a common set of values and beliefs that would have been encountered in every society. The Jewish traveller Benjamin of Tudela, who journeyed through much of the eastern Mediterranean in the later twelfth century, found the rabbis of Mosul and Tiberias practising astrology.[97] Jalal al-Din Khwarazmshah, who had just burst into the Caucasus when al-Ashraf's astrolabe was made, also employed astrologers (it was at his court that Ibn Bibi's mother began her career as a seer), and the Mongolians used Chinese astrologers, such as Yeh-lü Ch'u-ts'ai, who practised for Genghis Khan in the 1220s.[98] Thus Tamta was in a world infused with astrology at every step of her life and travels. The dominance of Arabic astrological literature in this period shows that the Arabic world was recognised as the leading centre for its study. There was thus an Arabic inflection to all astrological beliefs, even in Byzantium, which had a much older Hellenistic tradition (this had been overtaken in the course of the twelfth century by new texts from the Arabic world). This must have

---

[94] Conradus de Fabaria, 'Casus S. Galli Continuatio III', in *Monumenta Germaniae Historica: Scriptores*, vol. 2, ed. G. H. Pertz (Leipzig, 1829), 163–83, at 178.

[95] E. Savage-Smith, *Islamicate Celestial Globes: Their History, Construction, and Use* (Washington, DC, 1985), no. 3; RCEA X, 3924.

[96] Delpont, ed., *L'Orient de Saladin*, 127; Wieczorek, Fansa and Meller, eds., *Saladin und die Kreuzfahrer*, cat. B.37.

[97] Saliba, 'The Role of the Astrologer', 62; Benjamin of Tudela, *The Itinerary of Benjamin of Tudela*, ed. M. A. Signer, trans. M. N. Adler (Malibu, 1983), 45, 52, 80.

[98] I. de Rachewiltz, 'Yeh-lü Ch'u-ts'ai (1189–1243): Buddhist Idealist and Confucian Statesman', in *Confucian Personalities*, eds. A. F. Wright and D. Twitchett (Stanford, 1962), 189–216, at 194.

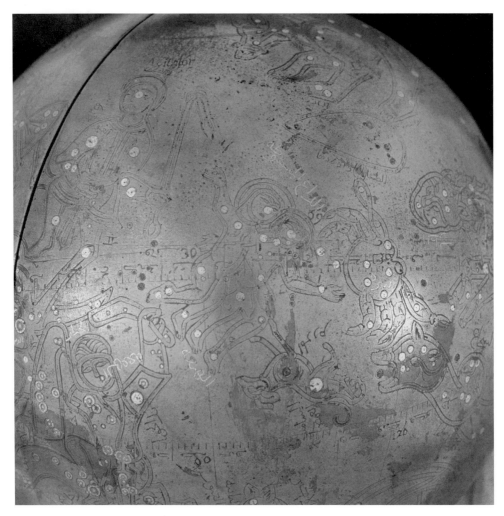

Figure 98 Detail of the celestial globe of Frederick II, Holy Roman Emperor, a gift from al-Kamil Ayyub, 1225/6, showing Gemini and Cancer, with Orion and Hydra below. Brass with gold and silver inlay (Naples, Museo di Capodimonte; diameter 22.1 cm)

given Tamta a sense of familiarity with this one major aspect of Ayyubid society before she ever arrived in Akhlat. It indicates a degree of cultural uniformity that crossed medieval societies in the thirteenth century. These shared beliefs never outweighed the greater cultural and religious differences that divided different communities and groups, but they do suggest a common aspect of societies that might have eased some transitions between groups.

The world of the palace was principally designed to evoke the interests and pastimes of the male elite that inhabited its spaces, indulged in its pleasures and were concerned by its beliefs. However, it was this same male world that was perhaps the most familiar to Tamta as she moved between courts during her lifetime. The common preoccupations of the ruler and his courtiers transcended cultural, religious and ethnic boundaries. They were perhaps the most important drivers of cultural convergence across the region. In each court the visual and verbal languages used to express the ideals varied, but all were united by a common understanding of the values that these buildings and objects espoused: all mixed the real and the fantastical, the earthly and the heavenly. It was a world that celebrated the display of wealth and pleasure. It co-opted both nature and man-made objects into its arsenal. Although there is no evidence that women were considered part of the audience for this art or that the range of imagery was in any way altered when it was made for women, it is nevertheless clear that this imagery had an important effect on the perception and self-perception of women. The imagery perpetuated the invisibility of women (other than dancers and musicians, whose status obviated any need for them to remain beyond the sight of men). It forced women to belong to a world in which male fantasies and male interests predominated.

10 | Akhlat, Builders and Buildings

Although the previous three chapters have examined Tamta's position in the Ayyubid world, a recurring issue has been how her life and actions compared to those of other women and Christians in equivalent roles in neighbouring societies. This has been necessary because of the way in which Tamta's life came at the intersection of different physical, political and cultural geographies. This overlap was partly determined by the coming together of Tamta's paternal and marital families; but it was also determined by the ambiguous location of the city in which she mostly lived: Akhlat. Whether we have studied her as a wife, as a Christian or as a courtier, we have seen that the position of each of these three groups was subtly but significantly different in the cultures that intersected at Akhlat. To what extent should Ayyubid Akhlat be seen in the context of the Jazira and Syria, where the rest of the Ayyubid confederacy lived and ruled? To what extent did the city's culture belong alongside that of Turkic Anatolia, within which it had existed for a century until its capture by the Ayyubids in 1207? And to what extent should the city be viewed within a Caucasian context, determined by its majority-Christian, Armenian population?

One final set of evidence may contribute to an understanding of these questions. This is the evidence of Akhlat itself. Little of Tamta's Akhlat survives: its early buildings were destroyed, if not by the invasions of the Khwarazmians and Mongols, then by the devastating earthquakes that periodically rocked the area. However, the buildings of the city survive in a different guise, or rather a different location. A series of buildings exist across Anatolia that all contain inscriptions proclaiming them to have been built by men from Akhlat. A study of these buildings allows us to establish which of the worlds that intersected in Akhlat its builders chose to emulate in their own buildings. This was the material culture that surrounded Tamta for most of her adult life. Studying these buildings also helps to establish the skills and training of builders in Akhlat, the types of building they were familiar with, as well as the styles and techniques that they exported with them. However, simply to see these buildings as a reflection of Akhlat itself is fraught with problems. To look at the tombs, caravanserais, mosques and hospitals by Akhlati builders that are spread across Anatolia is to see Akhlat at second hand; and to see it filtered through a series of additional intermediaries. The buildings set up by Akhlati masons outside Akhlat had to respond to local needs and the demands of local patrons who sought to present their own vision of their status, position and ambitions; they required the involvement of different groups of local workers and local building materials. Each of these had an impact on what the masons could build, and the freedom they had to introduce their own ideas to the building. There is also a danger in assuming that there is any direct association between the builders' city of origin and the particular style in which they worked, or that there should be any consistency in the style of buildings they erected. The employment of a *nisba* such as al-Khilati ('of Akhlat') may simply indicate someone's place of birth or family origin; although its repeated use by masons suggests that the city had a reputation for its prowess, with which these men wished to be associated.[1]

The dangers associated with an overly simplistic association of place and style become apparent if we examine the work of one Ayyubid architect from Damascus who worked in Anatolia in the 1220s, Muhammad bin Khawlan al-Dimashqi. His name is recorded at two major royal monuments in Anatolia, the Alaeddin Camii in Konya, the burial site of almost all the Seljuk Sultans, and the Sultan Han on the road between Aksaray and Konya. It is possible that Muhammad bin Khawlan first came to Seljuk Anatolia as part of the entourage that accompanied al-Ashraf's sister, Malika 'Adiliyya, on her marriage to Kaykubad I in 1219. Muhammad's inscription at the Alaeddin Camii is associated with the extensive work at the mosque that took place in 1219–20.[2] The impact of Syrian architecture is visible on the central portal that opens on to the courtyard [Fig. 99].[3] Its distinctive *ablaq* arch, with interlocking semi-arches in black-and-white marble set in a broad rectangular frame with a thick rectilinear design that encases a central disc, adapts Syrian forms more normally seen around the *mihrab*s of mosques and madrasas, such as that around the *mihrab* in Dayfa

---

[1] This is analogous to the use of al-Mawsili by metalworkers in the thirteenth century: see J. Raby, 'The Principle of Parsimony and the Problem of the "Mosul School of Metalwork"', in *Metalwork and Material Culture in the Islamic World: Art, Craft and Text. Essays Presented to James W. Allan*, eds. M. Rosser-Owen and V. Porter (London; New York, 2012), 11–85.

[2] *RCEA* X, 3855; *TEI*, 4025; van Berchem, 'Arabische Inschriften', no. 172.

[3] S. Redford, 'The Alaeddin Mosque in Konya Reconsidered', *Artibus Asiae* 51/1 (1991), 54–74, at 56, and 73 inscription 2. A series of inscriptions dated to 1218–19 claim the building variously for Kayka'us I and for Kaykubad I. It is impossible to know to which Sultan this mason's inscription belongs: *RCEA* IX, 3835, 3837 (Kayka'us); 3836, 3854, 3856, 3857, 3858, 3859 (Kaykubad).

Figure 99 North portal of the Alaeddin Camii, Konya, Turkey; 1219–20

Khatun's Firdaws madrasa in Aleppo of 1235–6.[4] It has been suggested that the prominent placement of distinctively Syrian elements on the exterior of the mosque was to give it an appropriately solemn air after the Caliph awarded Kaykubad new caliphal titles, but equally it may have been a more straightforward response to the presence of the Ayyubid bride and her architect in the city.[5]

The second work linked to Muhammad bin Khawlan is very different, and shows that there is no automatic correlation between the place of

---

[4] Tabbaa, *Constructions of Power*.
[5] Ibn Bibi, 101–4; Redford, 'The Alaeddin Mosque in Konya Reconsidered', 71.

Figure 100 Portal of the Sultan Han near Aksaray, Turkey; 1229 (photo by Gertrude Bell, 1907)

origin of a builder and the manner or style in which he built. His name appears in two hexagonal medallions on the main portal of the Sultan Han near Aksaray, dated June 1229, a decade after the work at Konya [Fig. 100].[6] Commissioned by Kaykubad I, this was one of the largest caravanserais to be built, and lay on the road between Aksaray and Konya, one of the principal commercial routes of the Seljuks. Its monumental entrance is very different from that of the Alaeddin mosque. The emphasis in the porch on verticality, the elaboration of the muqarnas niche over the doorway and the

---

[6] Erdmann, *Das Anatolische Karavansaray*, 89. For the donor inscriptions with date: *RCEA* XI, 4006, 4007; *TEI*, 2453, 2454.

extensive use of shallowly carved geometric interlace borders all fit squarely within the Anatolian tradition of porches, seen on caravanserais, mosques and madrasas. The two portals of Muhammad bin Khawlan do share some elements, notably the use of joggled masonry in the lintel over the door and the engaged columns carved with a zig-zag pattern that mark the corners of the portal recess. These two elements find their origins in Syria and Anatolia respectively. Architects were clearly adaptable, and capable of adapting, combining and altering the styles in which they worked to suit the requirements of their clients and particular building types.

We must therefore be very cautious in associating Akhlati masons solely with an 'Akhlati' style, and in recreating the buildings of Akhlat through these Akhlati buildings 'in exile'. While they may produce evidence for the possible impact of Akhlat on the arts of other cities in Anatolia, they cannot easily do the opposite: show the impact of other regions on Akhlat. It is conceivable, for example, that the Ayyubids imported builders from the Jazira and Syria into Akhlat, and used them to transform the appearance of the city. As we have seen with the extramural minaret in Mayyafariqin, al-Awhad and al-Ashraf brought a distinctively Syrian building type with them to the edges of Anatolia, and its design must have required the involvement of Syrian builders. The brothers may have set out to remodel the appearance of Akhlat in a similar vein. However, I will suggest in what follows that this is unlikely to have been the case – or if it was, it had no lasting impact on what Akhlati architects themselves built. We can establish this from the one group of medieval monuments that does survive in Akhlat, and which allow us to see the degree of overlap between masons' work in the city and elsewhere. A sequence of elaborately carved tombstones dating from the 1220s to the 1350s, and a small number of grander mausolea, the earliest of which dates to 1273, still stand in the Muslim cemetery to the west of the town. These, the only surviving element of the medieval city, allow us to see the extent to which common stylistic and technical solutions were being employed by Akhlati masons in the city in Tamta's lifetime and in the decades after her death. They can give us some confidence that Akhlati masons received a consistent technical and stylistic training over a number of generations.

The first point to note about all the buildings in this chapter is that they are all in Anatolia. There is no evidence that Akhlati masons worked further south, in Ayyubid territories. On the other hand, there is more evidence of other Syrian builders working in Anatolia. In addition to the work of Muhammad bin Khawlan, we know of an architect from Aleppo, Abu 'Ali al-Halabi bin al-Kattani, working on the fortifications at Alaiya (Alanya) and Sinop.[7] Given that all the surviving evidence from inscriptions suggests that the movement of masons seems to have been one way, from Syria to Anatolia rather than vice versa, we should assume that the experience of the Akhlati architects was limited to the types of building that predominated in the region: stone-built structures with external carved ornament, and often with conical domes.

Early Akhlati Buildings

The earliest surviving structures linked to builders from Akhlat confirm this assumption. These edifices were erected by men who had trained at Akhlat in the second half of the twelfth century. This was the period during which Akhlat itself had been extensively rebuilt by Shahbanu, the wife of Nasir al-Din Sökmen II, the Shah-i Armen of Akhlat (r. 1128–85).[8] Two monuments erected in the 1190s have been linked to a builder who signed his name as Tutbeg bin Bahram al-Khilati (i.e. from Akhlat). It is this builder who gives himself the title *al-najjar*, 'the woodworker', even though his only surviving works are in stone.[9] This highlights both the multifarious nature of the skill of these masons and craftsmen and the variety of media they could work in. Indeed, the earliest reference we have to a craftsman from Akhlat comes from an ebony *minbar* that was made for the Alaeddin Camii in Konya in 1155, naming its creator as Menku Birti al-Khilati.[10]

Tutbeg bin Bahram was an itinerant craftsman who worked for different dynasties around Anatolia. The earlier of the two buildings with which he is linked is the Alay Han, a caravanserai near Aksaray on the road to Kırşehir.[11] Built for the Seljuk Sultan Kılıç Arslan II (r. 1156–92), it is one of the earliest of all the known caravanserais in the region, and its design, with an open courtyard and enclosed hall, all within a protective windowless curtain wall, helped to establish the dominant form that the buildings took over the next half century.[12] The second building that names him is the Sitte Melik in

---

[7] Abu 'Ali al-Halabi bin al-Kattani: Sinop (1215): Redford, *Legends of Authority*, nos. 5, 6 (=*RCEA* VIII, 3774, 3761); Red and Tophane Towers at Alaiya (Alanya) (1231): S. Lloyd and D. S. Rice, *Alanya ('Alā'iyya)* (London, 1958), 15, 55. It is this inscription that provides the best reading of his name.

[8] Pancaroğlu, 'The House of Mengüjek in Divriği', esp. 54.

[9] Pancaroğlu, 'The House of Mengüjek in Divriği', 41–2.

[10] *RCEA* IX, 3200; Redford, 'The Alaeddin Mosque in Konya Reconsidered', 56.

[11] Erdmann, *Das Anatolische Karavansaray*, no.24; none of what follows can improve upon the recent analysis in Pancaroğlu, 'The House of Mengüjek in Divriği', 39–42.

[12] Yavuz, 'The Concepts That Shape Anatolian Seljuk Caravansarais'.

Divriği. This was the tomb of Shahanshah, the Mengujekid ruler of the city (1175–97), and is firmly dated 1196–7. Divriği stands on the remote headwaters of the Caltu Suyu, a tributary of the river Euphrates in the centre of Anatolia. Even today it is three hours by car on good roads from the nearest large town, but that isolation gave it importance in the thirteenth century as a stopping point on the north–south slave-trade route between the Black Sea and the Mediterranean. The Mengujekids vied with the Seljuks for control of this area, and so Tutbeg had had to cross a contested frontier in order to take work from each ruler.

Both the caravanserai and the tomb are finely crafted monuments in ashlar, showing the mastery of stonework achieved in Akhlat. Both are also innovative in their incorporation of architectural and decorative devices drawn from a range of sources around the region. The two buildings are rooted in Muslim culture: the caravanserai was introduced to Anatolia by the Seljuks, and the isolated mausoleum tower also came from the Islamic east.[13] The overall design of the Sitte Melik [Fig. 101], a squat octagonal tower topped by a pyramidal dome, looks to precedents in Azerbaijan and Iran (such as the tomb built for Mumine Khatun, the first wife of Jahan Pahlavan in Nakhchivan (Azerbaijan) in 1186) [Fig. 102], although it is also superficially similar to the domes of Armenian churches.[14] Aspects of both buildings suggest that other cultural influences can be found in their design. The porch of each is surmounted by elaborate muqarnas vaults; these are among the earliest occurrences of this form of vaulting in Anatolia. Its appearance here, as a structural element in stone, is very different from the use of muqarnas as a decorative element made from stucco seen before this in Iraq.[15] The transformation of the muqarnas into stone – indeed, the overall use of ashlar for the building of both monuments – reflected the predominance of this material in Anatolia and the Caucasus. The long tradition of building in stone across the region suggests that the indigenous people there, the Byzantines, Armenians and Georgians, may have been involved in the construction of these early stone buildings, as they had the craftsmen who had the centuries of expertise to undertake such complex work.[16] The appearance of two niches either side of the entrance of the Sitte Melik, one triangular in section, the other semi-circular, also seems to be

---

[13] R. Hillenbrand, *Islamic Architecture: Form, Function and Meaning* (Edinburgh, 1994), 253–68, 331–6.

[14] E. Jacobsthal, *Mittelalterliche Backsteinbauten zu Nachtschewân im Araxesthale, mit einer Bearbeitung der Inschriften von Martin Hartmann* (Berlin, 1899), 13–19, 21–2.

[15] Y. Tabbaa, 'The Muqarnas Dome: Its Origin and Meaning', *Muqarnas* 3 (1985), 61–74.

[16] Blair, *Monumental Inscriptions*, 7.

Figure 101 Sitte Melik, Divriği, Turkey; 1196. The tomb of Shahanshah, Mengujekid ruler of the city

an adaptation from Christian architecture in the region. Similar niches were frequently added to the façades of churches and monasteries to articulate the separate spaces of the interior on their otherwise undifferentiated exteriors. At the Sitte Melik, the niches have shrunk and are purely decorative; they enliven the faces of the tomb into which they are cut, but have no impact on, or relation to, the interior space. Thus, even before Tamta arrived in Akhlat, there is evidence that the city's masons were well aware of the different architectural forms produced by the Anatolian and Caucasian societies that surrounded the city to east and west. The collation of these motifs in the works of a single Akhlati mason for different clients across the region hints

Figure 102 Tomb of Mumine Khatun, Nakhchivan, Azerbaijan; 1186. Built for the first wife of Jahan Pahlavan, *atabeg* of Azerbaijan

at the complexities of the cultural relations that existed in Akhlat before the Ayyubids and then Tamta arrived.

Tercan

This is confirmed when we look at one slightly later building, the Mama Khatun complex in Tercan, a small town some 90 kilometres to the west of Erzurum on the road to Erzincan [Fig. 103].[17] The complex consists of a tomb set in a walled enclosure and a caravanserai, both on the north side of the main road, and it is linked with a builder from Akhlat, who inscribed his name on the façade of the tomb enclosure: 'The work of Abu'l Muna bin Mufaddal al-Awhal ... al-Khilati, the builder, may God pardon him, as well as his father and his mother'.[18] The buildings' association with Mama Khatun, the daughter of 'Izz al-Din Saltuk II, the Emir of Erzurum (r. 1132–68), is based on a long oral tradition, but no documentary support

---

[17] The key account of this complex remains S. K. Yetkin, 'The Mausoleum of Mama Khatun', *Yıllık Araştırmalar Dergisi* 1 (1956), 79–91, Turkish text: 'Mama Khatun Türbesi', 75–7; P. Paboudjian, 'Le mausolée de Mama Khatun à Terdjan et l'architecture arménienne', in *The Second International Symposium on Armenian Art*, vol. 2, ed. R. Zarian (Yerevan, 1978), 297–311.

[18] Khachatrian, *Korpus arabskikh nadpisei Armenii*, no. 116; *RCEA* XI, 4266; Paboudjian, 'Le mausolée de Mama Khatun' at 302.

Figure 103 Portal of mausoleum of Mama Khatun, Tercan, Turkey; early thirteenth century

survives. She died in 1201, and a date early in the thirteenth century is plausible for the two buildings. A surviving burial bearing the date 1203 in the tomb enclosure supports this.[19]

The caravanserai is a low rectangular building, with deep halls set around a central courtyard. Its exterior is unadorned apart from semi-circular buttresses set along the main façade; even the entrance has only a simple pipe moulding around its main arch. This plainness deflects attention to the tomb complex opposite, which is more strikingly organised and decorated. The design is unique for the thirteenth century: its octagonal tomb stands in the centre of a small compound, surrounded by a thick, low, circular wall that tightly hems in the tomb. Eleven deep niches in the outer wall provided space for extra sarcophagi to surround the central tomb, suggesting that the complex was designed as a long-term dynastic burial site for one family [Fig. 104]. Only the fourteenth-century Köşk Medrese outside Kayseri comes close to replicating this claustrophobic combination of tomb and surrounding wall.[20]

---

[19] Bates, 'Anatolian Mausoleum', 325.
[20] Gabriel, *Monuments turcs d'Anatolie I*, 67–70; it is dated 1339, at least a century after our monument. The courtyard mosques in some caravanserais, such as the Sultan Han near Kayseri, also place a small isolated monument within a courtyard, but these are much more spacious. For earlier incarnations of this form see Hillenbrand, *Islamic Architecture*, 274–5.

Figure 104 Ground plan of the mausoleum of Mama Khatun, Tercan, Turkey, early thirteenth century

Plate 29 Tree of Pearls mosaic in the conch of the *mihrab* in the mausoleum of Shajar al-Durr, Southern Cemetery, Cairo, Egypt, 1250–80

Plate 33 Cathedral (1000–1) and mosque of Minuchihr (twelfth–thirteenth centuries) seen from the west, at the edge of the ravine of the river Akurean, Ani, Turkey

Plate 70 The Annunciation and a polo match; details from the 'Freer' basin made for Najm al-Din Ayyub, Sultan in Cairo. Brass with silver and gold inlay; 1247–9 (Freer Gallery of Art, Smithsonian Institution, Washington, DC: purchase, F1955.10; height: 22.5 cm; diameter: 50 cm)

Plate 75 *Minai* bowl with a noblewoman listening to a musician, Iran, early thirteenth century (Freer Gallery of Art, Smithsonian Institution, Washington, DC: purchase, F1938.12; diameter 23 cm)

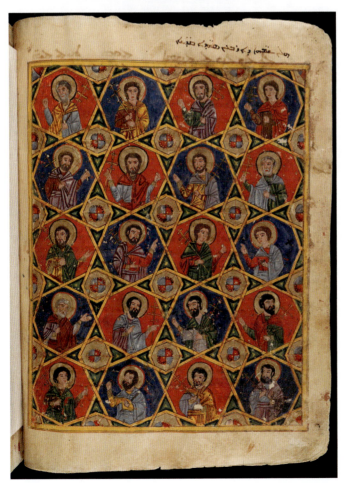

Plate 76 Twenty of the XL Martyrs of Sebaste, from a Syriac lectionary, copied at the monastery of Mar Mattai, near Mosul, Iraq; 1219–20 (Biblioteca Apostolica Vaticana, Syr. 559, fol. 93v; 43.5 × 33.5 cm)

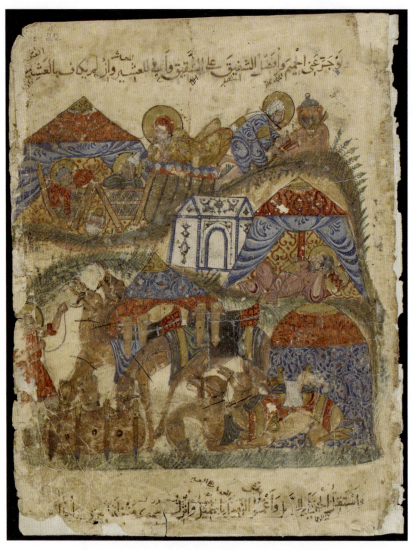

Plate 80 The tents of a caravan, from the fourth *Maqama* of al-Hariri, *c.* 1230 (St Petersburg, Institute of Oriental Studies, Ms c-23, fol. 12a; 25 × 19 cm)

Plate 88 Tiles from the Seljuk palace at Kubadabad on the edge of Lake Beyşehir, Turkey, built by the Sultan Kaykubad; 1220s

Plate 111 Tympanum over the west door of the zhamatun, Harichavank, Armenia; 1234

Plate 115 Polychrome vaulting in the zhamatun of the church of the Holy Apostles, Ani, Turkey; before 1217

Plate 116 Polychrome vaulting in the mosque of Minuchihr, Ani, Turkey; twelfth–thirteenth century

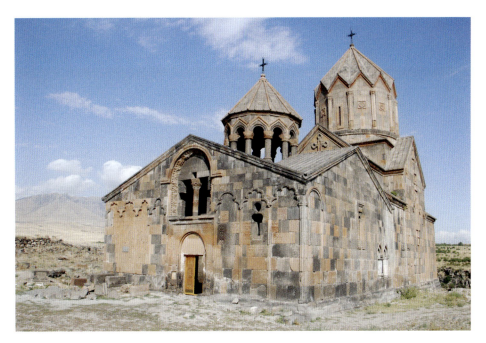

Plate 128 View from south-west of Hovhannavank monastery, Armenia; church (1215–21); zhamatun (1250–5)

Plate 135 *Minai*-ware dish showing a siege; *c.* 1210–20 (Freer Gallery of Art, Smithsonian Institution, Washington, DC: purchase, F1943.3; diameter: 47.8 cm)

Plate 139 Design for a fountain for cleaning hands, from al-Jazari's *Book of Knowledge of Ingenious Mechanical Devices;* 1206 (TSMK. Ahmet III, 3472, fol. 136a)

From the outside visitors face a blank circular wall which surrounds the actual tomb. Its only ornament appears on its porch. In common with most Anatolian buildings of this period (although not of the caravanserai opposite), the entrance is the most imposing feature of the exterior: a rectangular construction that rises above the walls to either side. Carved decoration is concentrated around the central door: this is flanked by two colonnettes, each covered in interlace decoration that support an arch decorated with Qur'anic verses in an elongated, simple Kufic lettering. The capitals of the columns have particularly elaborate pentagrams that include the names of the Prophet Muhammad and the first four Caliphs: Abu Bakr, Umar, 'Uthman and 'Ali.[21] The verticality of the porch is emphasised by a recessed moulding and a band of interlace that frames the central arch. However, unlike most contemporary Seljuk porches, the portal here is as wide as it is tall. Its outer flanks have deeply carved interlace bands which frame two tall triangular niches, which are purely decorative. The only parallels to them come from the Christian monuments of the Caucasus, such as the zhamatun of the church of the Holy Apostles in Ani, and the Akhlati-built Sitte Melik in Divriği. They provide further evidence of the way in which Caucasian motifs have been completely subsumed within the visual language of those who made and viewed these porches.

The tall entrance hides any view of the most extraordinary feature of the site, the tomb itself, which is only revealed on entering the small courtyard inside [Fig. 105]. The core design of the tomb, an octagonal drum surmounted by a conical dome, is traditional (compare the tomb of Malika 'Adiliyya [Fig. 64]), but its execution is something quite new among Anatolian tombs. Each face of the exterior is convex, creating an undulating, petal-like exterior, divided by a simple pipe moulding. This flower-like design is even more pronounced inside the tomb, as the eight internal walls are deep semi-circular niches whose cusps project into the centre of the tomb where they end in thin, attached colonnettes. These colonnettes rise up to form a ribbed vault in the centre of the dome above.

The result is a building that is full of movement both outside and in, with a gentle rhythm to encourage movement around. This is accentuated by the mismatch between the tomb and the surrounding wall: the entrances are not aligned, and the number of niches in the wall (fourteen, once the entrance and the fountain and stairs to either side of it are included) means that the two structures never achieve a settled relationship. The tomb complex is clearly a Seljuk entity, in terms of its overall function and its main

---

[21] Khachatrian, *Korpus arabskikh nadpisei Armenii*, no. 114.

Figure 105 Tomb of Mama Khatun, Tercan, Turkey; early thirteenth century

architectural elements, the tall entrance block and the tomb tower. However, the details of the buildings and their decoration do not find their parallels in the Seljuk heartlands of central Anatolia. Rather, we have to look to the east, to Mqargrdzeli-ruled Armenia. Like Akhlat and Erzurum, Tercan had a large Armenian population in the Middle Ages.

The cusped form of the mausoleum has a number of precedents in Armenian church architecture looking back to the tenth century in Ani, the first decades of the city's early prosperity under the Bagratunis. The church of St Gregory the Illuminator of Abughamrents has a hexagonal exterior, but a deeply cusped interior, similar to that at Tercan. However, a closer

Figure 106 Convent of the Virgin, Ani, Turkey, from the north; early thirteenth century

comparison comes from a building identified as the convent of the Virgin in Ani. It stands just above the river Akurean, close to the church of Tigran Honents [Figs. 106 and 107]. It is a small hexagonal building and, like Mama Khatun's tomb, it has convex faces on the exterior, and petal-like deep niches inside. The church has an upper storey, so there is a division in the masonry on both the exterior and interior which breaks the vertical unity of the ribs at Mama Khatun's tomb. The convent also has the umbrella dome so favoured by the Bagratunis and their later Mqargrdzeli imitators. The dating of the convent in Ani is controversial, but most scholars now think it belongs to the Mqargrdzeli period of the early thirteenth century, given

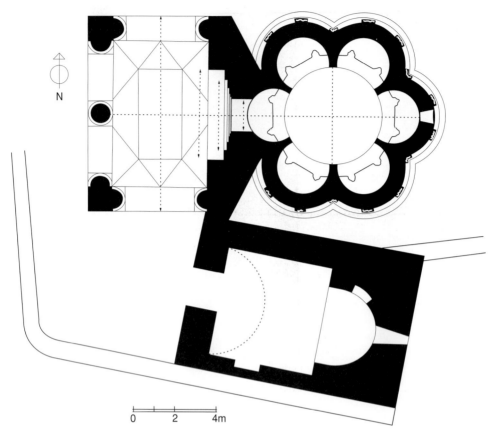

Figure 107 Ground plan of the convent of the Virgin, Ani, Turkey; early thirteenth century

the similarity of its exterior decoration to that of Tigran Honents' church of 1215.[22]

The picture painted by these buildings from the decades either side of the year 1200 is that the work of Akhlati masons fits within a milieu of Anatolian Seljuk architecture, but that it can equally be paralleled in Armenian buildings. It is not possible to assert the priority of one over the other; it was certainly not a one-way axis of artistic transfer. Rather, the evidence suggests a thriving world of artistic exchange, and as many ideas moved from Seljuk Anatolia to Armenia as vice versa. We have already seen the way in which

---

[22] Basmadjian, *Inscriptions arméniennes d'Ani*, no.9, is a graffito dated to 1156 on the church. However, this has not been seen by any other visitors. The external sculpture is very close to that of Tigran Honents' church, suggesting a thirteenth-century date: for full discussion see Thierry and Thierry, *L'église Saint-Grégoire*, 87–91; also Cuneo et al., *Ani*, 86–8.

Figure 108 Muqarnas stonework in the central vault of the zhamatun of the monastery of Harichavank, Armenia; c. 1224

the Mqargrdzeli caravanserai at Zor was designed within the broad framework of Seljuk caravanserais, with a similar layout and façade decoration. It is also evident in Armenian church design; an element of their design that was not discussed in Chapter 2.

The most obvious architectural form that was adopted in Armenian churches was the muqarnas vault. A fine example is the complex muqarnas that was used to build up the central vault of the zhamatun at Harichavank, which was added to the main church in the monastery by 1219 [Fig. 108].[23] The origin of this type of vaulting clearly comes from Islamic sources, but it is used very differently here. There are no comparable examples in the Islamic world of using it to form complete vaults with an oculus in the centre. Throughout Anatolia in this period muqarnas were used to form niche heads. It was used for domes elsewhere in the Islamic world, as at Nur al-Din Zangi's 1174 hospital in Damascus, but conceived very differently: the monastic muqarnas are structurally pendentives, whereas the Damascus dome is a succession of stucco squinches. A generation later the Armenian use of muqarnas was re-imported into the Muslim world, and buildings such as the Yakutiye Madrasa in Erzurum (1310) copied the idea of a muqarnas vault around an oculus [Fig. 109].

---

[23] Vardanyan, ed., 211; S. K. Mnatsakanian, *Arkhitektura armianskikh pritvorov* (Yerevan, 1952), 19, 53–4, 118, 125–6.

Figure 109 Muqarnas stonework in the central vault of the Yakutiye Madrasa, Erzurum, Turkey; 1310

Figure 110 West façade of the chapel of St Gregory, Goshavank, Armenia; 1237

Another echo of the Seljuk world appears in Armenian portal design. Here the idea of a rectangular porch containing an arched doorway was copied, but the greater height of most churches meant that the scale of the porch was reduced, and became just one element in façade design.[24] The façade of the chapel dedicated to St Gregory the Illuminator at Goshavank, built in 1237, includes a rectangular porch which was awkwardly incorporated into a façade that was otherwise designed around more traditionally Armenian blind arcading with arched and lobed heads [Fig. 110]. The

---

[24] For a survey of Armenian porches see S. R. Azatian, *Portaly v monumental'noi arkhitekture Armenii IV–XIV vv* (Yerevan, 1987).

Figure 111 Tympanum over the west door of the zhamatun, Harichavank, Armenia; 1234 (For the colour version, please refer to the plate section. In some formats this figure will only appear in black and white)

muqarnas hood that one would expect to find in such a porch in a Seljuk building is here replaced by a tympanum which provides a field for interlace decoration. Elsewhere in Mqargrdzeli Armenia the availability of multicoloured stone enabled the interlace to be accentuated with variation in colour, an adaptation of *ablaq* work to suit local materials, as on the entrance to the zhamatun at Harichavank [Fig. 111]. These designs continued inside the buildings, where they adorned the face of the altar platform, as at both at Harichavank and Makaravank (1205) [see Fig. 130]. Other technical devices were also shared, such as cantilevered staircases, which are ubiquitous in Anatolia and Armenia [Fig. 112; compare Fig. 54]. Even some Armenian inscriptions were made in imitation of Islamic forms. The donor inscription that runs around the cornice of the east façade at Harichavank, carved in relief, has small floriated tips to the letters, reviving floriated Kufic scripts used in the tenth century at Amid [Fig. 113].

Many of these overlaps come together in one building, the zhamatun that was added to the early eleventh-century church of the Holy Apostles in Ani some time shortly before 1217 (the earliest inscription on the building).[25]

---

[25] A date of around 1200 is supported by the similarity of the vaulting of the zhamatun of the monastery at Bagnayr, where the earliest inscription dates to 1201: Basmadjian, *Inscriptions arméniennes d'Ani*, no. 150.

Figure 112 Cantilevered staircase in the main church at Harichavank, Armenia; 1201

With its vertical columns of geometric interlace, its shallow, purely decorative niches, the muqarnas hood over the doorway, the east façade looks very Islamic, and is frequently mistaken for a Seljuk caravanserai in modern guidebooks (as well as the current tourist notice on the building itself) [Fig. 114]. The central vault of the interior has a muqarnas design with a central oculus, and the six square and twelve triangular vaults that surround it each has a different bi-coloured masonry structure [Fig. 115]. It is remarkably similar to the vaulting in the mosque of Minuchihr on the other side of the city [Fig. 116]. When all these different 'Islamic' features in Christian buildings are listed in this way, it becomes apparent how inadequate

Figure 113 Armenian inscription on east façade of main church at Harichavank, Armenia; 1201

the descriptive terminology is. Whilst features such as muqarnas and geometric interlace now appear to be intrinsically Islamic to modern eyes, it is clear that they did not have such unambiguous religious connotations in medieval eyes. The builders of Harichavank, Goshavank or Ani clearly

Figure 114 East façade of the zhamatun of the church of the Holy Apostles, Ani, Turkey; before 1217

Figure 115 Polychrome vaulting in the zhamatun of the church of the Holy Apostles, Ani, Turkey; before 1217 (For the colour version, please refer to the plate section. In some formats this figure will only appear in black and white)

saw no contradiction in using these features: they did not make the buildings in any way less Christian; nor, evidently, did they confuse the Christian Armenian identity that the churches undoubtedly proclaimed to their worshippers.

It is noticeable that all these examples come from within Mqargrdzeli-controlled lands. To the north, in the areas under the direct rule of the Kings and Queens of Georgia, there is much less evidence of an interweaving of stylistic motifs. Contemporary churches in Georgia, such as Pitareti, built in the reign of Giorgi IV Lasha (r. 1210–23), employ interwoven knot designs around windows and porches that are much more organic and sinuous in form than those seen in either Armenia or Anatolia. Even when interlace does appear in Georgia, as at Daba, dated to 1333, it forms part of larger vegetal designs.[26] Only a few works of art, such as the 1188 astrological treatise (Tbilisi NMC, A-65), show direct evidence of Islamic influence in Georgia in this period. This distinction further accentuates the differences between Georgian and Armenian buildings that were discussed in Chapter 2. Although the Mqargrdzelis were important figures at the Georgian court, it was only in exceptional cases, such as Ivane's burial church at

[26] R. O. Shmerling, 'Postroika molaret-uxucesa caria Georgiia Blistatel'nogo v cel. Daba, borzhomskogo raiona', *Ars Georgica* 2 (1948), 111–22; Eastmond, *Art and Identity in Thirteenth-Century Byzantium*, fig. 66.

Figure 116 Polychrome vaulting in the mosque of Minuchihr, Ani, Turkey; twelfth–thirteenth century (For the colour version, please refer to the plate section. In some formats this figure will only appear in black and white)

Akhtala, that they turned to Georgia for a visual language to express their piety. It would therefore seem that the architecture that Tamta encountered in Akhlat was likely to have been very familiar to her from what she had encountered throughout her life up until then. It would have been much more alien to her husbands.

Divriği

One final complex of buildings is associated with an architect from Akhlat. Like the Sitte Melik, it is in Divriği, but unlike it, this mosque–hospital complex is one of the most extraordinary buildings to have been erected in Anatolia in the thirteenth century. Housed within one structure, the two parts

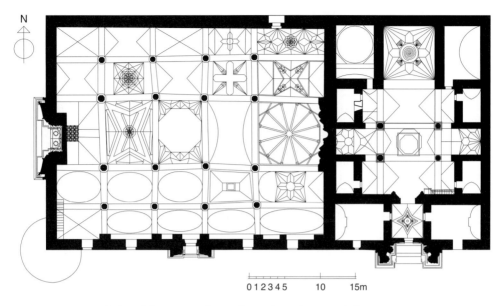

Figure 117 Ground plan of the mosque–hospital complex at Divriği, Turkey; 1229

of the building were funded separately. The mosque, which takes up the left-hand two-thirds of the building as it is approached up the hill from the modern town, was commissioned by the Mengujekid Emir of the city, Ahmadshah (r. 1229–42).[27] He was the grandson of Shahanshah who had been buried in the Sitte Melik tomb. The hospital, entered through the portal on the right-hand side of the main façade, was built by Ahmadshah's female cousin Turan Malik [Fig. 117].[28] The inscriptions make no mention of their relationship, but as the building is clearly all one great project and they must have been working together, it is generally assumed that they were married. The long, low building lies to the south of the citadel, which was also rebuilt by Ahmadshah. It was completed in 1229. The architect of the building is twice identified by inscription as Khurramshah b. Mughith al-Khilati.[29] It is therefore the one building that was definitely built during Tamta's time in Akhlat, although 1229 was the year that Akhlat itself faced the long and brutal siege of Jalal al-Din Khwarazmshah. Indeed, it may well have been the turmoil that Akhlat had faced for the previous four years that had encouraged Khurramshah to seek work elsewhere.

---

[27] *RCEA* X, 3999; XI, 4000, 4187; H. Edhem and M. van Berchem, *Matériaux pour un corpus inscriptionum arabicarum*, vol. 3 (Cairo, 1917), part 1: *Siwas et Divrigi*, nos. 41, 43, 48.

[28] *RCEA* XI, 4001; Edhem and van Berchem, *Matériaux*, no. 44; more properly she was his first cousin once removed.

[29] *RCEA* XI, 4003, 4004; Edhem and Van Berchem, *Matériaux*, nos. 46, 47.

Divriği is a baroque extravaganza, and the supreme example of the brilliance of the masons of Akhlat. Its portals are covered with a riot of carvings which adorn every stone, but at the same time seem to try to break away from the surface of the walls. Delicate tendrils fight for attention with stark, oversized geometric blocks, and architectural order clashes with sculptural exuberance. Many scholars have sought to trace the origins of the styles and motifs used at Divriği, proclaiming it to be a miraculous synthesis of motifs from a multiplicity of sources.[30] The portals defy attempts to describe them, let alone to analyse the details of their decoration. Four entrances were designed, each following the standard vertical rectangular format of mosques, madrasas and caravanserais in Seljuk Anatolia. The four were conceived radically differently from each other. The hospital has just one entrance, at the south end of the west façade, the mosque three entrances, one to the left of the hospital entrance, and one each on the north and east facades. That on the west is the most visible, but it is dwarfed by the entrance on the north side. Even though it is partly hidden by the slope of the hill into which the complex is cut, the north door was the principal entrance to the mosque as it faced the town's citadel. The ambition of the carving has often been criticised by modern scholars and visitors for the apparent lack of coordination between its elements, and the contrast between the grandiose elements and the fussy details [Fig. 118].

The complexity of the design of the north porch becomes apparent once you try to describe it, as listing the variety of details, the differences in scale of ornament and the multiplicity of surfaces becomes overwhelming: it is easy to lose the wood for the trees. The main door of the mosque, for example, is set back from the rest of the façade to produce a series of projecting concentric zones of decoration. The door is surmounted by a large hexagonal design, and flanked on either side by a series of large convex rhomboids [Fig. 119]. These create a grid between them of alternating squares and stars filled with boldly carved foliage and flowers. The background around the foliage is deeply drilled to provide a dark contrast to the foreground stonework. The heaviness of the rhombus design is cleverly undercut by a delicate tendril that rises up the side walls of the porch from a small tulip-shaped vase. The area above the central hexagon was reserved for the main donor's inscription, set apart from the rest of the decoration by a plain frame (although the background to the inscription is filled with a foliate scroll which occasionally erupts into a large flower or palmette). Even here the

---

[30] Y. D. Kuban, *Divriği Mucizesi: Selçuklar Çağında Islam Bezeme Sanatı Üzerine Bir Deneme* (Istanbul, 1997).

Figure 118 North portal of the mosque at Divriği, Turkey; 1229

Figure 119 Detail of rhombuses and foliate decoration on north portal of the mosque, Divriği, Turkey; 1229

craftsmen have played with contrasts of scale and texture in the stone: a plain moulded cornice above this frame appears to have a lace band hanging from it.

The transition between the inner door niche and the arch that frames it is filled with a band of octagons set within eight-pointed stars. Every segment receives a different design. The carving here is all of the same scale and depth, producing a more harmonious (but in the context of the portal as a whole, much less visible) zone of decoration. There is no muqarnas to fill the underside of the arch; instead, a small niche from which two carved bosses appear to hang. A second inscription, paying homage to the Seljuk

Figure 120 Detail of interlace medallions and palmettes on north portal of the mosque, Divriği, Turkey; 1229

Sultan Kaykubad, is barely visible just above these, hinting at the reluctant nature of the Mengujekid vassalship to the Seljuks that had existed since the beginning of the century.

Halfway up the door, the eight-pointed stars are hidden by large foliate scrolls that seem to have erupted from the main front of the porch in the most eye-catching and exuberant section of the decoration. Running in a band around the edge of the rectangular porch is a symmetrical sequence of medallions containing complex interlace patterns set between huge palmettes and other foliate elements [Figs. 120 and 121]. These stand proud of the surface of the porch by as much as 50 centimetres, and in

Figure 121 Detail of the depth of carving of the decoration on the north portal of the mosque, Divriği, Turkey; 1229

places are deeply undercut. The surface of the palmettes is then carved with further foliate decoration on a smaller scale. The outer edges of the porch are marked by very thin attached columns which support muqarnas capitals that swell alarmingly to act as the base for a thick cluster of columns above. These then slowly diminish to support a single attached column that rises to the top of the porch. However, even this single pier is thicker than that at the bottom of the porch, giving the whole edifice a disconcertingly top-heavy appearance. Beyond the porch itself is a final decorative flourish. In the corners where the projecting walls of the porch emerge from that of the mosque itself are thick pipe-like columns which rise the full height of

Figure 122 West portal of the mosque, Divriği, Turkey; 1229

the mosque wall. The cylindrical drum alternates with cubes carved with eight-pointed stars on their visible faces. As everywhere else on the façade, each level of stars has its own foliate design, part of the apparently ceaseless variety that fills the whole porch.

The other porches of the mosque–hospital at Divriği are equally idiosyncratic in their decoration, although never on the scale of the north porch. The west door into the mosque seems to present the lapidary equivalent of an Anatolian carpet, with its dense surface patterning [Fig. 122],[31] whereas the entrance to the hospital continues the playful variations on scale and depth of decoration seen on the north porch [Fig. 123]. Only the east façade entrance to the mosque, probably a door reserved for the ruler, which would have given access to a raised platform (*mahfil*) inside the building, has a more familiar muqarnas hood.

The interiors of both buildings continue the emphasis on variation. All nineteen vaults in the hypostyle mosque have different vaulting designs [Fig. 124], and the capitals and bases of all columns are also different. The *mihrab* has elements that copy the stucco used in Ayyubid mosques in Cairo – but here they are executed in stone, and combined with the oversized palmettes and top-heavy corbels seen on the exterior. The interior of the hospital is

---

[31] For example that in B. Brend, *Islamic Art* (London, 1991), fig. 61: Turk vs Islam Muzesi, inv. 685.

312 Tamta's World

Figure 123 West portal of the hospital, Divriği, Turkey; 1229

dominated by an iwan that lies beyond a central pool opposite the door; to either side are much smaller iwans [Fig. 125]. It too takes delight in its vaulting, not least a spiral groin vault over the main iwan. The west wall also has bulky star-like corbels that grow out from the thinnest of bases, reminiscent of the side columns of the north porch of the mosque.

It is possible to associate many of the technical and stylistic features at Divriği with Akhlat through their employment, albeit on a much smaller scale, on the hundreds of tombstones that survive in Akhlat's cemeteries. Ranging in height from 50 centimetres to over 2 metres, the tombstones were clearly made with similar workshop practices, starting with the density of decoration that completely covers every face. They also share the use of

Figure 124 Detail of a vault in the south-east corner of the mosque, Divriği, Turkey; 1229

multiple planes of carving on one surface and the contrast of scale and form, such as the use of heavy, bold foliate motifs that are set against intricate carving around them [Fig. 126].[32] These all suggest that the forms employed at Divriği still formed part of the repertoire of Akhlati masons over the next two generations.

Nowhere else in Anatolia was the extraordinary decoration employed by Khurramshah at Divriği adopted wholesale; but individual, isolated elements can be found. Tracing these allows us to build a network of relations that spans central and eastern Anatolia. Michael Rogers has noted extensive correspondences between the decoration in Divriği and that employed in the Çifte Minare Medrese in Erzurum, which he argues was being built at the time of the battle of Kösedağ in 1243 (the decoration was never completed).[33] He has noted the love of variety in vaults, columns and capitals, and the use of heavy torus mouldings.[34] Bold palmettes and interlace medallions also appear, as well as double-headed eagles and other birds on

---

[32] B. Karamağaralı, *Ahlat mezartaşları* (Ankara, 1972).
[33] J. M. Rogers, 'The Date of the Çifte Minare Medrese at Erzurum', *Kunst des Orients* 8/1-2 (1972), 77-119, at 99-111; Blessing, *Rebuilding Anatolia*, 123-42, argues for a date towards the end of the century.
[34] Rogers, 'The Date of the Çifte Minare Medrese'; J. M. Rogers, 'The Çifte Minare Medrese at Erzurum and the Gök Medrese at Sivas: A Contribution to the History of Style in the Seljuk Architecture of 13th Century Turkey', *Anatolian Studies* 15 (1965), 63-87.

Figure 125 Iwan of the hospital, Divriği, Turkey; 1229

the outside faces of the porch. By 1249 the rhomboids in the north porch of Divriği had been copied twice in Kayseri: on the portal of the madrasa of Mahperi's Huand Hatun complex (in place by 1237) [Fig. 127], and a decade later on the mosque–madrasa complex known as the Hajji Kılıc, founded by Abu'l-Kasim ibn ʿAli al-Tusi.[35] However, its use in Kayseri shows how bold the Divriği design is: the later version appears in a much more conventional, conservative porch design. Placed in the equivalent position on the side of the mosque, it is much smaller in scale, lacks the three-dimensionality of the original and is less mannered in its contrasts

---

[35] *RCEA* XI, 4314, 4315.

Figure 126 Detail of a tombstone at Akhlat; late thirteenth century

of scale and plasticity.³⁶ Other of the more playful features became more popular after the Mongol domination of Anatolia: for example, interlace in protruding medallions appears in the Buruciye Medresesi in Sivas of 1271.³⁷

This network continues into Mqargrdzeli Armenia. It is difficult to pin down whether we are seeing the movement of masons or motifs, but it is certain that architectural design was not confined by the political and religious frontiers of the region in the thirteenth century. The mosque–hospital at Divriği was erected at the same time as two monasteries in Armenia,

---

³⁶ Gabriel, *Monuments turcs d'Anatolie I*, 52–4.
³⁷ Blessing, *Rebuilding Anatolia*, figs. 2.13–2.15.

Figure 127 Side wall of the portal of the madrasa of the Mahperi Huand Hatun complex, Kayseri, Turkey; 1237

Hovhannavank and Saghmosavank. These lie 5 kilometres apart on the west side of a gorge cut deep into the earth by the Kasagh river, near Yerevan. Both monasteries were founded by Vache Vachutian (1213–32) in 1215–21; their zhamatuns were added by Vache's son, Kurd, in 1250 and 1255 respectively. The two main structures at each monastery therefore bracket the work at Divriği.[38]

---

[38] Hovhannavank: church of St John the Baptist, 1215–21, by Vache Vachutian; zhamatun added in 1250 by his son Kurd Vachutian (1235–54), in front of both his father's church and the fifth-century basilica to the north. Saghmosavank: Zion church, 1215; small church of Mother of God, 1235; library to south added by Kurd Vachutian and his wife Khorishah in 1255.

Vache was a vassal of the Mqargrdzelis, and his loyalty to them is proclaimed in an inscription he added to the north wall of the mausoleum at Hovhannavank, which is presented in their words:

> By the grace of beneficent God, in the reign of queen Tamar, daughter of the great Giorgi, in the year 642 (AD 1200), of the race of Torgom, we the brothers Zakaria and Ivane, sons of Sargis the great, son of Avag Zakaria, when the light of God's grace rose and entered Armenia and strengthened our weakness in the battle against the enemies of Christ's cross and destroyed their power and quenched their violence and the country of Ararat was delivered from the heavy yoke of their servitude, we wished to make offering and gave the tribute of grace to the Holy Forerunner of Hovhannavank…

Along with his mother Mamakhatun, Vache also gave donations to the Mqargrdzeli church at Harichavank in 1221.[39]

The inscription is also a reminder of the ostensible hostility between the Christians of the Caucasus and their Muslim neighbours to the west. Yet many architectural details at the two sites have their closest parallels only at Divriği. The west front of the zhamatun at Hovhannavank has a window in the centre of the façade to give light to the upper storey [Fig. 128]. The window rises above a rectangular porch, and is divided in two by a squat, heavy pier. An identical solution had been applied for the upper storey of the hospital porch at Divriği. Above the apse in the library building at Saghmosavank (1255) is a fan-tympanum that is identical to those in the main iwan of the hospital at Divriği (and which also appears in the lateral tympana of the entrance vault of the Sultan Han on the Kayseri–Sivas road, almost certainly built in about 1229 for Kaykubad I). The zhamatun at Hovhannavank employs different vaulting designs, including star-based ones similar to those in the mosque at Divriği. The façade of the zhamatun at Saghmosavank employs a five-point-star design similar to that over the entrance to the hospital at Divriği [Fig. 129]. The web of connections centred at Divriği even extends into the heart of Georgia itself. The wooden *minbar* in the mosque includes an inscription naming its maker as Ahmad ibn Ibrahim al-Tiflisi. His *nisba* indicates his origins in Tbilisi, the capital of Georgia.[40] At Makaravank (1205) the front of the apse stage has an interlocking design of octagons and eight-pointed stars containing vegetal designs, all of which appear on the north porch at Divriği [Fig. 130].

---

[39] Der Manuelian, 'The Monastery of Geghard', 101–2.
[40] *RCEA* XI, 4189; Edhem and van Berchem, *Matériaux*, no. 49.

Figure 128 View from the south-west of Hovhannavank monastery, Armenia; church (1215–21); zhamatun (1250–5) (For the colour version, please refer to the plate section. In some formats this figure will only appear in black and white)

Figure 129 Tympanum over the west entrance to the zhamatun at Saghmosavank monastery, Armenia; 1250–5

Figure 130 Altar platform in the main church at Makaravank monastery, Armenia; 1205

In every case the stylistic features that appear both in the work of Akhlati builders and in surviving structures across Anatolia and the Caucasus are isolated motifs. Normally motif-spotting exercises such as this are used to discern 'influences' and so argue for a hierarchy of creativity. However, the dating of the Armenian monasteries cited here is too close to that of the mosque–hospital, so to seek an order among them would be fruitless. There is not enough evidence to be able to propose a direct route of transmission, or to proclaim Akhlat as the centre of an architectural practice that dominated the region. However, the recurrence of these motifs in Christian and Muslim buildings, the consistent use of stone, and the interest in variation in vaulting techniques in particular, suggest that this group of buildings have much more in common than their diverse locations and functions might indicate.

More broadly, it is important to note how well the buildings by Akhlati masons can be fitted in to both Armenian and Anatolian contexts. Indeed, the association of Akhlati builders with architectural elements that are shared in both the Muslim west and the Christian east is remarkably consistent from the 1190s on. In many ways this should be unsurprising. It

Figure 131 *Mihrab* commissioned by al-Muzaffar Ghazi in the Ulu Camii at Mayyafariqin (Silvan), Turkey; 1227

suggests that the architecture reflects the cultural, religious and ethnic mix of the city of Akhlat, and that builders did not see any individual, isolated architectural motifs as traits exclusive to one religion or another.

This overview of Akhlati-built structures reveals some more specific points. The first is that there is little evidence of Ayyubid motifs being adopted. This suggests that Akhlat was relatively unaffected by work from the Jazira and Syria to the south. Whilst there may have been distinctively Syrian buildings at Akhlat, similar to the extramural minaret at Mayyafariqin, they were not copied. This may have been because the buildings were not impressive enough to attract attention (unlikely given the scale and quality of the minaret at Mayyafariqin), or it may be that the political and cultural associations of Syrian buildings with the Ayyubids made them inappropriate given the growing incursions of the Ayyubids in the region. However, it is more likely that architecture was conceived more along regional than political lines, and that it was determined by the local building materials available and the craftsmen able to work them. After al-Ashraf removed his brother al-Muzaffar Ghazi from Akhlat in 1224 he made him governor of Mayyafariqin. In this role al-Muzaffar Ghazi donated a new *mihrab* to the city's main mosque in 1227. He looked to local men to produce it and the result, carved in stone, fits local artistic traditions, rather than the Ayyubid forms they take in Syria [Fig. 131].[41] The minaret outside the city was much more unusual in its clear non-local regional affiliation.

The evidence that architecture was largely shared between Anatolia and the Caucasus, and continued to be so even after the Ayyubid conquest of Akhlat, suggests that the city lay largely on an east–west axis, rather than a north–south one that would link it to Ayyubid Syria. This lends support to the idea that Tamta too lived primarily on this east–west axis. As pointed out in Chapter 4, it was her Armenian and Georgian associations that gave her her value to al-Ashraf, and so it makes sense that she remained in this cultural world. It is too simplistic to see the buildings erected by men from Akhlat as straightforward confirmation of this, or to see Tamta's presence in the city as any kind of catalyst for the transmission of ideas between the Caucasus and Anatolia. However, both Tamta and Akhlat do appear as mediators in this world, linked to no single cultural tradition, but able to draw upon many.

[41] Gabriel, *Voyages archéologiques*, 344 inscription no. 124.

11 | Tamta and the Khwarazmians

> Jalal al-Din is close by, and if he takes Akhlat he will conquer the whole region.¹

Tamta's life as an Ayyubid regent in Akhlat was abruptly ended in the mid-1220s, when the city faced a brutal siege led by Jalal al-Din Minguburnu Khwarazmshah, the leader of a new invasion, this time from the east. If the responsibility for Tamta's first Ayyubid marriages can ultimately be laid at the feet of her father's military failure, then so too can the events that led up to her third, bigamous marriage in 1230 to the Khwarazmshah. This third marriage brought to an end Tamta's direct engagement with the Ayyubid world in the Jazira and Syria, and moved her more decisively into the Turkic–Persian world. Once again it was Ivane's military sloppiness that cost his daughter dearly. Although this was the briefest interlude in Tamta's life, it was probably the most traumatic.

The Battle of Garni

The latest invaders, the Khwarazmians, appeared in the Caucasus in 1225 at Garni. This site, in central Armenia, was a remarkable location for this first encounter with a new world from the east. Garni possesses the easternmost building of the Graeco-Roman world [Fig. 132]. Located above a gorge whose cliffs are formed of perfectly hexagonal basalt columns stands a peristyle temple probably erected in the first century AD. Its form, with a single central cell surrounded by twenty-four Ionic columns, which support a full entablature and an elegant pediment over the entrance façade, is instantly recognisable as classical in form, faithfully following the proportions and designs of Vitruvius' *Ten Books on Architecture*. It was probably dedicated to the sun cult of Mihr-Mithra.² Still standing in the thirteenth century, it had become part of a palace complex belonging to the Armenian Catholicos

---

[1] Sibt ibn al-Jawzi, quoted in Humphreys, *From Saladin to the Mongols*, 216.
[2] Donabédian and Thierry, *Les arts Arméniens*, 528–9.

Figure 132 Roman temple at Garni, Armenia; first century AD (rebuilt 1960s)

by the tenth century. On its conversion to Christianity, the temple was not structurally altered, its new religious allegiance being marked only by new texts inscribed on its doorframe. However, throughout the Middle Ages its status as a church was made obvious by the somewhat incongruous juxtaposition of a huge circular tetraconch church which was built right up against the side of the temple (in 879). The circular church was a conscious reworking of the great seventh-century circular church at Zvartnots, one of the defining monuments of the early Armenian Church.[3] An earthquake in 1679 destroyed all the buildings at the site, and it is revealing of the international kudos attached to the Classical that in the 1960s the Soviet authorities decided to rebuild just one structure at the complex: the temple.

It was in the shadow of this agglomeration of Graeco-Roman Classicism and indigenous Armenian architecture that Ivane Mqargrdzeli drew up his forces to face the Khwarazmian army in 1225. More than a decade after his brother Zakare's death, Ivane remained a key figure at the Georgian court. As well as ruling in the parts of Armenia that he had conquered with Zakare in 1199, he held the court title of chamberlain (*msakhurtukhutsesi*) at Queen Tamar's court in Georgia. On his brother's death he had also gained a new post, *atabeg* (tutor to the heir), copied from the title held by the

---

[3] W. E. Kleinbauer, 'Zvart'nots and the Origins of Christian Architecture in Armenia', *Art Bulletin* 54/3 (1972), 245–62.

Pahlavunis in neighbouring Azerbaijan. This had made him the personal adviser to Tamar's successor, Giorgi IV Lasha. His pre-eminence ensured that he was still in power when Giorgi IV died after a decade as King, to be succeeded by his sister Rusudan. Indeed, it is likely that it was thanks to Ivane's support that Rusudan was able to take power against Giorgi's illegitimate son, Davit Ulu.

As ever, the sources disagree about why the Georgians lost; although they all agree that it was Ivane's fault. The Georgian chronicle, *Kartlis Tskhovreba*, blamed Ivane's jealousy at the growing success of two rival generals, the Georgian brothers Ivane and Shalva Toreli-Akhaltsikheli.[4] They led the fight against Jalal al-Din whilst Ivane kept his troops in reserve in a strategic position on the ridge among 'a chaos of mountains' above the battlefield.[5] As the battle turned against the Georgians, the Toreli brothers sent messengers three times to Ivane, asking him to release his forces into the battle, but on each occasion he refused. Then, when there still may have been an opportunity for his men to turn the fight, Ivane ordered them to flee the battlefield, and this led to the slaughter of those that remained. This cautiousness may have been a lesson learned from his capture at Akhlat fifteen years earlier, but his care to avoid reckless action had now been replaced with equally dangerous inaction. The chronicle also reports that by this time Ivane had secretly become a monk, suggesting a further explanation for his shift away from military concerns.[6]

For Kirakos Gandzaketsi, defeat could be blamed, once again, on Ivane's decision to convert to Georgian Orthodoxy. His account of the battle matches that of the Georgian Chronicle, but he cites Ivane's misplaced boastful arrogance, rather than his jealousy, as the cause of the defeat. Ivane had made an agreement with the Georgian Queen, Rusudan, that all the Armenians under their rule would be forcibly converted to Georgian Orthodoxy (or killed) after their victory: 'This scheme, and the vow they made, took no account of God nor of His concern, nor did they ask the Lord who grants victory to whomever he pleases.'[7] Vardan Areweltsi also places theological disputes at the root of the defeat, but passes the blame through Ivane to his wife, Tamta's mother, Khoshak, and her 'new and alien evils'.[8] The account is obscure, but involves a dead Armenian priest called Parkesht, whose body had become a site of pilgrimage. For reasons unknown she had taken against this burgeoning cult, and ordered that the body be exhumed and burned, and she sacrificed a dog in mockery of those venerating the

---

[4] *Kartlis Tskhovreba*, 323–4.   [5] Al-Nasawi, 186.   [6] *Kartlis Tskhovreba*, 323.
[7] Kirakos, 112.   [8] Vardan, 214.

holy man. Those who had incited her into these actions had been struck by lightning, but God's larger wrath was taken out on Ivane and his whole army. Vardan's account mixes misogyny and anti-Chalcedonian sentiments in equal measure.

For others it was complacency rather than arrogance that was Ivane's downfall. Ivane and his fellow Georgian nobles simply did not believe that the Khwarazmians were a threat. They had written to Jalal al-Din on his arrival in the Caucasus to tell him that he was a spent force, reminding him of his various defeats by the Mongols. The very fact that he had come so far west to the Caucasus was testimony not to his fighting prowess, but to his lack of it, they thought. The Georgians had no idea what they were facing, and so were grossly underprepared when the battle came.

By the end of the battle the Georgian–Armenian army was largely destroyed, its best generals killed or captured, and huge numbers of soldiers forced over the cliff edge to plummet down the basalt columns to their deaths below. The Caucasus was now largely undefended. Queen Rusudan had to flee west to set up base in Kutaisi, protected from Kartli to the east by the Likhi mountains. Individual noble families retreated to their castles. This left the cities in the east to face the Khwarazmians on their own. Tamta's brother, Avag, was sent to negotiate terms with the invader, meeting at a bridge at Bjni over the river Hrazden (to the east of modern-day Yerevan), the new de facto border. This was in the heart of Mqargrdzeli territory. The negotiations foundered on that staple of diplomatic encounters, the royal marriage. Jalal al-Din demanded that Rusudan divorce her husband to marry him; she refused.[9] The Georgian nobility, already shocked by Ivane's actions at the battle, sided with their Queen (for once).

Between 1225 and 1229 Jalal al-Din repeatedly harried the Caucasus. He put Tbilisi, the capital of Georgia, to the torch twice, and captured Dvin from the Mqargrdzelis, although Ani resisted. He also invested the city of Akhlat, trying three times to capture the city, before he finally succeeded in April 1230. Jalal al-Din's determination to take Akhlat reflected the city's strategic importance – remember Husam al-Din 'Ali's warning from 1225: 'Jalal al-Din is close by, and if he takes Akhlat he will conquer the whole region.'[10] Arabic sources stress that he did not take any of the surrounding region or towns, only Akhlat, underlining the importance of this one site.

---

[9] See Jaba Samushia in B. Kudava, ed., *Istoriani: sametsniero krebuli midzghvnili Roin Metrevelis dabadebis 70 tslist'avisadmi* (Tbilisi, 2009), 232–49.

[10] Sibt ibn al-Jawzi, quoted in Humphreys, *From Saladin to the Mongols*, 216.

Ivane's failure of tactics (or nerve) at the battle of Garni gave the Khwarazmians their foothold in the Caucasus, but he was not the sole agent of his daughter's downfall. Responsibility can also be laid at the doors of others within the Ayyubid and Iranian worlds. Jalal al-Din's interest in Akhlat was encouraged by factions within the Ayyubid confederacy, indicating that some of the blame for Tamta's capture might also lie with her husband, al-Ashraf. As soon as the Khwarazmians had arrived in Iran, some of the Ayyubid brothers had looked to them as potential allies in their internal disputes, adapting that old adage 'my brother's enemy is my friend'. Al-Mu'azzam, al-Ashraf's brother in Damascus, had first sought an alliance with Jalal al-Din in 1226. He hoped that a Khwarazmian attack on Akhlat would force al-Ashraf to abandon his plans to expand south into Syria and return to defend his primary lands in the north.[11] He accepted a robe of honour from the Khwarazmshah, which he wore in front of al-Ashraf during al-Ashraf's imprisonment in the city, as a signal of his new alliance.[12] The alliance was then to be cemented by a marriage alliance between al-Mu'azzam's daughter, Khadija Khatun, and Jalal al-Din. However, Khadija Khatun never set off to meet her husband as her father died before the treaty was sealed, and Jalal al-Din was anyway too embroiled in suppressing a rebellion in Iran to come south to collect her.[13] It was because of this that she remained in Damascus, where she was to build the madrasa next to al-Ashraf's Dar al-Hadith in the 1240s.

On al-Mu'azzam's death in 1227, his son al-Nasir Dawud sent his tutor Shams al-Din Khusraushahi to try to revive the alliance. Al-Nasir Dawud was by now besieged in Damascus by his uncles al-Ashraf and al-Kamil, and so his need was great. Unlike a few years earlier, Jalal al-Din was now in a position to oblige, and launched the terrible siege of Akhlat that ran through the latter part of 1229 and into 1230 with its diet of rats that Ibn al-Athir reported.[14] So part of the responsibility for Akhlat and Tamta's fate in the late 1220s can also be laid at the door of her husband's by now obsessive desire to take control of Damascus.

The final cause of Jalal al-Din's wrath was one of his wives, Malika.[15] Malika was the daughter of the last Great Seljuk Sultan of Iran, Toghril Shah III (1177–94). She had first married Muzaffar al-Din Özbek, the *atabeg* of

---

[11] Humphreys, *From Saladin to the Mongols*, 176–7, 201.
[12] Humphreys, *From Saladin to the Mongols*, 184.
[13] Humphreys, 'Women as Patrons', no. 17.   [14] Ibn al-Athir, 3: 298.
[15] By 1224 he had already married Mu'mina (Malika) Khatun, the daughter of Sa'd, the Salghurid *atabeg* of Fars: R. Holod, 'Event and Memory: The Freer Gallery's Siege Scene Plate', *Ars Orientalis* 42 (2012), 194–220, at 205.

Azerbaijan, but her status as the daughter of the Shah of Iran clearly gave her power and influence in the region. Juvayni very clearly states that she was in charge in Tabriz when the Khwarazmians invaded: it was she who recognised that the city could not withstand a siege, and she who called together the emirs and notables of the town to negotiate the surrender.[16] She was also able to force her husband to divorce her in order to free herself to marry Jalal al-Din.[17] Malika clearly knew how to manipulate the institutions around her to promote her own policies.

The marriage to Jalal al-Din did not work out, however, and in 1227 Malika, possibly enticed by Husam al-Din ʿAli, al-Ashraf's chamberlain in Akhlat, fled from her husband and took refuge in the city, from where she orchestrated an attack on Azerbaijan.[18] Jalal al-Din's final reason to attack Akhlat, then, was to reclaim his wife and take revenge on the Ayyubid emir who had lured her away and was now possibly her lover.[19] The confusions of history are such that a second chronicle reports the same incident, but with different actors and motives.[20] Al-Makin ibn al-ʿAmid writes that Jalal al-Din's wife was the daughter of his vizier Jihan Hawaga, and that the *hajib* Husam al-Din ʿAli captured her and sent to al-Ashraf as a prisoner during his raids on Tabriz. When Jalal al-Din took the city, on 14 April 1230, Malika was gone, but Tamta remained behind to face the Khan's wrath, displayed in the most sexually aggressive means available to him: 'He entered the palace where he passed the night in the company of the daughter of Ivane, who was the wife of Malik Ashraf, and so assuaged his anger at the elopement of Malika.'[21] Rape was a common tactic of war, frequently alluded to in chroniclers' accounts of the fall of cities and a real danger to all women, but it was much rarer to employ it against female members of the elite. They were usually protected by the shared codes of belief and behaviour that bound the international fellowship of rulers together. As a result, those cases of rape against elite women, notably those of Tamta and Simonis in the thirteenth century, stand out as particular breaches of this unwritten international etiquette. The rapes also highlight the status of these women as ciphers for the states that they represented and the shifting balance in power relationships that enabled the rapes to take place. Tamta's rape simultaneously humiliated the Georgians, the Armenians and the Ayyubids.

Tamta's treatment was subsequently legalised by marriage, giving Tamta her third (and in this case bigamous) husband. The marriage only lasted

---

[16] Juvayni, 2: 424. [17] See Chapter 5.
[18] al-Dahabi, 222; Humphreys, *From Saladin to the Mongols*, 216.
[19] Juvayni, 2: 445. [20] Ibn al-ʿAmid, 40. [21] Juvayni, 2: 445.

four months, and for much of that time Jalal al-Din must have been preoccupied by the emerging alliance between al-Ashraf and Kaykubad, and the joint army they were building to fight him. After Jalal al-Din's defeat at Yassıçemen in August 1230, he retreated to Khoy via Akhlat, where he collected the rest of his men. If he took Tamta with him to Khoy, she must have been returned to al-Ashraf in Akhlat when the two parties agreed a truce.[22] Thereafter al-Ashraf immediately returned to Damascus (via Sinjar). Given that Tamta's next encounter was with the Mongols, we must assume that she remained behind in Akhlat, as the Mongols never reached Damascus. Jalal al-Din spent the final months of his life being chased round south-eastern Anatolia by the Mongols. The events in Akhlat in 1229–30 undoubtedly had an enormous impact both on the city of Akhlat and on Tamta. Chroniclers were not interested in Tamta's condition, however; they only recorded the state of the city. When al-Ashraf re-entered the city after the fall of Jalal al-Din he found it 'in ruins and totally abandoned'.[23]

It was easy for chroniclers, especially Christian ones, to demonise the Khwarazmians. They were violent, rapacious invaders who appeared as suddenly as a plague from a distant land. However, this was just one face of the Khwarazmian invasion. The Khwarazmians could be characterised in other ways as well. These alternative views presented features more familiar to the peoples of Anatolia. The Khwarazmians were a Turkic people who had long lived in a Persianate world. This had been intensified during their conquest of Iran at the beginning of the thirteenth century, and its ruling elite celebrated the great Persian myths of the *Shahname* as their own. They also professed Islam, and they promoted their religion against both Christianity and rival forms of Islam. However, the Khwarazmian army also included Kipchaq warriors hired from the lands to the north of Khwarazm, many of whom were not Muslim, or whose conversion was still largely superficial. These soldiers arrived at the Khwarazmian court with Jalal al-Din's grandmother, the powerful Kipchaq princess, Terkan Khatun. They became her emirs at the court, and remained loyal to her above their nominal ruler, the Shah. They brought a ferocity to fighting that terrified their enemies. The conquest of Iran gained the Khwarazmians a reputation for cruelty and violence that was to be confirmed by their atrocities in the Caucasus.[24] Some of the Ayyubids sought alliances with the Khwarazmians and played

---

[22] Ibn al-Athir, 3: 299–300.   [23] Abu'l-Fida, 107.
[24] C. E. Bosworth, 'The Political and Dynastic History of the Iranian World (AD 1000–1217)', in *The Cambridge History of Iran*, vol. 5: *The Saljuq and Mongol Periods*, ed. J. A. Boyle (Cambridge, 1968), 1–202, at 191.

down this reputation, believing that they could exploit these useful if potentially uncontrollable allies. The events leading up to the battle of Yassıçemen showed that the Khwarazmians could not be trusted; but even after Jalal al-Din's defeat and death, many of his men survived in the area, hiring themselves out as mercenaries in northern Iraq, or roaming the countryside as bandits. It was a Khwarazmian band that sacked Jerusalem in July 1244, ending the brief second kingdom of Jerusalem that Frederick II had established through treaty with al-Kamil in 1222, and the marauding soldiers left the city in terrible condition. It was the Kipchaqs who also tainted their Khwarazmian rulers with a reputation for other non-orthodox beliefs. The foreignness of the Kipchaqs should not be overestimated, however. In the early twelfth century the Georgians had already invited other Kipchaq tribes to cross the Caucasus mountains and settle in Georgia to help them fight against the Seljuks. The Georgian King Davit IV the Builder (r. 1089–1125) had even married a Kipchaq princess, Gurandukht; and one of the leading opponents of Queen Tamar at the start of her reign, Qubasar, is described in the Georgian chronicles as a 'former Kipchaq'.[25] As with all the groups in this book, Khwarazmian identity was a multi-faceted thing. Friends and foes picked out different aspects either to accentuate how much their cultures had in common or to highlight their foreignness and barbarity. Support for both of these opposing characterisations can be found in the limited material evidence of the Khwarazmian empire, which barely lasted two generations.

The Khwarazmians

Jalal al-Din's family had come to power in Khwarazm, the area of Transoxiana to the south and east of the Aral Sea, at the end of the eleventh century. His distant ancestor Anushtigin Gharacha'i, who rejoiced in the title of Keeper of the Royal Washing-Bowls to the Great Seljuk Sultan of Iran, Malik Shah (r. 1073–92), had been appointed governor of the region, and subsequent generations had been able to exert increasingly independent rule there, given its remoteness from the rest of Iran. By the end of the twelfth century they were competing with the Ghurids of Afghanistan for control of Khorasan in eastern Iran, and Jalal al-Din's father, Muhammad (r. 1200–20), pushed Khwarazmian power as far west as Tabriz. The move to take control of Iran had been facilitated by the political collapse of the Great Seljuks in the later part of the twelfth century.

[25] Thomson, *Rewriting Caucasian History*, 325, 327.

The conquest of Iran lasted just twenty years; it was ended by the arrival of the Mongols. In 1218 trade envoys from Genghis Khan were arrested at the Khwarazmian Silk Road city of Otrar (now in Kazakhstan) by the city's governor, Inalchuq Ghayir-Khan. The envoys were executed as spies and their caravan seized and sold in Bukhara. Genghis Khan sent an ambassador to demand that the governor be punished, but Inalchuq was Muhammad's uncle, and this second delegation was also executed. Genghis Khan took immediate revenge. The population of Gurgenj (Urgench), the main city of the Khwarazmians, was massacred; Muhammad had to flee to an island in the Caspian, where he died of pleurisy.[26] Likewise the city of Merv was destroyed:

> The Mongols ordered that, apart from four hundred artisans ... the whole population, including the women and children, should be killed, and no one, whether woman or man, be spared. To each [Mongol soldier] was allotted the execution of three or four hundred Persians. So many had been killed by nightfall that the mountains became hillocks, and the plain was soaked with the blood of the mighty.[27]

Jalal al-Din himself, after a fleeting victory against the Mongol army at the battle of Parwan, was pursued to the banks of the river Indus. His forces were wiped out and Jalal al-Din survived only by swimming the river to the far bank. His audacity at then calmly sitting on the river bank to taunt Genghis Khan to follow him became legendary; but whilst Genghis Khan is recorded as praising Jalal al-Din's bravery, it is evident that he did so in the knowledge that the Khwarazmian no longer represented a threat.

Jalal al-Din spent three years in exile in India before returning to Iran in 1224 and raising a new army, this time to seek new lands to the west, away from the Mongols. He campaigned through Iran to reconquer the northwest of the country, and then moved into Azerbaijan, establishing himself at Tabriz and Khoy. It was from there that he looked even further west, to Armenia. Jalal al-Din's arrival in the Caucasus was initially welcomed by his fellow Sunni Muslims in the region, who saw him as a liberator from Christian tyranny. However, his relationship to the rest of the Islamic world was an awkward one. On the one hand, he paid allegiance, albeit nominal, to the Abbasid Caliph in Baghdad. The reverse of Jalal al-Din's coins deferentially names the Caliph as 'Commander of the Faithful', but at the same time he continued his father's military campaigns against the Caliph, whose growing power he saw as a threat. In 1217 he launched an invasion of the Caliph's

[26] Al-Nasawi, 76–81.   [27] Juvayni, 1: 162.

lands in Iraq. His march on Baghdad was only stopped, as he was to be for so long at Akhlat, by unusually heavy snow.[28]

The Khwarazmians ruled in Urgench (now Dorye-Urgench, Old Urgench) on the Turkmenistan side of the Turkmen–Uzbekistan border in Central Asia. As evidence of their piety they could point to extensive patronage of religious institutions and buildings. The medieval city was comprehensively destroyed by Genghis Khan in 1221, and so little survives, but the known buildings, primarily madrasas and mausolea, fit exactly the same models of patronage that we have seen sponsored by the Ayyubids and Seljuks. The only real difference is the architectural form of the buildings, which adopted local materials and traditions. The 60-metre-high minaret of Gutluk Temir erected in the eleventh century, and the tomb of Tekesh, Jalal al-Din's grandfather, set up in 1200, bear witness to the thriving Iranian tradition of Muslim architecture there. The laying of bricks in complex patterns to create ornament within the brickwork of the buildings, the rich blue faience decoration, the wide diameter of the mausoleum dome, and the low profile of the square, ground-floor storey were all ideas taken from the buildings of the Great Seljuks of Iran.[29] More evidence survives from Iran and Afghanistan after the Khwarazmian conquest of the old Seljuk and Ghurid realms. In 1219 Jalal al-Din's governor in Zuzan, on the modern border between Iran and Afghanistan, built an enormous madrasa [Fig. 133].[30] With its huge scale, complex brickwork façades and three-coloured glazed tile work it provides evidence of how Khwarazmians continued to adapt their architecture to take on the trappings of those that they conquered, in this case the luxury arts of the Ghurids of Khorasan, who had been forced east from Khorasan and Afghanistan into India in the face of the Khwarazmian invaders.[31] It was almost certainly built by local builders from Herat, the main centre of artistic production in the region.

The Khwarazmians similarly absorbed other artistic forms from the region that they conquered. This is evident in an inlaid pen box of 1210–11, now in the Freer Gallery, which was made for Majd al-Mulk al-Muzaffar, the grand vizier of Jalal al-Din's father, 'Ala al-Din Muhammad. The box is signed by its maker, Shazi, who used the *nisba* al-Haravi on two other

---

[28] Juvayni, 2: 365; al-Nasawi, 47.
[29] R. Ettinghausen, O. Grabar and M. Jenkins-Madina, *Islamic Art and Architecture, 650–1250* (Harmondsworth, 2001), 105–16.
[30] S. Blair, 'The Madrasa at Zuzan: Islamic Architecture in Eastern Iran on the Eve of the Mongol Invasions', *Muqarnas* 3 (1985), 75–91.
[31] F. B. Flood, *Objects of Translation: Material Culture and Medieval 'Hindu–Muslim' Encounter* (Princeton, 2009).

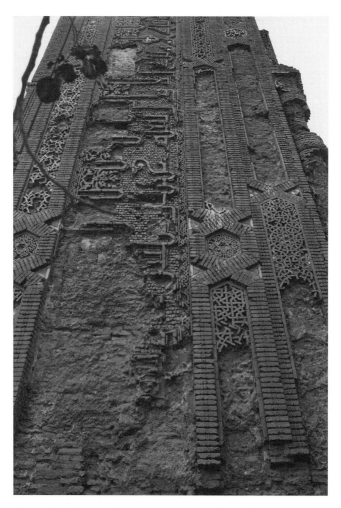

Figure 133 Detail of the ornate brick-and-tile work on the south iwan of the madrasa at Zuzan, Iran; 1218

objects he made, indicating his origins in Herat.[32] It must have been commissioned by the vizier during the conquest of Iran, before he returned to Merv (in modern Turkmenistan). The techniques required to inlay silver into the brass from which the pen box was made were first developed in Herat at the end of the twelfth century. The Mongol invasion of the region in the early 1220s then forced the craftsmen to flee west to Iraq, where they seem to have settled in Mosul.[33] They therefore introduced these techniques to the Near East, opening the way for the production of the great inlaid vessels from the 1230s on that were so admired by the Ayyubids (see

[32] Atil et al., *Islamic Metalwork*, cat. 14. [33] R. Ward, *Islamic Metalwork* (London, 1993), 74–80.

Chapters 8 and 9). The visual assimilation of Iranian Islamic culture by the Khwarazmians was undoubtedly a reason for the welcome that Jalal al-Din received among his co-religionists, and in the desire of al-Mu'azzam and others to forge alliances with him. Despite their patronage of such extraordinary objects and monuments, some Muslim chroniclers remained determined to cast the Khwarazmians as provincial outsiders. Ibn Bibi wrote that when Jalal al-Din's envoys came to Alanya in 1229 they fell to the ground with awe and amazement before the grandeur and wealth of the Seljuk palace.[34]

Khwarazmian piety was manifested in a second, more violent, way. This was in their reaction to religious art. Jalal al-Din's victories in the Caucasus in the 1220s were followed by the wholesale destruction of Christian religious images. This was in striking contrast to the relative tolerance of Christian images that existed in Ayyubid and Seljuk lands. Islam denounced the use of images in religious contexts and the danger of idolatry that surrounded them. The destruction of icons and wall paintings that followed was therefore in accordance with general Muslim teaching on idolatry, but the manner in which it was executed was uniquely Khwarazmian in its inventiveness and its cruelty. According to *Kartlis Tskhovreba*, after his capture of Tbilisi, Jalal al-Din forced its citizens to 'foul' icons of Christ and the Mother of God that he laid out beneath the destroyed dome of the Sioni church, the most prestigious church in the city.[35] Those who refused were decapitated without further ceremony. Jalal al-Din's sweep through the Caucasus and eastern Anatolia left little in its wake but destruction. There is evidence, however, that he was planning a more constructive future, and was beginning to re-establish a monetary economy for the region. This is evident from the speed with which he reopened mints in the areas he controlled. One copper ingot from the reign of Queen Tamar in the David Collection in Copenhagen was overstruck by Jalal al-Din to validate it for his new reign in 1226. After his departure from Georgia in 1228 it was overstruck once more by Queen Rusudan [Fig. 134].

The piety and violence of the Khwarazmians comes together with their adoption of Persian art forms in a most remarkable way on a plate now in the Freer Gallery in Washington DC [Fig. 135]. Measuring 47.8 centimetres in diameter, the plate is a magnificent example of *minai* ware (from the Persian for 'enamelled', to denote its multi-coloured technique). It presents a large field on which the ferocious siege of the city of Khalkhal is depicted. Mounted warriors attack the fortified city, which is defended by archers and catapults. The centre of the dish focuses on the encounter between the leader

---

[34] Quoted in Arık and Arık, *Tiles*, 281.   [35] *Kartlis Tskhovreba*, 327.

Figure 134 Copper ingot of Jalal al-Din Khwarazmshah counterstamped by Queen Rusudan of Georgia; 1228 (Copenhagen, David Collection, inv. C330; 49.2 g)

Figure 135 *Minai*-ware dish showing a siege; c. 1210–20 (Freer Gallery of Art, Smithsonian Institution, Washington, DC: purchase, F1943.3; diameter: 47.8 cm) (For the colour version, please refer to the plate section. In some formats this figure will only appear in black and white)

of the attackers, Muzaffar al-Sawla wa'l-Din, and his beaten opponent, who falls from the battlements, his body pierced by arrows. However, these two are hardly visible in the maelstrom of action – with charging horsemen, dismembered bodies, fleeing troops filling every space on the plate. The city is named in an inscription, as are eight of the (victorious) combatants, but none has been convincingly identified in other sources. It has recently been proposed that the dish represents an attack on an Assassin stronghold in eastern Azerbaijan by Jalal al-Din Khwarazmshah in about 1225.[36] The Assassins were a branch of Nizari Isma'ilis which had formed in the late eleventh century, centred on a series of castles in north-western Iran, most famously Alamut.[37]

The narrative is set out horizontally, so disregarding the shape of the bowl, leading to a confused design. This may suggest that the image derives from a manuscript or wall painting source (further evidence for the existence of large-scale narratives in Persian art), but it also helps to capture the chaos and fractured nature of war.[38] The plate encapsulates the ambivalent view of the Khwarazmians in Iran. The size of the plate, its luxurious manufacture, wealth of colours and detail all glorify the event and celebrate the eight men who are named in inscriptions. Their heroism is reflected in the mythical heroes from Persian epic who adorn the underside of the plate.[39] At the same time, the images of death and dismembered bodies, and the implicit fate of those still defending the city, are a reminder of the suffering and cruelty involved. This cannot be seen as an implicit critique of the warriors – accounts of victory from Christian and other Muslim sources all celebrated the violence of their victories (as we saw in Chapter 3). The Shi'a beliefs of the Assassins made them enemies of the Sunnis, and so the violence here is best seen as a celebration of Sunni orthodoxy. The paradoxical beauty of violence can be found in much medieval art. Nevertheless, the tension between the horror of the siege and the colourful beauty of its depiction is unsettling. The ambivalent relationship between the Muslim powers around the Mediterranean and the Khwarazmians is best summarised by Ibn Wasil's final verdict on Jalal al-Din:

> This man, with all we have recounted about his tyranny and bloodthirstiness, possessed vigour, determination, boldness and high resolve. He was a barrier between us and the Tatars, and by his ruin they were

---

[36] Holod, 'Event and Memory', 203–6.
[37] B. Lewis, *The Assassins: A Radical Sect in Islam* (New York, 1980).
[38] Atil, *Ceramics from the World of Islam*, no. 50.
[39] Atil, *Ceramics from the World of Islam*, no. 50; compare also Pope, ed., *A Survey of Persian Art*, pl. 706: the Iranians leaving the fortress of Furud.

established in Iraq, Rum, and the Jazira and were enabled to penetrate into Syria.[40]

These examples of pious foundations, attacks on Christians and the promotion of Sunni Islam allowed Muslim chroniclers to praise the Khwarazmians and to defend alliances made with them. However, the adherence to Islam papered over aspects of the Khwarazmian regime that were less palatable to other Muslims. They performed other religious practices that could not so easily be reconciled with the teachings of the Qur'an and the hadith. These elements of Central Asian shamanistic and occult beliefs had reached the Khwarazmian court with the large numbers of Kipchaq fighters who were recruited to the army. We have evidence of the impact of these non-Muslim beliefs from al-Nasawi's biography of Jalal al-Din, which gives two examples of these practices. Given al-Nasawi's sympathy for his subject, these cannot simply be the usual attempts by authors to denigrate unpopular rulers.

At the same time that Jalal al-Din was destroying Christian icons, he was also seeking to control the power contained in other magical images. Jalal al-Din's father had created a statue (*timthal*) and had buried it, probably in the grounds of the caliphal palace in Baghdad. What exactly this *timthal* was is unclear; it could be either a physical likeness or a symbolic representation (something bearing names, titles, insignia).[41] A *timthal* was imbued with powers deriving from the particular materials from which it was fashioned, enhanced by the auspicious rituals performed during its manufacture. All were governed by astrological readings.[42] The statue had been buried in Baghdad by Jalal al-Din's father during his wars when he faced the combined forces of the caliphate and the Assassins, with the aim of weakening their power. But now the statue was, like so many statues across the medieval world, acting capriciously and turning against those that made it. Rumours even claimed that it incited the Caliph to encourage the Mongol invasion of Khwarazm.[43] Jalal al-Din had to send an agent to try to retrieve it, but he was unable to find it, probably due to new building work in the palace. The power attributed to this particular statue derived from the esoteric knowledge of its maker, one Siraj al-Din Abu Yusuf Ya'qub al-Sakaki, who was believed to be able to bewitch the stars (in other words, he could not just read the future in the stars, but alter it), as well as having the power to reverse

[40] Quoted in Humphreys, *From Saladin to the Mongols*, 221.
[41] I. Miller, 'Occult Science and the Fall of the Khwarazm-Shah Jalal al-Din', *Iran* 39 (2001), 249–56.
[42] L. Thorndike, *A History of Magic and Experimental Science during the First Thirteen Centuries of our Era* (New York, 1923), 1: 661–6.
[43] Van Berchem, *Amida*, 223.

Figure 136 Black stone of Jalal al-Din Khwarazmshah; November 1230 (British Museum, inv. ME OA 1990.6–12.1; 47 × 29 cm)

the movement of the stars through the night sky; with his breath he could halt the flow of rivers.[44]

A second area of magical interest may be reflected in an extraordinary object now in the British Museum [Fig. 136].[45] It is a large black volcanic stone measuring 47 × 29 centimetres. Weighing 35 kilograms, it is too heavy to be lifted comfortably by one person. The front surface of the stone has been engraved with inscriptions that name Jalal al-Din as ruler and give the identity of the carver, Mahmud b. Muhammad, known as Rashid, a jeweller and a seal-cutter from the city of Nishapur, whose name survives in a number of other carvings. These inscriptions join two Qur'anic inscriptions, and all frame a pseudo-architectural niche that resembles nothing so much as a *mihrab*.

---

[44] Al-Nasawi, 249–50.

[45] V. Porter, R. G. Hoyland and A. D. Morton, *Arabic and Persian Seals and Amulets in the British Museum* (London, 2011), 12–13.

The stone's rounded back means that it cannot stand up by itself, and there are no marks on its back to indicate that it was ever set into a wall. It cannot, therefore, be a distance marker or commemorative plaque (and the inscriptions make no reference to any such function). We can only conclude that what was important is the stone itself: a large black monolith, a naturally occurring pebble of unnatural size. A basic meander pattern carved along the bottom in a much cruder technique (it looks to have been pounded with a small stone tool, rather than Rashid's precise chisel-and-drill work) suggests that the stone had a longer history, preceding Jalal al-Din's ownership. Was it a magical object in its own right, now harnessed to Islam by Rashid's carving?

Unusual stones were the object of occult belief in Central Asia and among the Khwarazmians in the early thirteenth century; beliefs shared by Jalal al-Din himself.[46] Al-Nasawi reports that after making peace with the Ayyubids and Seljuks after the battle of Yassıçemen in 1230 Jalal al-Din was in Valashjird, a village near Akhlat that was suffering from drought, heat and flies. He produced magic stones, and personally supervised the ceremonies whereby these stones produced rain, which immediately began to fall, to the delight of the villagers. (The delight proved to be short-lived as the rain became torrential and continued day and night. Jalal al-Din was unable to stop it, and the whole area became a sea of mud. His own women complained that they could barely reach the royal tent: 'You are the Lord of the World, but not in the art of making it rain, it seems, because you have caused so much damage to everyone in producing such a flood. Anyone else would not have done this; they would have produced just as much rain as was needed.')[47] Similar beliefs are also found further west: a polished stone by the Gate of Victory in Aleppo was believed to cure those suffering from bad nails when they rubbed their fingers against it.[48] Other medieval literature on rain stones suggests that they were usually small and easy to handle, so this giant pebble cannot be such an object; but its unusual completeness and size suggest that it was regarded as having a particular (possibly magical) value. The addition of Qur'anic inscriptions may have been an attempt to control its powers or legitimise its veneration or use.[49]

[46] For an overview of stone cults see F. W. Hasluck, *Christianity and Islam under the Sultans* (Oxford, 1929), 1: 179–220.
[47] Al-Nasawi, 396–7; J. A. Boyle, 'Turkish and Mongol Shamanism in the Middle Ages', *Folklore* 83/3 (1972), 177–93, esp. 189.
[48] Sibṭ ibn al-'Ajami, 3.
[49] Rashid al-Din, ed. Quatremère, 428–40 for more, see also 432–4; Y. Porter, 'Les techniques du lustre métallique d'après le Jowhar-name-ye-Nezami', *VIIe congrès international sur la céramique médiévale en mediterranée* (Athens, 2003), 427–436.

The date of the stone is as remarkable and perplexing as its function. It is inscribed with the month of Muharram 628 (November 1230). This is very close in time to al-Nasawi's story of the rain stones, but striking in terms of Jalal al-Din's own history. It was made in the winter after he was defeated at Yassıçemen, when he had had to abandon Tamta and his possessions in Anatolia to go on the run. During these months the Mongols arrived specifically to hound him to his death. It shows that even as a fugitive Jalal al-Din had the wherewithal to transport this cumbersome object with him, and the time and interest to lavish craftsmanship on such an awkward and apparently functionless stone.

The Khwarazmians' outward, Islamic condemnation of images, combined with their covert interest in, and fear of, the potential power of magical objects, was a potent blend. It recognised the power of images whilst at the same time accepting that this came from a sinister source. Jalal al-Din's interest in such supernatural powers obviously conflicted with the more orthodox Islamic attitude to images and the occult that lay at the core of an Islamic court. However, the opposition between orthodox and magical beliefs was a blurred one. Magic was as prevalent in all the Christian and Muslim cultures that Jalal al-Din encountered in eastern Anatolia, and was practised by the very richest in society. In 1241/2, a decade after Jalal al-Din's death, a metalworker, Muhammad ibn Khutlukh al-Mawsili (i.e. from Mosul), was employed to make an astonishingly elaborate geomantic instrument, now also in the British Museum.[50] As a computational device to tell the future it has no equal, but the execution of the work, particularly the interwoven foliage of the handle, is very close to that of al-Ashraf's astrolabe. The inscription on the front proclaims its power:

> I am the revealer of secrets; in me are marvels of wisdom and strange and hidden things. But I have spread out the surface of my face out of humility, and have prepared it as a substitute for earth ... From my intricacies there comes about perception superior to books concerned with the study of the art [of geomancy].[51]

Extensive handbooks were written in order to help interpret the signs, with many being compiled in the thirteenth century. Al-Malik al-Mas'ud, who

---

[50] All that follows is from E. Savage-Smith and M. B. Smith, *Islamic Geomancy and a Thirteenth-Century Divinatory Device* (Malibu, CA, 1980); and E. Savage-Smith and M. B. Smith, 'Islamic Geomancy and a Thirteenth Century Divinatory Device: Another Look', in *Magic and Divination in Early Islam*, ed. E. Savage-Smith (Aldershot, 2004), 211–76.

[51] J. W. Allan and A. T. Aron, *Metalwork of the Islamic World: The Aron Collection* (London; New York, 1986), 24–5, 66–9.

ruled in Amid in 1222–31, whilst Jalal al-Din rampaged in the countryside around him, commissioned 'Abd al-Rahim al-Jawbari to compile the *Kitab al-Mukhtar fi kashf al-Asrar* (The book of selected disclosure of secrets).[52] The book is an examination of the four divinatory arts: geomancy, aeromancy, hydromancy and pyromancy. His concern was not with the veracity of each of these sciences, but with the abuses to which they were subject in the hands of the unscrupulous. To weed out the frauds, deceptions and charlatans would strengthen the hand of those who could practise the magic. Later in the century two handbooks were written by the Iranian astronomer and philosopher Nasir al-Din al-Tusi (d. 1275), in addition to his studies of the astrolabe and his treatises on astronomy and religion.[53] These occult sciences were just as common in the Christian world. At the end of the twelfth century the Byzantine Emperor Andronikos I Komnenos had abandoned astrology 'as being both more common and more obscure in revealing future events', only to take up hydromancy in its place.[54]

After the Khwarazmians

After Jalal al-Din had been killed in 1231, the Mongol army that had been pursuing him returned to the east. Jalal al-Din's name remained potent, however, and rumours persisted that he had survived and would return to wreak havoc. One (presumably mad) man who claimed to be Jalal al-Din (saying that it was actually his servant who had been killed) so frightened those he met that he was taken to the Mongols and tortured to death in 1249.[55] Despite these scares, the serious threat from the Khwarazmians ended with their leader's death. This freed Tamta to return to her husband, al-Ashraf, and to Akhlat. Despite the devastation the Khwarazmians had caused, politics quickly resumed as normal across the region. The alliance that had brought the Seljuks and Ayyubids together quickly fell apart, and the involvement of Georgian troops in the Khwarazmian army at Yassıçemen briefly revived enmity between the Georgians and the Ayyubids, leading to fighting along their common frontier to the north-east of Lake Van. It does not seem as if any power in the region expected the Mongols to return; in any event they certainly made no preparations. It is only with the benefit of hindsight that we can see how mistaken a path this was. The one significant change in goal came from al-Ashraf. Having restored

---

[52] Savage-Smith and Smith, 'Islamic Geomancy', 213.
[53] Savage-Smith and Smith, 'Islamic Geomancy', 215–16.
[54] Niketas Choniates, 96 (ed. van Dieten, 168–9).   [55] Bar Hebraeus, 421–2.

Tamta to Akhlat he left the city and rode on to Sinjar, and then back to Damascus. He was never to return to Akhlat. He seems to have abandoned all interest in the city thereafter, preferring to concentrate instead on his new capital in Syria. Tamta's capture by the Mongols in 1236 shows that she cannot have travelled with al-Ashraf: she must have remained in Akhlat or returned to her family in Armenia. However, Akhlat was now in a very different position. With al-Ashraf showing no sign of interest in the city, the Seljuk Sultan Kaykubad I was easily able to take control of it. Thus in 1232 Akhlat was brought firmly back into the Turkic world of Anatolia, after the thirty-year interlude of Ayyubid rule. Kaykubad installed his *pervane* Kamyar as governor in the city, and he was to govern there until the city fell to the Mongols.[56] Given that the Mongols were eventually to return Tamta to Akhlat as its ruler, they clearly still understood her to have a close connection with the city a decade later, so it is possible that she remained in Akhlat during these years. A likely scenario is that she was employed in a similar way to that in which she had been used by al-Ashraf, as a Christian figurehead in the city, able to mediate between the Christian population and its Muslim rulers.

Once again this played on different facets of Tamta's identity. It might seem that this would be a recipe for conflict and disaster: who was Tamta's master now? But this was by no means uncommon, as we have already seen with the case of Basil Giagoupes and Tamar (sometimes identified as Gurji Khatun) in their church in Belisırma in Cappadocia, who acknowledged both a Christian and a Muslim master (Chapter 8). Today this looks like divided loyalties, but in the thirteenth century it was recognition of the different, overlapping (not competing) identities that people had. Byzantine Christianity required recognition of the Emperor as Christ's viceregent on earth; military service and political reality required recognition of the Sultan as the couple's temporal lord. Inscriptions discussed in earlier chapters show that this was the case throughout the thirteenth century. Thus it was possible for Tamta to shift allegiance without losing power.

[56] For the narrative of these years see Cahen, *The Formation of Turkey*, 59–65.

12 | Tamta and the Mongols

> They were more numerous than locusts,
> And more terrible than wasps,
> And worse than serpents,
> And more ferocious than devils.
>> Hymn on the sack of Tiflis 1220–1, attributed
>> to the Syriac poet Giwargis Warda[1]

In 1236 the general Chormaqan, leading an army of swift-moving Mongol cavalry, invaded the Caucasus.[2] Ögödei, the Great Khan, had charged him with the permanent conquest of the region. His advance was fast and devastating. Already weakened by the Khwarazmian invasion a decade earlier, and still fragmented by the internecine squabbles of the intervening years, cities and castles fell rapidly. When the army advanced further west into Greater Armenia and Anatolia in 1242–3, the different powers of the region formed a new alliance against the Mongols, but their combined army was crushed at the battle of Kösedağ (between Sivas and Erzincan), after which Mongol domination of the region was assured. We do not know exactly where Tamta was during this invasion – she may have been in Akhlat or with her brother Avag in his castle at Kayean, across the Debed gorge from Akhtala. Avag had succeeded his father Ivane as *msakhurtukhutsesi* and *atabeg* to Queen Rusudan of Georgia, and was now the leading courtier at the Georgian court. Kayean fell after only a brief siege early in the invasion in 1236, despite Avag's attempt to buy off the besiegers by sending his daughter Khoshak out of the castle to the Mongols as a hostage, 'wishing to win their goodwill'.[3] Akhlat fell not long after.[4]

---

[1] A. Pritula, 'A Hymn on Tiflis from the Warda Collection: A Transformation of the Muslim Conquerors into Pagans', in *Caucasus during the Mongol Period – Der Kaukasus in der Mongolenzeit*, eds. J. Tubach, S. G. Vashalomidze and M. Zimmer (Wiesbaden, 2012), 217–37, at 229–30.

[2] T. May, 'The Conquest and Rule of Transcaucasia: The Era of Chormaqan', in *Caucasus during the Mongol Period – Der Kaukasus in der Mongolenzeit*, eds. J. Tubach, S. G. Vashalomidze and M. Zimmer (Wiesbaden, 2012), 129–51.

[3] Kirakos, 126; May, 'The Conquest and Rule of Transcaucasia', esp. 133–9, although a problematic chronology of the invasion.

[4] It had already been attacked once by the Mongols during a raid in 1232: B. Dashdondog, 'The Mongol Conquerors in Armenia', in *Caucasus during the Mongol Period – Der Kaukasus in der*

Although Tamta does not appear by name in this period, she may well be present in the sources. The Georgian chronicles often refer to Avag, and mention him in the same sentence as a figure named only as 'the Sultan of Akhlat'.[5] Given the general lack of connection between Georgia and Akhlat, the Sultan's appearance here only makes sense if it is interpreted as a means of describing Avag's sister, Tamta; although why the chronicler should not be prepared to give her name is perplexing. The absence of gender in the Georgian language means that 'sultan' might equally refer to a man or woman, similar to the use of the non-gendered *mepe* (king) to apply to both Tamar and Rusudan, even though a gendered alternative (*dedopali*, queen) was available.

The chaos caused by the Mongols is reflected more generally in the various surviving sources, which conflate or confuse the dates and events of the next ten years, and frequently contradict each other. What follows presents one possible interpretation of events. After his surrender, Avag was sent to Batu, the grandson of Genghis Khan, who commanded the Mongol armies in the west from his base by the river Volga. Avag made formal submission to Batu, after which he was released to return to Armenia as a vassal.[6] To win his loyalty, Avag was given a Mongol bride, and in return he worked to secure the compliance of the other noble families in the region. He duly persuaded his cousin, Shahnshah Mqargrdzeli, the son of Zakare, as well as Vahram Pahlavuni and his son Aghbugha of the leading noble family in the region around Ani, Hasan Jalal al-Dola, the ruler of the eastern Armenian province of Khachen, 'and many others' to come over to the Mongols without fighting. When they submitted each was given back control of his lands, and a pardon – 'for the time being'.[7] At some point during this campaign Tamta was also captured and made a hostage, but her treatment was different from that of her brother. She was also sent to Batu's camp on the Volga, but instead of being returned to Armenia or Akhlat, she was then sent on to the court of the Great Khan, Ögödei, at Karakorum in Mongolia. Given her brother's importance in delivering Armenia to the Mongols, keeping Tamta as a hostage would have been a sensible means to ensure Avag's loyalty to the new regime; although given how little regard for Tamta the rest of her family ever publicly displayed, and given the ease with which Avag surrendered his daughter in 1236, we might wonder how much of a hold over Avag this gave the Mongols. It was to be nine years before Tamta saw Akhlat again.

Mongolenzeit, eds. J. Tubach, S. G. Vashalomidze and M. Zimmer (Wiesbaden, 2012), 53–82, at 61; *Kartlis Tskhovreba*, 334; Stepannos Episkopos in *Armianskie istochniki*, 40.
[5] *Kartlis Tskhovreba*, 335, 338.   [6] *Kartlis Tskhovreba*, 338.
[7] Kirakos, 130; Dashdondog, 'The Mongol Conquerors in Armenia', 70–1.

The portents for Tamta's treatment at the hands of the Mongols were not good. Those who survived the conquest of a city faced terrible treatment. Captives from the 1220s had been forced to march naked across Asia during the winter to the Mongol court; others (particularly Germans) had been put to work in the mines, extracting gold and making arms for their new masters.[8] One woman named Pascha (possibly Paquette), who arrived at Karakorum whilst Tamta was there, had come from Metz. She had been captured in Hungary after the battle of Mohi in 1241, and was made a slave of a Christian wife of Güyük Khan.[9] We are told only of the 'unheard of privations she had endured before she came to the court', but by the 1250s, when the Franciscan missionary William of Rubruck met her, she had given birth to three sons with a captive craftsman from the other end of Europe: a Russian builder who had carved out a comfortable living constructing houses for the Mongols, 'which is a profitable craft among them'. Members of the elite who survived were treated better, but still faced privations: the defeat of Muhammad Khwarazmshah in 1221 led to all the female members of the dynasty being shipped off to Mongolia.[10] Terkan Khatun, his formidable grandmother, was sent to Genghis Khan where, according to al-Nasawi, she lived luxuriously, but miserably, forced to wait on the Khan at table.[11] Similarly, when Muhammad's son Jalal al-Din was defeated in 1231, his harem was also transferred to Mongolia. One of his daughters, aged two when she was captured, was to remain in Karakorum for a quarter of a century, until she was finally returned to become the bride of al-Salih Isma'il, the son of the *atabeg* Badr al-Din Lu'lu', in 1258. By then her Islamic roots had been overlaid with a veneer of Mongolian upbringing. When she arrived in Mosul she was wearing Mongol costume,[12] and received 'a dowry after the Mongol custom', but she was married in accordance with Islamic rites.[13] We do not know who this girl's mother was: given her age, it is conceivable that it could have been Tamta.

Quite how much of all this Tamta experienced we cannot know. The selective reporting of all the surviving sources about the treatment of Christians among the Mongols means that their accounts are limited. Tamta is never mentioned, and neither is the fate of other women brought to the Mongolian court. However, although women hostages in Mongolia receive little attention, it is possible to reconstruct rather more about the lives that they led, and the ways in which visitors from Europe and the Near East constructed their encounters with the Mongols.

[8] William of Rubruck, 145–6. [9] William of Rubruck, 182–3.
[10] V. V. Bartol'd, *Four Studies on the History of Central Asia* (Leiden, 1956), 41–2.
[11] Al-Nasawi, 69. [12] Bar Hebraeus, 426. [13] Juvayni, 2: 468.

Who Were the Mongols?

The first problem that everyone who encountered the Mongols in the 1230s had to face was to decide who and what they were. People found this surprisingly difficult to answer, even though they had encountered them before. The aftermath of the defeat of Muhammad Khwarazmshah in 1220 had seen a Mongol raiding force sweep through the Caucasus in 1221, causing particular havoc as they raided in January, well outside the normal fighting season.[14] They were accompanied by worrying portents on the earth and in the sky:

> There was a terrible earthquake, and the elegantly decorated church at Mshakavank collapsed, on 11 January [1221] at lunchtime; four officiants were killed in the great loss of life. During the whole night there was visible to everyone a star in the sky in the shape of a lance. The two signs indicated the change from a peaceful world to the turbulence of enemies armed with lances.[15]

The Mongols were these 'enemies armed with lances'. Tamta's father, Ivane Mqargrdzeli, had led the resistance to that first invasion, drawing up his army at Khunani on the river Mtkvari. He was defeated and, more worryingly, Giorgi IV Lasha, the King of the Georgians, was seriously wounded. Not even the arrival of the royal banner, 'the blessed, the august, the famous standard of David, the instrument of triumph... which had never been defeated', could save the Georgians.[16] This first serious defeat of the Georgian army was one of the factors that enabled Jalal al-Din Khwarazmshah to conquer them five years later; and marked the beginning of centuries of misfortune for the Christians of the Caucasus, after the glories of the previous 130 years.

The speed of the invasion was such that the Georgians were left unclear both as to the identity of the invaders and their religion. The first Georgian account records only 'the arrival of a strange people speaking a strange language'.[17] As fuller descriptions appeared, the picture became no clearer:

> There appeared extraordinary people, alien in face, customs, manners and appearance, not spoken about in any ancient text; as for their language,

---

[14] D'Ohsson, *Histoire des Mongols*, 1: 327.

[15] Vardan, 213; compare a comet and earthquake leaving the earth leaking black water on the eve of Chormaqan's arrival from the anonymous annals from Sivas: Dashdondog, *The Mongols and the Armenians*, 19.

[16] *Kartlis Tskhovreba*, 287, 323; Kirakos, 100.

[17] *Kartlis Tskhovreba*, 318; Brosset, *Histoire de la Géorgie*, 492.

their appearance, their lives, all were astounding. They did not know the taste of bread, and fed themselves only on meat and mares' milk. They were full bodied, bold in their person, and strong on their feet, handsome and clean in their flesh, with small, narrow, dark eyes, with obvious and well-developed strength, their heads covered with thick black hair, flat-browed, with noses set so low that their cheeks stood out above their noses, their nostrils seemed just as small, their lips were small, their teeth even and clean, and they were completely without facial hair.[18]

The purpose of their arrival was also unclear. They seemed to have no interest in stealing gold or jewels, the usual aims of war, taking only horses.[19]

As to their religion, Giorgi IV's successor, Queen Rusudan (r. 1223–45), wrote to Pope Honorius III in 1223 in the aftermath of the invasion, saying that it had been assumed at first that they must be Christians because they had been fighting Muslims up until their arrival in the Caucasus.[20] Other rumours circulated that they had been seen with a portable tent-church and a miracle-working cross.[21] Whilst people soon realised how mistaken this was, and talk turned to the idol they venerated named Kunjit, confusion remained.[22] Even two decades later Smbat the Constable, brother of Hetum I, King of Armenian Cilicia, could write from Samarkand to King Henry I Lusignan of Cyprus that the Tatars were Christians who had saved the Crusader states: 'If God hadn't brought the Tartars who then massacred the pagans, they [the Saracens] would have been able to invade the whole land as far as the sea.'[23] It was this letter that encouraged Louis IX of France to send the Franciscan William of Rubruck to Mongolia to confirm the Mongols as Latin Christians and to make a permanent alliance against Islam.[24]

Of all the upheavals Tamta faced, her captivity in Mongolia was the longest and most gruelling. It involved travel far from her family and homeland, and into a world that had almost nothing in common with the cultures she had mostly moved between so far in her life. The Mongols embraced different religions, cultures and languages, all on a different continent. In Mongolia, identities played a different role: all those who arrived from the west were outsiders; therefore allegiances and identities were aligned a different way. Traditions inherited from the Graeco-Roman and Christian worlds now were in a minority, alongside groups from the Iranian and Chinese

---

[18] *Kartlis Tskhovreba*, 321; Kirakos, 134, was also struck by the absence of facial hair.
[19] Kirakos, 100.
[20] *Regesta Honorii*, 2: 246 no. 4979; M. Tamarati, *L'église géorgienne dès origines jusqu'à nos jours* (Rome, 1910), 416–17, or 414–30.
[21] Kirakos, 100.   [22] *Kartlis Tskhovreba*, 318.
[23] *Armianskie istochniki*, 64–6.   [24] Yule, 1: 162–3.

worlds. Nevertheless, it is possible to build up a vivid picture of the ways in which these groups interacted, and particularly about the relationship between the different Christian communities in the Mongol world – once again, art became a key force in the maintenance of identities and difference. The evidence for this covers the reigns of three successive Khans: Ögödei (r. 1229–41), who was Khan throughout the span of Tamta's captivity in Mongolia; his son Güyük (r. 1246–8), whose coronation was witnessed by all the rulers conquered by the Mongols; and Ögödei's nephew Möngke (r. 1251–9), under whom Mongol rule in Anatolia became increasingly structured and demanding.

Travel to Mongolia

As the crow flies it is more than 4,800 kilometres from Akhlat to Karakorum; on the ground, whether travelling on foot or on horseback, it is considerably longer. This was the journey that Tamta made twice, as she travelled to and from the capital of the Great Khan. She was probably away from Akhlat for between five and nine years. We have no information about what she did in Mongolia, or how she was treated; but we are able to piece together a clear picture of the position of captured Christians in the Mongol world, their internal squabbles and disputes, and their relations with other subjugated peoples and their Mongol overlords.

We have some idea of what Tamta's travels entailed from the accounts of those who undertook the same journey, albeit a decade after Tamta had completed hers. The earliest recorded is that of the Franciscan ambassador of Pope Innocent IV, John of Plano Carpini, who journeyed between 1245 and 1247. From a contemporary source we know that John was a companion of St Francis himself; he was also over sixty, extremely fat and in poor health.[25] To have survived the journey, much of it undertaken in the snows of winter, shows quite how tenacious the first friars were. A fuller account was penned by William of Rubruck, who was sent to Karakorum by King Louis IX of France in 1254. A third, briefer account recorded the route of King Hetum I of Armenia, who set out for Karakorum as William was on his return home.[26]

---

[25] Mary-Emily Miller, 'Giovanni da Pian del Carpini', in *Dictionary of World Biography II: The Middle Ages*, ed. F. N. Magill (Oxford, 2008), 206–9.

[26] The journey is recorded in Kirakos, 176–81; with commentary in J. A. Boyle, 'The Journey of Het'um I, King of Little Armenia, to the Court of the Great Khan Möngke', *Central Asiatic Journal* 9/3 (1964), 175–89.

By the time Hetum travelled, many rulers had already made the journey. All the subject rulers in the west had been required to attend the *kuriltai* (great meeting) of 1246 at which Güyük was installed as Great Khan. The roll call is impressive. Armenian Cilicia was represented by Smbat the Constable, Hetum's brother, and he was joined by all his near neighbours:

> From Khitai there came emirs and officials; and from Transoxiana and Turkestan the emir Mas'ud accompanied by grandees of that region. With the emir Arghun there came the celebrities and notables of Khorasan, Iraq, Lur, Azerbaijan and Shirvan. From Rum came Sultan Rukn al-Din and the Sultan of Takavor; from Georgia, the two Davits; from Aleppo, the brother of the Lord of Aleppo; from Mosul, the envoy of Sultan Badr al-Din Lu'lu'; and from the city of Peace, Baghdad, the chief qadi Fakhr al-Din. There also came the Sultan of Erzurum, envoys from the Franks, and from Kerman and Fars also; and from 'Ala al-Din of Alamut, his governors in Quhistan, Shihab al-Din and Shams al-Din. And all this great assembly came with such baggage as befitted a court; and there came also from other directions so many envoys and messengers that two thousand felt tents had been made ready for them: there came also merchants with the rare and precious things that are produced in the East and the West.[27]

Once at Karakorum they joined the defeated rulers from other parts of the Mongol Empire, including Yaroslav II of Vladimir, the Grand Prince of Russia, and people from China too, as well as ambassadors from the recently formed sultanate in Delhi. All these journeys – of Tamta, of the Franciscan missionaries and of the rulers attending the *kuriltai* – were conducted under the official sanction of the Mongols, and so were presumably easier than those endured by captured slaves. John of Plano Carpini recorded that he travelled with 'Batu's sealed letter and order saying that they [innkeepers and families on the route] were to provide us with horses and food, otherwise he would put them to death'.[28] Yet none had an easy journey. As Rubruck summarised: 'There is no counting the times we were famished, thirsty, frozen and exhausted.'[29]

Both Rubruck and Hetum travelled north around the Caspian and across the steppes to Karakorum (although Hetum would later return around the south side and through Iran). The first part of Hetum's journey in 1255/6 had to be undertaken in disguise as a cattle driver for fear of being captured by the Seljuks, who had declared him an enemy because of the alliance the

---

[27] Juvayni, 1: 249–50; discussion of Takavor as Trebizond in A. A. M. Bryer, 'The Grand Komnenos and the Great Khan at Karakorum in 1246', in *Itinéraires d'Orient: Hommages à Claude Cahen*, eds. R. Curiel and R. Gyselen (Bures-sur-Yvette, 1994), 257–61.
[28] *The Mongol Mission*, 71.   [29] William of Rubruck, 141.

Armenians in Cilicia had already forged with the Mongols, which meant that they had not provided any troops for the alliance at Kösedağ in 1243.[30] The scale of the enmity can be judged by the speed with which they travelled: they made it from Sis to Kars (i.e. across Seljuk territory from Cilicia to Mqargrdzeli-controlled Armenia) in just twelve days, averaging more than 60 kilometres per day.[31] Hetum even travelled separately from all the gifts he was preparing to give to the Mongols, and had to wait in Kars for their arrival.[32]

Hetum's speed in this early part of the journey was facilitated by the extraordinary road and caravanserai network that the Seljuks had built up since the 1220s (discussed in Chapter 6) – although, dressed as a cattle herder, it is more problematic whether he would have been able to stay in these establishments. Although caravanserais facilitated speedy and safe travel in Anatolia and its environs, we should not overestimate the sense of security they conveyed. Al-Hariri's *Maqamat* provides a scurrilous reminder of the dangers: the tales' anti-hero Abu Zayd and his son manage to drug all the guests at a caravanserai in order to rob them while they slept, only escaping punishment through his legendary rhetorical skills.[33] However, such dangers were nothing compared to those faced by sea voyagers. The Mongol princess Arpay Khatun, en route around the Black Sea to arrange a marriage to the Seljuk Masʿud II in 1279, was attacked by 'Frankish corsairs' – i.e. the Venetian or Genoese navy – and lost all her possessions.[34] Whilst overland travel could be dangerous, it was at least more under the control of the Mongols.

Once beyond the caravanserai networks the journey from the Caucasus to the Mongols became a slower and more arduous affair. It was still supported by a sophisticated infrastructure of stations, called *iam*s, where food and fresh mounts could be had, but lacked the grand masonry buildings of Anatolia. At times even this system failed, and William of Rubruck at one point travelled for three days without seeing a single other human being.[35] As these men and women travelled further east they moved beyond the limits first of the Graeco-Roman world and then the Iranian. Physiognomies, languages, religions and customs all began to change. The sights became stranger and the witnesses increasingly struggled to explain them.

---

[30] Smbat Sparapet in *Armianskie istochniki*, 49.
[31] Sis to Kars is 740 kilometres as the crow flies. [32] Hayton, 164.
[33] BNF arabe 5847, fol 89v: Maqama 29: Brend, *Islamic Art*, fig. 78.
[34] A. C. S. Peacock, 'Sinop: A Frontier City in Seljuq and Mongol Anatolia', *Ancient Civilizations from Scythia to Siberia* 16 (2010), 103–24, at 115, citing Baybars al-Mansuri.
[35] William of Rubruck, 110.

First Encounters: At Batu's Camp

The first sustained encounter with the Mongols took place on this route at the camp of Batu on the river Volga. Batu (d. 1255) was the grandson of Genghis Khan and led the most formidable of the Mongol armies in the west. He had destroyed the cities of Rus', and harried as far as west as Hungary in 1241. It was he who could authorise and facilitate travel further east. The road to Batu was already beyond most people's experience: when Avag travelled there, in the company of 'the sultan of Akhlat' (presumably Tamta), they 'went along unknown roads, which no one among the Georgians had ever walked before'.[36]

Seeing Batu's court, his *ordo*, set out on the Russian steppes with its sea of tents all carefully arranged around their leader's (but never to its south, where the entrance lay), William of Rubruck could only compare it to Moses' tabernacle in the book of Exodus – 'as among the people of Israel, where each one knew in which quarter from the tabernacle he had to pitch his tents, so these know on which side of the *ordo* they must place themselves when they set down their dwellings'.[37] As the site became more permanently settled, it was established as the town of Sarai, from the Persian for 'palace'.

Whilst Rubruck's account presented an alien scene through the familiar (although semi-legendary and therefore remote) language of the Old Testament, other customs could not be rationalised. Most striking of all were the Mongols' burial memorials that appeared alongside the tracks that Tamta and others travelled along. As well as reporting that they buried their worldly goods and servants, still alive, alongside the deceased, Kirakos Gandzaketsi gives an account of the memorials set above ground. Travellers encountered the ghostly presence of the dead man's now-empty tent, left as a marker of the grave site or, more alarmingly, a tomb marker made from an impaled horse rising out of the ground, the stake emerging through the horse's mouth.[38]

Batu's camp also provided the first insights into the living rituals and customs of the Mongols. Although Tamta had experienced many very different customs in her moves between the Georgians, Armenians, Ayyubids,

---

[36] *Kartlis Tskhovreba*, 335.   [37] William of Rubruck, 131.
[38] Kirakos, 135; William of Rubruck, 96. Image in J. A. Boyle, 'Kirakos of Ganjak on the Mongols', *Central Asiatic Journal* 8 (1963), 199–214; and for discussion: J. A. Boyle, 'A Form of Horse Sacrifice amongst the Thirteenth- and Fourteenth-Century Mongols', *Central Asiatic Journal* 10 (1965), 145–50; for recent archaeological evidence see W. T. Woodfin, Y. Rassamakin and R. Holod, 'Foreign Vesture and Nomadic Identity on the Black Sea Littoral in the Early Thirteenth Century: Costume from the Chungul Kurgan', *Ars Orientalis* 42 (2012), 155–87, at 159.

Khwarazmians and Seljuks, none could have prepared her for what she now encountered. Arriving visitors were compelled to walk between two fires in order to purify their souls and cleanse them so that they could then venerate the cult image of Genghis Khan that Batu erected after his grandfather's death in 1227. This image was described by another Franciscan emissary, Benedict the Pole, as taking the form of a golden statue.[39] Benedict was prepared to walk between the fires, but his religion forbade him from venerating what he regarded as a pagan idol. He was fortunate, and escaped with merely bowing his head; but Mikhail of Chernigov, one of the Russian princes brought before Batu, was not so lucky. He was condemned to death for his refusal to venerate the dead Khan's image. Unlike the three Hebrews who refused to venerate the idol of Nebuchadnezzar, God did not come to his aid, and he was martyred.[40] Other idols in human form, made of felt or silk by the senior women in the camp, were placed at the entrance to each tent.[41]

The appearance and position of Mongolian women was of great interest to the travellers. They were unsettled both by their appearance (too fat, too much make-up on their faces, noses too small), and by their prominence (women wore the same as their menfolk, so could not easily be distinguished from afar; they could shoot; they sat beside their husbands; they wielded much power). We will return to the importance accorded to Mongolian women in the next chapter.

One refrain that constantly recurs is the prohibition on standing on the threshold of a Mongolian tent. To do so meant instant execution. John of Plano Carpini and William of Rubruck repeat this warning no less than six times in their accounts.[42] Such an injunction was undoubtedly necessary to visitors from the west (regardless of their religious affiliation), as for them thresholds had a very different symbolic import. The Muslim rulers of Gandza buried captured Christian crosses under the threshold of their city gates precisely 'so that all passers-by would step on them', in just the same way that the cross from the cathedral of Ani had been sent to Nakhchivan to be trodden upon on the threshold of the city's mosque by all those coming to pray.[43] In Ayyubid Cairo pharaonic hieroglyphs had been subjected to the same contemptuous treatment.[44] Georgian kings had understood the symbolism of the threshold, but used it to different ends: King Davit the Builder (r. 1089–1125) had himself buried in the floor of the entrance gate

---

[39] *The Mongol Mission*, 80.   [40] *The Mongol Mission*, 10.   [41] *The Mongol Mission*, 9.
[42] *The Mongol Mission*, 11, 54, 63.   [43] Matthew of Edessa, 104; Kirakos, 117.
[44] Creswell, *The Muslim Architecture of Egypt*, 101.

of Gelati monastery so that visitors had to tread on his grave as they entered; a marker of his humility.[45] What had been a barrier that required physical interaction was now a symbolic marker that had to be acknowledged through avoidance.

Another problem that visitors from the west encountered was the Mongol diet. *Kumiss*, fermented mare's milk, rice wine and dried meat from 'unclean' animals were all unfamiliar and unappetising new tastes to acquire. When Avag had first been captured he had refused to try them: 'Christians are not accustomed to eat this food and drink this beverage, rather, they eat meat from clean animals which we have sacrificed, and they take wine to drink.'[46] Avag was fortunate that Chormaqan was willing to accede to his particular dietary demands. Another new foodstuff that was encountered was rhubarb. Its medicinal properties were recognised, but newcomers to Mongolia were unsure how to use it. A self-proclaimed Armenian monk at Karakorum named Sergius (on whom more later) infused it with holy water made by leaving a crucifix in water overnight, and succeeded in using it to cure Qotai Khatun, the wife of Ögödei Khan. But later he nearly killed a Parisian captive when he failed to distinguish between the safe and the poisonous parts of the plant.[47] Its value was such that when Genghis Khan captured the Chinese city of Ling-wu in December 1226 his astrologer, Yeh-lü Ch'u-ts'ai, asked for his share 'only a few books and two camel-loads of rhubarb'.[48]

Court Life in Mongolia

Once she was released by Batu, Tamta then had to continue her journey to Mongolia. John of Plano Carpini, a decade later, completed the trip to the *ordo* of the Great Khan at Karakorum in 106 days, covering some 4,800 kilometres (averaging 45 kilometres per day). He was able to complete the journey so fast as he was compelled to ride from dawn until well after dark each day. To manage this he had to change horses three or four times each day (occasionally seven changes), indicating the sophistication and frequency of the *iam*s, the post stations set up by the Mongols to ensure quick

---

[45] I. Khuskivadze and D. Tumanishvili, eds., *Gelati 900: Architecture, Murals, Treasures* (Tbilisi, 2007), 238–41, 295–6.
[46] Kirakos, 127.   [47] William of Rubruck, 217.
[48] I. de Rachewiltz, H.-l. Chan, H. Ch'i-ch'ing and P. W. Geier, eds., *In the Service of the Khan: Eminent Personalities of the Early Mongol–Yüan period (1200–1300)* (Wiesbaden, 1993), 146–7.

communications across the empire.⁴⁹ He often slept in the open air (having to kick his way through the snow to the frozen ground beneath on his return journey during the winter), only to find himself covered by snow in the morning. His only meal each day was in the evening, but that was frequently delayed until the following morning, so late did they travel each day.⁵⁰ Given his age, weight and health this was some achievement. Hetum undertook the same journey in 1253–4, taking five months.

These journeys across such vast, unknown swathes of land placed the travellers on the fringes of those legendary lands of which there were always rumours but rarely facts. The accounts are full of second- or even third-hand tales of the monstrous races, and other wonders of nature. John of Plano Carpini tells that 'we were told by the Russian clerics who live in the ordu with the emperor' about the Cyclopedes who, with only one arm and one leg, could move as fast as a horse by cartwheeling; they were rumoured to have made a treaty with the Khan.⁵¹ Equally, the dog-headed Cynocephali and the Parocitae who cannot eat but only drink, and 'inhale the steam of meat and fruit', become fact at fourth hand, told to us by the friar who jotted down Benedict the Pole's account of what others had told him they had seen.⁵² King Hetum also heard of men who took the form of dogs; he told Kirakos Gandzaketsi about them, as well as miraculous trees in Siberia.⁵³ Other wondrous rumours, such as idols so large that they could be seen at two days' distance, are now much less fantastical than they seemed to the early travellers; although with the recent destruction of the great Buddhas at Bamiyan, even these are now moving into the realm of legend rather than reality [Fig. 137].⁵⁴

When Tamta finally reached Karakorum, she found a new city emerging on the plain, the route of its walls only set out by Ögödei Khan in the spring of 1235.⁵⁵ The organisation of the Mongol camp at Karakorum was very different from Batu's on the Volga. Batu kept all his different envoys in isolation from each other; none was to learn about the presence or the plans of the others. At Karakorum they all mixed, allowing for much greater interaction.⁵⁶ By the time William of Rubruck arrived less than two decades later, there were 'twelve idol temples belonging to different

---

[49] *The Mongol Mission*, 55, 60–1; 58 for seven horses.   [50] *The Mongol Mission*, 61.
[51] *The Mongol Mission*, 31.   [52] *The Mongol Mission*, 80.
[53] Kirakos, 180; commentary in Boyle, 'Kirakos of Ganjak on the Mongols'.
[54] William of Rubruck, 152.
[55] E. Bretschneider, *Mediaeval Researches from Eastern Asiatic Sources: Fragments towards the Knowledge of the Geography and History of Central and Western Asia from the 13th to the 17th Century* (London, 1910), 1: 122, n.304: according to the Yüan shi annals.
[56] William of Rubruck, 183–4.

Figure 137 The great Buddha at Bamiyan, Afghanistan; sixth century AD (photo by Robert Byron, 1933/4)

peoples, two mosques [*mahumnerie*] where the religion of Mahomet is proclaimed, and one Christian church at the far end of the town'.[57] The Christians at Karakorum were among the first to encounter Buddhists and Mongol shamans. The Mongol court resounded to a cacophony of rival beliefs: Chinese fortune tellers now sought to foresee the future in competition with Mongol shamans (who divined using burned sheep shoulder-blades), Muslim astrologers armed with astrolabes and pseudo-Christian seers, including Sergius, the Armenian monk encountered earlier as a user of rhubarb. Sergius presented himself at court as a monk, although on closer questioning he turned out to be a cloth-worker from Ani who had taken the

---

[57] William of Rubruck, 221.

opportunity to reinvent himself once he had arrived in Mongolia.[58] He presumably arrived in Mongolia at about the same time as Tamta, after the capture of Ani in 1236, but stayed considerably longer. His self-appointed ecclesiastical title gave him high status, including privileged access to the Great Khan, which he used to enrich himself.

With a limited memory of Christianity, Sergius evolved his own beliefs and practices, which verged on Manichaeism. William of Rubruck, who provides the only history of this man, despaired of his faith. He only tolerated his behaviour and eccentricities because he was a co-religionist: 'He had a folding stool made for him of the type bishops generally have, and gloves, and a cap with peacock's feathers and surmounted by a little gold cross – I approved of the cross at least.'[59] His interpretation of the liturgy was decidedly unorthodox, involving filling the communion chalice with ashes, on top of which he placed a black stone for the Mongol queen, Qotai Khatun. He also worked with a Muslim geomancer. William was equally contemptuous of the Nestorian Christians, the dominant Christian confession at the Mongol court: 'The Nestorians there know nothing. They say their offices, and have the Holy Scriptures in Syriac, but they do not know the language, so they chant like those monks among us who know no grammar, and for this reason they are completely corrupt... For the lives of the Mo'als and even of the *tuins* (that is, the idolators) are more innocent than theirs.'[60] At times their views verged on heresy: 'those Nestorians and Armenians never make the figure of Christ on their crosses; they would thus appear to entertain some doubt of the Passion, or to be ashamed of it'.[61] Surviving pendants and tombstones, such as that found in modern Kyrgyzstan for a Nestorian man and his mother who died in 1261 (the date given according to both the Syriac and Chinese calendars: 1572, the year of the rooster) are indeed adorned with only a simple cross.[62]

The theological bickering between these different Christian confessions at the Mongol court now had to be put into perspective against a wider worldview. The court politics that took place around Tamta spanned the Eurasian world. At one end was the sinicised Khitan bureaucrat, Yeh-lü Ch'u-ts'ai, who instituted important administrative and tax reforms across

---

[58] His origin in Ani is presumed from his reference to coming from a city with a thousand churches: William of Rubruck, 197–8, 251.
[59] William of Rubruck, 199.   [60] William of Rubruck, 163–4.   [61] William of Rubruck, 196.
[62] D. Chwolson, *Syrisch-Nestorianische Grabinschriften aus Semirjetschie* (St Petersburg, 1897), 7, no. 5; for similar examples Roxburgh, ed., *Turks*, cats 18, 19 and 21; for pendants F. S. Drake, 'Nestorian Crosses and Nestorian Christians in China under the Mongols', *Journal of the Hong Kong Branch of the Royal Asiatic Society* 2 (1962), 11–25.

China in the 1220s for Ögödei.⁶³ At the same time he was the Khan's astrologer and employed forms of 'esoteric computation' to warn him against the actions that eventually killed him.⁶⁴ He also dabbled in other forms of divination. His vision of a unicorn (prosaically interpreted as a rhinoceros by modern rationalist scholars) led to Genghis Khan's withdrawal from India.⁶⁵ In opposition were Asian and Persian administrators, such as 'Abd al-Rahman, who replaced Ch'u-ts'ai after he fell from power in 1240. When 'Abd al-Rahman provoked too much opposition because of his excesses as a tax farmer in China he was in turn replaced by the Khwarazmian Mahmud Yalavach (d. 1254).⁶⁶ Rival factions formed around these figures, and they in turn were surrounded by envoys from across the world seeking peace, alliances with or favourable treatment from the Mongols. The leopards and greyhounds of the envoy from India mixed with gifts brought by ambassadors sent by the Caliph in Baghdad, and by envoys from the Greek Emperor of Nicaea. When all the historical sources are placed together, the tent of the Mongol Khan appears as the first truly global court, yet that is not how it was perceived by those who attended it. The travellers whose tales survive present curiously insular accounts in which they were obsessed by the local politics that they imported with them to Mongolia. The Christian reports rarely mention the Chinese and Asian figures at the court, and vice versa. Instead, we learn only that the Armenian monk Sergius tried to relive the battles of his youth. Echoing the long history of bloody warfare between the Armenians and the Muslims in Ani, he deliberately tried to stoke up Mongol hatred against the Muslims. He provoked arguments with them, calling them dogs, and even started fights; largely, it seems, without success.⁶⁷

The Visual World of the Mongols

The visual world of the Mongol court brought together art from across their empire. The Mongols seem to have been very keen to accumulate artists and craftsmen at their court. More than one account of the capture of a city concludes with the Mongols raping and then massacring all the inhabitants,

---

⁶³ De Rachewiltz, 'Yeh-lü Ch'u-ts'ai'.
⁶⁴ De Rachewiltz et al., eds., *In the Service of the Khan*, 137–75 for his biography; esp. 141–2 and 161; de Rachewiltz, 'Yeh-lü Ch'u-ts'ai', 194–5.
⁶⁵ De Rachewiltz et al., eds., *In the Service of the Khan*, 141–2.
⁶⁶ De Rachewiltz et al., eds., *In the Service of the Khan*, 122–8.
⁶⁷ William of Rubruck, 225.

but preserving the lives of artisans. Thus when Chormaqan besieged Ani in 1236, he reduced the city's walls to rubble with his catapults, and then murdered all the nobles even after they had surrendered (and after promising them clemency) 'and spared only a few women and children and some artisans whom they led into captivity'.[68] A decade earlier, the only people to survive the Mongol siege of Merv were the four hundred artisans that they took into captivity. All the other inhabitants were killed.

The range of objects encountered was truly eclectic: Chinese silks mixed with statues 'made in the French style'.[69] The throne made for the coronation of Güyük Khan in 1246, at which all the rulers of Anatolia (bar Tamta) were present, had been made by a Russian craftsman named Cosmas. It 'was of ivory, was wonderfully carved and there was also gold on it, and precious stones, if I remember rightly, and pearls'.[70] Cosmas also fashioned the Khan's great seal. The throne was housed in a tent plated in gold, with brocades covering the interior, and filled with silks, furs, armour and other gifts, which was described by a Chinese author, Hei-Ta Shih Luah: 'It is secured by more than a thousand ropes. It has one door. The threshold and doorposts are completely faced with gold. For this reason it is named "golden".'[71]

In front of the Khan's tent was a true wonder, made by a Parisian goldsmith named Guillaume Boucher. He had been captured in the aftermath of the battle of Mohi, and transported to Karakorum. Whilst he worked for the Great Khan, he believed that his brother, Roger, was still maintaining the family business on the Grand Pont in Paris almost 7,000 kilometres away.

> At the entrance to this great palace, since it was unfitting that skins of milk and other drink should be brought through there, Master Guillaume of Paris has constructed for him a large tree made of silver, with four silver lions at its roots, each one containing a conduit-pipe and spewing forth white mare's milk. There are four conduits leading into the tree, right to the top, with their ends curving downwards, and over each of them lies a gilded serpent with its tail twined around the trunk of the tree. One of the pipes discharges wine, a second *caracomos* [refined mare's milk], a third *boal* [a drink made from honey], and a fourth rice ale, known as *terracina*. Each beverage has its own silver vessel at the foot of the tree, ready to receive it. Between the four pipes, at the top, he made an angel holding a trumpet, and beneath the tree a cavity capable of concealing a man; and there is a pipe leading up to the angel through the very core of the tree.

---

[68] Kirakos, 128. John of Plano Carpini tells the same story: *The Mongol Mission*, 37–8.
[69] William of Rubruck, 215–16. [70] *The Mongol Mission*, 64–6.
[71] This from http://islamic-arts.org/2012/movable-palaces/.

(Originally he had constructed bellows, but they failed to blow with sufficient force.) Outside the palace there is a chamber where drink is stored and where stewards stand ready to pour when they hear the angel sound the trumpet. The branches, leaves and fruit of the tree are of silver.

So, when drink is required, the head butler calls to the angel to sound the trumpet. On hearing this, the man concealed in the cavity then blows strongly on the pipe that leads to the angel, the angel puts the trumpet to its mouth, and the trumpet gives out a very loud blast. When the stewards in the chamber hear this, each pours his drink into the appropriate pipe, and the pipes spurt it out, down into the vessels designed for the purpose; whereupon the butlers draw it up and convey it through the palace to the men and women.[72]

It was a marvellous fountain of drinks, with moving parts, blowing horns, flowing liquids. Such automata had been famous in the Byzantine and Islamic worlds of the tenth century; golden trees with singing birds and floating thrones are described at the court of the Byzantine Emperor Constantine VII and that of the Abbasid Caliph al-Muqtadir.[73] These machines were a well-established courtly tradition that drew gasps of wonder from all who saw them.[74]

William of Rubruck gives sole credit to Guillaume Boucher for this creation, which fits his Eurocentric view of the Mongol court. This European vision was recreated in the chinoiserie engraving that was made to accompany Pierre Bergeron's edition of William's travels published in France in 1735 [Fig. 138].[75] However, other evidence suggests that much of the credit may have lain elsewhere, as Rashid al-Din describes an automaton that was made for Ögödei Khan, when Tamta was present in Karakorum, but before the influx of western craftsmen including Guillaume Boucher after the battle of Mohi.[76] In the early thirteenth century the leading engineers of these kinds of automata came from the lands in which Tamta had lived: the Jazira. The most famous designer was Badi' al-Zaman ibn al-Razzaz al-Jazari, mathematician and engineer at the court of Nasir al-Din Mahmud, the Artuqid ruler of Amid (Diyarbakir) (r. 1201–22). Such men were

---

[72] William of Rubruck, 209–10.   [73] Ibn al-Zubayr, 50–5.

[74] For a twelfth-century fictional example see *Drosilla and Charikles* by Niketas Eugenianos in *Four Byzantine Novels*, 354.

[75] P. Bergeron, *Voyages faits principalement en Asie dans les XII, XIII, XIV, et XV siècles, par Benjamin de Tudèle, Jean du Plan-Carpin, N. Ascelin, Guillaume de Rubruquis, Marc Paul vénitien, Haiton, Jean de Mandeville, et Ambroise Contarini: accompagnés de l'Histoire des Sarasins et des Tartares, et précédez d'une Introduction concernant les voyages et les nouvelles découvertes des principaux voyageurs*, vol. 2 (La Haye, 1735), 95.

[76] Rashid al-Din, 62.

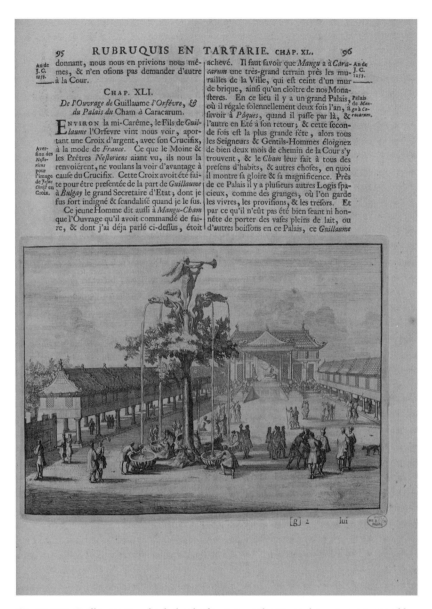

Figure 138 Guillaume Boucher's drinks fountain at the Mongol court, as imagined by Pierre Bergeron to accompany *Illustrations de voyages faits principalement en Asie* (Paris, 1735)

welcomed in the Mongol court: Nasir al-Din al-Tusi, one of the leading authorities on astrolabes and astrology, was quick to seek the patronage of Möngke's brother, Hülegü, when he came under Mongol rule, persuading the Khan to build him an observatory at Maraghu in 1259.

Al-Jazari's *Book of Knowledge of Ingenious Mechanical Devices* contains descriptions of complex automata, including fountains and clocks. The earliest manuscript of this was made during al-Jazari's lifetime in 1206 (Topkapı Sarayı, Sultan Ahmet III, MS 3472).[77] His designs include water clocks, fountains and other devices that have human figures with moving body parts like those on the Karakorum fountain. One basin for cleaning hands has a peacock that faces the user to pour water from its mouth, after which two slave figures emerge in turn to proffer soap and then a towel [Fig. 139: folio 136a].[78] Another, more frivolous, design is for a model boat to be set on a lake showing the ruler drinking with his companions.[79] It is doubtful that Guillaume worked alone on his fountain, despite the Eurocentric views of some modern scholars.[80]

Although she was among the first people from the ruling class to travel to Karakorum, Tamta was by no means the first Christian. In addition to its established Nestorian community, it held a number of Christians from Europe who had been there for fifteen years already.[81] More arrived during her stay; Karakorum was a centre that sucked in art and captives as spoils of war or as diplomatic gifts from across the world that the Mongols had conquered. As the threat and potential of the Mongols became evident both Christian and Muslim rulers began sending diplomatic gifts hoping to win the Khans over to their faith. On behalf of Louis IX, William of Rubruck carried illuminated manuscripts with him (although his best, a psalter from Louis' queen, Margaret of Provence, illuminated with gold, was seized by Batu's son, Sartach, en route to Karakorum).[82]

Earlier, in 1248, Louis IX had sent an embroidered tent–chapel with Christian scenes. It was described by Jean de Joinville:

> When sending the envoys back the king had sent with them, by his own envoys, a chapel made to his own orders of scarlet cloth. Moreover, to attract the Tartars to our faith, he had ordered a set of figures to be placed

---

[77] *Olağanüstü makanik araçların bilgisi hakkında kitap* = *The book of knowledge of ingenious mechanical devices* [Bilim vs Teknoloji Dizisi 2] (Ankara, 1990), facsimile edition of Topkapı Sarayı, Sultan Ahmet III, MS 3472.

[78] Al-Jazari, 149–52: Chapter 9 of Category III.   [79] Al-Jazari, 107–9: Chapter 4 of Category II.

[80] L. Olschki, *Guillaume Boucher: A French Artist at the Court of the Khans* (New York, 1946), 60.

[81] *The Mongol Mission*, 66.

[82] William of Rubruck, 114–18, 120. A. C. Moule, *Christians in China before the Year 1550* (London, 1930), 85 and n.15. One possible relic of the Franciscan mission is the so-called *Bibbia di Marco Polo*, a Latin Bible of the thirteenth century which was obtained at Ch'ang-chou in Chiang-su by P. Philip Couplet SJ towards the end of the seventeenth century, and is now in the Laurenziana Library at Florence: A. Tartuferi and F. D'Arelli, eds., *L'arte di Francesco: capolavori d'arte Italiana e terre d'Asia dal XIII al XV secolo* (Florence, 2015), cat. 81.

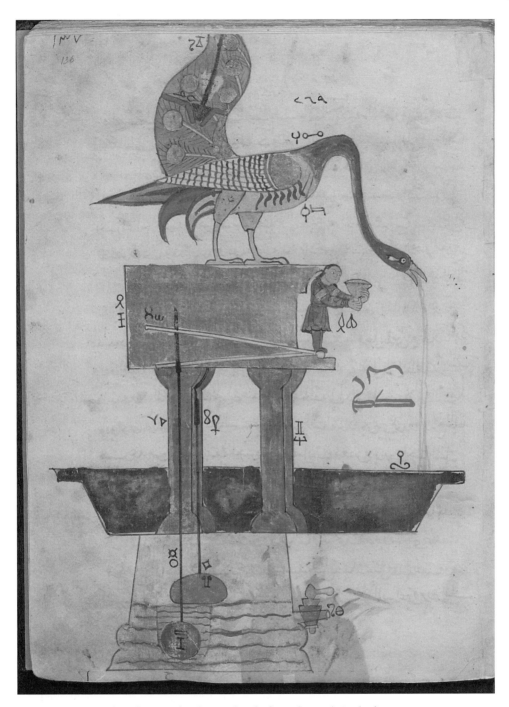

Figure 139 Design for a fountain for cleaning hands, from al-Jazari's *Book of Knowledge of Ingenious Mechanical Devices*; 1206 (TSMK. Ahmet III, 3472, fol. 136a) (For the colour version, please refer to the plate section. In some formats this figure will only appear in black and white)

in this chapel representing every point of our religion: the Annunciation of the Angel, the Nativity, the ceremony of our Lord's Baptism, all the stages of the Passion, the Ascension, and the coming of the Holy Ghost. With the chapel he had also sent cups, books, and everything necessary for the celebration of mass, and two predicant friars to chant the service before the Tartars.[83]

Five years later William of Rubruck described seeing a tent church near Möngke's *ordo*: 'an altar which has been really beautifully decked out. For there was embroidered on a cloth of gold an image of the Saviour, of the Blessed Virgin, of John the Baptist and of two angels, and the lines of the body and of the garments were marked out with pearls.'[84] Quite possibly these were the textiles sent by his king a few years earlier.

Later, in 1265 Maria Palaiologina, an illegitimate daughter of the Byzantine Emperor Michael VIII Palaiologos, was sent to marry Hülegü, Möngke's brother who was set up as the Ilkhan (junior Khan) in Iran; another case of a 'lesser' young woman sacrificed in the hope of world order. The Byzantine chronicler Michael Pachymeres records that Maria journeyed across Asia Minor well prepared. She was accompanied by the abbot of the Pantokrator monastery (Theodosios de Villehardouin), artists and a tent, richly embroidered with images.[85] The artists were employed to paint a church for her, and on their way back to Greece they were persuaded to paint a second church in northern Iraq for the local Syriac community. This they decorated with images of Ezekiel's chariot, prophets, the Evangelists, Church Fathers and the Virgin.[86]

Sending tents to Mongolia might seem like sending coals to Newcastle, but they provided a guaranteed way of inserting Christianity into the visual world of the Mongols.[87] John of Plano Carpini reports that Güyük permanently kept a Christian tent outside his own, their guy ropes intertwined.[88] And the Mongols always needed new and more impressive tents. The most significant such spoil was that captured from the Hungarians at the battle of Mohi in 1241. It was a tent large enough to hold 10,000 people, and was carried by naked Hungarian captives as it journeyed east to Batu's camp. This

---

[83] Joinville, chap XIII (trans. Shaw, 282–3). An almost identical description appears in chap XIII (trans. Shaw, 198).
[84] William of Rubruck, 173–4.   [85] Georgios Pachymeres, 1: 235 (II.3).
[86] J. M. Fiey, *Assyrie chrétienne: contribution à l'étude de l'histoire et de la géographie ecclésiastiques et monastiques du nord de l'Iraq* (Beirut, 1965), 433–4; J. M. Fiey, *Chrétiens syriaques sous les Mongols (Il-Khanat de Perse, XIIIe–XIVe s.)* (Louvain, 1975), 96.
[87] On tents in general see P. A. Andrews, *Felt Tents and Pavilions: The Nomadic Tradition and its Interaction with Princely Tentage* (London, 1999).
[88] *The Mongol Mission*, 68.

was larger than the tents used by the Mongols, and was displayed by Batu in his camp, where it was seen by William of Rubruck more than a decade later.[89]

The decorated Christian tents fitted with Mongol notions of tents as spiritual spaces. William of Rubruck describes the images linked to ancestor worship that he encountered inside Mongol tents, idols he describes as being like dolls, made of felt stuffed with wool.[90] Yet at the same time, with their detailed depictions of Christian saints and the life of Christ, the imported tents would have stood out from the other tents around them, which tended to draw their aesthetic from a different tradition; Möngke Khan's tent, for example, was

> constructed of cloths of splendid texture resembling the green cupola and a model of the highest vault, whereof the designs from the abundance of the embroidery and the beauty of the colouring appeared as a sky with the lights of the stars shining as lanterns, or as a garden wherein flowers and blossom were scattered like pearls. The floor of the tent, covered with carpets of all kinds in all varieties of colour, seemed to be a meadow full of every sort of fragrant herb... The interior was like the Garden of Iram and the exterior fair and pleasant.[91]

Tents could serve a variety of purposes. Louis IX's was certainly a missionary tent, sent to attract and convert the Mongols to Christianity; Maria Palaiologina's, on the other hand, seems to have been more defensive in nature: to provide her with a safe, enclosed space that could reinforce her faith in the face of the competing Christian confessions and rival religions that abounded at the Mongol court, particularly Islam, which, by the 1260s, was growing in influence in the Ilkhanid court. No tents such as Maria's survive from the thirteenth century, which means that everything we know about them comes second hand – from images and descriptions. In art and rhetoric, such tents are shown as more than just portable houses; they are silken metaphors. They are the visible manifestation of their owners' worlds, their exteriors a canvas for the display of power, piety or ambition, their hidden interiors closed worlds, sometimes hinting at erotic desire behind their carefully woven flaps.[92] Because they could move, all these messages could be projected abroad.

---

[89] Andrews, *Felt Tents and Pavilions*, for refs. 504.
[90] *The Mongol Mission*, 95–6, 141.   [91] Juvayni, 2: 570–1.
[92] M. Jeffreys and J. Anderson, 'The Decoration of the Sevastokratorissa's Tent', *Byzantion* 64 (1994), 8–18.

However, whilst such messages might be woven into the fabric of the cloth, art's power to impress or convert was limited, even when it had interpreters with it to help explain. The dangers of passing meanings via art were discovered by William of Rubruck when he first sought to bring Christian imagery before the Khan: 'The Khan [Möngke] had them bring our books – the bible and a breviary – and enquired keenly what the pictures meant. The Nestorians gave him whatever answer they chose, as our interpreter had not accompanied us inside.'[93] It did not matter what the art showed, if there was no one able to explain it. After 5,000 kilometres William's missionary goal was scuppered by having left a man outside the tent (they may have left him outside deliberately, as on the occasion of their previous meeting he had quickly become drunk on the local rice wine).[94] This failure is surely the best riposte to Gregory the Great's dictum that 'art is the bible of the illiterate'.

William of Rubruck lost the theological argument of his pictures because he lost control of the words that accompanied the imagery. For Louis IX the consequences of loss of control of the imagery were much more serious. His tent became not a vehicle for conversion, but evidence of submission. The Khan set the tent up before his entourage, proclaiming: 'My lords, the king of France has sued for mercy and submitted himself to us. Here you can see the tribute he has sent us. If you do not submit to us [like him], we will send for him to destroy you.'[95]

This, then, was the world in which Tamta moved and lived for somewhere between five and nine years. That it opened her eyes to new languages, cultures and religions is undoubted, but its impact upon her remains unknown. The evidence of the daughter of Jalal al-Din who was brought up at Karakorum and was later sent to Mosul in marriage suggests the extent to which some women's lives were transformed by spending their formative years in Asia. She had been brought up as a Muslim, but still arrived in Mosul attired according to Mongol custom. But for others, notably the rulers who travelled for the *kuriltai* of 1246 at which Güyük was acknowledged as Great Khan, it was surely a briefer experience, dominated by the thousands of miles that they had to travel to and from the event.

The cultural consequences of the Mongol invasions took even longer to be felt, no doubt because of the short-term disruption to life across the region that the destruction caused. It took another generation before aspects of east Asian culture became visible in the western lands that they had conquered. Although there had been many embassies that had travelled to

---

[93] William of Rubruck, 190.   [94] William of Rubruck, 178–9.
[95] Joinville, chap XIII (trans. Shaw, 287).

Figure 140 Tiles from the summer palace at Takht-i Sulayman, Iran; 1270s (Los Angeles County Museum of Art, Shinji Shumeikai Acquisition Fund, AC1996.115.1–4; each tile 24.8 cm high)

Karakorum and then returned to Iran, Anatolia and the Caucasus from the 1240s, it is only from the 1270s that we find evidence of them seeking to exploit the Chinese visual language that they saw there to express their own status. A new repertoire of imagery began to appear, weaving Asian features amongst a more familiar repertoire of designs. The Ilkhanid palace at Takht-i Sulayman in north-western Iran was adorned with tiles reminiscent of those that decorated Kaykubad's palace at Kubadabad, but among the animals and scenes from the *Shahname* new images began to appear, including phoenixes and dragons [Fig. 140].[96] And in Armenian Cilicia, John, the

---

[96] L. Komaroff and S. Carboni, eds., *The Legacy of Genghis Khan: Courtly Art and Culture in Western Asia, 1256–1353* (New York, 2002), 75–103.

Figure 141 John, bishop of Grner and brother of King Hetum II, consecrating a priest, from a Gospel book made in 1289 (Yerevan, Matenadaran 197, fol. 341v; 26.3 × 18 cm)

Armenian bishop of Grner and brother of King Hetum II, chose to depict himself consecrating a priest in a Gospel book made in 1289 (Matenadaran 197, fol. 341v). He wears an extraordinary concoction of Latin mitre, Orthodox omophorion, all worn over a silk tunic embroidered with a Chinese dragon [Fig. 141].[97] Judging from relief sculpture, Mongol fashions also

---

[97] Der Nersessian, *Miniature Painting in the Armenian Kingdom of Cilicia*, 96–7, fig. 645; D. Kouymjian, 'Chinese Motifs in Thirteenth-Century Armenian Art: The Mongol Connection', in *Beyond the Legacy of Genghis Khan*, ed. L. Komaroff (Leiden, 2006), 303–24.

began to appear in Greater Armenia in the later thirteenth century as well.[98] But whilst Tamta must have experienced such forms in Karakorum, neither she nor any of the other supplicants to the Mongol court in the first half of the thirteenth century was in a position to bring them back to the west on their return.

[98] R. Ward, ed., *Court and Craft: A Masterpiece from Northern Iraq* (London, 2014).

13 | Tamta as Ruler of Akhlat

> He brought her with him with orders from the Khan that whatever had been hers while wife of Malik Ashraf be given back to her. They obeyed the commands of their king and gave to her Khlat, and the districts surrounding it.[1]

The appearance of a Georgian ambassador at the court of the Mongol Khan presaged the final stage in Tamta's long and varied life. He gained Tamta's release, which came with the condition that 'whatever had been hers while wife of Malik Ashraf be given back to her. They obeyed the commands of their king and gave to her Khlat, and the districts surrounding it.'[2] Tamta's return represents the great turn-about in her life: she left her homeland as a captive and hostage, but returned as ruler. However, as we will see, this was by no means the fairy-tale ending that it might appear.

Kirakos Gandzaketsi names the envoy as Hamadola, presumably the Georgianised version of a name like Shams al-Dawla. He brought with him a letter from Rusudan, Queen of Georgia, in which she requested the return of Tamta, who had been a captive of the Mongols since 1236. The choice of Hamadola as Rusudan's envoy is a surprising one. The name occurs in only one other source, Grigor Aknertsi's *History of the Nation of the Archers*. When Grigor talks about the first battles between the Georgians and the Mongols in the early 1220s (i.e. before the main invasion of the 1230s), he mentions an 'accursed Hamidawla' who deliberately hamstrung Ivane Mqargrdzeli's horse at the moment fighting began, in order to throw the Georgians into confusion. The only explanation for this act of treachery is that it was 'because of some rancour' between the two men.[3] Ivane and his horse seem to have become a common thread in the military defeats of the Georgians in these decades. Hamadola is a very unusual name, and so it is likely that the two events concern the same man. Although the chronicler recorded the enmity between the men, it seems to have been forgotten by Queen Rusudan when she came to select Hamadola for this mission, unless perhaps his actions had earned him some credit among the Mongols.

---

[1] Kirakos, 145. [2] Kirakos, 145. [3] Grigor Aknertsi, 291–3.

Rusudan could certainly turn to other arguments to support her plea for Tamta's return, not least the loyalty the majority of Georgians had shown the Mongols at the battle of Kösedağ, at which the Georgian army had lined up with the Mongols against the Seljuks and their allies.

No account of Hamadola's mission survives; the return of Tamta is its only recorded outcome. We know that he was sent by Rusudan 'at the beginning of the second year after the flight of Sultan Giyath al-Din [Kaykhusraw II]', and this allows us to date Tamta's return to the year 1245, two years after the Seljuk Sultan's defeat at the battle of Kösedağ.[4] These years marked the Mongol consolidation of power in eastern Anatolia and western Armenia, matching the dominance that they had achieved in the Caucasus at the end of the 1230s.

The decision of the Mongols to return Tamta to Akhlat suggests that they believed that she still represented the Ayyubid government in Akhlat, even though no Ayyubid had been in control of the city for more than a decade. However, the fact that Queen Rusudan requested her return indicates that even after her years in captivity Tamta still possessed a complex, multi-faceted identity which enabled her to retain a value and relevance among the different groups across the region. Her existence as the daughter of Ivane and sister of Avag, two successive *atabeg*s to the Georgian throne, meant that she was related to some of the most powerful men at the Georgian court, and this must have been a significant factor in Rusudan's request. This is the one moment where we see the ties of kinship coming to Tamta's aid from the male members of her family. The fact that Tamta was able so quickly to resume power in Akhlat (or at least that no reports of revolts against her are known) indicates that to the Armenians and others in Akhlat she was still regarded as their ruler, although she now had to mediate between them and her Mongol overlords, rather than the Turkic and Arabic powers that had previously been in power. It was convenient for all sides to believe that Tamta had inherited rule of the city and its surroundings from her husband.

Working for the Mongols

In the face of the Mongol attacks, populations had two choices: to resist and face destruction, death or captivity; or to surrender and live, but live under oppressively heavy taxation.[5] Unsurprisingly, few chose to resist. After submitting, the Mongols generally reappointed many of the local nobles,

---

[4] Sebastatsi in *Armianskie istochniki*, 26. [5] Grigor Aknertsi, 313.

who now had to act as their agents. Tamta was just one example of the way in which the Mongols now sought to manipulate the government of the territories that they now controlled. In order to contain the power of Rusudan in Georgia, the Mongols released Davit Ulu, the illegitimate son of Giorgi IV Lasha, who had been sent to the court of Kaykhusraw II to be with his cousin Gurji Khatun (Tamar, the daughter of Rusudan), where he had been imprisoned in order to prevent him from threatening Rusudan's legitimacy.[6] He was crowned as king in Mtskheta in a service orchestrated by Tamta's brother, Avag. Davit Ulu's rise forced Rusudan to flee with her own legitimate son, Davit Narin, to Svaneti, the remotest corner of Georgia, high in the mountains of the Caucasus.[7] This policy was orchestrated by Ayltana Khatun, the wife of Chormaqan, who now held the khanate in the region after the death of her husband.[8] When Töregene Khatun summoned the *kuriltai* in 1246 to elect Güyük, the two Davits were required to attend to swear loyalty. They were ordered to share power in Georgia by the new Khan, but when they returned from Karakorum it was Tamta's brother Avag who was left to mediate between them.[9] To make it work, Avag effectively divided the country in two between the cousins, Davit Narin ruling to the west of the Likhi mountains that divide Georgia from north to south, Davit Ulu to the east. Elsewhere in the Caucasus, other families were given greater autonomy once they had demonstrated their loyalty to the Mongols.[10] The Jaqelis in Samtskhe (southern Georgia) and the Orbelians in Siunik (southern Armenia) both used this to build local power bases that were to gain increasing independence of their regions over the next century, contributing to the decentralisation and disruption of both states.

The Mongols imposed three main requirements on their vassals: to fight for them as and when required; to maintain order in their lands; and to collect taxes. This final requirement, with the increasingly onerous burden it imposed on everyone, made the second ever harder.

War

The Mongols required those who submitted to them to fight for them. In order to supplement the native Mongol troops, whose nomadic system

---

[6] *Kartlis Tskhovreba*, 328, 335–8 (exile), 343–4 (return).   [7] Kirakos, 143.
[8] Grigor Aknertsi, 315–17.   [9] Kirakos, 156–7.
[10] H. Conrad, 'Beobachtungen und Notizien zur Situation der armenischen Fürsten unter der Mongolenherrschaft', in *Caucasus during the Mongol Period – Der Kaukasus in der Mongolenzeit*, eds. J. Tubach, S. Vashalomidze and M. Zimmer (Wiesbaden, 2012), 83–105.

required constant movement to find pasture for their horses, the involvement of local men was important. This was particularly needed when there was the prospect of a prolonged siege. Conscription was imposed as soon as the submission was agreed. Although Tamta could not be made to fight herself, it is likely that she was required to supply troops from Akhlat and its surroundings for the Mongolian army. Tamta's brother, Avag, was very quickly involved in Mongolian warfare. Immediately after surrendering at his castle at Kayean in 1236 Avag was enrolled in the army of his besieger, the Mongol general Chormaqan, that marched on Ani.[11] Ani, once the most important city of the Mqargrdzelis, had been inherited by Avag's cousin Shahanshah (the eldest son of Zakare), but he was away from the city at his castle in Lore and the city elders were unsure how to proceed.[12] Whilst they debated, a mob seized the Mongolian ambassadors in the city and killed them, believing that the new walls built by Zakare and Ivane in the 1210s would protect them. Their faith was misplaced; the city was quickly captured and the citizens massacred or led into slavery. The fall of the city was lamented in the colophon of a Gospel book (Nor Julfa Library, MS 36/156) made the same year at the nearby monastery of Khtskonk:

> This was written in a bitter and difficult time, in the year when the mother of cities Ani was taken and innumerable souls perished in blood. Which mouth of tongue can relate the cruelty of the lawless Tatars in the year 685 [= 1236]?... Let us recount the God-sent wrath that came upon the lands of the Armenians and Georgians and Tajiks from the human-faced beasts the Tatars, the bitterness and turmoil of our times, since the mind cannot conceive and the tongue cannot tell the shedding of blood and the massacre of all... There is no count to the cities and regions that were ruined right up to our borders.[13]

Avag was then required to march on Kars immediately afterwards. Having seen the fate of its near neighbour, Kars tried to surrender, but this was ignored by the Mongols and a second massacre occurred. (And after the Mongols withdrew, the city was sacked for a second time by the Seljuk Sultan Kaykhusraw II, who took into captivity all those who had survived the Mongols.) The continuing favour shown by the Mongols to Avag in these years indicates that he fought well for his new masters, and was clearly prepared to attack and kill his compatriots in order to preserve his position. Such conflicts of interest must have been faced by all the new Armenian and Georgian vassals in these decades.

[11] Kirakos, 126–8. [12] Mutafian, 'Ani after Ani', 161.
[13] Vardanyan, ed., *Hoṙomos Monastery*, 344 n.52.

The Georgian and Armenian troops could be required to fight anywhere in the region. Most famously, Georgians and Armenians were called on by Möngke Khan to participate in his great campaigns in the 1250s. For seven years they fought to destroy the Assassins, the Isma'ili sect in northern Iran, a campaign led by the Mongols' Nestorian Christian commander Kitbugha.[14] This was followed by the siege of Baghdad in 1258, ordered by Möngke's successor, Hülegü Khan. The army included a contingent led by Zakare Mqargrdzeli, Shahanshah's son. Despite the size and wealth of the city, the siege lasted just twelve days before the city fell. Bar Hebraeus reports that the Georgians 'especially effected a great slaughter'.[15] The Georgians had already gained a strong reputation for fighting among the Mongols. When the Franciscan Benedict the Pole returned from his mission to the Mongols in the late 1240s, he reported:

> While they were staying there, they often met Georgians who lived among the Tartars and were highly respected by them as brave and warlike men. These people are called Georgians because they invoke St George in their wars and have him as patron and honour him beyond all other saints. They use the Greek version of Holy Scripture and have crosses on their camps and their carts. They follow the Greek rites in divine worship among the Tartars.[16]

The fall of Baghdad led to the death of the last generally recognised Caliph, al-Musta'sim (r. 1242–58), who was kicked to death rolled up inside a carpet or some sackcloth in order to avoid spilling royal blood onto the ground.[17] Marco Polo later provided a more poetic, alternative account of his end: Hülegü locked the Caliph up with all his gold, which he had refused to spend on the defence of the city: 'Now caliph, eat your fill of treasure for you will get nothing else.'[18] He died after four days.[19]

The fall of Baghdad was one of the defining moments of the Middle Ages, marking the close of an era in the Muslim world, as it ended the Abbasid caliphate which had been the primary source of Islamic Sunni legitimacy since the eighth century.[20] From the Mongol point of view it was just one more city to be conquered, albeit a particularly rich one. More often, the Georgian and Armenian troops in the Mongol army were involved in smaller-scale attacks, often fought in territories with large Armenian

---

[14] F. Daftary, *The Ismaʿīlīs: Their History and Doctrines* (Cambridge, 2007), 391–9.
[15] Bar Hebraeus, 431. [16] *The Mongol Mission*, 82. [17] Bar Hebraeus, 505–6.
[18] Marco Polo, 63–4. [19] Grigor Aknertsi, 335, combines the two accounts.
[20] The Abbasid caliphate was revived by the Mamluks in Cairo in 1261, but never again had the same authority.

populations. Grigor Aknertsi reports that in 1239 the city of Erzurum was attacked: 'They captured it and cruelly slaughtered and plundered the rich and beautiful town. Likewise they depopulated the monasteries of the country and the marvellous churches, taking captives and plundering.'[21] The Georgian and Armenian troops were being forced to attack and suppress their own populations. The chronicles make no mention of the ethical dilemmas that they must have faced; instead, they try to point out what could be gained. Grigor continues: 'Then the Armenian and Georgian princes took away many books – heortologia [books of religious festivals], martyrologia, the Apostolic works, lectionaries, Acts and the Gospels written in gold, rich adorned beyond comparison for the edification and adornment of the sons of the new Sion – and brought them to the eastern country and filled the monasteries with all the adornments of the Church.'[22] Kirakos has the same story.[23] Some of this redistribution was carried out openly, with the Christians in the army buying other books from the Mongol soldiers they fought alongside, before then donating these sacred texts to their home monasteries. Other efforts to support Christians within the captured cities, notably the ransoming of priests and clerics (whose release was perhaps seen as more of a threat by the Mongol authorities), had to be conducted more furtively.[24]

Perhaps the most extreme case came when Armenians, including Avag, his cousin Shahanshah and his vassal Hasan Prosh, were required to besiege Mayyafariqin, the northernmost Ayyubid base in the Jazira before the capture of Akhlat.[25] It took two years to reduce the city, leading to a situation far worse than that faced in Akhlat in 1229–30.

> They ate clean and unclean animals and then started to eat people when there was no more food. The strong ate the weak. When the [supply of] poor people was exhausted they turned against one another. Fathers ate sons, and women ate their daughters; and they did not spare the fruit of their wombs. Lovers renounced their loved ones and friends, their acquaintances. And the food supply had so diminished that one *litr* of human flesh sold for seventy *dahekans*. Men and food were entirely exhausted, and not just there [in the city], but danger threatened many other districts for those who were besieging the city harassed the land already subjugated by the Tatars with tax collecting and with conveying food and drink for them. Many people died from the extreme cold of the snow which covered the mountains in wintertime.[26]

---

[21] Grigor Aknertsi, 307. [22] Grigor Aknertsi, 307–9. [23] Kirakos, 138–9.
[24] Kirakos, 139–41. [25] Stepanos Orbelian, 228.
[26] Kirakos, 187–9 (trans. Bedrosian, 110).

The price of the almost meatless head of a donkey reached thirty dirhams, almost the equivalent of a month's salary for Saladin's astrologer.[27] Many of those forced to turn to cannibalism were Armenian Christians, kinsfolk of their besiegers. However, Armenian chroniclers tend to gloss over this inconvenient truth, and concentrate once more on what the besiegers gained from the fall of the city. When Mayyafariqin finally fell to the Mongols in 1260 the Armenian troops in the army rushed in to rescue Christian relics. The bones of martyrs of Diocletian's persecutions of the third century had been gathered in the city by its bishop, St Maruta (c. 399–410), giving the city its alternative name of Martyropolis, the 'City of Martyrs'.[28] The soldiers then gave these captured relics to their monasteries. Haghbat managed to acquire the hand of the Apostle St Bartholomew: 'And it really is still there.'[29] No longer, as this relic is now lost; but the importance of his cult in the region is well attested: Bartholomew was believed to have been martyred to the south-east of Lake Van (a monastery was built over the site in the thirteenth century), and the island monastery of Aghtamar was known as the seat of St Bartholomew. A silver gilt reliquary containing his staff, which was possibly originally made for that monastery in the tenth century, was treasured in the region (it was restored in the fifteenth century in a nearby village, and is now at the patriarchal seat in Echmiadzin).[30] Thus the arrival of the Mongols in eastern Anatolia perversely proved to be of great benefit to the monasteries in Greater Armenia itself. Whilst the cities and monasteries in western Armenia were ransacked, their booty was transferred further east to the old heartlands of the Mqargrdzelis and their allies.

Taxation

In addition to fighting for the Mongols, the Georgian and Armenian lords that they set up as their vassals had to maintain order in their own lands, and to collect taxes. These taxes were based on censuses that the Mongols conducted soon after they gained control. A census was conducted in Seljuk

---

[27] For the cost of the donkey: Grigor Aknertsi, 335; for the wages of Saladin's astrologer: Ashtor, *Histoire des prix et des salaires*, 264.

[28] The Muslim geographer Yaqut al-Hamawi (*Muʿjam al-Buldan: Jacut's Geographisches Wörterbuch: aus den Handschriften zu Berlin, St. Petersburg, Paris, London und Oxford*, ed. F. Wüstenfeld (Leipzig, 1866), VII/VIII, 350), was similarly aware of the power of these Christian relics, which he believed had prevented the fall of the city until this point.

[29] Grigor Aknertsi, 335–7.

[30] Durand et al., eds., *Armenia Sacra*, cat. 72; V. Nersessian, *Treasures from the Ark: 1700 Years of Armenian Christian Art* (London, 2001), cat. 22.

Figure 142 Coin of Tamta from Akhlat; *c.* 1250 (Tübingen no. 99–14–54)

Rum immediately after its capture in 1239. This was followed by a second major census conducted across the region by Möngke Khan in 1251. According to the *History of the Nation of the Archers*, men were charged at 60 spitaks (aspers) a head; those who hid to avoid the poll tax were beaten, and then given over to be eaten alive by dogs. The severity of this tax was likened to the devastation caused by a swarm of locusts.[31] Under Hülegü the taxes increased:

> Hülegü commanded that the tax called *taghar* be collected from each individual listed in the royal register. From such he demanded 100 *litrs* of grain, 50 *litrs* of wine, 2 *litrs* of rice and [of] husks 3 sacks, 1 spitak [silver coin], 1 arrow, to say nothing of the bribes; and of 20 animals they demanded 1, plus 20 spitaks. From those who could not pay they took their sons and daughters as payment.[32]

In order to supply the taxes local rulers needed to re-establish mints. Coins minted at Akhlat from 1245 on indicate that coinage was a key concern of Tamta's on her return to the city. She minted a series of coins in the city decorated with a horseman shooting an arrow backwards, and a series of Arabic inscriptions naming her Mongol overlord and proclaiming Allah [Fig. 142].[33] The dominance of Arabic on the coin reflected the need to re-establish a trusted monetary standard as quickly as possible by reviving old

---

[31] Grigor Aknertsi, 323–5.   [32] Kirakos, 182 (trans. Bedrosian, 107).
[33] A. Vardanyan, 'Some Additions to the Coins with the Inscription "Ulugh Mangyl Ulus (Ulush) Bek"', *Journal of the Oriental Numismatic Society* 190/1 (2007), 7–20, at 8 (Tübingen no. 99-14-54).

coinage; and this seems to have been standard practice in the region: Queen Rusudan of Georgia issued almost identical coins.[34]

Tax collection fell to local lords such as Tamta. It was their duty to ensure that the money and goods were collected and passed on to the Mongols. This drove a wedge between the aristocracy and those they ruled. If Tamta's survival in Akhlat over four decades had been because of the way that she could identify with the people she ruled as a Christian and an Armenian, and to mediate between them and their Muslim overlords, the new role of the nobility now required the opposite, and separated her from those she ruled. People were quick to realise that many noblemen used the opportunity to enrich themselves. Even Kirakos Gandzaketsi, normally a supporter of the Mqargrdzeli elite, was unable to condone their practices: 'furthermore the princes, the lords of the districts, became the Mongols' co-workers in harassing and demanding taxes for their own profit'.[35] Whilst the nobility had collected taxes to fund their own lives before the Mongol conquests, the increased level of taxation made the additional self-interested element very divisive. It also encouraged people to reflect once more upon the identity of those who ruled them. For Kirakos Gandzaketsi, it is clear that to become one of these Mongol-appointed local lords was to forfeit being an Armenian: 'The princes deprived and robbed the poor, and from this extortion they bought expensive clothing and they dressed, ate, drank and boasted greatly, as is the arrogant custom of the Georgians.'[36] Before, Tamta had succeeded by being able to shift her identity, now one particular identity was being thrust upon her.

Mongol taxation was not just a one-way enterprise, despite the impression given by chroniclers in the thirteenth century. There could only be taxes to collect if there was an economy to generate wealth. As a result, once the initial conquests had finished in the late 1230s, the Mongols began to reinstate the society that they had just destroyed in order to provide an economic base for them to tax. Immediately after the sack of Ani and Kars, those who survived (and had avoided captivity) were allowed to return from their refuges to rebuild their villages and towns, although they no longer had clothes or houses, or oxen to till the fields. Fortunately they had a mild winter and there was enough wild grain to feed them until the next spring. Kirakos notes that even 'the merciless Georgian people displayed much kindness and concern for the [Armenian] exiles reaching them'.[37] The process of reviving the agricultural economy became more serious with

---

[34] H. C. Evans, ed., *Byzantium: Faith and Power (1261–1557)* (New York, 2004), cat. 256H.
[35] Kirakos, 175.   [36] Kirakos, 158.   [37] Kirakos, 129.

the appointment of Hülegü as the Ilkhan (junior Khan) of Iran: '[Hülegü] began to rebuild the devastated places, and from each inhabited village he selected householders, one from the small, and two or three from the large villages, and he called them *iam*, and sent them to all of the destroyed places to undertake rebuilding'.[38]

There were also attempts by local Armenian and Georgian lords to reduce the burden of taxation. The series of tax reductions recorded on the church of the Holy Apostles in Ani that were discussed in Chapter 6 all refer to this period of Mongol/Ilkhanid fiscal persecution.

Rebellion

The rebellions that were fuelled by the Mongols' taxation put the Armenian and Georgian elites in impossible positions. Forced to support the invaders, they had to condemn their own people against their oppressors. The greatest beneficiaries of the arrival of the Mongols had been the Armenian elite in Cilicia. They had quickly sided with the Mongols in a bid to secure support against the Seljuks and the Ayyubids who oppressed them from the north and the east. This policy had been remarkably successful, but it came at a cost. In 1251 the Armenian Catholicos was forced to preach homilies condemning revolts by his Christian flock against their pagan tormentors, on the grounds that they were a threat to the Armenians in Cilicia and the survival of their state. The ethical questionability of such contorted logic marked a growing split between the Armenians in Greater Armenia and the King and Catholicos in Cilicia who supposedly led them.

The division between Greater Armenia and Cilicia, between the ruling class and those they taxed, further widened the splits that were fracturing Armenia. However, this was not simply the start of class warfare. Not all nobles were prepared to accept the new status quo. Zakare, the son of Shahanshah Mqargrdzeli, was one who could not live with the position that he found himself in. William of Rubruck met him on his return from Karakorum and concluded that 'the overlordship of the Tatars goes so much against the grain with him that although he owns an abundance of everything he would rather be an exile in a foreign land than endure their rule'.[39] He resisted the new census of 1254, and was later executed after leading

---

[38] Grigor Aknertsi, 345. *Iam* is usually taken to refer to the postal relay stations established by the Mongols.
[39] William of Rubruck, 269.

an attempted revolt in 1261.⁴⁰ He was buried in the family mausoleum church built by his father at Kobayr, a little further up the Debed gorge from Akhtala.⁴¹

Other attempts to displace the Mongols also failed. Grigor Aknertsi, writing of the year 1249, paints a cruel picture of the impotence of the Georgians and Armenians as, fuelled by too much food and drink, they boasted of the strength of their forces and drunkenly fantasised about their ability to defeat the Mongols. In the atmosphere of fear and retribution that pervaded during these years, one of their number quickly betrayed them to the Mongols. Many were arrested to answer charges of treason and sedition, including the Georgian King, Davit Ulu, and Tamta's brother, Avag. However, when Avag arrived on a litter as he was too ill to ride a horse, the Mongols quickly understood how empty the threat of rebellion was, and further punishment was suspended.⁴² Kirakos Gandzaketsi provides a different account of these events, implying that it was Avag who betrayed his fellow nobles and his King (who were all punished by being left bound hand and foot for three days), and that his mother Khoshak played a significant part in assuring the Mongols that Avag had always been loyal. Khoshak's apparent importance in this indicates the changing position of women under Mongol rule.

Women

What is most apparent from the Mongol invasion is that it drew Tamta back into the political world of Georgia and Armenia, after the decades which she spent as al-Ashraf's wife. During those years she almost certainly remained in Akhlat and was closely involved with the wider Armenian population, but there is no evidence that she played an active role in the politics of her homeland. In the last years of her life, however, once she was back in Akhlat as its Mongol governor, she seems to have become more involved. As throughout her life, Tamta's ability to re-enter the Georgian court was limited by her gender. In order to circumvent this, she needed to find a man to work through. Kirakos Gandzaketsi suggests that she found a promising candidate: the illegitimate son of her brother Avag.⁴³ Avag had no legitimate heir: he had a daughter, Khoshak, with his wife Gontsa (Guantsa in

---

⁴⁰ Mutafian, 'Ani after Ani', 162.
⁴¹ Kalandia and Asatiani, 'Koberis I da II sametsniero eskpeditsiis pirveladi shedegebi (sainpormatsio mimokhilva)', 184.
⁴² Grigor Aknertsi, 321–3.   ⁴³ Kirakos, 159.

Georgian; she was a noblewoman from the Kakhaberidze family in Racha in western Georgia),[44] but he certainly had an illegitimate son with another, unknown woman. When Avag died in 1250 he was buried at Akhtala, alongside his father Ivane, but his inheritance was confiscated and passed over to his cousin Zakare. Tamta took the illegitimate son to bring up in her own household. Presumably she hoped that he would eventually inherit Avag's lands, in the same way that Giorgi IV's illegitimate son, Davit Ulu, had been raised to the Georgian throne by Avag at the command of the Mongols. She is therefore a strong candidate for being responsible for rumours that began to circulate after Avag's death that the son was, in fact, legitimate.

In the end Tamta was to be thwarted in her hopes, as she faced a formidable opponent with ambitions to match her own: her sister-in-law Gontsa, Avag's widow.[45] Dispossessed of land on Avag's death, and with no male heir of her own to work through, Gontsa still managed to fight back. First she succeeded in reclaiming Avag's inheritance from Zakare, and was able to administer it in her own name; an inscription in the monastery of Goshavank records a tax remission to the monks secured 'under the government of Gontsa Khatun'.[46] In this she was probably supported by the Chalcedonian Christian faction at the Georgian court, which would have been unhappy to see those lands passed over to the side of the Mqargrdzeli family that still adhered to the Armenian Apostolic Church.[47] She then managed to fortify her position and secure her place at the heart of the court: she married the Georgian king, Davit Ulu, and so became joint queen of Georgia (their co-ruler Davit Narin, was married to another Georgian noblewoman, Tamar Amanelisdze; later he would marry an illegitimate daughter in the ruling Palaiologan family of Byzantium). Davit Ulu's lands, concentrated in the eastern half of Georgia, combined with those of Avag (now Gontsa's) immediately to the south, gave the couple a powerful and wealthy estate. Gontsa proceeded to try to extend her control further south into Armenia. This led her into conflict with the powerful local Orbelian family, who controlled the region of Siunik, and had preserved their territories by submitting to the Mongols as Avag had. Smbat Orbelian was forced to travel to Karakorum in 1251 to defend his right to his lands. He spent three years at the Mongol court, but finally succeeded in saving his lands after Möngke Khan witnessed a miraculous vision of the cross rise from

---

[44] *Kartlis Tskhovreba*, 351. [45] Conrad, 'Beobachtungen und Notizien', 95–6.
[46] Augé, 'Gošavank', no. 173.
[47] Vardan, 212 records that Zakare's son, Shahanshah, had been brought up as a Chalcedonian by Ivane's wife, Khoshak.

a reliquary in Smbat's tent (his earlier gift of a precious jewel to the Great Khan may also have been a factor in winning support).[48] Möngke gave him a golden *paiza* (passport) to expedite his return to Armenia, along with a *yarligh* (decree) confirming the extent of his territories and excising his name from the register of vassals to the Georgian King. Smbat's tomb at Noravank, the mausoleum church of the Orbelian family, even names him as King.[49] Ultimately, Gontsa's plans were abruptly ended in 1261/2, when she was executed in the aftermath of her husband's failed revolt against Hülegü, although *Kartlis Tskhovreba* says it was instigated by her daughter Khoshak, then married to the senior administrator of the Mongols, Shams al-Din (brother of the historian Juvayni), who had been effectively cut out of her inheritance by her mother.[50] These politically active women could present a sequel to this tale: the next generations of Mqargrdzeli women who built a life for themselves that shifted easily between cultures, adept at manipulating political circumstances to their ends and with a public presence at court, and in monumental inscriptions and buildings.

The absence of Tamta's name from all these intrigues featuring her brother and his wife reflects the chroniclers' continued lack of interest in her. It also suggests that being based in Akhlat away from the lands directly under the rule of the Kings and Queens of Georgia meant that she stood outside the immediate jockeying for power and position that the Mongol conquests opened up.

Women and the Mongols

The return of Tamta as ruler of Akhlat, the ability of Khoshak to intervene in politics, and the rise to dominance of Gontsa in the next generation are examples of the remarkable change in gender politics after the Mongol conquests. This must partly be explained by the very different attitudes that the Mongols had to women and power. The change is visible at a general level, but also in the precise circumstances around Tamta's release. The cultural traditions of the Mongol world accorded women much higher status and independent power than they received among the peoples they conquered to their west. The women who married into the family of Genghis Khan and his relatives possessed considerable rights. Each organised her own *ordo* (court) with multiple tents, transported on up to two hundred

---

[48] Stepanos Orbelian, 228–31.
[49] Stepanos Orbelian, pt 2: 97; Dashdondog, *The Mongols and the Armenians*, 77.
[50] *Kartlis Tskhovreba*, 359; Margarian, 'Ṣāḥib-Dīvān', 172–3.

carts, some of which required twenty-two oxen to pull them.⁵¹ They had independent wealth, could own property and conduct trade, all of which could be passed on to other women on their deaths; they could command armies and even fight; and they determined the faith and education of their children.⁵²

Töregene Khatun, the de facto ruler of Mongolia during much of Tamta's captivity, was the most formidable of these women. After the death of her husband, Ögodei Khan, in 1241, she had assumed rule until a successor was chosen. As her favoured son, Güyük, was too young to succeed his father, Töregene spun out the regency for five years until he was old enough to be elected at the *kuriltai* that Töregene then convened (this was the *kuriltai* to which Hetum of Cilicia, the two Davits of Georgia, the Seljuk Sultan, Badr al-Din Lu'lu' of Mosul and so many other vassal rulers were summoned). Sources, whether Christian, Arabic or Persian, all praise her wisdom and discretion.⁵³ Töregene initiated tax collections, redistributed fiefs among emirs,⁵⁴ and was involved in the reshuffling of senior ministers, such as Yeh-lü Ch'u-ts'ai, 'Abd al-Rahman and Mahmud Yalavach.⁵⁵ She also had coins minted in her name. At the same time she promoted other women to administer the empire alongside her, including a former slave called Fatima from Mashhad in Iran: 'her influence became paramount; so that she became the sharer of intimate confidences and the depository of hidden secrets, and the ministers were debarred from executing business, and she was free to issue commands and prohibitions'.⁵⁶

Töregene can be set in a pattern of powerful Mongolian women at the start of the thirteenth century, including her sister-in-law Sorghaghtani Beki (d. 1252), who became mother to two successive Great Khans, Möngke (r. 1251–9) and Kublai (r. 1260–94), as well as the first Ilkhan of Iran, Hülegü (1256–65). John of Plano Carpini, garbling the Mongolian, named her as Soroctan in his account of his travels, and said of her that 'among the Tartars this lady is the most renowned, with the exception of the Emperor's mother [Töregene], and more powerful than anyone else except Batu [Genghis Kahn's grandson and commander in the west]'.⁵⁷ She inherited her husband Tolui's *ordo* and his *ulus* (territorial inheritance) in Mongolia and northern

---

⁵¹ William of Rubruck, 74; *The Mongol Mission*, 17–18, 95, 117, 154.

⁵² For a full account of these see B. De Nicola, 'Unveiling the Khatuns: Some Aspects of the Role of Women in the Mongol Empire' (Ph.D. thesis, University of Cambridge, 2011). William of Rubruck, 76. T. T. Allsen, *Culture and Conquest in Mongol Eurasia* (Cambridge, 2001), 30.

⁵³ Bar Hebraeus, 410–11; Juvayni, 1: 239–44. ⁵⁴ Juvayni, 2: 507.

⁵⁵ M. Rossabi, 'The Muslims in the Early Yüan Dynasty', in *China under Mongol Rule*, ed. J. D. Langlois (Princeton, 1981), 257–95, at 267–8.

⁵⁶ Juvayni, 1: 245; Rashid al-Din, 176. ⁵⁷ *The Mongol Mission*, 26.

China when he died in 1229. She was heavily involved in the negotiations that led to Güyük Khan's election in 1246, and she later tried to thwart Güyük's attempt to attack his cousin Batu in Russia.[58] And she commanded his army after 1232.[59]

Tamta's return to Akhlat must be set against this background of female power in Mongolia. Her release was the result of a diplomatic encounter between two ruling women – Töregene and Rusudan – concerning a third woman about to resume a position of power. More generally, all sides in the negotiations were familiar with women holding power: in Mongolia their ability to exercise power was well established, and in Georgia a queen had been on the throne for almost fifty of the last sixty years (Tamar: 1184–1210; Rusudan 1223–45). The impact of this changing culture became more evident towards the end of Tamta's life as more women began to emerge in independent power in Mongol realms. In south-eastern Iran under Ilkhanid rule, Terkan Khatun was able to assume power in Kerman after the death of her husband, the local Emir, Qutb al-Din Muhammad in 1257. By forging links with the Mongol regime she managed to rule independently until 1281, gaining direct control of the army, and even, according to some sources, having her name pronounced in the *khutba*.[60] She was later succeeded by her daughter Padishah Khatun, who had spent a decade in Anatolia, and who maintained female power in the region for a further five years.

The position of women was not absolute, however. In every case these women came to power through men – either as widows, wives or regents – and it was this that gave them legitimacy. It seems that only the Queens of Georgia ever claimed power through their own blood in this period. Moreover, these Mongol women still faced opposition, much of which was presented in gendered terms. This was particularly true for women who did not come from within the limited number of noble families that provided the majority of the important wives that each of the Khans married. Fatima, the increasingly dominant adviser to Töregene, attracted particular opposition, and Töregene was unable to prevent her removal from the government. Unlike her male counterparts, who faced straightforward charges of bribery or treason as a means to disgrace them, Fatima's downfall involved more pernicious accusations, all determined by her gender. She was linked with prostitution and pimping, and charged with sorcery. After being stripped naked and tortured, she had her orifices 'upper and lower'

---

[58] Rashid al-Din, 185.   [59] De Nicola, 'Unveiling the Khatuns', 147.
[60] De Nicola, 'Unveiling the Khatuns', 110–13; A. K. S. Lambton, *Continuity and Change in Medieval Persia: Aspects of Administrative, Economic and Social History, 11th–14th Century* (New York, 1988), 281–2.

sewn up, was wrapped up in a felt blanket and was thrown into a river to drown.[61]

Mongols and Christians

The women in charge of Mongolia at the time of Tamta's release had one other quality which perhaps made them more amenable to the idea: they were Christians. Both Töregene and Sorghaghtani Beki professed Nestorian Christianity. Although William of Rubruck was very rude about the Nestorians in the account of his travels he wrote for Louis IX of France, it is clear that they were still far more sympathetic to their co-religionists of all confessions than to followers of other religions. The number of senior women in the Mongol world who professed Christianity may well have been one of the causes of the confusion that had flourished since the 1220s about whether or not the Mongols were Christian, and whether they would prove to be allies in the fight against the Muslim states. This was part of the enthusiasm that led to the missions of friars such as William of Rubruck. Even fifty years later the flame of hope was still being fanned. The *Flower of Histories of the East*, a polemical history written in 1307 by the nephew of the King of Armenian Cilicia, aimed to encourage a new crusade and tantalised its readers with the supposed deal between Hetum and Möngke Khan in the early 1250s, at which the Great Khan agreed to be baptised, to restore all Armenian lands and churches, to free the Armenians of taxation and to facilitate pilgrimage to the Holy Land.[62]

This was clearly a fantasy, but there was enough fact surrounding it to give it credence to the work's readers. This was most evident when Möngke died, to be succeeded by his brother Hülegü, who became the first Ilkhan of Iran. Hülegü's most favoured wife was Doquz Khatun, a fervent Nestorian Christian. She had a linen tent in the form of a church with a wooden clapper.[63] She certainly aided the Christians: after the fall of Baghdad in 1258 it was her orders that spared the lives of the Christians in the city.[64] The royal palace was handed over to the Nestorian Patriarch, Mar Makkikha – confirming the old fear recounted in Juvayni's *History* of a Christian Patriarch being installed in the Caliph's palace (although Juvayni had worried it would be the Georgian Catholicos).[65] To the delight of Christian

---

[61] Juvayni, 1: 246. [62] Hayton, 164–7. [63] Vardan, 217. [64] Kirakos, 184–6.
[65] J. M. Fiey, *Chrétiens syriaques sous les Abbassides surtout à Bagdad (749–1258)* (Louvain, 1980), 273–4; Fiey, *Chrétiens syriaques sous les Mongols*, 24; Juvayni, 2: 426.

commentators, Hülegü also passed a law requiring Muslims under his rule to feed and care for pigs, and then to eat the meat of the slaughtered animals. The Christians were relieved that his ferocity was aimed against others: 'he was a great shedder of blood, but he slew only the wicked and his enemies, and not the good or righteous. He loved the Christian people more than the infidels.'[66] Other Mongol princesses became patrons of churches in Armenia. In the 1250s Baiju's Nestorian wife funded the restoration of the monastery at Tatev in southern Armenia.[67]

The Armenian chronicler Stepanos Orbelian, writing towards the end of the thirteenth century, even celebrated Hülegü Khan and Doquz Khatun as a new Constantine and Helena, the first Christian Emperors.[68] This vision paralleled that of the Syriac Christians who gave Constantine and Helena clearly Mongol features in the Gospel Lectionary now in the Vatican (Syr. 559, fol. 223v) [Fig. 143].[69] For others, the Mongols' origins in the east encouraged different, but equally grand, religious associations. Christian attention was particularly focused on Kitbugha, Hülegü's Nestorian general who led the Mongol campaign against the new Mamluk dynasty that emerged in Syria and Egypt after the death of Shajar al-Durr in 1250. The Christians in the Holy Land saw him as a potential saviour against their Muslim enemies, and so began to weave myths around his faith and his origins. Hetum's *Flower of Histories of the East* describes Kitbugha as 'of the lineage of the three kings who had come to Bethlehem to adore the nativity of Our Lord', echoing the words of the New Testament that the Magi were 'wise men from the east' (Matt. 2:1).[70] However, this was not the first time the link between the Mongols and the Magi had been made. In the 1260s a Byzantine artist at St Catherine's monastery on Mount Sinai painted the epistyle for a templon screen in the monastery. The twelve scenes he painted included the Adoration of the Magi, and one of the three wise men is given distinctly Mongol features.[71] This has often been interpreted as visual praise of the Mongol general. He was involved in the sack of Baghdad, but was killed by the Mamluks at the decisive battle of 'Ayn Jalut in 1260, which prevented the Mongols from invading Syria.

There was therefore a degree of sympathy between the Christian Mongols and their co-religionists in the Caucasus and eastern Anatolia which was bolstered by the military support that the Georgians and Armenians offered to the Mongols during their campaigns, leading up to the assault

---

[66] Grigor Aknertsi, 344.   [67] Stepanos Orbelian, 231–2.   [68] Stepanos Orbelian, 234–5.
[69] Leroy, *Les manuscrits syriaques*, 297.   [70] Hayton, 174.
[71] K. Weitzmann, 'Icon Painting in the Crusader Kingdom', *DOP* 20 (1966), 51–83, at 63–4; Hunt, 'Eastern Christian Art', 341.

Figure 143 Sts Constantine and Helena with Mongolian features, from a Syriac lectionary, copied at the monastery of Mar Mattai, near Mosul, Iraq; 1219–20 (Biblioteca Apostolica Vaticana, Syr. 559, fol. 223v; 43.5 × 33.5 cm)

on Baghdad in 1258. This alliance would have made it easier to make a case for the return of Tamta to Akhlat. Her position would have been further strengthened by the attitude towards women and power that prevailed among the Mongols. This is not to say that there was some sisterhood to promote women, but simply that Tamta may well have been regarded differently by the Mongols than by the societies among which she had lived up until that point. However, the Mongols' support for Christianity was by no means exclusive. Juvayni reports that Sorghaghtani Beki also founded the Madrasa-yi-Khani in Bukhara, which housed up to a thousand scholars.[72] And Doquz Khatun is recorded as having offered to adopt an Ayyubid prince, al-'Aziz (great-great-grandson of al-Kamil), as her son.[73]

Tamta's Death

Tamta worked under the Mongol regime for a decade, before she died, probably in the year 1254.[74] This date, like so many of the facts associated with her life, is based on circumstantial rather than direct evidence. On her death, Tamta returned to anonymity. We do not know where she was buried.

As ever, the multiple identities that accompanied her through her life opened options for her on her burial. The Mqargrdzeli family have left at least four family mausolea in the lands they controlled: at Harichavank and Sanahin (both for Armenian Apostolic branches of the family); and at Akhtala, and further up the Debed gorge at Kobayr for the branches that converted to Georgian Christianity.[75] At Akhtala Tamta's brother, Avag, commissioned a chapel in 1250; and tombstones survive from Kobayr of at least sixteen members of the family descended from Avag's cousin, Shahanshah, as well as the bell-tower of 1279 built for Shahanshah's son Zakare III and his wife Vaneni [Fig. 144].[76] On the other hand, if she was buried in the style of rulers of Akhlat, other options became available. A series of tomb towers are known from the city, the earliest surviving being the Usta Sakirt Türbe of 1273 [Fig. 145]. It shows the continuing masonry traditions that had developed in Akhlat over the past century, although in a considerably more restrained manner than at Divriği a generation earlier. Although the forms of burial are distinct, they share many technical and visual features, highlighting the continuing artistic overlap between Armenians and Turks under Mongol rule. Given Tamta's apparent adherence to Christianity throughout her life, it is most probable that she was buried in a church rather than in an isolated tower. However, as with so much of her life, Tamta's death and burial went unrecorded by chroniclers, and any monuments are lost.

---

[72] Juvayni, 1: 108–9.
[73] R. Amitai-Preiss, 'Hülegü and the Ayyūbid Lord of the Transjordan', *Archivium Eurasiae Medii Aevi* 9 (1995–7), 5–16.
[74] Date given in Toumanoff, *Les dynasties de la Caucasie chrétienne*, 296, tab. 63:8, but without citing his source.
[75] Drampian, *Freski Kobaira*; Thierry, 'A propos des peintures'.
[76] Z. N. Aleksidze, 'Louvre – Akhtala', *Humanitaruli kvevebi tselitsdeuli* 5 (2014), 143–61; V. Silogava, 'Epigrapikuli etiudebi da shenishvnebi', *Macne* 4 (1990), 79–119, at 116.

Figure 144 Family mausoleum bell-tower for Zakare III and his wife Vaneni Mqargrdzeli at Kobayr, Armenia; 1279

Conclusion

Tamta's life covered the greatest period of change that Anatolia had seen since the arrival of the Turks in the eleventh century. She was personally linked to all the groups that witnessed or brought about that change. In many ways this was a unique moment, a point at which cultures in Anatolia were more diverse and yet more interconnected than ever before. Moreover, at this moment Anatolia was also more closely connected to the rest of the world, whether to the Latin west, through the Crusaders and missionary friars, or to the Asian east, through the armies and administrators brought in by first the Khwarazmians and then the Mongols. Janet Abu-Lughod has dated this first global economy to the century after the 1250s, but the decades before are perhaps more interesting for showing the ways in which one half of this global economy was formed.[77]

However, we should not overestimate the types of convergence that the Mongol Empire supposedly brought about. Economies were connected but not united. The evidence of coin hoards indicates that long-distance trade was split into many shorter legs: it was rare for merchants to undertake

---

[77] Abu-Lughod, *Before European Hegemony*.

Figure 145 Usta Sakirt Türbe, Akhlat, Turkey; 1273

the full journey between the Mediterranean and Mongolia that Tamta and her fellow rulers embarked upon. The coins are generally found on distinct routes, either moving east–west or north–south: traditional trade routes remained entrenched.

Similar restrictions are visible in the architecture and literature that Tamta encountered. The motifs and forms employed by Akhlati architects appear on buildings across Anatolia and the Caucasus, but not further south in Syria, where local traditions held sway. Equally, whilst Persian poetry, notably the *Shahname*, was translated into Arabic in these decades, its impact in the Arabic world was limited. In the Christian Caucasus, on the other hand, its influence on poetry and art was much greater.

The speed of all the changes in the first half of the thirteenth century enabled transformation, but also brought about its end. Conquests could not easily be maintained, and resistance could flourish, especially on the fringes of the Mongol world. The victory of the Mamluk Sultan Baybars over the Mongol forces of Kitbugha at ʿAyn Jalut on 3 September 1260 ended Mongol expansion in the region and established a clearer frontier between Arabic Syria and Turkish Anatolia, close to the lines of the current frontier between Syria and Turkey. But within Syria, the Ayyubid family had already lost power, and Cairo became the real centre of power for the next century. The division of the Mongol Empire into separate khanates that followed re-established other political divisions, allowing the Ilkhan in Iran to reassert his territories as the dominant power in the region. In the Caucasus the centrifugal forces of the nobility fought for autonomy as the centralising power of the Bagrationi kings waned. Georgia was divided between two kings, east and west, and Samtskhe in the south-west began to move towards independence; in Armenia the separate provinces once again asserted themselves. A similar fragmentation occurred in Anatolia.

Tamta's life came at a unique moment in the history of the region. Never again would so many different religions, factions, armies and cultures all appear in one lifetime. Her transformations from daughter to wife to widow, from diplomatic hostage to ruler (and back again, twice) show the dynamism with which a woman's experiences could change, and the opportunities that were available – although all too often masked by terrible hardship. Looking back on Tamta's life, it remains the case that we cannot begin to guess at her character or personality. Whether she ever mastered her situation at each change, or was swept along by it, must remain unknown and open only to speculation. What we can be more sure of, however, is how adaptable she must have been. To have survived in each of the courts and cultures in which she found herself she must have learned languages, whether Armenian and Georgian in her youth, Arabic during her marriages to al-Awhad and al-Ashraf, possibly Turkish and Persian to prosper with merchants in Anatolia, and Uighur to cope with her years as a hostage in Mongolia.

With no evidence to the contrary, I have assumed that Tamta remained Christian throughout her life, not least as we know that her Ayyubid husbands had given their permission for her not to convert. However, although she may always have been Christian, that is not to say that her faith did not change during the course of her life: her father's conversion from Armenian to Georgian Christianity may have come very early in her life, but thereafter she had to worship alongside many other Christian confessions

(Greek, Syriac, Latin, Nestorian), and was surrounded by Muslims for much of her life. Despite William of Rubruck's picture of the number of Christians at the Mongolian court, in her years there she encountered Buddhists and shamans as well. Each religion and the culture associated with it placed another layer onto Tamta's life. Her identity was formed by the accretion of these layers, and the steps she took to protect or adapt her public appearance in response. Like the silhouette of an Anatolian city in the thirteenth century, which became an ever denser mesh of different features, all of which combined to create the city's character, so too must these experiences have shaped Tamta's.

Tamta's greatest triumph was survival. As a woman and as a Christian the core feature of her identity must, in the end, have been her abilty to adapt, to take on new aspects of her identity to suit each new situation, whilst retaining the links to her past, to her family and that of her husbands, that enabled her to prosper and live out her final years as the ruler of Akhlat.

14 | Afterlife

Tamta Mqargrdzeli is literally a footnote in history. She was first noted by the extraordinary French linguist and historian Marie-Félicité Brosset in his 1849 translation of the Georgian chronicles, which he wrote whilst working at the Imperial Academy of Sciences in St Petersburg. Brosset reconstructed her life in a couple of footnotes and two *additions et éclaircissements* to the main text.[1] She remained marooned in these incidental annotations for more than a century before receiving minor walk-on parts in more recent scholarship.[2] Equally, Akhlat, the city where she spent so much of her life, is a little-noticed provincial town in eastern Turkey. Both the woman and her city stand on the margins of history and geography.

The margins are usually seen as peripheral and inferior. By their very definition they stand away from the great focuses of power that dominate regions, and studies of provincial locations almost always define them in relation to the centre to which they most closely relate.[3] The idea that there is a one-way relationship between the two is deeply entrenched, and most tartly expressed by Bernard Berenson in his 1930 publication *Studies in Medieval Painting*: 'I cannot shake off my convictions that fashions in top hat and cravats do, as a rule, go from Bond Street and the Rue de la Paix to the Congolese heart of Darkness and not the other way round.'[4] Whilst no-one would condone the racism explicit in his choice of example (and visible in Hergé's depiction of the Congolese published a year later – *Tintin in the Congo*), the underlying sentiment about centre and province remains widespread.

The parallel lives of Tamta and Akhlat highlight some of the problems that this worldview encapsulates. The most significant of these is that there is no single centre against which a province can be defined, and that a province

---

[1] Brosset, *Histoire de la Géorgie*, 500 n.1, 520 n.3; elaborated in Brosset, *Additions et éclaircissements*, 272, 428–9.

[2] Rogers, 'The Mxargrdzelis between East and West'; La Porta, '"The Kingdom and the Sultanate were Conjoined"', esp. 87–9; La Porta, 'Re-Constructing Armenia', 264–5.

[3] For critiques of this approach see A. Eastmond, 'Art and the Periphery', in *The Oxford Handbook of Byzantine Studies*, eds. E. Jeffreys, R. Cormack and J. Haldon (Oxford, 2008), 770–6; Safran, *The Medieval Salento*, introduction.

[4] B. Berenson, *Studies in Medieval Painting* (New Haven, 1930), x.

is not simply a cul-de-sac. Berenson's mistake was not just that he believed that culture moved in just one way down a street; it was that he could conceive of only one street (which could lead only from Western Europe). Akhlat lay along at least three different streets. It was roughly equidistant from the great cities of the eastern Mediterranean and Near East – Constantinople, Cairo and Baghdad. Janet Abu-Lughod has noted how these each lay at the heart of one of the medieval world's major economic and cultural circuits, encompassing the Mediterranean, the Middle East and Asia (the Silk Road).[5] On her map of the world it is striking that Akhlat lies at the intersection – the centre – of these three circuits. If we invert the map, we might argue that the margins – Akhlat – are actually now the centre. Clearly, as the events recounted in this book have shown, Akhlat was not a centre in a traditional way. It was not an economic, political or cultural powerhouse. More often it became key because it was in the way: a city that needed to be conquered before invaders could move on to the greater prizes that lay beyond.

It is a cliché of history writing to present particular cities, usually Venice or Constantinople, as 'crossroads' of culture. However, Akhlat has a better claim than most to the title. Primarily it is truly a crossroads: a settlement based around the meeting of different roads running east to west and north to south across Anatolia. The point about crossroads is surely that they are places of intersection that lead on to a point beyond, not ends in themselves. This is certainly true of Akhlat, which suffered so much from war in the thirteenth century precisely because it was in the way.

Similarly, Tamta's importance lies less in the woman herself (if only because we know so little about her) than in her role as the point of encounter between so many different people, religions, languages and cultures in the first half of the thirteenth century. Both Tamta and Akhlat can be defined as lying on the margins, but it is through such a definition that both gain their importance in understanding the rapidly changing world of the thirteenth century. By being on the margins of the many worlds that met in eastern Anatolia, they became the heart of networks that stretched through them all. It is therefore important to redefine the idea of a centre, and to replace the notion that a centre is a monocultural site with a pluralist vision of centres that interconnect with many surrounding cultures. Without being rooted in a single cultural sphere, Akhlat emerges as a dynamic point of exchange in which people, ideas, materials and technologies were moved rapidly between Anatolia and the Caucasus and beyond. Although it

---

[5] Abu-Lughod, *Before European Hegemony*, fig. 1.

is rather crude, it is possible to imagine Tamta as the personification of the city in which she spent so much of her life. The range of people that she was forced to engage with through her family, her marriages and her defeats all established Tamta as the centre of a network of encounters mirroring that visible in the material culture of Akhlat, and which stretches from the city across Anatolia, the Caucasus and Syria. Although the city and its female ruler lie at the heart of this marginal centre there is insufficient evidence to present them as the originators of all that has been presented in this book. Rather, it is better to see them as indirect facilitators of encounters that enabled men, women, ideas and technologies to move and be adapted so widely.

Modern Frontiers

Just as Tamta crossed medieval frontiers throughout her life, so too she crosses modern political and academic frontiers. She first moved between sites that now lie in the modern republics of Georgia, Armenia and Turkey. The latter two, of course, have had a very fraught relationship over the past century. Turkey has, with a few notable exceptions, minimised the role and presence of Armenians in its eastern provinces, and (as in Azerbaijan) many of its Armenian monuments have been destroyed in the century of Atatürk's republic. Armenians are similarly reluctant to place their culture within a broader framework of Islamic/Turkish culture, preferring a narrative of noble exceptionalism and difference.[6] Seen against the background of the tragedy of the Syrian civil war that erupted in 2011, the frontier between Turks and Arabs has once again come to the fore. It is now slightly further south than it was in the thirteenth century – Harran rather than Akhlat is on the border – but the distinction remains, echoing the warning that the city's inhabitants 'are averse to the Arabs' that Ibn al-Athir reported to al-Awhad's troops at the start of the thirteenth century.[7] Iran continues to hold itself apart from both Turks and Arabs, a mix of ethnic,

---

[6] This is most evident in their reluctance to lend objects from the modern republic of Armenia to exhibitions in which Armenia is to feature as a part of the larger Byzantine world, but their enthusiasm to lend to exhibitions that focus solely on Armenia: contrast the list of lenders to *The Glory of Byzantium: Art and Culture of the Middle Byzantine Era, AD 843–1261*, eds. H. C. Evans and W. D. Wixom (New York, 1997) and *Byzantium: Faith and Power (1261–1557)*, ed. H. C. Evans (New York, 2004) with those to *Treasures from the Ark: 1700 Years of Armenian Christian Art*, ed. V. Nersessian (London, 2001) and *Armenia Sacra: mémoire chrétienne des Arméniens (IVe–XVIIIe siècle)*, eds. J. Durand, I. Rapti and D. Giovannoni (Paris, 2007).

[7] Ibn al-Athir, 3: 122.

nationalist and religious difference (being predominantly Shi'ite). Equally, Uzbekistan and Turkmenistan, the modern states on the territory from which the Khwarazmians emerged, have both developed an ethnically based, nationalist government since the fall of the Soviet Union, largely defined in opposition to the states around them, notably through persecution of (Persian) Tajiks. Finally, Mongolia remains as distant and alien to most modern travellers as it did to medieval ones.

In academic terms, Tamta's life falls between the cultural history of the 'west' (into which the Christian art of Byzantium, Armenia and Georgia is generally subsumed, even if only just), that of the Islamic world, and that of Eurasia and eastern Asia. In London, where I wrote this book, these fall between separate academic institutions that divided the world between themselves in the first half of the twentieth century: a Western block, studying what is called the 'Classical tradition' – the Warburg Institute, the Courtauld Institute of Art and the Institute of Classical Studies – with the rest of the world handed over to the School of Oriental and African Studies. This is the curse of Area Studies, which this book shows are necessarily false and constricting. It is only now that all these institutions are seeking to regain a global perspective on their particular regional and intellectual interests; but whilst the divisions are beginning to fragment, their legacy remains in terms of subject specialisms among academics, demarcations in teaching and library purchasing policies.

Tamta's life also falls between different branches of historical enquiry. Primary sources are too sparse to allow for an old-fashioned biographical history drawn from written sources alone; the material evidence of art and archaeology are essential. Yet art history by itself cannot suffice: the creation of monumental art is too collaborative to risk seeing any one building as a true reflection of the personality or aims of its commissioner. Equally, to shift emphasis onto a wider cultural or social history of women in the thirteenth century runs the risk of diluting the focus on Tamta and becoming beset by generalisations. This book is a compromise between approaches and materials. Like the different dating systems employed by all the peoples encountered, and their habit of giving different names to the same individuals and places, it is a work of translation and synthesis, bringing together disparate views to try to build up a larger picture of the medieval world. Tamta, although so often frustratingly elusive in her own life story, does, I hope, emerge as a more substantial figure, in a much wider, more diverse and more connected world than we normally imagine. This was Tamta's world.

Bibliography

Primary Sources

Short titles used in the notes are given at the beginning of each entry in this section.

Arabic

'Abd al-Rahman ibn Isma'il Le livre des deux jardins: histoire des deux règnes, celui de Nour ed-Dîn et celui de Salah ed-Din', in *RHCHO*, vol. 5, French trans. C. Barbier de Meynard (Paris, 1872)

Abu'l-Fida Annales d'Abu'l-Fédâ', French trans. in *RHCHO*, vol. 1 (Paris, 1872), 1–165

al-Dahabi *Kitāb Duwal al-Islām (Les dynasties de l'Islam): traduction annotée des années 447/1055-6 à 656/1258)*, French trans. A. Nègre (Damascus, 1979)

Harawi 'Ali ibn Abi Bakr Harawi, *Guide des lieux de pèlerinage*, French trans. J. Sourdel-Thomine (Damascus, 1957)

Husayni Sadr al-Din 'Ali ibn Nasir Husayni, *The History of the Seljuq State: A Translation with Commentary of the 'Akhbār al-dawla al-saljūqiyya'*, English trans. C. E. Bosworth [Routledge Studies in the History of Iran and Turkey: 9] (Abingdon; New York, 2011)

Ibn al-'Amid al-Makin Ibn al-'Amīd, *Chronique des Ayyoubides (602–658/1205-6–1259-60)*, French trans. A.-M. Eddé and F. Micheau [Documents relatif à l'histoire des croisades publiés par l'Académie des Inscriptions et Belles-Lettres: 16] (Abbeville, 1994)

Ibn al-Athir 'Izz al-Din Ibn al-Athir, *The Chronicle of Ibn al-Athir for the Crusading Period from al-Kāmil fi'l-Ta'rikh*, ed. D. S. Richards, 3 vols. [Crusade Texts in Translation: 13, 15, 17] (Aldershot, 2006–8)

Ibn al-Furat *Tarikh Ibn al-Furat* (Beirut, 1936–42), 5 vols.

Ibn Jubayr *The Travels of Ibn Jubayr: Being the Chronicle of a Mediaeval Spanish Moor Concerning his Journey to the Egypt of Saladin, the Holy Cities of Arabia, Baghdad the City of the Caliphs, the Latin Kingdom of Jerusalem and the Norman Kingdom of Sicily*, English trans. R. J. C. Broadhurst (London, 1952)

Ibn Khallikan *Biographical Dictionary*, English trans. W. MacGuckin de Slane (Paris, 1843), 4 vols.

Ibn Shaddad	Baha' al-Din Ibn Shaddad, *The Rare and Excellent History of Saladin or al-Nawādir al-Sultāniyya wa'l-Mahāsin al-Yūsufiyya by Bahā' al-Dīn Ibn Shaddād*, English trans. D. S. Richards [Crusade Texts in Translation: 7] (Aldershot, 2002)
Ibn al-Shihna	*'Les Perles Choisies' d'Ibn ach-Chihna*, French trans. J. Sauvaget [Matériaux pour servir à l'histoire de la ville d'Alep: 1] (Beirut, 1933)
Ibn Wasil	*Mufarrij al-kurub fi akhbar Bani Ayyub* (Cairo, 1953), 5 vols.
Ibn al-Zubayr	Ahmad ibn al-Rashid Ibn al-Zubayr, *Book of Gifts and Rarities (Kitāb al-hadāya wa al-tuḥaf): Selections Compiled in the Fifteenth Century from an Eleventh-Century Manuscript on Gifts and Treasures*, English trans. G. H. Qaddūmī [Harvard Middle Eastern Monographs: 29] (Cambridge, MA, 1996)
'Imad al-Din al-Isfahani	*Conquête de la Syrie et de la Palestine par Saladin (al-Fath al-qussî fî l-fath al-qudsî)*, ed. H. Massé [Documents relatifs à l'histoire des croisades: 10] (Paris, 1972)
al-Jazari	Isma'il ibn al-Razzaz al-Jazari, *The Book of Knowledge of Ingenious Mechanical Devices (Kitāb fī ma'rifat al-ḥiyal al-handasiyya)*, English trans. D. R. Hill (Dordrecht; Boston, 1974)
Maqrizi	Ahmad ibn'Ali Maqrizi, *A History of the Ayyūbid Sultans of Egypt* [Library of Classical Arabic Literature: 5] (Boston, 1980)
al-Nasawi	Shihab al-Din Muhammad al-Nasawi, *Histoire du Sultan Djelal ed-Din Mankobirti, Prince du Khwarezm*, French trans. O. Houdas (Paris, 1895)
Nasr-e Khosraw	*The Book of Travels [Safarnama]*, English trans. W. M. Thackston [Persian Heritage Series: 36] (New York, 1986)
Nizam al-Mulk	*The Book of Government or, Rules for Kings: The Siyar al-muluk or Siyasat-nama of Nizam al-Mulk*, English trans. H. Darke [Persian Heritage Series: 32] (London; Boston, 1978)
al-Nuwayri	*Nihayat al-arab fi funun al-adab* (Cairo, 1923–), 33 vols.
Sibṭ ibn al-'Ajami	*'Les trésors d'or' de Sibṭ ibn al-'Ajami*, French trans. J. Sauvaget [Matériaux pour servir à l'histoire de la ville d'Alep: 2] (Beirut; Paris, 1950)

Armenian

Armianskie istochniki	*Armianskie istochniki o mongolakh: izvlecheniia iz rukopisei XII–XIV vv*, Russian trans. A. G. Galstian (Moscow, 1962)
Grigor Aknertsi	Blake, R. P. and R. N. Frye, 'History of the Nation of the Archers (the Mongols) by Grigor of Akanc'', *Harvard Journal of Asiatic Studies* 12 (1949), 269–399
Hayton	Hayton, 'La Flor des estoires de la Terre d'Orient', in *RHCHO*, vol. 2, ed. C. Kohler (Paris, 1906), 113–253

Kirakos	Kirakos Gandzakeci, 'Histoire de l'Arménie par le vartabed Kirakos de Gantzac', in *Deux historiens arméniens*, French trans. M. F. Brosset (St Petersburg, 1870), 1–194; *History of the Armenians*, English trans. R. Bedrosian (New York, 1986)
Matthew of Edessa	*Armenia and the Crusades, Tenth to Twelfth Centuries: The Chronicle of Matthew of Edessa*, English trans. A. E. Dostourian (Lanham, MD; New York; London, 1993)
Nerses of Lambron	*Explication de la Divine Liturgie*, ed. and French trans. I. Kéchichian (Beirut, 2000)
Stepanos Orbelian	*Histoire de la Siounie par Stéphannos Orbélian*, French trans. M. F. Brosset (St Petersburg, 1864); *Step'annos Orbelean's History of the State of Sisakan*, English trans. R. Bedrosian (New York, 2012–15), 2 vols.
Vardan	'The Historical Compilation of Vardan Arewelc'i', English trans. R. W. Thomson, *DOP* 43 (1989), 125–226

Georgian

Amiran-Darejaniani	'*Amiran-Darejaniani*': *A Cycle of Medieval Georgian Tales Traditionally Ascribed to Mose Khoneli*, English trans. R. H. Stevenson (Oxford, 1958)
Kartlis Tskhovreba	*Kartlis Tskhovreba: A History of Georgia*, English trans. R. Metreveli and S. Jones (Tbilisi, 2014); *Histoire de la Géorgie depuis l'antiquité jusqu'en 1469 de J.-C.*, French trans. M. F. Brosset (St Petersburg, 1849); *The Georgian Chronicle: The Period of Giorgi Lasha*, partial English trans. K. Vivian (Amsterdam, 1991); *Kartlis tskhovreba*, ed. S. Qaukhchishvili (Tbilisi, 1955, 1959)
Shota Rustaveli	Shot'ha Rust'haveli, *The Man in the Panther's Skin*, trans. M. Wardrop (London, 1912); *Vepkhistqaosani. Teksti da variantebi*, eds. A. Shanidze and A. Baramidze (Tbilisi, 1966)
Nikoloz Gulaberisdze	*Sak'itkhavi suetis tskhovelisay kuartisa sauploysa da katolike eklesiisa* (Tbilisi, 1908)

Greek

Anna Komnena	*Anna Comnène: Alexiade*, ed. and French trans. B. Leib (Paris, 1937–76)
De Administrando Imperio	Constantine VII Porphyrogennetos, *De Administrando Imperio*, English trans. G. Moravcsik and R. J. H. Jenkins [Dumbarton Oaks Texts: 1] (Washington, DC, 1967)

Ecloga	*A Manual of Roman Law: The Ecloga*, English trans. E. H. Freshfield (Cambridge, 1926)
Four Byzantine Novels	*Four Byzantine Novels* English trans. E. Jeffreys [Translated Texts for Byzantinists: 1] (Liverpool, 2012)
Georgios Pachymeres	*Georges Pachymérès Relations historiques*, ed. and trans. A. Failler and V. Laurent [Corpus Fontium Historiae Byzantinae (Series Parisensis): 24/1] (Paris, 1984)
Nikephoros Blemmydes	*A Partial Account*, ed. J. Munitiz [Specilegium Sacrum Lovanense Etudes et Documents: 48] (Louvain, 1988)
Nikephoros Gregoras	*Rhomäische Geschichte*, German trans. J. L. Van Dieten (Stuttgart, 1973–9), 6 vols.; *Byzantina Historia*, eds. L Schopen and I. Bekker (Bonn, 1829–55)
Niketas Choniates	*O City of Byzantium, the Annals of Niketas Choniates*, English trans. H. Magoulias (Detroit, 1984); *Historia*, ed. J. L. Van Dieten [Corpus Fontium Historiae Byzantinae (Series Berolinensis): 11] (Berlin, 1975)
PG	*Patrologiae Graecae, Patrologiae Cursus completus* (Paris, 1857–66), 161 vols.
Theognostus	*Treasury*, English trans. J. Munitiz [Corpus Christianorum. Series Graeca: 5] (Turnhout, 2013); *Theognosti Thesaurus*, ed. J. Munitiz [Corpus Christianorum. Series Graeca: 5] (Turnhout, 1979)
Typika	*Byzantine Monastic Foundation Documents: A Comparative Translation of the Surviving Founders' Typika and Testaments*, eds. J. Thomas and A. C. Hero [Dumbarton Oaks Studies: 35] (Washington, DC, 2000)

Hebrew

Benjamin of Tudela	*The Itinerary of Benjamin of Tudela*, ed. M. A. Signer, trans. M. N. Adler (Malibu, 1983)

Latin and Western Vernaculars

Chronica regia coloniensis	*continuatio IV* [Monumenta Germaniae Historica, Scriptores Rerum Germ. in Usum Scholarum: 18] (Hanover, 1880)
de Fabaria, Conradus	'Casus S. Galli Continuatio III', in *Monumenta Germaniae Historica: Scriptores*, vol. 2, ed. G. H. Pertz [Monumenta Germaniae Historica. Scriptores: 2] (Leipzig, 1829), 163–83
Du Chesne and Du Chesne	A. Du Chesne and F. Du Chesne, *Historiæ Francorum scriptores ab ipsius gentis origine* (Paris, 1645), 5 vols.
Hendrickx	B. Hendrickx, 'Régestes des empereurs latins de Constantinople (1204–1261/71)', *Byzantina* 14 (1988), 7–220

Joinville	*Vie de Saint Louis*, ed. and French trans. J. Monfrin (Paris, 1995); *Joinville and Villehardouin: Chronicles of the Crusades*, English trans. M. R. B. Shaw (Harmondsworth, 1963)
Marco Polo	*The Book of Ser Marco Polo the Venetian Concerning the Kingdoms and Marvels of the East: Third Edition, Revised Throughout in the Light of Recent Discoveries by Henri Cordier (of Paris)*, English trans. H. S. Yule (London, 1903)
The Mongol Mission	*The Mongol Mission: Narratives and Letters of the Franciscan Missionaries in Mongolia and China in the Thirteenth and Fourteenth Centuries*, English trans. C. Dawson (London; New York, 1955)
Pegolotti	Francesco Pegolotti, *La Pratica della Mercatura*, English trans. A. Evans [The Mediaeval Academy of America. Publication: 24] (Cambridge, MA, 1936)
Regesta Honorii	*Regesta Honorii papae III*, ed. P. Pressutti (Hildesheim; New York, 1978), 2 vols.
Rigord	'Gesta Philippi Augusti', in *Oeuvres de Rigord et de Guillaume le Breton, Historiens de Philippe Auguste*, ed. H. F. Delaborde (Paris, 1882), 1–167
William of Rubruck	*The Mission of Friar William of Rubruck: His Journey to the Court of the Great Khan Möngke, 1253–1255*, English trans. P. Jackson [The Hakluyt Society. 2nd Series: 173] (London, 1990)
Yule	Sir Henry Yule, *Cathay and the Way Thither*, 2nd edn, rev. H. Cordier (London, 1915), 2 vols.

Persian

Aflaki	Shams al-Din Aflaki, *The Feats of the Knowers of God (Manaqeb al-'arefin)*, English trans. J. O'Kane [Islamic History and Civilization. Studies and Texts: 43] (Leiden; Boston; Cologne, 2002)
Ibn Bibi	*Die Seltschukengeschichte des Ibn Bibi*, German trans. H. Duda (Copenhagen, 1960)
Juvayni	Ala al-Din Ata-Malik Juvayni, *The History of the World Conqueror*, English trans. J. A. Boyle (Manchester, 1958), 2 vols.
Rashid al-Din	*The Successors of Genghis Khan [Jāmiʿ al-Tawārīkh]*, English trans. J. A. Boyle (London; New York, 1971); French trans. *Histoire des Mongols de la Perse*, ed. E. Quatremère (Amsterdam, 1968)

Syriac

Abdishoʿ Bar Brikha	'Marganitha or Pearl: The Truth of the Faith', in *The Nestorians and their Faith*, vol. 2, ed. G. P. Badger (London, 1852), 380–422

Bar Hebraeus *The Chronography of Gregory Abu'l Faraj, the son of Aaron, the Hebrew Physician Commonly Known as Bar Hebraeus Being the First Part of his Political History of the World*, English trans. E. A. W. Budge (Oxford, 1932)

Michael the Syrian *Chronique de Michel le Syrien, patriarche jacobite d'Antioche (1166–1199)*, French trans. J.-B. Chabot (Paris, 1905), 3 vols.

Solomon of Basra *The Book of the Bee: the Syriac text edited from the manuscripts in London, Oxford, and Munich with an English translation*, ed. and trans. E. A. W. Budge [Anecdota Oxoniensia. Semitic Series: 1.2] (Oxford, 1886)

Secondary Sources

Abu-Lughod, J., *Before European Hegemony: The World System AD 1250–1350* (Oxford, 1991)

Aladashvili, N. A., and A. Vol'skaia, 'Fasadnye rospisi Verkhnei Svaneti', *Ars Georgica* 9 (1987), 94–120

Aleksidze, Z. N., 'Louvre – Akhtala', *Humanitaruli kvevebi tselitsdeuli* 5 (2014), 143–61

Allan, J. W., and A. T. Aron, *Metalwork of the Islamic World: The Aron Collection* (London; New York, 1986)

Allen, T., *A Classical Revival in Islamic Architecture* (Wiesbaden, 1986)

Allsen, T. T., *Culture and Conquest in Mongol Eurasia* (Cambridge, 2001)

Amiranashvili, S., *Beka Opizari* (Tbilisi, 1964)

   Gruzinskaia miniatura (Moscow, 1966)

   Istoriia gruzinskogo iskusstva (Moscow, 1963)

   Istoriia gruzinskoi monumental'noi zhivopisi, vol. 1 (Tbilisi, 1957)

Amitai-Preiss, R., 'Hülegü and the Ayyūbid Lord of the Transjordan', *Archivium Eurasiae Medii Aevi* 9 (1995–7), 5–16

Anderson, B., *Imagined Communities: Reflections on the Origin and Spread of Nationalism* (London; New York, 1991)

Andrews, P. A., *Felt Tents and Pavilions: The Nomadic Tradition and its Interaction with Princely Tentage* (London, 1999)

Arık, R., and O. Arık, *Tiles: Treasures of Anatolian Soil: Tiles of the Seljuk and Beylik Periods* (Istanbul, 2008)

Armstrong, J. A., *Nations before Nationalism* (Chapel Hill, NC, 1982)

Arutiunova-Fidanian, V. A., 'Les Arméniens Chalcédoniens en tant que phénomène culturel de l'Orient Chrétien', in *Atti del quinto simposio internazionale di Arte Armena* (Venice, 1992), 463–77

   'The Ethno-Confessional Self-Awareness of Armenian Chalcedonians', *Revue des études arméniennes* 21 (1988), 345–63

Ashtor, E., *Histoire des prix et des salaires dans l'Orient médiéval* (Paris, 1969)

Aslanapa, O., *Turkish Art and Architecture* (London, 1971)

Atil, E., *Ceramics from the World of Islam* [Freer Gallery of Art Fiftieth Anniversary Exhibition: 3] (Washington, DC, 1973)

'The Freer Bowl and the Legacy of the Shahname', *Damaszener Mitteilungen* 11 (1999), 7–12

Atil, E., W. T. Chase and P. Jett, *Islamic Metalwork in the Freer Gallery of Art* (Washington, DC, 1985)

Augé, I., 'Gošavank', un complexe monastique au regard des sources littéraires et épigraphiques', *Le Muséon* 125/3–4 (2012), 335–65

Azatian, S. R., *Portaly v monumental'noi arkhitekture Armenii IV–XIV vv* (Yerevan, 1987)

Babić, G., 'Les programmes absidaux en Géorgie et dans les Balkans entre XIe et le XIIIe siècle', in *L'Arte Georgiana dal IX al XIV secolo: Atti del Terzo Simposio Internazionale sull'arte Georgiana*, ed. M. Calo'Mariani (Bari, 1981), 117–36

Bacci, M., '"Mixed" Shrines in the Late Byzantine Period', in *Archeologia Abrahamica: issledovaniia v oblasti arkheologii i khudozhestvennoi traditsii iudaizma, khristianstva i islama*, ed. L. A. Beliaev (Moscow, 2009), 433–44

'A Sacred Shrine for a Holy Icon: The Shrine of Our Lady of Saydnaya', in *Hierotopy: The Creation of Sacred Spaces in Byzantium and Medieval Russia*, ed. A. M. Lidov (Moscow, 2006), 373–87

Baer, E., *Ayyubid Metalwork with Christian Images* (Leiden, 1989)

Balog, P., *The Coinage of the Ayyubids* [Royal Numismatic Society Special Publication: 12] (London, 1980)

Barrucand, M., 'The Miniatures of the Daqa'iq al-Haqa'iq (Bibliothèque Nationale Pers. 174): A Testimony to the Cultural Diversity of Medieval Anatolia', *Islamic Art* 4 (1990–1), 113–42

Barry, F., '*Disiecta membra*: Ranieri Zeno, the Imitation of Constantinople, the *Spolia* Style, and Justice at San Marco', in *San Marco, Byzantium, and the Myths of Venice*, eds. H. Maguire and R. S. Nelson (Washington, DC, 2010), 7–62

Bartol'd, V. V., *Four Studies on the History of Central Asia* (Leiden, 1956)

Basmadjian, K. J., *Les inscriptions arméniennes d'Ani, de Bagnaïr et de Marmachèn* (Paris, 1931)

Bassett, S. G., *The Urban Image of Late Antique Constantinople* (Cambridge, 2004)

Bates, Ü. Ü., 'The Anatolian Mausoleum of the Twelfth, Thirteenth and Fourteenth Centuries' (Ph. D. thesis, University of Michigan, 1970)

Bedrosian, R., 'The Turco-Mongol Invasions and the Lords of Armenia in the 13th–14th Centuries' (Ph.D. thesis, Columbia University, 1979)

Behrens-Abouseif, D., *Cairo of the Mamluks: A History of the Architecture and its Culture* (London, 2007)

Islamic Architecture in Cairo: An Introduction [Supplements to Muqarnas: 3] (Leiden; New York, 1989)

Berenson, B., *Studies in Medieval Painting* (New Haven, 1930)

Bergeron, P., *Voyages faits principalement en Asie dans les XII, XIII, XIV, et XV siècles, par Benjamin de Tudèle, Jean du Plan-Carpin, N. Ascelin, Guillaume de Rubruquis, Marc Paul vénitien, Haiton, Jean de Mandeville, et Ambroise Contarini: accompagnés de l'Histoire des Sarasins et des Tartares, et précédez d'une Introduction concernant les voyages et les nouvelles découvertes des principaux voyageurs*, vol. 2 (La Haye, 1735)

Beridze, V., 'Quelques aspects de l'architecture géorgienne à coupole de la seconde moitié du Xe siècle à la fin du XIIIe', in *Communication faite à Bergamo (Italie) le 29 juin 1974 au 'Primo simposio internazionale sull'arte Georgiana'* (Tbilisi, 1976), 74–96

Beridze, V., G. V. Alibegashvili, A. Vol'skaia and L. Xuskivadze, *The Treasures of Georgia* (London, 1984)

Blair, S. S., 'The Madrasa at Zuzan: Islamic Architecture in Eastern Iran on the Eve of the Mongol Invasions', *Muqarnas* 3 (1985), 75–91

The Monumental Inscriptions from Early Islamic Iran and Transoxiana [Studies in Islamic Art and Architecture: Supplements to Muqarnas: 6] (Leiden, 1992)

Blessing, P., *Rebuilding Anatolia after the Mongol Conquest: Islamic Architecture in the Lands of Rūm, 1240–1330* [Birmingham Byzantine and Ottoman Studies: 17] (Farnham, 2014)

'Women Patrons in Medieval Anatolia and a Discussion of Mahbari Khatun's Mosque Complex in Kayseri', *Belleten* 78 (2014), 475–526

Bloom, J. M., *Arts of the City Victorious: Islamic Art and Architecture in Fatimid North Africa and Egypt* (New Haven; London, 2008)

The Minaret [Edinburgh Studies in Islamic Art] (Edinburgh, 2013)

Minaret: Symbol of Islam [Oxford Studies in Islamic Art: 7] (Oxford, 1989)

Boase, T. S. R., *The Cilician Kingdom of Armenia* (Edinburgh, 1978)

Bolshakov, O. G., 'The St Petersburg Manuscript of the Maqāmāt by al-Ḥarīrī and its Place in the History of Arab Painting', *Manuscripta Orientalia* 3/4 (1997), 59–66

Bombaci, A., 'Die Mauerinschriften von Konya', in *Forschungen zur Kunst Asiens: In Memoriam Kurt Erdmann*, eds. O. Aslanapa and R. Naumann (Istanbul, 1969), 67–73

Bosworth, C. E., *The New Islamic Dynasties: A Chronological and Genealogical Manual* (Edinburgh, 1996)

'The Political and Dynastic History of the Iranian World (AD 1000–1217)', in *The Cambridge History of Iran*, vol. 5: *The Saljuq and Mongol Periods*, ed. J. A. Boyle (Cambridge, 1968), 1–202

Boyle, J. A., 'Dynastic and Political History of the Īl-Khāns', in *The Cambridge History of Iran*, vol. 5: *The Saljuq and Mongol Periods*, ed. J. A. Boyle (Cambridge, 1968), 303–421

'A Form of Horse Sacrifice amongst the Thirteenth- and Fourteenth-Century Mongols', *Central Asiatic Journal* 10 (1965), 145–50; reprinted in his *The Mongol World Empire 1206–1370* [Variorum Reprints] (London, 1977), Study XX

'The Journey of Het'um I, King of Little Armenia, to the Court of the Great Khan Möngke', *Central Asiatic Journal* 9/3 (1964), 175–89; reprinted in his *The Mongol World Empire 1206–1370* [Variorum Reprints] (London, 1977), Study X

'Kirakos of Ganjak on the Mongols', *Central Asiatic Journal* 8 (1963), 199–214; reprinted in his *The Mongol World Empire 1206–1370* [Variorum Reprints] (London, 1977), Study XIX

'Turkish and Mongol Shamanism in the Middle Ages', *Folklore* 83/3 (1972), 177–93

Brend, B., *Islamic Art* (London, 1991)

Brentjes, B., S. Mnazakanjan and N. Stepanjan, *Kunst des Mittelalters in Armenien* (Vienna; Munich, 1982)

Bretschneider, E., *Mediaeval Researches from Eastern Asiatic Sources: Fragments towards the Knowledge of the Geography and History of Central and Western Asia from the 13th to the 17th Century* (London, 1910), 2 vols.

Brisch, K., ed., *Museum für Islamische Kunst Berlin: Katalog* (Berlin-Dahlem, 1979)

Brockelmann, C., *Geschichte der arabischen Literatur*, vol. 1 (Leiden, 1943)

Brosset, M. F., *Additions et éclaircissements à l'Histoire de la Géorgie* (St Petersburg, 1851)

Description des Monastères Arméniens d'Haghbat et de Sanahin par l'archimandrite Jean de Crimée [Mémoires de l'Académie Impériale des Sciences de St-Pétersbourg, VIIe série: VI, no. 6] (St Petersburg, 1863)

'Ire livraison: 3e Rapport: Edchmiadzin, Ani', in *Rapports sur un voyage archéologique dans la Géorgie et dans l'Arménie exécuté en 1847–48* (St Petersburg, 1849), 1–120 with 'Excursion à Ani, en 1848' by M. N. Khanykof, 120–52

Les Ruines d'Ani, capitale de l'Arménie sous les rois Bagratides, aux Xe et XIe siècles: histoire et description (St Petersburg, 1860)

Bryer, A. A. M., 'A Byzantine Family: The Gabrades, c. 979–c. 1653', *University of Birmingham Historical Journal* 12 (1970), 164–87; reprinted in his *The Empire of Trebizond and the Pontos* [Variorum Reprints: 117] (Aldershot, 1980), Study IIIa

'The Grand Komnenos and the Great Khan at Karakorum in 1246', in *Itinéraires d'Orient: Hommages à Claude Cahen*, eds. R. Curiel and R. Gyselen [Res Orientalis: 6] (Bures-sur-Yvette, 1994), 257–61

'Last Judgements in the Empire of Trebizond: Painted Churches in Inner Chaldia', in *Mare et Litora: Essays Presented to Sergei Karpov for his 60th Birthday*, ed. R. Shukurov (Moscow, 2009), 519–52

Cahen, C., 'La Djazira au milieu du treizième siècle d'après 'Izz ad-din ibn Chaddad', *Revue des études islamiques* 8 (1934), 109–28

The Formation of Turkey. The Seljukid Sultanate of Rum: Eleventh to Fourteenth Century (London, 2001)

Pre-Ottoman Turkey (London, 1968)

'Un traité d'armurerie composé pour Saladin', *Bulletin d'études orientales* 12 (1948), 103–63

Carboni, S., *Following the Stars: Images of the Zodiac in Islamic Art* (New York, 2005)

Chevedden, P. E., 'The Citadel of Damascus' (Ph.D. thesis, UCLA, 1986)

Chwolson, D., *Syrisch-Nestorianische Grabinschriften aus Semirjetschie* (St Petersburg, 1897)

Cincadze, V., 'Der Königspalast in Geguti', in *L'Arte Georgiana dal IX al XIV secolo: Atti del Terzo Simposio Internazionale sull'arte Georgiana*, ed. M. Calo'Mariani (Bari, 1981), 105–10

Clarence-Smith, W. G., 'Same-Sex Relations and Transgender Identities in Islamic Southeast Asia from the Fifteenth Century', in *Sexual Diversity in Asia, c. 600–1950*, eds. R. A. Reyes and W. G. Clarence-Smith (New York, 2012), 67–85

Conrad, H., 'Beobachtungen und Notizen zur Situation der armenischen Fürsten unter der Mongolenherrschaft', in *Caucasus during the Mongol Period – Der Kaukasus in der Mongolenzeit*, eds. J. Tubach, S. G. Vashalomidze and M. Zimmer (Wiesbaden, 2012), 83–105

Cormack, R., 'But Is it Art?', in *Byzantine Diplomacy*, ed. J. Shephard and S. Franklin [Society for the Promotion of Byzantine Studies. Publications: 1] (Aldershot, 1992), 218–36

Cowe, P. S., 'Models for the Interpretation of Medieval Armenian Poetry', in *New Approaches to Medieval Armenian Language and Literature*, ed. J. J. S. Weitenberg (Amsterdam; Atlanta, GA, 1995), 29–46

'The Politics of Poetics: Islamic Influence on Armenian Verse', in *Redefining Christian Identity: Cultural Interaction in the Middle East since the Rise of Islam*, eds. J. J. van Ginkel, H. L. Murre-van den Berg and T. M. van Lint [Orientalia Lovaniensia Analecta: 134] (Leuven; Paris; Dudley, MA, 2005), 379–403

Crane, H., 'Notes on Salǧuq Architectural Patronage in Thirteenth Century Anatolia', *Journal of the Economic and Social History of the Orient* 36 (1993), 1–57

Creswell, K. A. C., *The Muslim Architecture of Egypt*, vol. 2: *Ayyūbids and Early Baḥrite Mamlūks, AD 1171–1326* (Oxford, 1959)

Cuneo, P., A. Zarian, G. Uluhogian, J.-M. Thierry and N. Thierry, *Ani* [Documenti di Architettura Armena: 12] (Milan, 1984)

Ćurčić, S., *Architecture in the Balkans, from Diocletian to Süleyman the Magnificent* (New Haven; London, 2010)

D'Ohsson, C., *Histoire des Mongols, depuis Tchinguiz-Khan jusqu'à Timour Bey ou Tamerlan* (Amsterdam, 1852), 4 vols.

Dadoyan, S., 'A Case Study for Redefining Armenian–Christian Cultural Identity in the Framework of Near Eastern Urbanism – 13th Century: The Nāṣirī Futuwwa Literature and the Brotherhood Poetry of Yovhannēs and Konstandin Erzěnkac'i – Texts and Contexts', in *Redefining Christian Identity: Cultural Interaction in the Middle East since the Rise of Islam*, eds. J. J. van Ginkel, H. L. Murre-van den Berg and T. M. van Lint [Orientalia Lovaniensia Analecta: 134] (Leuven; Paris; Dudley, MA, 2005), 237–64

Daftary, F., *The Ismaʿīlīs: Their History and Doctrines* (Cambridge, 2007)

Dashdondog, B., 'The Mongol Conquerors in Armenia', in *Caucasus during the Mongol Period – Der Kaukasus in der Mongolenzeit*, eds. J. Tubach, S. G. Vashalomidze and M. Zimmer (Wiesbaden, 2012), 53–82

The Mongols and the Armenians (1220–1335) [Brill's Inner Asian Library: 24] (Leiden; Boston, 2010)

de Callataÿ, G., 'La grande conjunction de 1186', in *Occident et Proche-Orient: contacts scientifiques au temps des Croisades*, eds. I. Draelants, A. Tihon and B. van den Abeele [Réminiscences: 5] (Leuven, 1997), 369–84

De Nicola, B., 'Unveiling the Khatuns: Some Aspects of the Role of Women in the Mongol Empire' (Ph.D. thesis, University of Cambridge, 2011)

de Rachewiltz, I., 'Yeh-lü Ch'u-ts'ai (1189–1243): Buddhist Idealist and Confucian Statesman', in *Confucian Personalities*, eds. A. F. Wright and D. Twitchett (Stanford, 1962), 189–216

de Rachewiltz, I., H.-L. Chan, H. Ch'i-ch'ing and P. W. Geier, eds., *In the Service of the Khan: Eminent Personalities of the Early Mongol–Yüan period (1200–1300)* [Asiatische Forschungen: 121] (Wiesbaden, 1993)

Dédéyan, G., 'Les colophons de manuscrits arméniens comme sources pour l'histoire des Croisades', in *The Crusades and their Sources: Essays Presented to Bernard Hamilton*, eds. J. France and W. G. Zajac (Aldershot, 1998), 89–110

Deichmann, F. W., 'I pilastri acritani', *Rendiconti Atti della Pontificia Accademia Romana di Archeologia* 50 (1980), 75–89

Delpont, É., ed., *L'Orient de Saladin: l'art sous les Ayyoubides* (Paris, 2002)

Der Manuelian, L., 'The Monastery of Geghard: A Study of Armenian Architectural Sculpture in the Thirteenth Century' (Ph.D. thesis, Boston University, 1980)

Der Nersessian, S., *Miniature Painting in the Armenian Kingdom of Cilicia from the Twelfth to the Fourteenth Century* [Dumbarton Oaks Studies: 31] (Washington, DC, 1993)

Diez, E., 'Ein Seldschukischer Türklopfer', *Zeitschrift für bildende Kunst* 56 (1921), 18–20

Donabédian, P., and J.-M. Thierry, *Les arts Arméniens* (Paris, 1987)

Drake, F. S., 'Nestorian Crosses and Nestorian Christians in China under the Mongols', *Journal of the Hong Kong Branch of the Royal Asiatic Society* 2 (1962), 11–25

Drampian, I., *Freski Kobaira* (Yerevan, 1979)

Durand, J., I. Rapti and D. Giovannoni, eds., *Armenia Sacra: mémoire chrétienne des Arméniens (IVe–XVIIIe siècle)* (Paris, 2007)

Eastmond, A., 'Art and Frontiers between Byzantium and the Caucasus', in *Byzantium. Faith and Power (1261–1557): Perspectives on Late Byzantine Art and Culture*, ed. S. T. Brooks (New Haven; London, 2007), 154–69

Art and Identity in Thirteenth-Century Byzantium: Hagia Sophia and the Empire of Trebizond [Birmingham Byzantine and Ottoman Monographs: 10] (Aldershot, 2004)

'Art and the Periphery', in *The Oxford Handbook of Byzantine Studies*, eds. E. Jeffreys, R. Cormack and J. Haldon (Oxford, 2008), 770–6

'Diplomatic Gifts: Women and Art as Imperial Commodities in the Thirteenth Century', in *Liquid and Multiple: Individuals and Identities in the Thirteenth-Century Aegean*, eds. G. Saint-Guillain and D. Stathokopoulos [Centre de recherche d'Histoire et Civilisation de Byzance, Monographies: 35] (Paris, 2012), 105–33

'Gender and Patronage between Christianity and Islam in the Thirteenth Century', in *Change in the Byzantine World in the Twelfth and Thirteenth Centuries*, eds. A. Ödekan, E. Akyürek and N. Necipoğlu (Istanbul, 2010), 78–88

'Inscriptions and Authority in Ani', in *Der Doppeladler: Byzanz und die Seldschuken in Anatolien vom späten 11. bis zum 13. Jahrhundert*, eds. N. Asutay-Effenberger and F. Daim [Byzanz zwischen Orient und Okzident: 1] (Mainz, 2014), 71–84

'"Local" Saints, Art and Regional Identity in the Orthodox World after the Fourth Crusade', *Speculum* 78/3 (2003), 707–49

'Other Encounters: Popular Belief and Cultural Convergence in Anatolia and the Caucasus', in *Islam and Christianity in Anatolia and the Caucasus*, eds. A. C. S. Peacock, B. De Nicola and S. N. Yıldız (Farnham, 2015), 183–213

Royal Imagery in Medieval Georgia (University Park, PA, 1998)

'Royal Renewal in Georgia: The Case of Queen Tamar', in *New Constantines: The Rhythm of Imperial Renewal in Byzantium, 4th–13th Centuries*, ed. P. Magdalino [Society for the Promotion of Byzantine Studies. Publications: 2] (Aldershot, 1994), 283–93; reprinted in *Languages and Cultures of Eastern Christianity: Georgian*, eds. S. H. Rapp and P. Crego [The Worlds of Eastern Christianity, 300–1500: 5] (Aldershot, 2012), Study XIV

'Un'eco della leggenda del Mandylion nell'Islam', in *Intorno al Sacro Volto: Genova, Bisanzio e il Mediterraneo (secoli XI–XIV)*, eds. A. R. C. Masetti, C. D. Bozzo and G. Wolf [Collana del Kunsthistorisches Institut in Florenz, Max-Planck-Institut: 11] (Florence, 2007), 175–80

Eastmond, A., and Z. Skhirtladze, 'Udabno Monastery in Georgia: The Innovation, Conservation and Reinterpretation of Art in the Middle Ages', *Iconographica: Rivista di iconografia medievale e moderna* 7 (2008), 23–43

Ecker, H., and T. Fitzherbert, 'The Freer Canteen Reconsidered', *Ars Orientalis* 42 (2012), 176–93

Écochard, M., and C. Le Coeur, *Les bains de Damas* (Beirut, 1942–3), 2 vols.

Edhem, H., and M. van Berchem, *Matériaux pour un corpus inscriptionum arabicarum*, vol. 3 (Cairo, 1917)

Ekhtiar, M., P. Soucek, S. Canby and N. N. Haidar, *Masterpieces from the Department of Islamic Art in the Metropolitan Museum of Art* (New York, 2011)

Enukidze, T. P., V. I. Shoshiashvili and N. Sologava, *Kartuli historikuli sabutebi XI–XIII s* (Tbilisi, 1984)

Erdmann, K., *Das Anatolische Karavansaray des 13. Jahrhundert*, vol. 1 [Istanbuler Forschungen: 21] (Berlin, 1961)

Eremian, S. T., 'Agartsinskaia nadpis 1184g.', in *Issledovania po istorii kultury narodov vostoka: sbornik v chest' akademika I. A. Orbeli* (Moscow, 1960), 78–87

Ettinghausen, R., O. Grabar and M. Jenkins-Madina, *Islamic Art and Architecture, 650–1250* (Harmondsworth, 2001)

Evans, H. C., 'Kings and Power Bases: Sources for Royal Portraits in Armenian Cilicia', in *From Byzantium to Iran: Armenian Studies in Honor of Nina G. Garsoïan*, eds. R. W. Thomson and J.-P. Mahé (Atlanta, GA, 1997), 485–507

Evans, H. C., ed., *Byzantium: Faith and Power (1261–1557)* (New York, 2004)

Evans, H. C. and W. D. Wixom, eds., *The Glory of Byzantium: Art and Culture of the Middle Byzantine Era, AD 843–1261* (New York, 1997)

Fiey, J. M., *Assyrie chrétienne: contribution à l'étude de l'histoire et de la géographie ecclésiastiques et monastiques du nord de l'Iraq* [Recherches publiées sous la direction de l'Institut de Lettres Orientales de Beyrouth: 22, 23] (Beirut, 1965)

Chrétiens syriaques sous les Abbassides surtout à Bagdad (749–1258) [Corpus Scriptorum Christianorum Orientalium: 420, Subsidia: 59] (Louvain, 1980)

Chrétiens syriaques sous les Mongols (Il-Khanat de Perse, XIIIe–XIVe s.) [Corpus Scriptorum Christianorum Orientalium: 362, Subsidia: 44] (Louvain, 1975)

Fleck, C. A., 'Crusader Spolia in Medieval Cairo: The Portal of the Complex of Sultan Ḥasan', *Journal of Transcultural Medieval Studies* 1/2 (2014), 249–99

Flood, F. B., *Objects of Translation: Material Culture and Medieval 'Hindu–Muslim' Encounter* (Princeton, 2009)

'Umayyad Survivals and Mamluk Revivals: Qalawunid Architecture and the Great Mosque of Damascus', *Muqarnas* 14 (1997), 57–79

Folda, J., *Crusader Art in the Holy Land, from the Third Crusade to the Fall of Acre, 1187–1291* (Cambridge, 2005)

Frenkel, M., 'Constructing the Sacred: Holy Shrines in Aleppo and its Environs', in *Egypt and Syria in the Fatimid, Ayyubid and Mamluk Eras: Proceedings of the International Colloquium Organized at the Katholieke Universiteit Leuven*, vol. 6, eds. U. Vermeulen and K. D'Hulster [Orientalia Lovaniensia Analecta: 183] (Leuven, 2010), 63–78

Gabriel, A., *Monuments turcs d'Anatolie I: Kayseri–Niğde* (Paris, 1931)

Monuments turcs d'Anatolie II: Amasya–Tokat–Sivas (Paris, 1934)

Voyages archéologiques dans la Turquie orientale (Paris, 1940)

Galatariotou, C., 'Holy Women and Witches: Aspects of Byzantine Conceptions of Gender', *Byzantine and Modern Greek Studies* 9 (1984), 55–94

Garsoïan, N. G., 'The Early-Medieval Armenian City: An Alien Element?', *Journal of Near Eastern Studies* 16–17 (1984), 67–83

Geopp, M., C. Mutafian and A. Ouzounian, 'L'inscription du régent Constantin de Papeṙōn (1241): redécouverte, relecture, remise en contexte historique', *Revue des études arméniennes* 34 (2012), 243–87

Georganteli, E., 'Transposed Images: Currencies and Legitimacy in the Late Medieval Eastern Mediterranean', in *Byzantines, Latins, and Turks in the Eastern Mediterranean World after 1150*, eds. J. Harris, C. Holmes and E. Russell (Oxford, 2012), 141–79

—— 'Trapezuntine Money in the Balkans, Anatolia and the Black Sea, 13th–15th Centuries', in *Trebizond and the Black Sea*, ed. T. Kyriakides (Thessaloniki, 2010), 93–112

George, D., 'Manuel I Komnenos and Michael Glykas: A Twelfth-Century Defence and Refutation of Astrology', *Culture and Cosmos* 5/1 (2001), 3–48; 5/2 (2001), 23–51; 6/1 (2002), 23–43

Giuzal'ian, L. T., 'Otryvok iz Shahname na glinianykh izdeliiakh XIII–XIV vv', *Epigrafika Vostoka* 4 (1951), 40–55 and 5 (1951), 33–50.

—— 'Persidskaia nadpis' Key-Sultana Sheddadi v Ani', in *XLV Akademiku N.Ia.Marru*, ed. I. I. Meshchaninov (Moscow; Leningrad, 1935), 629–41

Gomelauri, I., 'Khurotmodzghvruli dzegli sopel abeliashi', *Matsne* 1 (1968), 255–74

Grabar, O., 'The Illustrated Maqamat of the Thirteenth Century: The Bourgeoisie and the Arts', in *The Islamic City: A Colloquium*, eds. A. H. Hourani and S. M. Stern [Papers on Islamic History: 1] (Oxford, 1970), 207–22

—— *The Illustrations of the Maqamat* (Chicago, 1984)

Grube, E. J., and J. Johns, *The Painted Ceilings of the Cappella Palatina* [Islamic Art Supplement: 1] (Genoa; New York, 2005)

Grumel, V., *Traité d'études byzantines*, vol. 1: *La chronologie* (Paris, 1958)

Gunther, R. T., *The Astrolabes of the World: Based upon the Series of Instruments in the Lewis Evans Collection in the Old Ashmolean Museum at Oxford, with Notes on Astrolabes in the Collections of the British Museum, Sir J. Findlay, Mr. S. V. Hoffman, the Mensin Collection, and in Other Public and Private Collections*, vol. 1: *The Eastern Astrolabes* (Oxford, 1932)

Harrak, A., *Syriac and Garshuni Inscriptions of Iraq* [Recueil des inscriptions syriaques: 2] (Paris, 2010), 2 vols.

Hartner, W., 'The Principle and Use of the Astrolabe', in *A Survey of Persian Art from Prehistoric Times to the Present*, vol. 3, ed. A. U. Pope (London; New York, 1939), 2530–54

Hasluck, F. W., *Christianity and Islam under the Sultans* (Oxford, 1929), 2 vols.

Hasrat'yan, M., and J.-M. Thierry, 'Le couvent de Ganjasar', *Revue des études arméniennes* 15 (1981), 289–316

Heidemann, S., 'The Citadel of al-Raqqa and Fortifications in the Middle Euphrates Area', in *Muslim Military Architecture in Greater Syria: From the Coming of Islam to the Ottoman Period*, ed. H. Kennedy [History of Warfare: 35] (Leiden, 2006), 122–50

Heidemann, S., J.-F. de Laperouse and V. Parry, 'The Large Audience: Life-Sized Stucco Figures of Royal Princes from the Seljuq Period', *Muqarnas* 31 (2014), 35–72

Hennessy, C., 'A Child Bride and her Representation in the Vatican *Epithalamion*, cod. gr. 1851', *Byzantine and Modern Greek Studies* 30/2 (2006), 115–50

Images of Children in Byzantium (Aldershot, 2008)

Hewsen, R. H., 'The Historical Geography of Baghesh/Bitlis and Taron/Mush', in *Armenian Baghesh/Bitlis and Taron/Mush*, ed. R. G. Hovannisian [Historic Armenian Cities and Provinces: 2] (Costa Mesa, CA, 2001), 41–58

Hill, B., *Imperial Women in Byzantium 1025–1204: Patronage, Power and Ideology* (Harlow, 1999)

Hillenbrand, R., 'The Art of the Ayyubids: An Overview', in *Ayyubid Jerusalem: The Holy City in Context, 1187–1250*, eds. R. Hillenbrand and S. Auld (London, 2009), 22–44

Islamic Architecture: Form, Function and Meaning (Edinburgh, 1994)

Islamic Art and Architecture (London, 1999)

'The Schefer Ḥarīrī: A Study in Islamic Frontispiece Design', in *Arab Painting: Text and Image in Illustrated Arabic Manuscripts*, ed. A. Contadini [Handbook of Oriental Studies, Section One: The Near and Middle East: 90] (Leiden; Boston, 2010), 117–34

Hilsdale, C. J., 'Constructing a Byzantine Augusta: A Greek Book for a French Bride', *Art Bulletin* 87/3 (2005), 458–83

'Gift', *Studies in Iconography* 33 (2012), 171–82

Hoffman, E. R., 'Christian–Islamic Encounters on Thirteenth-Century Ayyubid Metalwork: Local Culture, Authenticity, and Memory', *Gesta* 43/2 (2004), 129–42

Holod, R., 'Event and Memory: The Freer Gallery's Siege Scene Plate', *Ars Orientalis* 42 (2012), 194–220

Hopwood, K., 'Byzantine Princesses and Lustful Turks', in *Rape in Antiquity: Sexual Violence in the Greek and Roman Worlds*, eds. S. Deacy and K. F. Pierce (London, 1997), 231–42

Hourani, A. H., 'Introduction: The Islamic City in the Light of Recent Research', in *The Islamic City: A Colloquium*, eds. A. H. Hourani and S. M. Stern [Papers on Islamic History: 1] (Oxford, 1970), 9–24

Humphreys, R. S., *From Saladin to the Mongols: The Ayyubids of Damascus, 1193–1260* (Albany, 1977)

'Women as Patrons of Religious Architecture in Ayyubid Damascus', *Muqarnas* 11 (1994), 35–54

Hunt, L.-A., 'Eastern Christian Art and Culture in the Ayyubid and Early Mamluk Periods: Cultural Convergence between Jerusalem, Greater Syria and Egypt', in *Ayyubid Jerusalem: The Holy City in Context, 1187–1250*, eds. R. Hillenbrand and S. Auld (London, 2009), 327–47

'A Woman's Prayer to St Sergius in Latin Syria: Interpreting a Thirteenth-Century Icon at Mt Sinai', *Byzantine and Modern Greek Studies* 15 (1991), 96–145

Jacobsthal, E., *Mittelalterliche Backsteinbauten zu Nachtschewân im Araxesthale, mit einer Bearbeitung der Inschriften von Martin Hartmann* (Berlin, 1899)

Jacoby, D., 'Crusader Acre in the Thirteenth Century: Urban Layout and Topography', *Studi Medievali* series 3, 20/1 (1979), 1–45

Jacoby, Z., 'The Medieval Doors of the Church of the Nativity at Bethlehem', in *Le Porte di Bronzo dall'Antichità al Secolo XIII*, ed. S. Salomi (Rome, 1990), 121–34

James, B., 'Les Kurdes au Moyen Âge', in *L'Orient de Saladin: l'art sous les Ayyoubides*, ed. É. Delpont (Paris, 2002), 24

Javakhishvili, I., *Kartveli eris istoria*, vol. 3 (Tbilisi, 1982)

Jayyusi, S. K., 'Arabic Poetry in the Post-Classical Age', in *The Cambridge History of Arabic Literature*, vol. 6: *Arab Literature in the Post-Classical Period*, eds. R. Allen and D. S. Richards (Cambridge, 2006), 25–59

Jeffreys, E., *Digenis Akritis: The Grottaferrata and Escorial Versions* [Cambridge Medieval Classics: 7] (Cambridge, 1998)

Jeffreys, M., 'The Vernacular εἰσιτήριοι for Agnes of France', in *Byzantine Papers: Proceedings of the First Australian Byzantine Studies Conference* (Canberra, 1981), 101–15

Jeffreys, M., and J. Anderson, 'The Decoration of the Sevastokratorissa's Tent', *Byzantion* 64 (1994), 8–18

Jones, D., and G. Michell, eds., *The Arts of Islam* (London, 1976)

Jones, L., *Between Islam and Byzantium: Aght'amar and the Visual Construction of Medieval Armenian Rulership* (Aldershot, 2007)

Kalandia, G., and K. Asatiani, 'Koberis I da II sametsniero eskpeditsiis pirveladi shedegebi (sainpormatsio mimokhilva)', *Saistorio krebuli* 2 (2012), 170–91

Kalantarian, A. A., *Dvin: histoire et archéologie de la ville médiévale* [Civilisations du Proche-Orient. Hors Série: 2] (Neuchâtel; Paris, 1996)

Karamağaralı, B., *Ahlat mezartaşları* [Selçuklu Tarih ve Medeniyeti Enstitütüsü. San'at tarihi serisi: 1] (Ankara, 1972)

'Ani Ulu Cami (Manucehr Camii)', in *9th International Congress of Turkish Art, Summary of Contributions* (Ankara, 1995), 323–38

Karamağaralı, H., 'Kayseri'deki Hunad Camiinin Restitüsyonu ve Hunad Manzumesinin Kronolojisi Hakkında Bazı Mülahzalar', *A.Ü. Ilahiyat Fakültesi Dergisi* 21 (1976), 199–243

Katzenstein, R. A., and G. D. Lowry, 'Christian Themes in Thirteenth-Century Islamic Metalwork', *Muqarnas* 1 (1983), 53–68

Kennedy, H., 'How to Found an Islamic City', in *Cities, Texts and Social Networks, 400–1500: Experiences and Perceptions of Medieval Urban Space*, eds. C. Goodson, A. E. Lester and C. Symes (Farnham; Burlington, VA, 2010), 45–63

Kerner, J. J., 'Art in the Name of Science: The Kitāb al-Diryāq in Text and Image', in *Arab Painting: Text and Image in Illustrated Arabic Manuscripts*, ed. A. Contadini [Handbook of Oriental Studies, Section One: The Near and Middle East: 90] (Leiden; Boston, 2010), 25–40

Kévorkian, R. H., *Ani: capitale de l'Arménie en l'an mil* (Paris, 2001)

Khachatrian, A. A., *Korpus arabskikh nadpisei Armenii* (Yerevan, 1987)

Khanykof, M., 'Quelques inscriptions musulmans, d'Ani et des environs de Bakou', *Bulletin de la classe des sciences historiques, philologiques et politiques de l'Académie Impériale des Sciences de Saint-Pétersbourg* 6/13–14 (1849), 193–200; reprinted in *Mélanges Asiatiques tirés du Bulletin Historico-Philologique de l'Académie Impériale des Sciences de Saint-Pétersbourg*, vol. 2 (St Petersburg, 1856), 70–8

Khoshtaria, T., 'The Wall Paintings of the Chapel–Martyrium Motsameta in the Rock-Cut Monastery Complex of Udabno David-Gareji', *Inferno: University of St Andrews School of Art History Postgraduate Journal* 9 (2004), 15–22

Khs-Burmester, O. H. E., *A Guide to the Ancient Coptic Churches of Cairo* (Giza, 1955)

Khuskivadze, I., and D. Tumanishvili, eds., *Gelati 900: Architecture, Murals, Treasures* (Tbilisi, 2007)

Khuskivadze, L. Z., *The Khakhuli Triptych* (Tbilisi, 2007)

Kirion, B., *Akhtal'skii monastyr'* (Tbilisi, 2005)

Kleinbauer, W. E., 'Zvart'nots and the Origins of Christian Architecture in Armenia', *Art Bulletin* 54/3 (1972), 245–62

Komaroff, L., and S. Carboni, eds., *The Legacy of Genghis Khan: Courtly Art and Culture in Western Asia, 1256–1353* (New York, 2002)

Korobeinikov, D., 'A Greek Orthodox Armenian in the Seljukid Service: The Colophon of Basil of Melitina', in *Mare et Litora: Essays Presented to Sergei Karpov for his 60th Birthday*, ed. R. Shukurov (Moscow, 2009), 709–24

Kotandjian, N., 'Les décors peints des églises d'Arménie', in *Armenia Sacra: mémoire chrétienne des Arméniens (IVe–XVIIIe siècle)*, eds. J. Durand et al. (Paris, 2007), 137–44

Kouymjian, D., 'Chinese Motifs in Thirteenth-Century Armenian Art: The Mongol Connection', in *Beyond the Legacy of Genghis Khan*, ed. L. Komaroff (Leiden, 2006), 303–24

Krabbenhöft, N., 'A Veneer of Power: Thirteenth-Century Seljuk Frescoes on the Walls of Alanya and Some Recommendations for their Preservation' (MA thesis, Koç University, 2011)

Krstic, T., 'The Ambiguous Politics of "Ambiguous Sanctuaries": F. Hasluck and Historiography on Syncretism and Conversion to Islam in 15th and 16th Century Ottoman Rumeli', in *Archaeology, Anthropology and Heritage in the Balkans and Anatolia: The Life and Times of F. W. Hasluck, 1878–1920*, ed. D. Shankland (Istanbul, 2013), 247–62

Kuban, Y. D., *Divriği Mucizesi: Selçuklar Çağında Islam Bezeme Sanatı Üzerine Bir Deneme* (Istanbul, 1997)

Kudava, B., ed., *Istoriani: sametsniero krebuli midzghvnili Roin Metrevelis dabadebis 70 tslist'avisadmi*, (Tbilisi, 2009)

Kuehn, S., *The Dragon in Medieval East Christian and Islamic Art* [Islamic History and Civilization. Studies and Texts: 86] (Leiden; Boston, 2011)

La Porta, S., 'Conflicted Coexistence: Christian–Muslim Interaction and its Representation in Medieval Armenia', in *Contextualizing the Muslim Other in Medieval Christian Discourse*, ed. J. C. Frakes (London, 2011), 103–23

'"The Kingdom and the Sultanate were Conjoined": Legitimizing Land and Power in Armenia during the 12th and Early 13th Centuries', *Revue des études arméniennes* 34 (2012), 73–118

'Lineage, Legitimacy and Loyalty in Post-Seljuk Armenia: A Reassessment of the Sources of the Failed Ōrbēlean Revolt against King Giorgi III of Georgia', *Revue des études arméniennes* 31 (2008–9), 127–65

'Re-Constructing Armenia: Strategies of Co-Existence amongst Christians and Muslims in the Thirteenth Century', in *Negotiating Co-Existence: Communities, Cultures and Convivencia in Byzantine Society*, eds. B. Crostini and S. La Porta [Bochumer Altertumswissenschaftliches Colloquium: 96] (Trier, 2013), 251–72

Lambton, A. K. S., *Continuity and Change in Medieval Persia: Aspects of Administrative, Economic and Social History, 11th–14th Century* [Columbia Lectures on Iranian Studies: 2] (New York, 1988)

Lane Poole, S., *Catalogue of Oriental Coins in the British Museum* (London, 1875–90), 10 vols.

Laurent, V., 'L'inscription de l'église Saint-Georges de Bélisérama', *Revue des études byzantines* 26 (1968), 367–71

Layard, A. H., *Discoveries in the Ruins of Nineveh and Babylon: with travels in Armenia, Kurdistan and the desert: being the result of a second expedition undertaken for the trustees of the British Museum* (London, 1853)

Le Strange, G., *The Lands of the Eastern Caliphate: Mesopotamia, Persia, and Central Asia from the Moslem Conquest to the Time of Timur* (New York, 1905)

Leiser, G., 'Observations on the "Lion and Sun" Coinage of Ghiyath al-Din Kai-Khusraw II', *Mésogeios* 2 (1998), 96–114

Leroy, J., *Les manuscrits syriaques à peintures conservées dans les bibliothèques d'Europe et d'Orient* (Paris, 1964)

Les regestes des actes du patriarcat de Constantinople, vol. 1: *Les actes des patriarches; fasc. 4: Les regestes de 1208 à 1309* (Paris, 1971)

Levanoni, A., 'Šağar al-Durr: A Case of Female Sultanate in Medieval Islam', in *Egypt and Syria in the Fatimid, Ayyubid and Mamluk eras*, vol. 3, eds. U. Vermeulen and J. Van Steenbergen [Orientalia Lovaniensia Analecta: 102] (Leuven, 2001), 209–18

Lewis, B., *The Assassins: A Radical Sect in Islam* (New York, 1980)

'The Coming of the Steppe People: 2: Egypt and Syria', in *The Cambridge History of Islam*, vol. 1A, eds. P. M. Holt, A. K. S. Lambton and B. Lewis (Cambridge, 1970), 175–230

Lidov, A. M., 'L'art des Arméniens Chalcédoniens', in *Atti del quinto simposio internazionale di Arte Armena* (Venice, 1992), 479–95

The Wall Paintings of Akhtala: History, Iconography, Masters (Moscow, 2014)

Livingston, J. W., 'Science and the Occult in the Thinking of Ibn Qayyim al-Jawziyya', *Journal of the American Oriental Society* 112/4 (1992), 598–610

Lloyd, S., and D. S. Rice, *Alanya ('Alā'iyya)* [Occasional Publications of the British Institute of Archaeology at Ankara: 4] (London, 1958)

Lordkipanidze, M., *Georgia in the XI–XII Centuries* (Tbilisi, 1987)

Loris'-Kalantar', A., 'Razvaliny drevniaiu karavansaraia', *Khristianskii Vostok* 3 (1914), 101–2

Lowick, N. M., S. Bendall and P. D. Whitting, *The 'Mardin' Hoard: Islamic Countermarks on Byzantine Folles* (London, 1977)

Lynch, H. F. B., *Armenia: Travels and Studies* (London; New York, 1901), 2 vols.

Lyons, M. C., and D. E. P. Jackson, *Saladin: The Politics of Holy War* (Cambridge, 1982)

MacEvitt, C., *Rough Tolerance: The Crusades and the Christian World of the East* (Philadelphia, 2008)

Macip Tekinalp, V., 'Palace Churches of the Anatolian Seljuks: Tolerance or Necessity?' *Byzantine and Modern Greek Studies* 33/2 (2009), 148–67

Magdalino, P., *The Empire of Manuel I Komnenos, 1143–1180* (Cambridge, 1993)

'Theodore Metochites, the Chora, and Constantinople', in *The Kariye Camii Reconsidered*, eds. H. A. Klein, R. Ousterhout and B. Pitarakis [Istanbul Araştırmarları Enstitüsü Yayınları: 14] (Istanbul, 2011), 169–87

Mahé, J.-P., 'L'étude de P. M. Muradyan sur les inscriptions géorgiennes d'Arménie', *Bedi Kartlisa* 38 (1980), 295–309

'Les inscriptions de Horomos', in *Le couvent de Horomos d'après les archives de Toros Toramanian*, eds. A. Baladian and J.-M. Thierry [Monuments et mémoires. Fondation Eugène Piot: 81] (Paris, 2002), 147–213

'Le testament de Tigran Honenc': la fortune d'un marchand arménien d'Ani aux XIIe–XIIIe siècles', *Comptes Rendus de l'Académie des Inscriptions et Belles-Lettres* 145/3 (2001), 1319–41

Mahé, J.-P., N. Faucherre and B. Karamağaralı, 'L'enceinte urbaine d'Ani (Turquie Orientale): problèmes chronologiques', *Comptes Rendus de l'Académie des Inscriptions et Belles-Lettres* 143/2 (1999), 731–56

Makariou, S., ed., *Islamic Art at the Musée du Louvre* (Paris, 2012)

Maksimović, L., 'War Simonis Palaiologina die fünfte Gemahlin von König Milutin?', in *Geschichte und Kultur der Palaiologenzeit*, ed. W. Seibt [Veröffentlichungen der Kommission für Byzantinistik: 8] (Vienna, 1996), 115–20

Manandian, H., *The Trade and Cities of Armenia in Relation to Ancient World Trade* (Lisbon, 1965)

Mango, C., 'Antique Statuary and the Byzantine Beholder', *Dumbarton Oaks Papers* 17 (1963), 55–75; reprinted in his *Byzantium and its Image* [Variorum Collected Studies: CS191] (Aldershot, 1984), Study V

The Art of the Byzantine Empire 312–1453 (Englewood Cliffs, NJ, 1972)

Margarian, H., 'Ṣāḥib-Dīvān Šams al-Dīn Muḥammad Juvainī and Armenia', *Iran and the Caucasus* 10/2 (2006), 167–80

Marr, N. I., *Ani: Knizhnaia istoriia goroda i raskopki na meste gorodishcha* (Leningrad; Moscow, 1934); French trans. *Ani: rêve d'Arménie*, trans. Aïda Tcharkhtchian (Paris, 2001)

'Arkaun, mongol'skoe nazvanie khristian, v sviazi s voprosom ob armianakh-khalkedonitakh', *Vizantiiskii Vremennik* 12 (1906), 1–68

'Freskovoe izobrazhenie parona Khutlu-bugi v' Akhpat' (hAibatp)', *Khristianskii Vostok* 1/3 (1912), 350–53

'Nadpis Epifaniia, katalikosa Gruzii (iz raskopok v Ani 1910 g.)', *Izvestiia Imperatorskoi Akademii Nauk* 4 (1910), 1433–42

'Nadpis' Sanahinskaiu mosta', *Khristianskii Vostok* 4 (1915), 191–2

'Novye materialy po armianskoi epigrafike', *Zapiski vostochnogo otdeleniia imperatorskogo russkogo arkheologicheskogo obshchestva* 8 (1894), 69–103

Martin-Hisard, B., 'Christianisme et église dans le monde géorgien', in *Histoire de Christianisme des origines à nos jours*, vol. 4, eds. J.-M. Mayeur, C. Pietri, L. Pietri, A. Vauchez and M. Venard (Paris, 1993), 549–603

'La vie de Jean et Euthyme et le statut du monastère des Ibères sur l'Athos', *Revue des études byzantines* 49 (1991), 67–142

Matevosyan, K. A., 'Scriptoria et bibliothèques d'Ani', *Revue des études arméniennes* 20 (1986–7), 209–21

Mathews, K. R., 'Other Peoples' Dishes: Islamic Bacini on Eleventh-Century Churches in Pisa', *Gesta* 53/1 (2014), 5–23

Mathews, T. F., and R. S. Wieck, eds., *Treasures in Heaven: Armenian Illuminated Manuscripts* (Princeton, 1994)

May, T., 'The Conquest and Rule of Transcaucasia: The Era of Chormaqan', in *Caucasus during the Mongol Period – Der Kaukasus in der Mongolenzeit*, eds. J. Tubach, S. G. Vashalomidze and M. Zimmer (Wiesbaden, 2012), 129–51

Mecit, S., *The Rum Seljuqs: Evolution of a Dynasty* [Routledge Studies in the History of Iran and Turkey: 10] (Abingdon; New York, 2014)

Meinecke, M., 'Das Mausoleum des Qala'un in Kairo: Untersuchungen zur Genese der mamlukischen Architekturdekorationen', *Mitteilungen des Deutschen Archäologischen Instituts. Abteilung Kairo* 27 (1971), 47–80

'Der Survey des Damaszener Altstadtviertels aṣ-Ṣāliḥīya', *Damaszener Mitteilungen* 1 (1983), 189–241

Meri, J. W., *The Cult of Saints among Muslims and Jews in Medieval Syria* (Oxford, 2002)

Mernissi, F., *The Forgotten Queens of Islam* (Cambridge, 1993)

Meskhia, S., *Sashinao politikuri vitareba da samokheleo tsqoba XII saukunis sakartveloshi* (Tbilisi, 1979)

Metreveli, R., *Mepe tamari* (Tbilisi, 1991)

Micheau, F., 'Les médecins orientaux au service des princes latins', in *Occident et Proche-Orient: contacts scientifiques au temps des Croisades*, eds. I. Draelants, A. Tihon and B. van den Abeele [Réminiscences: 5] (Louvain, 1997), 95–115

Miller, I., 'Occult Science and the Fall of the Khwarazm-Shah Jalal al-Din', *Iran* 39 (2001), 249–56

Minorsky, V., 'Caucasica [I] in the History of Mayyafariqin', *Bulletin of the School of Oriental and African Studies* 13 (1949), 27–35

Studies in Caucasian History (London, 1953)

Mitsani, A., 'The Illustrated Gospel Book of Basil Meleniotes (Caesaria, 1226)', *Deltion tes Christianikes Archaiologikes Hetaireias* 26 (2005), 149–64

Mnatsakanian, S. K., *Arkhitektura armianskikh pritvorov* (Yerevan, 1952)

Mols, L. E. M., *Mamluk Metalwork Fittings in their Artistic and Architectural Context* (Delft, 2006)

Moule, A. C., *Christians in China before the Year 1550* (London, 1930)

Mousheghian, K. A., A. Mousheghian and G. Depeyrot, *History and Coin Finds in Armenia: Inventory of Coins and Hoards (7th–19th c.)* [Collection moneta: 29, 35] (Wetteren, 2002, 2003), 2 vols.

Mulder, S., 'The Mausoleum of Imam al-Shafi'i', *Muqarnas* 23 (2006), 15–46

Mutafian, C., 'Ani after Ani, Eleventh to Seventeenth Century', in *Armenian Kars and Ani*, ed. R. G. Hovannisian [Historic Armenian Cities and Provinces: 10] (Costa Mesa, CA, 2011), 155–70

Le Royaume arménien de Cilicie, XIIe–XIVe siècle (Paris, 2002)

Nadwi, M. A., *al-Muḥaddithāt: The Women Scholars in Islam*, 2nd edn. (Oxford, 2013)

Nelson, R. S., 'The History of Legends and the Legends of History: The Pilastri Acritani in Venice', in *San Marco, Byzantium, and the Myths of Venice*, eds. H. Maguire and R. S. Nelson (Washington, DC, 2010), 63–90

Nersessian, V., 'Armenian Christianity', in *The Blackwell Companion to Eastern Christianity*, ed. K. Parry (Oxford, 2007), 23–46

Nersessian, V., ed., *Treasures from the Ark: 1700 Years of Armenian Christian Art* (London, 2001)

North, J. D., 'Opus quarundam rotarum mirabilium', *Physis* 8 (1966), 337–72

Stars, Minds and Faith: Essays in Ancient and Medieval Cosmology (London, 1989)

Novikoff, A., 'Between Tolerance and Intolerance in Medieval Spain: An Historiographic Enigma', *Medieval Encounters* 11/1–2 (2005), 7–36

O'Kane, B., ed., *The Treasures of Islamic Art in the Museums of Cairo* (Cairo, 2006)

Olschki, L., *Guillaume Boucher: A French Artist at the Court of the Khans* (New York, 1946)

Orbeli, I. A., 'Armianskie nadpisi na kamne', in *Izbrannye Trudy* (Yerevan, 1963), 469–76

Corpus Inscriptionum Armenicarum, vol. 1 (Yerevan, 1966)

Özbek, Y., 'Women's Tombs in Kayseri', *Kadın/Woman 2000* 3/1 (2002), 65–85; Turkish text 86–114

Paboudjian, P., 'Le mausolée de Mama Khatun à Terdjan et l'architecture arménienne', in *The Second International Symposium on Armenian Art*, vol. 2, ed. R. Zarian (Yerevan, 1978), 297–311

Pahlitzsch, J., 'The People of the Book', in *Ayyubid Jerusalem: The Holy City in Context, 1187–1250*, eds. R. Hillenbrand and S. Auld (London, 2009), 435–40

Pancaroğlu, O., 'The House of Mengüjek in Divriği: Constructions of Dynastic Identity in the Late Twelfth Century', in *The Seljuks of Anatolia: Court and Society in the Medieval Middle East*, eds. A. C. S. Peacock and S. N. Yıldız (London; New York, 2013), 25–67

'The Mosque–Hospital Complex in Divriği: A History of Relations and Transitions', *Anadolu ve Çevresinde Ortaçağ* 3 (2009), 169–98

Papadopoulos-Kerameus, A., 'Symbolai eis tin istorian Trapezountos', *Vizantiiskii Vremennik* 12 (1906), 132–47

Patton, D., *Badr al-Dīn Lu'lu', Atabeg of Mosul, 1211–1259* [Middle East Center, Jackson School of International Studies, University of Washington. Occasional Papers: 3] (Seattle; London, 1991)

Peacock, A. C. S., 'Georgia and the Anatolian Turks in the 12th and 13th Centuries', *Anatolian Studies* 56 (2006), 127–46

'An Interfaith Polemic of Medieval Anatolia: Qāḍī Burhān al-Dīn al-Anawī on the Armenians and their Heresies', in *Islam and Christianity in Anatolia and the Caucasus*, eds. A. C. S. Peacock, B. De Nicola and S. N. Yıldız (Farnham, 2015), 233–61

'Sinop: A Frontier City in Seljuq and Mongol Anatolia', *Ancient Civilizations from Scythia to Siberia* 16 (2010), 103–24, 537

Pentcheva, B. V., *Icons and Power: The Mother of God in Byzantium* (University Park, PA, 2006)

Pope, A. U., ed., *A Survey of Persian Art from Prehistoric Times to the Present* (London; New York, 1938–9), 6 vols.

Porter, V., and M. A. S. Abdel Haleem, eds., *Hajj: Journey to the Heart of Islam* (London, 2012)

Porter, V., R. G. Hoyland and A. D. Morton, *Arabic and Persian Seals and Amulets in the British Museum* [British Museum Research Publication: 160] (London, 2011)

Porter, Y., 'Les techniques du lustre métallique d'après le Jowhar-name-ye-Nezami', *VIIe congrès international sur la céramique médiévale en méditerranée* (Athens, 2003), 427–36

Pouzet, L., *Damas au VIIe/XIIIe siecle: vie et structures religieuses d'une métropole Islamique* (Beirut, 1991)

Preusser, C., *Nordmesopotamische Baudenkmäler altchristlicher und islamischer Zeit* [Wissenschaftliche Veröffentlichung der Deutschen Orient-Gesellschaft: 17] (Leipzig, 1911)

Pringle, D., *The Churches of the Crusader Kingdom of Jerusalem: A Corpus* (Cambridge, 1993–2009), 4 vols.

    Pilgrimage to Jerusalem and the Holy Land, 1187–1291 [Crusade Texts in Translation: 23] (Farnham, 2012)

Pritula, A., 'A Hymn on Tiflis from Warda Collection: A Transformation of the Muslim Conquerors into Pagans', in *Caucasus during the Mongol Period – Der Kaukasus in der Mongolenzeit*, eds. J. Tubach, S. G. Vashalomidze and M. Zimmer (Wiesbaden, 2012), 217–37

Privalova, E., *Rospis' Timotesubani* (Tbilisi, 1980)

Qaukhchishvili, T. S., *Berdznuli tsartserebi sakartvelo*, vol. 1 (Tbilisi, 1951)

Qenia, M., *Upper Svaneti: Medieval Mural Painting* (Tbilisi, 2010)

Raby, J., 'Nur al-Din, the Qastal al-Shu'aybiyya and the "Classical Revival"', *Muqarnas* 21 (2004), 289–310

    'The Principle of Parsimony and the Problem of the "Mosul School of Metalwork"', in *Metalwork and Material Culture in the Islamic World. Art, Craft and Text: Essays Presented to James W. Allan*, eds. M. Rosser-Owen and V. Porter (London; New York, 2012), 11–85

Rapp, S. H., 'The Coinage of Tamar, Sovereign of Georgia in Caucasia: A Preliminary Study in the Numismatic Inscriptions of Twelfth- and Thirteenth-Century Georgian Royal Coinage', *Le Muséon* 106 (1993), 309–30

    'Georgian Christianity', in *The Blackwell Companion to Eastern Christianity*, ed. K. Parry (Oxford, 2007), 137–55

Rapp, S. H., ed., *K'art'lis c'xovreba: The Georgian Royal Annals and their Medieval Armenian Adaptation* (Delmar, NY, 1998)

Rapti, I., 'La peinture dans les livres (IXe–XIIIe siècle)', in *Armenia Sacra: mémoire chrétienne des Arméniens (IVe–XVIIIe siècle)*, eds. J. Durand et al. (Paris, 2007), 176–83

Rayfield, D., *Edge of Empires: A History of Georgia* (London, 2012)

    The Literature of Georgia: A History, 3rd edn. (London, 2010; 2nd edn. Oxford, 2000)

Raymond, A., 'The Spatial Organization of the City', in *The City in the Islamic World*, vol. 1, eds. R. Holod, A. Petruccioli and A. Raymond (Leiden; Boston, 2008), 47–70

Redford, S., 'The Alaeddin Mosque in Konya Reconsidered', *Artibus Asiae* 51/1 (1991), 54–74

    'The Inscription of the Kırkgöz Han and the Problem of Textual Transmission in Seljuk Anatolia', *Adalya* 12 (2009), 347–60

    Landscape and the State in Medieval Anatolia: Seljuk Gardens and Pavilions of Alanya, Turkey, [BAR International Series: 893] (Oxford, 2000)

Legends of Authority: The 1215 Seljuk Inscriptions of Sinop Citadel, Turkey (Istanbul, 2014)

'Paper, Stone, Scissors: 'Alā' al-Dīn Kayqubād, 'Iṣmat al-Dunyā wa l-Dīn, and the Writing of Seljuk History', in *The Seljuks of Anatolia: Court and Society in the Medieval Middle East*, eds. A. C. S. Peacock and S. N. Yıldız (London; New York, 2013), 151–70

'The Seljuqs of Rum and the Antique', *Muqarnas* 10 (1993), 148–56

'Sinop in the Summer of 1215: The Beginning of Anatolian Seljuk Architecture', *Ancient Civilizations from Scythia to Siberia* 16 (2010), 125–49, 538

'Words, Books, and Buildings in Seljuk Anatolia', in *Identity and Identity Formation in the Ottoman World: Essays in Honor of Norman Itzkowitz*, eds. B. Tezcan and K. K. Barbir (Madison, WI, 2007), 7–16

Redford, S., and G. Leiser, *Victory Inscribed: The Seljuk Fetihnāme on the Citadel Walls of Antalya, Turkey* [Adalya Supplementary Series: 7] (Antalya, 2008)

Reitlinger, G., 'Medieval Antiquities West of Mosul', *Iraq* 5 (1938), 143–56

Rice, D. S., 'The Aghānī Miniatures and Religious Painting in Islam', *Burlington Magazine* 95/601 (1953), 128–35

'Inlaid Brasses from the Workshop of Ahmad al-Dhaki al-Mawsili', *Ars Orientalis* 2 (1957), 283–326

'Medieval Ḥarrān: Studies on its Topography and Monuments, I', *Anatolian Studies* 2 (1952), 36–84

'A Seljuq Mirror', in *Proceedings of the First International Congress of Turkish Art* (Ankara, 1961), 288–90

Richard, F., *Catalogue des manuscrits persans I: Anciens fonds. Bibliothèque Nationale, Département des manuscrits* (Paris, 1989)

Rogers, J. M., 'The Çifte Minare Medrese at Erzurum and the Gök Medrese at Sivas: A Contribution to the History of Style in the Seljuk Architecture of 13th Century Turkey', *Anatolian Studies* 15 (1965), 63–87

'The Date of the Çifte Minare Medrese at Erzurum', *Kunst des Orients* 8/1–2 (1972), 77–119

'The Mxargrdzelis between East and West', *Bedi Kartlisa* 34 (1976), 315–25

'Waqf and Patronage in Seljuk Anatolia: The Epigraphic Evidence', *Anatolian Studies* 26 (1976), 69–104

Rossabi, M., 'The Muslims in the Early Yüan Dynasty', in *China under Mongol Rule*, ed. J. D. Langlois (Princeton, 1981), 257–95

Roux, J.-P., ed., *L'Islam dans les collections nationales* (Paris, 1977)

Rowson, E. K., 'Homoerotic Liaisons among the Mamluk Elite in Late Medieval Egypt and Syria', in *Islamicate Sexualities: Translations across Temporal Geographies of Desire*, eds. K. Babayan and A. Najmabadi [Harvard Middle Eastern Monographs: 39] (Cambridge, MA, 2008), 204–38

Roxburgh, D. J., ed., *Turks: A Journey of a Thousand Years, 600–1600* (London, 2005)

Safran, L., *The Medieval Salento: Art and Identity in Southern Italy* (Philadelphia, 2014)

Saliba, G., 'The Role of the Astrologer in Medieval Islamic Society', *Bulletin d'études orientales* 44 (1992), 45–67

Sarre, F. P. T., and E. Herzfeld, *Archäologische Reise im Euphrat- und Tigris-Gebiet* [Forschungen zur islamischen Kunst: 1] (Berlin, 1911), 4 vols.

Sarre, F. P. T., and M. van Berchem, 'Das Metallbecken des Atabeks Lulu von Mosul in der Königlichen Bibliothek zu München', *Münchner Jahrbuch der bildenden Kunst* 1 (1907), 18–37

Sauvaget, J., 'Un bain damasquin du XIIIe siècle', *Syria* 11/4 (1930), 370–80

Sauvaget, J., and M. Écochard, *Les monuments ayyoubides de Damas, etc.* (Paris, 1938–48), 4 vols. in 1

Sauvaire, H., 'Description de Damas', *Journal Asiatique*, IXe série II: 3 (May–June 1894), 385–501; VI: 5 (May–June 1895), 377–411; VII: 6 (September–October 1895), 221–313

Savage-Smith, E., *Islamicate Celestial Globes: Their History, Construction, and Use* [Smithsonian Studies in History and Technology: 46] (Washington, DC, 1985)

Savage-Smith, E., and M. B. Smith, *Islamic Geomancy and a Thirteenth-Century Divinatory Device* [Studies in Near Eastern Culture and Society: 2] (Malibu, CA, 1980)

'Islamic Geomancy and a Thirteenth-Century Divinatory Device: Another Look', in *Magic and Divination in Early Islam*, ed. E. Savage-Smith (Aldershot, 2004), 211–76

Schregle, G., *Die Sultanin von Ägypten: Šaǧarat ad-Durr in der arabischen Geschichtsschreibung und Literatur* (Wiesbaden, 1961)

Shanidze, A., *Etlta da shwidta mnatobtatwis. Astrologiuri tkhzuleba XII saukunisa* (Tbilisi, 1948)

Sharashidze, K., *Sakartvelos sakhelmtsipo muzeumis kartul khelnatserta aghtseriloba: qopili saeklesio muzeumis khelnatserebi (A kolektsia)*, vol. 4 (Tbilisi, 1954)

Sharlet, J., 'Public Displays of Affection: Male Homoerotic Desire and Sociability in Medieval Arabic Literature', in *Islam and Homosexuality*, ed. S. Habib (Santa Barbara, CA, 2010), 37–56

Shmerling, R. O., 'Postroika molaret-ukhutsesa tsaria Georgiia Blistatelnogo v tsel. Daba, borzhomskogo raiona', *Ars Georgica* 2 (1948), 111–22

Shukurov, R., 'Churches in the Citadels of Ispir and Bayburt: An Evidence of "Harem Christianity"?', in *Polidoro: Studi offerti ad Antonio Carile*, ed. G. Vespignani (Spoleto, 2013), 713–24

'Harem Christianity: The Byzantine Identity of Seljuk Princes', in *The Seljuks of Anatolia: Court and Society in the Medieval Middle East*, eds. A. C. S. Peacock and S. N. Yıldız (London; New York, 2013), 115–50

'Iagupy: tiurkskaia familiia na vizantiiskoi sluzhbe', in *Vizantiiskie Ocherki: Trudy rossiiskikh uchenykh k XXI Mezhdunarodnomu kongressu vizantinistov* (St Petersburg, 2006), 205–29

Silogava, V., 'Epigrapikuli etiudebi da shenishvnebi', *Macne* 4 (1990), 79–119

Sims, E., *Peerless Images: Persian Painting and its Sources* (New Haven; London, 2002)

Skhirtladze, Z., 'Another Portrait of Queen Tamar?', in *Anadolu Kültürlerinde Süreklilik ve Değişim, Dr. A. Mine Kadiroğlu'na Armağan*, eds. C. Erel, B. Işler, N. Peker and G. Sağir (Ankara, 2011), 505–23

Smith, A. D., 'National Identities: Modern and Medieval?', in *Concepts of National Identity in the Middle Ages*, eds. L. Johnson, A. V. Murray, and S. Forde [Leeds Texts and Monographs, New Series: 14] (Leeds, 1995), 21–46

Snelders, B., *Identity and Christian–Muslim Interaction: Medieval Art of the Syrian Orthodox from the Mosul Area* [Orientalia Lovaniensia Analecta: 198] (Leuven, 2010)

Soifer, M., 'Beyond Convivencia: Critical Reflections on the Historiography of Interfaith Relations in Christian Spain', *Journal of Medieval Iberian Studies* 1/1 (2009), 19–35

Sokhashvili, G., *Samtavisi: Masalebi tadzris istoriisatvis* (Tbilisi, 1973)

Sourdel, D., 'Rūḥīn, lieu de pèlerinage musulman de la Syrie du Nord au XIIIe siècle', *Syria* 30 (1953), 89–107

Spatharakis, I., *The Portrait in Byzantine Illuminated Manuscripts* (Leiden, 1976)

Strayer, J.R., 'The Crusades of Louis IX', in *A History of the Crusades*, vol. 2, eds. R. L. Wolff and H. W. Hazard (Madison; Milwaukee; London, 1969), 487–518

Sublet, J., 'La folie de la princesse Bint al-Ašraf (un scandale financier sous les Mamelouks Bahris)', *Bulletin d'études orientales* 27 (1974), 45–50

Tabbaa, Y., 'Circles of Power: Palace, Citadel, and City in Ayyubid Aleppo', *Ars Orientalis* 23 (1993), 181–200

Constructions of Power and Piety in Medieval Aleppo (University Park, PA, 1997)

'Dayfa Khatun, Regent Queen and Architectural Patron', in *Women, Patronage, and Self-Representation in Islamic Societies*, ed. D. F. Ruggles (Albany, NY, 2000), 17–34

'The Muqarnas Dome: Its Origin and Meaning', *Muqarnas* 3 (1985), 61–74

The Transformation of Islamic Art during the Sunni Revival (Washington, DC, 2001)

Tamarati, M., *L'église géorgienne dès origines jusqu'à nos jours* (Rome, 1910)

Taqaishvili, E., 'L'évangile de Vani', *Byzantion* 10 (1935), 655–63

'Gruzinskiia nadpisi Akhtaly', *Sbornik materialov dlia opisanie mestnostei i plemen Kavkaza* 29 (1901), 138–45

'L'inscription d'Épiphane, Catholicos de Géorgie', *Revue de l'Orient Chrétien* 30 (1935–6), 216–24

Tartuferi, A., and F. D'Arelli, eds., *L'arte di Francesco: capolavori d'arte Italiana e terre d'Asia dal XIII al XV secolo* (Florence, 2015)

Taylor, A., 'Armenian Art and Armenian Identity', in *Treasures in Heaven: Armenian Art, Religion and Society*, eds. T. F. Mathews and R. S. Wieck (New York, 1998), 133–46

Temir, A., *Kırşehir emiri Caca oğlu Nur el-Din'in 1272 tarihli Arapça-Moğolca vakfiyesi = Die arabisch-mongolische Stiftungsurkunde von 1272 des Emirs von Kırşehi Caca Oğlu Nur el-Din* (Ankara, 1959); German summary, 281–301

Texier, C., *Description de l'Asie Mineure faite par Ordre du gouvernement français de 1833 à 1837* (Paris, 1839–49), 3 vols.

Thierry, J.-M., 'À propos de quelques monuments chrétiens du vilayet de Kars (IV)', *Revue des études arméniennes* 19 (1985), 285–323

Thierry, J.-M., and N. Thierry, *L'église Saint-Grégoire de Tigran Honenc' à Ani (1215)* (Louvain; Paris, 1993)

'Peintures de caractère occidental en Arménie: l'église Saint-Pierre et Saint-Paul de Tat'ev', *Byzantion* 38 (1968), 180–242

Thierry, N., 'Le Jugement dernier d'Axtala: rapport préliminaire', *Bedi Kartlisa* 40 (1982), 147–85

'À propos des peintures de la grande église de Kobayr', *Revue des études géorgiennes et caucasiennes* 2 (1986), 223–6

Thomson, R. W., 'The Eastern Mediterranean in the Thirteenth Century: Identities and Allegiances. The Peripheries: Armenia', in *Identities and Allegiances in the Eastern Mediterranean after 1204*, eds. J. Herrin and G. Saint-Guillain (Farnham, 2011), 197–214

The Lawcode [Datastanagirk'] of Mxit'ar Goš [Dutch Studies in Armenian Language and Literature: 6] (Amsterdam; Atlanta, GA, 2000)

'Medieval Chroniclers of Ani: Hovhannes, Samvel, and Mkhitar', in *Armenian Kars and Ani*, ed. R. G. Hovannisian [Historic Armenian Cities and Provinces: 10] (Costa Mesa, CA, 2011), 65–80

Rewriting Caucasian History: The Medieval Armenian Adaptation of the Georgian Chronicles. The Original Georgian Texts and the Armenian Adaptation (Oxford, 1996)

Thorau, P., 'Shadschar ad-Durr, Sultanin von Ägypten', in *Saladin und die Kreuzfahrer*, eds. A. Wieczorek et al. (Mannheim, 2005), 167–69

Thorndike, L., *A History of Magic and Experimental Science during the First Thirteen Centuries of our Era* (New York, 1923), 6 vols.

Toumanoff, C., *Les dynasties de la Caucasie chrétienne de l'Antiquité jusqu'au XIXe siècle: tables généalogiques et chronologiques* (Rome, 1990)

Trapp, E., ed., *Prosopographisches Lexikon der Palaiologenzeit* (Vienna, 1976–96)

Turan, O., 'Selçuk devri vakfiyeleri III: Celaleddin Karatay, vakıfları ve vakfiyeleri', *Belleten* 12 (1948), 17–171

Ulbert, T., and R. Degen, *Der kreuzfahrerzeitliche Silberschatz aus Resafa-Sergiupolis* [Resafa: III] (Mainz am Rhein, 1990)

Ulubabian, B., and M. Hasratian, *Gandzasar* [Documenti di Architettura Armena: 17] (Milan, 1987)

Ünal, R. H., 'Iğdir yakmlannda bir selçuklu kervansarayi ve Doğubayazit–Batum kervan yolu hakkmda notlar', *Sanat Tarihi Yıllığı* 3 (1970), 7–15 van Berchem, M., *Amida: matériaux pour l'épigraphie et l'histoire musulmanes du Diyar-Bakir* (Heidelberg, 1910)

'Arabische Inschriften', in *Inschriften aus Syrien, Mesopotamien und Kleinasien gesammelt im Jahre 1899*, ed. N. von Oppenheim [Beiträge zur Assyriologie und semitischen Sprachwissenschaft: 7] (Leipzig; Baltimore, 1909), 1–156

van Berchem, M., and H. Edhem, *Matériaux pour un Corpus Inscriptionum Arabicum*, Part 1, *Egypte* I(i) (Paris, 1903)

Van Cleve, T. C., 'The Crusade of Frederick II', in *A History of the Crusades*, vol. 2, eds. R. L. Wolff and H. W. Hazard (Madison; Milwaukee; London, 1969), 429–62

Vardanyan, A., 'Some Additions to the Coins with the Inscription "Ulugh Mangyl Ulus (Ulush) Bek"', *Journal of the Oriental Numismatic Society* 190/1 (2007), 7–20

Vardanyan, E., ed., *Hoṙomos Monastery: Art and History* [Collège de France – CNRS Centre de recherche d'histoire et civilisation de Byzance. Monographies: 50] (Paris, 2015)

Vasiliev, A. A., 'The Foundation of the Empire of Trebizond', *Speculum* 11 (1936), 3–37

Virsaladze, T., 'Freskovaia rospis' khudozhnika Mikaela Maghlakeli v Matskhvarishi', *Ars Georgica* 4 (1955), 169–231; reprinted in her *Izbrannye trudy* (Tbilisi, 2007), 145–224

von Folsach, K., *Art from the World of Islam in the David Collection* (Copenhagen, 2001)

Vryonis, S., 'Another Note on the Inscription of the Church of St George of Beliserama', *Byzantina* 9 (1977), 11–22

The Decline of Medieval Hellenism in Asia Minor and the Process of Islamization from the Eleventh through the Fifteenth Century (Berkeley; Los Angeles; London, 1971)

Ward, R., 'The Inscription on the Astrolabe by 'Abd al-Karim in the British Museum', *Muqarnas* 21 (2004), 345–57

Islamic Metalwork (London, 1993)

'Style versus Substance: The Christian Iconography on Two Vessels Made for the Ayyubid Sultan al-Salih Ayyub', in *The Iconography of Islamic Art*, ed. B. O'Kane (Edinburgh, 2005), 309–24

Ward, R., ed., *Court and Craft: A Masterpiece from Northern Iraq* (London, 2014)

Weitzmann, K., 'Icon Painting in the Crusader Kingdom', *Dumbarton Oaks Papers* 20 (1966), 51–83

Werthmuller, K. J., *Coptic Identity and Ayyubid Politics in Egypt, 1218–1250* (Cairo; New York, 2010)

Whelan, E. J., *The Public Figure: Political Iconography in Medieval Mesopotamia* (London, 2006)

'Representations of the Khāṣṣakīyah and the Origins of Mamluk Emblems', in *Content and Context of the Visual Arts in the Islamic World*, ed. P. Soucek (University Park, PA; London, 1988), 219–53

Wieczorek, A., M. Fansa and H. Meller, eds., *Saladin und die Kreuzfahrer* [Publikationen der Reiss-Engelhorn-Museen 17] (Mannheim, 2005)

Wolf, C. O. M., '"The Pen Has Extolled her Virtues": Gender and Power within the Visual Legacy of Shajar al-Durr in Cairo', in *Calligraphy and Architecture in the Muslim World*, eds. M. Gharipour and I. C. Schick (Edinburgh, 2013), 199–216

Wolff, R. L., 'The Lascarids' Asiatic Frontiers Once More', *Orientalia Christiania Periodica* 15 (1949), 194–7

'The Latin Empire of Constantinople, 1204–1261', in *A History of the Crusades: 2*, eds. R. L. Wolff and H. W. Hazard (Madison; Milwaukee; London, 1969), 187–233

Wolper, E. S., 'Princess Safwat al-Dunya wa al-Din and the Production of Sufi Buildings and Hagiographies in Pre-Ottoman Anatolia', in *Women, Patronage, and Self-Representation in Islamic Societies*, ed. D. F. Ruggles (Albany, NY, 2000), 35–52

Woodfin, W. T., Y. Rassamakin and R. Holod, 'Foreign Vesture and Nomadic Identity on the Black Sea Littoral in the Early Thirteenth Century: Costume from the Chungul Kurgan', *Ars Orientalis* 42 (2012), 155–87

Wroth, W., *Catalogue of the Coins of the Vandals, Ostrogoths and Lombards and of the Empires of Thessalonica, Nicaea and Trebizond in the British Museum* (London, 1911)

Yalman, S., 'Building the Sultanate of Rum: Memory, Urbanism and Mysticism in the Architectural Patronage of 'Ala al-Din Kayqubad (r. 1220–1237)' (Ph.D. thesis, Harvard University, 2010)

Yarnley, C. J., 'Philaretos: Armenian Bandit or Byzantine General?', *Revue des études arméniennes* 9 (1972), 331–53

Yavuz, A. T., 'Anatolian Seljuk Caravanserais and their Use as State Houses', in *Turkish Art: Proceedings of the 10th International Congress of Turkish Art*, eds. F. Déroche, C. Geneguard, G. Renda and J. M. Rogers (Geneva, 1999), 757–65

'The Concepts That Shape Anatolian Seljuk Caravanserais', *Muqarnas* 14 (1997), 80–95

Yetkin, S. K., 'The Mausoleum of Mama Khatun', *Yıllık Araştırmalar Dergisi* 1 (1956), 79–91; Turkish text: 'Mama Khatun Türbesi', 75–77

Yıldız, S. N., 'Manuel Komnenos Mavrozomes and his Descendants at the Seljuk Court: The Formation of a Christian Seljuk–Komnenian Elite', in *Crossroads between Latin Europe and the Near East: Corollaries of the Frankish Presence in the Eastern Mediterranean (12th–14th centuries)*, ed. S. Leder [Istanbuler Texte und Studien: 24] (Würzburg, 2011), 55–77

'The Rise and Fall of a Tyrant in Seljuq Anatolia: Saʿd al-Din Köpek's Reign of Terror, 1237–8', in *Ferdowsi, the Mongols and the History of Iran: Studies in Honour of Charles Melville*, eds. R. Hillenbrand, A. C. S. Peacock and F. Abdullaeva (London, 2013), 92–103

Yoltar-Yıldırım, A., 'Raqqa: The Forgotten Excavation of an Islamic Site in Syria by the Ottoman Imperial Museum in the Early Twentieth Century', *Muqarnas* 30 (2013), 73–93

Index

'Abd al-Rahim al-Jawbari, author, 340
'Abd al-Rahman, Mongol administrator, 356, 381
Abelia church, 92
ablaq, 300
Abu Ali al-Halabi bin al-Kattani, architect, 286
Abu Bakr, *atabeg* of Azerbaijan (1186–1210), 86, 89, 92, 108, 175, 213
Abu Salim bin Abil-Hasan al-Samman, Armenian-Syriac physician, 210
Acre, 269
'Adhara Khatun, sister of Saladin, 189
al-'Adil, Ayyubid Sultan in Egypt and Syria (1193–1218), 5, 7, 80, 81, 100, 173
Aghtamar, Church of the Holy Cross, 75, 374
Ahmad ibn 'Umar al-Dhaki, metalworker, 255
Ahmadshah, Mengujekid emir of Divriği (1229–1242), 305
Akhlat, 1, 9, 14, 18, 27, 64, 66, 73, 81, 124, 186, 282, 312, 369
   cemeteries, 158
   citadel, 150
   economy, 159
   taxation, 161
   Usta Sakirt tomb, 386
Akhtala church, 28, 29, 45, 59, 379
   inscription, 37, 43
   St Nino, 114
Alanya, 136, 142, 166, 196, 207, 286, 333
Aleppo, 133, 248, 252, 286
   citadel, 152
   Firdaws madrasa, 111, 121, 185, 186, 284
   Great Mosque, 134, 147
Alfonso X, King of Castile (1252–1284), 277
'Aliabad castle, 9, 103
Amberd
   castle
      inscription, 27
   church, 50
Amid, 133, 136, 140, 154, 273, 300
   Great Mosque, 212

Amin al-Dawla Abu al-Karim Sa'id, Syriac physician, 209
Amiran-Darejaniani, 259
Anatolia, 148, 185
Andronikos I Komnenos, Emperor of Byzantium (1183–1185), 340
Andronikos II Palaiologos, Emperor of Byzantium (1282–1328), 89, 209
Ani, 50, 76, 126, 127, 153, 156, 260, 357, 371, 376
   bathhouses, 189
   Church of St Gregory the Illuminator of Abughamrents, 294
      inscription, 64
   Church of St Gregory the Illuminator of Tigran Honents, 38, 133, 169
      inscription, 60
      miracles of St Nino, 61, 114
   Church of the Holy Apostles, 163, 169, 293, 300, 377
      inscription, 164
   citadel, 130
      inscription, 26
   city walls and towers
      inscriptions, 142
      Lion Gate, 130: inscription, 161
      Mamkhatun's tower, 142, 144, 233
   convent of the Virgin, 295
   massacre of Easter Sunday (1210), 67
   mosque of Abu Ma'maran, 130, 153, 161
   mosque of Minuchihr, 130, 152, 153, 301
Anna Komnena, Byzantine princess and historian (d.1153), 106
Antalya 140, 146
   Kirkgöz Han, 152, 191
Antiochos VIII, Seleukid king (121–96 BC), 149
Anton Glonistavisdze, Georgian archbishop of Chqondidi (d.1202), 55, 73
apotropaic images and objects, 150, 152, 232
Arjish, 76
Arpay Khatun, Mongol princess, 349

Arslan Shah I, Zangid ruler of Mosul
    (1193–1211), 7
Artsakh, 186
Artsruni dynasty, 27
Aruch caravanserai, 169
Arzu Khatun, Mqargrdzeli vassal, 186, 217
al-Ashraf Musa, second husband of Tamta, and
    Ayyubid Sultan in Harran, Akhlat and
    Damascus (1207–37), 6, 8, 12, 76, 79,
    81, 101, 104, 110, 134, 173, 175, 184,
    194, 233, 243, 250, 273, 321, 326, 340
'Ashura Khatun, Ayyubid wife of al-Nasir
    Dawud, 87
Assassins [Isma'ili sect], 335, 372
astrolabes, 273, 277, 279, 339
    al-Ashraf (Oxford Museum for the History
    of Science), 273
astrology, 270, 275, 279, 340, 356
atabeg, 26, 108, 140, 173, 181, 323
automata, 358, 360
al-Awhad, first husband of Tamta, and
    Ayyubid ruler of Akhlat (d.1210), 1, 5,
    75, 78, 79, 81, 88, 100, 133, 146, 239
Aybak, Mamluk Sultan (1250–57), 119
'Ayn Jalut, battle (1260), 384, 389

bacini, 146
Badi' al-Zaman ibn al-Razzaz al-Jazari, 358,
    360
Badr al-Din Aqsunqur, Sökmenid ruler of
    Akhlat (1193–1197), 212
Badr al-Din Lu'lu', *atabeg* of Mosul
    (1234–1259), 88, 119, 170, 194, 224,
    233, 258, 344
Baghdad
    buried *timthal* in, 336
    siege of 1258, 70, 372, 383, 384
    Talisman Gate, 232
Bagratuni dynasty, 27, 50, 134
Baiju, Mongol general, 202, 384
Baldwin II, Latin Emperor of Constantinople
    (1228–1273), 206
Bamiyan Buddhas, 353
Bar Hebraeus, Syriac chronicler, 20, 202, 243,
    271, 372
Basiani, battle (1202), 73, 77, 85, 91, 213
Basil Giagoupes, Christian emir of the Seljuks,
    209, 341
Basil of Malatya, Christian notary of the
    Seljuks, 209
bathhouses, 189
    Ani, 189
    Damascus, Sitti 'Adhra baths, 189
    Dvin, 189

Batu Khan, Mongol ruler (d.1255), 350, 352,
    363, 382
Baybars, Mamluk Sultan (1260–77), 160, 167,
    389
Bayburt, 140, 142, 146
Beg-Temür, Emir of Akhlat (d.1207), 5,
    103
Benedict the Pole, Franciscan missionary, 351,
    372
Benjamin of Tudela, Jewish traveller, 279
Bertubani monastery, 42
    donor portrait of queen Tamar, 116
Betania monastery, 42
Bethlehem
    Church of the Nativity, 218
    inscription, 219
bridges, 188, 271
    Cizre, 239
    Malabadi, 239
    Sanahin, 191
    Tokat, 192
    Yeşilırmak, 191

Cairo, 220, 351
    al-Nasir Muhammad mosque complex,
    269
    al-Salih Ayyub madrasa, 147
    Haret al Rum, Church of the Virgin,
    133
    Imam al-Shafi'i mausoleum, 186, 234
    Roda Island palace, 245
    Shajar al-Durr mausoleum, 119
Camii. *See* mosques
caravanserais, 166, 188, 191, 210, 233, 285, 290,
    301, 349
    Alay Han, 287
    al-Han, 170
    Aruch caravanserai, 169
    Chrplu caravanserai, 169
    Hatun Han
        inscriptions, 191
    Karatay Han, 167
    Kirkgöz Han, 150, 191, 197
    Kotrets caravanserai, 170
    Selim Han, 169
    Sultan Han, 167, 283, 317
    Talin caravanserai, 169
    Zor caravanserai, 169, 297
castles
    'Aliabad castle, 9, 103
    Amberd, 27
    Kayean castle, 13, 342, 371
    Kiz castle, 63
celestial globe, 279

ceramics, 146, 160, 229, 266
   lustreware dish, Metropolitan Museum of Art, New York, 94
   minai plate, Freer Gallery of Art, Washington, 333
Chormaqan, Mongol general (d.1241), 12, 13, 342, 357, 370, 371
Christian confessions, 4, 54, 130, 185, 209, 355, 360, 383, 386
Chrplu caravanserai, 169
Church Council of Chalcedon (451), 25, 60
Church Council of Lore (1205), 57
Church Council of Nicaea (325), 48
churches
   Abelia church, 92
   Aghtamar, Church of the Holy Cross, 374
   Akhtala church, 29, 37, 43, 45, 59, 114, 379
   Amberd church, 50
   Ani, Church of the Holy Apostles, 163, 293
   Ani, convent of the Virgin, 295
   Ani, Holy Apostles, 300
   Ani, St Gregory the Illuminator of Abughamrents, 294
   Ani, St Gregory the Illuminator of Tigran Honents, 38, 60, 114
   Bertubani monastery, 42, 115
   Betania monastery, 42
   Bethlehem, Church of the Nativity, 218
   Constantinople, Chora monastery, 268
   Dadivank monastery, 186, 195
   Deir Mar Benham monastery, 207
   Gandzasar monastery, 51
   Garni, 322
   Goshavank (Nor Getik) monastery, 31, 59, 126
      chapel of St Gregory the Illuminator, 299
   Gtchavank monastery, 51
   Haghartsin monastery, 4, 27, 47, 51, 55
   Haghbat monastery, 30, 31, 43, 51, 59, 62
   Haret al Rum, Church of the Virgin, 133
   Harichavank monastery, 35, 47, 51, 58, 297
   Horomos monastery, 91, 153
   Hovhannavank monastery, 51, 188
   Jerusalem, Holy Sepulchre, 140, 214, 217
   Jerusalem, Monastery of the Holy Cross, 214
   Khtskonk monastery, 50, 371
   Kirants church, 38
   Kobayr monastery, 38
   Makaravank monastery, 59, 317
   Marmashen monastery, 50
   Mount Sinai, St Catherine's monastery, 384
   Noravank monastery, 62, 380
   Odzun church, 30
   Pitareti monastery, 303
   Qintsvisi monastery, 42
   Saghmosavank monastery, 188
   Samtavisi church, 34
   Sanahin monastery, 30, 51
   Tatev monastery, 384
   Tegher, church of Mamakhatun Vachutian, 188
   Timotesubani monastery, 42
      Church of St George, 42
   Udabno monastery, 69
   Vardzia monastery, 41, 62, 115
   Venice, San Marco, 267
Cilicia, 23, 24, 57, 202, 365, 377
citadels, 208
   Akhlat, 150
   Aleppo, 152
   Amid, 152
   Ani, 26, 130
cities, 73, 124, 127
   design, 127
   layout, 124, 127, 153
city, 54
city gates
   Amid, 213
   Ani, Kars gate, 136
   Ani, Lion Gate, 130, 139, 161
   Baghdad, Talisman Gate, 232
   Constantinople, Golden Gate, 149
   Kayseri, Yeni Kapı, 198
   Konya, 148
   Mayyafariqin, Gate of Deliverance, 161
city walls and towers, 136, 144, 233
   Alanya, Red Tower, 136
   Amid, 141
      Ulu Baden, 136
   Ani, 136
      inscriptions, 139
      Mamkhatun's tower, 142, 144
   Ankara, 148
   Antalya, 140
   Bayburt, 142
   Damascus, 136
   Kars, 140
      inscription, 143
   Konya, 148
   Mayyafariqin, 146
   Sinop, 141
coinage, 165, 212, 239, 271, 333, 375
coins. *See* coinage

Constantine IX Monomachos, Emperor of
  Byzantium (1042–1055), 50
Constantine the Great, Emperor (303–337),
  149
Constantinople, 149, 266
  Blachernae monastery, 225
  Chora monastery, 268
  Golden Gate, 149
  spolia, 266
conversion, 4, 7, 22, 27, 28, 45, 46, 47, 55, 60,
  133, 206, 209, 225, 383, 386
cosmic iconography, 271, 277
court culture, 172, 242, 256, 266, 352
cultural contact, 225, 227, 230, 233

Daba monastery, 303
Dadivank monastery, 186, 195, 217
al-Dahabi, Arabic chronicler, 6, 193
Damascus, 193, 229, 233, 268, 297
  ʿAdiliyya Sughra madrasa, 194
  al-Salihiyya district, 181, 184
  Atabakiyya madrasa, 181, 195
  Dar al-Hadith of al-Ashraf Musa, 181, 184,
    326
  Khadija Khatun madrasa, 184
  Sitti ʿAdhra baths, 189
  Terkan Khatun ribat, 181
Davit IV the Builder, King of Georgia
  (1089–1125), 329, 351
Davit Soslan, husband of queen Tamar
  (c.1187–1207), 71, 91, 113
Davit VI Narin, King of Georgia (1254–1293),
  85, 370
Davit VII Ulu, King of Georgia (1247–1270),
  370, 379
Dayfa Khatun, wife of Ayyubid ruler al-Zahir
  Ghazi, 7, 10, 93, 110, 121, 154, 185, 212
Deir Mar Benham monastery, 207
Didgori, battle (1121), 72
Divriği, 186, 306, 317
  mosque hospital complex, 304
    inscription, 308
  Sitte Melik tomb, 288, 293
Diyarbakir. See Amid
Doquz Khatun, wife of Hülegü Khan, 383, 384
Dunaysir, 136
Dvin, 22, 24, 62, 68, 71, 76, 125, 160, 260, 325
  bathhouses, 189

Eghbayrik, Armenian merchant, 143
Erzincan, 3, 12, 71, 75, 76, 93, 163, 290, 342
Erzurum, 3, 6, 71, 75, 76, 77, 87, 155, 168, 294
  Yakutiye Madrasa, 297

Eudokia Palaiologina, the Byzantine wife of
  John II Grand Komnenos, Emperor of
  Trebizond, 99
ʿEyn al-Dowla, artist, 226

Farrukhshah, cousin of al-Ashraf Musa, 185
Fatima, influential Mongol slave, 381, 382
female virtue, 178
  modesty, 178
  patronage, 189, 195
  piety, 180, 194
foundation texts, 195
fountains, 189
Francesco Pegolotti, Florentine merchant, 166
Frederick II, Holy Roman Emperor
  (1220–1250), 215, 277, 329
futuwwa, 88

Gandza, 71
Gandzasar monastery, 51
  inscription, 216
gardens, 245, 247, 253
Garni
  Battle (1225), 9, 322, 326
  Roman temple and monastery, 322
Gelati monastery, 352
Genghis Khan, Great Khan of the Mongol
  Empire (1206–1227), 330, 344, 350,
  352
Gevher Nesibe, sister of Kaykhusraw I, 185,
  201
Georgian Chronicle, 27, 101, 324
Georgian saints, 114
Getik monastery, 126, 217
Giorgi III, King of Georgia (1156–1184), 4, 24,
  26, 69, 71, 77, 112, 154
Giorgi IV Lasha, King of Georgia (1210–1223),
  9, 24, 26, 101, 115, 303, 324, 345, 370
Gontsa Kakhaberidze, wife of Avag then Davit
  Ulu, 379
Goshavank (Nor Getik) monastery, 31, 59,
  126
  chapel of St Gregory the Illuminator, 299
  inscription, 379
graffiti, 217
Grigor Aknertsi, chronicler, 373, 378
Gtchavank monastery, 51
Guillaume Boucher, goldsmith, 357
Gurandukht, Kipchaq wife of Davit IV of
  Georgia, 329
Gurji Khatun (Tamar), Georgian wife of Seljuk
  Sultan Kaykhusraw II, 99, 174, 186,
  192, 198, 226, 240, 370

Güyük Khan, Great Khan of the Mongol Empire (1246–1248), 347, 348, 357, 362, 364, 370, 381

Haghartsin monastery, 47
  inscription, 4, 27, 51, 55
Haghbat monastery, 30, 31, 43, 51, 59, 62, 217, 374
hajib, 107, 176
Hamadola, Georgian ambassador, 368
Han. *See* caravanserais
al-Harawi, Arabic geographer, 231
Harichavank monastery, 35, 195, 297, 300, 386
  donor portrait, 51, 58
  inscription, 47, 300
Harran, 7, 81, 101, 107, 135, 147, 155, 180, 183, 231, 233, 252
Harun al-Rashid, Abbasid caliph (766–809), 204
Hetum I, King of Cilicia (1226–1269), 63, 219, 346, 347, 353
Hisnkeyf, 118, 133, 270
Honorius III, pope (1216–27), 116, 346
Horomos monastery, 153
  funerary chapel, 91
hospitals, 282
  Damascus, hospital of Nur al-Din Zangi, 297
  Divriği, mosque-hospital complex, 304, 311
  Kayseri, Çifte Medrese, 201
  Sivas, Şifaiye Medrese, 201
Hovhannavank monastery, 51, 316
  inscription, 317
Hromkla, 23, 24
Hülegü Khan, Mongol ruler (1256–1265), 362, 372, 375, 381, 384
Husam al-Din 'Ali, Ayyubid *hajib* (chamberlain) of Akhlat, 8, 10, 107, 176, 211, 327
al-Husayni, Arabic chronicler, 71

Ibn al-Athir, Arabic chronicler, 69, 74, 86, 91, 108, 326
Ibn Bibi, Persian historian, 197, 257
Ibn Hawqal, Arabic geographer, 76
Ibn Jubayr, Arabic traveller, 154, 166, 179, 189, 213
Ibn Khallikan, Arabic biographer, 176, 204, 243
Ibn Shaddad, Arabic scholar and writer, 231, 243, 253
Ibn 'Unayn, Arabic poet, 176

Ibn Wasil, Arabic historian, 83, 93, 109, 111, 212, 247, 335
icon, 54, 225, 229, 333
  Christ (Anchiskhati), 55, 227
  Christ (mandylion), 227
  Mother of God (Blachernitissa), 225, 227
  Mother of God (Hodegitria), 227
  Mother of God (Khakhuli), 55, 72
  Mother of God (Saidnaya), 228
  Mother of God (Vardzia), 55
Innocent IV, pope (1243–54), 241, 347
inscriptions, 140, 155, 170, 191, 194, 210, 258, 290, 300
  alphabet, 144
  language, 144
Ismat al-Dunya wa 'l-Din, wife of Seljuk Sultan Kaykubad I, 191, 196
Iurii Bogoliubskoi, Russian husband of queen Tamar, 113, 252
iwan, 249
'Izz al-Din Saltuk II, Emir of Erzurum (1132–1168), 77, 87, 91, 290

Jahan Pahlavan, *atabeg* of Azerbaijan (d.1187), 108, 175, 288
Jalal al-Din Khwarazmshah, Khwarazmian ruler (d.1231), 9, 11, 72, 98, 103, 108, 155, 215, 220, 279, 305, 322, 326, 328, 333, 345, 364
Jalal al-Din Rumi Mevlana, Persian poet and Sufi mystic, 226
James of Vitry, Latin bishop of Acre, 214
Jaqeli family, 370
Jazira, 237, 249, 273, 277, 282, 286, 320, 322, 358, 373
Jean de Joinville, French chronicler, 247
Jerusalem, 217
  Holy Sepulchre, 214, 217
  Monastery of the Holy Cross, 214
Jigda Khatun, wife of Georgian king Davit VII Ulu, 92
John, Armenian archbishop of Grner, 365
John II Grand Komnenos, Emperor of Trebizond (1280–1297), 99
John III Vatatzes, Emperor of Byzantium (1221–1254), 106
John Komnenos Mavrozomes, *emir* at the court of Kaykubad II, 208
John of Plano Carpini, Franciscan missionary, 2, 347, 351, 362, 381

Kaluyan-e Naqqash, painter, 227

al-Kamil, Ayyubid Sultan in Egypt (1218–1238), 87, 101, 154, 180, 215, 244, 245, 279, 329
Kamyar, Seljuk *pervane*, 341
Karakorum, 13, 353, 358, 360, 377
Kars, 140, 143, 371, 376
Kayean castle, 13, 342, 371
Kayka'us I, Seljuk sultan of Rum (1211–1219), 94, 174, 201
    inscription, Antalya, 140
Kaykhusraw II, Seljuk sultan of Rum (1237–1246), 99, 150, 174, 198, 200, 206, 225, 239, 370, 371
Kaykubad I, Seljuk sultan of Rum (1219–1237), 7, 11, 12, 99, 142, 174, 196, 200, 255, 258, 283, 341
Kayseri, 190
    baths of Mahperi Khatun, 157
    Çifte Medrese, 201
    Hajji Kılıc mosque and madrasa, 185, 314
    Karatay Han, 167
    Köşk Medrese, 291
    Mahperi Huand Hatun complex, 185, 198, 264, 314
        inscriptions, 200
    Sultan Han, 167
    Yeni Kapı, 198
Khadija Khatun, sister of Ayyubid ruler al-Nasir Dawud, 184, 326
Khalisat al-Dunya wa'l-Din, Megujekid princess, 142
Khawanrah Khatun, wife (?) of Badr al-Din Lu'lu', 224, 264
khatchkars, 67, 139, 158, 192, 218, 234
Khorishah, Armenian pilgrim, 216–17
Khoy, 10, 12, 76, 109, 328, 330
Khtskonk monastery, 50, 371
Khurramshah b. Mughith al-Khilati, architect, 305, 313
khutba, 111, 118, 196, 382
Khutlukhatun, Armenian noblewoman, 91
Kılıc Arslan, Seljuk sultan of Rum (1156–1192), 87, 128, 179, 287
Kipchaqs, 329
Kirakos Gandzaketsi, Armenian historian, 8, 22, 35, 69, 82, 84, 106, 172, 204, 210, 217, 232, 324, 350, 353, 368, 373, 376, 378
Kirants church, 38
Kitbugha, Christian Mongol general, 374, 384, 389
Kiz castle
    inscription, 63

Knight in the Panther's Skin, 176, 253, 259
Kobayr monastery, 38, 378, 386
Konya, 148, 156, 186, 258, 260, 266
    Alaeddin Camii, 201, 207, 283, 287
    Church of St Plato or St Amphilochios, 207
Kösedağ, battle (1243), 13, 99, 202, 313, 342, 349, 369
Kublai Khan, Great Khan of the Mongol Empire (1260–1294), 381
kumiss, 352

Lake Van, 8, 10, 18, 23, 27, 73, 74, 99, 125, 340, 374
    citadel, 152
liturgy, 34, 58
Louis IX, King of France (1226–1270), 346, 360, 364
love poetry
    Ayyubid, 176

madrasas, 183, 184, 190
    'Adiliyya Sughra madrasa, 194
    Aleppo, Firdaws madrasa, 111, 121, 185
    Cairo, Al-Salih Ayyub madrasa, 147
    Damascus, Atabakiyya madrasa, 181, 195
    Damascus, Khadija Khatun madrasa, 184
    Erzurum, Yakutiye Madrasa, 297
    Kayseri, Mahperi Huand Hatun complex, 314
    Sivas, Buruciye Medresesi, 315
    Sivas, Şifaiye Medrese, 201
    Zuzan madrasa, 331
magic, 337, 339
magical statues, 149, 336
Mahmud Yalavach, Mongol administrator, 356, 381
Mahperi Khatun, Armenian wife of Seljuk Sultan Kaykubad I, 99, 175, 186, 190, 191, 196, 197, 200, 204, 264
Maimonides, Moses, rabbi and physician, 209
Makaravank monastery, 59, 217, 300, 317
Malik Shah, Great Seljuk sultan of Iran (1073–1092), 329
Malika 'Adiliyya, Ayyubid wife of Seljuk Sultan Kaykubad I, 174, 196, 197, 202, 283, 293
    tomb, 202
Malika, wife of Muzaffar al-Din Özbek *atabeg* of Azerbaijan, 108, 326
Mama Khatun, daughter of 'Izz al-Din Saltuk II, Emir of Erzurum, 290
Mamakhatun Vachutian, Mqargrdzeli vassal, 188, 317

Mamkhatun, Armenian noblewoman, 142
Manuel I Komnenos, Emperor of Byzantium (1143–1180), 271
Manuel I Megas Komnenos, Emperor of Trebizond (1238–1263), 166
manuscripts
  astrological treatise, Tbilisi, National Center of Manuscripts A-65, 275, 303
  Book of Knowledge of Ingenious Mechanical Devices, Istanbul, Topkapı Sarayı Sultan Ahmet III MS 3472, 360
  Daqa'iq al-Haqa'iq, Paris, BNF Pers 174, 234
  Epithalamion, Rome, Vatican Library Vat. gr. 1851, 96
  Gospel Lectionary, Rome, Vatican Syr. 559, 384
  Gospels ('Haghbat Gospels'), Yerevan, Matenadaran 6288, 53, 266
  Gospels ('Red Gospels of Gandzasar'), Chicago, Goodspeed MS 949, 38, 209
  Gospels ('Vani Gospels'), Tbilisi, National Center of Manuscripts A-1335, 111
  Gospels, Athens, Gennadios Library MS Gr.1.5, 209
  Gospels, Nor Julfa Library MS 36/156, 371
  Gospels, Rome, Vatican Library Vat. Syr. 559, 234
  Gospels, Yerevan, Matenadaran 197, 366
  Gospels, Yerevan, Matenadaran MS 8321, 239
  Kitab al-Aghani, Cairo, Egyptian National Library Ms Farsi 579, 264
  Kitab al-Diryaq, Paris, BNF arabe 2964, 277
  Kitab al-Diryaq, Vienna, Nationalbibliothek MS A.F. 10, 264
  Maqamat of al-Hariri, Paris, BNF arabe 5847, 249
  Maqamat of al-Hariri, St Petersburg, Russian Academy of Science S-23, 245
  al-Tabsira fi 'l-Hurub of Saladin, Oxford, Bodleian Library MS Huntington 264, 137
al-Maqrizi, Egyptian scholar, 93
Marco Polo, merchant traveller, 74, 372
Maria Palaiologina, illegitimate daughter of Byzantine emperor Michael VIII Palaiologos, 362
Marmashen monastery, 50
marriage, 84
  ceremonies, 92
  control of land, 89
  diplomatic, 85
  rhetoric, 94
  symbolism, 89, 94
  wives, 109, 123, 172, 174
  women and power, 92, 103, 104, 107, 109, 111, 264, 381
masons, movement of, 283, 285, 286, 290, 296
al-Mas'ud, Artuqid ruler of Amid (1222–31), 273, 339
mausolea. *See* tombs
Mayyafariqin, 101, 135, 139, 210, 232, 233, 239, 286, 320, 373
  inscription, 100, 134, 146, 161
Merv, 330, 332
metalwork, 172, 221, 236, 254, 258, 266
  basin of al-'Adil II, 1238–40 (Louvre, 5991), 254
  basin of Najm al-Din Ayyub, 1247–9 (Freer Gallery of Art, F1955.10), 221
  dish of Badr al-Din Lu'lu', 1234–59 (Munich), 224
  inlaid pen box of Majd al-Mulk al-Muzaffar, 1210–11 (Freer Gallery of Art), 331
  Seljuk bronze mirror, 272
Michael Glykas, Byzantine court poet, 271
Michael Pachymeres, Byzantine chronicler, 362
Michael VIII Palaiologos, Emperor of Byzantium (1259–1282), 85, 362
mihrab, 208, 283, 311, 321, 337
minarets, 101, 130, 134, 135, 136, 286, 321, 331
Mkhitar Gosh, Armenian monk, jurist and theologian, 23, 31, 59, 62, 126
Mohi, battle (1241), 344, 357, 358, 362
monasteries. *See* churches
Möngke Khan, Great Khan of the Mongol Empire (1251–1259), 347, 363, 372, 375, 379, 381
Mongols, 236, 282, 330, 340, 343, 345, 349, 350, 362, 369, 372
monsters of the east (mythical), 260, 353
mosques
  Aleppo, Great Mosque, 134, 147
  Amid, Great Mosque, 212
  Ani, mosque of Abu Ma'maran, 130, 153
  Ani, mosque of Minuchihr, 130, 301
  Cairo, al-Nasir Muhammad mosque complex, 269
  Damascus, Great Mosque, 121
  Divriği, mosque-hospital complex, 304, 311
  Kayseri, Hajji Kılıc, 314
  Konya, Alaeddin Camii, 201, 207
  Mayyafariqin, 101, 135
  Niğde mosque, 169
  Sivas, Ulu Camii, 136
  Uluborlu, Ulu Camii, 196

Mosul, 224, 254, 266
Mount Sinai
  St Catherine's monastery, 384
Mqargrdzeli, 3, 21, 26, 77, 82, 93, 128, 163, 168, 173, 186, 277, 294, 317, 376
  Artashir, 253
  Avag, brother of Tamta (d.1250), 3, 9, 13, 325, 342, 350, 369, 371, 378, 386
  Ivane, father of Tamta (d.1227), 1, 2, 4, 9, 19, 21, 26, 27, 39, 46, 58, 62, 66, 73, 74, 76, 79, 82, 91, 92, 133, 303, 322, 345, 368
  Khoshak, daughter of Avag, 342, 378, 380
  Khoshak, mother of Tamta, 2, 324, 378, 386
  Khuandza, great niece of Tamta, 163
  Sargis, grandfather of Tamta (d.1187), 26
  Shahanshah, son of Zakare (d.12??), 377, 386
  Shahanshah, son of Zakare (d.1261), 371
  Zakare, uncle of Tamta (d.1210), 21, 26, 47, 54, 57, 67, 73, 76, 82, 133
al-Muʿazzam, Ayyubid Sultan of Syria (1218–1229), 9, 13, 103, 213, 214, 215, 219, 258
Muhammad bin Khawlan al-Dimashqi, Ayyubid architect, 283, 286
Muhammad Khwarazmshah (1200–20), 329, 344–5
Muin al-Din Sulayman, Seljuk *pervane* (d.1277), 192
muqarnas, 167, 181, 190, 248, 288, 297, 308
music, 172, 176, 211, 242, 255, 264
al-Mustaʿsim, Abbasid caliph of Baghdad (1242–1258), 117, 372
Muzaffar al-Din Özbek, *atabeg* of Azerbaijan (1210–1225), 87, 108
al-Muzaffar Ghazi, Ayyubid Sultan of Akhlat and Mayyafariqin (1220–1247), 9
al-Muzaffar Mahmud, Ayyubid ruler of Hama (d.1244), 221

Nagorno-Karabagh. *See* Artsakh
Najm al-Din Alpi, Artuqid ruler of Mardin (1152–1176), 149
Nakhchivan, 351
  Mumine Khatun tomb, 288
Nasir al-Din al-Ṭusi, Iranian astronomer and philosopher, 340, 359
Nasir al-Din Artuq Arslan, Artuqid ruler of Mardin (1184–1200), 277
Nasir al-Din Bahramshah, Mengujekid emir of Erzincan (1165–1225), 85
al-Nasir Dawud, son of al-Muʿazzam and ruler of Kerak, 87–8, 268, 326
Nasir al-Din Mahmud, Artuqid ruler of Amid (1201–1222), 358
Nasir al-Din Sökmen II, Sökmenid Shah-i Armen of Akhlat (1128–1185), 71, 77, 83, 154, 287
al-Nasir Salah al-Din Yusuf. *See* Saladin, Ayyubid Sultan (1174–1193)
Nasr-e Khusraw, Persian writer and traveller, 74
Nikephoros Blemmydes, Byzantine monk, 105
Nikoloz Gulasberidze, Georgian catholicos, 61
Nizam al-Mulk, Book of Government, 104, 189
Noravank monastery, 62, 380

Odzun church, 30
Ögödei Khan, Great Khan of the Mongol Empire (1219–1241), 12, 342, 343, 347, 352
Orbelian family, 370, 379, 380

palaces, 242, 249
  Akhlat palace, 245
  Aleppo palace, 248
  Aleppo, Palace of Glory, 253
  Aleppo, Palace of Pictures, 253
  Amid, Artuqid palace, 258, 261
  Ani, palace of the baron, 252
  Beyşehir, Seljuk palace, 260
  Geguti palace, 251
  Konya, 207
  Kubadabad, Seljuk palace, 157, 255, 266, 365
  Palermo, Palace of Roger II, 256
  Raqqa, 245, 247
  Roda Island palace, 245
  Sinjar, Guʾ Kummet, 250
  Takht-i Sulayman, Ilkhanid palace, 365
patronage, 189, 193, 195, 205
physicians, 209–210
pilgrimage, 213, 216, 228, 232
Pitareti monastery, 303

qadi of Ani, 62, 126, 210
Qintsvisi monastery, 42
Qotai Khatun, Mongol queen, 355, 359
Qutb al-Din Ghazi II, Artuqid ruler (1176–1184), 149

Rabiʿa Khatun, sister of Saladin, 184
Rafiqa, 255
rain stones, 337, 338
Resafa hoard, 241
rhubarb, 352

ribats, 189
    Damascus, Terkan Khatun ribat, 181
Rukn al-Din Suleymanshah II, Seljuk Sultan of Rum (1197–1204), 77, 90
Rustavi, 262
Rusudan, Queen of Georgia (1223–1245), 9, 14, 26, 86, 90, 99, 101, 111, 116, 174, 225, 324, 333, 346, 368, 376

Saghmosavank monastery, 316, 317
Saidnaya monastery, 228, 233
Saints
    Ekvtime Mtatsmindeli, 43
    Evagre, 43
    Giorgi Mtatsmindeli, 43
    Gregory the Illuminator, 45, 61
    Hilarion Kartveli, 43
    Ioane Shuvamdinareli, 43
    Jacob of Nisibis, 45
    Nino, 43, 61, 114
    Shio Mghvimeli, 43
    Stephen the Younger, 44
Saladin, Ayyubid Sultan (1174–1193), 1, 5, 22, 67, 75, 76, 77, 79, 110, 213
Saljukshah, sister of Seljuk Sultan Kılıç Arslan, 154, 179, 213
Samtavisi church, 34
Samtskhe, 370, 389
Sanahin monastery, 30, 51, 386
    inscription, 195
Sayf al-Din Begtimur, Sökmenid ruler of Akhlat (1183–1193), 212
Sergius, Armenian 'monk' at Karakorum, 354
Shahanshah, Mengujekid ruler of Divriği (1175–1197), 288, 305
Shahbanu, wife of Shah i-Armen Nasir al-Din Sökmen II, 77, 188, 287
Shahname of Firdowsi, 257, 259, 328
Shajar al-Durr, Ayyubid wife of Ayyubid Sultan al-Salih Ayyub, 117, 194, 221, 270, 384
    mausoleum, 119
    inscription, 120
Shamkhori, battle (1195), 73, 77
Shams al-Din, brother of Juvayni, 253, 380
Shams al-Din Ildeguz, *atabeg* of Azerbaijan (1136–1175), 86
Shams al-Din Yusuf, astrologer, 273
Sheikh of Surmari, 62
Silvan. See Mayyafariqin
Sinjar, Gu'Kummet, 250
Simonis, Byzantine wife of Serbian king Stefan III Milutin, 89

Sinop, 287
    inscription, 144
Siraj al-Din Abu Yusuf Ya'qub al-Sakaki, Khwarazmian astrologer, 336
Sitt al-Sham, sister of Saladin, 178
Sivas, 201, 258
Smbat II, King of Ani (977–989), 51
Smbat Orbelian, 379
Smbat the Constable, 346, 348
spolia, 147, 149, 266
    Ankara, 148, 149
    Konya, 148, 149
Stefan III Milutin, King of Serbia (1282–1321), 89, 99
Stepanos Orbelian, Armenian historian, 36, 67, 384
stucco, 254, 260, 262, 297

Tabriz, 9, 10, 76, 108, 109, 166, 168, 327, 329
Talin, 169
Tamar. See Gurji Khatun
Tamar, Queen of Georgia (1184–1210), 3, 14, 24, 26, 44, 55, 66, 73, 77, 85, 86, 90, 92, 111, 214, 252, 323
Taron, 8
Tatev monastery, 384
taxation, 161, 211, 212, 370, 374
    inscription, 161, 163, 165, 212, 379
Tbilisi, 34, 45, 160, 189, 262, 317, 325, 333
Tegher
    Church of Mamakhatun Vachutian, Mqargrdzeli vassal, 188
tents, 56, 93, 245, 357, 360, 362, 363, 388
Tercan
    Mama Khatun complex, 290, 293
Terkan Khatun, grandmother of Jalal al-Din Khwarazmshah, 328, 344
Terkan Khatun, ruler in Kerman, 382
Terkan Khatun, Zangid wife of Ayyubid Sultan al-Ashraf, 7, 173, 181, 185, 193, 254
Theognostes, 105
Thietmar, German pilgrim, 214, 229, 245
Tigran Honents, Armenian merchant, 38, 60, 133, 143, 154, 156, 166, 295
tiles, 157, 172, 255, 257, 261, 266, 331
Timotesubani monastery, 42
    Church of St George, 42
Toghril Shah III, Seljuk sultan of Iran (1177–1194), 108, 175, 326
Tokat, 190
tombs, 286, 293
    Akhlat, Usta Sakirt, 386
    Akhtala church, 28, 29, 379

tombs (*cont.*)
    Cairo, mausoleum of Shajar al-Durr, 119, 120
    Damascus, Atabakiyya madrasa, 181
    Divriği, Sitte Melik, 288, 293
    Gelati monastery, 351
    Harichavank monastery, 195
    Horomos monastery, 91
    Kayseri, Köşk Medrese, 291
    Kayseri, Mahperi Huand Hatun complex, 198
    Kobayr, 378
    Konya, 186
    Konya, Alaeddin Camii, 283
    Nakhchivan, Mumine Khatun, 288
    Noravank monastery, 380
    Sivas, Şifaiye Medrese, 201
    Tercan, Mama Khatun complex, 290
    tomb of Malika ʿAdiliyya, Ayyubid wife of Seljuk Sultan Kaykubad I, 202
Töregene Khatun, wife of Ögödei Khan, 381
trade routes, 76, 77, 165, 168, 170, 213, 288, 388
Trebizond, 133
    Shrine of St Athanasios, 231
Tughrilshah, Emir of Erzurum (d.1225), 3, 6, 82, 91, 140, 198
Turan Malik, cousin of Ahmadshah of Divriği, 186, 305
Turanshah, son of Shajar al-Durr, 118
Tutbeg bin Bahram al-Khilati, architect, 287

Udabno monastery, 69
Uluborlu
    Ulu Camii
        inscription, 196
Urgench, 330–1

Vache Vachutian, Mqargrdzeli vassal (1213–1232), 188, 316
Vaneni, Armenian princess, 106
Vardan Areweltsi, Armenian chronicler, 69, 76, 132, 324
Vardzia monastery, 41, 62
    donor portrait of queen Tamar, 115
Venice
    San Marco, 267

wall paintings, 35, 37, 54, 60, 69, 116, 260, 333, 335
waqf, 160, 167, 190, 193, 195
war, 66, 370, 372
    aims and functions, 67, 71
    economics, 71, 72
    taxation, 376
Wilbrand of Oldenburg, Latin pilgrim, 214
William of Rubruck, Franciscan friar, 66, 213, 244, 344, 346, 347, 350, 353, 360, 363, 377, 383
wives. *See* marriage
women and power. *See* marriage

Yağibasan, Danishmendid ruler of Malatya (1142–1164), 87
Yassıçemen, battle (1230), 12, 220, 328–9, 338–9, 340
Yeh-lü Ch'u-ts'ai, Mongol governor, 279, 352, 355, 381

Zahida Khatun, wife of Jahan Pahlavan, *atabeg* of Azerbaijan, 108, 175
al-Zahir Ghazi, ruler of Aleppo (1186–1216), 93, 110, 185, 248, 253
Zahra Khatun, sister of Ayyubid Sultan al-Ashraf, 194
Zor caravanserai, 169